SECOND EDITION

S. WATSON DUNN

Head, Department of Advertising
University of Illinois

ADVERTISING
ITS ROLE IN MODERN MARKETING

HOLT, RINEHART AND WINSTON, INC.

New York / Chicago / San Francisco / Atlanta
Dallas / Montreal / Toronto / London / Sydney

PREFACE

Like the previous edition this book is designed to introduce students to the complex, ever-changing world of advertising. It is aimed both at the student who may eventually practice advertising, or one of its many related fields, and at those who are curious to find out how this mysterious force called "advertising" really works. I suspect that the book's blending of theory and practice will appeal also to many professionals who want to reexamine advertising's role in today's society.

Advertising is worthy of more serious academic attention than it sometimes receives. Like psychology, political science, and economics, it deals with people and how they react to the world about them. Whether one examines advertising as an influence on consumption patterns, as a means of communication, as a marketing tool, or as a social institution, it will be discovered that advertising is one of the most pervasive forces in the world today.

This book, like its predecessor, is built around the major problems of modern advertising and promotion—those which are central and continuing. Among these we must include the following: (1) the social and economic role of advertising; (2) the proper use of controls over advertising; (3) planning the campaign on a step-by-step basis; (4) the role of research and other methods of gathering information both before and after the campaign; (5) creating messages that are keyed to today's changing needs, wants, and attitudes; (6) the growing complexity of media strategy; (7) the relationship of advertising to such established disciplines as psychology and sociology; (8) coordination with other elements of the marketing and communications mix; and (9) how to cope with the growing pains inherent in moving internationally. In covering these I have tried to keep the language simple, and at the same time provide an accurate picture of advertising and promotion as they really are. Both to emphasize the importance of tracking down facts in analyzing problems and to make complex concepts more easily understood, I have made extensive use of charts, tables, and other illustrative material. Throughout the book I have made an effort to practice what I have preached regarding effective communication.

Those familiar with the previous edition will note that certain changes have been made both in approach and organization. The coverage of the social, ethical, and economic problems of advertising has been expanded to two chapters instead of one. Two chapters rather than one are devoted to the behavioral science underpinnings of advertising planning. In addition, extensive behavioral-science material has been added in other relevant sections of the book. A chapter on sales promotion has been added to provide special emphasis for this important form

V

of marketing and communications. Considerably more emphasis has been given to the problems of merging advertising and promotion into the marketing and communications program. The chapter on the growing area of international advertising has been greatly expanded. Greater emphasis has been placed on the planning and creation of television commercials, with extensive examples of each. In general, I have attempted to provide as strong an analytical framework as possible for the serious student of advertising.

Part 1 covers the framework in which advertising operates — looking at it from a social, economic, ethical, and institutional viewpoint. Part 2 emphasizes the role of facts, the life blood of intelligent analysis and use of advertising and promotion. Part 3 is devoted to creative strategy; Part 4 to media strategy; and, beginning with chapter 29, to such problems as retail and international advertising, public relations, and measuring advertising's effectiveness. There is an effort to combine theory and practice and to focus on general principles and the managerial viewpoint rather than the specific techniques of advertising. For example, students taking an introductory course in advertising need not learn all the details of producing a television commercial or an advertisement, but they should know enough to work effectively with the specialists who handle such production problems.

I am indebted to numerous educators who have taken the time to read and criticize portions of the book and especially to those who have used the first edition and have passed on to me suggestions for this revision. I am indebted also to the many organizations and individuals who have supplied me with statistics, case histories, and copies of individual advertisements which are included in this book. Acknowledgment is due also to Charles L. Whittier, one of the real statesmen of advertising, for allowing me to include illustrations and examples which appeared first in his book, *Creative Advertising*.

S. Watson Dunn

January 1969

CONTENTS

PART 1

BACKGROUND FOR ADVERTISING AND PROMOTION

1

An Introductory Look at Advertising and Promotion

Most people who read this book will already have formulated some specific ideas about advertising, promotion and the people who practice them. Advertising, unlike other aspects of business such as accounting or production or purchasing, calls consistent attention to itself—to its sins as well as to its accomplishments. It has been aptly said that advertising men publish their mistakes for everyone to see and hear.

People like to pretend that it is always the other fellow who is influenced by methods of modern promotion. Some make fun of it. There are people who discuss novels, poetry, news stories, musical compositions, personal letters, and other creative works in all seriousness who would not think of giving the same consideration to creative advertising.

Some people are highly critical of all forms of promotion on social or economic grounds. Almost everyone will admit, however, that advertising is a vigorous form of communication that, for better or for worse, influences us all.

People who work in advertising are aware that their efforts are often criticized by those who do not understand how advertising works. They are concerned because adverse books and articles seem to make more of an impression than attempts to counter these attacks. The

3

layman would never speak so authoritatively about physics or geology as he does about the advertisement in today's newspaper or the commercial on television. The student who begins a course in almost any science will spend a lot of time familiarizing himself with basic concepts and terminology and will be reluctant to express his opinion.

Everyone is continually exposed to advertising, a state of affairs which can be helpful or harmful. It is helpful in that it gives everyone a basis for relating what he sees in the advertisements to his everyday life. It can be harmful in that a little learning is a dangerous thing. Because a person reads ads in the newspapers or sees commercials on his favorite television program, he may think he understands the advertising field. We tend to see a particular field in terms of our own experience. If we see an advertisement we believe is untrue, we damn advertising. If, on the other hand, we gain some useful information, we are enthusiastic. Even a businessman will judge advertising according

FIG. 1.1 *Outstanding public service advertisement keyed to a national problem of the time.* COURTESY INTERNATIONAL PAPER COMPANY.

to whether he thinks it increases *his* profits. If his quotas have been met he will tell his friends, "It pays to advertise."

Everyone, for his own sake, should know something about modern promotional methods, because they tell him much of what he knows about the goods and services that are for sale. On the basis of this information, he spends—wisely or foolishly—his precious dollars. From promotion come the images we form of brands and types of products and of the companies that make them. From promotion come many of our ideas in fields not related to commerce—of political candidates, of social mores, of charitable organizations, and of public service ideas ("The life you save may be your own"). Advertising and promotion are inextricably woven into our social and economic fabric, and, as the United States moves along in the last half of the twentieth century, promotion becomes more and more complex, and takes on more functions.

SOME VIEWPOINTS ON ADVERTISING

Sir Winston Churchill:

Advertising nourishes the consuming power of men. It creates wants for a better standard of living. It sets up before a man the goal of a better home, better clothing, better food for himself and his family. It spurs individual exertion and greater production. It brings together in fertile union those things which otherwise would never have met.

Franklin Delano Roosevelt:

If I were starting my life over again I am inclined to think I would go into the advertising business in preference to almost any other.

Historian David Potter, in *People of Plenty:*

One might read fairly widely in the literature which treats of public opinion, popular culture, and the mass media in the United States without ever learning that advertising now compares with such long-standing institutions as the school and the church in the magnitude of its social influence. It dominates the media, it has vast power in the shaping of popular standards, and it is really one of the very limited group of institutions which exercise social control. Yet analysts of society have largely ignored it.

Aldous Huxley:

It is far easier to write ten passably effective sonnets, good enough to take in the not-enquiring critic, than to write one effective advertisement that will take in a few thousand of the uncritical buying public.

Sovetskaya Kultura (Soviet Culture Magazine):

The purposes of advertising in Soviet Russia are the following: (1) to educate public taste, (2) to develop demand, (3) to help consumers quickly find what they want to buy, (4) to help them buy it easily, and (5) to tell them the price.

Advertising Agency Chairman Arthur E. Meyerhoff:

The techniques of persuasion by which the Russians seek to subvert governments, win the allegiance of new countries, and turn every political situation to their own advantage, are fundamentally the same psychological devices that we apply daily in selling products to consumers, and selling ideas at home.

Sociologist David Riesman, in *The Lonely Crowd:*

Academic and professional people are frequently only too pleased to be told that those horrid businessmen, those glad-handing advertisers, are manipula-

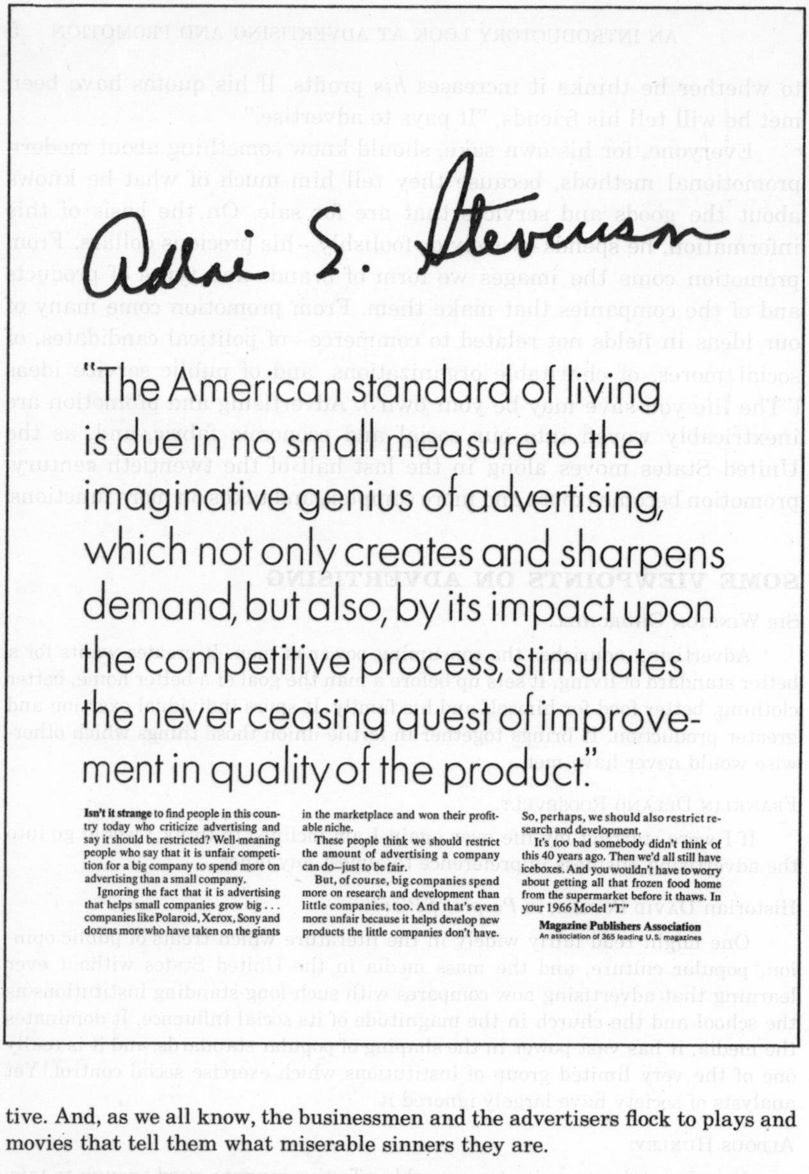

Adlai E. Stevenson

"The American standard of living is due in no small measure to the imaginative genius of advertising, which not only creates and sharpens demand, but also, by its impact upon the competitive process, stimulates the never ceasing quest of improvement in quality of the product."

Isn't it strange to find people in this country today who criticize advertising and say it should be restricted? Well-meaning people who say that it is unfair competition for a big company to spend more on advertising than a small company.

Ignoring the fact that it is advertising that helps small companies grow big . . . companies like Polaroid, Xerox, Sony and dozens more who have taken on the giants in the marketplace and won their profitable niche.

These people think we should restrict the amount of advertising a company can do—just to be fair.

But, of course, big companies spend more on research and development than little companies, too. And that's even more unfair because it helps develop new products the little companies don't have.

So, perhaps, we should also restrict research and development.

It's too bad somebody didn't think of this 40 years ago. Then we'd all still have iceboxes. And you wouldn't have to worry about getting all that frozen food home from the supermarket before it thaws. In your 1966 Model "T."

Magazine Publishers Association
An association of 365 leading U.S. magazines

FIG. 1.2 *Testimonial to the effectiveness of advertising from a noted public figure.* CLIENT: MAGAZINE PUBLISHERS ASSOCIATION; AGENCY: J. WALTER THOMPSON COMPANY.

tive. And, as we all know, the businessmen and the advertisers flock to plays and movies that tell them what miserable sinners they are.

Advertising Agency Chairman DAVID OGILVY:

Every advertisement must be considered as a contribution to the complex symbol which is the brand image. . . . The manufacturers who dedicate their advertising to building the most favorable image, the most sharply defined *personality* for their brands are the ones who will get the largest share of these markets at the highest profit—in the long run.

VANCE PACKARD, in *The Hidden Persuaders*:

The men and women who hold up these glowing images, particularly the professional persuaders, typically do so with tongue in cheek. The way these persuaders—who often refer to themselves good naturedly as "symbol manipulators"—see us in the quiet of their interoffice memos, trade journals and shop talk is frequently far less flattering, if more interesting. Typically they see us as bundles of daydreams, misty hidden yearnings, guilt complexes, irrational emotional blockages. We are image lovers given to impulsive and compulsive acts. We annoy them with our seemingly senseless quirks, but we please them with our growing docility in responding to their manipulation of symbols that stir us to action.

MARTIN MAYER, in *Madison Avenue, U.S.A.*:

Only the very brave or the very ignorant (preferably both) say exactly what it is that advertising does in the market place. The relative efficiency of advertising as a selling tool is arguable on the national scene and within specific industries. But advertising to the millions is unquestionably more efficient—less expensive per dollar of sales produced—than the old methods which saw individual salesmen working over individual customers. There can be no return to personal selling; capitalism is finally committed to the intensive use of advertising.

Economist JOHN KENNETH GALBRAITH, in *The New Industrial State*:

Management requires extensive access to means of communication—newspapers, billboards, radio and especially television. To insure attention these media must be raucous and dissonant. It is also of the utmost importance that this effort convey an impression however meretricious, of the importance of the goods being sold. The market for soap can only be managed if the attention of consumers is captured for what otherwise is a rather incidental artifact. Accordingly, the smell of soap, the texture of its suds, the whiteness of textiles treated thereby and the resulting esteem and prestige in the neighborhood are held to be of the highest moment. Housewives are imagined to discuss such matters with an intensity otherwise reserved for unwanted pregnancy and nuclear war.

A Trade Advertisement for Leo Burnett Company:

If you draw your conclusions from the self-styled experts in the field these days, advertising and selling are pretty sneaky stuff.

To hear these boys talk, you'd think advertising was one part psychiatry, to two parts brain washing, with a couple of dashes of henbane and dragonwort thrown in.

We happen to think that most people buy things because they need, want, and can use them.

And that people, regardless of their libidos or ids, like the kind of advertising that shows arresting pictures of these products and delivers fresh, truthful, interesting words about them.

SOME USEFUL DEFINITIONS

To the housewife, advertising can mean the advertisement in the Thursday newspaper telling her of the weekly specials at the supermarket; to her husband, it can mean the advertisement for the new Chevrolet "hardtop" he would like to buy; to their small children, it can mean the animated commercials for breakfast food that they see on television. To the teenager, it may mean the jingle he hears every evening on his radio.

All of these viewpoints focus on the *advertisement* rather than on *advertising*. In this book we shall take a comprehensive look at *advertising*, and analyze it from many viewpoints: those of the businessman, the social scientist, the consumer, and others. Consequently we shall use the following definition:

Advertising is paid, nonpersonal communication through various media by business firms, nonprofit organizations and individuals who are in some way identified in the advertising message.

Note that certain key words ("paid," "nonpersonal," "media," and "identified") are used to distinguish advertising from the many other forms of communication.

Promotion and *sales promotion* are terms that have caused much confusion in the marketing field. On the one hand, we have companies that have a "promotion manager" in charge of all those activities (except personal selling) that help to build demand for the products or services. He is responsible for advertising and publicity in the mass media as well as such supporting activities as point-of-sale displays, contests, premiums, and the like. Similarly, in the retail field, the coordinator of all forms of advertising and promotion is often called the "sales promotion manager." On the other hand, we have many firms which include functions like merchandising, cents-off deals, contests, premium offers, and such, under the heading of promotion and in this book this meaning will be used. In other words promotion includes all the other forms of communication which call attention to the promotional idea or in some way reinforce what is said in the advertising. For example, an automobile manufacturer will introduce its new model with a heavy barrage of both advertising and promotion. Advertisements

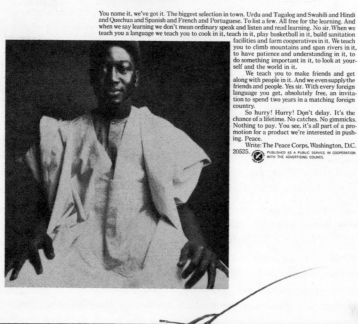

We'll teach you to speak a foreign language in thirteen weeks. Free!

You name it, we've got it. The biggest selection in town. Urdu and Tagalog and Swahili and Hindi and Quechua and Spanish and French and Portuguese. To list a few. All free for the learning. And when we say learning we don't mean ordinary speak and listen and read learning. No sir. When we teach you a language we teach you to cook in it, teach in it, play basketball in it, build sanitation facilities and farm cooperatives in it. We teach you to climb mountains and span rivers in it, to have patience and understanding in it, to do something important in it, to look at yourself and the world in it.

We teach you to make friends and get along with people in it. And we even supply the friends and people. Yes sir. With every foreign language you get, absolutely free, an invitation to spend two years in a matching foreign country.

So hurry! Hurry! Don't delay. It's the chance of a lifetime. No catches. No gimmicks. Nothing to pay. You see, it's all part of a promotion for a product we're interested in pushing. Peace.

Write: The Peace Corps, Washington, D.C. 20525. PUBLISHED AS A PUBLIC SERVICE IN COOPERATION WITH THE ADVERTISING COUNCIL.

FIG. 1.3 *One of a series of Peace Corps advertisements prepared by a volunteer task force of agency people for use in magazines. Supporting advertisements were prepared for newspapers, television, radio, and car cards.* COURTESY, THE ADVERTISING COUNCIL.

will be prepared for newspapers, magazines, television, radio, outdoor posters, and car cards. Promotion might consist of a dealers' get-together at which the new models are introduced with considerable fanfare; perhaps a contest in which the public is invited to write the last line of a jingle, or sponsorship of a road race for boys. There would be displays at major shows around the country. The company's dealers will also use both advertising and promotion, including among the latter such means as a city-wide auto show, an open house during the introductory period and a free gift to anyone who test-rides one of the new models.

Advertising and promotion are both considered forms of *communication*. This term, much abused at times, helps emphasize that there is more to both advertising and promotion than just the sending of messages. Unless there is someone to receive the message, we do not really have communication. Advertising is only one of many means of transmitting messages — a paid, nonpersonal means.

Another approach is that of the *marketing* program. The marketing-program approach, like the communication concept, focuses on the entire program and the use of a "mix" of elements. In marketing, we look at advertising in relation to personal selling, pricing, packaging, and other marketing tools that may be used to accomplish our marketing objective.

Most advertising is intended to lead eventually to a sale. Some, like mail order advertising, is designed to produce that sale immediately.

Some people call advertising "salesmanship in print," although that definition seriously shortchanges advertising. Much of today's advertising should more properly be called image-producing. It is designed to build or perpetuate a brand or corporate image.

There is an unfortunate tendency in some businesses to say "Let's charge it to advertising" whenever an unexpected expenditure arises. Such an attitude fails to draw a clear line between advertising and similar functions. Confusion has become more prevalent as advertising has moved into new areas of marketing and communication and as its functions and influence have spilled over into related areas.

Publicity, for example, may easily be confused with advertising or promotion. Like advertising, publicity is nonpersonal, is exposed in the media, and is used persuasively. There are, however, important differences — publicity is not paid for at established rates, and the sponsor is not identified. Usually, publicity appears — unidentified as such — in the editorial or news columns of printed media or in the noncommercial portion of radio or television programs.

Many companies supplement their advertising with publicity. For example, when one of the automobile manufacturers brings out a new model, it will inaugurate a big advertising campaign, and it will also prepare news releases in the hope that newspapers and television stations will use them in whole or in part when the new car is introduced.

A broader term than publicity, but one that is sometimes confused with publicity, promotion and advertising, is *public relations*. It has resulted in a plethora of definitions, but most practitioners agree that public relations involves the many practices used to build good relations with various sectors of the public. Public relations may, therefore, utilize advertising (particularly institutional advertising), publicity, or any other tools that might be appropriate. The automobile company that introduces a new model will conduct a continuous public relations program to build good will with its employees, its stockholders, its dealers, the owners of its cars, and so on. Public relations involves both good works and good communication.

SOME METHODS OF CLASSIFYING ADVERTISING

Advertising can be divided in various ways. Considered according to its audiences, there is one set of classifications; according to its functions or its media, there are others.

Audience. When Ivory Soap is advertised to the people who are going to use it, we have *consumer* advertising. If Ivory Soap's advertisements are directed to dealers, it is *business* advertising. The two most important audiences for business advertising are dealers and manufacturers. Some would classify advertising directed to farmers as farm advertising; others would include it under the heading of business advertising.

We might look at advertising audiences in terms of whether they are *mass* or *class* audiences. If you are advertising Ivory Soap, the chances are you will talk to a large, heterogeneous audience—a mass audience. However, if you are selling a soap that is very expensive or one with qualities that appeal only to a select group, you will probably address your advertisements to certain *classes* of people.

Type of Advertiser. There are two major types of advertisers who do most of the consumer advertising—*national* (general) and *local* (retail) advertisers. When the General Electric Company urges us, through magazines, television, radio, or some other medium, to buy a GE refrigerator, this is general or national advertising. On the other hand, if our local appliance dealer urges us to buy the refrigerator at his store, it is a retail advertisement. We may have advertising of both types for the same product in a single copy of our newspaper. In most cases the general advertiser pays higher rates for a given unit of space or time than the retail advertiser does.

The general advertiser seeks to persuade people to buy his brand wherever they may find it. The retail advertiser is eager to persuade them to buy at his store. The general advertiser emphasizes the product, the retailer emphasizes the store.

The national advertiser need not cover the entire country with his advertising. Some advertisers, such as General Electric and General Motors, do. The Oscar Mayer Company, however, had distribution only in certain areas of the country, although it is a general advertiser. Standard Oil Company (New Jersey) is a general advertiser, but it often advertises regionally because its heaviest distribution is in the eastern United States.

Media. Advertising can also be discussed on the basis of the media used to transmit the message. Thus we have newspaper advertising, radio advertising, television advertising, and many others.

Functions. Some people look at advertising in terms of what it does. On this basis we have, first of all, *product* and *institutional* advertising. When the Buick Division of General Motors runs an advertisement describing the virtues of the new Buick, this is obviously a product ad. However, when General Motors wants to enhance its corporate image through a description of its research facilities, it will use institutional advertising. The former is designed to sell the product, the latter to sell the institution.

Another way of looking at advertising functionally is on the basis of *direct-action* and *indirect-action* advertising. When the local drugstore ad shouts at you, "Come in today—Save at our one-cent sale!" it is using *direct-action* advertising. Virtually all the advertising in the Sears, Roebuck catalog is direct action. But when Cadillac suggests subtly, almost whispers, to you, "They'll take the Cadillac tonight," it is much less direct. Indirect advertising might be called the "soft sell"—direct advertising, the "hard sell."

Drowning...how can you save a child like Steve Berry?

One warm, sunny day, two-year-old Steve Berry was splashing around in his little backyard pool. His mother, thinking he was perfectly safe, went into the house to answer the phone. In those few unguarded minutes, Steve fell over. When Mrs. Berry returned, she found him face down in the water, limp and motionless.

She immediately started mouth-to-mouth rescue breathing—and saved her son's life.

Every year thousands drown—many of them children. Some of these tragedies are the result of carelessness and panic. Some, because children either don't know or don't obey the rules of water safety. And some happen because nobody present knows—as Steve's mother did—how to restore breathing. (Directions at right.)

America's drowning toll could be drastically cut if parents would take these precautions:

If there's a baby in your family, never leave him alone in a tub or basin—not even for the few seconds it takes to answer the doorbell. Very young children often have no fear at all of water, and when they're in even the shallowest of pools, constant supervision is vital.

If you're a child around three or four, it's not too early to start his swimming lessons. If you're not qualified to teach him yourself, get someone who is.

After a child learns to swim, forbid him to swim alone or at unsupervised beaches or pools, including even small backyard pools.

Warn him against playing pranks in the water. Jokingly calling for help and other such antics cause confusion and may lead to accidents of one sort or another.

Also make it clear that the one thing a swimmer in trouble should *never* do is panic or thrash around wildly. Your child should know how to conserve his strength and stay afloat until help arrives.

Metropolitan has published a booklet—*Panic or Plan?*—that covers a number of potential threats to your family's health and safety and tells you how to be prepared for them.

For a free copy, write to Metropolitan Life Insurance Company, Dept. A-66, One Madison Avenue, New York, N.Y. 10010.

How to give rescue breathing

1. Place one hand under victim's neck and lift. Tilt head back as far as possible by holding the crown of the head with your other hand.

2. Pull chin upward until the head is tilted back fully. This is essential for keeping the air passage open.

3. Place your mouth tightly over victim's mouth. Pinch nostrils shut. Breathe hard enough to make the chest rise. For babies and very young children, cover both nose and mouth tightly with your mouth. (For an adult, breathe vigorously about 12 times a minute. For a small child, take relatively short breaths, about 20 per minute.)

4. Remove mouth. Listen for sound of returning air. If you don't hear it, recheck head position. Breathe again. If you still get no air exchange, turn victim on side and slap between shoulders to dislodge foreign matter. Repeat breathing, removing mouth each time for escape of air. Don't give up. If possible call a physician.

Metropolitan Life
INSURANCE COMPANY

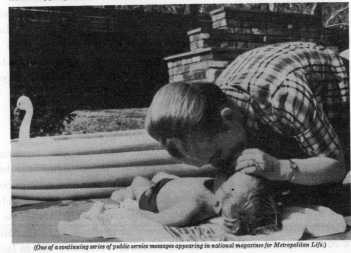

(One of a continuing series of public service messages appearing in national magazines for Metropolitan Life.)

FIG. 1.4 *Effective use of advertising to disseminate important information to a wide audience.* COURTESY OF METROPOLITAN LIFE INSURANCE COMPANY.

One other functional classification includes *primary* and *selective* advertising. The American Dairy Association announces, "You Never Outgrow Your Need for Milk." This is primary advertising, designed to promote a type or class of product rather than a particular brand. Pet Milk, however, is concerned with getting us to prefer Pet, so they talk about "double-rich, delicious Pet." Primary advertising promotes the class of product; selective advertising promotes a particular brand.

THEORY VERSUS PRACTICE

Advertising is more complicated than it might seem to the uninitiated. It is not possible to trace cause and effect in advertising as under the controlled conditions of the physical sciences. A chemist wanting to determine the effect of a certain compound he has formulated is able to control all the factors that might influence the outcome of his experiment. He can, therefore, attribute any effect he observes to the test ingredient.

The advertising man is less fortunate. Suppose he is advertising a soft drink and wants to observe the effect of an advertising campaign. He tries out the campaign in a test market and observes the effect in terms of sales. He finds that sales go up during this campaign, and he is optimistic. Then he starts examining other factors. He finds that one of the food chains had decided to run a special price deal on his product during the campaign. Furthermore, the area had an unusually hot spell and everyone, it seems, wanted soft drinks. All these are factors that he cannot control or scientifically evaluate. Nevertheless, he must try. If he is persistent and careful, he can add little by little to his store of knowledge about advertising, its theory, its practice, and its results. (The precariousness of thinking in terms of simple cause and effect is illustrated by a story told by researcher Alfred Politz. It concerns a man who "discovered" that soda water made him drunk. He changed all the other factors. He used whiskey with soda, brandy with soda, and many other combinations. But he got drunk every time. Since the soda was the only constant, it had to be the soda that made him drunk.)

Much of what we know comes from abstracting. In advertising, certain of our more imaginative analysts have looked at the available data and findings and come up with ideas. Some of these ideas are hypotheses that can be tested for accuracy. Many are still theories that are not provable. It is from these theories, though, that the pathways of progress are laid out in advertising, as in any endeavor.

ART VERSUS SCIENCE

People often ask whether advertising should more properly be termed an art or a science. Neither the practitioners nor the academicians have ever agreed on an answer, mainly because advertising has some of both. In general, creative people prefer to regard it as an art and themselves as artists who can, through their own innate creative ability, come up with effective ways of communicating advertising ideas. For example, a book of conversations with five top advertising writers (William Bern-

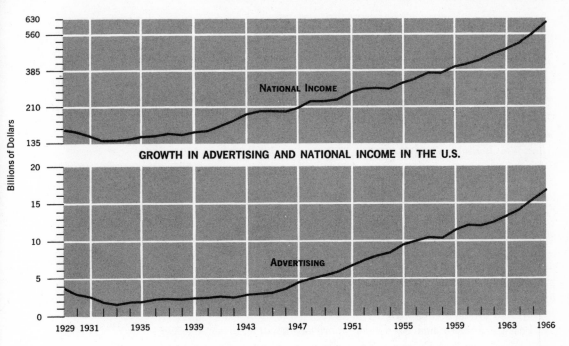

GROWTH IN ADVERTISING AND NATIONAL INCOME IN THE U.S.

FIG. 1.5 *Note how closely advertising expenditures tend to follow income over the long run.*

bach, Leo Burnett, George Gribbin, David Ogilvy, and Rosser Reeves) bore the title *The Art of Writing Advertising*.[1]

However, people who work in any of the areas of advertising closely related to marketing are likely to emphasize the science of advertising. Today's researchers, backstopped by great advances in research methodology and by computers, have come up with a mass of facts and have systematized much of what we know about advertising. From these facts have arisen principles which some will call "scientific," and some will not. But most persons will agree that they are useful guidelines for improving our practice. Scientists can test the product of the artist of advertising and tell how well it can accomplish its communication job.

Whether a person prefers to emphasize art or science, he must concede that advertising is constantly becoming more scientific. However, because it deals with people, and its main products are artistic expressions of human creativeness, it will never be an exact science.

HOW BIG IS ADVERTISING?

Advertising became big business in the United States in the years between World War I and World War II. Since 1946 it has become bigger and more influential than ever. For example, the total volume of advertising in 1967 was estimated by one authority as approximately $16,844,000,000 and by another as $17,300,000,000—about four and one-half times what it was in 1946.[2] Since World War II, advertising

---

[1]William Bernbach *et al., The Art of Writing Advertising* (Chicago: Advertising Publications, Inc., 1965).

[2]See *Marketing/Communications*, March 1968, and *Advertising Age*, April 8, 1968.

ADVERTISING EXPENDITURES
AND GROSS NATIONAL PRODUCT
AROUND THE WORLD

TABLE 1.1

	ADVERTISING EXPENDITURES		GROSS NATIONAL PRODUCT	
	Total (In millions of dollars)	Per Capita (In dollars)	Total (In billions of dollars)	Per Capita (In dollars)
United States	17,300.0	87.86	743.3	3,775
West Germany (inc. West Berlin)	1,853.5	31.05	119.6	2,004
Great Britain	1,550.0	28.11	105.3	1,916
Japan	1,276.0	12.90	97.5	986
France	831.0	17.03	101.4	2,052
Canada	830.0	41.29	53.3	2,660

SOURCE: *Advertising Age,* June 17, 1968, pp. 82, 88.

and related expenditures have been rising faster than gross national
product, national income, carloadings, or almost any barometer of
business activity. (See Figure 1.5) The reasons for this growth will be
explored in the next chapter.

Postwar growth has been even more spectacular in some other
countries. As western Europe and the Far East, for example, recovered
from the ravages of World War II, and companies started competing for
mass markets, advertising and promotion became essential parts of the
new economy. Large corporations like Unilever Limited and General
Motors have long been active all over the world, but since 1946 many
small and medium-sized companies have become international. Most
large advertising agencies in the United States, western Europe and
Japan have offices in several countries. In fact, the largest American
agency has more than one third of its billing and its offices outside the

Denmark   United States   Caribbean Area

United States. Media like *Reader's Digest* and *Paris Match* are circulated around the world, and satellites promise to make broadcasting truly international within a few years. Even socialist countries encourage the use of advertising by the managers of state-owned companies.

Slightly more than one half the world's advertising expenditure comes from the United States. However, during the 1960s expenditures have been increasing more rapidly in some other countries. As Table 1.1 indicates, expenditures per capita vary substantially even among well-developed countries.

One might also consider advertising in terms of the number of people it employs. The exact number of persons who work full time in some phase of advertising is not known. However, the American Association of Advertising Agencies estimated that in 1966 about 200,000 were employed in the four major areas of advertising: (1) agencies, (2) media, (3) advertisers, and (4) suppliers and special services. About half are employed as specialists in advertising. The 3,500 advertising agencies listed in national directories employ a total of nearly 70,000 men and women. The AAAA estimates that these four major branches will need a total of at least 20,000 new advertising specialists a year, 7,000 of them in advertising agencies alone.

FIG. 1.6 One of the most successful international advertising campaigns of recent years. Note how closely the advertisements in each market follow the original U.S. version. CLIENT: STANDARD OIL COMPANY OF NEW JERSEY; AGENCY: MCCANN-ERICKSON, INC.

We could also regard advertising in terms of its large users. For example, in 1967 Procter & Gamble spent more than $200,000,000 on various forms of advertising, and General Motors an estimated $160,000,000. The most heavily advertised product was Chevrolet, for which approximately $75,000,000 was spent. Or we might consider the agencies that represent the advertisers and place their advertising in the various media. The largest of the 3,500 agencies in the United States as well as the world in 1967 was J. Walter Thompson, which placed for its clients $590,600,000 of advertising ($363,600,000 of this in the United States) and employed 7,468 people in 56 offices around the world.

Belgium   Finland   Italy

SUMMARY

Most people have pronounced views, however erroneous, about advertising and promotion. In this chapter we have emphasized advertising as a paid, nonpersonal instrument of communication, and promotion as a supplementary activity to make advertising more effective.

To understand advertising we categorize it in these ways: retail or general, product or institutional, direct or indirect, primary or selective. We have seen that it is part theory, part practice, part art, part science. We should also think of advertising in terms of its size in dollars and personnel, and in terms of the variety of institutions that use it.

QUESTIONS FOR DISCUSSION

1. Why is advertising so difficult to define? Give four definitions of advertising as it exists today.
2. To what extent is modern advertising a science? To what extent is it an art?
3. How do you account for the internationalizing of advertising?
4. Name and explain four functions of advertising.
5. Collect from current periodicals examples of the best in modern advertising. Why do you consider these good advertisements?

2 | The Evolution of Modern Advertising and Promotion

An examination of the growth of advertising will help to clarify its social and economic functions. Without a look at its history some of its functions may seem strange. (For example, one might consider it curious that advertising agencies work only for the advertiser, yet receive the bulk of their income from the media. However, when considered historically, the practice makes sense.) In this chapter we shall try to capture some of the color and vitality of advertising as it grew. We shall try to identify some of the basic forces that made this growth possible. Efforts to persuade men to buy or trade something can be traced back thousands of years; the tools, the specialization, and the institutions that carry out this intention came later and have been refined to their present state largely since 1900.

EARLY PERIOD OF GROWTH

Street Criers, Signs, and Guilds. At first all advertising was vocal. In ancient Greece, town criers sold slaves and cattle, made public announcements, and chanted advertising rhymes that sounded something like today's singing commercials. A few years ago *Advertising Age* quoted this quatrain, said to have been used in ancient Athens:

For eyes that are shining, for cheeks like the dawn,
For beauty that lasts after girlhood is gone,
For prices in reason, the woman who knows,
Will buy her cosmetics of Aesclyptos.

The streets of ancient Rome and Carthage were also filled with barkers.

In England it was "What d'ye lack, sir?" or "Come, buy." Our own nursery rhyme books include the familiar

One-a-penny, two-a-penny, hot-cross buns!
One-a-penny, two for tuppence, hot-cross buns!

Some of the London criers used hyperbole: "Sprats as big as herrings, sprats all live, ho!" Others kidded their product: "Stinking shrimps today. Lor! 'Ow they do stink today, to be sure!" Some used humor: "My pretty little 'tater for a halfpenny stick, or a penny stick, or a stick to beat your wives or dust your cloths!" A few tried misrepresentation, like the vendor whose cry sounded like "Three hundred fifty songs for a penny!" but turned out to be "Three under fifty songs for a penny!"

According to James P. Wood, early New York was filled with such cries as

Clams! My clams I want to sell today,
The best of clams from Rockaway![1]

One of the well-known criers in pre-Revolutionary Philadelphia was a woman who sat in front of a toy shop, a basket of dried leaves and lavender on her lap, singing, "Lavender! Two cents a cup! Two cents for lavender." Other early Philadelphia street criers were, "Catfish! Catfish! Buy any catfish? Catfish!" and "Rags! Any rags? Any wool rags?" Criers seem to have come into their own again in radio and television.

The system of brand and trademark differentiation has its roots in the Middle Ages. Originally goods were sold in the immediate area where they were produced and there was no need for differentiating them. Later, however, marks were developed to identify the maker. When the medieval guild controlled quality, the mark became a great asset. For example, Osnabrück linen was carefully controlled for quality and commanded a price 20 percent higher than other Westphalian linens.[2] As production became more centralized and markets became more distant, the mark or identifying name took on more significance.

After the criers came signs. Most of the signs in ancient and medieval Europe and Asia were symbolic. A goat was the sign of a dairy in Rome, a mule driving a mill meant a bakery, and a boy being whipped was the sign for a school. In medieval England a coat of arms designated an inn, three nuns embroidering meant a draper's, a gilt arm wielding a hammer signified a goldbeater, and three pigeons and a scepter meant a thread maker.[3] The first cigar store Indians were carved in London by ships' carpenters from lengths of masts.

[1]James Playsted Wood, *The Story of Advertising* (New York: The Ronald Press Company, 1958), p. 21.

[2]Neil H. Borden, *The Economic Effects of Advertising* (Homewood, Ill.: Richard D. Irwin, Inc., 1942), p. 28.

[3]Wood, pp. 23–24.

Early English Advertising. In the early seventeenth century an important new medium gave advertising a substantial push forward. The first English newspaper, *The Weekly Newes*, was published in 1622 by Nicholas Bourne and Thomas Archer. One advertising historian, Henry Sampson, cites as the first bona fide newspaper advertisement one that appeared in 1650 in *Several Proceedings in Parliament.* It offered a reward for the return of twelve stolen horses. However, another historian, Frank Presbrey, asserts the first ad was an announcement in *Mercurius Britannicus* in 1625 of the publication of a book.

Both Joseph Addison and Richard Steele were devotees of advertising. In 1710 Addison wrote:

It is my Custom in a Dearth of News to entertain myself with those Collections of Advertisements that appear at the End of all our public Prints. These I consider as Accounts of News from the little World, in the same Manner that the foregoing Parts of the Paper are from the great. If in one we find the Victory of a General, in the other we see the Desertion of a private Soldier. I must confess, I have a certain Weakness in my Temper, that is often very much affected by these little Domestic Occurrences, and have frequently been caught with Tears in my Eyes over a melancholy Advertisement.[4]

Addison tried to develop certain principles of advertising. In one of his letters to the *Tatler* he included this advice to copywriters: "The great art in writing advertising is the finding out the proper method to catch the reader, without which a good thing may pass unobserved, or be lost among commissions of bankrupts. Of late years the N.B. has been much in fashion."

Addison and Steele joined forces in the *Spectator* when the *Tatler* was put out of business by the government. In the new publication one could find advertisements for tea, coffee, chocolate, auction sales, books, houses, patent medicines, and assignations. In 1710 the *Spectator* promoted a dentifrice as "the Incomparable Powder for cleaning of Teeth, which has given great satisfaction to most of the Nobility and Gentry in England."

In 1712 advertising in England was dealt a harsh blow when the government imposed a tax of a halfpenny on every newspaper or magazine sold, and an additional tax of a shilling on every advertisement published. This move was made to silence press criticism, not to raise money. But, in spite of the tax, advertising became very much a part of life in the eighteenth century. The Duke of Montague was convinced that one could make people believe literally anything in advertising. His friend Lord Chesterfield wagered that no one would believe it if Montague promised in an advertisement to present in a theater a man who would play "the music of every instrument now in use" on a walking cane and would go into "a common Wine Bottle" and sing. The ad appeared in several London papers in 1749. Montague was proved right. The house was jammed. However, the disappointed audience did not appreciate the joke; they tore the theater apart.

Advertising did not escape the all-encompassing eye of the eighteenth-century sage, Dr. Samuel Johnson. He wrote in the *Idler* in 1759:

---

[4]This and the following two excerpts by Addison and Steele are from the *Tatler*, September 14, 1710.

"Advertisements are now so numerous that they are very negligently perused, and it is therefore become necessary to gain attention by magnificence of promise and by eloquence sometimes sublime and sometimes ridiculous." Dr. Johnson's statement, "The trade of advertising is now so near perfection that it is not easy to propose any improvement," is often cited to indicate how naïve even a very wise man could be about advertising potential. Not so frequently quoted is the sentence which followed: "But as every art ought to be exercised in due subordination to the public good, I cannot but propose as a moral question to these masters of the public ear, Whether they do not sometimes play too wantonly with our passions?"

John Walter founded the now venerable *London Times* in 1788. He felt that "a News-Paper . . . ought to resemble an Inn, where the proprietor is obliged to give the use of his house to all travellers who are ready to pay for it and against whose person there is no legal or moral objection." During this period people used newspaper ads to announce what they wanted to buy or sell. Many ads were of the classified type—appeals for positions, places to live, friends of the opposite sex and offers of household goods for sale.

Mathew Carey, a militant Irishman and editor of the anti-English Dublin newspaper, *Volunteers Journal*, in 1784 made a strong solicitation for advertisers, using sales arguments similar to the ones that we hear today—wide circulation and heavy readership.

Early American Advertising. The first issue of colonial America's first successful newspaper, published in 1704, contained an advertisement promoting the newspaper as a medium for advertisers. In 1729, Benjamin Franklin, often regarded as the father of American advertising, began publishing his *Gazette*. As Wood points out, "Advertising and public relations, especially self-advertising and publicity, were as natural to Franklin as his curiosity, restless intelligence, and practicality. Franklin, in all his roles and on behalf of all his varied activities, was always the untiring promoter. He put advertising before editorial in the masthead of the first issue of the *Pennsylvania Gazette*."[5] Franklin's first issue contained a soap advertisement. The *Gazette* soon had the largest circulation and the largest advertising volume of any paper in colonial America. In it one could find ads for ship sailings, quills, books, wine, tea, chocolate, and many other commodities. In 1864 a biographer wrote about Franklin, "I think we must admit . . . that it was Franklin who originated the modern system of advertising. It is certain that he was the first man who used the mighty engine of publicity, as we use it now."[6]

Franklin was a copywriter as well as advertising manager, salesman, publisher, and editor. Perhaps his most famous piece of advertising copy was for the Pennsylvania Fireplace (the Franklin stove):

Fireplaces with small openings cause draughts of cold air to rush in at every crevice, and 'tis very uncomfortable as well as dangerous to sit against any

[5]Wood, p. 46.
[6]James Parton, *Life and Times of Benjamin Franklin* (New York: Mason Brothers, 1864).

such crevice. . . . Women, particularly from this cause (as they sit so much in the house) get cold in the head, rheums and deflexions which fall into their jaws and gums, and have destroyed early, many a fine set of teeth in these northern colonies.

Franklin, like today's more sophisticated copywriters, emphasized the rewards derived from the product (health and comfort) rather than the product itself. He was one of the principal colonial spokesmen against the hated tax on periodicals and advertising, levied in England in 1712 (it was not enforced in the colonies until 1765) and was successful in lining up support for his stand from powerful British politicians such as Edmund Burke and William Pitt.

Like Franklin, Paul Revere was a man of versatility. He was an engraver, a silversmith, a goldsmith, a manufacturer of gunpowder and false teeth — and an advertiser of these products. This advertisement for his wares appeared in 1768:

WHEREAS many Persons are so unfortunate as to lose their Fore-Teeth by Accident, and otherways, to their great detriment, not only in Looks, but speaking both in Public and Private:—This is to inform all such, that they may have them re-placed with artificial Ones that looks as well as the Natural, & answers the End of Speaking to all Intents, by PAUL REVERE, Goldsmith, near the Head of Dr. Clarke's Wharf, Boston.

George Washington was both an advertiser and a buyer of advertised products. He advertised in an attempt to attract settlers to his land. In a letter dated January 29, 1789, he wrote for some "superfine American Broad Cloths" and "London Smoke" as described in an advertisement in the *New York Daily Advertiser*.

RISE OF MASS PRODUCTION

Early Nineteenth-century Advertising in America. Newspaper advertising prospered in early nineteenth-century America. The more conservative newspapers (*Massachusetts Spy*) avoided front-page advertisements while others (*Providence Gazette*) devoted all or most of the first page to advertising. Many papers carried full inside pages of advertisements.

Most of the ads during this period were classified ads (wives looking for wandering husbands, owners looking for runaway slaves, householders looking for servants). However, there were a few insertions by advertisers well known today in national advertising. For example, Pierre Lorillard, who opened his tobacco factory in 1760, advertised snuff, "segars," and plug tobacco in American newspapers before the turn of the nineteenth century. By 1830, many advertisers were using broadsides (large folders which when opened became a poster-style advertisement) as well as newspapers.

The advent of the penny newspaper, with its increased circulation, made the newspaper even more desirable as an advertising medium. A twenty-three-year-old job printer, Benjamin H. Day, founded the first of these in 1833, the *New York Sun*. He was the first publisher to hire advertising solicitors to contact prospects, and boys to sell newspapers to the public. Like his penny competitors, the publishers of the *Tran-*

script and the *Herald,* he took all the advertising he could get, including patent medicine advertising.

James Gordon Bennett, colorful publisher of the *New York Herald*, was not dismayed when readers complained about the quantity and quality of his advertising. He replied "Business is business—money is money." Horace Greeley, publisher of the *New York Tribune*, suggested that people who had complaints about the patent medicine advertising should address them to the advertisers themselves.

Magazine publishing in America began in the early eighteenth century. Many of our first magazines were pamphlets or booklets, designed to influence opinion or to raise cultural standards. Until 1860, approximately 60 percent of all magazines expired within a year after they started publication.

The publishers of early American magazines did not think of them as advertising media. The first successful magazine in America, *Godey's Lady's Book*, was a class fashion magazine in the style of today's *Vogue* or *Harper's Bazaar*. It used color illustrations to display its fashions but did not carry advertising. The *Southern Literary Messenger*, edited briefly by Edgar Allan Poe, carried one notice labeled "Advertisement" in its issue of July 1844. In the early nineteenth century there was little reason to stimulate the masses to buy. It was difficult enough to manufacture what the consuming public already wanted.

Origins of the Advertising Agency. The idea of agencies to handle advertising for clients is usually attributed to the great French essayist, Montaigne. In 1588 he proposed that anyone "who had pearls to sell or wanted a servant or company on a trip to Paris" could make his needs known to "an officer" appointed for that purpose. This was far different from today's agency, but the officer was, in a sense, an advertising agent.

FIG. 2.1 *Nineteenth-century patent medicine advertisement.*

Some people see a moral in the fact that the first advertising agency head in the United States went mad. According to a contemporary, Volney Palmer was "a capital story teller, wore gold spectacles, carried a gold handled cane and was a first class canvasser. . . . He had more self-possession and assurance than any man I ever knew."[7]

After soliciting advertising for various newspapers, Palmer set himself up as an agent in Philadelphia in 1841. In 1845 he established a branch office in Boston and one in New York in 1849. After preparing advertising for various advertisers, he collected 25 percent of the cost of the advertising from the newspapers and the rest from the advertisers.

A farm boy from New Hampshire, George P. Rowell, was the most important of the early and mid-nineteenth-century advertising agents. Although Volney Palmer's concern was primarily a newspaper agency, Rowell developed his agency to sell advertising space at wholesale. Rowell anticipated the needs of the advertisers, bought space in large quantities, and resold it in smaller lots. He saw the profit opportunities in taking over certain risks of publishing. The publishers were happy to sell him large blocks of space at reduced rates. He could then sell the space to advertisers at lower rates than they could find elsewhere and still make a profit for himself. He was thus a middleman. Not surprisingly, other agents copied his mode of operation when they noted his success.

Historians agree that the early advertising agency played a vital role in developing advertising and all of American business. Historian Ralph Hower says, in summarizing the role of the agency from 1841 to 1869:

> The advertising agency came into existence because the ignorance of both publisher and advertiser, together with their genuine economic need for assistance, presented an opportunity for profit. The agency facilitated the purchase and sale of space. . . . In a larger sense, however, the agency's chief service in this early period was to promote the general use of advertising, and thus to aid in discovering cheaper and more effective ways of marketing goods.[8]

The modern agency, which plans and prepares advertising campaigns for an advertiser-client, did not become common until the latter part of the nineteenth century.

The Civil War Period. Immediately before and after the Civil War, there began a great era of business expansion in the United States. Technological discoveries made it possible to expand production significantly and to replace hand labor with power-driven machinery. This increased enormously the goods available for marketing.

The unrestricted excesses of the period are much in evidence in advertising and communication practices of the time. Consider, for example, the most flamboyant communicator of the period, Phineas Taylor Barnum, who was more publicity agent than advertising man. His first coup involved Joice Heth, a woman he featured in 1835 as the 161-year-old nurse of George Washington. She was totally blind and

[7]Earnest Elmo Calkins and Ralph Holden, *Modern Advertising* (New York: Appleton-Century-Crofts, 1905), p. 16.
[8]Ralph M. Hower, *The History of an Advertising Agency*, rev. ed. (Cambridge, Mass.: Harvard University Press, 1949), p. 19.

had no teeth, but she had been coached to repeat the cherry tree story and say, "I raised him." Barnum flooded New York with handbills, posters, and stories for the newspapers. He was undaunted by the fact that when Joice Heth died at the height of her highly successful career, an autopsy showed that she was only about eighty years old. Barnum ran a series of articles proclaiming his good faith in the whole matter.

Throughout his spectacular career, Barnum used advertising as an integral part of his showmanship. He defrauded the public again and again, but there was no Federal Trade Commission to bother him. Unlike some of his latter-day counterparts, he admitted to most of his frauds, and the people loved him for it.

The dominant newspaper advertising medium in the mid-nineteenth century was the *New York Herald*. Editor James Gordon Bennett's sensationalism and exposure of various frauds paid off in what was a huge circulation in pre-Civil War days—30,000 to 40,000 daily. Bennett was one of the first newspapermen to realize that people buy papers for the advertisements as well as the news items. He had access to the huge, growing New York market, and the expanding traders and manufacturers needed his medium. He specified that all advertising be run in solid columns (no display). No advertisement was allowed to break the column rule. Many tried subterfuges in their attempts to attract attention, but most were stopped by the vigilance of Bennett and his business staff.

The Civil War crushed the last powerful aristocracy in this country. At the close of the Civil War the middle class became the ruling class. As critic Norman Foerster says, "The new kings had machines for their scepters." Factories rose in the cities, and industrial production shot up.

Borden has noted the dearth of manufacturers' advertising before 1880. He says:

> Manufacturers' brands were frequently mentioned in retailers' advertisements, but the number of advertisements placed by manufacturers, excepting those producing books and medicines, were relatively few. After the eighties the number of manufacturers who carried their messages to consumers increased rapidly. At the same time, retailers also made increased use of advertising.[9]

Era of Bold Enterprise. During the period 1875–1905, advertising, like other businesses, was bold and vigorous. This was a period of laissez-faire, and few questions were asked of the successful entrepreneur. There were, for the first time, national markets, a transcontinental railroad, and major urban centers. New York had only 200,000 people in 1840, but in 1870 it had almost 1,500,000 and 3,500,000 by 1905. Centers such as Chicago, Pittsburgh, Cleveland—even Kansas City, and Omaha—became major cities during this period. This growing urban concentration helped industrial technology to operate more efficiently. Industry, in turn, made life easier for city dwellers.

In the post-Civil War period John Wanamaker, with the help of advertising and shrewd merchandising, was able to build in Philadelphia the largest men's retail clothing establishment in the United

[9]Borden, p. 34.

FIG. 2.2 This advertisement appeared in the Woman's Home Companion *in 1890.*

States. He had signs one hundred feet long posted along the Pennsylvania Railroad tracks leading into Philadelphia. He used newspaper advertising consistently. In 1876 he established the Wanamaker department store. Wanamaker was delighted with the success of his advertising. "Advertising," he said on one occasion, "is no game for the quitter. Advertising does not jerk — it pulls."

Artemus Ward, both a philosopher of sorts and a highly successful copywriter, wrote the Sapolio Soap ads. Ward made the advertising copy light, amusing, and quotable. In 1900 Ward launched his famous Spotless Town pictures and verses. According to Calkins and Holden, these were the first successful advertising jingles:

> This is the maid of fair renown
> Who scrubs the floors of Spotless Town,
> To find a spec when she is through
> Would take a pair of specs or two
> And her employment isn't slow
> For she employs Sapolio.

For the Lackawanna Railroad, Earnest Elmo Calkins wrote a series of advertisements about the immaculate Phoebe Snow. For example:

> Says Phoebe Snow
> About to go
> Upon a trip
> To Buffalo:
> "My gown stays white
> From morn till night
> Upon the Road of Anthracite."

Some time prior to 1905, Calkins prepared what he believed was the first national advertising plan. The plan was developed for the Gillette Safety Razor. In a letter to Professor P. D. Converse, Calkins tells of it "with all phases described, and illustrated with graphs, charts, rough sketches of advertisements for magazines, newspapers, trade journals, posters, window cards, booklets, window displays."[10]

An advertising man who summed up the opportunities of this period very astutely and acted accordingly was Francis Wayland Ayer.

[10]Quoted in Paul D. Converse, *The Beginning of Marketing Thought in the United States* (Austin: University of Texas, 1959), p. 30.

In 1869 he founded N. W. Ayer and Son, still one of America's largest agencies. He came from a simple rural home where thrift, hard work, and Puritan asceticism were emphasized.

Rapid expansion, feverish activity, ceaseless change, alarming complexity in every walk of life—how in all this confusion could an inexperienced youth chart a course of action? To a timid man the prospect must have seemed bewildering. But to a man of courage and enterprise, the very enlargement of economic life meant opportunity. In the economic organization that was growing up in America after the Civil War, the role of advertising was to become a vital one. There was to be almost unlimited opportunity as well as profits commensurate with the risks and efforts involved.[11]

The Ayer agency started advertising in eleven religious papers, to which it expected to confine its efforts. Ayer bought the entire space in these and sold it for what he could get. Then, sometime between 1880 and 1895, the agency began to prepare copy for its clients. It was, according to Hower, among the first, if not *the* first, to supply service as well as sell space. It became the forerunner of today's general advertising agency.

Era of Reexamination. In Chicago a confident ex-Texan, Albert Lasker, built an agency primarily around the function of copywriting. He had as his helpers two of the greatest copywriters in advertising history—John E. Kennedy and Claude C. Hopkins. During his career as head of this agency, Albert Lasker made (according to his own estimate) $40,000,000 or $60,000,000; he was not sure which.

Hopkins studied people at some length and decided early in his career that people liked to buy. Furthermore, he found that they wanted reasons for buying—preferably selfish reasons. He is the father of "reason-why copy." At Lasker's behest, Hopkins applied this idea to the selling of such products as Dr. Shoop's Restorative, Schlitz Beer, and Liquozone. When he was working on the Schlitz account, for example, he went through the brewery, where he was impressed by the fact that the bottles were cleaned with steam. This process was used by every leading brewery, but Hopkins thought of it as a possible reason for buying Schlitz beer. He featured the purity of Schlitz, attributing it to the use of the live steam used to clean Schlitz beer bottles. He never said that Schlitz alone did this. But competitors hesitated to point out that they too used steam. They feared they would be accused of "me-tooing" Schlitz.

Hopkins made one of the first market surveys. He sent interviewers from door to door to find out whether people baked their own beans. (He found that they did.) As a result, his agency, Lord and Thomas, launched a campaign for Van Camp's Pork and Beans, claiming that home-baked beans were hard to digest and mushy, and supplying reasons why Van Camp's were superior (Fig. 2.3).

During the first two decades of the twentieth century, advertising continued its phenomenal growth, but occasionally it was forced to justify itself. This was a period of trust busting, and many looked askance at certain business practices.

[11]Ralph M. Hower, *The History of an Advertising Agency*, rev. ed. (Cambridge, Mass.: Harvard University Press, 1949), p. 27.

How to Bake Beans

We have no secrets, madam. We are going to tell how you—if you had the facilities—could bake Pork and Beans exactly as good as Van Camp's.

Get the choicest of Michigan beans, picked over by hand. Get only the whitest, the plumpest, the fullest-grown. Have them all of one size.

You will need to pay from six to eight times what some beans would cost, but they're worth it. Soak the beans over night, then parboil them.

Now comes the impossible. The beans must be baked in live steam, and you lack it. That steam must be superheated to 245 degrees.

Dry heat won't do. You can't supply enough dry heat without burning the beans to a crisp.

Then the beans must be baked in small parcels — we bake in the cans. That's so the full heat of the oven can attack every particle. Otherwise the beans will not be digestible. They will ferment and form gas, as do your home-baked beans now.

Bake the tomato sauce with the beans — bake it into them. That's how we get our delicious blend.

When the beans are baked until they are mealy, surround the can with cold water. That stops the baking instantly, and sets the blend and savor.

Then you will have beans that are wholly digestible. All beans will be baked alike, yet not a skin will be broken. The beans will be nutty because they are whole.

Then the tomato sauce — that's impossible for you. It must be made from whole, vine-ripened tomatoes, picked when the juice fairly sparkles.

When you buy the sauce, you rarely know what you are getting. If it is made from tomatoes picked green, it lacks zest. If made of scraps from a canning factory, it lacks richness.

Some tomato sauce is sold ready-made for exactly one-fifth what we spend to make ours.

Our point is this: It isn't your fault that home-baked beans are mushy and broken — crisped on the top and half-baked in the middle. That they are neither nutty nor mealy — nor even digestible. That they always ferment and form gas. It is simply your lack of facilities.

Van Camp's PORK AND BEANS

The best way is to let us cook them for you. We have all the facilities. Let us furnish the meals—fresh and savory—ready for instant serving.

Think how unwise it is to bake your own beans when you can get Van Camp's. Here is Nature's choicest food — 84 per cent nutriment. More food value than meat at a third the cost. A food you should serve at least three times a week. Think what you are missing, and what your people are missing when you spoil such a dish as that.

Leave the choice to your people. Ask them which beans they want. And be glad of their choice. For, if they like Van Camp's, see the bother you save. And see what you save on your meat bills.

Three sizes: 10, 15 and 20 cents per can.

The Van Camp Packing Company, Established 1861 Indianapolis, Ind.

FIG. 2.3 *This* Ladies Home Journal *advertisement of 1908 is typical of the Claude Hopkins long-copy, reason-why technique.*

Reforms and exposés were fashionable in the early 1900s, and it is not surprising that advertising was caught in the cleanup movement. The focal point of attack was the patent medicine ad. The religious papers, strangely enough, were among the worst offenders in accepting questionable patent medicine advertising. One could find ads in them that promised to cure almost any disease. Some magazines accepted the ads because they were on the verge of bankruptcy and could not afford to be particular.

In 1903 the Scripps-McRae League of Newspapers was sufficiently stirred by attacks to appoint a censor to scrutinize advertising copy. According to Willard G. Bleyer, $500,000 of advertising was refused during the first year.[12]

[12]Willard G. Bleyer, *Main Currents in the History of American Journalism* (Boston: Houghton Mifflin Company, 1927), p. 417.

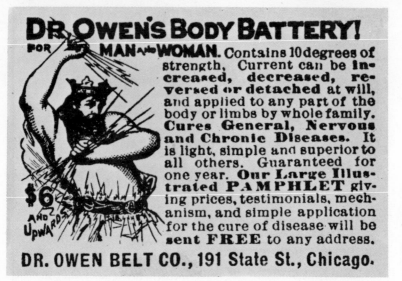

FIG. 2.4 *This advertisement, first published in 1888, is all too typical of medical and proprietary advertising of the late nineteenth century.*

The Associated Advertising Clubs of America, later to become the Advertising Federation of America, helped to launch a campaign for truthful and ethical advertising. The association drew up a code for ethical advertising in 1911 and adopted the slogan: "Truth in Advertising."

The magazine of the advertising industry, *Printers' Ink*, joined the fight. The publisher of *Printers' Ink* had a lawyer draw up a model state law that would penalize false and misleading advertising. This was the famous Printers' Ink Statute (Fig. 7.3).

In 1910 Cyrus Curtis, a successful magazine publisher, published the Curtis Advertising Code, which set forth in specific terms the kind of advertising that would not be handled by Curtis publications (for example, "knocking" copy, medical or curative copy, and advertisements for alcoholic liquors).

Psychologist Walter Dill Scott was one of the first to approach advertising as an academic discipline. In his *Theory of Advertising* (1903) Scott wrote, "There should be a theoretical basis for every important practical undertaking."[13] He pointed out that leading advertisers were asking for fundamental principles on which a "rational theory of advertising" could be constructed.

RISE OF MASS MARKETING AND MASS COMMUNICATION

Era of Salesmanship. During World War I much advertising, like other business activities, was directed to the service of our country. Government advertisements said, "I Want YOU for the U.S. Army." Individual companies used war themes in their ads (Kodak's "Ask Your Soldier Boy or Sailor Boy to Send Pictures to You").

[13]Walter Dill Scott, *The Theory of Advertising* (Boston: Small, Maynard & Co., 1903), p. 48.

FIG. 2.5 *A new word—
"Halitosis"—is added to
our vocabulary.*

The 1920s was a period of fantastic growth for advertising. Total expenditures, only $2,282,000,000 in 1919, rose to $3,426,000,000 in 1929. It is not surprising that advertising flourished in this colorful era. Wood describes it thus:

> The period from the end of World War I until the stock market crash of 1929 was a period of extremes, of cynicism and enthusiasm, of reckless optimism and romantic despair, of flaming youth and the lost generation, of impatience with everything that was old and a fever for what was new. It was the period of the bobbed-hair flapper and John Held's cartoons, of the sharpies and the "final hoppers," of T. S. Eliot's *The Waste Land* and the early novels of Hemingway, of *Main Street* and *Babbitt*, of the discovery and exploitation of sex, of bathtub gin, companionate marriage and Rotary. Greenwich Village was so self-consciously wicked it hugged itself in ecstasy; the Algonquin wits were dazzled by their own brilliance; Edna St. Vincent Millay sang the vitality and weary disillusionment of the flapper in her lyrics, and Vachel Lindsay happily thumped out his booming verse.[14]

For the first time, not only was marketing (including advertising and selling) respectable—it was considered equal in importance to production. The high-pressure salesman and the high-pressure advertising man were the darlings of the 1920s. Both helped the growth of the mass markets needed to support our mass-production facilities.

Gerald B. Lambert has written that he once feared his tombstone would bear the inscription, "Here Lies the Body of the Father of Halitosis." Another disease that advertising men "discovered" in the 1920s

[14]Wood, p. 364.

FIG. 2.6 *Typical of the early advertisements in one of advertising's most successful campaigns.*

was "athlete's foot." That disease enabled the W. F. Young Company to sell millions of bottles of Absorbine, Jr. The manufacturers and marketers of Ipana discovered "pink tooth brush"; the Pepsodent men (and Claude Hopkins) discovered "film on teeth."

Edward S. Jordan, president of a motor car company and an experienced advertising man, wrote one of the most influential ads of the 1920s. It appeared in *The Saturday Evening Post* on June 23, 1923, and was surprisingly like some of today's auto advertisements. It bore the heading "Somewhere West of Laramie" and started this way:

SOMEWHERE WEST of Laramie there's a broncho-busting, steer-roping girl who knows what I'm talking about. She can tell what a sassy pony, that's a cross between greased lightning and the place where it hits, can do with eleven hundred pounds of steel and action that's going high, wide and handsome.

Unlike most auto ads of the time it was "image-building" rather than "reason why."

The car that probably aroused more excitement than any car before or since was introduced in 1927. This was the Ford Model A. After months of suspense built up by rumor, carefully leaked bits of news, and coyness on the part of Henry Ford, the following ad announced the big event:

IMPORTANT FACTS ABOUT

The New Ford Car

The new Ford has exceptional beauty of line and color. It is in every respect, a new and modern car, designed and created to meet modern conditions. . . . The new Ford has unusual speed and power. It will do 55 and 60 miles an hour with ease and has run 65 miles an hour on road tests. . . .

In addition to the accomplishments mentioned earlier, Albert D. Lasker and his client, George Washington Hill, head of American Tobacco Company, promoted smoking among women and lovers of sweets and helped convince doubting businessmen that advertising really paid. Lucky Strike sales boomed, and advertising appropriations rose to $19,000,000 in 1931. According to *Advertising Age*, Lasker paid one of his copywriters a bonus of $10,000 for "So round, so firm, so fully packed, so free and easy on the draw."

The J. Walter Thompson Company discovered that movie star testimonials helped to sell Lux Soap. Other agencies soon followed the pattern.

A major new advertising medium, radio, was added during the 1920s. At first most of the radio ads were indirect, in that there was no plea for sales, just a mention of the product ("brought to you through the courtesy of . . ."). *Printers' Ink* and Herbert Hoover, then Secretary of Commerce, opposed the idea of making radio an advertising medium.

It was soon evident, however, that it would take a great deal of money to support radio. There were alternative means of support, but advertising was the quickest and handiest. WEAF, the first commercial radio station, opened in 1922. In 1924 N. W. Ayer produced the first sponsored broadcast (the Eveready Hour) over a network. By 1928 radio

FIG. 2.7 *A famous image-building advertisement of the 1920s.*

accounted for $10,500,000 of the advertising in the United States. Two classes of advertisers dominated early radio, just as they dominate much radio and television advertising today: makers of low-priced, mass-consumption items, such as cigarettes, soft drinks, and toothpaste; and makers of major durable items, such as appliances and automobiles. Radio was, in fact, the most rapidly growing advertising medium during the 1920s. By 1930, more than 50 percent of the homes in the United States had radios.

The Depression Years. The depression of the 1930s brought about a searching examination of the economic system that had allowed such a debacle to happen. The professional critics and the public looked for scapegoats. One of the favorite targets was advertising. The attacks on advertising in the 1930s were different from previous ones. The attacks were more bitter and far-reaching. The attackers struck at the very existence of advertising, rather than at its excesses or the products advertising promoted. Best-selling books such as *100,000,000 Guinea Pigs* and *Skin Deep*, as well as *Eat, Drink and Be Wary*, "exposed" advertising as the unscrupulous exploiter of the consumer. Consumer's Research and Consumers Union were formed to provide unbiased information for consumers. Any organization that promised to save money for people found a ready audience in the 1930s.

Some of the opposition to advertising crystallized in the form of restrictive laws. The proposed Tugwell Bill, for example, called for compulsory grade labeling of canned goods, drugs, and cosmetics. A much modified version of the bill was passed in 1938 as the Federal Food, Drug and Cosmetics Act. The Wheeler-Lea amendments to the Federal Trade Commission Act (1938) granted to the FTC added power over false advertising. It was designated as an "unfair or deceptive act or practice in commerce." The new law called for special vigilance in the advertising of foods, drugs, and cosmetics.

What was the effect of restrictive laws? Otis Pease, after a careful study of advertising during the 1920s and 1930s, concluded, "The increase in the powers and in the regulatory activity of the FTC which occurred in the summer of 1938 was in all probability only the culmination of a larger sequence of factors which over the course of the previous decade, had tended to encourage greater honesty and accuracy in a large number of national advertisements."[15] The Wheeler-Lea amendments, in other words, took effect when the worst abuses of public confidence had begun to abate.

Not surprisingly, the appeal to thrift was especially effective in advertising during the depression years. George Washington Hill brought back Bull Durham, famous earlier as a chewing tobacco, with "Roll Your Own and Save Your Roll." Popular cigarettes, selling at fourteen and fifteen cents a pack in 1932, were challenged by relatively unadvertised ten-cent brands. In December 1932, at the height of their popularity, the ten-centers accounted for 23.17 percent of total cigarette sales.

[15]Otis Pease, *The Responsibilities of American Advertising* (New Haven, Conn.: Yale University Press, 1958), p. 108.

The sales resistance of consumers during the depression forced advertising men to turn to research as they seldom had before. Perhaps the researchers could find out why people bought one brand rather than the other, or did not buy at all. And what radio programs did people listen to? Why? Researchers such as A. C. Nielsen, George Gallup, Arch Crossley, and Daniel Starch established companies to find answers to questions such as these. Research business, in general, prospered during the depression years.

Modern Advertising. During World War II advertising turned once again to government and institutional advertising. The War Advertising Council, supported and manned by advertising men, planned and executed public service campaigns during the war. The Council worked with the Treasury Department to help sell war bonds, with the Navy to recruit women for the WAVEs (enlistments, according to the Council, doubled), and with the Public Health Service to get volunteer cadet nurses. For the Army, it said to soldiers: "Take care of your equipment and your equipment will take care of you."

Probably the most famous World War II advertisement was prepared for the New York, New Haven & Hartford Railroad. It carried the headline: "The Kid in Upper Four." The copy started this way:

It is 3:42 a.m. on a troop train. Men wrapped in blankets are breathing heavily, two in every lower berth, one in every upper. This is no ordinary trip. It may be their last in the United States until the end of the war. Tomorrow they will be on the high seas. . . .

Although advertising boomed during the 1940s and 1950s, so did criticism of it. *The Hucksters*[16] and *The Hidden Persuaders*,[17] were high on the best-seller lists for months. Both painted a picture of the advertising world that disturbed many observers and aroused latent criticism. Again, advertising was called on to justify its existence and to clean house, where necessary.

Television, another mammoth medium, had been added to the advertising world. Television expenditures were computed for the first time by *Printers' Ink* in 1949—$57,800,000. By 1967 they had risen to $2,923,000,000, and more than 10 percent of the homes in the United States had color television. During the 1940s and 1950s motivation researchers like Ernest Dichter and Burleigh Gardner probed man's subconscious in their search for successful advertising themes. Other researchers experimented with linear programming and fed masses of data into computers in their attempt to make promotional decisions more accurate.

THE FORCES BEHIND THE FACTS

The phenomenal growth of advertising during the past century and a half is irrefutable. It is not quite so clear, however, just what forces lie beneath that growth. Certain aggressive, bright individuals have had much to do with it. Advertising is a highly personal business. Yet there

[16]Frederick Wakeman, *The Hucksters* (New York: Rinehart & Company, 1946).
[17]Vance Packard, *The Hidden Persuaders* (New York: D. McKay & Co., 1957).

were certainly nonpersonal forces at work which contributed to this
phenomenon:

1. Growth in productivity per worker. An efficient way had to be
   found to stimulate demand.
2. Technological developments. These made improvements in
   production and distribution and communication systems.
3. Increase in income. A prosperous population is an attractive
   market for the advertiser.
4. Growth of the middle class. The prosperous middle class,
   growing steadily as a percentage of the total population, became the bulk of the advertiser's audience.
5. Growth of transportation. This made national markets and
   central producing points feasible.
6. Increase in education. A literate, better educated populace is
   eager to live better and can be more easily influenced by advertising.
7. Decline of personal selling. Advertising can do many kinds of
   selling more cheaply and efficiently.
8. Growth of specialized advertising organizations. Advertising
   agencies helped institutionalize and professionalize the advertising industry and helped convince business of the usefulness
   of advertising.
9. Growth in research. This made advertising more productive
   and helped lessen the guesswork.
10. Growth of brands and variety of merchandise. Advertising tries
    to build preference for certain brands.
11. Growth of large-scale manufacturing and servicing.
12. Remoteness of manufacturer from the consumer. Advertising
    provides communication.
13. Growth of self-service retailing. Advertising tries to presell the
    consumer.
14. Growth and public acceptance of consumer credit.

QUESTIONS FOR DISCUSSION

1. How has patent medicine advertising changed from the early
   examples shown in this chapter? How do you account for this
   change?
2. What is the relation between advertising and economic development?
3. Why has advertising developed more rapidly in the United States
   than in other countries of the world?
4. What media are available to advertisers today that were not available a century ago? What influence has the development of new
   media had on the growth of advertising?
5. How has automobile advertising changed in character since the
   period before World War I? How do you account for this change?
6. Why does the nature of advertising change when a nation is engaged in a major war?

7. On the basis of what you have read in this chapter, what predictions would you make regarding the future of advertising and promotion?

SUGGESTED READINGS

Borden, Neil H., *The Economic Effects of Advertising*. Homewood, Ill.: Richard D. Irwin, Inc., 1942. Chapter 2.

Brink, Edward L., and William T. Kelley, *The Management of Promotion*. Englewood Cliffs, N.J.: Prentice-Hall, Inc., 1963. Chapter 2.

Calkins, Earnest Elmo and Ralph Holden, *Modern Advertising*. New York: Appleton-Century-Crofts, 1905. Chapter 2.

Gunther, John, *Taken at the Flood: The Story of Albert D. Lasker*. New York: Harper & Row, Publishers, 1960.

Hopkins, Claude C., *My Life in Advertising*. New York: Harper & Row, Publishers, 1927.

Hower, Ralph M., *The History of an Advertising Agency*, rev. ed. Cambridge, Mass.: Harvard University Press, 1949.

Lambert, Gerald B., *All Out of Step*. New York: Doubleday & Company, Inc., 1956.

Pease, Otis, *The Responsibilities of American Advertising*. New Haven, Conn.: Yale University Press, 1958.

Presbrey, Frank S., *The History and Development of Advertising*. New York: Doubleday & Company, Inc., 1929.

Wood, James Playsted, *The Story of Advertising*. New York: The Ronald Press Company, 1958.

3 | The Marketing Approach

One of the most fruitful ways to approach the study of advertising and promotion is in terms of the advertiser's marketing program. Since World War II many companies have inaugurated the "marketing concept" and insisted that advertising's functions be reexamined in terms of marketing. However, to approach advertising from the marketing standpoint, we must answer the question, "What do we mean by marketing?"

This question is not as easy to answer as it might seem, because both the businessman's and the academician's concept of marketing has changed within recent years. At one time marketing was thought of simply as selling. Later it became "all business activities involved in the flow of goods and services from physical production to consumption.[1] Experience has shown that both of these descriptions are too limiting, and in the latter case too mechanistic. Marketing people were forced to come up with a more realistic definition in terms of today's practice.

Although many marketers have their favorite definition, most would probably accept the one agreed on by a group of marketing experts at *Life's* Marketing Round Table:

[1]Harold H. Maynard and Theodore N. Beckman, *Principles of Marketing*, 4th ed. (New York: The Ronald Press Company, 1946), p. 3.

Marketing is the total of all activities needed to convert consumer purchasing power into effective demand.

Therefore some of the major marketing activities include the planning and development of products; the formulation of policies on channels of distribution; working out advertising, promotional, and personal selling plans; and making decisions on pricing. Advertising, promotion, and personal selling are the major communications aspects of marketing.

Notice how the definition of marketing has broadened. This broadening, in turn, has encouraged companies to make the marketing director one of the firm's top executives in charge of planning and coordinating the various marketing functions. In the words of one top marketing executive "advertising, selling and promotion must be thought of not as separate functions but as integral parts of a larger function—marketing." In many companies the "advertising plan" has been replaced by a "marketing plan." This emphasis has also resulted in the addition of marketing executives to the staffs of advertising agencies. Since World War II marketing has been defended, damned, investigated, and studied as never before. Terms like "The New Marketing Concept," "The New Philosophy of Marketing," and "The Marketing Revolution" have become common in the titles of trade articles and speeches at conventions.

This chapter will explore the role of advertising and promotion in the marketing program and attempt to assess their proper functions in that program. The next chapter will relate them to communications.

NEW DIMENSIONS IN MARKETING

The modern marketing concept, which is not as revolutionary as some of its more zealous advocates seem to believe, has helped emphasize certain principles that are basic in understanding marketing and advertising. The following are worth special note.

Marketing Emphasizes the Consumer. One large agency advises that the

. . . modern marketing concept is first and foremost a basic frame of mind, a philosophy of doing business. It is a deep conviction that as the company serves the consumer, it serves itself. Under the modern marketing concept, planning starts with the consumer. Thus understanding the consumer becomes a first order of business. Regardless of the kind of marketing decisions being made . . . whether it be product packaging, advertising or even distribution policy . . . the modern marketing man constantly asks himself, "Would more value be communicated to the consumer if we did it this way or that way?"[2]

The marketing vice-president of a large manufacturer says, "The entire organization (research, engineering, production, and marketing) must work together to determine what the customer wants, how best to produce it, how to motivate its sale, and how to deliver it."

If production people, for example, regard the consumer as someone who complicates their problems, the "marketing concept" is not in

[2]*The Modern Marketing Concept and the Changing Role of the Advertising Agency* (New York: McCann-Erickson Communications Workshop, n.d.).

operation. On the other hand, if they see him as someone to be served as well as to guide their operations, the firm can be said to be marketing-minded. Consumers help plan the product and help design the package the company uses. The consumer therefore holds veto power over what the company does in such fields as product styling, production scheduling, inventory control, and pricing. The marketing-minded firm starts its planning with the consumer.

Marketing Includes Many Interacting Activities. Sometimes, an advertiser will say, you run a brilliant advertising campaign and sales go down. At another time, you run a poor campaign but sales go up. Why? Today's marketing-minded executive will say the answer lies in the interaction of other marketing factors.

> The product may not be right.
> The price may not be right.
> The distribution may not be right.
> The selling technique may not be right.

This is only a partial list of many factors that can influence a sale. Some marketing authorities consider more than a hundred such factors in appraising a firm's marketing "mix."

Marketing Is a Flow Process. One of the characteristics that make it so difficult to trace cause and effect in marketing activities is the continuous flow of the marketing process. Marketing is dynamic. The way one major marketer has charted this flow is illustrated in Figure 3.1. As this diagram indicates, the logical way of coping with this flow of activities is to have a plan — or still better, various plans — for various purposes. These plans should incorporate your marketing strategy.

Why has the marketing concept caught on? Many reasons are given for the increased interest in marketing and advertising's place in it. A

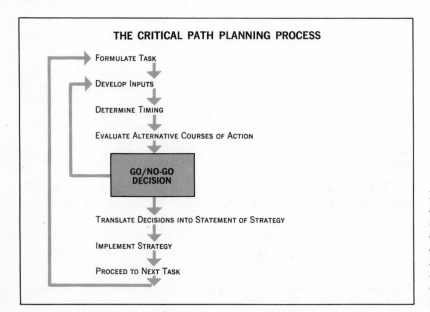

THE CRITICAL PATH PLANNING PROCESS

FORMULATE TASK

DEVELOP INPUTS

DETERMINE TIMING

EVALUATE ALTERNATIVE COURSES OF ACTION

GO/NO-GO DECISION

TRANSLATE DECISIONS INTO STATEMENT OF STRATEGY

IMPLEMENT STRATEGY

PROCEED TO NEXT TASK

FIG. 3.1 *Plan for stepped-up flow of marketing information devised by marketing executive Remus Harris. Note the circular nature of the planning process.* COURTESY MARKETING INSIGHTS MAGAZINE.

leading marketing executive, G. Maxwell Ule, attributes the growth of interest to five factors.

1. The need for better prediction and estimation in modern business as the result of today's high break-even point.
2. The need for minimizing business risks. Ninety-five percent of the new products and brands introduced either are unsuccessful or do not meet sales expectations.
3. The need for increased efficiency in distribution and selling. In the total sales and administrative budget of the top twenty U.S. advertisers, approximately forty cents out of every dollar goes for advertising and promotion.
4. The new technology arising out of the behavioral and mathematical sciences. For instance, mathematics has produced a revolution in sampling procedures.
5. The new breed of administrator in business. He is objective, wants proof, is disciplined.[3]

Marketing Draws on Many Disciplines. From such diverse fields as economics, psychology, sociology, anthropology, cultural ecology, demography, and political science have come significant contributions to marketing knowledge and practice. The relation of marketing to other areas of knowledge and its influence on our culture have been the subjects of much friendly and unfriendly analysis during the 1950s and 1960s.

The Marketing Plan: Its Triad. In many advertising agencies and manufacturing concerns it has become standard procedure to require a complete marketing plan each year. However, the concept of serious, methodical planning is a surprisingly recent one. Maynard Phelps and J. Howard Westing point out that:

Only within the past two or three decades has there been evidence of substantial progress in the use of scientific methods in the development of sound techniques in the solution of problems in marketing management. Even yet, in many marketing organizations planning is a groping and uncertain procedure and rule-of-thumb methods are habitually used.[4]

No one would pretend for a minute that any plan — no matter how good — assures the success of a marketing or advertising campaign. Yet such planning helps the campaign get started right and improves its chances of eventual success. If the plan is right, the chances are good that the strategy that follows will also be right.

Specifically, a good, well-thought-out marketing plan has the following advantages:

1. It forces marketing and advertising personnel to analyze background facts and bring them up to date.
2. It assembles all the facts and thinking on which the year's plan is based.

[3]From a speech presented at the annual meeting of the American Association of Advertising Agencies (April 1958), and reprinted in *Advertising Age*, July 28, 1958.
[4]D. Maynard Phelps and J. Howard Westing, *Marketing Management* (Homewood, Ill.: Richard D. Irwin, Inc., 1960), p. 5.

3. It makes available to new personnel working on a product, both within the agency and in the advertising department of the advertiser, all the information and thinking necessary to familiarize them with the status and problems of the product.

4. It forces all those involved in charting marketing strategy to justify their thinking at least once a year. This challenge is highly desirable, because it helps minimize the chances of continuing a marketing strategy that is not proving itself.

5. It helps to integrate the various elements of marketing strategy into a single unit. These elements should always be considered in relation to one another, because no single one can be evaluated intelligently without consideration of its effect on the other elements. Each of the elements of the "marketing mix" can thus be evaluated on the basis of the integrated plan.

What are the characteristics of a workable plan? Marketing research executive Henry Bund suggests that all plans should be "well integrated . . . well rounded-out in terms of quality, quantity, people, space and time." Mr. Bund recognizes, however, that such qualities are easier to specify than to achieve. He says further:

Now, these are principles to which many managements are willing to give lip service. But it is surprising how many top executives miss the ramifications of planning. For example, I know of quite a few companies that have thought they could set the stage for planning by changing a few titles around and giving the vice president in charge of sales the title of marketing manager. Then they expect miracles to happen. A company cannot have marketing planning without marketing, and it cannot have marketing without a considerable amount of spadework. Generally speaking, I would say that one test of whether a company really means business on this score is whether it is willing to so organize and equip the marketing department that it can answer questions and provide judgments on a broad range of problems—problems that overlap into engineering, production, financial and other company areas.[5]

Almost all agree that the marketing plan should be in writing. However, no two agree completely on what should be included in the ideal plan. Some advise the journalistic formula of "who, what, when, where." Others include a great many more elements. To keep our discussion brief and to the point, we shall settle on three elements (our marketing triad):

1. Analysis of background material on the company, product, and prospective customers.
2. Objectives: long-range, intermediate, and short-range.
3. Marketing mix needed to carry out these objectives.

Let us look at an example. When the H. J. Heinz Company introduced its new Campside Beans, it worked on the basis of a marketing plan. According to the company, these beans were so named because of their smoky, woodsy flavor, which was achieved by grinding smoked bacon into tomato sauce. An analysis of background material showed

[5]Henry Bund, "Steps in Successful Marketing Planning," in David W. Ewing, ed., *Effective Marketing Action* (New York: Harper & Row, Publishers, 1958), p. 300.

that 75 percent of all canned beans were bought by 25 percent of American families. It also showed that 52 percent of housewives "doctor up" canned beans by adding bacon, molasses, sugar, and the like. The objective was to tap the market that does not buy beans regularly.

The company used several marketing elements in its introductory campaign. Advertising was used in 136 daily newspapers in 102 markets. These were later augmented by radio spot announcements, color pages in consumer magazines, black-and-white ads in sports magazines, and TV commercials. Sales promotion in the form of a "buy two and get one free" offer was used. Factory-assembled units of three cans in a cardboard sleeve carton were supplied to retailers for end displays and floor stacks. A handling allowance was given to the retailer to cover the free can. The price was 2 cents a can higher than their regular beans, but this did not worry the company. According to the company's vice-president in charge of marketing, "Consumers are able to pay for better-flavored foods and will do so when the foods have appetite-appeal."

ANALYSIS OF BACKGROUND MATERIAL

Before background information can be analyzed, it must be collected and organized. This raises the question of what kinds of information we are looking for when building a marketing plan. Like everything else connected with the plan, such information will vary according to individual situations. The following are some of the most important elements:

1. *What is the sales history of the product, year by year?* For maximum clarity the history should be in tabular form, but explanatory comments should be added to point out significant trends and explain sharp deviations from the norm.
2. *What is the historical trend of consumer sales?* This should be a chronological picture, showing sales in units and dollars and, if possible, in share of the market through the period studied.
3. *What is the history of the product itself?* This might include such factors as quality problems encountered, successive product improvements, and consumer preferences.
4. *What are the principal products with which you have to compete?* How successful are they compared with yours? Is your competition local, regional, or national; from distributors' or manufacturers' brands? What are your advantages over your competition? What are theirs over yours?
5. *What is the market?* This has a direct bearing on your marketing objectives. Who are your present customers? Who are your best potential customers? What do you know about them from past experience?
6. *What are consumer attitudes toward your product?* How do consumers compare your product with that of your competitors? What are the attributes of your product that have led people to buy it in the past? What have you found out from consumer surveys?

7. *What is your strength in various areas?* Is your strength fairly uniform throughout the country, or is it made up of strong, medium, and weak territories? Is there a difference in strength by city size or type of major industry?

8. *What is the trend of your distribution?* Is there some indication that inadequate distribution is a deterrent to satisfactory sales progress on a national or regional basis? What kind of distributor markets your product best? Is extensive or intensive distribution more successful?

9. *What is your profit history?* How much profit has your business earned for a significant number of years—in dollars, in amount per unit sold, and in percent of net sales?

10. *What is the history of your advertising expenditures?* This should be in both dollars and percent of sales.

11. *What is the history of your selling expense?* This should be shown year by year, in dollars and percent of sales.

12. *What is the history of other marketing expenses?* This should include such expenses as display, promotions, packaging, branding, merchandising, and public relations—again shown by dollars and percent of sales.

13. *What is the history of your marketing strategy?* What kinds of strategy have worked best, and which have failed? What has the success of various marketing mixes been?

Once these data are collected, they can be analyzed to show significant trends and major problems. They should point the way to the formulation of logical objectives.

MARKETING OBJECTIVES

Suppose you are president of a medium-sized corporation and an inquisitive reporter asks you what your company's objective is. Your first impulse might be to stare at the questioner for asking such an obvious question. "Of course," you'd say, "our objective is to make a profit."

If you are thinking of long-range objectives, the chances are you are right, because this is the ultimate objective of any business. However, you might prefer to emphasize short-range objectives; for example, those of the coming year. Then you might say, "Our objective is to sell a million units of our product," or "Our objective is to gain first position in the field for our brand." Such objectives also focus attention on marketing problems.

Specific objectives are most helpful to the market planner. These grow out of the general or broad objectives, but they furnish actual market targets, something on which the marketer can set his sights.

Specific marketing objectives are probably best expressed in terms of consumer types. No business needs to sell to everybody. Some, such as the producer of *pâté de foie gras*, can make a tidy profit selling to small markets. Some, such as the producer of a breakfast cereal, aim at mass markets. An essential part of the marketing plan is a clear definition of the potential consumer. We start with *potential consumers* (or groups of them) and end with *consumers* when the sale is made to them.

Test yourself.
She's in the _____ generation.

The drink? Cold, bold, clean-tasting _____.

_____-Cola grew up with her,
matched her tastes and her pace.

**No wonder _____ is the official drink
of her generation.**

Yours, too.

**Come alive!
You're in the _____ generation!**

FIG. 3.2 *Effective attempt to involve the reader in the advertising message. Note that the name of the advertiser, "Pepsi-Cola," does not appear in the advertisement.* CLIENT: PEPSICO, INC.; AGENCY: BATTEN, BARTON, DURSTINE & OSBORN, INC.

We might, for example, say we are attempting to reach the teen-age market. This is a very large market (an estimated 25,000,000 in the United States in 1968), and it is a market with special characteristics. It is a market based on age—one of the frequently used *demographic factors*. Other factors commonly used in defining markets are income, race, religion, place of residence, and occupation.

On the other hand, we might say we are trying for the upper middle-class market. If this is so, we are talking about a *sociological* instead of a demographic class. This, then, is a class market, one based primarily on such factors as family background, education, source of income, and personal possessions.

Finally, we might say we are trying for the hypochondriacs or the "venturesome"—discussed by researcher Alfred Politz in a study he made for *Better Homes and Gardens*. In either situation we are thinking of people in terms of *psychological* classes.

Communication executive's office. Carpet: deep-pile Margate® Wilton in Poppy. 100% Bigelow Approved wool face. Accent rug: Fortune's Wheel from our Custom Carpet collection.

A title on the door rates a Bigelow on the floor

For every place of business, every public building, every home, Bigelow
has or can readily create the perfect carpet. We've done it since 1825.

FIG. 3.3 *Advertisement designed to build the status of the product.*
COURTESY BIGELOW RUGS AND CARPETS.

Objective may also be stated in terms of what it is we want to tell people. These are, as we shall see in the next chapter, our communication objectives. For example, our marketing plan might call for capturing a certain percentage of the teen-age market during the next year. Our communication plan would outline specifically what we want to communicate to this market in order to capture this percentage (a brand or corporate image). Furthermore, the plan should outline the strategy (copy and layout, media, and the like) for getting this idea to the desired audience.

In summary, then, we are concerned with three types of objectives. First we formulate our long-range objectives. On the basis of these and our appraisal of all available information, we are then in a position to formulate two other types of objectives: marketing objectives and communication objectives (see Chapter 4).

FIG. 3.4 *Advertisement designed both to enhance the status of Equitable representatives and to attract to the business promising young men who might like to be representatives.* CLIENT: A NATIONAL ADVERTISEMENT OF THE EQUITABLE LIFE ASSURANCE SOCIETY OF THE UNITED STATES; AGENCY: FOOTE, CONE & BELDING.

THE MARKETING MIX

Makers of proprietary medicine often market their product without the help of a sales force. Instead, they depend heavily on advertising to "pull" the product through the retail outlets. They use advertising to build a demand among consumers. In other words, they do little to get the retailers to "push" their product.

Contrast this method with that of the maker of heavy machinery, who customarily puts only a small percentage of sales into advertising and, instead, relies heavily on his well-trained sales force and the sales force of his distributors.

One manufacturer of a leading toothpaste spends approximately 20 percent of each sales dollar for advertising. Another company spends virtually nothing on advertising and sells most of its output to a large retail chain, which markets the toothpaste under its own brand name.

That company receives a steady profit for its efforts, but it has little incentive to advertise. Instead, it has to concentrate on keeping price and quality in line to satisfy its customers.

One retailer of men's clothes, located in the main shopping center of a city, regularly spends 3 percent of each sales dollar for advertising. He features the latest in men's fashions and depends on men and their wives to drop in when they are downtown. He has a loyal, steady clientele for his medium-to-higher-priced merchandise.

Another men's store is located on the outskirts of a main shopping area. The manager spends 6 cents of every sales dollar to tell potential customers of "low overhead" and bargain prices for men's merchandise. This store depends more on bargain hunters and less on regular customers.

These are examples of variations in the "marketing mix" used by various business adminstrators. No single mix is, in itself, right or wrong. Instead, successful mixes vary widely from one product to another. They even vary from product to product within the same class, because objectives, manufacturers and consumers vary. The astuteness of a marketer can be judged—partly at least—by his skill in adjusting the ingredients of his mix to the conditions of the market. As conditions change, he should change the mix. Naturally, there has to be a certain amount of experimentation—preferably augmented by intuition and creative imagination.

INGREDIENTS OF THE MARKETING MIX

Advertising. Table 3.1 shows the relative importance of certain elements in the marketing mix of selected manufacturers.

In such product classifications as drugs and tobacco, the percentage of sales spent for advertising is substantially higher than that spent for personal selling. For these products advertising is obviously a very important part of the mix. Here masses of consumers must be reached cheaply, and the product must be "pulled" through the trade. It is possible to build a strong preference for a particular brand through advertising. The characteristics of a product that make people prefer it to another can best be exploited through advertising. Drugs, toilet articles, and tobacco products are consumed by almost everyone and are often bought on impulse.

On the other hand, manufacturers of home furnishings and agricultural equipment emphasize personal selling. People do not buy these items on impulse, although they may be influenced by advertising to prefer a certain brand. For the most part, the product is not sold until the local dealer explains to the customer how this brand will best fit his needs.

In all types of retail stores the expenditure for personal selling is significantly higher than for advertising. Department and specialty stores spend a higher percentage for advertising than do food and variety stores. The latter are steady, day-after-day advertisers who have to keep selling their stores to the public. The food chain concentrates its advertising on certain days of the week, and the variety store tends to

TABLE 3.1   RELATIVE IMPORTANCE OF THE ELEMENTS OF MARKETING COMMUNICATIONS*

SALES EFFORT ACTIVITY	INDUSTRIAL GOODS	CONSUMER DURABLES	CONSUMER NONDURABLES
Sales management personal selling	69.2	47.6	38.1
Broadcast media advertising	0.9	10.7	20.9
Printed media advertising	12.5	16.1	14.8
Special promotional activities	9.6	15.5	15.5
Branding and promotional packaging	4.5	9.5	9.8
Other	3.3	0.6	0.9
Total	100.0	100.0	100.0

*The data are the average point allocations of 336 industrial, 52 consumer-durable, and 88 consumer-nondurable-goods producers. Nine responses are excluded because of point allocations that did not equal 100. Each respondent manufacturer was asked to allocate 100 points among the activities according to the estimated contribution of each to the marketing success of his product.

SOURCE: Jon Udell, "The Perceived Importance of the Elements of Strategy," *Journal of Marketing,* January 1968.

stress price rather than steady patronage. (See Chapter 14 for a more complete listing of percentages spent for advertising.)

The emphasis on advertising will depend, too, on the "advertising communication mix" itself (the type of copy needed, the frequency of insertions, and the media used). These problems will be treated in the next chapter as part of the "communication concept."

Personal Selling. The salesman who can talk the retailers' language is worth a great deal to the head of his company. A good salesman understands concepts important to the dealer, such as percent markup, stock turnover (how many times the average inventory turns over in a year), cost of shelf space, sales per square foot, and investment in store and warehouse. The salesman can show the retailer how the company's products fit his needs and can contribute to his net profit. Although advertising treats everyone as part of the mass, the salesman treats each customer as an individual and adapts his message to that person.

Suppose you are selling turret lathes. They are expensive, and each potential customer will need advice in fitting them into his own production setup. You will need some engineering know-how, as well as selling skill, if you are to convince the customer to buy your product.

In the retail field the salesperson helps the potential customer choose the right dress, find the correct size in shoes and understand the workings of an electrical appliance. In spite of all the self-service retailing, personal selling is still an important part of the retailer's mix.

Advertising and personal selling often work together. Advertisements in magazines and newspapers turn up leads that salesmen can follow. They make selling easier for the salesman by opening doors that would otherwise be closed to him. Similarly, the salesman will remind dealers or potential customers that the manufacturer is working for them by placing ads in the mass media. He may help them prepare a local advertising campaign. The retail salesperson may remind the customer of the advertised "specials."

Price Policy. To illustrate how price is determined, an economist usually uses a model. He sets up a demand schedule (the quantity of a product people will buy at various prices) and a supply schedule (the amount producers are willing to put on the market at various price levels). When these two schedules are plotted on a graph, they usually look like an open pair of scissors. The point at which the demand line crosses the price line is supposed to be the price of the product.

Economists use this model only to illustrate the interaction of supply and demand. They, like the marketers, realize that in today's market price is not determined quite so easily. One of the major factors in setting price is the extent to which it will be important in selling the product. Sometimes price is an important factor in product sales, sometimes it does not seem to make much difference, and occasionally you can sell even more at a high price than at a low one. Let us look at some examples.

In the 1920's Henry Ford cut the price of his Model T car by 10 percent. The number of cars sold went up much more than 10 percent, so price was apparently important in the sale of these cars. In the late 1950s many United States automobile manufacturers maintained that the price of a car was not really so important in this prosperous age. Then came sharp increases in the sale of both foreign and domestic economy cars. The other American manufacturers took another look, got their market researchers on the job and brought out their own lines of economy (compact) cars.

The marketer of bread, however, might find the effect of price quite different. Suppose he decides to experiment by offering it first at the prevailing price. Then he lowers the price and finds that he sells only slightly more. He will probably conclude that the demand for his product is relatively inelastic. If, however, his price had been quite high in the first place, the situation might have been different—the importance of price as an appeal varies from one price level to the next.

Finally, consider the marketing problem of a cosmetics manufacturer. He markets a brand of face powder at $1.00 a box because this price will provide a fair profit. However, he decides to experiment by selling it at $2.00 a box. He finds that he sells more boxes at the high price than at the lower one. This situation is not unusual in the case of products such as cosmetics and proprietary medicines, where consumers are sometimes suspicious of the quality of a low-priced product.

Discount houses thrive on price appeal, and they generally find advertising a primary tool in telling people about their low prices. "Nationally advertised appliances," they will say in their advertisements, "at 50 percent of list prices."

Some manufacturers are very eager to prevent retailers from offering their products at less than the set prices. In some states their feeling is backed by law (Fair Trade law), and price-maintenance contracts between a manufacturer and any one retailer in the state make it mandatory that other retailers sell at that price. Manufacturers have had mixed success in enforcing such contracts, even though small retailers tend to favor them on the basis that such contracts give them a chance to compete with larger retailers.

The setting of price and its importance in the marketing mix are indeed complex. They depend partly on the appraisal of consumer behavior toward possible prices. In discussing pricing of a household cleaner, Neil H. Borden points out, "Consumer behavior towards price for such an article . . . ordinarily reflects a complex of influences — the

FIG. 3.5 *Effective use of what could be a problem — the high price of the tire — as the main selling point of the advertisement.*
CLIENT: UNIROYAL;
ADVERTISEMENT
PREPARED BY DOYLE DANE
BERNBACH INC.

influence of customary price, of prices of competing soap products, and of opinions or attitudes as to the cost of the new product."[6] Ordinarily there is conflict between price and product quality. If a product is the best in the field, the chances are that a firm cannot make it the least expensive as well.

Product Planning. The industrial revolution put the emphasis on making a product more cheaply than one's competitors. The trouble was that a competitor could often copy manufacturing advantages and make the product just as cheaply. Recently, we have seen the emphasis turn to making the finished product a better, rather than a cheaper, one. Usually this means higher production costs and higher selling costs. Consequently, the marketer has to adjust the quality of the product to the price people are willing to pay.

A product is *better* than its predecessor or the competition only if it better satisfies some want or need. Furniture factories still manufacture a type of chair designed by Hepplewhite in the eighteenth century. However, no shoe manufacturer today produces the high-button shoes that were designed to satisfy tastes of the early twentieth century. A product may go unchanged for years and satisfy the public, but it is safe to assume that it is not likely to continue to. Nylon stockings replaced those made of silk. Lipstick that would not "kiss off" superseded that which smeared. Baker's bread replaced homemade, and sales of baking powder declined as sales of cake mixes skyrocketed. Smaller houses have been built because people wanted them. Straight razors have been relegated to barber shops, and electric razors at $20 each compete very well with safety razors at $1.00 or less.

Some companies put continual emphasis on product planning as part of their marketing mix. These companies are known for their new products. Others depend more on price and remain satisfied to copy the leaders and let others do the innovating. This is especially well illustrated in the world of fashion, where certain companies are fashion leaders and charge very high prices to the few who buy their "fashion firsts." These customers can, of course, be the fashion leaders of the community. Many other manufacturers concentrate on copying the style when they are sure it will be a hit.

FIG. 3.6 *"Believe it or not—this is hamburger,"* a voice-over announcer says of the finished dish on the right. The commercial starts with Kraft Foods' Velveeta for the "cheddary-flavored" cheese sauce. COURTESY KRAFT FOODS, CHICAGO, ILLINOIS; AGENCY: J. WALTER THOMPSON COMPANY.

[6]Neil H. Borden, *Economic Effects of Advertising* (Homewood, Ill.: Richard D. Irwin, Inc., 1942), p. 76.

Brand Policy. Many products that were bought only in bulk a generation or so ago are now packaged and sold by brand. To the customer the brand provides an index to assure him that the quality is satisfactory. To the manufacturer, it represents a means of attaining customer loyalty by building a consumer franchise around his particular brand. Brand policy is an important part of marketing strategy. Companies such as Procter & Gamble and General Foods have brand managers, who are important executives in charge of the advertising and promotional programs of individual company brands. Advertising people are very much concerned about building the brand image for a certain product and measuring the extent to which it is communicated to the consuming public.

The question each marketer must ask himself is this: "To what extent do I want to emphasize brand in marketing?" You might assume that every marketer would want to go as far as possible in pushing brand. This is not always true. The cost may be too great—because it is

FIG. 3.7 *Effectively designed display cylinder which holds 10 cases of Top Job.* COURTESY THE PROCTER & GAMBLE COMPANY, OF WHICH TOP JOB IS A REGISTERED TRADEMARK.

FIG. 3.8 *Promotion to dealer which ties in "whiter teeth" theme of the consumer advertising, price appeal to the dealer, and the convenience of the point-of-purchase display.* COURTESY BEECHAM PRODUCTS INC.

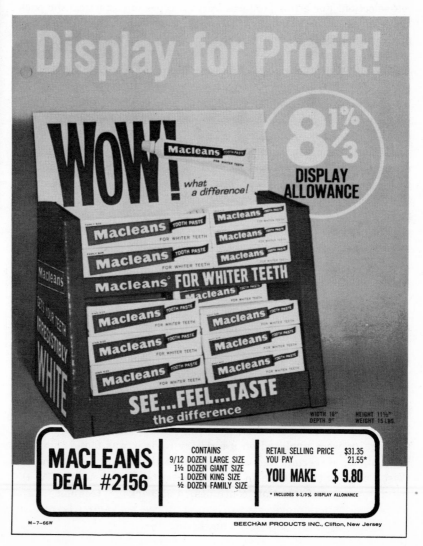

uneconomic to sell the brand beyond a certain point of diminishing return or because distribution presents problems, or for some other reason. Some marketers do not go in for brand promotion because they like the stability achieved by selling their products to someone else to market under his own brand. Many small canneries, for example, sell their entire output to food chains and have no worry about advertising, distribution, sales promotion, or other marketing problems. The chain in turn sells the canned food under its own brand name.

Sometimes a marketer decides that making his brand a mass brand requires too much money. So he calls off the heavy promotion and tries to preserve the identity of his brand with a small and, he hopes, loyal segment of the market.

Packaging. Packaging is often an important part of the marketing mix, although its importance varies with the product. In many industries the package is a powerful selling force, because it is in constant competition for the customer's attention as the result of self-service and self-selection. For a few products (certain types of cosmetics) the package costs more and is frequently more important than the product itself in inducing potential customers to buy.

Many questions arise in connection with packages. What size should be used? What colors? Shapes? Layouts? Closures? Packaging material?

One marketing strategy employed extensively since World War II is the addition of a larger package size to an established line. For example, three manufacturers of three nationally distributed items marketed a large size in their line (a drugstore item, a food item, and a nonfood item). Two of the large sizes were well established on a national scale in the 1950s, though the third had by that time attained distribution in only three market territories. The sales share of each of these large sizes as a part of the total market (large, medium, and small) in the entire United States during a nine-year period was as follows:

PERCENTAGE OF TOTAL MARKET   **TABLE 3.2**

Product	Period I	Period II
Commodity A (drug)	23.0	45.6
Commodity B (food)	22.9	35.0
Commodity C (nonfood)	9.7	32.2

SOURCE: *Nielsen Researcher*, published by A. C. Nielsen Co.

Note how much more the marketers of Commodity C gained by the addition of the large size than the marketers of the other two. (When these gains were analyzed on a territory basis it was found that they were higher in certain territories, such as the Pacific Coast and the West Central States, than in most other parts of the country.) As the trend toward self-selection continues, and package technology and package design improve, we can expect to see packaging become an even more important part of the marketing mix.

Promotion. As we pointed out in Chapter 1, sales promotion is a much-abused term but has usually come to denote activities that supplement advertising and personal selling. The most common of these are premiums, contests, couponing and cross-couponing, special price offers, consumer incentives, dealer incentives, point-of-purchase displays, and special deals of all kinds.

If a company gives away cigarette lighters to important buyers, it is carrying on a sales promotion effort. If a manufacturer supplies retail stores with advertising folders (known as envelope "stuffers") to send out with their monthly bills, that is sales promotion. If an advertiser works out a plan of related selling that will be used by stores all over the country, it is a sales promotion effort, also.

Sales promotion can be used to increase sales to wholesalers, retailers, and the general public. To increase sales to *wholesalers*, concessions are sometimes given. For example, there is the "count-and-recount deal." The incentive is an extra discount on all sales made during a certain period. The deal begins on a specified date. Before that date, a salesman goes into a wholesaler's warehouse and counts the stock. At the expiration of the special discount period, the salesman returns and recounts the stock. The invoices will then tell how many units of the product he has purchased between the two dates, and the recount will show the volume of sales on which he is entitled to the extra discount.

A "baker's dozen" offer may be used to get larger-than-usual orders from *retailers*. For a limited period, if a retailer orders a certain amount of merchandise, he will receive thirteen items for every twelve he purchases.

Increased sales to *consumers* may be gained (temporarily) by offering coupons that are worth money toward the purchase of a product.

Sales promotion usually begins with a company's salesmen. Most well-organized sales forces are supplied with sales manuals—books that give salesmen complete information about the products they sell and suggestions for selling the products most effectively. Companies also supply salesmen with sales portfolios, which give the circulation reached by the company's advertising, reproductions of some of the advertisements themselves, and other information about the advertising program. Salesmen show them to retailers to impress upon them the impact made on the public and to emphasize the public franchise that is being sustained and enlarged for the product they are selling.

Premiums have become an important form of sales promotion. Roughly, premiums fall into two categories—those given free and those for which the consumer pays. A free premium may be a cutout on a package—a funny mask, small cowboys and Indians, or it may be a premium that is packed with the product, such as a washcloth in a box of detergent. A premium may be separate from the package and given by the dealer to customers when two or more packages are purchased. It may consist of a "banded deal": a small package of one product banded to the larger package of another that the consumer gets free by paying only the price of the large package. Or it may be a bargain in which the consumer is offered a set of knives worth $1.50 for 59 cents and two box-tops. The 59 cents usually represents the cost of the premium plus the cost of handling and mailing and costs the company nothing. This is known as a "self-liquidating" premium; that is, for every premium the company mails out, it gets its out-of-pocket costs back.

Window displays range from simple cards printed by the thousands and sent out to all stores handling the product, to elaborate sets costing several hundred dollars. Very expensive window displays are not given general distribution. They are handmade in limited quantity and are scheduled for use only in selected stores. They are booked ahead of time, as vaudeville acts used to be. A display period for each store is about a week, at the end of which time the display is sent on to the next store.

Inside display materials can be back-bar strips in drugstores, shelf strips in grocery stores, counter displays, floor displays, or complete display racks. The most widely used sales promotion material is this kind of "point-of-sale" display.

There are few sales programs in which promotion is not an important part of the mix. For some products—Hershey's Chocolate, for example—promotion is more important than advertising.

Channels of Distribution. The marketer has a choice of several methods of distribution. He can sell direct to consumers as does Fuller Brush. He can sell direct to retailers (as do the automobile companies) and become his own wholesale organization. He can utilize manufacturers' agents. He can follow the traditional route of selling to wholesalers, who in turn sell to retailers.

In the wholesale field he has a choice between such widely varied institutions as brokers, who never own or possess the goods, and full-function wholesalers, who take both possession and ownership of the goods.

In the retail field he has a choice of many types of stores. Among the standard classifications are department stores, variety stores, food stores, and men's and women's specialty stores. He must be alert, however, to the changing patterns in these standard classifications. We have seen the variety store, for example, change from the "five-and-ten," with its low-priced merchandise, to a store carrying high-priced jewelry and TV sets. We have seen the corner grocery become a supermarket that carries, even in a small town, products ranging from smoked oysters to men's shirts.

The marketer may decide on extensive or intensive distribution—or something in between. Automobile companies generally prefer to limit the number of dealers in an area, whereas soap companies allow their products to be sold through any number of stores. Even within the same product category, policies will differ. One candy company makes distribution an important part of its marketing mix. It owns and operates the stores that sell its candy, all of which are located in the main shopping centers of larger cities. Another company prefers to deal through established wholesalers and retailers, but helps retailers merchandise the candy by making point-of-purchase material available to them.

Service. Some marketers emphasize service. Others offer little or no service. Many insurance companies make a sales point of the "quick settlement of claims" or of "friendly service." Some prefer to stress the low cost of their policies. Automobile companies often feature their service policies or promote the service offered by their dealers. To a lesser extent, makers of appliances emphasize service, but usually the manufacturer who promotes service will not have the lowest price to promote. In the retail field, we have, on the one hand, the "discount house," which may even emphasize its lack of service ("carry it home with you") and, on the other, the full-service retailer ("we'll charge and deliver it").

MARKETING AND PROMOTIONAL DECISION MAKING

It is apparent from our discussion in this chapter that the process of working out a marketing mix is complicated and that few marketers can be sure they have found just the right mix. Robinson and Luck have suggested that the process would be greatly improved and systematized if marketers would follow what they call a "reference structure," known as the "Adaptive Planning and Control Sequence" (APACS). The following eight steps are suggested:

1. Define problem and set objectives.
2. Appraise over-all situation.
3. Determine tasks and identify means.
4. Identify alternative plans and mixes.
5. Estimate expected results.
6. Review and decision by management.
7. Feedback of results and postaudit.
8. Adapt program if required.[7]

Neil Borden, who has done much through the years to popularize the concept of the marketing mix, suggests that marketers can best determine the proper mix of ingredients if they will keep in mind these four forces once they have determined their objective:

1. Consumer buying behavior.
2. Trade behavior.
3. Competitors' position and behavior.
4. Government behavior—control over marketing.[8]

He adds that the skillful marketer is one

who is a perceptive and practical psychologist and sociologist, who has keen insight into individual and group behavior, who can foresee changes in behavior that develop in a dynamic world, who has the creative ability for building well-knit programs because he has the capacity to visualize the probable response of consumers, trade, and competitors to his moves.

He recognizes that marketing decision making, like many business activities, is part science and part art.

Kotler suggests that

the notion of a marketing mix can be conveyed in the form of a vector notation. Suppose the firm produces a product currently priced (P) at \$20 and backed by

[7]Patrick J. Robinson and David J. Luck, *Promotional Decision Making: Practice and Theory* (New York: McGraw-Hill, Inc., 1964), p. 4.

[8]Neil H. Borden, "The Concept of the Marketing Mix," *Journal of Advertising Research,* 4, no. 2 (June 1964), pp. 4–5.

an annual advertising budget (A) of \$20,000 and distribution expenditures (D) of \$30,000. The company's mix at time (t) can then be summarized as

$$(\$20, \$20,000, \$30,000)$$

In more general terms, the company's marketing mix at time (t) is

$$(P, A, D)t$$

For example, suppose the company's price is constrained by competitive factors to lie somewhere between \$16 and \$24, and both its advertising and its distribution expenditure are constrained by budget limitations to lie somewhere between \$10,000 and \$50,000 (to the nearest \$10,000) each. The company can then choose one of nine possible prices and one of five possible budgets for advertising and distribution respectively, or 225 ($9 \times 5 \times 5$) marketing-mix combinations in all. The large number of possible marketing mixes makes it apparent why the optimal mix is so hard to discover.[9]

The success of any marketing lies in the skill with which its various parts are integrated. The objectives determine the target and the mix of elements implements these objectives. The skillful marketer must not only visualize the probable response of consumers to each mix of elements but also use the same predictive ability in working out ways to weld the elements into a workable program and seeing that the plan is carried out.

SUMMARY

Modern marketing has at least three distinguishing characteristics: emphasis on the consumer, interaction of activities, and the flow of functions. Like all business activities, it works much better if it has behind it a well-organized, written plan. The marketing plan should include these elements: an analysis of background material, a definition of marketing objectives, and the mix needed to carry out these objectives.

Among the more important ingredients in the typical marketing mix are the following: advertising, personal selling, pricing, product planning, brand policy, packaging, sales promotion, channels of distribution, and service. Once the mix has been decided on, the problem is to integrate the various elements and make sure the plan is carried out effectively.

QUESTIONS FOR DISCUSSION

1. Why has the marketing concept become popular since World War II?
2. What is the relation of advertising to the other ingredients of the "marketing mix"?
3. To what extent does marketing depend on such areas as economics and psychology for its conceptual framework?

---

[9]Philip Kotler, *Marketing Management: Analysis, Planning and Control* (Englewood Cliffs, N.J.: Prentice-Hall, Inc., 1967), pp. 326–327.

4. Why do some marketers use very little advertising, compared with personal selling, whereas others put little stress on personal selling?

5. Can we properly say that there is a "theory of marketing"?

6. Summarize an article from the *Journal of Marketing* or the *Journal of Marketing Research* that discusses advertising's relation to marketing.

SUGGESTED READINGS

Borden, Neil H., and Martin V. Marshall, *Advertising Management: Text and Cases.* Homewood, Ill.: Richard D. Irwin, Inc., 1959. Chapters 1–3.

Boyd, Harper W., Jr., and Joseph W. Newman, *Advertising Management: Selected Readings.* Homewood, Ill.: Richard D. Irwin, Inc., 1965. Part I.

Crain, Edgar, *Marketing Communications.* New York: John Wiley & Sons, Inc., 1965. Chapters 1–3.

Howard, John, *Marketing Management: Analysis and Planning,* 2d ed. Homewood, Ill., Richard D. Irwin, Inc., 1963.

Kotler, Philip, *Marketing Management: Analysis, Planning and Control.* Englewood Cliffs, N.J.: Prentice-Hall, Inc., 1967.

McCarthy, E. Jerome, *Basic Marketing,* rev. ed. Homewood, Ill.: Richard D. Irwin, Inc., 1964.

Matthews, John B., Jr., *et al., Marketing: An Introductory Analysis.* New York: McGraw-Hill, Inc., 1964.

Phelps, D. Maynard, and J. Howard Westing, *Marketing Management.* Homewood, Ill.: Richard D. Irwin, Inc., 1963.

Robinson, Patrick J., and David J. Luck, *Promotional Decision Making: Practice and Theory.* New York: McGraw-Hill, Inc., 1964. Chapters 1–2.

4 | The Communications Concept

In the previous chapter we examined advertising in terms of the broad picture—that of the firm's marketing program. In this chapter we will narrow the picture somewhat by focusing on the position of advertising in the communications program. We will provide a framework for appraising alternative communications strategies and for making decisions. This approach will be called the "communications concept" although it might also be termed a "concept of marketing communications."

WHAT IS COMMUNICATION?

There are few sounds or gestures that are not attempts to communicate. Some communication is intentional, some is not. When a candidate for the United States Senate makes a speech advocating higher tariffs, he is consciously using communication. When, however, he says nothing on an important issue, his silence also communicates, although in a more subtle manner. Some of our communication takes the form of words, much does not. The clothes a person wears, the car he drives, and the way he walks, tell us a lot about him. Every time someone receives a message there is communication.

The word *communication* comes from the Latin *communis*, meaning common. The basic ingredient of communication is "common-ness." This idea is graphically emphasized by the overlapping of the two ovals in Figure 4.1. Only if the medium of the message is common to both the sender and the receiver is there really a communication.

Let us take an example. You are a communication source (copywriter) of information about a new bath soap that contains a "miracle" ingredient. Your job is to tell people about this new soap and the ingredient that distinguishes it from competing soaps. What kind of message will you send? You may use illustrations of people made more beautiful or happy by the soap. You may use words such as "new" or "amazing" or "miracle ingredient." All of these represent attempts on your part to

FIG. 4.1 *Graphic portrayal of the process of encoding and decoding messages.* SOURCE: WILBUR SCHRAMM, ED., THE PROCESS AND EFFECTS OF MASS COMMUNICATION. (URBANA, ILL.: UNIVERSITY OF ILLINOIS PRESS, 1954), P. 6.

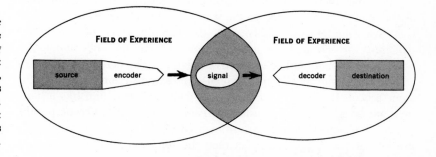

encode a message. But these attempts do not necessarily produce communication. The message communicates successfully only if it means the same thing to (or overlaps the field of experience of) the people you address as it does to you. The illustration, the word, the phrase that seemed so clear to you may not fall within the field of experience of your audience. Through pictures and music you can communicate across national boundaries, but your words must usually be translated—made common to the people of another country.

Wilbur Schramm tells of an American teacher in Africa who was dismayed to find that students laughed the first few times she called the roll of names in class. Consequently, she worked desperately hard to learn to pronounce the names correctly, because she thought they were laughing at her accent. However, when she became very skillful, they laughed all the harder. Finally she learned that they were laughing out of friendliness and pleasure at how hard she was trying and how well she was doing. In *her* frame of reference a laugh at that point meant derision; in *their* frame of reference it meant just the opposite.[1]

THE FRAMEWORK OF COMMUNICATION

One approach to analyzing the process by which people communicate with one another is the 5–W approach—*who* says *what* to *whom*

[1]Wilbur Schramm, "Communication Research in the United States," in Wilbur Schramm, ed., *The Science of Human Communication* (New York: Basic Books, Inc., 1963).

through *which channel* with *what effect*.[2] Although the model is over-simplified, it provides a useful structure for organizing the alternatives facing any communicator and for making decisions. The *who* is the communication source—an official of a company or a copywriter in an advertising agency, for example. The *what* is the message itself—a collection of words, pictures, and white space on the printed page or electronic impulses over the broadcast media. The *whom* is the audience the communicator hopes to reach; perhaps one person, perhaps millions. The *which* (channel) may be a newspaper or a television station. The *what* (effect) may be measured in terms of how many saw or listened to the message, how much of the message the readers recall, how the message changed their attitudes, or the extent to which it impelled them to buy the product or service advertised.

Another approach is to examine communication in the framework of the meanings attributed to the words, pictures, sounds, and the like that are communicated. Basically, the meanings are of two kinds: *denotative*, which is the common dictionary meaning, and *connotative*, which is the emotional or evaluative meaning. The denotations will be roughly the same for all people who use the same dictionary or go to the same school. However, a word like "Republican" or a sign like a hammer and sickle will have different connotations for different people.

We find that meanings are influenced by the context in which they are spoken, by the relation between the sender and receiver, and by many variables. For example "Good morning," or its counterpart in any other language, is not really used to describe the weather but to establish a bond of friendship. An advertising message urging people to drive carefully will be interpreted in one way when the sender is an auto insurance company with a financial interest in safer driving and in another when the sender is a bank with a less direct interest.

Any framework we use to organize our communication makes the process of communication seem simpler than it really is, and almost any communication between sender and receiver is influenced by a host of variables. Joseph Klapper summarizes some of these in the following:

> More recent studies, both in the laboratory and the social world, have documented the influence of a host of other variables, including various aspects of contextual organization; the audiences' image of the source; the simple passage of time; the group orientation of the audience member and the degree to which he values group membership; the activity of opinion leaders, the social aspects of the situation during and after exposure to the media; the degree to which the audience member is forced to play a role; the personality pattern of the audience member; his social class, and the level of his frustration; the nature of the media in a free enterprise system; and the availability of "social mechanisms" for implementing action drives.[3]

[2]See Harold Lasswell, "The Structure and Function of Communication in Society," in Lyman Bryson, ed., *The Communication of Ideas* (New York: Harper & Row, Publishers, 1948). Other general models for analyzing communication are described by Bruce H. Westley and Malcolm M. MacLean, Jr., "A Conceptual Model for Communications Research," *Journalism Quarterly* (Winter 1957), and Wilbur Schramm, "How Communication Works," in Wilbur Schramm, ed., *The Process and Effects of Mass Communication* (Urbana, Ill.: University of Illinois Press, 1954).

[3]Joseph T. Klapper, "What We Know about the Effects of Mass Communications: The Brink of Hope," *Public Opinion Quarterly*, Winter 1957–1958, p. 455.

COMMUNICATION VERSUS MARKETING

In the last chapter we defined marketing as "the total of all activities needed to convert consumer purchasing power into effective demand." The success of the marketing program is determined on the basis of how successful the conversion was—that is, sales of the company's product. Advertising is only one of many marketing elements that contribute to this ultimate objective. Specifically, its contribution is to communicate a message from the advertiser to the potential consumer—not just to expose people to a message but to deliver a message that may contribute to action.

For example, suppose that the marketing goal of a particular soap company is to increase its share of industry sales from 8 percent to 10 percent. Advertising will be only one of several forces helping to perform this job. Distribution, packaging, and many of the other marketing elements we discussed in Chapter 3 will also be important. The job of advertising will be to communicate the sales message that will help achieve the marketing objective. For example, we might have the following:

Marketing Objective: to increase the share of the market from 8 percent to 10 percent in three years.

Advertising Objective: to convey the message that our soap will keep your skin soft for a longer time than competing soaps will.

We are able through research to be even more specific. It is possible to find out how many of our prospective consumers now identify our soap as the one that will keep their skin softest. Let us say that we find that 10 percent of our potential consumers so identify our brand. Then we may define as our advertising goal:

To increase from 10 percent to 20 percent the number of women in the twenty-to-forty-five-year age bracket who are persuaded that our soap will keep their skin soft for a longer time than competing soaps.

The emphasis in marketing is on sales, and the emphasis in advertising communication is on the transmission of a message that may contribute to sales.

In advertising, as in all forms of mass communication, the medium is interposed between the communicator and his potential audience. Although the media provide a much more economical method of reaching large audiences than person-to-person communication does, they create certain problems for the communicator. Among the most important of these are the following:

Mass Communication Is Mainly One-Way. When a salesman attempts to sell you a new suit, there can be a give-and-take exchange of comments. You can ask questions ("Will it hold a crease?" or "What is the material in the suit?"), and he can answer. When you read about the same merchandise in the mass media you do not have that opportunity to comment or question. As we shall see later, communication research provides a sort of feedback to overcome this problem. The astute communicator will try to anticipate the reaction of his audience as much as possible through research or some other source of information. However, the emphasis in mass communication is *toward* the audience.

Mass Communication Emphasizes Selection. There is a buyer's market in communication, because everyone is surrounded by far more material than he can possibly absorb. Few people, for example, read more than a fraction of the daily paper or note more than a small portion of the material to which they are exposed on the broadcast media. Audiences are constantly selecting certain communications and rejecting others. It is little wonder that advertisers have to try so hard to attract the attention of audiences. We shall examine the principles of selection in more detail in a later chapter.

Audience Predispositions Heavily Influence Communication Effectiveness. Many studies confirm the importance of predisposition (the social or psychological state of the audience at the beginning of the communication). For example, people who are well-disposed toward a

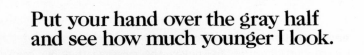

Put your hand over the gray half and see how much younger I look.

Cover the gray hair in the photo and the years go. Cover the dark hair and the years come clumping back.

Young/old/young/old/young/old/young/old—it happens every time you shift your hand. Which goes to prove just one thing. Gray hair makes you look older. And dark hair makes you look younger.

But we suspect you've known that all along. Then how come you didn't do something about it before now?

We suspect you know the answer to that one, too.

The embarrassment.

The embarrassment of having to stand in a crowded drugstore and ask for a bottle of women's haircoloring "for-uh-your wife."

The embarrassment of having friends (and unfriends) kid you about it—"Hey, fellows, look —Charley dyed his hair."

And finally, there was the biggest embarrassment of all—the funny feeling that doing something to your gray was too flashy, too "show biz," not for a "regular fellow."

GREAT DAY® For Men

Well, let's take the last worry first. Because if we can get you over that one, we have a new product that *solves all the other problems.* (It's called *"Great Day."* From Clairol Research. More about it later.)

More Men Than You Think

It may have been true ten years ago that only a few actors colored their hair. But since then a

minor, and somewhat surprising, revolution has taken place. Today it's estimated that over 2,000,000 men from all walks of life have broken with tradition and have done something about their gray hair—bankers, farmers, longshoremen, teachers and police officers do it. Without blushing.

They all have one thing in common: they don't want to look old before their time.

No Embarrassment

Now, finally there's a product designed especially for men—a product that won't embarrass you in any way. Great Day. With Great Day a man can return his graying hair to a soft, rich, natural-looking color in the privacy of his own bathroom, or have it done in any good barbershop. Without any of the worries.

We Give It To You Straight

Great Day works like a shampoo. Once every two weeks or so, you pour it on—*straight from the bottle.* (No mixing.) Lather it in, let it sit, rinse it off. No complications. Leave it on a few minutes each time, and you color the gray gradually. If you want to take the plunge all at once, just leave it on longer before rinsing.

Nobody Notices

Great Day doesn't change your natural hair color. It only works on the gray. The change is subtle. Amazingly, even though *you're* very conscious of what you've done, experience has shown that most people don't even notice the difference in color. Only the effect. "Say, Charley, you look great. Did you lose weight or something?"

Your Pillow Won't Talk

Great Day goes inside your gray hair shafts. So it can't rub off on your collar, or on the pillow. It contains no peroxide in any form. It doesn't harm your hair in any way. (Actually, it leaves your hair in better condition.) It doesn't affect the texture of your hair at all. But just by making it darker, it does make it look somewhat fuller. (Nobody will mind *that* extra benefit.)

Great Day is made by Clairol, the world's leading authority on women's haircoloring. Now, after years of laboratory work and thousands of tests on gray-haired men, Clairol can say, "Hair color so natural only his *barber* knows for sure."™ And unless your barber applied it to your hair himself, even *he* won't be absolutely certain.

Muster up your courage a little—and do something about your gray hair.

It's nice to look young.

FIG. 4.2 *Excellent use of visual and verbal elements of the advertisement to communicate the message.* *TM © COPYRIGHT 1965, 1966 CLAIROL INC.; ADVERTISEMENT PREPARED BY DOYLE DANE BERNBACH INC.

particular political party will normally give more attention to publicity from that party than to that coming from an opposing party. They will tend to accept as "facts" partisan political material from their own party and to misread or distort material from the opposing party.[4] Furthermore, people respond more favorably to a communication that is in line with their predispositions — when it tells them what they want to be told. Similarly, if the position taken by a persuasive message is fairly close to the predispositions of the audience, it is fairly easy to change opinions. For example, in one of the studies reported by Carl I. Hovland, an attempt was made to change the opinion of people regarding alcoholic-beverage regulation.[5] It was found that when a wet position was espoused, 28 percent of the middle-of-the-road subjects were changed to the position of the communicator, compared with only 4 percent of the drys. When a dry position was espoused, 14 percent of the middle-of-the-roaders were changed, whereas only 4 percent of the wets were changed.

Audiences Generally Have to Pay for Mass Communication. There is an old saying that "talk is cheap." However, people must pay for most of what they get from their mass media. In radio and television, they pay for the sets, not directly for the message. Research by Scripps-Howard newspapers indicates that people today spend about the same percentage of their income for mass media (about 2.4 percent) that they spent in 1880.[5] In the depression years of the 1930s the percentage increased to 2.6 percent of income.

Mass Communication Is Heavily Institutionalized. Mass communication is impersonal in that it is the product of institutions — the various media, the business firms who use them, and the agencies that plan the programs and prepare the messages. It cannot, like person-to-person communication, be attributed to an individual.

ADVERTISING VERSUS OTHER MASS COMMUNICATIONS

There are, of course, many forms of mass communication. For example, the news reporter or the producer of a television show communicates to mass audiences. Here are some of the ways in which advertising differs from other forms of mass communication:

Advertising Is Primarily Persuasive. Every advertiser has some definite purpose in mind when he buys space or time. He may want to build a certain image. He may be looking for immediate sales. But he always tailors his campaign to fit a certain objective.

Advertising Content Is Not Controlled by the Medium. The advertiser buys his space and time and decides (within certain limits, of course) what he will put into it. Publicity releases, however, that come from that same advertiser may go into the editor's wastebasket if he does not see fit to use them.

Advertising Is Commercial. To the advertiser, his advertising is a business expense that must be justified. It must make a contribution

[4]Bernard Berelson and Gary A. Steiner, *Human Behavior* (New York: Harcourt, Brace & World, Inc. 1964), p. 537.
[5]Berelson and Steiner, p. 541.

to his net profit. To the medium, advertising is the primary source of revenue (approximately 68 percent of total revenue for United States newspapers and magazines, virtually 100 percent for radio and television).

PLANNING THE COMMUNICATION PROGRAM

The advantages of planning need not be repeated. It is sufficient to emphasize that it is as important to plan the communication as it is to plan the marketing program. One might argue that it is even more important to plan communications, because the pathways to effective communication are so hard to follow, so little charted.

Ideally, our communication plan should have four parts—the first three are reminiscent of the marketing triad described in the last chapter.

1. Analysis of appropriate background information.
2. Communication objectives.
3. The "communication mix."
4. Feedback.

ANALYSIS OF BACKGROUND INFORMATION

The information-gathering process—in communication as in marketing—is the systematic application of research, experience, and judgment to the solving of communication problems. It might be useful to elicit certain types of information that are likely to be especially useful in this respect.

Communicators.   What types of communicators are most effective in telling your story? To what extent should they work in combination and to what extent alone? What makes a communicator creative?

Content.   Under what conditions are illustrations likely to tell your message more effectively than words? What is the relative readership of various types of content? What is the relation between a particular type of advertising content and the medium that transmits it to consumers?

Audiences.   Who reads (or listens to or watches) the message? How intensively do they pay attention to the message? Why do they read or not read it? What predisposes them to select one message and reject another?

Media.   What media are most effective for reaching particular audiences? What are the images people have of particular media? To what extent do media audiences overlap?

Effects.   What effect, if any, did a particular message or campaign have on an audience? To what extent is this effect the result of other influences than advertising? What is the nature of this effect (attention, change in attitude, and the like)?

COMMUNICATION OBJECTIVES

Although the ultimate purpose of most advertising is to make a sale, its immediate purpose is a more limited one that can best be defined in terms of communication. More specifically, the purpose is to communicate a message to a particular audience. As Russell Colley points out, "The purpose of advertising is to bring about a change in a state of mind toward the purchase of a product."[6] The need for a better definition of objectives was dramatically illustrated in a study made by Professor Harry Dean Wolfe for the National Industrial Conference Board. The companies interviewed gave ninety-one different marketing communication objectives for their advertising.[7] Among the most important were the following: creating awareness, creating a favorable image, increasing sales, and soliciting requests for information.

As in marketing, good communication objectives are both *specific* and *measurable*. Thus the planners have a goal to work toward in their strategy, and they can tell afterward just how successful they have been. Colley illustrates this effectively by dividing advertising objectives into four stages of "commercial communication":[8]

Awareness. The prospect must be made aware of the existence of a brand or company.

Comprehension. He must comprehend what the product is and what it will do for him.

Conviction. He must arrive at a mental disposition or conviction to buy the product.

Action. Finally, he must take action.

As Colley points out, it is possible to measure the accomplishment of such objectives *before* and *after* advertising. Let us suppose, for example, that we are advertising a food product and that we hope to measure the awareness, comprehension, conviction, and action resulting from our campaign. We might obtain the following information:

	BEFORE THIS ADVERTISING CAMPAIGN	AFTER THIS ADVERTISING CAMPAIGN
	(In percentages)	
Awareness of our brand name, key message	25	35
Comprehension of image we are trying to communicate	10	20
Belief in our key message or slogan	6	12
Action taken	2	4

The objective of many advertising campaigns is to communicate a brand image to prospective consumers. Agency president David Ogilvy, describing his company's image-building advertising for Rolls-Royce, said, "We were called on to perform a miracle analogous to the Miracle

[6]Russell H. Colley, *Defining Advertising Goals for Measured Advertising Results* (New York: Association of National Advertisers, Inc., 1961), p. 39.
[7]Harry Dean Wolfe, *Measuring Advertising Effectiveness* (New York: National Industrial Conference Board, 1961).
[8]Colley, p. 38.

"I don't know who you are.

I don't know your company.

I don't know your company's product.

I don't know what your company stands for.

I don't know your company's customers.

I don't know your company's record.

I don't know your company's reputation.

Now—what was it you wanted to sell me?"

MORAL: Sales start before your salesman calls—with business publication advertising.

McGRAW-HILL
market-directed®
PUBLICATIONS

FIG. 4.3 *An advertisement used again and again by McGraw-Hill to dramatize the communication objective of business publication advertising.* COURTESY MCGRAW-HILL PUBLICATIONS.

of the Loaves and the Fishes."[9] He referred here to the problem of advertising the Rolls-Royce with a budget that was a small fraction of those of competitors such as Cadillac, Imperial, and Continental. The agency men decided that its objective would be to make the car a symbol of aristocratic living and fine workmanship (Fig. 17.2). At the same time, it wanted people to feel comfortable with the Rolls-Royce or, as Ogilvy put it, "lower the pedestal that Rolls-Royce is on without upsetting it." In addition to the small budget, the agency faced the problems of the average American's ignorance of Rolls-Royce and the reluctance of well-to-do families to have cars that were different from those of other families in the neighborhood. A final problem was a trend toward inverted snobbery using a battered station wagon as a symbol of the I-don't-care attitude. Despite these handicaps, sales indicate that the desired image is being achieved.

Pierre Martineau has provided one of the best descriptions of a brand image: "The halo of psychological meanings, the associations of

[9]"Rolls-Royce: Can a U.S. Ad Agency Sell a Symbol of Aristocracy to Americans?" *Printers' Ink,* June 27, 1958, pp. 34–35, and Gilbert Burck, "Rolls-Royce Stoops to Sell," *Fortune,* December 1958, pp. 82ff.

FIG. 4.4 *Effective use of advertising in a rapidly changing field to communicate factual information for 1966.* COURTESY NEW YORK STOCK EXCHANGE.

feeling, the indelibly written esthetic messages over and above the physical qualities."[10]

In discussing image building, researcher Ben Gedalecia says, "The image and the reality must be synonymous. If they are not, no words can long stand against deeds."[11] Like most communication experts, he emphasizes the importance of defining objectives: "Objectives, I feel, will remove a lot of the anecdote-type glamor from our operations. . . . Are we aiming at all people or designated groups? Are we presenting just any information at all? Just working for any attitude change?"

To a company's public relations director, objectives may mean the building of a certain corporate image. Some companies like to be thought of as "progressive," some as "safe," some as "public-spirited." When the desired image is decided on, advertising, publicity, speeches, and all other communications can be focused on achieving it.

[10]Pierre Martineau, *Motivation in Advertising* (New York: McGraw-Hill, Inc., 1957), p. 146.
[11]Ben Gedalecia, "The Importance of Prior Planning," *Evaluating Public Relations* (Madison: The University of Wisconsin Press, 1959).

To the manager of a retail store, communication objectives are the creation of desirable store images. What sort of store image does the public look for? Martineau offers this explanation:

> One of the most important functions in the housewife's role is to know the store. She learns to single out certain cues in the advertising which will tell her about the store's status, its sense of styling, its policies on returns and credit, its general atmosphere, its customer body, even its physical qualities; and then she decides intuitively whether this is where she fits in. Far more than by any explicit claims about the store, by the store, her intuitive judgments are formulated by nonrational symbols: the type, the whiteness or fullness of the ad, the general tone, the sophistication of the art—in other words by the totality of the advertising style.[12]

There are those who say that the objective is to communicate facts—facts about the company or about the product. This puts things in reverse order. When one talks about facts one is talking about what is *given out*. A communication program has a lot more focus when attention is directed to what is *taken in* and objectives are expressed on this basis.

Obviously objectives do not spring from a vacuum. They come from a careful study of background information. They involve the creative use of such facts—creative, that is, in the same sense that a scientist uses data to formulate his hypotheses or an artist examines his subject and creates a painting.

THE COMMUNICATION MIX

The third step is a rigorous appraisal of the alternative means of carrying out these objectives. From this should come our "communication mix." The expression "marketing mix" has become part of the modern business idiom. Why not, then, have a mix of communication activities?

In one respect the word "mix" applied to communication can lead to confusion. Do we mean a mix of the media? Or of the audiences? Or of some other phase of communication? The answer is that we mean *all* of these. If we consider again our framework—who says what, to whom, through what channel, with what effect—we shall see that we have to evaluate alternatives in each of these areas. Thus someone has to evaluate which of the alternative communicators available he will utilize, which of the alternative forms of content he will use, which of the alternative audiences he will attempt to reach, and which of the alternative media he will use in trying to reach them. (Formulating the objective involves an appraisal of alternative effects.) The optimum result is an integrated plan consisting of the various activities.

The Communicators. The word "communicator" can be used to describe either a large organization like General Electric or the people who prepare the message. The focus here will be on the latter interpretation. These people can in turn be divided into two general categories—the mass communicators and the person-to-person communicators.

[12]Pierre Martineau, *Motivation in Advertising* (New York: McGraw-Hill, Inc., 1957), p. 175.

Mass Communicators. These are the professionals who put together the message and speed it on its way. It is they who staff the advertising departments and agencies, the public relations departments and agencies, and the media. Sometimes advertisements are the work of one person working alone, but more frequently they are the product of a team of people working together. Consequently, there is often a problem in finding the right "mix" of communicators to put together an advertisement or campaign most effectively. Advertising agencies, for example, emphasize the range of talents they can offer. The client is invited to put together almost any mix his inclinations or commercial purposes might dictate. Agencies can usually provide not only copywriters and artists, but also merchandising specialists, package-goods specialists, animation specialists, and many others.

The trend is more and more toward specialization. A study by Ernest A. Sharpe of various "mixes" of copywriters and artists indicated that the growth of specialization within advertising means that more talent is brought to bear on advertising a particular brand. But the individual contributions of these specialists must be harmonized and unified or the effect is likely to be a fuzzy brand image that was never intended. In communicating a clear-cut brand image, the more the communicator team tends to "level and sharpen" the concept of the brand image, the more it tends to communicate the brand image intended. In Sharpe's study "leveling and sharpening" was defined as the degree to which the communicators in the team concentrated meaning and importance on a limited number of qualities.[13]

Person-to-Person Communicators. Many effective communicators are nonprofessionals who spread a message by word of mouth. One interesting study of person-to-person communicators was reported in *Fortune* by William H. Whyte, Jr.[14] In studying the spread of air-conditioning ownership in Philadelphia he found that while a certain neighborhood as a whole might show an average of ten air conditioners in a block, one block might have three and the next block eighteen. He investigated further and found clusters within blocks. He concluded that these clusters in a homogeneous neighborhood of identical houses were the symbols of a communication network. The influence seemed to flow up and down the block and across the alley, rather than across the street, following the pattern of communication among families. Communicators in the block were spreading information and influence.

A comprehensive study of the flow of personal communication was reported on by Katz and Lazarsfeld.[15] They found, for example, that women looked to unmarried girls for fashion information, but to women with large families for information and advice regarding food. They found that the communicators who influenced people in a certain class

[13]Ernest A. Sharpe, *Effects of Encoder-Team Variables upon Decoder Perception* (Unpublished Ph.D. Thesis, University of Wisconsin, 1964).
[14]William H. Whyte, Jr., "The Web of Mouth," *Fortune*, November 1954, pp. 140ff. See also Robert C. Brooks, Jr., "'Word-of-Mouth' Advertising in Selling New Products," *Journal of Marketing*, October 1957, for a summary of several studies.
[15]See Elihu Katz and Paul Lazarsfeld, *Personal Influence* (New York: The Free Press, 1955), and Everett M. Rogers, *The Diffusion of Innovations* (New York: The Free Press, 1962).

were likely to be members of the group, rather than of a remote class. The study thus implied that influence of testimonials by movie or sports stars or even of professional experts may be overrated.

We have a lot to learn about these amateur opinion leaders or "influentials." We know, however, that they are greater readers of the mass media than are the people whom they influence. It is not clear whether or not the information they obtain from the media results in their influence over other people. But we know that they get information from sources other than the media.

The role of the amateur communicator and his relation to the over-all communication mix was demonstrated in a study of the acceptance of new ideas by Iowa farmers.[16] Researchers found that changes that involved new skills or techniques required the longest periods of time for acceptance and that most decisions were made after many contacts with various communication sources. A typical farmer seemed to go through the following stages in learning about and adopting new ideas:

Awareness (knows that the idea exists, but knows little about it)
Interest (looks for more information)
Evaluation (weighs the pros and cons)
Trial (usually on a small scale)
Adoption

Mass media made the greatest impact during the awareness and interest stages. Neighbors and friends were the most important influences during the evaluation stage; and agricultural agencies, neighbors, friends, dealers, and salesmen during the trial stage.

In this study, farm people were divided into four groups. These groups and the major sources of influence on each were as follows:

Innovators (university and other technical sources)
Community adoption leaders (agricultural agencies, farm media, innovators)
Local adoption leaders (agricultural agencies, community adoption leaders, mass media)
Later adopters (local adoption leaders)

The findings in this and related studies suggest that the mass media are most effective in creating awareness, whereas person-to-person communications are most effective in influencing evaluation. Both appear to play a relatively minor role in the trial stage because their importance lies mainly in showing the consumer how to use the item correctly. As an innovation moves from the trial to the adoption stage personal communications become more and more important.[17]

The communicator mix is inevitably complicated. The alternatives are intertwined, and the evidence on which to base decisions is

[16]See George M. Beal and Joe Bohlen, *The Diffusion Process* (Ames: Iowa Agricultural Experiment Station, 1957).
[17]See Gerald Zaltman, *Marketing: Contributions from the Behavioral Sciences* (New York: Harcourt, Brace & World, Inc., 1965), pp. 28–31, for a discussion of this point.

sketchier than it is in any other phase of communication. Companies interested in communicating will probably continue to depend on a mix of professional creative people from their communication departments and agencies. They should not overlook, however, the possibility of reaching influential amateurs, who may in turn help to communicate about the products and services they sell.

Content of the Message. The core of the communication program is the message itself. This message is composed of two parts—the visual and the verbal. These are the two means the communicator uses to symbolize what he has to say. The ultimate effectiveness of any advertisement will depend on how well the elements are created and arranged.

Until the invention of movable type in the fifteenth century the emphasis was on pictures. In early advertising the emphasis was on words. During the 1920s and 1930s advertising copy became important. Albert Lasker commented in the 1930s that only three things of major importance had ever happened in the history of the advertising business: the *original* N. W. Ayer contract, the discovery of copy as the most important element in advertising, and the injection of sex into advertising.[18]

Today the advertisers are divided. On one hand, we have certain practitioners who believe that the magic of advertising lies primarily in words and that the picture people have gone too far. (This point of view is mostly among practitioners who have had extensive mail order or retail experience.) On the other hand, the case for the visual is stated dramatically by Pierre Martineau:

> In advertising the typical journeyman wordsmith seems quite insensitive to the fact that illustrations, color, and design can by themselves alone be powerful channels of communication to the inner man. . . . Most attempts to generate mood with the language of advertising jargonese end up as shallow and unconvincing. To take another example, pictures will convey ideas with a completeness and clarity that words can never attain. Try to describe a pretty girl and see how hopelessly inadequate is any word report by comparison to a picture.[19]

Advertising presentation is not so circumscribed as these two general points of view might imply. We have in the print media, for example, type-face design, white space, and signatures as alternatives that we may use to communicate. In the electronic media, sound effects, visual effects such as dissolves and wipes, and even silence are alternatives that might be considered.

Some business executives are so used to thinking verbally that they have difficulty in rationally considering the other alternatives of the content mix. Some are even doubtful that something is worth communicating until they see it in words. How else, they will say, can you discuss it in a committee meeting? Verbalization is good as a device to organize thinking, but the communicator may get into trouble by assuming that the audience will absorb a message *only* in verbal form. Suppose a company finds out that people believe it is backward (com-

---

[18]James Webb Young, *The Diary of An Adman* (Chicago: Advertising Publications, 1944), p. 101.
[19]Martineau, p. 175.

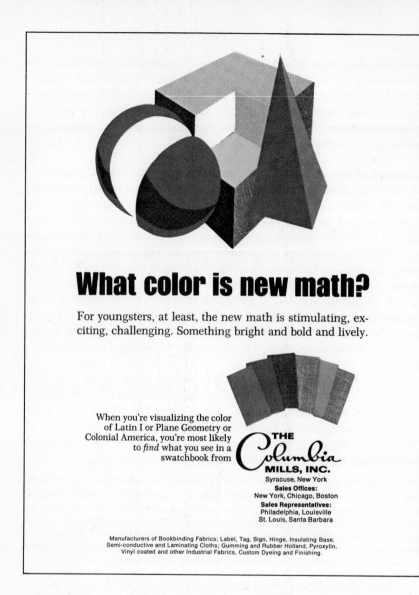

What color is new math?

For youngsters, at least, the new math is stimulating, exciting, challenging. Something bright and bold and lively.

When you're visualizing the color of Latin I or Plane Geometry or Colonial America, you're most likely to *find* what you see in a swatchbook from

THE *Columbia*
MILLS, INC.
Syracuse, New York
Sales Offices:
New York, Chicago, Boston
Sales Representatives:
Philadelphia, Louisville
St. Louis, Santa Barbara

Manufacturers of Bookbinding Fabrics; Label, Tag, Sign, Hinge, Insulating Base,
Semi-conductive and Laminating Cloths; Gumming and Rubber Holland, Pyroxylin,
Vinyl coated and other Industrial Fabrics, Custom Dyeing and Finishing.

FIG. 4.5 *Advertisment (originally printed in color) emphasizing the ability of color to communicate.* CLIENT: THE COLUMBIA MILLS, INC.; AGENCY: MARCH ADVERTISING INC.

pared with its competitors) in research. It has many alternative methods of saying, in effect, "We are a progressive, up-to-date business organization." S. C. Johnson and Sons commissioned Frank Lloyd Wright to design a building that was so unusual (yet functional) that it said this. General Electric depends heavily on words in its ads. Container Corporation was a pioneer in using abstract art in consumer ads.

In general, communicators who appeal to man's logical nature depend more on the verbal than on the visual. A glance at the pages of the business press will help to confirm this. Note how heavily the advertisements depend on words. On the other hand, an appeal to emotion is more likely to utilize the visual.

Audiences. When we talk about communication, we talk in terms of audiences. However, in marketing we talk primarily about market groups. One might inquire whether they are the same. Actually they are not, although many media buyers think of the two as almost identical (they buy media to cover a specific market). The difference is in focus. "Audiences" emphasizes the direction of a message to a specific group. "Market" emphasizes the selling of a product or service to a group.

Although we speak of *mass* communication (and *mass* marketing), we never reach more than a fraction of our potential audience. According to Nielsen figures, over 20,000,000 American families tuned in to the movie, *The Birds*, on television in 1968. Our largest circulation magazine, *Reader's Digest*, had an adult audience of approximately 34,000,000 in mid-1968. The New York *Daily News* ranked first in United States newspaper circulation with an average daily circulation of more than 2,000,000. These audiences may be fragmented into more specialized audiences for advertisements and editorial material.

In no other area of communication does the practitioner find such a plethora of data as he does in the audience field. Much of it is supplied to him by media that claim certain audiences as their own. Some of these treat audiences as synonymous with markets, so that, to them, the upper-income market is the upper-income audience. It is an obvious advantage for the advertiser to have audience figures that coincide with markets he is interested in reaching. Many studies supply information covering both audiences and markets in terms of classifications such as food, medicine, and recreation. We can also study both audiences and markets on social and psychological bases. We might call these "audience-market" classifications. They are discussed in Chapter 12.

But we have also a choice of alternatives that are strictly media-oriented. Suppose that we want to build a corporate image of solidarity for a bank with the upper-income people in our community. We find that these people are a mix of "hi-fi"–radio listeners, financial-page readers, boating-magazine readers, and watchers of late movies on television. Here is an audience mix that delivers the market and is consistent with our objective.

Audiences may be classified in terms of the media (such as newspapers, magazines), the types of material they choose (such as variety-show audience, sports-page audience), the intensity of listening, viewing, or reading (the avid viewer, the casual viewer, and the like), or the time of day (the afternoon audience, the noontime audience, in radio and television). Any audience classification that clearly outlines possible alternatives might help one to decide on the "mix."

One problem is the overlapping of audiences. Some people are such avid communications fans that they turn up in almost every classification—they're western fans, classical music fans, mystery drama fans, financial page readers. Although this complicates the picture, it by no means destroys the usefulness of audience classifications.

Channels. As we saw earlier, we have a choice between mediated and nonmediated channels of communication. In the two-step process of communication we have a combination of *both* mediated and person-to-person communication. Let us look at a case in point. Where would doctors expect to find out about a new drug? As Table 4.1 indicates, this may well depend on what stage of the adoption process we are describing. This table summarizes the sources of information mentioned by physicians in connection with their decision to adopt the new "miracle drug," Gammanym. In the early stages, person-to-person communication was most important but diminished in importance as the adoption process progressed. Note that mass media became more important as person-to-person communication decreased in importance.

	STAGE 1	STAGE 2	STAGE 3
Salesmen	52	27	5
Colleagues and meetings	13	19	36
Direct mail	22	16	14
Journal articles	6	21	21
Drug house periodicals	3	11	21
Other media	4	7	3
Total mentions	(87)	(131)	(87)

SEQUENCE OF SOURCES OF INFORMATION MENTIONED BY PHYSICIANS IN CONNECTION WITH THE DECISION TO ADOPT GAMMANYM
(In percentages)

TABLE 4.1

SOURCE: Elihu Katz, "The Social Itinerary of Technical Change: Two Studies on the Diffusion of Innovation," in Harper W. Boyd, Jr., and Joseph Newman, *Advertising Management: Selected Readings* (Homewood, Ill.: Richard D. Irwin, Inc., 1965), p. 139.

We have several standard classifications of mass media to help us in selecting which to use. We have, first of all, the *type of medium* (newspapers, magazines, television, and so on). The print media in turn can be divided into classes on the basis of *frequency of issue* (weekly, monthly), *area of interest* (such as women's, sports, antiques), or *area of coverage* (local, national, regional). The electronic media may be categorized on the basis of such classifications as *power* (wattage), *type of frequency* (uhf-vhf), *community* (metropolitan, rural), and ownership (network, independent).

Schramm recommends the following useful scale for differentiating channels:

1. *Space-time.* The space media seem to offer better facilities for communicating complex information — information that the respondent should think over. On the other hand, we are fairly sure that the time media (mainly radio and television) offer certain advantages for rote learning.
2. *Participation.* The scale of participation will range from personal conversation at the top, with maximum participation, to magazines and books where there is little audience participation.
3. *Speed.* Radio and television are right at the top in speed or timeliness. It is not unusual these days to see pedestrians on the street or coeds strolling the campus, carrying transistor radios. Books and magazines are much less immediate.
4. *Permanence.* Books are quite permanent. Radio and television messages are not.[20]

In formulating alternative media mixes we are handicapped by gaps in our research data, even regarding leading mass media. We have

[20]Schramm, pp. 87–90.

substantial information on how many people read, or subscribe to, or watch our media; very little information on how they *feel* about alternative channels of communication (what do they expect to get from television as compared with newspapers? Under what conditions do they look to opinion leaders?). Not surprisingly, different advertisers with similar objectives will develop quite different mixes. One regional oil company spends most of its advertising appropriation in newspapers and television, whereas a competitor spends all of its advertising money in radio and television. Most media experts will admit in their more candid moments that they have to use a good deal of intuition in making final media decisions.

INTERRELATION OF ELEMENTS OF THE MIX

Our concept of the communication mix might be easier to understand if we spelled out what has so far been only implied—the interrelation between the various steps. For example, the message mix will be influenced by the channel that is to carry it as well as by the general objective. Obviously, it would be inappropriate to publish in *Harper's Bazaar* or *Vogue* the editorial and advertising material you find in pulp magazines.

Similarly, communication researchers have long recognized the interrelation between audience and content. The audience sees in the message what it wants to see and filters the material through its own feelings and drives, which act as a kind of protective net. The Chevrolet owner, for example, sees in the Chevrolet ad a reinforcement of his own good judgment; the prospective owner sees an image of himself.

Obviously, a message might be appropriate for one type of communicator and not for another. We don't expect Tiffany or Rolls-Royce to shout their wares, and we should be unpleasantly surprised if either did. Research tells us that the opinion leader is more effective if his message reinforces groups' norms or advocates only minor changes. His effect in promoting major changes can be overestimated.

The various "W" elements ("Who" says "What" to "Whom" through "What channel" with "What effect") must be considered as a whole in terms of the communication objective.

THE FEEDBACK

Another important element in the communication process is the feedback. In conversation with a friend the feedback is obvious, because the friend may frown, nod his head in agreement, or interrupt in violent disagreement. In conversation we even get feedback from our own messages. We hear our own voices and correct our mispronunciations. We see the words we write and correct misspellings or awkward constructions.

The feedback for mass communication must be in terms of averages. Audience research supplies our feedback by telling us that 200,000 viewers were exposed to our commercial or that 10 percent of the magazine's readers read at least 50 percent of our copy. We have to settle for audience norms as feedback.

In many respects our feedback techniques in mass communication are still fairly primitive. An advertiser can get only the haziest idea of the feedback he is most anxious to learn about—consumer sales. Although sales data are plentiful, it is only in isolated instances that we can trace a real cause and effect—a relation between a communication (or campaign) and the sales of the product advertised. Consequently, feedback techniques still fall mainly in the indirect category. Because we cannot measure the sales impact of the message, we measure factors that we hope correlate with sales. Readership and listenership are, of course, outstanding cases in point. Attention, however, is now turning to more sophisticated areas (depth interviewing, multivariate analysis, and the like).

SUMMARY

The communications concept (like the marketing concept) emphasizes the establishing of objectives and alternative means of achieving them. In both concepts a framework for decision making is provided.

We have seen that communication works best when it is planned. The four-part plan suggested consists of an analysis of background information, definition of communication objectives, the communication mix, and provision for feedback. The mix is perhaps the trickiest of these in that the possible alternatives are so interwoven. If, however, we evaluate our alternatives on the basis of the five-W framework we may analyze them in an organized manner.

Whether the five-W framework or some other is used, it is most important that advertising itself be considered as a part of the whole communication program of an advertiser.

QUESTIONS FOR DISCUSSION

1. What are the principal differences between person-to-person communication and mass communication?
2. Select five advertisements from current advertising media and attempt to define the communication objectives of these advertisements.
3. To what extent is the communication function of advertising related to our knowledge of psychology?
4. What is the diffusion process? Explain its relation to the use of advertising.
5. Select two advertisements from a current magazine or newspaper. Explain as precisely as you can what you believe are the communication objectives of each advertisement, and how these objectives differ from their marketing objectives.

SUGGESTED READINGS

Arndt, Johan, *Word of Mouth Advertising*. New York: Advertising Research Foundation, 1968.

Berelson, Bernard, and Morris Janowitz, eds., *Reader in Public Opinion and Communication*. New York: The Free Press, 1966.

THE COMMUNICATIONS CONCEPT 77

————, and Gary A. Steiner, *Human Behavior*. New York: Harcourt, Brace & World, Inc., 1964. Chapter 13.

Bettinghaus, Erwin P., *Persuasive Communications*. New York: Holt, Rinehart and Winston, Inc., 1968.

Boyd, Harper W., Jr., and Joseph W. Newman, *Advertising Management: Selected Readings*. Homewood, Ill.: Richard D. Irwin, Inc., 1965. Part II.

Colley, Russell H., *Defining Advertising Goals for Measured Advertising Results*. New York: Association of National Advertisers, 1961.

Dunn, S. Watson, *Advertising Copy and Communication*. New York: McGraw-Hill, Inc., 1956. Chapter 2.

Hovland, Carl I., Irving Janus, and Harold E. Kelley, *Communication and Persuasion*. New Haven, Conn.: Yale University Press, 1953.

Katz, Elihu, and Paul F. Lazarsfeld, *Personal Influence*. New York: The Free Press, 1955.

Martineau, Pierre, *Motivation in Advertising*. New York: McGraw-Hill, Inc., 1957. Chapters 1, 2, 6, and 11.

Sandage, C. H., and Vernon Fryburger, eds., *The Role of Advertising*. Homewood, Ill.: Richard D. Irwin, Inc., 1960. Part II.

Schramm, Wilbur, ed., *The Process and Effects of Mass Communication*. Urbana, Ill.: University of Illinois Press, 1954.

———— ed, *The Science of Human Communication*. New York: Basic Books, Inc., 1963.

5 | Economic Effects

Before we examine how advertising and promotion work, it is important to ask ourselves a few questions. Does advertising make goods or services more expensive? Is advertising good or bad for our economy? Is promotion generally truthful?

These and many other questions are raised by the critics of advertising and promotion and are important enough to deserve the most objective answers we can provide. Whether we are consumers beset by doubts regarding advertising, practitioners whose living depends on it, or businessmen who use it as a business tool, we are continually confronted by troublesome questions. In this chapter we shall deal with some of the most important economic questions asked by critics of advertising; in the next chapter we shall concentrate on questions that are primarily social or ethical in nature.

HOW DO ECONOMISTS VIEW ADVERTISING?

Economists have either ignored advertising or have viewed it with skepticism. It does not fit neatly into the theories constructed by leaders of economic thought. For example, Alfred Marshall, father of the neo-classical school of economics, divided advertising into two categories, "informative" and "persuasive."[1] He admitted the benefit of providing information about new products, but he objected to "persuasive" advertising because he thought that it merely shifted demand from one brand to another without serving any socially useful function. He and other neoclassicists did not recognize the "added value" derived from advertising or that advertising may increase primary demand for a class of products.

Advertising has not fared particularly well with modern economists either. Many of them believe that persuasion is antithetical to the concept of an "economic man" who should make his decisions rationally rather than emotionally. Paul A. Samuelson emphasizes the disadvantages of promotion but admits certain economic advantages:

> Business research and advertising are expensive and their results cumulative, success tends to breed success, and profits tend to breed more profits. Therefore small business claims that it cannot always effectively compete with such firms. In other words, industrial research may be subject to economies of large scale which small businesses cannot enjoy.
>
> The instances of beer, cigarettes and soap remind us that advertising and research are quite different things. Budweiser beer sales may stay large because a national audience has been persuaded of its merits. Much soap advertising is aimed more to solidify the sales of one brand than to expand total soap use and cleanliness. Yet in many cases it will not be easy to decide whether a certain bit of applied industrial research is for the purpose of technical improvement or for market improvement.[2]

One of the most articulate and widely read of modern economists, John Kenneth Galbraith, accuses his colleagues in the economics field of being behind the times in their analysis of advertising:

> The present disposition of conventional economic theory to write off annual outlays of tens of billions of dollars of advertising and similar sales costs by the industrial system as without purpose or consequence is, to say the least, drastic. No other legal economic activity is subject to similar rejection. The discovery that sales and advertising expenditures have an organic role in the system will not, accordingly, seem implausible.
>
> The general effect of sales effort, defined in the broadest terms, is to shift the locus of decision in the purchase of goods from the consumer where it is beyond control to the firm where it is subject to control. This transfer, like the control of prices, is by no means complete. But again what is imperfect is not unimportant.[3]

Although he concedes that industrialists occasionally stub their toe and find it impossible to manipulate demand (as Ford did, for instance, in the case of the ill-fated Edsel), he maintains that "means can almost always be found to keep exercise of consumer discretion within workable limits."[4] He finds this situation socially dangerous, yet maintains that advertising has a social function:

> This extends from the management of demand, the necessary counterpart of the control of prices, to the conditioning of attitudes necessary for the operation

[1]Alfred Marshall, *Principles of Economics* (London: Macmillan & Co., Ltd., 1890).
[2]Paul A. Samuelson, *Economics: An Introductory Analysis*, 6th ed. (New York: McGraw-Hill, Inc., 1964), p. 500.
[3]John Kenneth Galbraith, *The New Industrial State* (Boston: Houghton Mifflin Company, 1967), p. 205.
[4]Galbraith, p. 207.

and prestige of the industrial system. For advertising men it has long been a sore point that economists dismissed them as so much social waste. They have not quite known how to answer. Some have doubtless sensed that in a society where wants are psychologically grounded, the instruments of access to the mind cannot be unimportant. They were right. The functions here identified may well be less exalted than the more demanding philosophers of the advertising industry might wish. But none can doubt their importance for the industrial system given always the standards by which that system measures achievement and success.[5]

DOES ADVERTISING MAKE GOODS MORE EXPENSIVE?

To analyze the effects of advertising or other promotion on the cost of goods we look at price setting from two standpoints: the *costs* involved in producing and marketing, and the *demand* for the goods. The price may go up if advertising increases the total cost of making and marketing the product. On the other hand, the price may go up even though the cost remains the same, if the marketer believes that the use of advertising has made the demand greater. Let us look at each of these situations more closely.

Advertising's Effect on Costs. Advertising's effect on total cost has long puzzled professional economists and businessmen as well as consumers. The economist wants to know whether advertising makes our economy operate more efficiently. The businessman wants to know if advertising makes it possible for him to produce and market his goods more cheaply. Many consumers, wonder if the goods they buy might be cheaper if advertising money were left unspent. Why not, some ask, give us this money in lower prices?

Effect on Production Cost. Although advertising expense, like shipping or delivery expense, is obviously part of the cost of producing a product, many maintain that advertising ultimately makes the product cheaper. For many products they are right; for others they are wrong. To understand what happens, we must examine the nature of production costs. Ordinarily, these are composed of three basic costs—labor, materials, and overhead. In certain industries, such as the shoe industry, where a great deal of work is done by hand, labor cost is high in proportion to other costs. In an industry such as steel or automobiles, overhead cost is relatively high, labor cost low.

The claim is often made that advertising lowers the overhead cost per unit if it increases the sales of the product. The point is that overhead may remain the same, while the number of items produced increases. If overhead cost is $100,000 and you produce 100,000 items, your overhead cost per item will be $1.00. However, if you boost your sales to 200,000 units, and your overhead remains the same, overhead cost has been cut to $0.50 a unit. The same idea might apply to labor and material costs. Increased sales volume could make it feasible to install a labor-saving machine and cut labor cost or it might encourage buying raw materials by the carload instead of in smaller lots.

In practice the situation is not quite so simple. Let us look at the hypothetical candy corporation whose production cost is shown in Table

[5]Galbraith, p. 210.

5.1. It is evident that this firm has an optimum point of production. At this point (50,000 cases a year), production cost is lowest. However, costs are highest at the 10,000-cases-a-year rate. At the 20,000-cases-a-year rate we have a substantial cut in overhead cost per case and some in materials, because we can now buy ingredients in larger quantities. When 30,000 cases a year are produced, costs are still lower but the drop is not so large. However, when we go to 40,000 cases our costs per case rise instead of fall. We have to buy new machinery, or add a new section to the factory. The small saving in labor cost is not enough to take care of the increased overhead. However, an increase to 50,000 cases a year brings us to the lowest costs of all. This is our optimum.

TABLE 5.1   ADVERTISING'S EFFECT ON PRODUCTION COSTS

YEARLY RATE OF PRODUCTION	COST PER CASE Overhead	COST PER CASE Labor	COST PER CASE Materials	TOTAL PRODUCTION COST PER CASE
10,000	$0.75	$0.25	$0.20	$1.20
20,000	0.50	0.25	0.15	0.90
30,000	0.40	0.25	0.15	0.80
40,000	0.45	0.23	0.15	0.83
50,000	0.40	0.20	0.15	0.75

Our optimum rate of production will change as new equipment, new staff and new facilities are added. However, there is always some point at which the addition of new facilities becomes pointless.

Certain types of industries are more easily adaptable to mass production than others are. It would be very expensive to make automobiles, television sets, or refrigerators by any method other than mass production. On the other hand, dressmaking, home building, and other types of businesses are much less adaptable to mass production.

Advertising may also cut production costs if it makes possible the stabilization of demand. Stabilization can become particularly important in a product that has a highly seasonal demand. Certain soft-drink makers, for example, are eager to stimulate sales in the winter months to round out the seasonal cycle.

Production cost is only one aspect of the cost picture. We must also consider marketing cost, because it is included in the price the consumer must pay for the product.

Effect on Marketing Cost. Let us examine what might happen to selling costs at each production level of our candy corporation. These cost comparisons are shown in Table 5.2. Note that our 50,000-cases-a-year level does not look quite so good now. We find that our marketing cost at that level is so high that our total cost is slightly higher than it was at the 40,000-cases-a-year rate. The advertising and extra sales effort required to push sales up to the 50,000-case level were so expensive that they vitiated the savings in production cost. This situation is not unusual, because marginal sales (above the optimum point) are often very expensive.

We might expect that increased advertising, by increasing demand, would have cut down other selling costs and reduced total marketing

ADVERTISING'S EFFECT ON MARKETING COSTS   **TABLE 5.2**

YEARLY RATE OF PRODUCTION	COST PER CASE Advertising	COST PER CASE Display	Selling	TOTAL MARKETING COST PER CASE
10,000	0.40	0.10	0.50	1.00
20,000	0.30	0.08	0.45	0.83
30,000	0.20	0.08	0.43	0.71
40,000	0.20	0.08	0.42	0.70
50,000	0.23	0.08	0.44	0.75

cost. Again, this depends on a host of variables. It may, for instance, depend on the age of the industry. In an exhaustive investigation of the relation between advertising and marketing costs, Borden found that

in relatively new industries in which various producers are attempting to build demand and in which the tendency towards similarity of competing products has not progressed far, advertising costs are often relatively high. Such is the case, for example, in the various electrical household appliance fields and in grocery specialty fields.[6]

More recently we can see this happening with regard to television sets and certain packaged food products. These are situations in which the increase in advertising cost per unit is often less than the per unit reduction in overhead and other costs resulting from the increase in demand.

Effect of Demand. Let us consider next what effect consumer demand is likely to have on the price of the goods. We must remember that a businessman is interested primarily in making a maximum profit and sets his production and pricing schedules accordingly. We noted that the candy corporation's total marketing cost per case was lowest at the 40,000-cases-a-year rate. Is that the rate our businessman will decide on? His decision will hinge on demand as well as cost.

In Figure 5.3 we have set up a demand schedule, to show the amount we think the entrepreneur can get per case at each level. If this estimate is correct, it is apparent that the best level of production is the 50,000-level. Although profit and estimated selling price per case are both a little lower at this level, the *total* profit is highest here.

We can say, then, that advertising, by stimulating demand, has helped make this candy cheaper to the consumer. However, if the maker had tried to boost demand above the 50,000-level, he might have found selling cost so high and demand so inelastic that his total profit would have dropped.

The role of demand in price determination has been the concern of both economists and consumers. British economist F. P. Bishop points out how difficult it is to evaluate the role of demand because "goods that are advertised are not the same goods as would be produced without advertising."[7] He notes that manufacturers continually search for *nonprice* features that will help to differentiate their products and make it difficult for consumers to make price comparisons. Bernard De Voto asked why he should pay $1,500 for a high-fidelity radio-phonograph

[6]Neil H. Borden, *The Economic Effects of Advertising* (Homewood, Ill.: Richard D. Irwin, Inc., 1942), p. 445.
[7]F. P. Bishop, *Economics of Advertising* (London: Robert Hale, Ltd., 1944), p. 24.

TABLE 5.3 | ADVERTISING'S EFFECT ON TOTAL PROFIT

YEARLY RATE OF PRODUCTION	TOTAL COST PER CASE	ESTIMATED PRICE PER CASE	PROFIT PER CASE	TOTAL PROFIT
10,000	$2.20	$3.20	$1.00	$10,000
20,000	1.73	2.56	0.83	16,600
30,000	1.51	2.21	0.70	21,000
40,000	1.53	2.18	0.65	26,000
50,000	1.50	2.10	0.60	30,000

combination when he could buy one "using only parts that the big manufacturers make" for about $175.[8] He compared this to buying parts from General Motors and putting them together in the form of a car that outperformed the Cadillac. However, business executive Richard Weil replied that Mr. De Voto would probably not like the stripped-down hi-fi he got for $175. Instead, he would probably prefer the mahogany cabinet, the testing, and the guarantee he would get with the advertised model that came from a nationally-known manufacturer. Each marketer has to make his own assessment of the demand for his product, and he may well decide that profits will be greatest if he maintains his selling price even after he has made substantial profits and reduced his manufacturing costs. He may decide that he can make more money by competing on a quality or some other nonprice basis.

We have to conclude then, as have Borden and others, that the evidence in this area is indeterminate.[9] As he pointed out, for production and marketing costs, the evidence is just too sketchy to justify generalization. We find certain highly advertised products (television sets, power mowers) priced lower than they were in the early days of production. Advertising appears to have played a significant role in this decrease. On the other hand, we find certain products, also highly advertised (cosmetics, soap, cigarettes), have not shown any appreciable reduction in price, although there may have been an increase in quality. Jules Backman points out that "for many new products, for which advertising costs are relatively the greatest, prices often decline — a trend which is made possible by the mass markets developed through various methods including advertising."[10] However, he points out:

On the other hand, in the declining phase of the life cycle of a product, unit costs would tend to rise as demand declines. Under such conditions, it is usually impossible to recover these rising costs out of higher prices. Clearly each situation must be examined separately to determine the impact on unit costs.

O. R. Firestone has called the gains resulting from advertising expenditures "social net costs."[11] If, for instance, advertising expands the market, making possible mass production and/or mass marketing, or if

[8]See "The Professor's Complaint" and "An Answer from Macy's," in Editors of *Fortune, The Amazing Advertising Business* (New York: Simon and Schuster, Inc., 1957).
[9]Borden, chaps. 17–21.
[10]Jules Backman, *Advertising and Competition* (New York: New York University Press, 1967), p. 143.
[11]O. R. Firestone, *Economic Implications of Advertising* (London: Methuen & Company, Ltd., 1967), pp. 130–131.

it allows the replacement of more costly selling methods with advertising, the "net cost" is the amount saved. Although it is difficult to translate this into precise terms, it is by no means impossible to make rough estimates of the savings.

DOES ADVERTISING INFLUENCE OUR NATIONAL INCOME?

The influence of advertising on national income (or gross national product) has been debated for many years by critics and friends of advertising. Most critics concede that it has an effect, but they feel that it has been at the wrong time or for the wrong products. For example, some of them contend that advertising accentuates a downturn in the business cycle or uses money that could contribute more to our income if spent in some other manner. The friends of advertising attribute a good deal of the increase in our national income to the influence of advertising. Some of them believe it should be used to offset recessions in the business cycle.

Undoubtedly the best evidence of advertising's relationship to national income during the period before World War II was compiled by Neil Borden and published in his *Economic Effects of Advertising*. He concluded:

> The analysis indicates that advertising has not, in itself, been a causative factor of appreciable moment in cyclical fluctuations. However, as used, it has tended to accentuate fluctuations because expenditures for advertising have varied directly with business activity. As an employer of men and materials, advertising has been subject to the same fluctuations as business generally. As a stimulant to demand for products and services, it has been most extensively used in boom times and most lightly used in depressions. Thus employed, it has tended to accentuate the swings in demand. Indirectly it may have had some influence on fluctuations in so far as its use has accompanied inflexible prices, but the effect here is not deemed significant.[12]

It is true that one of the easiest budget cuts for a businessman to make when he sees trouble ahead is advertising and promotion. However, there is evidence since World War II that many businessmen have realized the futility of this and have tried to use advertising to restimulate demand for their products. In the post-Korea depression of 1952, for example, advertising expenditures increased approximately 10 percent over the previous year although business in general declined. In 1958, a recession year, advertising expenditures fell only 0.1 percent, whereas industrial production fell 9 percent and capital spending declined 17.3 percent.

Charles Yang studied the relation between advertising expenditure and sales for the tax years 1949–1950 through 1958–1959.[13] He found that advertising expenditures generally followed sales. However, he discovered that advertising expenditures followed sales more closely in some categories than in others. In general, he found fluctuations mildest in sales and advertising expenditures for consumers' nondurable goods, producers' goods and consumers' durable goods in that order. He

[12]Borden, pp. 734–735.
[13]Charles Y. Yang, "Variations in the Cyclical Behavior of Advertising," *Journal of Marketing*, 28 (April 1964), pp. 25–30.

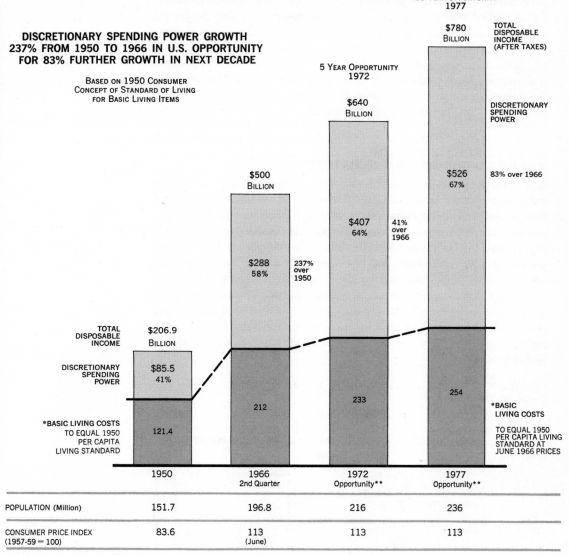

**DISCRETIONARY SPENDING POWER GROWTH
237% FROM 1950 TO 1966 IN U.S. OPPORTUNITY
FOR 83% FURTHER GROWTH IN NEXT DECADE**

BASED ON 1950 CONSUMER
CONCEPT OF STANDARD OF LIVING
FOR BASIC LIVING ITEMS

10 YEAR OPPORTUNITY
1977

$780
BILLION

TOTAL
DISPOSABLE
INCOME
(AFTER TAXES)

5 YEAR OPPORTUNITY
1972

$640
BILLION

DISCRETIONARY
SPENDING
POWER

$500
BILLION

$526
67%

83% over 1966

$407
64%

41%
over
1966

$288
58%

237%
over
1950

TOTAL
DISPOSABLE
INCOME

$206.9
BILLION

DISCRETIONARY
SPENDING
POWER

$85.5
41%

233

254

*BASIC
LIVING COSTS

212

*BASIC LIVING COSTS
TO EQUAL 1950
PER CAPITA
LIVING STANDARD

121.4

TO EQUAL 1950
PER CAPITA LIVING
STANDARD AT
JUNE 1966 PRICES

	1950	1966 2nd Quarter	1972 Opportunity**	1977 Opportunity**
POPULATION (Million)	151.7	196.8	216	236
CONSUMER PRICE INDEX (1957-59 = 100)	83.6	113 (June)	113	113

*Basic living costs of food, clothing, shelter.
**Based on production potential $940 billion by 1972 and $1150 billion (over one trillion dollars) by 1977.

FIG. 5.1 *Opportunity for advertising to tap discretionary spending power in the United States.* COURTESY J. WALTER THOMPSON COMPANY.

also found fewer fluctuations in the large than in the small and medium-sized companies. One factor that may account for this is the tendency of a corporation to shift from magazines (a somewhat flexible medium) to network television (a medium in which long-range commitments must be made) as it grows.

Where there are minor declines, in cyclical activity, advertising may well help support consumer confidence. There is some evidence that that was what happened in 1957–1958, when consumers had money to buy but their confidence was low. In the depression of the 1930s, on the other hand, purchasing power virtually disappeared in major segments of our population, and neither advertising nor any other form of promotion could make people who had no money buy. In an interesting attempt to determine the promotional elasticity of advertising (the relation of advertising to the gross national product), Yang studied the years 1950–1963.[14] He determined that it was 0.1 percent, meaning that an increase of 1 percent in advertising expenditures over the rate of increase in the gross national product can produce an increase in consumption of one-tenth of 1 percent. This increase in consumption leads to increased investment and increased income; thus the additional dollar of advertising investment can, according to Yang's predictions, "create $16 of additional income."

DOES ADVERTISING ADD VALUE TO GOODS AND SERVICES?

It is obvious that a new package or a new ingredient can increase the value of a product in a consumer's mind; but how about advertising? Can advertising alone enhance the product? There is evidence that it not only can but frequently does. This point is demonstrated in the use of placebos, pills of no medicinal value. When people are told that the placebo is a headache cure, the placebos will actually "cure" the headaches of some people. Suggestion (an ingredient of advertising) creates a certain value for an otherwise worthless product. There are examples in cosmetic advertising that are almost as dramatic. Women who buy unadvertised brands of cosmetics because they are cheaper feel they are unglamorous; they buy the same product, heavily advertised, and feel devastating.

[14]Charles Y. Yang, "$1 in Ads Generates $16 in Income," *Advertising Age*, December 29, 1965, pp. 1, 39.

THE ADDED CONSUMER VALUE OF MAJOR ADVERTISED BRANDS

Example: Tea Bags

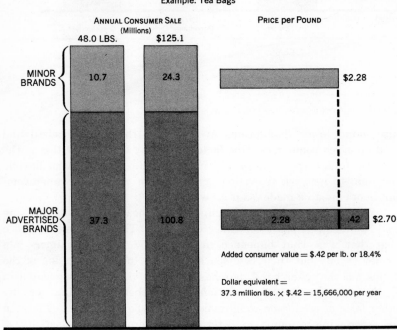

FIG. 5.2 *Demonstration of the value of the advertised brand of tea as compared with the unadvertised brand. Consumers pay 18.4 percent more for the advertised brands.* SOURCE: A. C. NIELSEN COMPANY.

How much more are consumers willing to pay for advertised products? This varies from product to product. Let us examine an instance based on the Nielsen Food Index. Recently consumers purchased 48,000,000 pounds of tea bags at a total price of $125,100,000 during one year. Minor brands accounted for $24,300,000 at an average price of $2.28 a pound, major advertised brands accounted for $100,800,000, or 37,300,000 pounds at an average price of $2.70 a pound. This difference of 42 cents a pound divided by $2.28 (the average price paid for the minor brands) results in a figure of 18.4 percent as the added value to the consumer for nationally advertised brands (see Figure 5.2).

We can also express this added value in terms of dollars. If, 37,300,000 pounds of advertised brands of tea bags were sold at a price differential of 42 cents a pound, the dollar equivalent of the added consumer value of advertised brands of tea bags amounted to $15,666,000 a year. This is a good example, because tea is a product in which the consumer has a choice between unadvertised and advertised brands at most food stores. In many food chains the store's brand is frequently promoted at the point of purchase much more heavily than nationally advertised ones.

As Vincent Norris points out, the "value added" concept is especially appropriate in analyzing modern promotion.

> In today's opulent economy, a small and ever-decreasing portion of consumers' incomes is spent to acquire the necessities of survival and minimal comfort. That portion which is spent to obtain psychological satisfaction is large and is growing. As a result, the allocation of resources has been constantly readjusted in the direction of greater creation of utilities intended to provide these psychological satisfactions. By the same reasoning, the utility added by advertising has increased as psychological characteristics of goods have become more important to consumers, and this addition of utility by advertising will probably become a more dominant factor in the market place for goods with the anticipated rise in the standard of living.[15]

To some people this concept of added value may seem wasteful. Actually, it accentuates something people do naturally. They look for products that will satisfy their wants. They put values on these products and are willing to pay accordingly. It is extremely difficult to apply objective standards of judgment to individual valuations of products and services. Some persons find a particular brand of automobile more valuable than others. Our market place is based, in part, on the idea that people have differing standards of value. These standards are subjective and are not readily measured by any objective yardstick.

DOES ADVERTISING NARROW
THE RANGE OF CONSUMER CHOICES?

Advertising inevitably leads manufacturers to make their product different from their competitors. They try to convince us that their soap is "whiter" or that it "kills bacteria faster." Perhaps we are convinced; perhaps we are skeptical. However, certain critics claim that the power

[15]Vincent Norris, "Advertising and Value Added," C. H. Sandage and Vernon Fryburger, eds., *The Role of Advertising* (Homewood, Ill.: Richard D. Irwin, Inc., 1960), p. 154.

possessed by the giants of advertising will narrow our choice to a few well-advertised brands. What are the facts?

For one thing, we know that from the days of the medieval linen makers in Osnabrück merchants have tried to differentiate their products. Consumers in Adam Smith's day realized that products were not identical. Modern advertising did not start product differentiation; it merely accelerated the search for different features as the number of merchants became larger and competition stiffer. Borden estimates that more than a million different brands of products have been marketed simultaneously. A current *Milwaukee Journal* Consolidated Analysis indicates that 53 brands of coffee, 43 brands of pretzels, and 132 brands of hardwood floor cleaners are bought in that city.

A brand, then, represents an attempt on the part of a manufacturer to gain control of a market. If his brand satisfies consumers, he can probably expect brand loyalty. And if consumers are loyal enough to insist on his brand, the retailer will find it necessary to carry the brand. The retailer may, as Borden points out, get by with one or two brands of sugar, because people do not have strong brand preferences for sugar, but he will have to carry ten or fifteen brands of prepared cereal.[16]

Consumers see brands as a speedy way to select or reject merchandise. If you liked the last can of Green Giant peas you bought you will probably select the same brand at your next purchase. If you happen to see a Green Giant ad (and research indicates you are more likely to notice it if you use the product) your confidence in the brand is reinforced.

Borden found evidence to indicate that "advertising in itself has been a force tending to bring uniformities of demand."[17] Advertising has led consumers to focus on a smaller array of brands than probably would have been present were advertising not a strong influencing factor. This happens when big national advertisers or distributors gain strong consumer acceptance. The trend is dramatically illustrated by the number of brands of domestic automobiles there are today, as compared with twenty years ago.

On the other hand, frequently advertising has increased requirements. As economist Walter Taplin points out, the consumer is generally the master and "the producer and advertiser is ultimately the slave." He points out:

If the consumer disliked being faced with a large gap between detergents and soap flakes and would like something which combines the chemical activity of one with the "gentle" action of the other, then sooner or later and probably sooner, some producer tries to fill that gap.[18]

In his study of advertising and competition, Jules Backman found that advertising was only one of many factors influencing a firm's management to enter or not to enter a specific market.[19] He points out:

The situation for each product must be examined together with all the factors which affect entry before deciding that advertising is *the* significant

[16]Borden, chap. 10.

[17]Borden, p. 638.

[18]Walter Taplin, *Advertising: A New Approach* (Boston: Little, Brown & Company, 1963), p. 106.

[19]Backman, p. 79.

barrier. Capital requirements, lack of production and/or marketing know-how, prospective profits, lack of availability of adequate distribution facilities, failure to have a line of related products—these and other factors play a vital role in the decisions of firms to enter a product market and hence may provide important barriers to entry.

SUMMARY

Advertising and promotion, which are maligned or ignored by economists, have both good and not-so-good effects on our economy. This chapter has attempted to analyze certain important economic issues without glossing over advertising's inequities. Some of the problem areas result from current promotional practices and should be remedied; but some are inevitable in a system of capitalistic enterprise.

We have seen that advertising can produce some savings in business costs. Comparisons are extremely difficult, because the product advertised is not usually the same as that produced without advertising. Furthermore, it is difficult to find satisfactory base periods for comparison. However, there is considerable evidence that advertising has cut production costs (particularly overhead costs) and that it also cuts marketing costs.

Advertising appears to add increased product value. It does not appear to narrow the range of consumer choices in general, but it apparently does in certain selected areas.

QUESTIONS FOR DISCUSSION

1. Why have so many economists ignored advertising or criticized its role in our economy?

2. Try to find a heavily advertised product whose price to consumers has decreased during the past ten years. To what extent do you think advertising has helped to decrease this price? Try to find a product whose price has remained fairly constant during the past ten years. Why has advertising not been able to lower the price of this item? Has there been any increase in quality during this period?

3. To what extent do you believe our standard of living might have suffered during the past century if all advertising had been prohibited?

4. Backman says: "The expenditures for advertising do not represent a net cost to the economy, however that cost is measured." Do you agree? Why?

5. To what extent should the federal or state governments encourage businessmen to increase their advertising during a recession or depression? What form should such encouragement take?

6. Does an advertised product have more value than an unadvertised product that has the same physical characteristics?

SUGGESTED READINGS

Readings for Chapters 5 and 6 are given at the end of Chapter 6.

Social
and
Ethical Problems

Almost every form of promotion has at some time been criticized for its social or ethical effect. The average consumer or lay critic is often reluctant to analyze promotion in terms of technical areas, but few hesitate to voice their opinions regarding questions of ethics or morals. It is difficult for objective analysts to evaluate such opinions because their values are often so nebulous. Ethical standards vary among cultural, religious, racial, and other groups. What one person deems epicurean indulgence, another will regard as almost spartan. Before we examine some of the major social and ethical issues raised by promotion, we shall attempt to assess the social importance of such issues.

HOW IMPORTANT ARE ETHICAL AND MORAL ISSUES?

Any serious student of history knows that a hundred years ago businessmen operated by ethical standards that we should now consider very low. Advertisements like the one in Figure 6.1 were typical in the post-Civil War period. A certain amount of trickery was expected, and buying was a sort of contest between buyer and seller. As a result of more sophisticated buyers, an increase in business stability, a growth in branding, and the growth of both governmental and consumer bodies, times have changed. How important does the public think these issues are?

Through the years many studies have been made of the public's attitude toward advertising. Several of these have been summarized by Neil Borden in his *Economic Effects of Advertising*.

In spite of the shortcomings of many of these opinion surveys, including the Harvard Study, and in spite of doubt as to the exact meaning of the replies, the general tenor of the responses found in all the studies should give and undoubtedly has given advertisers food for thought. They show that although a substantial majority of consumers are not unfriendly to advertising, nevertheless a considerable group of people do not bear goodwill toward advertising. Or, if the general attitude of many consumers is not unfriendly, the unfavorable opinions, directed against exaggeration, poor taste, or lack of information, provide a fertile background for further destruction of confidence in advertising as an economic tool.[1]

Probably the most searching and comprehensive examination of the public's attitude toward advertising was underwritten by the American Association of Advertising Agencies and supervised by a committee of academic and agency researchers. Analysis of the data was completed in 1965. The study was based on a national probability sample of 2000 Americans. Intending to represent the population eighteen years of age and upward, the study came up with the following major findings:

1. To the average American, advertising is a matter of secondary importance. When he complains about advertising he does not mean it in the same sense that he does complaints about children, family life, religion, and the like.
2. Of all the advertisements the individual sees, only 15 percent are classified as "Informative, Enjoyable, Annoying or Offensive." Of the two negative classifications, the average consumer was more likely to call an advertisement "Annoying" than "Offensive."
3. A consumer is more likely to call advertising for his favorite brand "Informative" or "Enjoyable" and less likely to call it "Annoying" or "Offensive."
4. Of the 78 product classes studied, 73 produced at least one advertisement that was "Annoying," 50 at least one "Offensive."
5. People were likely to classify advertisements as "Annoying" when they contradicted experience with and knowledge of the product; when unreal or disturbing methods of presentations inflated product importance; when they talked down and used undue repetition (especially in the case of television commercials).
6. People were likely to classify advertisements as "Offensive" because they had moral reservations about the product class per se and resented unreal presentation and undue repetition.[2]

There was evidence to indicate that consumers were not as interested in advertising as many copywriters liked to think. There was evidence that they ignored much of the advertising, and what they did

[1] Neil H. Borden, *The Economic Effects of Advertising* (Homewood, Ill.: Richard D. Irwin, Inc., 1942), pp. 798–799.
[2] Donald Kanter, "A Preliminary Report on the AAAA Study on Consumer Judgment of Advertising." An address before the National Conference of American Marketing Association, June 1–15, 1964, and *The AAAA Study on Consumer Judgment of Advertising* (New York: American Association of Advertising Agencies, 1965). Mimeographed.

see or hear was viewed through a self-protecting veil of skepticism, caution, and realism.

We should look not only to the voice of the people but also to the opinions of our intellectual, ethical, and moral leaders. Many of these have been caustic indeed in their criticisms. Jacques Barzun has called advertising "florid nonsense," Clifton Fadiman "raucous ballyhoo," and Henry Steele Commager "the nadir of vulgarity." There is obviously real need to look more deeply into some of the social and ethical implications of advertising. Some of the more important of these will be discussed in this chapter.

DOES ADVERTISING TELL THE TRUTH?

There is no simple answer to the complex question: does advertising tell the truth? Yet it is probably the most important question raised in this chapter. Advertising must have consumer confidence if it is to perform its communication job effectively.

To answer this question, we must first decide what we mean by "tell the truth." Do we mean the literal truth? Do we mean does advertising give a true impression? Here is what the Supreme Court said regarding misleading and fraudulent advertising:

> Advertising as a whole must not create a misleading impression even though every statement separately considered is literally truthful.
> Advertising must not obscure or conceal material facts.
> Advertising must not be artfully contrived to distract and divert readers' attention from the true nature of the terms and conditions of an offer.
> Advertising must be free of fraudulent traps and stratagems which would induce action which would not result from a forthright disclosure of the true nature of the offer.

Judged by these criteria, more than 97 percent of the thousands of advertisements inspected annually are satisfactory without investigation to the government's principal policing agent, the Federal Trade Commission. In a normal year, the FTC issues about 270 complaints against "deceptive practices" in labeling and advertising. Less than one-fourth of the advertisements investigated require any action. From time to time, the FTC changes its interpretation of these rules. For example, the FTC ruled at one time that it was deceptive for book clubs to advertise "free" bonus books, but some years later it reversed itself.

Relatively few businessmen deliberately set out to delude the public. There was, however, this ad in the "Help Wanted" column of a midwestern newspaper: "Three Young Actors—To play three nights a week, selected audience. Call for appointment." The local Better Business Bureau found that the ad was inserted by a company seeking door-to-door salesmen to work on commission, selling cookware. This ad was clearly a trap. Most of us would agree that the advertisement reproduced in Figure 6.1 is overenthusiastic. It would be stopped today.

One company advertised that its product would turn a lawn green in "just 60 seconds! . . . and keep it green 365 days of the year!" This claim was true enough, but the company did not say in the ad that its product contained a water-soluble dye. To have a green lawn 365 days a year one would have to make repeated applications. Even then, if one

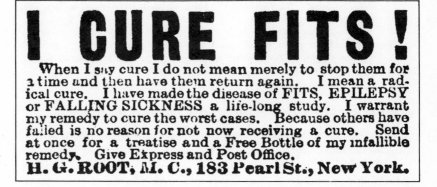

FIG. 6.1 *A nineteenth-century claim that would be clearly illegal today.*

walked across a wet lawn one's shoes would turn green. The impression in the ad was clearly misleading, although the statements were true, if taken separately.

Other means by which advertisers sometimes stretch the truth include testimonials from people who are not bona fide users of the product and "bait" advertising (presenting a product at a ridiculously low price in order to attract people to a store).

The Federal Trade Commission believes some poetic license is permissible in advertising copy. The commission assumes that you do not take every advertising statement literally any more than you accept everything the retail salesperson tells you. As Otis Pease points out, "[The] question of literal truth or falsity is largely irrelevant, since the appeal of the advertisement lies not in factual assertions but in the association which it sets up in the mind of the reader."[3] The important question, for both the FTC and the general public, is the impression an ad or a series of ads makes on people's minds.

The FTC must take special precautions in policing advertising for such products as foods, drugs, cosmetics, and therapeutic devices —products which may affect people's health. If, for example, a drug advertiser claims his product cures some ill, he must have positive proof. However, he probably can present testimonials from people who said they felt better after they used his product, because these are subjective statements of opinion. Under current regulations an advertiser will probably be stopped if he devises a television commercial that features a white coated model advising people to use his medicine.

Any untruth in advertising does a disservice to honest advertisers who want only to communicate to the masses certain truthful benefits of their product. Fortunately, there is a built-in brake on untruthfulness that is sometimes overlooked. Advertising in print puts the statement on record, inviting scrutiny that tends to keep dishonest men from using advertising regularly. The vigilance of government and business and the wariness of consumers help to regulate advertising.

Professor Raymond Bauer, who helped supervise the AAAA Study described earlier in this chapter, points out:

[3]Otis Pease, *The Responsibilities of American Advertising* (New Haven, Conn.: Yale University Press, 1958), p. 201.

These data strongly suggest that the issue of truth involves annoyance as well as moral concern.

It is my guess that there is a hard core of concern with genuinely misleading advertising. However, included with this, in undetermined proportion is — I think — a certain amount of condescending contempt which, if articulated, would take the form: "Who do they think they are kidding?"[4]

IS ADVERTISING OFFENSIVE OR IN BAD TASTE?

We have seen that the public classifies some (though not much) advertising as offensive. However, it is even more difficult to define terms like "offensive" or "in bad taste" than it is to define "truthful." College students, for example, are not easily offended. They find amusing or artistic certain material that brings cries of outrage from the general public. This is also true in art, literature, and the motion pictures. The television industry has generally operated on the premise that material of a questionable nature, which would be inappropriate on a telecast earlier in the day, can be used on a late evening show like "Tonight."

Criticisms of taste in advertising are provoked as much by products as by the manner of presentation. The National Association of Broadcasters has, for example, decided that certain intimate products, meritorious though they may be, should not be advertised on television, because any commercial messages about them, no matter how carefully written, would offend large numbers of people. Some people are offended by any liquor advertisement, no matter how innocuous. Some products are not offensive per se, but questionable advertising is frequently used to promote them. Motion pictures and books are good examples. Marketers of both tend to overemphasize their sensational aspects on the basis that this is what makes the sales. The sales success of such books as "Tropic of Cancer" and "Candy" would seem to bear them out. Ohrbach's, a leading New York department store, ran a full-page ad at Mother's Day featuring an obviously pregnant woman with the large headline "She's Entitled." *Advertising Age* took an informal poll of its readers and found that 55.4 percent saw nothing wrong with the ad, but that 40.1 percent thought it was in bad taste.

The techniques that most often offend people are those emphasizing sex, violence, or body functions. Some of these are not necessarily offensive the first time people see them, but they become so when watched repeatedly on television, particularly when the family is gathered around the set. And, as we have seen in the AAAA study, some people consider any unreal or unbelievable presentations "offensive."

We conclude that the question of taste will continue to be one of the most baffling in advertising. There is always the temptation for an eager creative person to gain attention by shocking people. Because copywriters are normally rather sophisticated, they can easily underestimate the shock value of a particular ad that seems only mildly shocking to their own circle. It is probably unrealistic to expect the industry to free advertising of everything that someone may consider in bad

[4]"Sources of Support and Criticism of Advertising," in *The AAAA Study on Consumer Judgment of Advertising* (New York: American Association of Advertising Agencies, 1965).

The Sun Fighter

Bronze Lustre's the name. Protects you while
you tan soft, tan deep, tan smooth. Fights sun-
damage, sun-aging with an exclusive Revlon sun-
screen. And it's loaded with special moisturizers;
acts like a night cream in the sun to guard against
sun dryness and wrinkles.
     Two formulas: Regular and Extra-protective,
both in gelée, lotion or foam. And for your lips
—Bronze Lustre Sun Sticks in Pink Gloss, Peach
Gloss, Tan Gloss, Coral Gloss, Natural Gloss.
     New! Bronze Lustre After Sun Silk – to
sleek on all over at sundown. It moisturizes,
softens and smooths; helps prevent flaking and
peeling. Makes even a little tan look like a lot.
     So go ahead. Expose those wide open spaces.
Bronze Lustre's got you covered all the way.

FIG. 6.2 *Relevant use of
sex appeal in advertising.*
COURTESY REVLON INC.

taste or even to expect it to be a crusader in elevating taste. On the
other hand, society can expect admen to abide by the accepted rules of
decency and taste of the audience they expect their advertisement to
reach.

DOES ADVERTISING INFLUENCE ELECTIONS?

Although advertising men have long been active in political campaign-
ing, they have been under special fire since the Presidential elections of
1952 when television spot announcements represented a major part of
the Eisenhower campaign. Agency chairman Rosser Reeves, who helped
plot the 1952 advertising strategy and wrote many of the spot commercials, is quoted as saying:

> What I did with the Eisenhower spots was to apply the mechanics of adver-
> tising to the expenditure of money. It's a question of two mathematical factors.
> First, spots versus network speeches; you get a larger audience with spots.

Second, recall; you get 8 percent on a Stevenson speech, 91 percent on an Eisenhower spot.[5]

Since 1952 many politicians have come to accept the necessity of strong advertising support. The fact that Eisenhower won convinced many that advertising was a necessary part of any campaign, local or national. The mass invasion of the United States by television sets made it possible to reach most families through this intensely personal medium. At the same time, advertising men began to take more interest in politics. One, Maurice McCaffrey, wrote a book on how to use advertising in politics. He says,

(Political) fighters and workers . . . need the assistance of strong advertising to succeed. It doesn't just happen. It is not enough to deserve the identity, although it must be deserved to sell, but the message must be expertly conveyed to the voters. When the average voter is alone within the isolated confines of the voting booth he hardly knows the names of all the candidates on the ballot, so he cannot be expected to absorb a barrage of appeals and carry them into the booth. It takes all of the force of advertising to get one point across.[6]

Many critics are disturbed by what they consider the infiltration of advertising men into the field of politics. Some politicians have been cynical enough to make a political issue out of the use of "Madison Avenue techniques" by their opponents, while taking full advantage of advertising techniques themselves to get this point across. Many serious critics have been concerned about advertising's oversimplification of complicated issues. How, they say, can you explain foreign policy or monetary issues in a 60-second commercial? The defenders point out that with or without advertising, politicians have always oversimplified complicated issues and they will undoubtedly continue to do so. Critics complain that the candidate with the most pleasing television personality has a big advantage although he may not be the best qualified for office. Though there is some validity to this criticism, it should be emphasized that an attractive personality has always been considered an important asset — whether presented on television or in person at the county fair.

What is the proper role of advertising? Martin Mayer points out that we should distinguish between advertising and public relations.

Advertising supplements the content of the media by means of advertising pages or paid commercial announcements; public relations seeks to direct and if necessary distort the media's supposedly undirected and undistorted content.

He believes that only three of the jobs performed by advertising men for a political campaign can be regarded as advertising:

1. The preparation of actual print ads or announcements.
2. The selection of media for commercial messages.
3. The measurement by research of how well the message is coming across.[7]

[5]Martin Mayer, "On Politics," in C. H. Sandage and Vernon Fryburger, eds., *The Role of Advertising* (Homewood, Ill.: Richard D. Irwin, 1960), p. 329.
[6]Maurice McCaffrey, *Advertising Wins Elections* (Minneapolis: Gilbert Publishing Company, 1962), p. 6.
[7]Mayer, p. 327.

We must conclude that both advertising and public relations in politics are here to stay. Their influence is vastly overestimated by some of their more zealous critics, but they do help the candidate to project his personality to large numbers of voters. They probably make a difference in the outcome only in close elections. No serious analysts claim that any advertising or public relations techniques could have elected Barry Goldwater president in 1964 or Adlai Stevenson in 1956. Also, there is no evidence that they can elect a bad candidate over a good one—any more than they can effectively promote a bad product over a good one. There is evidence that our electorate will be better informed if the issues are presented. It does not seem reasonable in this era of mass communications to deny political candidates the assistance of our most skilled communications experts—the professional advertising and public relations specialists.

DOES ADVERTISING CREATE CONFORMITY?

To sociologist David Riesman conformity connotes a sort of "other-directedness" (looking to the ideas one gets from friends, friends of friends, or the mass media, instead of looking within one's self for direction). To some, conformity is man's desire to live in a ranch house just like his neighbors, and read the same magazines as everyone else. To some it is the desire to be an "organization man" in a "gray flannel suit." William Whyte, in his incisive analysis of this latter type, somewhat facetiously describes the aptitude tests used by many modern corporations as "tests of conformity."[8] Sometimes the critics seem to be talking about the problem of status symbols and status striving. Vance Packard says:

> Most of us surround ourselves, wittingly or unwittingly, with status symbols we hope will influence the raters appraising us, and which we hope will help establish some social distance between ourselves and those we consider below us. The vigorous merchandising of goods as status symbols by advertisers is playing a major role in intensifying status consciousness.[9]

There is little concrete evidence that we have any more conformity today than fifteen years ago. It is true that economic prosperity has improved the condition of the country's lowest economic groups, that our educational levels have been raised, and that certain distinctions, such as urban versus rural, seem much hazier than a few years ago. In these respects there is more homogeneity than there used to be. However, the same influences that have brought homogeneity have made it possible for differences to grow—more subtle differences, perhaps, but differences all the same. A prosperous society has the time, money and inclination to indulge its individual tastes. Even the much-maligned "organization man" has a remarkable degree of individual freedom.

In fact, advertising appears to decrease rather than increase conformity. As pointed out in the previous section, advertising thrives on

[8]See William H. Whyte, Jr., *The Organization Man* (New York: Doubleday & Company, Inc., 1957), chap. 10.
[9]Vance Packard, *The Status Seekers* (New York: David McKay Company, Inc., 1959), p. 7.

THIS IS A
DECIMAL POINT!
It's Getting In The Way
Of Industrial Peace In The Bell System

NEGOTIATIONS BETWEEN CWA — the Communications Workers of America — and Western Electric will be in serious difficulty unless this big decimal point obstruction can be cleared away.

We are concerned because Bell System management shows little interest in clearing this barrier to agreement.

The decimal point symbolizes the 3.2 per cent national wage 'guidelines'. That 3.2 figure is wrong from the standpoint of economic theory and of practical labor-management relations. It will hinder, not help, the settlement of differences.

In our bargaining with Western Electric's Installation Division, as in all our negotiations, CWA believes in the value of flexible guidelines to help labor and management reach agreements that will benefit each other and the public we all serve.

But a decimal point phobia, in which government decree takes the place of free collective bargaining, carries definite dangers for all of us.

That's why we are deeply concerned that the idea of a helpful, flexible guideline has become, for some government economists, a rigid, inflexible reliance on 'three-decimal-point-two' per cent as a *maximum* package for wages and benefits.

That won't work.

As CWA President Joseph A. Beirne told the union's convention last month:

"This year Bell management has made clear it would like to strangle us with a 3.2 guideline. And we say . . . we are not going through all the hard work of collective bargaining just to arrive at 3.2. There are real economic

problems that must be solved. A decimal point won't solve them."

* * *

Here's the situation at Western Electric Installation! CWA is bargaining in New York City for a new national contract to replace the three-year agreement that ends this July 28.

About 22,000 Western Electric installers are involved, in just about all the 50 states. These highly skilled workers are the men with the technical know-how to install the complex new central office telephone equipment that's going in around the country.

These are the men who installed and maintain the Washington-Moscow "hot line." Many worked on the DEW line in northern Canada . . . our sentry against surprise air attack. Others work on the sophisticated special communications network of the Strategic Air Command.

Our country needs these men and their skills. The men need fair wage increases to provide decent incomes. They need improved pensions, with no deduction from the retiree's pension check of the money he gets from social security. They need company-paid health and hospitalization as in most other big industries. They need security for their union, to promote responsible labor-management relationships.

These matters will require hard bargaining, with a give-and-take between union and company.

That guideline decimal point won't provide the answers . . . and it gets in the way of an agreement.

That's why it's getting in the way of industrial peace.

COMMUNICATIONS WORKERS OF AMERICA, AFL-CIO
The Community-Minded Union
1925 K Street, N.W., Washington, D. C. 20006

Joseph A. Beirne
President

Patrick J. Morgan
*CWA National Director
W. E. Installation*

W. A. Smallwood
Secretary-Treasurer

FIG. 6.3 *Use of advertising to communicate the labor union's point of view.* COURTESY COMMUNICATIONS WORKERS OF AMERICA.

differences (brands, colors, constructions, and so forth). Through advertising, our modern consumer is encouraged to explore various ways of indulging his tastes. Our industrial and marketing revolutions have succeeded almost too well. They have made the consumer so prosperous that he is no longer satisfied with his mass-produced car. He demands difference in color or style. He wants new styles in clothing and furniture. Some will claim that our new middle class looks to such status symbols because of insecurity in its new-found prosperity. The middle class is looking for symbols to reveal who belongs to which class. The reasons are not important here. The point is that advertising does not change people but mirrors them. Advertising men are not reformers.

SHOULD ADVERTISING OFFER THE FACTS WITHOUT PERSUASION?

Most critics concede that consumers are eager to find out about the week-end specials at the local supermarket and that they are interested in knowing the specifications and uses of a new product. Most accept advertising as a prime source of such facts. However, critics sometimes overlook the importance of communications that are not factual but are nevertheless informative. For example, people are usually interested in the psychological and esthetic associations of products and services. They wonder whether they would feel at home with a certain kind of furniture. They wonder what kind of people smoke a certain brand of cigarette. They wonder whether people would admire them or criticize them if they bought a certain brand of automobile. These are the kinds of information people seek. It is natural therefore that advertisements should attempt to provide it.

The amount of factual information included in an ad is limited by two additional factors: the reluctance of consumers to read or listen to facts unless they are sugar-coated, and the space and time limitations of ads. Americans, it seems, are wary of data as such. Advertisers have found, through research, that they can get better readership of their ads by dramatizing relatively few features rather than by trying to cover many. However, although advertising people have frequently failed to exercise ingenuity in presenting facts, some very long copy is thoroughly and widely read because it was written with skill and imagination.

But what about persuasion? Advertising, in any form, contains an element of persuasion.

Advertising that is purely informative is often all that is needed to persuade a reader or listener to buy the product. In periods when some consumer goods have been very scarce, such as silk and nylon hosiery during World War II, an announcement by any local merchants that a shipment of nylons had been received was enough to produce a rush for the store. There is much persuasion in the one word "fire" when shouted with sincerity and truth to persons in a burning building.[10]

People appear to seek analysis and guidance as well as facts. Consider, for example, the popularity of news analysts who supply background to the broadcast news, newspapers, and the news magazines that interpret current happenings. People also take it for granted that those with a particular point of view—editorial writers, politicians, and salesmen, for example—will be free to persuade the public to think or act in a certain manner. Consequently, they do not regard persuasion in advertising as an evil but as a perfectly normal part of society. Most would agree that it is necessary for progress, and certainly all would regard it as preferable to, and quite different from, force.

It is true that many advertisements are too persuasive, too "hard sell." Others may not be persuasive enough. It is one function of the copywriter to determine the appropriate approach for his particular ad's objectives. Preconceived notions that facts are either always good or always bad for consumers may mislead him.

DOES ADVERTISING CAUSE PEOPLE TO BUY THINGS THEY DO NOT REALLY NEED?

In *The Hidden Persuaders*, Vance Packard raised the following questions in connection with the use of research techniques:

[10]C. H. Sandage and Vernon Fryburger, *Advertising Theory and Practice,* 7th ed. (Homewood, Ill.: Richard D. Irwin, Inc.), 1967, p. 86.

. . . a good many of the people-manipulating activities of persuaders raise profoundly disturbing questions about the kind of society they are seeking to build for us. Their ability to contact millions of us simultaneously through newspapers, TV, etc., gives them the power, as one persuader put it, to do good or evil "on a scale never before possible in a very short time." Are they warranted in justifying manipulation on the ground that anything that increases the gross national product is "good" for America; or on the ground that the old doctrine "Let the Buyer Beware" absolves them of responsibility for results that may seem to some antisocial?[11]

The average businessman would not deny that he does his best to make people dissatisfied with their present possessions. However, he would differ with Mr. Packard and other critics on both the ethics and the success of his efforts. If businessmen catered only to people's needs they

[11]Vance Packard, *The Hidden Persuaders* (New York: David McKay Company, Inc., 1957), p. 221.

How to build trouble-free concrete driveways

News and notes from the field

A concrete driveway lends an unmistakable touch of distinction to a home. More important, perhaps, is its exceptional durability. A properly designed, well-constructed concrete driveway can be as durable as the best of the nation's highways.

Faulty driveways, on the other hand, can be a source of more complaints than any other construction error because the owner lives with the problem day after day. And there's no excuse. It's just as easy to build a long-wearing concrete driveway as it is to "botch" the job—and a lot more satisfying in the long run.

Before the concrete is delivered

To insure durability, order concrete with a slump of 3-4 inches. For areas subject to freezing and thawing, ask for air entrained concrete. Specify 4-8 per cent air with ¾ in. max. size coarse aggregate, or 3½-6½ per cent air with 1-in. max. coarse aggregate.

Remove all sod, vegetation, and soft spots, and loosen all hard spots. Then compact the entire surface uniformly with a tamper or roller. If the subgrade is not well drained, use a six-inch layer of crushed stone, gravel or cinders.

Be sure to dampen the subgrade before the concrete is placed so that it won't suck water from the concrete. But, don't create puddles. Make sure forms are level with the desired finished grade of the driveway, and oil them before the concrete is placed.

Placing the concrete

Be sure the crew at the job-site is ready to place the concrete when it is delivered. Extended periods of mixing in the truck drum after the water is added causes a reduction in the entrained air, a decrease in slump, and an ultimate loss of overall strength.

Place the concrete in the forms to the full depth, spading along the sides to reduce honeycombing. Push the concrete into place with a shovel, but be careful not to mix it with the subgrade material.

Strike off the excess concrete by screeding in a saw-like motion. However, don't over-work it.

Finishing, making joints

After all bleed water has disappeared, smooth the concrete with a magnesium float. Start edging when all water sheen has left the surface, and the concrete has started to stiffen. After edging, begin placing joints.

Cut all contraction joints to a depth of no less than ½ the thickness of the slab, and place them no further than 10 ft. apart. If the driveway is 20 ft. or more in width, place an expansion joint along the entire length. To do this

efficiently, place one half of the driveway at a time, using a bulk head for the center joint. After the second half is placed, replace the bulk head with a premolded bituminous jointing material.

This expansion joint material should also be used wherever the new concrete contacts a rigid object, such as the garage, sidewalk, curb, etc.

It is seldom necessary to steel trowel finish an outdoor driveway. A textured surface, produced by drawing a broom over it, is usually preferred.

Curing

This is probably the most important step in the entire operation and is the key to durability.

One of the most commonly used methods of curing exposed concrete is the sprayed-on curing membrane. Your local construction supply can advise on the best type for your particular job.

Wet burlap or canvas, or straw can also be used. Straw is especially good if the concrete is exposed to subfreezing temperatures during the first seven days because it serves as an insulator as well as a means of retaining moisture.

In any case, be sure to keep the concrete damp for at least seven days.

When you buy concrete

When you buy concrete, you are buying more than the material itself. You're buying the experience, dependability and quality capability of the ready mix concrete producer. So look beyond price, and consider the added quality assurances, including the right mix for the job. You'll save a lot of concrete.

Reprints of this "News and Notes" ad are available free.

PORTLAND CEMENT COMPANY
Alpha Building, Easton, Pennsylvania

FIG. 6.4 *Almost solid copy, this Portland Cement advertisement scored a high 43 percent noted in an Ad-Gage readership study. Good demonstration of the power of advertising to inform.* COURTESY ALPHA PORTLAND CEMENT COMPANY.

would be selling tents instead of ranch houses, horses instead of automobiles, and animal skins instead of high fashions. It is the wants and desires people have — not only their needs — that make advertising and business in general prosper.

The question, then is not whether advertising attempts to make people buy things they don't need, but whether the attempt is successful. Critics like Mr. Packard would have us believe that advertisers, through modern research, have almost unlimited power in this area. Some advertising practitioners, particularly those who are trying to convince prospective clients, take this same line (for different reasons, of course). The evidence shows that advertising, although it is becoming more efficient all the time, is often overestimated in this respect. Advertising does have the power to awaken desires, conscious and subconscious, but there is no black magic in its approach.

DOES ADVERTISING CREATE INSECURITY IN ORDER TO SELL GOODS?

Advertising is accused of causing people to worry about tooth decay, body odor, lack of self-confidence, and many other ills. The implication is that the advertiser claims that his product will reduce these worries. The charge is true, at least in part. Advertising men take people as they are and attempt to find out how products will satisfy them. There is no evidence that advertising can create a fear where no seeds of anxiety exist. However, advertising can magnify latent fears. Gerald Lambert exploited this when he hit on "halitosis" to sell Listerine in the early 1920s. Insurance salesmen must exploit anxiety in their sales talks to sell life or fire insurance. Not all attempts to create insecurity are successful. Many fail, and we are more likely to hear about success stories (such as that of "Halitosis," "pink tooth brush," "cleans your breath while it cleans your teeth") than failures.

Although advertising may accentuate people's worries about social or physical shortcomings, it does offer solutions. The girl with pimples may feel more confident at the next party after having used a product advertised as a complexion aid. That the product will not transform her from a wallflower to the belle of the party is no reason for condemnation of the advertising. In assessing the argument that advertising creates insecurity we must balance the relative value of assuaging people's fears against advertising's tendency to accentuate latent fears.

DOES ADVERTISING INFLUENCE THE PRESS?

Recently the president of a major automobile company severely criticized newspapers for lambasting the automotive industry in editorial columns when millions of dollars were being spent by the car makers in newspaper ads. He said:

Frequently I have observed that our advertisements and those of other domestic automotive advertisers were in direct competition with a considerable amount of editorial material printed free of charge extolling the supposed virtues of the foreign-built product and deprecating those which we manufacture. . . . How could car manufacturers as advertisers buy enough space to counteract such comments? Why should we subsidize with our advertising dollars publications which continually deprecate the products in which we expect the public to have confidence if the public is to buy them?

A few years earlier a nationally known advertising executive, speaking to the annual meeting of the Advertising Federation of America, recommended that advertising people find out

whether, while pocketing the advertiser's money and publishing his advertising, it [the press] is permitting its editorial writers or its columnists or commentators to discredit business and businessmen, and to lend insidious assistance —consciously or unconsciously—to those who would destroy our economic and social system.

Such outbursts might give the impression that our press is in danger of becoming "kept." There is little evidence to support that impression. The American press is probably the freest in the world, although there are occasional attempts to influence the press (some of them perhaps successful).

The main weapon of the advertiser or agency against the press is cancellation or threatened cancellation of advertising. One of the most publicized cancellations in recent years was $250,000 of advertising in the *Wall Street Journal* by General Motors, the country's second largest advertiser, principally because the corporation did not think the newspaper should have published drawings of the company's forthcoming models. This action had no influence on the paper's editorial policy.

An advertiser may, from time to time, be interested in any of the following: omission or "burying" of a news story embarrassing to him; coloring of a news story involving him; extra publicity on some item favorable to him; or shading of opinion expressed in editorials to agree with his opinion.

The accusation that advertisers exercise undue control over the press is based largely on the methods by which the media are financed. Although a small minority of magazines and newspapers are financed without any advertising revenue, the majority of them depend heavily on it. According to *Editor and Publisher*, a "50,000-circulation" daily newspaper received in 1967 about 79 percent of its revenue from advertising (49 percent from local advertising, 11 percent from national, and 19 percent from classified). Most radio and television station revenue come entirely from advertising. However, if we look at the *total* revenue flowing in to support these media (set sales and service, as well as station revenue) we find that advertisers supply between 30 and 40 percent of total revenue.

There is some evidence that the small, financially insecure newspaper is more likely to be influenced than the large, financially stable one. A thorough study of influences on the nation's press was made by the Commission on Freedom of the Press. "The evidence of dictation of policy by advertisers," said this Commission's report, "is not impressive. Such dictation seems to occur among the weaker units. As a newspaper becomes financially stable, it becomes more independent and tends to resist pressure from advertisers."[12]

[12]Commission on Freedom of the Press, *A Free and Responsible Press* (Chicago: University of Chicago Press, 1947), p. 62.

In his history of the N. W. Ayer organization, Ralph M. Hower points out the disputes with the press in the earlier and lustier days of advertising, and concludes:

> Agencies do not often have occasion to protest, but the absence of protests or direct threats does not mean that advertising has ceased to influence content or treatment of reading matter. Editors have learned to make precautionary expurgations to forestall criticism. Actually the result is seldom serious. Minor items of news are toned down or ignored and problems which ought to be freely discussed are sometimes softpedaled. But no advertiser, regardless of the extent of his advertising, can suppress or minimize big news. . . . Other groups such as pressure groups are really much more powerful.[13]

The fact that the majority of newspapers editorially support Republican candidates in many elections is sometimes cited as an example of business influence over the press. A more likely explanation seems to be the community of interest between the editor-publisher and the businessman. Both tend to be politically conservative and are probably less likely than the average person to support major social and economic changes.

Fortunately, there are certain built-in checks against undue influence on the media by advertisers. Perhaps the strongest is the self-interest of the media owner. He cannot afford to ignore news of interest to his readers or listeners, and expect to retain public confidence. As he builds public confidence and good will, he can expand his medium and make it more valuable as an advertising medium. If he can provide the needed coverage of his trading area and show that he has public confidence, no space or time buyer can afford to ignore him, whether or not their political or economic ideologies harmonize.

Another check is the fact that the advertiser usually needs the medium even more than his money is needed by the medium. Except for some financially weak newspapers and radio and television stations, the withdrawal of advertising would probably hurt the advertiser more than it would hurt the medium. Also, organizations such as Consumers Union and Consumer's Research act as a check against undue influence by advertisers. They do not accept advertising and are certainly free to print anything they want or to editorialize about a product in any manner they like.

We can conclude that the press is probably much less "kept" than most people think. He who pays the piper does not necessarily call the tune.

DOES ADVERTISING IMPLEMENT FREEDOM OF SPEECH?

In the last section we asked whether advertising influenced the press. Now we shall discuss the question of whether it *implements* our freedom of speech.

Suppose you have an idea or point of view that you think a large number of people should know about. Because you can reach only a

[13]Ralph M. Hower, *The History of an Advertising Agency* (Cambridge, Mass.: Harvard University Press, 1939), pp. 626–627.

small number of people through personal contact, you would like to communicate with them through the mass media. In these media you can reach people in either of two ways: through the news (and editorial) columns or through advertising. If you are a newsworthy person or if you couch your message in dramatic terms, you may be fortunate enough to get publicity in the news columns.

However, more and more individuals, organizations of all kinds and corporations are turning to advertising in print and broadcast media to promote their points of view. Our mass media have become the modern counterpart of the town hall, where everyone can speak his piece. For example, in several labor disputes, unions have used advertising space and time to tell the public why the workers thought a strike was necessary. Most frequently employers also used the mass media to tell their side. Both have complete freedom to tell the public their stories; the public is then free to read or reject the messages, to believe or disbelieve.

SUMMARY

We have seen that social and ethical issues, although important, do not loom so large among the general public as some critics would have us believe. Perhaps the most important of these problems is that of truth. Although advertising usually tells the truth, it does not necessarily always tell the whole truth. Some advertising is considered offensive, but exact standards are hard to determine because they are so subjective.

Outcomes in close political elections are sometimes influenced by advertising, although that influence is vastly overrated by people who confuse advertising and promotion with publicity. There is little evidence that advertising has contributed to conformity in any meaningful sense of that much abused term.

Advertising uses both persuasion and selected facts to convince people to buy things they want but do not really need. There is nothing diabolic in this practice unless we believe that there is something immoral in wanting something. Advertising does not appear to have influenced the press to any substantial degree, although of the questions considered in this chapter, this is perhaps the most difficult to analyze objectively.

QUESTIONS FOR DISCUSSION

1. What are the two most important social or ethical problems facing the advertising industry at the present time?
2. What guidelines would you suggest to an advertiser or an agency endeavoring to write a truthful but persuasive advertisement?
3. Is it possible for an advertisement to be both persuasive and completely truthful?
4. What should be the public policy regarding advertising by candidates for political office?
5. Under what conditions might advertising influence the news content or editorial policy of an advertising medium?

6. Does advertising contribute more to conformity or to individualism? Under what conditions is it most likely to contribute to conformity?

SUGGESTED READINGS

Bauer, Raymond A., and Stephen A. Greyser, *Advertising in America: The Consumer View*. Boston: Harvard Business School, 1968.

Borden, Neil H., *The Economic Effects of Advertising*. Homewood, Ill.: Richard D. Irwin, Inc., 1942.

Brink, Edward L., and William T. Kelley, *The Management of Promotion*. Englewood Cliffs, N.J.: Prentice-Hall, Inc., 1963. Chapters 17–19.

Firestone, O. J., *Economic Implications of Advertising*. London: Methuen & Co., Ltd., 1967.

Packard, Vance, *The Hidden Persuaders*. New York: Pocket Books, Inc., 1958. Chapter 23.

Pease, Otis, *The Responsibilities of American Advertising*. New Haven, Conn.: Yale University Press, 1958.

Potter, David, *People of Plenty*. New Haven, Conn.: Yale University Press, 1954. Chapter 8.

Sandage, C. H., and Vernon Fryburger, eds., *The Role of Advertising*. Homewood, Ill.: Richard D. Irwin, Inc., 1960 Parts I and III.

Taplin, Walter, *Advertising: A New Approach*. Boston: Little, Brown and Company, 1963.

Wright, John, and Daniel Warner, eds., *Speaking of Advertising*. New York: McGraw-Hill, Inc., 1962.

7 | Formal and Informal Controls

Controls are becoming increasingly important in modern advertising. There are many reflections of this trend: in the growth in size and operating budgets of government agencies policing advertising; in the increasing amount of attention devoted to advertising's social and economic problems; and in the resultant clamor for more controls to regulate excesses. We shall examine in this chapter the growth of controls and analyze in some detail how they work.

GROWTH OF CONTROLS

Nineteenth-century America came as close as any major economy in history to a real laissez-faire state—one characterized by a general absence of controls. Carlyle called laissez faire "anarchy plus the constable." One result, in the United States at least, was a century of great material progress within an environment of individual freedom. However, grave excesses abounded in all phases of business activity, including advertising. It is hardly surprising that there was public outcry during the turn of the century, for more stringent regulation. Because excesses in advertising were more obvious than those in other business activities, it bore a substantial amount of the criticism. The result was a great increase in federal and state regulation, particularly under the

Federal Trade Commission Act of 1914. The industry itself cooperated in setting up these regulations, through its magazine, *Printers' Ink*, and its most potent organization, the Associated Advertising Clubs of America (now American Advertising Federation).

The next big reform came in the depression years of the 1930s, when our sick economy was undergoing serious examination. Advertising again resorted to excesses in an attempt to cajole recalcitrant consumers into buying goods and services. Three major pieces of federal legislation that involved the regulation of advertising were enacted during this period.

In the 1950s and 1960s advertising men were again subjected to substantial criticism. Laws to tax advertising, increase the police powers of the Federal Trade Commission, restrict the placing of billboards along highways, and prohibit subliminal advertising were suggested. A worried and much criticized broadcasting industry took away the right to display the National Association of Broadcasters' TV code seal from offending stations.

Historically, each step in regulation has actually been a compromise. This is true of both legal regulation and regulation by the industry itself. Although some industry leaders favored the Federal Trade Commission Act before it was passed, many considered it dangerously radical. On the other hand, many critics thought it did not go far enough in eliminating "unfair and deceptive practices in commerce." The same can be said for most other laws and for the self-regulatory codes enacted by the advertising industry.

In a sense, the increase in controls is a tribute to advertising's power. Of course, some critics greatly overestimate the power of advertising and cause advertising people to hope for the day when advertising will really be as powerful as the critics think it is. It is well to remember that almost every business activity has experienced an increase in controls as they have grown more complicated and our economy more complex.

And what about the future? History suggests that we can expect continued increase in advertising controls. However, history adds a note of caution. It tells us that either unyielding opposition to controls or unyielding clamor for them is likely to end in defeat. Economic systems must be flexible enough to accommodate themselves to accumulated pressures and social changes. Technological and economic innovations are constantly changing our communication systems, and practices must keep up with these changes.

TYPES OF PROBLEMS

An examination of some specific problems for which controls have been devised may serve as a frame of reference for our analysis of the control mechanisms.

Content of the Advertisement. A substantial percentage of present and proposed regulation involves control of the content of the ad itself. The more commonly recurring problems tend to fall into the following areas:

FIG. 7.1 *In this television commercial the "diagram" talks about the man instead of vice-versa.* CLIENT: ALKA-SELTZER, MILES LABORATORIES, INC.; AGENCY: JACK TINKER & PARTNERS INC.

Truth. There is a great deal of concern (and rightly so) about truthfulness in the advertising message. Difficult as it is to determine truth in specific instances, there is agreement among the public and advertising practitioners that advertising should tell the truth. The Federal Trade Commission considers untrue advertising one of the "unfair methods of competition in commerce," and thus actionable under the provisions of the Federal Trade Commission Act and the Wheeler-Lea amendment to it.

Obscenity and Bad Taste. Obscenity is difficult to define. In an exhaustive examination of this problem, Zechariah Chafee, Jr., concluded, "The upshot of the foregoing discussion is that no legal definition of obscenity is very satisfactory. Indeed, I am forced to the conclusion that no attempt to frame a definition which will work in all situations is likely to succeed."[1] Bad taste is just as difficult to assess. Most people would agree that a recent advertisement picturing a babe-in-arms with these words coming out of his mouth, "I am so glad my mother smokes —————— cigarettes," was in bad taste. On the other hand, some advertisements might be in bad taste in a children's magazine but perfectly all right in a medium read primarily by adults.

Lottery. Gambling and lotteries are illegal in interstate commerce and within most states. Advertisements that promote contests or giveaways sometimes run afoul of the lottery laws. Legally, there is a lottery only if three elements are present in the offer: *prize, consideration,* and *chance.* If any one of these is absent, the offer does not constitute a lottery. However, certain states (and people) interpret these criteria differently. Take, for example, the matter of *consideration*—a frequent cause of confusion. In some states a contest that requires you

[1]Zechariah Chafee, Jr., *Government and Mass Communications* (Chicago: University of Chicago Press, 1947), vol. 1, p. 210.

to go to a certain store to enter the contest is illegal because this action constitutes a consideration.

Right of Privacy. Sidney Diamond, an attorney, has pointed out that "the right of privacy . . . is a legal doctrine with special relevance to the world of advertising. It is the principle that prohibits the use of the name or picture of a living person without consent and thus makes it necessary to get a signed release even from a professional model."[2] It is sometimes argued that professional models, actors, or persons regularly in the public eye have no real right of privacy, but the courts have ruled that they cannot be used for commercial publicity without their consent. Some have talked about their "right of publicity."

Libel. What is libel? Chafee says,

Anything . . . is libelous if it is defamatory, and the word "defamatory" has been carefully defined as follows: "A communication is defamatory if it tends so to harm the reputation of another as to lower him in the estimation of the community or to deter third persons from associating with him."[3]

Advertisers should take every precaution to avoid libelous material.

Copyright. The National Association of Broadcasters warns its members, "A copyright owner need only write, compose, paint or otherwise create something that is original with him — it need not be novel or new. While he cannot copyright an idea, he may achieve protection for the way he expresses that idea." Suppose that someone sat in his room one day and dreamed up a clever jingle advertising Chevrolets or wrote a highly original headline for a Chevrolet ad. If this work is truly original, he is the owner of a common-law copyright. Now put yourself in the place of an advertising executive. An unsolicited letter comes in the mail and you open it. You thank the sender for the idea, but explain in a letter that the company's agency prepares all the advertising and uses only original work. Two years later the agency prepares a campaign that looks or sounds much like the one suggested. Your company has a lawsuit on its hands. Because of risks such as this, most advertisers and agencies refuse to look at, listen to, or read proposed material until the person submitting it has signed a release. Before using original material from *any* source, they secure written permission to use it, because a copyright suit can be time-consuming and expensive.

Trademarked Material. Advertising neophytes sometimes confuse trademarks with copyrights. According to the Lanham Trade-Mark Act, which went into effect in 1947, the term includes "any word, name, symbol or device or any combination thereof adopted and used by a manufacturer or merchant to identify his goods and distinguish them from those manufactured or sold by others." An advertiser who has spent money and time building up a distinctive mark to identify his product is naturally anxious to protect the mark. Under present law not only a mark but "names, symbols, titles, designations, slogans, character names, and distinctive features of radio or other advertising" are specifically protected. Procter & Gamble thus protects "Camay," and

---

[2]Sidney A. Diamond, "Changing Concepts of the Right of Privacy," *Advertising Age,* January 17, 1966, p. 134.
[3]Chafee, p. 77.

Schlitz protects "The beer that made Milwaukee famous." According to the National Association of Broadcasters, some program titles, attention-getting symbols, characteristic sounds, and even distinct personalities may be protected. For example, "Bonanza" and the NBC chimes are registered as "service marks."

Type of Product Advertised. Many people feel that hard liquor (or even beer and wine) should not be advertised. Some people would prohibit the sale of many types of patent medicines. We could list innumerable products that are morally or socially objectionable to one group or another. Certain products are regulated voluntarily. However, the United States Supreme Court has said that if an industry or activity is legal, it is legal to advertise that business or industry.

Excessive Amounts of Advertising.   There are doubtless some people who think that any advertising at all is too much. Most, however, accept advertising but, at some stage, rebel at its overuse. We have all objected to the piling of one commercial upon another in a radio or television program. Many people object to an excessive number of billboards on highways and want them prohibited on certain scenic roads. Newspapers too are faced with the constant problem of determining the proper balance between advertising and editorial material.

Vertical Cooperative Advertising.   When the dealer and the manufacturer share the cost of the advertising (vertical cooperative advertising), all sorts of legal problems arise. Because such advertising amounts to more than a billion dollars a year, its problems are discussed in detail in Chapter 29. Let us merely say at this point that cooperative advertising allowances may be used as hidden price concessions to retailers, although this practice is illegal.

Labeling. In labeling foods, drugs, and cosmetics the marketer faces special problems. For example, what is not included (when *not* to use the product) may be as important as what is included.

Political and Public Service Advertising. Political and public service advertising presents ticklish problems for media sales managers. Should a manager refuse to accept advertising because he wants to stay clear of political involvements? Should he accept advertising for a cause he believes unworthy? Laws and rulings set forth specifically what radio and television stations can and cannot do, but the other media have to judge each situation separately.

Monopoly. In 1967 the United States Supreme Court decided that the acquisition of the Clorox Company by Procter & Gamble approximately ten years earlier was illegal. One of the principal considerations involved in this decision was the fact that the huge advertising outlay of Procter & Gamble and the advertising expertise it has at its disposal substantially reduced competition in the liquid bleach industry. According to the Court, it would be difficult for another company to compete against the P & G – Clorox combination. The Court also emphasized the fact that advertising and sales promotion are "vital" in the marketing of liquid bleach and soaps and detergents.[4]

TYPES OF CONTROL

Control of advertising and promotion—like control of any business activity—can be direct or indirect. The direct controls are more important and much easier to describe. They are of two main types—self-regulatory, or informal, controls instituted by the advertising industry itself, and regulation by law, or formal controls, enforced by governmental agencies at the federal, state, or local level. Emphasis here will be on the various types of direct controls, because indirect controls are understandably difficult to pinpoint. (Who can tell, for example, what motivated a copywriter to modify a wild claim he had considered including in his copy? Was it fear of legal action? Was it the possibility of arousing ill will on the part of consumers? Was he worried about an adverse report by a consumer-testing organization?)

SELF-REGULATION

Better Business Bureaus. The U.S. Department of Commerce calls Better Business Bureaus "one of the most unusual and effective instruments of self-regulation ever developed by the private enterprise system."[5] As the department points out, the Better Business Bureaus have been established so long and are so highly respected that many people think of the BBB as a semiofficial agency. The local bureaus are financed by business firms who want to stamp out unfair competition. Complaints may come from individuals or businesses. For example, an ad in your daily paper may offer a late model used car at a very low price. When you contact the dealer he tells you that the car has been sold and tries to sell you a higher-priced model. You suspect that the advertised car never existed and that the ad was placed merely as "bait." You report your suspicions to the Better Business Bureau. The Bureau investigates your charge, and if it finds your suspicions correct, tries to persuade the dealer to stop his "bait" advertising. If he refuses, or if he agrees but does not stop, publicity may be used as a weapon to stop him. If publicity does not work, legal action may be taken.

In 1967 there were 122 separate bureaus—108 local bureaus in major United States cities, nine in Canada, one each in Puerto Rico, Mexico, Venezuela, and Israel, and the National Better Business Bureau in New York City. They were supported by more than 100,000 firms whose total membership dues or subscriptions exceed $6\frac{1}{2}$ million a year. However, each bureau is organized as an independent, nonprofit corporation usually supported by a diversity of business interests in the community (such as retailing, manufacturing, investment). The board of directors of each local bureau appoints a manager and authorizes the addition of a staff. Typically a local BBB has three main divisions:

[4]"High Court Backs FTC; Orders P & G to Drop Clorox," *Advertising Age*, April 17, 1967, p. 1.
[5]U.S. Department of Commerce, *Self-regulation in Advertising* (Washington, D.C.: U.S. Government Printing Office, 1964), p. 50.

1. *Merchandise Division*, which is concerned with the advertising, selling and delivery of goods and services.
2. *Financial Division*, which deals with advertising and selling in the field of investments and securities, real estate, business opportunities, schools, insurance, or any other type of business that involves investments by the public.
3. *Solicitations Division,* which investigates campaigns aimed at securing contributions for charitable, philanthropic, propaganda, social, or economic causes, advertising in or subscriptions to various types of magazines and publications of "puff sheets" with a charitable, civic, patriotic, or religious appeal.[6]

The National Better Business Bureau deals with national advertisers according to the same principles employed in other BBB operations. However, it takes on additional jobs. It frequently assists new industries in developing codes and standards of practice such as the one

[6]*Self-regulation in Advertising*, p. 51.

FIG. 7.2 *Advertisements sponsored by the AAAA Interchange of Opinion on Objectionable Advertising. Consumers are invited to report objectionable advertising to the member agency whose name appears in the advertisement.* SOURCE: AMERICAN ASSOCIATION OF ADVERTISING AGENCIES.

described later in this chapter. It is a central source of information for advertisers, agencies, and media. It researches problems of regulations and helps advertisers keep out of trouble. One of its most important contributions is the publication of *Do's and Don'ts in Advertising Copy*. This is a loose-leaf manual that covers problem areas and legislation, court decisions, administrative rulings, and industry standards on a variety of products and marketing situations. Its purpose is not to censor but to help advertisers and agencies determine what they may say and what should be avoided. For example, we find the following under "Vacuum Cleaners":

> No false or misleading copy, layouts or illustrations shall be employed in advertising used or rebuilt vacuum cleaners. No sales practices or methods shall be used by salesmen to discourage, hinder or prevent the prospective customer's freedom of purchase of advertised machines nor shall sales clerks "knock" advertised machines. Advertised machines shall not be used merely as "bait" to attract customers for the purpose of switching them to something else.

Be
Eagle-
eyed

WHEN YOU SEE (OR HEAR) OBJECTIONABLE ADVERTISING REPORT IT TO

In print. Clip the advertisement and note where it appeared.
On the air. Make a note of sponsor, message, time and station.

A dealer featuring the sale of certain used or rebuilt machines shall have on hand a quantity of the advertised machines adequate to meet reasonably expected demand.

The Better Business Bureaus have rightfully been called "the most significant single element in the entire structure of advertising self-regulation."[7]

Advertising Agencies. The agencies, both individually and as a group, through the American Association of Advertising Agencies, exercise control over the advertising they produce. Cooperative efforts of agencies will be discussed later, with other advertising organizations. However, the individual agencies do a good deal of self-policing, and this is likely to increase now that agencies, as well as their clients, are legally liable for misleading or fraudulent claims in their advertisements. Some exercise careful surveillance to make sure that the copy they turn out meets acceptable standards. Most have legal counsel. Some refuse to handle advertising for certain products (liquor, cigarettes, proprietary medicines).

Advertising Media. A substantial portion of the self-regulation of advertising is carried on by the media, both individually and through their associations.

Newspapers. Many newspapers have become famous for their refusal to accept questionable advertising. *The New York Times*, for example, for more than fifty years has had a strict set of standards administered by its own Advertising Acceptability Department. This department will not accept a claim like "the finest dress we have ever seen" but may permit "the finest dress we have ever sold." The *Chicago Tribune* has a comprehensive review by a three-man board of censors. One of the most comprehensive codes is that of the *Detroit News* which bans advertisements of persons seeking introduction to members of the opposite sex, those offering homework for pay, or selling habit-forming drugs. A few years ago the *Milwaukee Journal* turned down thousands of dollars in the advertising of Hadacol, a patent medicine with a high alcoholic content, at a time when Hadacol was in great demand. It did so, even though the product had not been adjudged harmful by the Food and Drug Administration.

Television and Radio. The fleeting nature of television and radio messages makes it especially difficult to police this type of copy. Much of it is never written at all but ad-libbed by an announcer. Many stations are quite selective about what they accept. Others complain, however, that the advertiser who has a questionable product or piece of copy will always find another station that is not so particular.

The patterns and methods of self-regulation in television and radio differ in certain respects from those of newspapers and magazines: (1) they rely more heavily on industry codes virtually unknown in the print field; (2) they involve many matters of technique and presentation as well as claims; (3) they are more concerned than is print with controlling volume as well as content of advertising. In general, these differences grow out of the fact that these are government-licensed media.

---

[7]*Self-regulation in Advertising*, p. 55.

Control over television advertising is usually exercised through either of two types of self-regulatory machinery: continuity acceptance departments of stations and networks; and the Television Code and the Code Authority of the National Association of Broadcasters.

Most commercials that appear on the air are prechecked and prescreened at the network or station level by a department called the "continuity acceptance department," "clearance department," and the like.

The TV Code has been in effect since 1952, and it has gone through many revisions. The Code lists certain types of advertising that are not acceptable on television. Among these are "bait" advertising, advertising for tip sheets, race track publications, fortune tellers, and astrologists. Among the products banned are feminine hygiene products and liquor.

Among the types of presentation considered unacceptable under the code are "those not in courtesy and good taste," "disturbing or annoying material," "appeals involving matters of health which should be determined by physicians," and "appeals to help fictitious characters in television programs by purchasing the advertiser's product or sending in a premium."

In its early days television was plagued by a rash of actors dressed as doctors, so the "Men in White" clause was adopted. The 1959 version of the Code forbade the use of any but actual doctors or dentists in television commercials. However, the more recent (1967) version forbids the employment of "physicians, dentists, nurses, or actions representing physicians, dentists, or nurses."

The Code also limits the amount of broadcast time that may be devoted to commercials. In prime time (popular evening hours) not more than 17.2 percent (10 minutes in a 60 minute-period) can be devoted to "nonprogram" material – advertising, billboards, public service announcements, and so on. For other time the maximum in any 60-minute period is approximately 26 percent, or 16 minutes. The Code provides for a maximum of one interruption in a 5-minute program, and two in any program from 10 minutes to a half hour. Not all stations, however, subscribe to the Code.

Magazines. Unlike broadcasting, magazines have no over-all advertising code. However, many individual magazines have stringent rules. For example, *Good Housekeeping* tells us that it has a staff of 100 technicians and spends more than $1,000,000 a year testing products in the *Good Housekeeping Institute* to check claims made in advertisements submitted for insertion. It guarantees to refund the money paid for any product that does not live up to the advertised claim. *The New Yorker* exercises "a type of advertising control which has been termed not only 'tougher, more rigid' than that of any other magazine but also on occasion, 'more arbitrary, more arrogant and more bluenosed.'"[8] It will not accept advertisements for feminine hygiene products, products for self-medication (including aspirin), women's foundation garments showing a live model, or cut-rate retail store advertising. In *The New*

[8]*Self-regulation in Advertising*, pp. 66–67.

Yorker ads no mention may be made of competitors. Before it would accept an advertisement from a manufacturer of women's electric shavers it made him cut one-half inch off the photograph of bare female legs. The magazine considers that use of models who resemble famous people is in poor taste, and it has ruled out advertisements with models resembling Presidents Kennedy and Johnson.

Direct Mail. Most of the self-policing of direct mail is carried out by the Direct Mail Advertising Association. It bans sending unsolicited merchandise, vulgar or immoral matter, and gambling devices. It works through a Standards of Practice Committee.

Outdoor Ads. Outdoor advertising, unlike the other media, is concerned with the construction and maintenance of poster panels, painted bulletins, and spectaculars. Most of the self-regulation occurs through the organized sections of the industry because the unorganized section depends entirely on a variety of standards and sporadic self-control. The principal trade association for the outdoor industry, the Outdoor Advertising Association of America, has, like other media groups, adopted a code of acceptable practice. It is particularly concerned with such problems as zoning, design and construction of the displays, and placement of billboards.

Publications of the Advertising Industry. The advertising industry is blessed with a vigorous press of its own, which is not afraid to spotlight excesses in its field. *Printers' Ink*, for example, was a force in getting the Federal Trade Commission Act passed and sponsoring the Printers' Ink Model Statute (which we shall discuss later in this chapter). In the 1930s and the early 1950s the magazine struck out against the excesses that had provoked criticism. Publisher C. B. Larrabee said in 1952, "We at *Printers' Ink* are worried about the mounting criticism of advertising coming from responsible leaders of American thought. They do not question the value of advertising as an economic necessity, but they are repelled by its shortcomings."[9] *Advertising Age,* which has the largest circulation of any of the advertising publications, has also waged a consistent battle for more truthful and tasteful advertising. It has criticized advertising people for trying to put pressure on the media, changing agencies often and for trivial reasons, and for the poor taste of some advertising. It has popularized a feature, "Advertising We Can Do Without," which reports copy objected to by readers or editors.

Individual Advertisers. Most individual advertisers are concerned with either obedience to the law or matters of public taste or interest. As they become more concerned with their corporate image, they pay increased attention to advertising that is associated with their company or brand. For example, at Procter & Gamble all basic facts about a product's performance are presented to both its advertising copy section and its legal section. The copy section then works with the company's agencies in the development of copy. The advertising is submitted to the legal section for review. At Lever Brothers much the same policy is followed. At General Foods, all product claims of performance, quality, and value must be approved by an advertising policy committee. Block

[9] C. B. Larrabee, "Thunder on the Right," *Printers' Ink,* March 7, 1952, p. 39.

Basis for state laws on truth in advertising— the Printers' Ink Model Statute

- How the laws came into being
- Better Business Bureau relations
- Revised statute
- States that do not have such laws

One of the great landmarks in the fight for decent advertising was the creation of the honest advertising law is the PRINTERS' INK Model Statute which has served faithfully since 1911.

Today the statute, substantially as originally written by Harry D. Nims, is in use in 26 states and the District of Columbia and 17 other states have adopted variations of it, variations which PRINTERS' INK believes to be of a weakening nature. Thus 43 of the 48 states plus the District of Columbia have endorsed the principle of the P.I. Model Statute. The five states that don't have such laws are: Arkansas, Delaware, Georgia, Mississippi, New Mexico.

It is the law from which the Better Business Bureau movement stems and on which Better Business Bureaus operate. Without it or some similar piece of legislation, the Bureaus would find themselves hopelessly handicapped in their splendid and unremitting fight for honest advertising. To anyone who will contrast advertising as it is today with what it was in 1911, the very fact that the original P.I. Model Statute has served so well and is serving so well today is all the more amazing.

Any law, however, no matter how carefully drawn, lives by its judicial interpretation. Also, few laws drawn in 1911 and dealing with a business so complicated and progressive as advertising do not need some sort of revision.

Because of our study of certain court cases based on the P.I. Model Statute and because of our knowledge of how the statute is being applied under modern conditions, we felt that it would be desirable to investigate the operations of the old law, to determine how far it met present merchandising practices and how it had fared in the decisions of the courts.

We learned that a number of Better Business Bureau executives were asking themselves similar questions. As a result, at the annual meeting of the National Association of Better Business Bureaus in Cleveland in June 1945, PRINTERS' INK asked for the cooperation of Better Business Bureaus in a further study. A committee of Better Business Bureau executives was appointed to act with us in the study.

We engaged the late Isaac W. Digges, member of the New York Bar, to head the investigation and to suggest such revisions as seemed suitable and necessary after consultation with Bureau executives, Bureau lawyers, enforcement officers and businessmen generally. We chose Mr. Digges because of his intimate knowledge of law as it applies to merchandising practices.

Loopholes

We discovered several problems in the enforcement of the P.I. Model Statute and several loopholes through which a few local advertisers were continuing to mislead the public. With this experience behind us, we then rewrote the original law. No better tribute can be made to the original statute than the mere fact that a few minor changes make it completely adaptable to present-day conditions.

The statute with these revisions, which have been approved by the National Association of Better Business Bureaus, appears below.

We believe that it is highly desirable that advertising people in the states that have no advertising statute get behind a move to enact the revised statute.

Advertisers in those states having a form of the statute with certain weakening clauses should make every effort to remedy the situation. Since 1953 laws in 5 states have been strengthened.

Revised Printers' Ink Model Statute

(Italics indicate the changes made in 1945)

Any person, firm, corporation or association or agent or employee thereof, who, with intent to sell, *purchase* or in any wise dispose of, *or to contract with reference to* merchandise, real estate, service, *employment*, or anything offered by such person, firm, corporation or association, or agent or employee thereof, directly or indirectly, to the public for sale, *purchase*, distribution, *or the hire of personal services*, or with intent to increase the consumption of *or to contract with reference to any merchandise, real estate, securities, service, or employment*, or to induce the public in any manner to enter into any obligation relating thereto, or to acquire title thereto, or an interest therein, or to make any loan, makes, publishes, disseminates, circulates, or places before the public, or causes, directly or indirectly, to be made, published, disseminated, circulated, or placed before the public, in this state, in a newspaper, magazine or other publication, or in the form of a book, notice, circular, pamphlet, letter, handbill, poster, bill, sign, placard, card, label, or over any radio or television station or other medium of wireless communication, or in any other way *similar or dissimilar to the foregoing*, an advertisement, announcement, or statement of any sort regarding merchandise, securities, service, *employment*, or anything so offered *for use, purchase or sale*, or the interest, terms or conditions upon which such loan will be made to the public, which advertisement contains any assertion, representation or statement of fact which is untrue, deceptive, or misleading, shall be guilty of a misdemeanor. ●

FIG. 7.3 *The* Printers' Ink *Model Statute as revised in 1945—law in twenty-seven states and adopted partially by seventeen others.* SOURCE: PRINTERS' INK.

Drug submits television copy and storyboards to the networks and to the NAB in addition to its own review committee. In problems of taste, most advertisers have advertising reviewed on a case-by-case basis. However, Falstaff Brewing has a specific list of "Do's and Don'ts" which include avoidance of appeals to children, emphasis on sex and "cheesecake," and implications that beer will give people a "lift."

Individual Industries. Industry self-regulation involves an agreement on the part of companies in the same industry to abide by certain standards of advertising practice. However, competing firms have to be careful that they do not run afoul of the antitrust laws when they make such agreements and try to enforce them. In general, industries that have a particular problem, or are new, are most likely to adopt codes. For example, seat belt and distilling industries have drawn up such codes but steel and soap industries have not.

Many codes are strongly influenced by the Federal Trade Commission, which prepares and publishes the following: *Federal Trade Practice Rules*, which are issued after a conference between the Commission and members of the industry involved; *Federal Trade Practice Guides*, which are restatements of the law in language of the laymen as decided by the Commission; and *Federal Trade Regulation Rules*, which are based on studies and reports made available to the Commission.

An interesting example of an industry code is that of the distilling industry. The code goes beyond federal or state requirements regarding the promotion of distilled spirits. For example, it prohibits advertising of liquor on radio or television, advertising in a publication bearing a Sunday dateline, and advertising on outdoor posters near a military or naval base. The Wine Institute code prohibits advertisements featuring athletes, appeals to children, and suggestions that wine is associated with religion.

In an effort to avoid legal regulation of its advertising copy, the cigarette industry adopted an advertising code in 1964 and hired ex-governor Robert Meyner of New Jersey to see that it was enforced. For example, terms such as "neat," "clean," and "smooth" were abandoned. Chesterfield was encouraged to change "They satisfy" to "Chesterfield people smoke satisfied." Fancy names for filters were banned. Cigarette advertisers were encouraged to avoid television shows with strong appeal to younger people, to discontinue advertising in college publications and in comic books. Entertainers and athletes were banned as endorsers, and models (male or female) were to be at least twenty-five years of age.

Advertising Associations. At least three major advertising associations—the American Advertising Federation, the American Association of Advertising Agencies, and the Association of National Advertisers—have helped regulate advertising. The AAF (a federation of advertising organizations) helped establish the Federal Trade Commission, and the Better Business Bureaus grew out of early "vigilance committees." Because most local advertising clubs belong to the AAF it is in a particularly good position through its emphasis on Truth in Advertising to influence local practices. Its emphasis has been on compliance with laws rather than matters of taste.

The AAAA exercises control through its ability to refuse membership to prospective agencies not considered ethically qualified. Through its Standards of Practice and its Creative Code it insists that members not engage in such practices as "false or misleading statements, testimonials which do not reflect the real choice of a competent witness, statements or pictures offensive to public decency."

Perhaps the most interesting activity of the AAAA is its Interchange Program (Interchange of Opinion on Objectionable Advertising), which it conducted independently until 1960 and has since operated jointly with the Association of National Advertisers, which represents the clients of its member agencies. The Interchange is a reviewing procedure whereby advertisements of questionable taste or truth are referred to a committee of twenty executives; ten from agencies, ten from the advertisers. Complaints are circulated among members of the committee, together with a voting form. If the majority considers the advertising "objectionable" or "serious," the advertiser and agency are notified. In "serious" situations a reply is required. No publicity is given to citations or to action taken as a result of it.

GOVERNMENT REGULATION

Much of the control in advertising is by law; thus an advertising man's best friend may be a lawyer. However, the advertising man, himself, must know enough about the law to prevent a possible illegality before it occurs. He should realize that there are laws that control advertising directly (the Wheeler-Lea amendments) and others that control it indirectly (the Communications Act of 1934 and some tax laws). The operation of both direct and indirect control can be best discussed if we analyze regulation in terms of those agencies that administer the legislation.

Federal Government. *Federal Trade Commission.* The FTC is the most powerful and active of the regulatory agencies. It was established by the Federal Trade Commission Act of 1914 to "stop unfair competition before such practices became illegal within the proscription of the Sherman Act."[10] During its early years the Commission was handicapped by the vagueness of the phrase "unfair competition." However, in the Beech-Nut Packing Company case (1922) the Court affirmed the right of the Commission to regulate manufacturers' representation to dealers, which was the same as advertising in the eyes of the Commission. In the Winsted Hosiery Company case (1922) the Court affirmed the Commission's right to regulate false labeling and advertising as unfair methods of competition.

The Wheeler-Lea amendments to the Federal Trade Commission Act (1938) extended significantly the powers of the Commission to regulate advertising. The most important changes were these:

1. They extended "unfair methods of competition" to include "deceptive acts or practices."
2. They gave the Commission power to issue a cease and desist order that automatically became a final and binding order sixty days after issuance. The Commission could thus cite a defendant for contempt if he did not comply with the order within that time.
3. They gave the Commission specific jurisdiction over false advertising of foods, drugs, cosmetics, and therapeutic devices. False advertising here includes false representation; as well as the failure to reveal material facts.
4. The Commission was empowered to issue an injunction to halt improper advertising of food, drugs, and cosmetics while hearings were in progress on the basis that such advertising might be harmful to health.

[10]Max Geller, *Advertising at the Crossroads* (New York: The Ronald Press Company, 1952), p. 123. (See also chapter 6 of this book for a discussion of the background and work of the Federal Trade Commission.)

The Commission reviews television and radio advertising, as well as that in the print media. All media can be considered by legal definition to be included under "interstate commerce." In 1958 the FTC set up a liaison with the Federal Communication Commission under which the FCC was provided with copies of complaints and orders involving broadcasters or broadcast advertising. In 1960 the two agencies extended the cooperation by making it possible for personnel of each to have access to confidential files of the other. The agencies also agreed to inform each other when they obtained investigation leads of mutual interest.

The Federal Trade Commission is also responsible for administering certain other laws affecting advertising. One example is the Fur Products Labeling Act, which prevents the calling of rabbit (or other plebeian fur) by a more exotic name. Another is the Robinson-Patman Act of 1936, which was designed to protect small retailers against larger outlets that could, because of their size, get a substantial price advantage. This involves the use of cooperative advertising allowances to dealers; it will therefore be discussed in more detail under that heading in Chapter 29.

Ordinarily, complaints come from competitors, the public, or one of FTC's own monitors. After investigation by field agents, a preliminary report is prepared in the FTC Bureau of Investigation. This report is forwarded to the Bureau of Litigation. Only after this bureau decides a complaint is justified, does the case go to the Commission. FTC's course of action varies according to the seriousness of the offense, the past record of the offender, and his willingness to cooperate. The FTC may turn the case over to its Division of Stipulation for the negotiation of informal settlement. On the other hand, it may send the case to the Bureau of Litigation, where a formal complaint is issued.

When a complaint is issued, the respondent has thirty days to reply. In litigated cases hearings are held before a trial examiner employed by the FTC but not under Commission discipline. His initial decision can be appealed to the FTC by either side. The Commission affirms or modifies the order, or the case may be dismissed. However, the decisions of FTC (like those of other government regulatory agencies) are appealable to any federal court of appeal.

The Federal Trade Commission has five weapons at its disposal:

1. *Letter of compliance.* This is the least formal of the weapons and involves a written promise to discontinue a disputed practice.
2. *Stipulation.* After investigators have recommended punitive action, a signed agreement is negotiated. It is a recorded public action and can be used as evidence in future cases, although it does not constitute an admission of guilt.
3. *Consent order.* This is a short-cut settlement after a formal complaint has been issued. However, a consent order still does not constitute an admission of guilt.
4. *Cease and desist order.* This is a finding of "guilty" after trial. Like a consent order, it is legally enforceable, although it is appealable to court.

5. *Publicity.* FTC publicizes all judicial activities, just as courts publicize their operations. For example, all complaints are announced in FTC press releases, and the full text of the complaint is available to the press. Also FTC issues releases summarizing replies received from respondents, initial decisions by examiners and final decisions by the Commission.

The Federal Trade Commission is making its influence felt more and more in areas that were once considered outside its province. For example, it has contended that agencies as well as clients are liable for false or misleading advertising, and, in several cases the courts have borne this out. It adopted a rule in 1965 that would require cigarette companies to include in their advertisements a warning that smoking might be dangerous. As a result, Congress passed a law requiring such a warning on the package, but not in the advertisement. In 1965 it moved into the controversial area of broadcast audience ratings and recommended guides for program promotion. Ira M. Millstein has warned that the FTC may be treading on dangerous ground:

> There are . . . and will continue to be areas involving problems of social values. The point is not that the FTC must ignore cases that fall within these areas, but that in considering them, it must make a conscious effort to avoid passing upon the "rightness" or "wrongness" of the appeal, and must concentrate on whether a promise has been made that is not true, and whether the promise is such as may induce people to act.[11]

The Clorox case referred to earlier in this chapter represented the FTC's increased interest in possible monopolistic effects of advertising. The FTC's contention that Procter & Gamble's advertising and promotional facilities were so great that competitors would be discouraged from entering the household bleach field was upheld by the United States Supreme Court. However, within a few weeks of this landmark decision, Jules Backman's *Advertising and Competition* was published. The book's conclusion is that advertising does more to stimulate competition than to create monopoly.[12]

Food and Drug Administration. The Pure Food and Drug Act of 1906 prohibited shipment in interstate commerce of adulterated and misbranded food and drugs. The Pure Food, Drug, and Cosmetics Act of 1938 represented an attempt to eliminate some of the weaknesses and ambiguities of the original legislation. Its most important contributions were: it made failure to reveal material facts on a label an element of misbranding and thus a misdemeanor; it made clear that this act covered only *labeling*, which includes literature that accompanies the product or is shipped as a booklet or folder, apart from the product. The law is administered by the Food and Drug Administration.

Federal Communications Commission. Under the Communications Act of 1934, the Commission is empowered to operate our telecommunications system in the "public interest, convenience and necessity."

---

[11]Ira M. Millstein, "The Federal Trade Commission and False Advertising," *Columbia Law Review*, vol. 64 (March 1964), p. 449.

[12]Jules Backman, *Advertising and Competition* (New York: New York University Press, 1967).

These are the main criteria for awarding operating licenses to television and radio stations and for renewing them. The Commission thus wields indirect control over advertising, in that certain types of advertising and advertising practices are not considered in the "public interest, convenience and necessity."

More specifically, here are some of the problems that cause the FCC trouble in television and radio commercials: misleading statistics and demonstrations, the patriotic appeal, the physiological commercial, intermixing of program and advertising content, and propaganda in commercials. Other advertising problems of concern to the Commission are the length of commercials, number of commercials, piling up of commercials, middle commercials in a program, sponsored versus sustaining programs, and lotteries. (Lotteries fall within the statutes of the United States Criminal Code rather than the Communications Act, but the Commission enforces this part of the Criminal Code.)

The FCC has no power of censorship and does not check on individual programs or commercials unless complaints have been received. Instead, each station is required to keep a complete log of all programs and commercials, and these may be examined at the time a license renewal is due. The FCC also works with the FTC and exchanges confidential information with regard to advertising problems, particularly those concerning false advertising and sponsored programs not identified as such. At a NAB convention, response to a question concerning how this liaison worked, Federal Communications Commissioner Lee said,

> Where the Federal Trade Commission makes a final determination that certain advertising is deceptive or has some other fault, the continued broadcasting of such advertising would raise some questions in our mind with respect to the public interest.

Commissioner Lee also said that the FCC would advise the station if the FTC had found there was some basis for taking formal action in connection with advertising carried over that station.

Post Office Department. The activity of the Postal Service with regard to advertising is mainly in the fields of obscenity, lottery, and fraud. With respect to obscenity, advertisements for books or motion pictures are among the types commonly questioned. In 1959, for example, the Post Office stopped certain advertising for the movie "The Naked Maja" from going through the mails.

In cases of fraud, the Post Office operates in the same area as the Federal Trade Commission. However, Geller points out that "while the Federal Trade Commission's interest is centered solely upon the bad practice to be remedied, the Post Office Department is concerned not only in the elimination of the evil but also in protecting itself from providing the means, through its own service, of bilking the public."[13] He contends that control over fraudulent advertising should eventually be integrated, either by statute or by voluntary action.

In policing lotteries, the Post Office Department, like the FCC, uses the three-part test — prize, consideration, and chance.

[13]Geller, p. 238.

Alcohol Tax Unit. In 1935 a Federal Alcohol Tax Administration was created as a division of the Treasury Department to control practices (including advertising) in the brewing and liquor industry. In 1940 the Federal Alcohol Tax Unit in the Bureau of Internal Revenue took over these powers. This unit grants licenses to permit the manufacturer or producer of alcoholic beverages to carry on his business. Thus it has a stick to wield over recalcitrant advertisers.

Actually, the liquor industry is so conscious of its public relations problem that it is not likely to indulge in advertising excesses. The Distilled Spirits Institute has kept its own house in order. Also the Alcohol Tax Unit has an advisory service for distillers and bottlers; thus they can secure prepublication advice on the propriety of advertisements.

Seed Act Division. This is a branch of the Department of Agriculture. As far as advertising is concerned, its main duty is to check deceptive seed advertisements and take appropriate action when necessary.

United States Patent Office. Trademarks, service marks, slogans, and other material protected under the Lanham Trade-Mark Act should be registered with the United States Patent Office. According to Sandage and Fryburger:

Such registration serves as (1) constructive notice of claim of ownership, (2) prima-facie evidence of registrant's exclusive rights to use the mark in commerce, and (3) conclusive evidence of registrant's exclusive right to use the mark in commerce under certain circumstances. The incontestable right in a mark is secured after the mark has been filed with the Commissioner of Patents within the time prescribed, and providing there are no actions pending which contest the registrant's claim to ownership.[14]

Obviously, everyone who has developed a trademark, a slogan, or a service mark of any sort will try for this "incontestable right." An advertiser who is slow to register his mark is in danger of losing these rights.

Library of Congress. The Library of Congress enforces the copyright laws, as set forth in the United States Code.

Securities and Exchange Commission. This commission examines all printed promotional material of stock and bond offerings. One of its prime concerns is to make sure full and accurate information on the company is divulged in the security offering.

State Regulation. In 1911, at the request of *Printers' Ink*, a group of advertising men worked out a "Model Statute" designed to make advertising more truthful. At their convention in Boston that year, the Affiliated Advertising Clubs of the World passed a resolution urging every state to adopt the statute. The statute said that any person who placed before the public an announcement that "contains assertions, representations, or statement of fact which is untrue, deceptive or misleading, shall be guilty of a misdemeanor."

This statute, in much the same form as originally proposed, has been adopted by all but three states. However, according to agency chair-

[14]C. H. Sandage and Vernon Fryburger, *Advertising Theory and Practice,* 7th ed. (Homewood, Ill.: Richard D. Irwin, Inc., 1967), p. 360.

man Kenneth Laird "the very severity of this law operates to prevent its enforcement. It is a criminal statute . . . and the average prosecutor knows that juries are unlikely to convict under a criminal statute, and he concludes he should use his limited staff to prosecute more serious crimes. Thus, the advertising shyster has an easy time moving around inside this legal vacuum."[15] According to Otis Pease, "Prosecutions under the statute (to World War II) remained few in number, but its principal value was as a deterrent in the hands of the Better Business Bureaus and other voluntary agencies which sought to dissuade offenders rather than punish them."[16]

Many states have laws defining lotteries. It is possible that a contest legal in certain states may be considered a lottery in others. Some states also regulate the use of people's names in testimonials and the advertising of certain types of products such as alcoholic beverages.

However, most advertising is interstate, and federal laws are therefore the more important ones.

TAXATION AS A CONTROL

It is recognized that taxes may be used as controls as well as for raising money. Sometimes lawmakers find that they can achieve a combination of the two objectives in one law. Advertising is not generally taxed at present, but federal, state, and municipal legislators have made increasing attempts to tax it in recent years.

Advertising has been taxed at the national level only a few brief times in American history. The first time was in 1765, when a Stamp Tax of two shillings was assessed on each advertisement, regardless of its size or the amount paid for it. That law was repealed in 1766. During the five years of the Civil War a federal tax on advertising was in effect. It was repealed after the war.

At present, advertising is tax exempt under the Internal Revenue Code, on the basis of its being an ordinary expense of business. However, the Internal Revenue Service and other government agencies have made rulings that modify this situation. In one instance, the IRS ruled that advertising by utilities designed to emphasize the advantages of privately operated utilities over government-controlled utilities was "lobbying" and not deductible as an ordinary business expense. In another, the Federal Power Commission disallowed expenditures for institutional advertising by private utilities as a factor in fixing the rates of that company.

Another problem has arisen regarding the levying of excise taxes. The question is, "Should the excise tax be levied on the full price of the merchandise or on the price of the merchandise less the rebate for cooperative advertising?" Until 1958 IRS policy held that this allowance given by manufacturers to retailers (mainly for local advertising) was not part of the price. However, it was then ruled that it was part of the price and therefore subject to the tax. This was a blow to local

[15]"Update False Ad Law Model: Laird to AAF," *Advertising Age,* July 15, 1968, p. 72.
[16]Otis Pease, *The Responsibilities of American Advertising* (New Haven, Conn.: Yale University Press, 1958), p. 46.

media, which can sell more advertising to dealers if the dealers receive an allowance from manufacturers.

Both states and municipalities have made efforts in recent years to levy taxes directly and indirectly on advertising. A tax on advertising in Baltimore was ruled unconstitutional on the basis that it was "a violation of the due process clause of the Constitution because it was vague, indefinite and ambiguous." Some states and cities have sales taxes that are applied to advertising or advertising materials as well as to other goods and services that are sold. In Arizona, for example, newspapers must pay the sales tax on all general and local advertising and on all circulation revenue. In Georgia the sales tax is applied to newspaper circulation but not to advertising.

The advertising industry is understandably disturbed at the idea of taxes on advertising. The industry bases its opposition on Chief Justice John Marshall's dictum that "the power to tax is the power to destroy" and on the First Amendment to the Constitution. It is possible, no doubt, that taxation could be used to silence a critical press. However, advertising people will undoubtedly have to continue trying to defend their tax-free position. Legislatures and city councils faced with a mounting need for additional revenue are bound to cast covetous eyes on the advertising industry.

INDIRECT CONTROLS

Indirect controls work in subtle ways and are more difficult than direct controls to describe precisely. However, two indirect controls that deserve mention are product-rating services and consumer education.

Product-Rating Services. The two leading testing organizations are Consumers Union and Consumer's Research. Each offers a testing and rating service for its subscribers, to whom it reports its conclusions with a specific rating as "Best Buy," "Acceptable," etc. Their conclusions do not always agree with each other or with other independent testing laboratories. They deal in claims that can be proved true or false, not in esthetic associations or matters of individual taste. They cannot test a brand image, and this is often very important in consumer selection.

Consumer Education. There has been a trend in recent years toward training both students and adults to be better consumers. Consumer education courses in high schools, colleges, and vocational schools often include such topics as selection of merchandise, quality judging, and budgets. Consumer education exerts an indirect influence on advertising forcing the advertising industry to appeal to a more perceptive consumer who will less easily be misled by wild claims. (In many areas the advertising industry cooperates actively in the conduct of such courses.)

EFFECTIVENESS OF CONTROLS

The inevitable question is, "How effective have these controls been?" Any answer must be qualified. It seems evident that both self-regulation and legal regulation eliminate many excesses. Both act to discourage the more zealous violators. Occasionally, the regulators will crack the whip over violators; more often, the velvet glove of persuasion is used. Pease seems unduly pessimistic when he concludes that "the structure of internal control . . . operated with effectiveness to curb only behavior found objectionable by those within the industry and even in this relatively narrow sphere of action the forces for internal control were generally of small effect."[17] The Federal Trade Commission has said that "considering the great increase in (advertising) volume, an amazingly small percentage is questionable."

There is, however, room for improvement in all the areas of control covered in this chapter. Unless industry members assume responsibility for curbing the excesses in the field and unless they work with government regulators and with legislators, they are likely to find government regulation stepped up sharply in coming years. One leading executive, William Colihan, has warned the industry that time may be limited.

The middle and upper middle managements of Washington lack the informational facilities and guidance that even the lower middle managers of our business can muster and deploy . . . .the Washingtons have to balance what we tell them with what the unions tell them and what the NAM tells them and what the ADA tells them and what their mother in law tells them.[18]

SUMMARY

In this chapter we have seen how controls have increased during the last one hundred years. In general, the most pressing problems of advertising content concern truth, obscenity and bad taste, lotteries, the right of privacy, libel, the protection of ideas through copyright, and the trademark laws. Other problems include the control of vertical cooperative advertising, labeling, and public service advertising.

Control of advertising may be either direct or indirect. There is considerable indirect control, but it is more difficult to trace than direct control. Direct controls are exerted by both the advertising industry itself and legal agencies. The principal vehicles of self-regulation are the Better Business Bureaus, the agencies, the media, advertising publications, advertisers, and advertising organizations. In the federal government are controls by the Federal Trade Commission, Food and Drug Administration, Federal Communications Commission, Post Office Department, Alcohol Tax Unit, Seed Act Division, Patent Office, Library of Congress, and the Securities and Exchange Commission. State regulation is accomplished mainly through variations of the Printers' Ink Model Statute.

QUESTIONS FOR DISCUSSION

1. Which of the agencies involved in federal regulation of advertising seems to you to be the most effective? What can be done to improve the effectiveness of some of the other agencies?

[17]Pease, p. 201.
[18]William J. Colihan, Jr., "Relating to Washington, or Thoughts on the Shuttle," Talk before the 1967 AAAA Meeting, White Sulphur Springs, Va., April 20, 1967.

2. Compare self-regulation with government regulation on the basis of their influence on growth of industry.
3. Check your local newspaper to see whether any advertisements fail to meet the standards of the Better Business Bureaus.
4. Check a cross section of current television commercials to find out whether any of them fail to meet the standards of the National Association of Broadcasters or the Wheeler-Lea amendments.
5. To what extent is it in the interests of agencies, advertisers, and media to regulate their own advertising?
6. Write a letter that might be sent to your congressman or United States senator outlining the extent to which he should support either *more*, or *less*, federal regulation over advertising.

SUGGESTED READINGS

Brink, Edward L., and William T. Kelley, *The Management of Promotion.* Englewood Cliffs, N.J.: Prentice-Hall, Inc., 1963. Chapters 20–21.

Chafee, Zechariah, Jr., *Government and Mass Communications.* Chicago: University of Chicago Press, 1947. Chapters 1–13.

Digges, I. W., *The Modern Law of Advertising and Marketing.* New York: Funk & Wagnalls, 1948.

Dunn, S. Watson, *Advertising Copy and Communication.* New York: McGraw-Hill, Inc., 1956. Chapter 18.

Geller, Max, *Advertising at the Crossroads.* New York: The Ronald Press Company, 1952.

Howard, Marshall C., *Legal Aspects of Marketing.* New York: McGraw-Hill, Inc., 1964.

Millstein, Ira M., "The Federal Trade Commission and False Advertising," *Columbia Law Review,* 64 (March 1964), 439–499.

National Better Business Bureau, *Do's and Don'ts in Advertising Copy.* New York: National Better Business Bureaus, 1968.

Pease, Otis, *The Responsibilities of American Advertising.* New Haven, Conn.: Yale University Press, 1958.

United States Department of Commerce, *Self-Regulation in Advertising.* Washington, D. C.: U.S. Government Printing Office, 1964.

8 | The Institutions of Advertising: The Agency

Most advertising or promotion can be divided into three parts. One is the *agency* that plans and prepares the campaign. Another is the *advertiser* (general or retail) who pays the bills and whose name usually appears in the advertisement. And finally there are the *media* that carry the message to the public. In this chapter we shall examine the first of these, the agency, and in the next chapter the advertisers and the media.

To the public, advertising frequently means Madison Avenue in New York City or Michigan Avenue in Chicago. In the Madison Avenue area of mid-town New York are between 25,000 and 30,000 agency people—more than three times the number in any other area of the United States. Of the 55 United States agencies that handled billing of more than $25,000,000 in 1967 reported by *Advertising Age*, 37 had their official headquarters in New York, 8 in Chicago, and 3 in Detroit. However, of the 15 largest agencies listed in Table 8.1, all except 2 are headquartered in New York.

We should not, however, lose sight of the fact that agencies are scattered throughout the United States and that there are few cities of any business importance which do not have at least one agency listed in the *Standard Directory of Advertising: The Agency List*.

128

TABLE 8.1

ESTIMATED TOTAL BILLINGS OF TOP U.S. ADVERTISING AGENCIES
(Dollar totals in millions*)

*Figures shown in this table represent the best information available to *Advertising Age* and are constructed either from answers to questionnaires (sometimes revised on the basis of other information) or on the best data available.

1967 BILLING RANK World	U.S.		WORLD BILLING 1967	1966	U.S. BILLING 1967	1966	Data for U.S. Only SPACE/TIME 1967	1966
1	1	J. Walter Thompson Co.	590.6	580.8	363.6	379.8	332.5	352.6
2	4	McCann-Erickson, Inc.**	476.0	465.0	281.0	283.0	235.0	–
3	2	Young & Rubicam	430.3	406.7	326.4	320.2	220.4	222.2
4	3	Batten, Barton, Durstine & Osborn	313.5	328.3	298.7	308.7	241.7	247.4
5	8	Ted Bates & Co.	301.0	265.0	190.0	177.0	163.3	147.8
6	7	Foote, Cone & Belding	268.6	262.0	207.0	201.3	192.0	190.1
7	5	Leo Burnett Co.	261.3	222.5	250.0	212.2	216.5	186.8
8	6	Doyle Dane Bernbach	245.4	211.5	218.7	191.5	185.9	163.7
9	9	Grey Advertising	200.0	174.0	170.0	154.0	164.0	147.0
10	15	Ogilvy & Mather International	183.2	166.3	114.2	97.7	99.4	–
11	14	Compton Advertising	175.0	137.0	120.0	105.0	95.8	85.0
12	11	Benton & Bowles	173.2	168.9	144.7	156.1	113.0	119.2
13	10	Dancer-Fitzgerald-Sample	160.2	151.6	156.0	148.7	150.0	–
14	12	Campbell-Ewald Co.	136.8	144.3	131.7	139.1	97.5	–
15	13	William Esty Co.	131.0	128.0	131.0	128.0	121.0	–

BILLING RANK World	U.S.		Data for U.S. Only CAPITALIZED FEES 1967	1966	GROSS INCOME 1967	1966	TOTAL EMPLOYES 1967	1966
1	1	J. Walter Thompson Co.	31.1	27.2	–	–	2,642	2,520
2	4	McCann-Erickson, Inc.**	25.0	–	–	–	1,002	1,978
3	2	Young & Rubicam	23.1	25.6	47.8	47.3	2,412	2,481
4	3	Batten, Barton, Durstine & Osborn	18.0	16.5	44.1	45.5	2,033	2,082
5	8	Ted Bates & Co.	0.7	1.2	28.8	26.3	1,300	1,126
6	7	Foote, Cone & Belding	4.7	2.7	39.1	38.5	1,300	1,300
7	5	Leo Burnett Co.	4.1	3.0	–	–	1,589	1,388
8	6	Doyle Dane Bernbach	8.8	6.9	32.1	27.5	1,398	1,198
9	9	Grey Advertising	6.0	7.0	–	24.6	1,197	1,250
10	15	Ogilvy & Mather International	53.4	–	17.1	–	830	767
11	14	Compton Advertising	3.5	2.0	18.0	15.7	818	793
12	11	Benton & Bowles	11.7	–	21.3	23.0	911	1,166
13	10	Dancer-Fitzgerald-Sample	3.0	–	–	–	893	885
14	12	Campbell-Ewald Co.	5.5	–	–	–	897	961
15	13	William Esty Co.	–	–	–	–	727	708

**Part of Interpublic Group of Companies, whose agency units billed an estimated world aggregate of $721,500-000 in 1967 ($685,000,000 in 1966).

EVOLUTION OF THE MODERN AGENCY

Until about 1869 the advertising agency business in the United States was unstable. Fly-by-night operations were frequent. Price cutting and private deals were common during this period. There was not even a directory of media and rates for agencies or advertisers to use for reference.

In 1869 George P. Rowell added a note of stability when he published the first accurate list of the nation's newspapers. Then, in 1875, N.W. Ayer offered an "open contract" that gave advertisers access to true rates charged by newspapers and religious journals. Ayer made it clear that his agency worked for the advertiser rather than for the medium, and he began to de-emphasize space selling and explore ways of helping the advertiser sell more goods. This was the beginning of advertising service. Another step forward was the emphasis on advertising copy made by Albert Lasker.

Services provided by agencies began to expand steadily. The perfection of halftone engravings, development of four-color printing, market, media, and copy research, and radio and television, added greatly to the amount of service needed to handle accounts.

Each of these developments also added to the agency's cost of doing business. Even today, the increase in the number of services offered by agencies is causing considerable concern among advertising agency managements. In the average agency today, about two thirds of total income is paid out for payroll. The remaining third covers rent, traveling expenses, taxes, profit, and so on. In 1967 the average agency that belonged to the American Association of Advertising Agencies made 3.7 percent of gross income as profit.

WHY TODAY'S ADVERTISERS USE AGENCIES

There are good reasons why most general advertisers (and some retailers) prefer to use an agency to handle at least part of their advertising.

Specialized Skills. An agency retains high-priced, highly skilled specialists whom a single client could not afford. Some agencies specialize in a single type of business.

Objectivity of Viewpoint. A company has difficulty in analyzing its own problems objectively. It is valuable to an advertiser to have available a perspective not subject to internal company politics, prejudices, or limited viewpoints.

The Commission System. Because agencies receive a commission (usually 15 percent) on space and time bought from the media, the advertiser would have to pay full card rates if he bought space and time direct.

HOW BIG IS THE AGENCY BUSINESS?

It is difficult to say just exactly how many agencies there are because definitions of the word "agency" differ. According to the Census Bureau, in 1963 there were 7,423 advertising agencies, 4,816 of which were more than one man operations. Receipts of these agencies surpassed

TABLE 8.2

TEN-YEAR RECORD OF ADVERTISING AGENCIES' COSTS AND PROFITS
(Percentage of gross income unless otherwise stated)

	1957	1958	1959	1960	1961	1962	1963	1964	1965	1966
Number of agencies represented	222	239	240	245	237	239	238	234	226	239
Rent, light, and depreciation	7.01	7.52	7.24	7.34	7.52	7.52	7.54	7.22	6.81	6.80
Taxes (other than U.S. income)	1.71	1.72	1.91	2.18	2.22	2.33	2.45	2.36	2.23	2.58
Other operating expense	13.60	14.19	13.82	14.02	14.06	13.87	14.32	14.29	14.41	14.28
Total payroll	69.86	70.30	69.18	68.94	69.35	68.51	67.99	67.01	67.14	66.05
Payments into pension or profit-sharing plans	1.31	1.17	1.27	1.31	1.32	1.39	1.63	1.98	1.93	2.00
Insurance for employee benefit	0.42	0.45	0.52	0.56	0.62	0.65	0.70	0.76	0.78	0.80
Total expenses	93.91	95.35	93.94	94.35	95.09	94.27	94.63	93.62	93.30	92.51
Profit before U.S. income tax (as percentage of gross income)*	6.09	4.65	6.06	5.65	4.91	5.73	5.37	6.38	6.70	7.49
U.S. income taxes	1.98	1.42	1.79	1.79	1.45	1.76	1.67	1.62	1.77	2.00
Net profit (as percentage of gross income)*	4.11	3.23	4.27	3.86	3.46	3.97	3.70	4.76	4.93	5.49
Profit before U.S. income tax for incorporated agencies (as percentage of gross income)*	6.09	4.28	5.94	5.56	4.41	5.62	5.17	6.23	6.40	7.42
U.S. income tax for incorporated agencies	2.55	1.89	2.17	2.12	1.92	2.23	2.13	2.00	2.15	2.44
Net profit for incorporated agencies (as percentage of gross income)*	3.54	2.39	3.77	3.44	2.49	3.39	3.04	4.23	4.25	4.98
Net profit for incorporated agencies (as percentage of sales—i.e. billing)	0.58	0.42	0.67	0.60	0.44	0.61	0.55	0.83	0.81	0.98

*Gross income comprises commissions, agencies' service charges, and fees.

SOURCE: Annual studies of advertising agencies' costs and profits conducted by American Association of Advertising Agencies. Figures are averages for agencies of all sizes. *Advertising Age,* July 1, 1967, p. 56.

$5,700,000,000.[1] The American Association of Advertising Agencies uses a more precise definition and estimates approximately 3,500 agencies (with independent payrolls), including branch offices in the United States.[2] These are estimated to employ more than 70,000 people to serve national and regional advertisers.

During the years between 1958 and 1968 net profit for incorporated

[1]"Major Sources of Agency Receipts for Selected Metro Areas," *Advertising Age,* August 2, 1965, p. 86.
[2]Career Opportunities in Advertising (New York: American Association of Advertising Agencies, 1965), p. 21.

advertising agencies was less than 3 percent of gross income in two years and reached a high of approximately 5 percent in 1966.[3] It must be remembered, however, that these are percentages of sharply rising dollar amounts. In these ten years total agency billings nearly doubled. In 1967 a little more than half the AAAA member agencies increased their billings. Interestingly, the greatest increase in billings was in the $5 to $10 million billings category.

Agency chairman Paul Foley has predicted that by 1975 or 1980 there will be at least four or five agencies with billings of more than a billion dollars a year and that one may well be a Japanese agency.[4] He also predicts that the idea of public ownership of agency stock will grow and that at least fifty will be in some form of public ownership by 1980.

TYPES OF AGENCY ORGANIZATION

Because of the highly personal nature of the advertising agency business it is difficult to make generalizations about agency organizations. Even more than most businesses, they are organized according to the personal preferences of the management. Most large and medium-sized agencies follow one of the two main systems: the group system or the departmental system—some combine them.

The Group System. Under the group system, writers, artists, media buyers, and other specialists are assigned to a group of accounts. All are under the general direction of an account executive or a group head. In a single agency you may find several such groups, each able to function like a complete agency. A principal advantage of the group system is the concentrated application of the skills or specialists to a common set of problems. These people are seldom diverted to work on other accounts.

Departmental System. Under the departmental system, specialists are grouped in the same department. All the writers are in the copy department, the artists are in the art department, and so on. These people are not directly responsible to account executives but to their own department heads, who usually have the authority to make major decisions. A writer or a researcher might work on four accounts, each headed by a different account executive. Assignments to accounts are made by the department head, not by the account executive.

One of the advantages of the department system is that it places responsibility on the specialists (the department heads) rather than on account executives. Even the ablest account executive cannot be expert in all the facets of advertising. The department system also broadens the experience of staff members, because they can gain experience on varied accounts. The department heads are normally key members of the agency's plans board. Whenever this board meets to review a client's problem, it has the benefit of the knowledge and experience of the best specialists in the agency.

[3]John Crichton, "Address of the President," Annual Meeting, American Association of Advertising Agencies, April 25, 1968.
[4]Paul Foley, "On a Clear Day You Can See Like Crazy," address before Western Region Annual Meeting, American Association of Advertising Agencies, November 1, 1965.

Decentralized Organization. A good example is Interpublic which has been decentralized to increase its billings and clients and to offer a large number of services. Nine advertising agencies and seven othes types of organization have been brought together. The largest of these, McCann-Erickson, had 1967 billings of $476,000,000 and had 1,002 employees in the United States and Canada, and another 3,097 outside the United States. By having such a decentralized organization, an agency can serve all types of clients (large or small, consumer or industrial) and can offer all types of services.

Smaller-Agency Organization. Most smaller agencies cannot afford either the group or the department system. Instead, their personnel is expected to handle a variety of jobs. The account executive, for example, is likely to write his own copy, specify his own production, and perhaps work out his own media schedule. The president of the small agency may act as an account executive on some of its accounts.

WHAT ADVERTISING AGENCIES DO FOR THEIR CLIENTS

According to the American Association of Advertising Agencies, an agency's service to a client consists in "interpreting to the public, or to that part of it which it desires to reach, the advantages of a product or service."[5] More specifically, this interpretation is, according to the AAAA, based upon the following:

1. A study of the client's product or service in order to determine the advantages and disadvantages inherent in the product .itself, and in its relation to the competition.
2. An analysis of present and potential markets for which the product or service is adapted.
3. A knowledge of the factors of distribution and sales and their methods of operation.
4. A knowledge of all the available media and means that can profitably be used to carry the interpretation of the product or service to consumer, wholesaler, dealer, contractor, or others.
5. Formulation of a definite plan and presentation of this plan to the client.
6. Execution of this plan through (a) writing, designing, and illustrating the advertisements; (b) contracting for the space, time, or other means of advertising; (c) incorporation of the message in mechanical form and forwarding it to the media; (d) checking and verifying insertions, display, and so forth; (e) auditing and billing for the service, space, and preparation.
7. Cooperation with the client's sales force.

These are generally accepted as the basic definitions of agency service. However, many agencies branch out, offering their clients service in package designing, sales research, sales training, preparation

[5]Frederic R. Gamble, "What Advertising Agencies Are—What They Do and How They Do It." Lecture delivered at Columbia, Missouri, February 27, 1959.

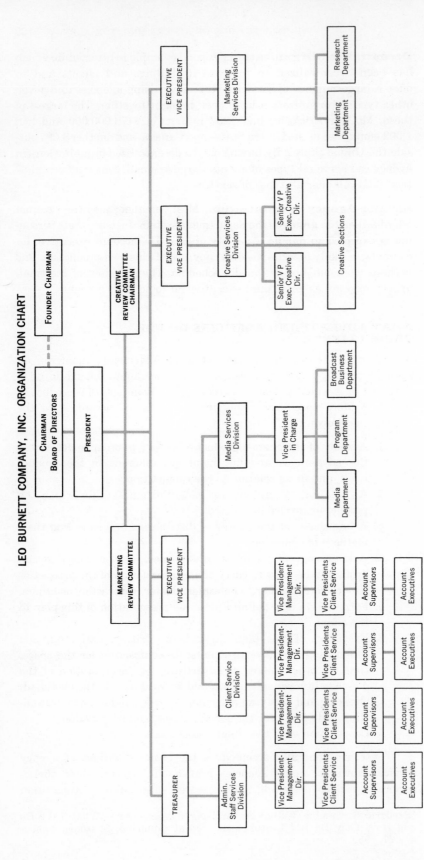

LEO BURNETT COMPANY, INC. ORGANIZATION CHART

FIG. 8.1 *Organization of a large agency with head office in Chicago. It had 1,440 employees in 7 offices and $261,000,000 in billings in 1967.*

COURTESY: LEO BURNETT COMPANY, INC.

of sales and service literature, design of merchandise displays, public relations and publicity.

Note that the seven standard services include two that involve study, two that involve knowledge on the part of agency personnel, and three that involve the use of research and knowledge in behalf of specific products or services. In the next section we shall see how the modern agency is organized to provide these services.

FUNCTIONS OF THE MODERN AGENCY

From popular advertising novels, you might get the idea that agencies exist primarily to write clever slogans and buy martinis for thirsty clients. Actually, any agency, regardless of its size or general philosophy of organization, must include a variety of skilled specialists. Although the number of specialized departments will vary widely from agency to agency (even those doing the same volume of business), the following are functions one would find in almost any agency:

Planning. If you are a client you can expect your agency to make recommendations regarding the objectives and strategy of your advertising campaigns. The agency should also indicate how it intends to use its skills in carrying out strategy and tactics. Many agencies accomplish this through a plans board or planning committee, some through informal meetings. An important part of planning is preparation of the budget.

Copy. To at least one veteran agency executive, "Copy is still the backbone of advertising." In most agencies the copy department is one of the largest departments. Its function is usually the planning and preparation of advertising copy in all media, although some agencies have separate departments for preparing television and radio commercials. Note that the two copy departments, the art department, and production department are placed under a creative head at Burnett (Figure 8.1).

Art. The principal art function of an agency is to lay out advertisements. This consists in arranging various elements so that the ad will attract the attention of the right audience and communicate what the planners had in mind. In television the "storyboard" corresponds to the layout of the printed advertisement, in that it visualizes for the agency, the client, and often a film company, the subject matter of the commercial. The art department will also arrange for finished art work, most of it ordinarily prepared by outside art studios.

Media Selection. In many agencies (for example, Young & Rubicam, which employs about 200 people in media) the media department is the largest department in the agency. Its primary job is the selection and evaluation of media. It is expected to come up with a media mix that will carry out the campaign's communication objectives. This means media experts must know all about the various media and their coverage as well as the audiences the advertiser is attempting to reach. After the agency makes its recommendations, it prepares a schedule of advertising, showing the publications and dates of printing of the ad and the times and stations of television or radio appearances. It then makes contracts, and finally pays the bills from the media.

Research. Research has grown rapidly in importance in recent years. Both agency planners and clients have a constant need for facts that will help them. Every agency does some basic research, but the large agency may include among its functions facilities for handling field surveys and, coding and tabulating the findings.

Contact. A person who acts as liaison officer — who coordinates the activities of the agency and maintains contact with clients — is known as an "account executive." He should be the captain of the account team, inspiring the best work the agency is capable of doing and then getting this work approved by his clients. He need not be a specialist in all phases of advertising but should be able to tell a good creative effort from a bad one. Obviously the contact people work closely with clients and should know as much as possible about their clients' business.

Production. After the copy has been written and the layout and illustration approved, the advertisement is turned over to the production department. This department maintains contacts with printers, typographers, photoengravers, and other suppliers. The production department will order an engraving of an illustration, arrange to have the copy set in type, and assemble them in the final ad. The department may then offer proofs for client approval before matrices or electrotypes (printing plates) are made.

Television and Radio Production. An agency may produce its own programs and commercials for the broadcast media. Agency men may, for example, direct, write the script, select the talent, cast them, and then rehearse and produce the show or commercial announcement. However, many outside organizations offer these services. In recent years agencies have come to depend more and more on these organizations.

Merchandising. The agency often works with advertisers and dealers in planning retail promotions, point-of-purchase material, and any other promotional devices that make the advertising more productive. A merchandising department may create sales-promotion material and work with the sales and marketing managers to get it to salesmen and dealers.

Public Relations. Many agencies will help a client work out his public relations program. Public relations may involve anything from publicity about a new product to a full-blown campaign to build a new corporate image. If the agency is to function truly as a communication agency, it is logical that it offer public relations assistance to its clients.

Accounting. The only way any business can make money is to pay out less than it takes in. The accounting department keeps track of expenses and revenue. It is responsible for paying the agency's bills. It takes care of taxes and collects bills due the agency from clients. It handles "job envelope" invoices, such as purchase orders and bills from artists or other suppliers. It controls the payroll and the agency's internal operating budget.

New Business. There is a continual turnover of accounts in the advertising agency business. One major beer account has shifted agencies four times in as many months. On the other hand, the American Telephone and Telegraph account has been with the same agency for more than fifty years. There need be, however, nothing unethical in the

A TYPICAL AGENCY ORGANIZATION CHART
BY FUNCTIONS

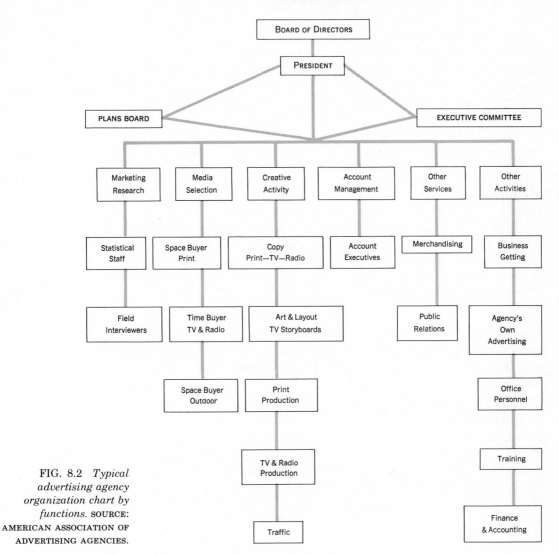

FIG. 8.2 *Typical advertising agency organization chart by functions.* SOURCE: AMERICAN ASSOCIATION OF ADVERTISING AGENCIES.

solicitation of new business. In order to grow, an agency must either gain new accounts or develop its present accounts. Most agencies expect to do both. In general, the larger agencies frown on speculative solicitations for new business (those that present a complete campaign for approval) in the belief that a new agency cannot know a client's problems until it has the account. However, there is evidence that agencies do present ideas and describe what the agency can offer.[6] The new-business people are, in effect, the agency's sales department.

[6]For a detailed description of how several agencies solicited two accounts, see Thomas P. Murphy, "How to Find an Agency," and Spencer Klaw, "More Smooch in the Pooch," in the *Amazing Advertising Business* (New York: Simon and Schuster, 1957).

ORGANIZATION OF A SPECIFIC AGENCY

Figure 8.1 (p. 134) shows how one large advertising agency has been organized to serve its clients. At the beginning of 1968 the company reported United States billings for the preceding year at more than $261,000,000 and international billings of $11,000,000. The agency had 1,440 employees in 7 offices (including 1,264 employees in Chicago alone). Leo Burnett established the agency in 1935 with three accounts and eight associates. He had also the hope that the depression would soon be over. Billings for the first year were $900,000. From the beginning the agency emphasized creative work. The majority of Leo Burnett's collected speeches and memoranda through the years, reprinted in *Confessions of an Advertising Man*, concern creativity.[7] This emphasis is reflected in the present organization.

All creative work is centralized in the agency's main office in Chicago in the belief that each account will then have the attention of the agency's top people. All this work is screened through the Creative Review Board, which is headed by the executive vice-president for creative services and attended by Mr. Burnett and most of the top creative people. Note that the two other major divisions are client services and marketing services.

HOW AGENCIES ARE COMPENSATED

Agencies are normally compensated in three ways—*commissions, percentage charges* on materials and services purchased for clients, and *fees.*

Commissions from Media. According to the American Association of Advertising Agencies, about two thirds of agency income is derived from media commissions. This is unusual in the business world (although not unique) and has been the subject of much discussion in recent years. The system is a holdover from the early days of advertising when agents were primarily space brokers. This is the way it works:

Suppose you operate an agency and prepare a full-page magazine advertisement for your client. The card rate for this page is $10,000. However, because your agency is "recognized" by this medium, you are entitled to the commission of 15 percent (almost all media except outdoor pay 15 percent). Furthermore, there is a cash discount of 2 percent on the amount due if the bill is paid in ten days. You therefore collect $9,830 from the client and pass on $8,330 to the publisher, keeping $1,500 for your commission.

Card rate for full page in Magazine X	$10,000
Agency commission	1,500
Gross amount agency owes medium	$ 8,500
Less cash discount of 2 percent (of $8,500)	170
Net amount agency owes medium	$ 8,330
Net amount advertiser owes agency (card rate less discount for cash of $170)	$ 9,830

[7]Leo Burnett, *Confessions of an Advertising Man* (Chicago: Leo Burnett Company, 1961).

Note that the cash discount is computed on the amount your agency owes the medium ($8,500) rather than on the full card rate.

Agency Charges. There are other out-of-pocket costs to the agency besides the cost of space or time. For print media an agency may buy art work, typographic composition, and electrotypes from outside suppliers. With broadcast media it is likely to have expenditures for talent, production, free-lance writers, and filming or taping. What is done about these charges? Practices vary widely on this point.

As Table 8.3 indicates, the agency is less likely to charge for a service such as rough layouts (usually made in the agency's art department) than for finished art (usually purchased outside). Where the agency adds a percentage, as it often does in the case of engravings and talent, the rate is usually either 15 percent or 17.65 percent of net, which would equal 15 percent of gross.

Fees. Agency income is also derived from fees charged by the agency. If, for example, a market survey or a mailing piece is prepared by the agency, there is no agency commission involved. The agency may charge the client a flat fee based on agency costs. On the other hand, the agency may decide (if the account is a particularly profitable one in other respects) to absorb the cost.

A variation of the fee system is the charging of an annual or monthly "minimum fee." If you have an agency, you may have certain accounts that involve space and time and whose card rates are so low that the commission will not compensate you for your effort. In order to do the account justice, you may charge a minimum fee to the account (say $1,000 a month). You may then credit all commissions against these fees. Retail and industrial accounts are often handled this way.

TABLE 8.3   METHODS OF COMPENSATING AGENCIES FOR SPECIFIC SERVICES
(In percentage of total advertisers reporting)

SERVICE	NUMBER OF ADVERTISERS REPORTING	MEDIA COMMISSION ONLY	FEE PLUS COMMISSION	FEE MEDIA COMMISSION CREDITED	FLAT FEE	COST TO AGENCY	COST TO AGENCY PLUS PERCENTAGE
Copy (magazines, newspapers, etc.)	2719	66.5	17.6	4.3	3.7	2.2	5.7
Copy (direct mail)	1906	21.5	15.0	3.9	23.9	9.7	26.0
Rough layouts	2477	27.3	12.9	2.8	16.0	18.5	22.5
Comprehensives	2259	23.5	15.9	2.9	12.8	14.0	30.9
Finished art	2517	9.0	17.1	1.0	14.0	12.4	46.5
Marketing research	1113	9.0	9.1	.6	41.6	19.7	20.0
Publicity	1346	8.2	8.5	1.2	40.6	24.0	17.5
Engravings, typography	2369	10.5	13.2	1.1	8.3	13.0	53.9
Radio-TV commercials	1167	39.6	17.1	.7	7.0	5.2	30.4
Radio-TV shows (package)	629	46.4	26.4	2.4	7.3	2.1	15.4
Radio-TV shows (agency produced)	409	32.0	38.9	1.0	4.9	3.9	19.3
Radio-TV talent	579	17.1	14.7	.9	6.7	25.6	35.0
Dealer aids	1057	12.0	13.4	1.9	19.2	12.2	41.3
Salesmen's aids	977	10.8	11.3	1.6	20.5	15.0	40.8
Exhibits and shows	562	11.4	11.4	.9	22.6	20.8	32.9

SOURCE: Albert W. Frey and Kenneth Davis, *The Advertising Industry* (New York: Association of National Advertisers, Inc., 1958), p. 222.

PROBLEMS IN AGENCY COMPENSATION

There has been considerable concern about the ethics and economics of the system by which agencies are compensated. The extensive Frey-Davis report on the advertising industry disclosed a great deal of dissatisfaction with the present compensation system, especially among the larger clients. Less than half the companies that spend more than $5,000,000 a year for advertising consider the present system "satisfactory."[8] However, if you combine those who consider the present system "satisfactory" with those who consider it "not satisfactory but most practical" you find that the system is endorsed to some extent by more than 80 percent of the respondents.

One of the main reasons that the commission system has been so durable is its simplicity. It is easy to compute agency commissions. Thus there is less reason for haggling, so the emphasis in competition is on nonprice factors rather than on the price of services rendered. The system is more flexible than it might seem at first glance, because the agency may include many services without extra charge if the account is a particularly profitable one; conversely, it may provide only basic copywriting, artwork, and media selection for the commission for a less profitable account.

In recent years many advertisers have spoken out against the agency system and even some of the agency leaders have criticized it. One difficulty is that it may tempt an agency to recommend an advertising program using expensive media or another in which few services are provided. It is often true that the time spent on an account is not necessarily in proportion to the dollar expenditures of that account. For example, a $50,000 page in a magazine may not require any more agency effort and time than a $500 one in a trade paper. A most articulate critic is agency head David Ogilvy, who has called it "an old-fashioned anachronism." His agency, Ogilvy & Mather, is handling several accounts on a fee rather than a commission basis and is making money on accounts that were, at best, marginal.[9] Another critic is the chairman of Batten, Barton, Durstine and Osborn, who says, "The commission system may be around for a long time, but is a dying sacred cow."[10] However, even these two agencies handle a substantial part of their business on a commission (or modified commission) basis, and most large agencies still depend on commissions for the majority of their income.

Recognition. To qualify for commissions, an agency must be "recognized" by the media. The recognition system is supposed to prevent you (or any other would-be agency entrepreneur) from collecting commissions until you have proved yourself to the media. How do you prove yourself? In general the following are the important requirements for recognition:

1. Freedom from financial control by an advertiser or the owner of a medium.

[8]Albert W. Frey and Kenneth Davis, *The Advertising Industry* (New York: Association of National Advertisers, Inc., 1958), pp. 240–241.
[9]See Spencer Klaw, "Is Ogilvy a Genius?" *Fortune*, (April 1965).
[10]Klaw, p. 166.

**You're entitled to only one face.
Try to get one you can be proud of.**

Every company has a face. It earns it by the things it does. If it is a good face, truthful advertising will propagate it. If it is not, false advertising cannot save it. **Young & Rubicam**

FIG. 8.3 *Advertisement used in trade publications to promote a large advertising agency.* SOURCE: YOUNG & RUBICAM, INC.

2. Financial resources sufficient to meet obligations to media owners.
3. Personnel of sufficient experience and ability to serve general advertisers.

As manager of a fledgling agency you will probably first turn to the local media for recognition — newspapers, radio, and television. Then, as billings grow and the area you serve widens, you will turn to outside media.

The United States government has, at times, questioned the legality of the recognition system. In 1955 the Department of Justice charged that certain practices of the American Association of Advertising Agencies and five of the leading media associations were illegal under the Sherman Anti-Trust Act. Specifically, it questioned the uniform standards for recognizing agencies (all media seemed to use the same criteria), the refusal to grant commissions to nonrecognized agencies, and the uniformity of the 15 percent commission.

In 1956 the AAAA and the media associations entered into a consent decree with the Department of Justice and the charge was dropped. These groups agreed to restrain from "fixing, establishing, or stabilizing agency commission." This means, among other things, that the agencies and the media cannot take action as a *group*, but are free to act as they see fit on their own. Consequently, the associations do not take an active part in recognition procedures (as all but the AAAA did prior to 1956); however, the procedure in practice is much the same as it was before, because few media have deviated from past procedures.

House Agencies. Recognition is granted only to agencies—never to advertisers. If an advertiser prefers to prepare advertising for his own company, why should he not collect a commission? The defenders of the commission system maintain that this would undermine the present system and result in an inferior grade of advertising. However, it is well known (though not publicly proclaimed) that some advertisers get around this by establishing "house agencies." Though such organizations do not measure up to the first requirement for recognition listed above, many of them are granted recognition. Some are little more than company advertising departments set up as separate corporate entities; while others accept outside accounts even though their primary affiliation is to the parent company. One of the nation's largest advertisers uses its house agency in addition to three regular agencies.

Rebating. Some media insist, as a requirement for recognition, that the agency not "rebate" any of its commission to the client. The rationale here is that this would constitute a form of price cutting and that agencies should compete on a quality rather than price basis. It is felt that the agency should keep the entire commission if it is to do an adequate job. This position is generally sound, but it may at times be unnecessarily rigid. The Frey-Davis report on the advertising industry concluded that "there seems to be no sound reason why agency compensation should be taboo as a matter of individual negotiation in each client-agency relationship. On the contrary, there seems to be sound reason why there should be such individual negotiation."[11]

William King has suggested a flexible system of compensation whereby agencies and clients would negotiate contracts for compensation based on the amount of risk involved.[12] In new product situations where there is low agency participation the agency would receive costs plus a negotiated fixed fee. If, on the other hand, there is high agency participation in connection with this new product, the rewards would be shared on a cost-plus-incentive fee basis, thereby assuring the agency that its costs will be covered, but also that it will share in the profits.

Source of the Compensation. Why, some critics ask, should the agency be compensated by the *medium* rather than the *advertiser*? N. W. Ayer has long objected to this arrangement. In 1875 it devised the "open contract" system to emphasize its allegiance to the advertiser. Under this system clients were charged *net* rather than *gross* rates

[11]Frey and Davis, p. 396.
[12]William King, "A Conceptual Framework for Ad Agency Compensation," *Journal of Marketing Research*, May 1968.

—the agency's compensation was then added to the agency net, so that payment would clearly be made by the advertiser. One may argue that the advertiser is really paying the agency under the conventional system, because he pays to the agency the gross rates from which the agency's compensation is subtracted. In any event, the present system seems too well entrenched to be radically changed (Ayer itself finally accepted it).

HANDLING COMPETING ACCOUNTS

An agency will not ordinarily handle competitive accounts. Because of the confidential nature of the business an agency should be free to devote its full efforts to each client. Consequently, an agency that has an automobile account does not usually handle another automobile account. But what about truck and automobile accounts? It will probably depend on whether the original client thinks the new account would be competitive. This does not mean that a national agency would avoid a local sausage account, which it could handle out of its San Francisco office, because it had another sausage account with distribution only in the east. A national agency is thus limited in the accounts it can solicit. For example, Young & Rubicam can take on less than a dozen new accounts. Except for these, its expansion must come from the growth of existing business.

The American Association of Advertising Agencies has suggested that the "ideal agency client policy on account conflict is one which is based on individual product category rather than the total line of products of any given client."[13] Under such a policy an agency would not handle brands that are directly competitive for more than one client. However, it would be allowed to handle an automobile account for one client and a refrigerator account for another client, even though the automobile client happened to make and advertise a competing brand of refrigerators. The AAAA also points out that some agencies handle competing accounts by having autonomous full-service offices in different cities. One office may handle the account for product "A" and a second office act as the agency for product "B". Other possibilities include having separate account groups in the same office and setting up separate agencies with a common ownership.

SUMMARY

Within a century the advertising agency has developed from a space wholesaler to a major institution in our society. It is a business organization, offering clients a complete range of communication and marketing services. As clients demand more services, it can be confidently predicted that the agencies will offer them, if the clients are willing to pay for them.

Although the two main types of agency organization are *group* and *departmental*, there are almost as many variations as there are agen-

[13]"The Ideal Agency-Client Policy on Account Conflicts" (New York: American Association of Advertising Agencies, 1967).

cies. However, certain functions, such as copy, art, research, and the like are fairly standard, regardless of the type of organization.

Agencies receive about two thirds of their income from media commissions, the balance from fees and other charges. Although the commission system has been under heavy attack, it is unlikely that it (or the system of "recognition") will be radically changed in the near future.

QUESTIONS FOR DISCUSSION

1. Why has the commission system of compensating agencies been questioned? What system of compensation is likely to be predominant in twenty years?
2. Why has the agency business become so centralized in our larger cities?
3. Discuss the pros and cons of the departmental versus the group system of agency organization. What effect does the size of the agency have on the way it is organized?
4. What is the proper relation between the research department and the various creative departments (primarily copy and art)?
5. Why are retailers less likely to call on the services of an agency than are general advertisers? What is the likelihood of the retailer increasing his use of advertising agencies?
6. Does it seem logical to you that agencies should have to turn down an account if it already has a competitive account? Is this situation any different from that of the newspaper or television station that sells space or time to competing advertisers?

SUGGESTED READINGS

Barton, Roger, *Advertising Agency Operations and Management*. New York: McGraw-Hill, Inc., 1955.

Editors of *Fortune*, *The Amazing Advertising Business*. New York: Simon and Schuster, Inc., 1957. Chapters 7 – 10.

Frey, Albert W., and Kenneth Davis, *The Advertising Industry*. New York: Association of National Advertisers, Inc., 1958.

Gamble, Frederic, *What Advertising Agencies Are — What They Do and How They Do It*, 4th ed. New York: American Association of Advertising Agencies, 1963.

Groesbeck, Kenneth, *Advertising Agency Success*. New York: Harper & Row, Publishers, 1958.

Hower, Ralph M., *The History of an Advertising Agency*, rev. ed. Cambridge, Mass.: Harvard University Press, 1949.

Mayer, Martin, *Madison Avenue, U.S.A.* New York: Harper & Row, Publishers, 1958. Part 2.

Ogilvy, David, *Confessions of an Advertising Man.* New York: Atheneum Publishers, 1963.

Sandage, C. H., and Vernon Fryburger, *Advertising Theory and Practice*, 7th ed. Homewood, Ill.: Richard D. Irwin, Inc., 1967. Chapter 29.

9 The Institutions of Advertising: Advertisers and Media

In this chapter we shall examine the other two major institutions in the advertising and promotion field—the company or retailer that pays the bill and the medium that carries the communication to the public. In both cases activities are likely to be centralized in one department, headed by an advertising or sales promotion manager.

Virtually every business organization uses some form of advertising or promotion. It is true that there are manufacturers who make a profit selling unbranded products to stores for sale under that store's brand. There are corner groceries that never buy space in the local paper. But even these write sales letters or use point-of-sale promotion from time to time. However, we are concerned here mainly with the regular advertiser, whether he is a *general* advertiser (does not sell directly to the ultimate consumer) or a *retail* advertiser (sells to the ultimate consumer).

The General Advertiser. The general advertiser accounts for about 60 percent of the nation's advertising expenditures. Usually he spends this money through an agency.

Although there are thousands of general advertisers, promoting many thousands of brands, a handful of product groups accounts for a disproportionate percentage of total expenditures. According to *Adver-*

tising Age, the 125 leading advertisers (see Table 9.1 for top 10) accounted for more than $4,500,000,000 in 1966. However, expenditures were heaviest in the following groups:

Food: Of the top 125 advertisers, 22 were companies with food lines. They invested approximately $816,500,000 in advertising, the highest of any product category.

Drugs and Cosmetics: Twenty-one companies spent $721,000,000.

Automobiles: Five automobile companies were in the top 125. Two automobile companies were among the top 10.

Soap and Cleansers: Five companies selling soap and cleansers were among the top 125, 2 in the top 10.

Tobacco: Six tobacco companies in the top 125 advertisers invested $311,733,322.

The Advertising Manager. In a few exceptionally advertising-minded companies such as Procter & Gamble (where the last two presidents have risen via the advertising route) the advertising manager is one of the top executives in the company. In most companies, however, he is not really on a policy-making level.

A study of advertising managers was made by *Printers' Ink* and reported by Professor Dale Houghton.[1] The results were tabulated from 200 questionnaires completed by a selected list of 570 advertising managers. The study covered everything from salaries to duties. Here are a few of the findings: Salaries ranged from $5,000 a year to $70,000, with the median salary $16,000. Those who received the highest salaries did not always head the largest advertising departments.

The 200 replies listed 34 different titles. Those mentioned by 4 or more respondents were

Advertising manager	76
Director of advertising	31
Advertising and sales promotion manager	26
Vice-president – advertising	9
Director of advertising and sales promotion	7
Director of advertising and public relations	6
General advertising manager	4
Publicity and advertising manager	4

Almost half of these advertising managers reported to the president, vice-president, executive vice-president, general manager or other executive whose title did not indicate that he was directly responsible for advertising. The departments ranged in size from 1 to 200 employees.

Duties of the Advertising Manager. The specific duties of the advertising manager vary widely according to the size of the firm, the importance of its advertising, and the nature of the product. Certain duties, however, are common to most advertising managers.

1. Planning the campaign is probably the most important job the manager has. He cannot delegate it completely to the agency or to another executive. He must engage in long- and short-range planning.

[1]See "How Much Are Ad Managers Paid?" in *Printers' Ink Advertisers Guide to Marketing for 1958*, p. 112.

TABLE 9.1   ESTIMATED ADVERTISING EXPENDITURES OF TOP TEN U.S.
ADVERTISERS*

ADVERTISER	TOTAL 1967 EXPENDITURES (In thousands of dollars)	PERCENTAGE OF 1967 SALES
Procter & Gamble Co.	280,000	11.1
General Motors Corp.	184,000	1.1
General Foods Corp.	148,000	9.8
Bristol-Myers Co.	121,000	16.5
Ford Motor Co.	106,500	2.0
Colgate-Palmolive Co.	105,000	22.5
Sears, Roebuck & Co.†	97,000	1.3
American Home Products Corp.	81,500	9.8
R. J. Reynolds Tobacco Co.	81,000	4.2
Warner-Lambert Pharmaceutical Co.	81,000	18.3

*Totals are for domestic operations only.

†Percentage would be more than doubled if Sears' $130,000,000 in local advertising were added to the $97,000,000 general advertising total.

SOURCE: Reprinted with permission from the August 26, 1968, issue of *Advertising Age.* Copyright 1968 by Advertising Publications, Inc.

To accomplish this, he must, according to one of the country's best-known advertising and agency executives, Clarence Eldridge, be a marketing man as well as an advertising man. Mr. Eldridge says:

I think it is not too much to say that unless *he qualifies* himself to be considered a marketing man, and unless he assumes responsibilities as broad as the entire marketing concept—unless he does these things, the adoption of the marketing concept in management and in business will inevitably down-grade the advertising function. . . . Perhaps the most cogent reason why the advertising man should be a marketing man has to do with planning.[2]

2. He supervises the carrying out of this plan by both his subordinates and the agency.

3. He helps select and evaluate the work of the agency. In the selection he will probably have to work with the management of the company, certainly with the top marketing executives.

4. He informs the top executives of advertising matters and advises them on all matters that touch on advertising. This means that he is called in on all the company's marketing and communication problems and must therefore know all phases of marketing and communication.

5. He coordinates advertising and other marketing functions. He must work closely with the sales manager and his staff. He should, for example, make sure that the company's advertising stresses the most salable features of its products and that the ads appear in the media that will be most helpful to the sales personnel. He may help prepare portfolios that the company's salesmen will use, and sales promotion material (envelope stuffers, newspaper mats, and the like) which dealers may use in advertising to consumers. He and his assistants may be called on to develop enthusiasm among lagging salesmen and dealers at sales

[2]Clarence Eldridge, "The Job of the Advertising Manager," in David Ewing, ed. *Effective Marketing Action* (New York: Harper & Row, Publishers, 1958).

conventions. He may be responsible for preparing instructional booklets and labels for use by the sales department.

6. He works with the production department. If, for instance, he thinks a product should be made in a different color, the production department will decide whether this is practicable.

7. He works with the public relations department in planning and executing the communication program. In institutional advertising, he will certainly need the help of the public relations people. In one large soap company, the public relations director passes on all ads (product as well as institutional), primarily to make sure that they contribute to the desired corporate image.

8. He coordinates the work of other departments with that of the advertising department. In a proposed contest he checks with the legal department for possible violations of the Federal Trade Commission regulations or of the lottery laws. He may work with the accounting department in connection with media or advertising production costs or to see that bills are paid.

9. He works out the budget. This, of course, will be a joint effort with the agency and some of the other top executives (particularly marketing) of the company.

The Committee System. Some companies have a committee to keep a watchful eye on the work of the advertising department. However, the advertising manager is commonly the chairman of such a committee. The reasons for forming the committee are the same as those for appointing an agency plans board: a pooling of viewpoints so that the best brains of the company will be applied to the forming of advertising policy and the execution of that policy.

Brand Management. There has been a decided increase in the popularity of the brand management concept in recent years. A company that markets several brands may want to encourage the competition of these brands within the company itself. Management may feel that it can gain a larger share of the total market for a product if it maintains two or three brands instead of one. The brands will usually have different advertising agencies and different advertising budgets, each headed by a brand manager. These men compete just as vigorously with other brand managers within the company as they do with outside companies.

The brand manager is, in effect, the advertising manager for a brand. He works with the agency and sales departments and makes most of the advertising decisions for his brand. The company's general advertising manager can then operate with a comparatively small department, because he is primarily concerned with policy decisions.

Advertiser-Agency Relations. Some advertising people like to think there is a "marriage" between the agency and the client. Almost all practitioners agree that the nature of the advertiser-agency relation can be extremely important in the success of any advertising campaign. We should like to quote in part two excellent analyses of this relation by veteran advertising men.

Clarence Eldridge[3] suggested the following at an advertising meeting in Minneapolis in 1960:

That in a great many cases the relationship is far from ideal, I think no one will seriously deny. The frequency of account-shifts is one index of dissatisfaction on one side or the other. But account changes alone do not tell the whole story. There is, in varying degree, a lack of mutual confidence and respect as between the client and the agency. On the one side, the client is likely to criticize the agency for its lack of skill or judgment or objectivity — frequently believing, even if it does not openly say so, that the agency's recommendations are slanted in favor of those activities that will be most profitable to the agency.

On the other side, there is a fairly prevalent feeling on the part of agencies that the client is frequently unreasonable in his demands upon the agency; that the marketing people with whom they have to deal are stupid, that they are not empowered to make any but the most routine decisions, that the higher-ups who do make the important decisions are unapproachable — and that therefore the agency recommendations, and the reasons therefore, never get the consideration they are entitled to.

Now there are undoubtedly many reasons for the unsatisfactory and unsettled state of client-agency relationships, some of which have nothing to do with the matter of compensation or profits. Yet I believe that an important factor in the situation is the traditional system by which agencies are compensated.

This subject has become fraught with such emotional overtones that it is almost impossible to consider it rationally, logically or emotionally. . . . It is my belief that a change in the system of compensation, arrived at through collaboration of all parties in interest — advertisers and agencies together — and as a result of an objective study of the entire situation, would be more likely to result in an increase rather than a reduction in compensation, and one which could conceivably go a long way toward removing the suspicions that now tend to poison the client-agency relationship.

Don C. Miller, marketing vice-president of B. F. Goodrich Company and former agency executive, in addressing a meeting of the Association of National Advertisers, said,

My main theme is that very few companies are actually getting full value from their advertising dollars. My minor theme, closely related to the first, is that at least 90 percent of all agencies know how to prepare better advertising than the great majority of their work that actually gets into print and on the air.

If this is true, it may represent one of the greatest areas of waste in business. The present cost of advertising is right around $10 billion per year. For many companies, it is the largest single item of expense. To the extent that advertising falls short of delivering the results it should, our whole economy is being unnecessarily handicapped. . . .

Why does this problem exist and more to the point, what can be done to solve it? Certainly I have no magical solutions. But I do have a few thoughts for your consideration, the result of years of working with and learning how agency people think and react, and how they get themselves into positions where they cannot do the work they know how to do and are paid to do.

As a starting point, there is a widespread agreement among agency people that a need exists for clear, simple, measurable objectives as to just what the advertising is supposed to do, and exactly what responsibility the agency has for achieving them. Advertising objectives can easily become so broad, so fuzzy and so confused with general objectives of the business, completely outside the function of advertising, that they become meaningless. . . .

[3]Mr. Eldridge has been a practicing attorney, sales manager of a large automobile corporation, vice-president of Young & Rubicam, Inc., vice-president of General Foods, executive vice-president of Campbell Soup Company and senior consultant with Lennen and Newell.

The next point for your consideration is that it is easy for agencies to over-promise — to over-promise on the services they are prepared to render. . . .

The next point is that individual thinking and individual responsibility for both the preparation and approval of advertising has been too broadly superseded by the modern ritual of "decision by committee."

Professor Alfred Oxenfeldt suggests that one way of keeping the client-agency marriage a happy one is for the advertising manager to insist that the agency put new people on an account when agency account people appear to be going stale rather than wait until the work disintegrates and a switch is almost inevitable.[4]

Ryan and Colley, both authorities in agency relations, suggest that the best solution to the problem of client-agency rifts is a program of performance audits. They concluded after a series of studies of agency conflicts that the causes of unsatisfactory performance are identifiable and are correctible in the great majority of cases. The fundamental purpose of the audit is to "search for improvement opportunities, to spot weaknesses in performance and relationships, and to take corrective action before deterioriation sets in."[5]

Examples of Advertising Department Organization. The examples provided in Figures 9.1–9.4 are based on data collected by the Association of National Advertisers, an organization to which most general advertisers belong. They were reported by the former chairman of ANA, Edward Gerbic, vice-president of Johnson and Johnson, at a marketing conference.[6] Among the companies included were Johnson

[4]Alfred R. Oxenfeldt, "Management of the Advertising Function" in Alfred R. Oxenfeldt and Carroll Swan, eds., *Management of Advertising* (Belmont, Calif.: Wadsworth Publishing Company, Inc., 1964).

[5]M. P. Ryan and Russell H. Colley, "Preventive Maintenance in Client-Ad Agency Relations," *Harvard Business Review*, September-October 1967, pp. 66–74.

[6]"Has Advertising Kept Pace with Changing Sales Methods?" *Broadening Horizons in Marketing* (New York: American Management Association, 1956), pp. 46–49.

SMALL ADVERTISING DEPARTMENT ORGANIZED BY FUNCTION

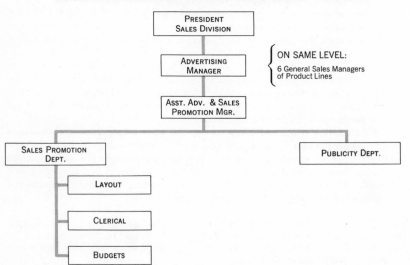

FIG. 9.1

SMALL ADVERTISING DEPARTMENT ORGANIZED BY PRODUCT LINE

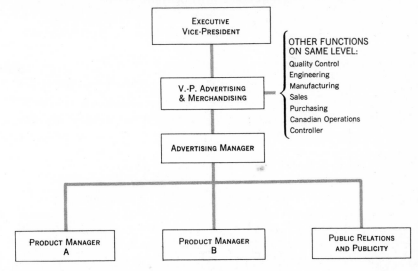

FIG. 9.2

and Johnson, Bristol-Myers, du Pont, Eastman Kodak, Ford, General Foods, General Mills, Kraft, and Thomas J. Lipton.

Note the difference between the two examples of small advertising departments. The first is a simple and widely used form in which the central advertising department serves the general managers of several product sales divisions. The advertising department is organized according to three major functions: media, which are the responsibility of the advertising manager; sales promotion; and publicity.

In the second small department, a vice-president combines advertising and merchandising functions with the simplest product-manager type of organization, plus one functional activity (public relations and publicity), and reports to the advertising manager.

LARGE DIVERSIFIED COMPANY—CENTRALIZED ADVERTISING

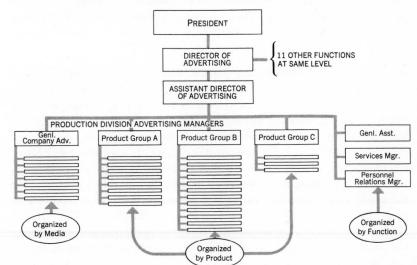

FIG. 9.3

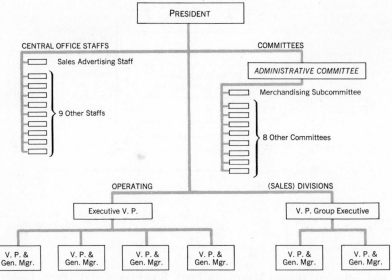

LARGE COMPANY—ADVERTISING DECENTRALIZED AT DIVISION LEVEL WITH CENTRAL STAFF

FIG. 9.4

The large diversified company shown here manufacturers a long line of consumer and industrial goods. Advertising is one of the twelve functions under the chief executive. The size and diversity of this company call for divisional advertising managers, product group advertising managers under them, and sometimes brand managers under them. Certain services are provided centrally. In Figure 9.3 note that company advertising is organized by media, and other advertising operations are organized by product and function.

In the final example, sales and advertising are among ten staff functions that report to the president. A committee setup is used with a merchandising subcommittee having final authority over broad advertising policies and budget approval. This is a centralized company. Each sales division has its own operating vice-president. Advertising is one of four functions under the direction of an assistant general sales manager. The advertising department is organized under three coordinators of product advertising and one functional position, a coordinator of budgets and cooperative advertising.

International Advertising and Promotion Manager. There is some discussion currently, regarding just how a company should organize to take best advantage of the sales potential of foreign markets. Much of the discussion focuses on the problem of decentralization. Should you try to run an advertising operation from a main office, or should you allow each foreign market to plot its own strategy? Many companies are moving toward a multinational concept where there is no domestic or foreign organization as such but merely a central office for world-wide operation. In such a structure there is a tendency to centralize the advertising-sales operation in the home office. On the other hand, many companies find that the decentralized advertising operation works better. R. J. McGorrin, coordinator of international operations for Quaker Oats, says,

Because of the vastness of the territory covered by our international operations and the ever-increasing attention required by each important market, we recognize that our world organization may be decentralized to a certain degree. Many people have referred to our organization as being decentralized centralization, in that we have divided the world into three areas of responsibility.[7]

The problems of international advertising and promotion are discussed in more detail in Chapter 31.

THE RETAIL ADVERTISER

Almost every store uses advertising in some form at some time. The following types of stores account for most of the dollars invested in retail advertising:

1. Appliance dealers	7. Jewelry stores
2. Department stores	8. Men's specialty shops
3. Drugstores	9. Music shops
4. Furniture stores	10. Shoe stores
5. Food stores	11. Stationery stores
6. Hardware stores	12. Women's specialty stores

Why Retailers Seldom Use Agencies. The retail advertiser, unlike his counterpart in general advertising, is not a regular user of advertising agencies. Instead, retailers frequently prepare their own advertising or, with smaller stores, depend heavily on the media for help. This reluctance to use agencies stems from four characteristics of retail advertising:

1. A heavy percentage of it goes into newspapers at retail rates. Because these are ordinarily lower than general rates and not commissionable, any agency that handled the account would charge a fee for its services. Many agencies have found it difficult to get stores to pay such a fee.
2. The retailer ordinarily operates on a day-to-day basis. If you work in a retailer's advertising department, you are probably working today on the ad that will appear in the newspaper the day after tomorrow, or on the television commercial that may be on tonight's late news. A sudden change in merchandising policy or in the weather — or some other late development — may cause you to revise the ad at the last minute. A department in the store, close to buyers and merchandise managers, is in a better position to adapt quickly to such changes than is an outside organization.
3. Retail stores, unlike manufacturers, usually handle a wide variety of products. In a department store we may find thousands — or tens of thousands — of different items sold by the one advertiser. Although it is true that only a fraction of the store's offerings would be advertised on any one day, there may still be ten or twenty items in a single ad. How can an agency ac-

[7]R. J. McGorrin, "Case History of a Decentralized International Advertising Operation," in S. Watson Dunn, ed., *International Handbook of Advertising* (New York: McGraw-Hill, Inc., 1964), p. 675.

count executive (or copywriter) get to know these items well? The account executive who handles a product for a manufacturer comes to know the product and the market intimately.

4. Retailers depend heavily on manufacturers and the media for free help in their advertising. A high percentage of their advertising consists of matrices (mats) supplied by the manufacturers of products they sell. They often have to use these mats as furnished if they are to qualify for cooperative deals, whereby the manufacturer pays a share (usually at least 50 percent) of the cost of the advertising.

The Retail Advertising Organization.

Large Stores. In going through the advertising department of a large department or specialty store (more than $10,000,000 annual gross), you are struck by the completeness of the organization. The advertising department is really an agency within the store. You will note in the organization chart shown in Figure 9.5 the completeness of services offered by this one department store ($40,000,000 – 50,000,000 annual gross).

The head of a large store's advertising department may be called a publicity director, a sales promotion director or manager, or simply the advertising manager. The planning is ordinarily done by the store's top advertising and merchandising executives, but the actual execution of the plan is likely to be in the hands of the store's advertising department. Such specialties as finished art, however, are frequently handled by outside free-lance help.

The large store's production department makes sure that the advertisement gets into print. It will specify kinds of type and engravings to be used and proofread the final ad.

Most advertising departments of large stores are geared to handling newspaper and direct-mail advertising. However, they sometimes call on an agency for help in the planning and execution of radio and television campaigns. One study of 33 large department stores indicated that 18 called on an agency for at least some help in producing their television shows and that 17 used some agency help in producing the commercial copy (7 depended entirely on the agency for commercials).[8] Another problem arises with respect to direct mail. Some stores handle this advertising through their regular department; some set up a special department; and some use the help of an agency or letter shop.

Small Stores. In general, the smaller store (under $10,000,000 gross and usually specializing in one line) uses less advertising (as a percentage of its sales) than the larger store does. Some of these stores do not possess the knowledge of how advertising is used and what it can do. Some are located in big cities where media rates are high, and they are willing to let the big stores attract business to the trading area. Some draw from such small trading areas that they do not buy space in the media.

[8]Howard P. Abrahams, "TV Advertising for the Retail Sponsor," in Irving Settle and Norman Glenn, eds., *Television Advertising and Production Handbook* (New York: Thomas Y. Crowell Company, 1953), p. 92.

GIMBELS MILWAUKEE—SALES PROMOTION DIVISION ORGANIZATION CHART

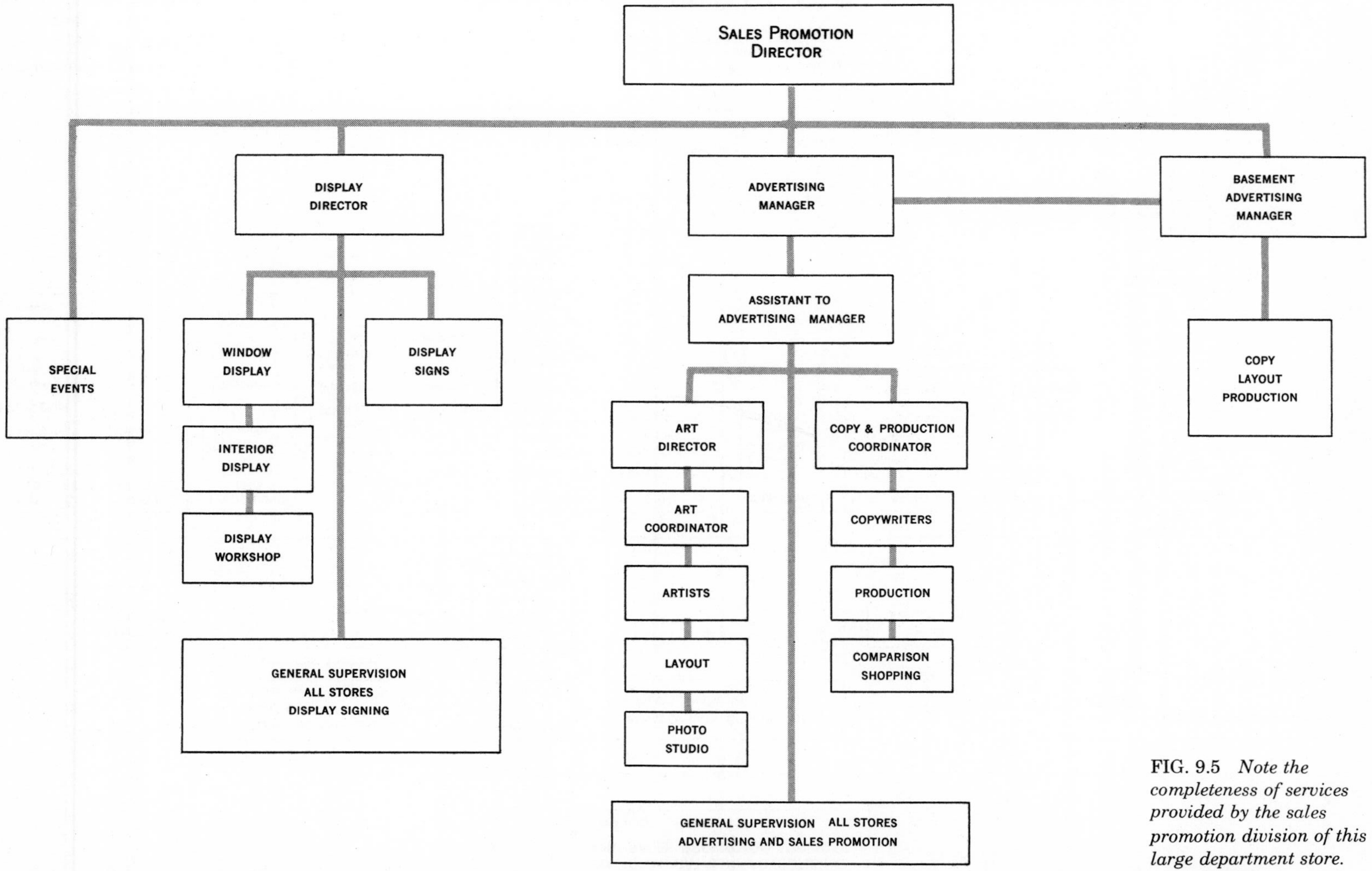

FIG. 9.5 *Note the completeness of services provided by the sales promotion division of this large department store.* SOURCE: GIMBELS.

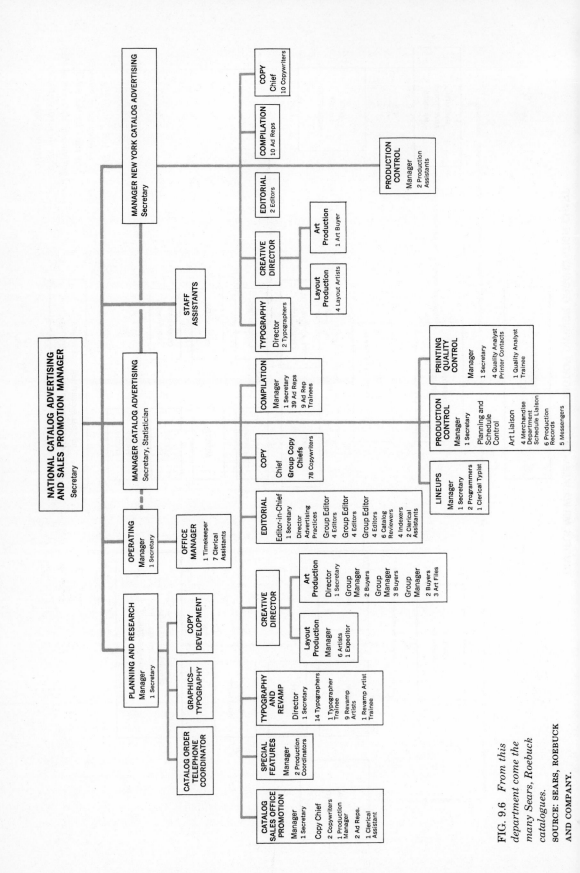

FIG. 9.6 *From this department come the many Sears, Roebuck catalogues.*
SOURCE: SEARS, ROEBUCK AND COMPANY.

The advertising department in the small store usually consists of few people. In many, there is no advertising manager; the store manager is the advertising manager. Whether the store has a small advertising department or no department at all, the manager is likely to call on certain outside sources for fairly regular help:

1. *Media.* Newspapers and the radio and television stations will help him plan his campaign, lay out his ad, and write his copy. All this is normally done free of charge.
2. *Manufacturers.* Manufacturers of brands sold by a particular retailer will frequently supply him with mats, point-of-purchase display material, films or transcriptions for the broadcast media, display materials, and even planning guides.
3. *Syndicated mat services.* Certain companies produce mats that they sell to retailers and to newspapers. A retailer who does not want to prepare his own copy and layout can send for the proof book which shows a wide variety of advertisements (all shapes and sizes and all types of merchandise). All he has to do is order those he wants to use in whole or in part. Because most newspapers subscribe to one or more of these services, he may use the service offered by the paper.
4. *Trade associations.* Most retailers belong to at least one trade association. Many of these supply copy ideas and layouts to their members and make suggestions that their retail members may use in putting together advertising plans.

MAIL ORDER HOUSE

Many retail stores do a sizable volume of business by mail, depending on their ads in newspapers, radio, television, or special catalogues. They consider mail order a supplement to their main business. There are a number of businesses that are primarily mail order houses. Some (Sears, Roebuck and Company, for example) began as mail order operations but have since developed into retail businesses with even greater volume. Unlike the retail store, the mail-order house depends entirely on the catalogue as its medium. It hires a large staff of advertising people to put these catalogues together. At Sears, Roebuck the catalogue is prepared by its National Catalog Advertising and Sales Promotion Department (see Figure 9.6). A beginner in the department is given a short training period and then assigned to a merchandise department. He works with professional layout artists, art directors, typographers, editors, and production specialists, who provide technical assistance. The copywriter, however, is responsible for certain catalogue pages and interprets the merchandise plan worked out by the sales managers. He works with buyers and merchandise managers in preparing the advertisements.

Although there are catalogue sales offices in many Sears retail stores, the mail-order advertising department does not prepare local retail ads. Instead, the local store manager (like the manager of most chain stores) depends heavily on mats supplied by the district office, but he may make changes in these mats or decide to use such media as radio and television.

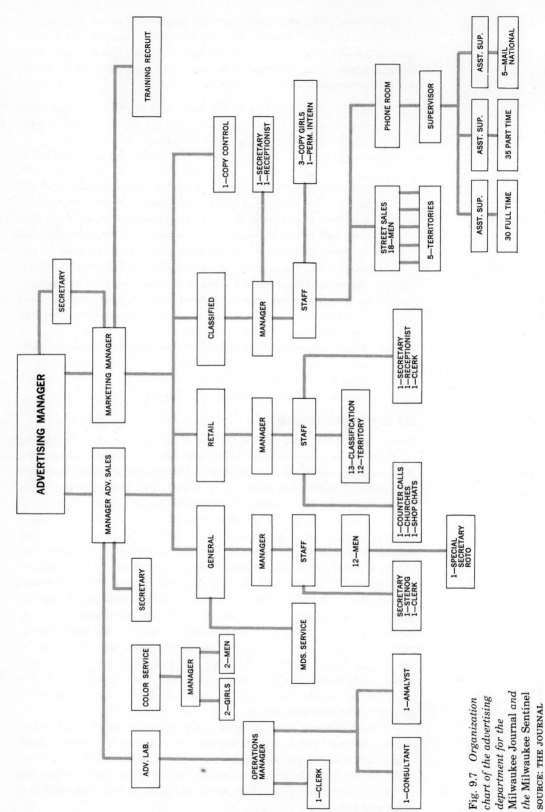

Fig. 9.7 *Organization chart of the advertising department for the* Milwaukee Journal *and the* Milwaukee Sentinel

SOURCE: THE JOURNAL COMPANY.

MEDIA ADVERTISING AND SALES PROMOTION DEPARTMENT

The third major type of advertising institution is the medium that carries the ad. The advertising department of any medium is primarily a sales department, and people who work for it or for the medium's national representative are primarily salesmen. In fact, the head of the advertising department is often called the "advertising sales manager" or, in the case of broadcast media, simply "sales manager."

There are perhaps 2,500 media salesmen in New York City alone, according to Martin Mayer.

Alone among advertising men they owe no debt of fealty to a brand name or to a manufacturer; they work as individuals with individual records of accomplishment and failure; and they can usually prove with facts and figures the value of their selling services. Like account executives and salesmen in other industrial fields, they tend to be personable, articulate, and highly convincing while they are talking.[9]

If you are a space salesman, you need facts to back up your sales claims. Consequently, most media sponsor research, which they look on as a form of promotion. You have to provide certain services to the people who buy your space. Therefore the typical media advertising department is set up to perform three principal functions—*selling, fact gathering,* and *account servicing.*

Newspapers. Newspaper advertising departments vary in size from the one-man department in the small town weekly to metropolitan departments that have more than 500 employees. McClure and Fulton list the following as typical units of a large newspaper advertising department:

Retail advertising department (also known as local display): sells display advertising to retail stores, to other local business firms, to organizations, and to individuals and gives them helpful advice.

General advertising department (national): works independently or in conjunction with publisher's representative, to sell space and service accounts.

Classified department: sells, prepares, and serves classified advertising to individuals and business firms.

Creative (copy service, copy and layout): plans and prepares display advertisements for retailers and other local firms.

Merchandising department: services and merchandises general advertising, persuades local retailers to tie in with national campaigns.

Research department: gathers data about the newspaper, its advertisers, and its market.

Promotion department: plans promotional events for the paper, handles public relations, and prepares sales solicitations material.

Production department: orders or prepares type, engravings, mats, etc.

Public service department: gives free or nominal-cost services to the public.

Order department: records space orders.

Planning department: forecasts business and market changes and trends as a basis for future planning.[10]

In the advertising department of *The Milwaukee Journal* (daily circulation 370,000; Sunday 571,000), one of the six top papers in the

[9]Martin Mayer, *Madison Avenue, U.S.A.* (New York: Harper & Row, Publishers, 1958), pp. 142–143.
[10]Leslie W. McClure and Paul C. Fulton, *Advertising in the Printed Media* (New York: Crowell—Collier and Macmillan, Inc., 1964), pp. 65–69.

United States in total advertising linage, the organization varies somewhat from this pattern. Heading the department is the advertising manager. Reporting to him are the marketing manager and the manager of advertising sales, with the managers of general, retail, and classified advertising working with both. The retail and classified advertising managers have top-level assistants who work closely with them. The classified department (57 members) is the largest segment of the advertising department. It handles building, real estate, and most of the used-car advertising in addition to the conventional want-ad type of advertising. The next largest is the retail department with 27 members. The *Journal's* general advertising department (12 members) maintains a three-man service wing called the merchandising service department for the promotion of national advertising campaigns.

Many of the functions often found in a newspaper's advertising department are performed instead by the *Journal's* research and promotion department. Here one will find copy and layout, research, market planning, and public relations. Naturally, this department must work very closely with the advertising department.

A medium-sized newspaper's advertising operation will not ordinarily provide such a variety of services but will concentrate on the department's basic function—the selling of general, retail, and classified advertising. The *Cedar Rapids Gazette* (daily circulation, 72,000) has managers for each of these. So does Madison (Wisconsin) Newspapers, Inc., which publishes two newspapers (daily circulations, 66,000 and 45,000). The Madison operation also includes a copy-service department and a small research and promotion unit.

In the small daily newspaper one man may have to perform all the advertising services. In the small weekly, the one-man advertising department may also write an occasional news story or help in the "back shop."

Television and Radio Stations. Because the local television or radio station operates much like the local newspaper, we need not describe the advertising operation in detail. Like the newspaper, the station will ordinarily have managers for both retail and general advertising, and will offer the buyer of time some help in copy and layout, merchandising, and research. Some stations offer a substantial amount of help in promoting programs sponsored by local advertisers and by network advertisers. There is no counterpart to the classified department in the local station.

Where television and radio stations operate under the same management, the executives must decide to what extent the sales staffs of the two media will work together. The tendency is to keep them separate, so that each salesman can concentrate on a single medium in spite of the fact that he may be competing with others in his own company. Similarly, managements who own both newspapers and radio or television stations generally prefer to keep the advertising operations quite separate.

Radio and television sales personnel may have to do even more for their retail advertisers than their newspaper counterparts do. As indicated earlier in this chapter, retailers are better adapted to handling their own newspaper and direct-mail advertising than their television or radio advertising.

Television and Radio Networks. The network concentrates its selling program on the general advertisers (particularly those that have national distribution). The salesman (or account executive) works for a sales manager. He has at his disposal a myriad of services to persuade the prospective time buyer. Whatever the advertiser's problems may be, the salesman can provide something to fit his needs — everything from a completely packaged program series to desired time clearances (agreement by local stations to use the program). He has research data to help the buyer and, incidentally, to indicate what a good buy his network is; he may throw in free merchandising if the account is a particularly desirable one. The network employs promotional writers to prepare material publicizing the network.

Independent Program Producers. Independent producers create, produce, and distribute programs for television. As such, they form an important part of the industry. Some have become multimillion dollar corporations; some have branched out into the ownership of stations. Most of them, however, direct their efforts toward providing commercial program fare for networks and stations.

According to a report of the House Committee on Interstate and Foreign Commerce, independent program activities can be described under four headings: (1) syndication; (2) production and distribution of "live" programs; (3) production and distribution of "film programs" for network exhibition; and (4) distribution of "theatrical" films for television stations.[11] Several of the companies that supply independent programs confine their activities to one of these categories, some engage in several, and a few companies offer all four services. This report describes syndication as

. . . a highly organized and often lucrative business. The companies involved vary greatly in size. Some are organized to seek national distribution of their programs. Others are virtually "one man" operations. The larger companies maintain offices and sales forces in principal cities throughout the country, and distribute several programs simultaneously. They maintain direct contact with the stations and seek to sell their film in as many markets as possible. The price at which a film is sold in a market depends on the complex of competitive factors which are present in that particular market at the time of the sale.

Magazines. Like newspapers and the broadcast media, magazines (whether consumer or business) provide three major types of services to the national advertiser: *personal help* with his advertising problems, *research*, and *merchandising*. Like the networks, they deal directly with advertisers and agencies rather than through representatives. Most magazine business offices are located in New York or Chicago, and those that are not have sales offices there. From these central offices the salesmen call on their prospects. The salesmen are usually well trained

---

[11]*Network Broadcasting: Report of the Committee on Interstate and Foreign Commerce*, House Report No. 1297, January 27, 1958 (Washington, D.C.: U.S. Government Printing Office, 1958).

How to court 6 million cultivated women

FIG. 9.8 *Trade advertisement for* Time. *Note how much color adds to this advertisement in the color plates.* COURTESY TIME INC.

and well paid, and most of them have had experience in local media, agencies, or advertising departments.

The media salesmen are aided by a wealth of promotion material, prepared mostly by people who work for the magazine. Copywriters may create direct-mail pieces, which are sent out regularly to space buyers in agencies. Other promotional people put together selling aids to be used in presentations. . . . Figure 9.8 is representative of *Time* magazine's multiphased promotional program. Space ads of this type are often converted to direct-mail promotion and scheduled to coincide with magazine insertion dates. (See Plate 1 in color section between Chapters 20 and 21 for full-color reproduction of this particular ad.)

The magazine's research department works closely with salesmen and promotion personnel. However, many of the larger research studies are made by outside organizations, because they can be more objective.

Hence their findings are not suspect. The Alfred Politz firm, for example, has conducted several major studies of media audiences.

Extensive merchandising services are a newer development. *Life*, for example, has a merchandising staff of more than thirty people. The primary job of merchandising representatives is to visit stores around the country to tell them about *Life* and its importance to retailers. Mainly they encourage them to feature products bearing the tag "As Advertised in *Life*" in store displays and local advertising. The Curtis publications also do an extensive merchandising job.

Outdoor. The important unit in the outdoor advertising industry (posters, painted bulletins, and spectaculars) is the local plant operator. He leases promising sites for his units and places boards on these sites. Then (either through his own salesmen or the industry-wide sales organization) he sells the space to agencies or directly to advertisers. Like other good media salesmen, he is armed with assorted information that emphasizes the strong points of his medium.

A major part of the work of the plant operator is keeping his plants in good physical condition. Most operators will offer help in the preparation of copy and layout if the buyers want it.

MEDIA REPRESENTATIVES

Media representatives sell most of the newspaper space and the television and radio time that is bought by national (general) advertisers. These representatives handle only one paper or station in a market and have exclusive rights to sell their paper or station at the national level. They are the only regular contact most media buyers in agencies and advertisers have with the local medium. Exceptions are the New York newspapers (which handle their own national advertising sales to Madison Avenue agencies), certain regional magazines, and those few newspapers (the *Chicago Tribune*) which have New York sales offices.

Newspaper Representatives. The economic justification for a newspaper representative is that a salesman representing a number of papers can do a better job at less cost than the newspaper or station could do by itself.

The "media rep" has a threefold job: to sell newspapers (or radio or television) as a medium, to sell the markets in which his media operate, and to sell his medium in that market against the competition. In cities with only one newspaper, the second job is likely to be the big one. The "media rep" may sell the city as "the fastest growing market in the Southeast," or as an ideal test market for new products or campaigns, or he may stress the high per capita income in the area.

In selling his newspaper against the competition he operates like the salesman back home. He may sell it as cheaper than the competition. He may sell the high quality of its audience, or the merchandising help it offers, or the sheer number of people it reaches. It is interesting that we can sometimes find two newspapers in a given area, both claiming (truthfully) to reach the largest audience. For example, according to an ad in the Standard Rate and Data Service, the *Pittsburgh Press* is "Number One in Daily and Sunday Circulation." On the other hand, the *Pittsburgh Post-Gazette* points out that "two-thirds of the market's three million people live outside the central city zone" and that it is "the only paper which covers the surrounding area plus the city zone."

The Hearst Advertising Service, which is a national representative for some Hearst newspapers, supplies national advertisers with "an operating sales control" for its markets. It includes complete detailed maps of each city and its suburbs subdivided into sales districts according to traffic flow, with the different kinds of stores clearly marked. Mayer points out that

> . . . experience has taught the Hearst people that by keeping an eye on a few of these districts a manufacturer can predict what will happen throughout the entire city; if desired (for a small fee), the Hearst merchandising man, checking through a retail store, finds that an advertiser's product is out of stock, he will kindly call the distributor; if he finds the advertiser's point-of-sale posters and display cartons reposing quietly in their shipping box, he will (bullying the retailer if required) put them up himself.[12]

Television and Radio Representatives. The sale of television and radio time to national advertisers is handled in much the same way as newspaper space. There are, however, some differences worth noting.

Networks maintain "spot sales" organizations, primarily for the stations they own and operate. These organizations also handle spot sales for some of the key affiliated (but independently owned) stations. The regular national representatives believe — as does the House Committee on Interstate and Foreign Commerce — that the networks have an unfair advantage in that independent stations are sometimes forced to accept representation to gain affiliation, which is essential in most television operations.

A second difference lies in the nature of the coverage offered. If a buyer wants to reach the entire newspaper-reading public in a certain multinewspaper community, he will have to buy space in all the newspapers. However, because audiences tune in and out of a television or radio station it is possible to reach most of the people with a saturation schedule of spot commercials on one station.

A third difference lies in the time orientation of television and radio, compared with newspapers. It is easy to expand the number of pages in a newspaper as extra advertising is sold. The station, however, has a limited amount of time it can sell. There is some flexibility in the number of spot announcements stations can sell, but most stations are reluctant to devote more than seven minutes of each hour to advertising.

Compensation. National representatives may work on either a commission or a salary basis. According to some authorities all the representatives of small papers work on commission, ranging from 10 to 15 percent.[13] However, among the larger papers the payment, in most instances, is on a salary or fee basis. This salary is less, as a percentage of total sales, than the commissions (some were as low as 3 percent of sales). Two papers which maintain their own branch offices report costs

[12]Mayer, pp. 158–159.
[13]McClure and Fulton, p. 141.

of between 5 and 7 percent of sales. Mayer noted a tendency for newspaper representatives to receive less than broadcasting representatives. The House Committee report specifies commissions in the broadcasting industry as ranging from 5 to 15 percent of sales, both on new accounts and on renewal of old ones.

MEDIA ASSOCIATIONS

Much of the basic job of building acceptance for a medium is taken over by the media associations. Unlike the local salesmen or the media representatives, people who work for these associations have to sell the idea that their type of medium is superior to the others. Some of the leading associations are given below:

American Newspaper Publishers Association. The ANPA is the leading national organization of daily newspapers. It serves the advertising industry through its Bureau of Advertising, which in turn has five divisions: retail, national, research, promotion, and creative, each headed by a vice-president.

National Association of Broadcasters. This association serves the television and radio broadcasters in much the same way that the ANPA does the newspaper publishers. It represents the industry on legislative matters and acts as a clearinghouse for industry matters.

Television Bureau of Advertising. The purpose of this bureau is to promote television as a medium and assist stations in their own promotion.

Radio Advertising Bureau. This bureau promotes radio as a medium and helps stations with promotion.

Magazine Publishers Association and *Periodical Publishers Association.* These groups represent the magazine industry.

Associated Business Publications. This organization is an association of industrial, trade, and professional publications, all of which are members of the Audit Bureau of Circulations. Its counterpart in the controlled (free) circulation field is *National Business Publications,* which accepts members from both the paid and controlled field.

Direct Mail Advertising Association. This association promotes the interests of users, producers, and suppliers of direct-mail advertising in all its forms.

Agricultural Publishers Association. This association represents the farm press.

Outdoor Advertising Association of America. This group is the trade organization for outdoor advertising. (The promotional arm for this industry, however, is the *Institute of Outdoor Advertising.*)

SUMMARY

We have seen that advertisers are of two main types—general and retail. Although organization may vary substantially, the advertising manager is usually the top man in advertising policy and execution. He may be one of the company's top executives, but he is more likely not to be. He must work with the other executives in his company and with the agency.

Variations of the advertising organization that are becoming somewhat more common are the committee and the brand management systems. Since World War II, there has been a noticeable trend toward decentralization.

The retailer depends less on the agency and, within the store, performs most of the agency's normal functions. If the store is small, it may rely largely on help from manufacturers, mat services, trade associations, and the local media. The mail order house's advertising operation is geared primarily to producing effective catalogues.

We find the advertising departments of all the media strongly sales-oriented. In almost any media department there is some provision for the following: selling time or space; gathering facts that will be useful to both the medium and prospective customers; and providing service to keep the customers happy. In the larger media we are likely to find people who perform such additional services as merchandising and preparation of sales presentations.

The local media (newspapers, television, and radio) provide their own staffs for selling and servicing local accounts, but their national representatives sell the national advertisers and their agencies. These representatives have exclusive rights to the local medium and will handle only one paper or station in a given market.

The third type of selling organization (besides the media and the media representatives) is the media association, which not only attempts to build demand for the medium but may also help with research, public relations, or legislative activities.

QUESTIONS FOR DISCUSSION

1. List and explain briefly the major functions of the advertising department of a manufacturer.
2. To what extent should an advertising manager or members of his staff concern themselves with checking the work of their advertising agency?
3. Why is the advertising manager more likely to delegate to his agency responsibility for media advertising than responsibility for sales promotion activities?
4. To what extent can you say the advertising department of a retail store or of a mail order house is a miniature advertising agency?
5. To what extent is the practice of advertising by an advertiser a profession? To what extent the practice by an agency?
6. To what extent does the size of a general or retail advertising budget influence the type of organization developed to spend that budget?
7. What are the principal sales tools used by a person who represents an advertising medium?

SUGGESTED READINGS

Brink, Edward L., and William T. Kelley, *The Management of Promotion.* Englewood Cliffs, N.J.: Prentice-Hall, Inc., 1963. Chapter 23.

Edwards, Charles, and Russell A. Brown, *Retail Advertising and Sales Promotion*. Englewood Cliffs, N. J.: Prentice Hall, Inc., 1959. Chapter 2.

Frey, Albert W., and Kenneth Davis, *The Advertising Industry*. New York: Association of National Advertisers, Inc., 1958.

McClure, Leslie, and Paul C. Fulton, *Advertising in the Printed Media*. New York: Crowell – Collier and Macmillan, Inc., 1964.

McGorrin, R. J., "Case History of a Decentralized International Advertising Department," in S. Watson Dunn, ed., *International Handbook of Advertising*. New York: McGraw-Hill, Inc., 1964.

Mayer, Martin, *Madison Avenue, U.S.A.* New York: Harper & Row, Publishers, 1958. Chapter 9.

Sandage, C. H., and Vernon Fryburger, *Advertising Theory and Practice*, 7th ed. Homewood, Ill.: Richard D. Irwin, Inc., 1967. Chapters 29 – 30.

Seehafer, E. F., and J. W. Laemmar, *Successful Television and Radio Advertising*. New York: McGraw-Hill, Inc., 1959. Chapters 2 – 3.

Wright, John, and Daniel S. Warner, *Advertising*, 2d ed. New York: McGraw-Hill, Inc., 1967. Chapter 6.

PART 2 | # PLANNING THE CAMPAIGN

10

The Information Revolution

Claude Hopkins was one of the earliest advertising men to appreciate the importance of facts. He credited much of his success at the beginning of the century to his early poverty and his willingness "to talk to laboring men, to study housewives who must count their pennies, to gain the confidence and learn the ambitions of poor boys and girls." He had only scorn for advertising people who "gained their impressions from golf-club associates." He was a great believer in what he called "data"—from prospective customers and the testing of products to be advertised.

In Hopkins' day copywriters who went out and talked to consumers—no matter how unscientific the sample might be statistically—had a decided advantage over those who did not. Today, facts and the use of sophisticated methods in obtaining them are taken for granted in American business. At Procter & Gamble one in every ten employees is engaged in some form of research. Richard H. Brien and James E. Stafford point out three compelling reasons why marketing information systems must be upgraded: (1) the growing complexity of the areas to be managed; (2) the expansion of marketing effort across existing environmental frontiers—geographic, economic, and social; and (3) the explosion of the world's store of knowledge, allegedly doubling during the

1958–1968 decade.[1] Observers speak of the mushrooming "knowledge industry." Economist Fritz Machlup estimated that the knowledge industry (education, mass media, movies, research and development education, and the like) increased 43 percent between 1958 and 1963 and accounted for 36 percent of our nonfarm employed.[2] *Fortune* has called it our biggest growth industry.

The production of measurable knowledge goes on expanding faster than the economy because it generates as well as feeds on economic growth. People spend more and more for information they feel or hope will help them cope with a rapidly changing and increasingly complex world, and they also spend more and more for information whose value to their economic well-being is marginal and tenuous. They can afford this increased outlay only because the economy is expanding faster than the population, and because their living standards are consequently rising. And by a happy but logical coincidence, the biggest single factor in the nation's rising productivity is the growth of the knowledge industry.[3]

CONTRIBUTIONS OF THE COMPUTER

Many people contend that the information revolution really started when computers appeared in force during the early 1950s. They made it possible for everyone interested in information—businessmen, scientists, government officials, and educators—to process huge quantities of unrelated data and find meaningful relation. The computer has provided what Isaac Auerbach calls an "information window." He maintains that "there is as big a difference between the perspective afforded by this information window and our normal view of things as there is between the earthbound view of the moon and the photographs taken by the Ranger space vehicle. . . . What's more the window has just started opening and the information revolution is still in its early phases."[4]

The case for computers was offered by Gilbert Burck in *Fortune* magazine:

Knowledge is power and control, provided it is timely, ample, and relevant. Only a businessman who knows what is happening inside his company as soon as it happens can truly adjust his means to his aims; and only one who understands what is happening in the marketplace as soon as it happens can really make sound decisions about his aims. . . .

Today's advanced electronic computer enables a man to control his business and to assess its environment with incomparable effectiveness because it enables him both to lay hands on relevant facts swiftly and to understand their changing relationships.[5]

In no other business is it as important to have information promptly and abundantly as in the field of advertising and sales pro-

---

[1]Richard H. Brien and James E. Stafford, "Marketing Information Systems: A New Dimension for Marketing Research," *Journal of Marketing*, July 1968, pp 19–23.

[2]Fritz Machlup, *The Production and Distribution of Knowledge in the United States* (Princeton, N.J.: Princeton University Press, 1964).

[3]Gilbert Burck, "Knowledge: The Biggest Growth Industry of Them All," *Fortune*, December 1964, p. 129.

[4]Isaac L. Auerbach, "Information—A Prime Resource," *New York Times*, Information Revolution Supplement, June 14, 1965, p. 4.

[5]Gilbert Burck, "'On Line' in 'Real Time,'" *Fortune*, April 1964, p. 141.

The computer with a future is still expanding.
IBM introduces the new System/360
Model 25.

It's a system to grow with. IBM engineers say Model 25 is bigger than it looks. It sets a new price-performance standard for a system of its size.

The reasons are simple. To reduce Model 25's size, price and power requirements, we built control units for many peripheral devices right into the central processing unit.

To boost performance, we introduced a new high-speed working storage area.

This growth system has the same instruction set and flexibility as the larger models. For example, Model 25 can use most System/360 input-output devices with whatever combinations of tape, disk and card systems you need.

Flexibility means Model 25 will even run existing IBM 1401, 1440 and 1460 programs without reprogramming. It means Model 25 can use high-level operating systems as well as PL/I, FORTRAN and COBOL—the same program languages used in larger systems. It means utility programs are ready and waiting in IBM's program library—as are System/360 application programs tailored for such industries as finance, manufacturing, process and distribution.

It all adds up to this: as your business grows, your System/360 will be able to grow with it. Programmers will be more productive. Your installation investment will be lower. And you'll see results faster.

That's Model 25... a system to grow with.

IBM

FIG. 10.1 *Advertisement promoting a new computer system — more and more the indispensable tool of the modern advertising researcher.*
SOURCE: INTERNATIONAL BUSINESS MACHINES CORPORATION.

motion. Computerized information will have a lasting impact on this area of decision making.

WHAT KINDS OF FACTS DO WE NEED?

In Chapters 3 and 4 we dealt with advertising in relation to the larger picture — its role in marketing and communications. It was stated that both approaches put advertising in its proper perspective and help you to take advantage of its many potentialities. It was emphasized that you cannot build your marketing-communications plan without facts.

Then arises the problem: what kinds of facts do you need? You will probably use the same facts, whether you consider advertising and promotion in the broad context of marketing (converting consumer purchasing power into demand) or in the narrower one of communication (getting your message to one or more people). So you need not worry about whether you have "marketing" or "communication" facts.

One logical approach to deciding what kind of information we need is to determine the kind of decisions we have to make in planning a campaign. These can generally be consolidated into five general categories: the relative importance of *market segments*; the behavior and attitudes of *consumers*; the images and characteristics of the *products* or *services* we are promoting; the content of the *messages* we are to use; and the combination of *media* that can best accomplish our objective.

Market Segments. Suppose you are advertising a soft drink. You will want to know which segment of the total market represents your best potential—teen-agers, high or middle social class, and so forth. You will also want to know the importance of these markets and how they can best be reached by your promotional campaign. The following chapter discusses the problem of market segmentation.

Consumer Behavior and Attitudes. This is the complex area of why people behave and think as they do. Why, for instance, do they like or not like your soft drink? What motives or attitudes can be tapped to influence their future behavior? What are their habits and their preferences? Chapters 12 and 13 explore this area in detail.

Product Images and Characteristics. Some products and services have inherent drama and are easy to advertise. A new automobile or a revolutionary new food preparation are good examples. More common, however, is the prosaic, unglamorous product that is much the same year after year. For such a product the planner really has to dig if he is to conceive of a good advertising campaign.

Content of the Message. What kinds of copy should be used? Long copy? Short copy? Color? Black and white?

Media. There is no shortage of information about media. The problem is to sift out usable and accurate information.

SCIENTIFIC APPROACH TO COLLECTING AND USING INFORMATION

Earlier in this book we agreed that the scientific approach would be used wherever possible. This does not mean that nothing but research is to be used. It does mean, however, that campaign planning should be approached in an orderly manner. There are some in advertising who sigh for the good old days before science came on the scene—but their ranks are thinning. There are some who are concerned because facts are misused. And there are some who are honestly confused because fact gathering (especially when it is done by professional researchers) is sometimes surrounded by a veil of mysticism and unintelligible jargon.

A scientific approach to the collection and use of information that can be helpful in solving marketing problems might include defining the problem, researching information, diagnosing the results, and deciding what action to take.

Defining the Problem. If a problem is not clearly and sharply defined, how can you know what facts to look for? Suppose you are advertising a brand of men's shirts—a product that has no obvious features to differentiate it from your competition's (price, distribution, for example). But you do have some hunches (scientifically known as *hypotheses*). You suspect that the shirts are considered ill-fitting by some customers—or they are bought by older men and shunned by

FIG. 10.2 *Advertisement promoting data-processing service to advertising and marketing researchers.* SOURCE: STATISTICAL TABULATING CORPORATION.

younger buyers, or that the buttons stay on longer. These hypotheses can be proved or disproved by collecting the right data.

There are times when it pays not to define a problem too precisely. There are times, for instance, when you have only a hazy idea about what the real problem is and therefore more data have to be collected than will probably be needed; then you sift through the collected data to discover more about your problem. There are times when it pays simply to dream a little—in a disciplined way, that is. Some companies, for example, are working on research programs to investigate the pure nature and purpose of advertising. Some are delving into basic marketing and advertising forces rather than merely finding answers to specific questions. There is a place in advertising for the disciplined dreamer, for today's dreams may be tomorrow's realities.

Digging for Information. If you ask a plans board member what facts he thinks are needed for planning a campaign, he is more likely to reply, "Everything you can get." He would be reflecting the insatiable thirst for information that characterizes today's advertising man. He digs for everything that even shows promise of relating to a problem. The following are some suggested sources:

Research. Research is the most scientific method of digging. But your research need not always start from scratch. It is just as profitable (and a great deal cheaper) to take advantage of someone else's digging — to research the research. There are times, however, when secondary data will not do the job and firsthand (or primary) research is needed. Then it may be necessary to survey a goodly sample of the people you are trying to influence. Or you may want to conduct experiments in the laboratory or in the field where attempts are made to control the exposure of subjects to a particular message or combination of media.

Both survey and experimental research are extremely valuable as sources of planning data, but their effectiveness depends in part on how the data are used. Research has been called "the strong man's tool and the weak man's refuge." It should not be looked on as a substitute for judgment. Some people lean too heavily on it and allow it to make their decisions for them. They use research as a shield to protect their opinions with someone else's statistics. You should learn to think of research as *data*, not as dogma.

Some people refuse to use research data unless field or experimental conditions are practically perfect. However, researcher Seymour Banks points out that the world in which goods are sold is incredibly complex and businessmen are shortsighted if they avoid using scientific experimentation. He asserts that conditions need not be perfect, because "in almost all situations in which experiments are used, the fundamental interest is in a comparison of alternatives, not in the establishment of absolute values. Seldom, if ever, are we asked to measure a single value like the speed of light or the pull of gravity."[6]

Research should be used to stimulate thought but never to supplant thinking. It should be used in the formulation of judgment, but never as a substitute for judgment.

One of the problems any advertising man faces is distinguishing good research from bad. Here is a guide suggested by the Advertising Research Foundation:

1. Under what conditions was the study made? Problems. Sources of finances. Names of organizations participating. Period of time covered. Date of report. Definition of terms. Questionnaire and instructions to interviewers. Collateral data. Complete statement of methodology.

2. Has the questionnaire been well designed? Dangers of bias. Unreasonable demands on memory. Poor choice of answers. Monotonous questions. Lack of space for answers. Was it pre-tested?

3. Has the interviewing been adequate and reliably done? Familiarity with prescribed interview procedure. Training. Maturity. Were spot checks made to check accuracy?

4. Has the best sampling plan been followed? Random sample is preferable. Quota sample is more likely to be satisfactory for collecting *qualitative* than *quantitative* data.

5. Has the sampling plan been fully executed? Substitutions or other variations may destroy validity of data.

[6]*Experimentation in Marketing* (New York: McGraw-Hill, Inc., 1965), p. 1.

6. Is the sample large enough? If probability sample is properly designed, reliability of results can be determined mathematically. In other samples it is much more difficult to determine adequate sample size.

7. Was there a systematic control of editing, coding, and tabulating?

8. Is the interpretation forthright and logical? If one factor is interpreted as cause, all others must be held constant. All basic data which underlie interpretations should be shown. Validity of respondent's memory should not be over-emphasized. Small differences should not be emphasized. Analysis should be clear and simple.[7]

Personal Observation. One large agency, Cunningham and Walsh, has built a trade promotional campaign around the fact that its employees spend at least one week each year working in the field where they can observe the consumer firsthand. One will work in a retail store that handles some of the client's products; another in a service station

[7]*Criteria for Marketing and Advertising Research* (New York: Advertising Research Foundation, 1953).

FIG. 10.3 *A new word, "Computermanship," is coined by a research firm.*
PREPARED BY WITT-FRANCIS, INC.

pumping the client's gasoline and talking to customers. This practice is followed by many agencies. It is a sound idea that people working on an account pick up impressions and facts about the product or even just the "feel" [nebulous as that may be] of consumer reaction.

Committees. The committee is an integral part of today's complex business organization and can, at best, be a fruitful source of data and ideas. (It may, at worst, be a crutch for weak leadership or just a misdirected bull session).

Intuition. We know that certain facts and the interpretation of them are stored in our subconscious. Trained intuition may bring them out. Creative people emphasize the role of intuition or inspiration in helping them unearth "facts" and impressions and, perhaps more important, effective ways of using them. One study of practicing copywriters indicated that the ideas they "use most often" came more often from "my own inspiration" (over 85 percent listed it as their prime source) than any other source.[8]

Pierre Martineau calls intuition "raw, direct, immediate, preconscious, prelogical, nonrational perception. We grasp an idea, judge a person, make a decision, size up a situation in a flash."[9] We must distinguish intuitive digging from the logical, step-by-step procedure we have mentioned before. Through intuition we can dip into reservoirs of facts, impressions and ideas below the conscious level. People who read a great deal, or are especially perceptive, store great quantities of material in their subconscious. Many great minds do not really know where their ideas come from—they merely know that some sort of synthesis takes place in their subconscious.

Diagnosing the Facts. It is easier to gather facts than to determine what they mean. Some Freudian-oriented researchers may look for moral implications or sexual imagery in the research data they collect. Ernest Dichter, for example, says in discussing foods:

> Certain foods are considered morally bad, while others are considered morally good. . . . For example, Quaker Oats, which is emotionally associated in the consumers' mind with a time of sacrifice, virtue and idealism has acquired a virtuous character among morning cereals. . . .
> Many Americans tend to develop a guilt feeling toward any food that is too rich or fancy. . . .
> Rice is considered feminine, but potatoes are masculine; tea is feminine, but coffee is strongly masculine.[10]

Sociologically oriented analysts may look for status symbols or "other-directedness" (the extent to which actions or attitudes are related to peer groups). Freudians and sociologists often use the same techniques and come up with the same data; however, their diagnosis may be quite different.

Data gathered through projective techniques (Rorschach inkblot tests, sentence completion, and thematic apperception) are tricky to

[8]S. Watson Dunn, *Advertising Copy and Communication* (New York: McGraw-Hill, Inc., 1956), pp. 80–81.
[9]Pierre Martineau, *Motivation in Advertising* (New York: McGraw-Hill, Inc., 1957), p. 20.
[10]Martin Mayer, *Madison Avenue, U.S.A.* (New York: Harper & Row, Publishers, 1958), p. 220.

diagnose, and even experts may disagree on what certain data mean. On the other hand, some data may be handled easily by dividing the findings into significant categories; and combining (scientists prefer "synthesizing") the various parts into a complex whole in the hope that you can come up with a decision.

Some persons are wary of small samples and want a large survey or long series of experiments before they are satisfied with the data.

Deciding What Action to Take. In deciding what action to take, a creative executive is most valuable. He evaluates the facts and uses them as *bases* for judgment, not as a substitute.

Facts do not make decisions. Facts do not write an ad. Agency president Charles Brower humorously points out this danger when he says:[11]

> If Christopher Columbus, the well-known sailor from Genoa, had applied modern advertising research methods to his proposed voyage, a consumer jury test would have told him in advance that the world was flat; depth interviews with expert seamen would have revealed the impressive monsters that awaited him hungrily at the end of the sea, motivational studies would have shown that his crew were interested in money; Ferdinand and Isabella would have cancelled the appropriation; America would never have been discovered, and *you* would all be *Indians*.

According to *Advertising Age*, the inspiration for one prizewinning advertisement came to agency president Bill Bernbach after a lunch with executive vice-president Ned Doyle, at which the problem of introducing El-Al's jet-prop Britannia—two and one-half hours faster to London—was discussed. *Advertising Age* says, "As they were walking back to their office, Bill said, 'I know what I'll do. I'm gonna take the ocean and cut off 20%.' That was the beginning."[12]

However, these so-called intuitive decisions are not nearly so rash as they may seem to be in trade paper articles and stories that we hear. A capable executive has spent many years learning the discipline of rational thinking and intellection. He has absorbed general facts about the company he works for, the advertising policies, and the products. He can—in fact has to—make decisions based on a combination of the mechanistic appraisal of facts and his intuition. He may be unable to explain his logic or the rationale of his decision. Yet the chances are that the decision is a wise one. When management makes an outlay for plant expansion, or for a new product line, there are facts alone; in addition, there is the creative use of them.

TECHNIQUES FOR CREATIVE USE OF INFORMATION

Some organizations believe in special techniques to stimulate the flow of ideas. Perhaps the most famous of these is "brainstorming," popularized by Batten, Barton, Durstine & Osborn. In a "brainstorming" session everyone involved in a problem-solving situation comes up with all the ideas and solutions he can think of, no matter how absurd or irrelevant. These are recorded without criticism. Later all the ideas are sifted, and the most promising one selected.

[11]"The Growing Pains of Advertising," *Broadcasting-Telecasting*, January 17, 1955.
[12]See "Copy Impact Brought DDB Agency to $22,000,000-a-Year-Billings Level," *Advertising Age*, June 1, 1959.

Joie de vivre, joie de savourer l'existence. Plaisir de fumer une cigarette généreuse, comme seule la Marlboro peut l'être. Parce qu'à chaque bouffée, elle prouve ce qu'elle est: une authentique américaine.

Une vie exaltante — une cigarette exaltante!

La cigarette de prestige signée Philip Morris

Soyez dans la course!

Marlboro

Son goût en a fait un succès mondial

FIG. 10.4 *Example of use in another country of information and experience gained by marketing this product in the United States.* COURTESY PHILIP MORRIS INTERNATIONAL.

Many firms believe that an individual or product group should sift through facts and work out decisions and then defend their decisions before a plans board or committee. The advertisement in Figure 10.4 (one of a highly successful series) is an example of work by such a group.

Another approach is based primarily on the individual. Says Doyle Dane Bernbach's copy chief, Phyllis Robinson, "We have no brainstorming, no great group meetings, no plans board. At every level, an ad is the product of a copywriter and an art director working together and the spark can come from either of them."

The advocates of yet another approach — *synectics*[13] — maintain that the only way to learn about creative action is to try to gain insight into the underlying, nonrational, free associatory concepts in man's preconscious mind. Synectics theory holds that the creative efficiency of people in any field can be markedly increased if they understand the psychological process by which they operate, and that in the creative process the emotional is more important than the intellectual, the irrational more important than the rational.

[13]See William J.J. Gordon, *Synectics: The Development of Creative Capacity* (New York: Harper & Row, Publishers, 1961).

SUMMARY

This chapter has stressed the revolutionary changes in collecting information for planning the campaign. The most important facts fell within five major categories — consumers, markets, product, advertising content, and media. A scientific approach to collecting facts and analyzing an advertising problem might include the 4 D's — defining the problem, digging for facts, diagnosing the facts, and deciding what to do.

With this background we can investigate in more detail some of the types of information and approaches that will be helpful in planning. These will be covered in the next four chapters.

QUESTIONS FOR DISCUSSION

1. Compare the role of research in advertising planning with that of other methods of gathering information.
2. What has been the influence of computers on the gathering of information?
3. Would you call intuition a scientific method of collecting information?
4. What are the requirements of a good research program?
5. Is there any difference between a research program and the sort of questioning any good newspaper reporter does before he starts to write a story?
6. Why do some people in the advertising and promotion field believe that research will inhibit their creative processes? Do you agree with this point of view?

SUGGESTED READINGS

Banks, Seymour, *Experimentation in Marketing*. New York: McGraw-Hill, Inc., 1965. Chapters 1–2.

Bliss, Perry, ed., *Marketing and the Behavioral Sciences*, rev. ed. Boston: Allyn and Bacon, Inc., 1968. Part I.

Boyd, Harper W., Jr., and Joseph W. Newman, eds., *Advertising Management: Selected Readings*. Homewood, Ill.: Richard D. Irwin, Inc., 1965. Parts I–II.

Crespi, Irving, *Attitude Research*. Chicago: American Marketing Association, 1965.

Dichter, Ernest, *Handbook of Consumer Motivation*. New York: McGraw-Hill, Inc., 1964.

Ghiselin, Brewster, *The Creative Process*. Berkeley, Calif.: University of California Press, 1954.

Hovland, Carl I., *et al*, *Communication and Persuasion*. New Haven, Conn.: Yale University Press, 1953.

Lucas, Darrell B., and Steuart H. Britt, *Measuring Advertising Effectiveness*. New York: McGraw-Hill, Inc., 1963. Chapters 1–2.

Nafziger, Ralph O., and David M. White, eds., *Introduction to Mass Communications Research*. Baton Rouge, La.: Louisiana State University Press, 1963.

Wright, John S., and Daniel S. Warner, *Advertising*. New York: McGraw-Hill, Inc., 1962. Chapter 16.

11

Locating
and
Forecasting
the Market

Common sense tells us that we cannot please everybody. We know that a person who tries to win the friendship of everyone is likely to have few friends, because he will lack any real individuality and be considered insincere. Businessmen face a similar problem. If they attempted to sell to everybody, they, too, would probably fail. No business needs to sell to *all* potential customers. A fraction of the market is all most firms have to try for. The trick is to select the types of customers representing the most desirable market. Once the groups have been located, a company can mobilize all its forces (content mix, media mix, and so on) to reach them. In this chapter we should explore some of the ways in which the potential worth of markets is differentiated and evaluated.

CRITERIA FOR MARKET SEGMENTATION

In setting up criteria we should keep the following in mind: (1) they should reflect group differences that will decide or at least affect what actions the businessman should take, and (2) they should apply to a particular product in the specific markets in which it is being sold. John G. Myers and Francesco M. Nicosia point out that although there are hundreds of approaches to classifying markets, two major approaches can be identified:

The first consists of postulating one or more qualities or dimensions chosen on the basis of a theory, as relevant to develop a classification. Combinations of different values of such dimensions generate a priori or theoretical classes. Empirical observations are then taken to test whether such theoretical classes are found in nature. . . .

The second major strategy is essentially the opposite of the first. For example, a variety of empirical observations on many subjects are first collected and through computational procedures some dimensions are identified. These are then used for segmenting or classifying the subjects into subgroups.[1]

We are likely to find one or more of the following bases helpful in classifying markets: demographic, sociological, cultural, psychological, and product-usage factors.

Demographic Factors. The researcher's traditional method of dividing markets is by demographic factors. Consequently, many of our available data on both markets and media audiences are broken down by demographic classifications.

Income. No two families spend money in exactly the same way. However, if you know a person's income you can predict with some accuracy what his wants are likely to be and how he is likely to satisfy them. Or, you can estimate how much of your product you should sell if you know how many households in your market are in each income group. Fortunately, we have a great deal of data on the relation of income to purchasing patterns.

The data in Figures 11.1 to 11.5 are based on a comprehensive study of expenditure patterns of the American family conducted by the National Industrial Conference Board. The study was designed to "provide a statistical profile of how America lives" by showing the demand for 700 individual products and services, by various demographic groups. Approximately 12,000 American families were included in the sample.

According to this study, the importance of income is shown by the fact that real income jumped 15 percent during the decade from 1952 to 1962. This difference meant that a significant portion of families moved from the "necessity" to the "discretionary" spending bracket. In the early 1950s only a third of total buying was accounted for by households earning $7,500 or more, but by the 1960s that income group purchased half of all goods and services.

In some product categories, expenditures rise with income, whereas in others they do not. For example, the amount spent for automobiles increases very sharply up to $7,500 annual income. At that point the rate of rise is more modest, although larger than the rate of increase in family income. At $15,000 a year and above, the percent of the family's income that goes into automobiles remains relatively constant.

Tobacco expenditures rise with family earnings most sharply in the lower-income brackets and at a slower rate as one moves up the scale. They then widen sharply at the $10,000-a-year level. Food expenditures also rise with family income, but not so sharply as many other types of

[1]John G. Myers and Francesco M. Nicosia, "On the Study of Consumer Typologies," in *Journal of Marketing Research*, May 1968, pp. 182–193.

expenditures. In lower-income groups, families spend more for tobacco than alcoholic beverages, but the reverse is true in upper-income brackets ($10,000 a year and above).

Among product categories most sensitive to income increases are home furnishings, appliances, automotive, and recreation, according to this and other studies. Among the less sensitive categories is food.

Education. In general, the higher a person's education, the more likely he is to have a higher income. Consequently, for many types of products it does not make much difference whether you divide the markets by income or by the education of the head of the household. However, most studies indicate that the more highly educated spend more on the average than the poorly educated on housing (rent, mortgage, school and land taxes), communications (for example, telephone, newspapers), and such recreation materials as cameras and other photographic equipment.

In the NICB study, weekly smoking expenditures rose from $1.12 for those with a grade-school education or less to $1.59 for persons with some high school. However, the figure dropped to $1.56 for high school graduates and persons with some college, and to $1.23 for college graduates.

The importance of keeping abreast of education trends has been emphasized by economist Arno Johnson. He states that between 1940 and 1966 the percentage of high school graduates in the United States population twenty years and older increased from 27 percent to 53 percent. He predicts that by 1976 it will be 62 percent. The percentage of college graduates has also increased with the estimated number of college graduates in 1976 3 ¾ times the number in 1940.[2]

Occupation. Occupation, like education, is related to income in that certain occupations are traditionally better paid than others. The differential between "white-collar" and "blue-collar" incomes has been steadily decreasing. The craftsman-foreman, for example, spends almost as much in total as the clerical-sales person, although this does not mean that their spending patterns are the same. For example, the white-collar, clerical-sales person spends substantially more for clothing and home furnishings than the craftsman-foreman does, although both spend approximately the same for recreation.

Age. There are two methods of analyzing markets by age. One is to divide the population into age groups and analyze the wants and needs of each group. The other is to examine households in terms of the age of the household head. If we use the first approach, we find certain identifiable spending patterns. Consider the so-called "Teen-Age Group," defined by the Bureau of the Census as boys and girls aged thirteen through nineteen.

What are the characteristics of the teen-age market? One study summarizes it this way:

Teen-agers live in a world of their own. A world that industry tries to understand. Teens are a homogeneous group. They act, dress, live, and talk the same in all sections of the country. It is an experimental group willing to give

[2]Arno H. Johnson, "Consumption Lag Threatens Growth," *Advertising Age,* May 22, 1967, p. 53.

new things a try. Almost all mass buying trends originate in this market. Trends or fads that reach the adult market have their beginnings here.

Psychologically, teen-agers tend to consider as necessity what most adults generally regard as luxuries, for example, cars, hi-fi, vacations. Teen-agers are highly fashion conscious, not price conscious, usually agreeable to trading-up. They are acutely brand conscious. Their brand loyalty is relatively easy to capture, not so easy to keep. . . . They veer from fad to fad. This faddishness reflects insecurity and a strong urge to conform. . . . They like being considered as adults, hate condescension and being talked down to.[3]

In the NICB study the age bracket from thirty-five to forty-four spent the greatest amount a week for cigarettes ($1.76), and those sixty-five or older, the smallest amount (48 cents). For food expenditures, which are family-oriented, the age of the head of the household appears to be more useful in discriminating among market groups than the age of the person making the purchase. The households with the head of the family between thirty-five and forty-four spent more for food than families in any other age group.

In general, the United States population since 1940 has been characterized by a rapid increase in the very young and the very old. Between 1940 and 1967 the number of Americans under ten years of age increased 87 percent, those sixty-five years of age increased 109 percent, although the total population increase was only 51 percent.[4]

Life Cycle. Several demographers and marketing specialists have suggested the "family life cycle" as a variable holding great promise in segmenting markets. For example, Lansing and Kish have divided consumers into the following eight stages in the life cycle: young single, young married with no children, young married with youngest child under six, young married with youngest child six or older, older married with children, older married with no children, older single, and others.[5] After investigating the relation of the life cycle to six characteristics (home ownership, indebtedness, working wife, income in excess of $4,000, recency of car purchase and purchase of television) they concluded:

For each of these characteristics it (family life cycle) proved itself superior in "explanatory" power to age classes. This result is consistent with social theory since the FLC (family life cycle) should be a better reflection than age of the individual's social role.

Advantages of the family life cycle over age probably can be shown for many economic, social, political and psychological variables as well as for the few shown here. Of course, contrariwise, there are characteristics for which age is a better explanatory variable: mortality and morbidity come to mind immediately. Laws and contracts are often written in terms of age. But we believe that the life cycle should be adopted more widely as an independent variable to be used in place of or parallel to age.[6]

Households with small children represent particularly good markets for products such as prepared mixes, major appliances, and household waxes and cleaners, in addition to the more obvious goods such as

[3]*The Teen-Age Market* (New York: Modern Talking Picture Services, Inc., 1959).
[4]Johnson, p. 53.
[5]John B. Lansing and Leslie Kish, "Family Life Cycle as an Independent Variable," in Harper W. Boyd and Joseph W. Newman, eds., *Advertising Management: Selected Readings* (Homewood, Ill.: Richard D. Irwin, Inc., 1965), p. 196.
[6]Lansing and Kish, p. 203.

baby powder, cereals, and toys. Households with older children spend more on clothing — especially women's and girls' clothing.

Urbanization. In the NICB study families living in the urban fringe of cities spent more for food and cigarettes than those in other areas did. The city family spends more than its rural counterpart for goods and services, and more than twice as much on home operation and improvements. In general, the rural and small-town household accounts for a disproportionately small share of total expenditures; yet in certain product groups (gasoline and oil) its expenditures are more than the average.

Geographical Location. Most studies show regional differences in spending patterns. For example, market surveys show that the southern household (both metropolitan and nonmetropolitan) has less money to spend than households in other sections of the country have. Families in the northeast spend more for food than do people in other parts of the United States. Note in Figure 11.1 how brand preferences vary not only region by region but also city by city.

However, the importance of regional patterns can easily be overestimated. When they are analyzed in detail, we find that spending patterns are heavily influenced by characteristics such as urbanization, age, occupation, or race, rather than by the region itself. The northeast, for example, is much more urbanized than the south.

Race. Attention has been given during recent years to race as a market variable — particularly to the question of whether the Negro market is different. Bauer, Cunningham, and Wortzel have reviewed a large number of studies regarding Negro spending behavior to determine whether the Negro market is different from other lower-income,

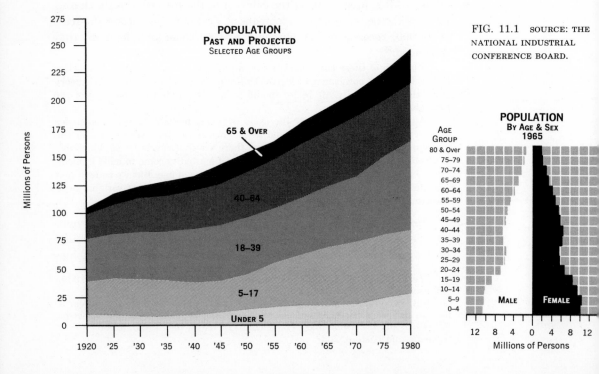

FIG. 11.1   SOURCE: THE NATIONAL INDUSTRIAL CONFERENCE BOARD.

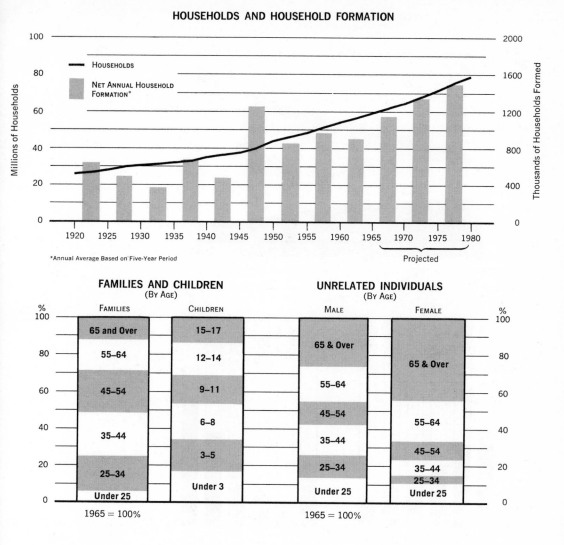

HOUSEHOLDS AND HOUSEHOLD FORMATION

*Annual Average Based on Five-Year Period

Projected

FAMILIES AND CHILDREN
(By Age)

UNRELATED INDIVIDUALS
(By Age)

1965 = 100%

1965 = 100%

FIG. 11.2 SOURCE: THE NATIONAL INDUSTRIAL CONFERENCE BOARD. lower-educated, and geographically concentrated groups[7] They have concluded that it is different. They found that certain products symbolize high status to the Negro. For example, Negro per capita consumption of Scotch is three times as high as that of whites, and there is evidence that it is regarded as a high-status drink. On the other hand, some products (like facial tissues) appeared to have no discernible symbolic value to the Negro.

They found that Negroes were split between "strivers" and the "nonstrivers." It is expected that a growing number of Negroes will become strivers as their expectations rise with regard to a fuller place in American life. The authors concluded that

> Compared with whites, Negroes show more concern, more anxiety, and more ambivalence. . . . What the women liked most (to a greater degree than white women) about shopping was getting things, and what they liked least was spending money.

[7]See Raymond A. Bauer, Scott M. Cunningham, and Lawrence H. Wortzel, "The Marketing Dilemma of Negroes," *Journal of Marketing*, 29 (July 1965), 1–6.

EDUCATIONAL ATTAINMENT
YEARS OF SCHOOL COMPLETED, PERSONS 25 AND OVER

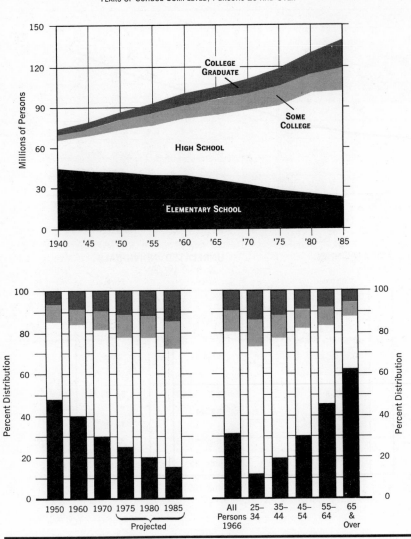

FIG. 11.3 SOURCE: THE NATIONAL INDUSTRIAL CONFERENCE BOARD.

CHANGING PROFILE OF INCOME DISTRIBUTION
ALL FIGURES IN 1965 DOLLARS

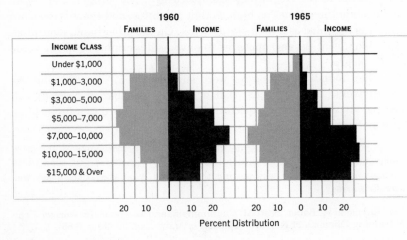

FIG. 11.4 SOURCE: THE NATIONAL INDUSTRIAL CONFERENCE BOARD.

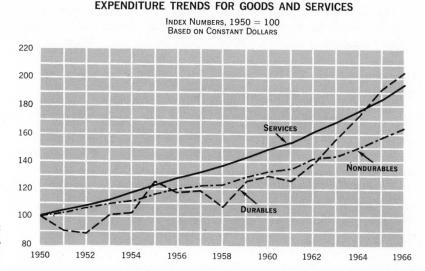

EXPENDITURE TRENDS FOR GOODS AND SERVICES

INDEX NUMBERS, 1950 = 100
BASED ON CONSTANT DOLLARS

SERVICES

NONDURABLES

DURABLES

FIG. 11.5 SOURCE: THE NATIONAL INDUSTRIAL CONFERENCE BOARD.

Sociological Factors. Advertisers and assorted marketers have for many years been interested in the idea of segmenting markets on the basis of social class. Some became disenchanted with social stratification as a useful guide in promotion when they ran into difficulty in applying it to specific problems. Others are enthusiastic. For example, Pierre Martineau says,

There is certainly a rough correlation between income and social class. But social class is a much richer dimension of meaning. There are so many facets of behavior which are explicable only on a basis of social class dynamics. For instance, an analysis of the purchase of household appliances in Chicago over a four-year period shows a very different picture by income and by class. . . .

Income analysis shows that the lowest income group represents an understandably smaller market, but nevertheless a market. Social-class analysis highlights a fundamental difference in attitude toward the home between the two lower classes. The Upper-Lower Class man sees his home as his castle, his anchor to the world, and he loads it down with hardware—solid heavy appliances—as his symbols of security. The Lower-Lower Class individual is far less interested in his castle and is more likely to spend his income for flashy clothes or an automobile.[8]

Social class appears to be more important in some markets than it is in others. The middle-class consumer is likely to buy a General Electric refrigerator at a discount house because he feels he is safe with such a dependable brand. He is not impressed with the advertising of the carriage-trade department store asking him to buy this refrigerator there. However, it is a different matter when he buys furniture or clothes. Brand names in these fields are not quite so well known as in appliances. Matters of taste and style are more important in these areas; so the consumer will probably go to a store in which he has confidence.

How, then, do we differentiate meaningfully among the various social classes so that we may learn their spending behavior? The six-class

[8]Pierre Martineau, "Social Classes and Spending Behavior," *Journal of Marketing*, (October 1958), 125–126.

system advocated by Paul Lunt and Lloyd Warner is one of the most widely accepted by marketing people: the Upper-Upper (old, rich, and socially established families); Lower-Upper (newly rich); Upper-Middle (mainly professionals and successful businessmen); Lower-Middle (mainly the white-collar salaried); Upper-Lower (wage earner and skilled worker); and Lower-Lower (unskilled labor).[9]

In studying the spending behavior of a probability sample of Chicago families (3,880 households), Martineau followed the Warner-Lunt approach in classifying respondents.[10] The social status of each household (Index of Status Characteristics) was computed numerically. The data were as follows: Occupation (1–7 categories); Sources of Income (1–7 types); and Housing Type (1–7 types). Occupation was weighted by 5, Sources of Income by 4, and Housing Type by 3. The sum of the individual's weighted scores was then converted to social class as follows:

ISC Scores	Social-Class Placement
0–11	Upper-Upper Class
12–21	Lower-Upper Class
22–37	Upper-Middle Class
38–51	Lower-Middle Class
52–66	Upper-Lower Class
67–84	Lower-Lower Class

Martineau emphasizes three conclusions:

1. There is a social-class system operative in metropolitan markets that can be isolated and described.

2. There are far-reaching psychological differences between the social classes.

3. Consumption patterns operate as prestige symbols to define class membership, which is a more significant determinant of economic behavior, than mere income is.

Coleman contends that "the role of social class has too often been misunderstood or oversimplified and that, if the concept is applied in a more sophisticated and realistic fashion, it will shed light on a great many problems to which, at first glance, it has not seemed particularly relevant.[11] He points out that the market for quality goods and brands is not necessarily drawn from the traditional "Quality Market" or Upper-Middle and Upper-Class people nor even from the highest income categories but rather from "those people within each social level who have the most discretionary income available for enjoying life's little extras above and beyond the requirements of their class." He

[9]Paul Lunt and Lloyd Warner, The Social Life of a Modern Community (New Haven, Conn.: Yale University Press, 1950); and W. Lloyd Warner, Marchia Meeker, and Kenneth Eells, Social Class in America (Chicago: Science Research Associates, 1949).
[10]Martineau, pp. 121–130.
[11]Richard P. Coleman, "Family Life Cycle as an Independent Variable," in Harper W. Boyd, Jr., and Joseph W. Newman, eds., Advertising Management (Homewood, Ill.: Richard D. Irwin, Inc., 1965), p. 205.

FIG. 11.6 *Appeal to the rapidly–growing do–it–yourself market.*
COURTESY STANLEY TOOLS.

points out that automobiles and color television sets are symbols, more of high status ("class within class") than symbols of higher status per se. Sometimes products thought to be status symbols (air conditioners in the South and the like) are bought on the basis of mere physical comfort rather than status.

Some of the difficulty in applying the social-class concept stems from the vagueness of the concept itself. Berelson and Steiner point out that "people are put into classes by other people in the society, but the determination is only seldom made individual, as is true, for example, in the case of purely moral judgments."[12] Instead, classifying judgments are typically based on conventional criteria that distinguish broad social groups (immigrants, the rich), holders of certain offices or positions (clergy, doctors), or members of organizations (college faculties, army officers). They state that the major criteria for social stratification are the following:

[12]Bernard Berelson and Gary A. Steiner, *Human Behavior* (New York: Harcourt, Brace & World, Inc., 1964), p. 454.

Authority

Power (political, economic, military)

Ownership of property, relation to the means of production, control over land (the feudal estates)

Income — amount, type, and sources

Consumption patterns and style of life

Occupation or skill and achievement in it

Education, learning, and wisdom

Divinity, "control" over the supernatural

Altruism, public service, and morality

Place in "high society," kinship connections, and ancestry

Associational ties and connections

Ethnic status, religion, and race

Which characteristics become the basis for social stratification depend on what is considered important by the stratifying society. The values most highly prized in the society are taken as the central bases of the system. If the society is ruled by a military class, the social classes will be based on military prowess; if by an educational elite, education becomes more important.

Cultural Factors. As marketers eye the rich untapped markets around the world and even groups within the United States such as Negroes or opera-goers, they try to reach particular cultural groups. It has become common to refer to international advertising as "cross-cultural" advertising.

Although social scientists and marketers agree that people are divided into various cultures and subcultures, they have had great difficulty in deciding just what constitutes a "culture." Two distinguished anthropologists, Kroeber and Kluckhohn, analyzed 164 definitions of culture and decided that they would forego the addition of the 165th definition.[13] However, they did decide that a culture is "a product, is historical, includes ideas, patterns and values, is selective, is learned, is based upon symbols, and is an abstraction from behavior and the products of behavior."

Most students of culture agree that it is one of the primary links between individuals. Some equate it with communication, believing that people who communicate with one another become members of the same culture. Edward T. Hall builds an interesting theory on this basis. He contends that culture is communication and as such consists of ten systems.[14] It thus "speaks" in ten different ways or ten "silent languages" that advertising people might use in communicating with various groups. He implies that someone interested in communication might categorize cultural groups on the basis of these "Primary Message Systems":

1. Interaction: writing, speaking, etc.
2. Association: gathering in groups, clubs, etc.

[13]Alfred L. Kroeber and Clyde Kluckhohn, "Culture: A Critical Review of Concepts and Definitions," *Papers of the Peabody Museum*, 47, no. la. 1952.
[14]Edward T. Hall, *The Silent Language* (New York: Fawcett Publications, Inc., 1961), chap. 3.

3. Subsistence: means by which an individual's livelihood is obtained.
4. Bisexuality: concepts of masculinity and femininity.
5. Territoriality: physical boundaries for work, play, etc.
6. Temporality: the life cycle.
7. Learning: adoption, innovation, etc.
8. Play: choice of leisure-time activities.
9. Defense: methods of defending self, body, etc.
10. Exploitation: new and improved ways of doing things.[15]

Hall contends that these ten message systems communicate at formal, informal, and technical levels.

For the marketer confused by the plethora of definitions and descriptions of culture, criteria based on communication promise the greatest help. He segments potential markets on the bases of factors that are meaningful in the context of marketing—communication factors. It is also apparent that cultural factors are related to buying habits, to consumer needs, and to the use of the communications media. As such they offer real promise as a means of segmenting markets.

Psychological Factors. Our behavior is oriented toward fulfilling various drives or needs. These motivating forces are related to both the direction and the intensity of our actions. Advertising and marketing people, as well as psychologists, have long recognized these facts. They also know that some people have stronger drives than others have, though basic drives exist in everyone. To what extent can this variation in drives be used to classify people?

At a meeting of the American Marketing Association, researcher Arthur Koponen reported on an experimental study of psychological response patterns among 5,000 families in his agency's consumer panel. The researchers used for this measurement a standard psychological test set up to measure responses to fifteen basic needs (heterosexual, aggression, achievement, dominance, exhibition, change, autonomy, dependence, endurance, analysis, assistance, association, self-depreciation, order, and compliance).

Dr. Koponen reported that men who bought a certain product, for example, were above average in needs such as heterosexuality, aggression, achievement, and dominance, but significantly below average in compliance, order, self-depreciation, and association. The implication is that the best market for the product was among those who are not conservative or timid. He also found users of a new product high in dominance and achievement, users of an older product higher in aggression and autonomy (needing independence and resenting authority). He found, too, that responses varied according to age, sex, income, education, city size, and religion. However, he cautioned the audience on interpreting his results too literally, a point emphasized by an experiment conducted just before this by a large agency that had a major drug account. Researchers in this agency hypothesized that there must be certain psychological differences between heavy users and nonusers of the product. However, even after trying a number of psychological tests, the agency did not find any differences that appeared very promising for predicting product usage.

[15]Hall, pp. 45–62.

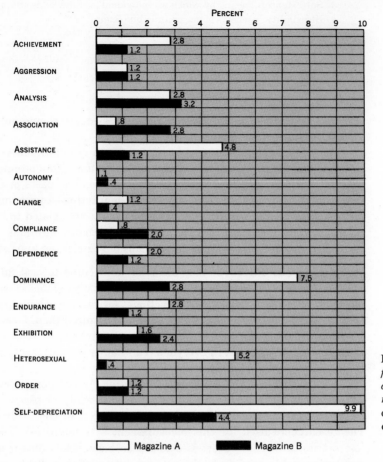

MAGAZINES
(MALE)

PERCENT

	0 1 2 3 4 5 6 7 8 9 10
ACHIEVEMENT	A: 2.8 / B: 1.2
AGGRESSION	A: 1.2 / B: 1.2
ANALYSIS	A: 2.8 / B: 3.2
ASSOCIATION	A: .8 / B: 2.8
ASSISTANCE	A: 4.8 / B: 1.2
AUTONOMY	A: .1 / B: .4
CHANGE	A: 1.2 / B: .4
COMPLIANCE	A: .8 / B: 2.0
DEPENDENCE	A: 2.0 / B: 1.2
DOMINANCE	A: 7.5 / B: 2.8
ENDURANCE	A: 2.8 / B: 1.2
EXHIBITION	A: 1.6 / B: 2.4
HETEROSEXUAL	A: 5.2 / B: .4
ORDER	A: 1.2 / B: 1.2
SELF-DEPRECIATION	A: 9.9 / B: 4.4

☐ Magazine A   ■ Magazine B

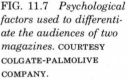

FIG. 11.7 *Psychological factors used to differentiate the audiences of two magazines.* COURTESY COLGATE-PALMOLIVE COMPANY.

Grey Advertising's *Grey Matter* calls the use of psychological factors "psychographic market segmentation" and points out that it "breaks across the boundaries of these traditional market sectors and discovers a homogeneity of linkage among people who have been considered as belonging to diverse markets."[16] For example, a family in its middle forties and of middle-income status may have the same outlook and youthful attitude that a young newly formed family unit has. What might appear to be a small unimportant market might therefore become a large one. The marketers of Maclean's toothpaste reasoned that because 70 percent of the population is concerned with tooth decay, it would be sound strategy to aim at that part of the remaining 30 percent of people who are psychologically or emotionally more concerned with "whiteness" or the cosmetic effect of brushing their teeth than with cavities (see Figure 3.8). The success of this strategy has been, according to *Grey Matter*, "beyond their expectations."

In *The Lonely Crowd*, David Riesman suggested that people should be divided on the basis of "tradition-directed," "inner-directed" and

[16]*Grey Matter*, November 1965 (New York: Grey Advertising Agency).

"other-directed."[17] Subsequent studies have shown that these classifications have wider application than was generally realized. For example, an experimental study by Harold H. Kassarjian indicates that inner- and other-directed subjects exhibited significantly different reactions to specially designed advertisements. He concludes that a social character typology such as the one suggested by Riesman "may well be a meaningful variable in communication and persuasion processes."[18]

Seymour Banks has suggested the following psychological variables that should be considered by researchers: intelligence, verbal and symbolic facility, extroversion-introversion, acceptance or rejection of their role in life, and acceptance of impersonal versus personal communication. He further suggested these sociological variables: status and responsibility within the family; position within a communication network; self-evaluation of class status; and acceptance or rejection of personal and impersonal authority.[19]

Usage of the Product. Another approach is to classify markets according to the extent of product usage. Thus advertising may be directed to the heavy users of a product on the basis that they represent the people who are already presold on the product. According to Norton Garfinkle, his firm's studies confirm that one third of the households that can be identified as heavy users of a specific product category frequently account for two thirds of the total product consumption. In categories such as car rental, air travel, hair coloring, and dog food, less than 20 percent of the population accounts for more than 80 percent of usage. Even in such widely used products as soft drinks and coffee, 50 percent of the households account for almost 90 percent of usage.[20]

SOURCES OF MARKET DATA

Much information about market groups used for forecasting comes from studies of buying behavior. The two best known and most useful are the retail store audit (best exemplified by the work of the A. C. Nielsen Company), and the various consumer panel studies, many of which are supported by local advertising media.

Retail Store Audit. The oldest and most successful of the marketing organizations, the Nielsen Company, was started in 1923 as an engineering consulting firm. In the late 1920s the company began to make market studies of industrial goods for its engineering clients. In 1933 it launched its *Drug Index*, consisting of data collected from a panel of drugstores that were representative of the nation's drugstores as a whole. A year later the service was extended to food products and

[17]See David Riesman, *The Lonely Crowd* (New Haven, Conn.: Yale University Press, 1950).

[18]Harold H. Kassarjian, "Social Character and Differential Preference for Mass Communication," *Journal of Marketing Research*, May 1965, pp. 146–153.

[19]Seymour Banks, *"Where ARF Ought to Go from Here,"* address given at the Third Annual Conference of the Advertising Research Foundation, New York City, November 14, 1957.

[20]Norton Garfinkle, "How Marketing Data Can Identify Your Target Audience," speech before Eastern Annual Conference of the American Association of Advertising Agencies, October 25, 1966.

grocery stores. By 1967 Nielsen was auditing 1,600 grocery stores servicing 500,000 families, and 700 drugstores servicing 750,000 families. Its clients included most of the important food, drug, soap, and toiletries companies in the nation, some of which were paying over $500,000 a year for this service.

Mr. Nielsen emphasizes the usefulness of his firm's data by recounting how a number of marketing problems were once proposed to executives in several large corporations. Each executive was asked to tell how he would resolve these problems without benefit of research. The answers given by the executives were later compared with facts revealed by comprehensive marketing research. The executives were right in only 58 percent of their decisions.

Like a large manufacturing organization that divides the United States into sales districts, Nielsen divides it into nine districts: New England, Metropolitan New York, Middle Atlantic, East Central, Metropolitan Chicago, West Central, Southeast, Southwest, and Pacific. Grocery stores included in the *Food and Drug Indexes* fall into three ownership classifications: corporate chain (every major chain in the country except A & P is included), voluntary chain, and independent.

A store audit makes it possible for a manufacturer to know fairly accurately and at regular periods how consumers are reacting to his marketing and promotional efforts and to his various brands. Because most manufacturers sell to chains and to wholesalers, they have no way of knowing from their own records how goods are moving into consumers' hands. Inventories in chain and wholesale warehouses and in stores fluctuate so widely from month to month that the amount of orders received in any given month may vary greatly from the amount of goods moved into the hands of consumers across retail counters. In addition to providing continuous, bimonthly data on the movement of food products to consumers, the *Nielsen Food Index* also provides continuous information on the following:

1. The movement of goods *into* retail stores.
2. Retail inventories and the number of days' supply on hand.
3. Retailers who are out of stock (the percentage of retailers who regularly stock a product but do not have it in stock at the time the bimonthly audit is made).
4. Special sales prices.
5. Dealers' use of displays.
6. Premium use.
7. Redemption of coupons.
8. Response to trade deals.
9. Cooperative advertising.

Special studies may also be made of such factors as stock location, shelf position, and shelf facings (number of items visible at a given time).

The data compiled by Nielsen permit an advertiser to

1. Distribute advertising and merchandising effort correctly among territories, urban vs. rural markets, seasons, etc.
2. Separate profitable copy, media, displays, and so forth from the unprofitable.

3. Detect marketing weaknesses and keep track of the results of efforts to correct them.
4. Provide advance warnings of sales declines, competitive inroads, and need for a change in product or package.
5. Reveal causes of sales declines and point way to remedies.
6. Detect gain or losses in dealer good will.
7. Determine the most profitable price levels.
8. Predict results of proposed promotional expenditures.
9. Reduce risk in marketing new products.
10. Keep track of what the competition is doing.

Certain other research firms and some of the large advertising agencies also maintain panels of retail stores and make regular audits of the movement of products by brand.

National Consumer Panels. Another approach is to locate potential markets by collecting data directly from consumers. The dominant organization in this area is the Market Research Corporation of America, which maintains a continuing panel of approximately 7,000 households scattered around the United States. These are selected on the basis of an area probability sample (modified to compensate for the fact that certain households that appear in the mathematical sample refuse to keep a diary of their purchases). Ideally, each household fills in its diary (including price and package size) so that purchases by all members of the family are included. Diaries are mailed back to MRCA every week with a Sunday night or Monday morning postmark.

Within the panel families keep daily diaries mailed out every night, reporting their purchase of food, household supplies, drugs, and many other products. Each member of the household signs the weekly diaries, and is paid in "points" redeemable for catalogue merchandise. According to Martin Mayer, the dropout rate for panel members is roughly 1,100 families a year, and replacements are chosen from the same neighborhood.[21] To help retain the sample, MRCA increases the payment per diary for every year the family is in the panel. Payment begins immediately when a family joins the panel, but data from that family are not included in the totals until thirteen weekly diaries have been filled in.

The panel, although not as objective as the dealer audit, has the advantage of providing data on who buys what. Subscribers can tell what members of the family bought each brand, and how frequently they bought it, and can study buying by age, size of family, income, and other factors.

Local Consumer Studies. In several areas, newspapers collect data on consumer buying. A few, such as the *Chicago Tribune*, the *Pittsburgh Press*, and the *Cleveland Press*, have occasionally operated panels much like that of MRCA in their local area for continuous buying data.

Much more common is the type of study pioneered by the *Milwaukee Journal*—a consumer analysis. In this method a questionnaire is mailed to a sample of households in the area. Included are questions on

[21]Martin Mayer, *Madison Avenue, U.S.A.* (New York: Harper & Row, Publishers, 1958), pp. 229–232.

general buying ("Do you buy paste floor wax?") and specific buying ("What brand did you buy last?"). Questionnaires are completed and returned in person to the newspaper, where they are checked by auditors. The respondent is given a grocery bag full of food products at the end of the interview. The *Milwaukee Journal* and twenty other newspapers have now joined forces, using the same research methods, so that advertisers may have comparable data from each of these marketing areas. Summaries show the number of families using a particular product, the number of brands in the area, relative rating of brands, and number of users by income groups.

Some newspapers collect local market information through a home inventory or "pantry count." Interviewers, with the cooperation of the housewife, check the storage areas and record what brands are stocked there. Data may be tabulated by income, occupation, age of housewife, and so on. However, there is no information on frequency of purchase, so that the dollar volume for the various market groups cannot be estimated as it can with the retail audit or the consumer panel.

Food product companies sometimes test the reaction of consumers to their products by leaving two versions of particular products with a housewife and asking her to use as much of either or both, as she prefers. A measurement of how much has been used of each will provide a measure of her comparative preference. This is one of many ways of observing behavior directly when variables are at least partially controlled.

MATHEMATICAL MEASURES OF MARKET POTENTIALS

Suppose we know that a product sells well in Chicago and New York and not so well in Minneapolis or San Francisco. Or we find out that the market lies more in the upper income groups than in the lower and lower-middle groups. In both cases, copy approach, budgeting, media, and other plan elements would be much more accurate if we knew *how much greater* the potential was in Chicago than in Minneapolis, and in the upper- than the lower-income groups.

It is possible to make quantitative comparisons of the potential of various markets. Such comparisons are based on the concept that there is a relation between a known variable (such as population) and one that is unknown (sales of your product, for example). In other words, we assume that if one city has twice the population of another, the sales potential is twice as great. We may be basing our idea of this relation between population and sales on common sense or some empirical data we have collected—in either event, the approach is the same.

Single-factor indexes are the simplest kinds of measures. They are based on only *one* factor and are measures of general buying power rather than the special characteristics of a product.

One of the pioneers in developing today's sophisticated buying power indexes was L. D. H. Weld, for many years research director of McCann-Erickson advertising agency. He based the agency's early buying-power index on these factors: (1) number of income-tax returns (to indicate the level of affluence among consumers); (2) number of domestic lighting customers (to indicate level of urbanization); (3) bank deposits (an indication of wealth); and (4) combined circulation of four leading magazines (a measure of people's general awareness of their surroundings).

One of the most widely used general buying power indexes is computed and published annually by *Sales Management* in *Survey of Buying Power*. In the 1968 edition, New York, the nation's largest market, had an index of 4.5918. San Francisco had 0.5468, and Madison, Wisconsin, 0.0909. In each case the index is given as a percent of the total United States potential. In other words, if we have a nationally distributed product, we might spend 5.0633 percent of our national advertising budget in the New York market five-county area, because that represents its share of the national potential.

This index is based on the number of people in a market area, their buying habits as revealed in total retail sales, and the amount of money they have to spend. These are weighted in this manner: an area's percent of the United States population $\times$ 2; the area's percent of total United States retail sales $\times$ 3; and its percent of the total United States buying income $\times$ 5. Because the weighting factors total 10, the sum is divided by that number.

We may, however, be marketing a product that does not follow general buying trends. We find that sales are high in certain areas where the index shows they should be low. There are two possibilities: either our sales and advertising effort is particularly strong in those areas, or other variables not included in the general index are closely related to our sales. The manufacturer of a cosmetic found his sales were especially high in certain areas where the potential indicated they should be low. On investigation he found that the product was preferred by certain racial groups. When the racial mix was considered as a factor in computing the index, the index succeeded in predicting sales potential.

The construction of a buying-power index is a complex affair and should be undertaken only by one who understands what can and cannot be done with statistics. However, once an index is constructed and has been proved a satisfactory predictor of sales potential, it can be used by any advertising practitioner. It can be used to set sales quotas for a territory and the promotion budget for one territory as compared with another. It can be used to direct sales effort and executive attention to the right places at the right time.

SALES FORECASTING

Business executives are understandably concerned about what their firm's sales are likely to be in the coming years. Knowledge of the market potential does not tell them what share of the market they will actually get. The preparation of sales forecasts is usually—but not always—the job of the company's marketing research department.

We should distinguish first of all between a general business forecast and a sales forecast. A general business forecast is usually the task of an economist and is an attempt to estimate broad trends in general business activity. On the other hand, a sales forecast involves only the expected sales of a single firm. The general business forecast should be a guide in the preparation of the sales forecast. Actually, it is more difficult to make a reliable general business forecast, and would-be sales forecasters should not be discouraged by the poor batting average of economists in predicting the ups and downs in business activity. The sales forecaster works within a narrower field than that of the economist. He is concerned only with the expectations of a single industry and then the expectations of a single, individual company within that industry; the economist has to worry about the entire economy — the sum of all the industries, some of which may be on the upgrade, others on the downgrade.

Researcher Richard Crisp recommends that the sales forecaster follow these six steps:

1. Determine the purposes for which the forecast is intended.
2. Subdivide the forecasting task.
3. Prepare a preliminary sales forecast.
4. Relate the forecast to advertising, selling, and promotional plans.
5. Review competitive activities and trends.
6. Review and revise in the light of experience.[22]

The sales forecast becomes valuable only after something is done about it. It will not make itself come true. One of the best ways of making sure that it is implemented is to spell out as specifically as possible in the marketing plan what is to be done — and when — once the sales forecast has been accepted as valid.

According to Brink and Kelley, there are five major elements to be considered in making a sales forecast: (1) past patterns of the company's sales and its sales goals; (2) sales of competitors and their plans and intentions; (3) level and trend of consumer spending, in total and for the products; (4) general trend of the industry; and (5) general economic conditions — past, present, and future.[23]

SUMMARY

The purpose of this chapter has been to explore the methods of differentiating among significant market groups, to analyze the methods of gathering data on them, and to estimate their relative sales potential.

The four principal criteria for differentiating among classes are demographic, sociological, cultural, and psychological. The first of these has been widely used for many years, although studies like the excellent one by NICB have shed new light on it. We still have much to learn about sociological, cultural and psychological criteria, although all show promise of indicating meaningful differences among the consuming public.

Many marketers attempt to put the market potential in mathematical terms in order to compare one area or market group with another.

[22]Richard D. Crisp, *Marketing Research* (New York: McGraw-Hill, Inc., 1957), pp. 497–502.
[23]Edward L. Brink and William T. Kelley, *The Management of Promotion* (Englewood Cliffs, N.J.: Prentice-Hall, Inc., 1963) pp. 219–221.

Another extremely valuable tool in the preparation of the marketing plan is the sales forecast.

QUESTIONS FOR DISCUSSION

1. Why is it more useful for an advertiser to direct his message to members of a specific market instead of to heterogeneous masses?
2. How can trends in income or education influence the selection of magazines or television programs by an advertiser?
3. How can cultural factors be used to define markets in the international advertising and promotion field?
4. What is the advantage of using social class rather than income or education to define markets? What are the disadvantages?
5. Why is there an increased interest in the use of psychological criteria for market segmentation?
6. Clip a current advertisement whose primary appeal is to each of the demographic groups discussed in this chapter.

SUGGESTED READINGS

Berelson, Bernard, and Gary A. Steiner, *Human Behavior*. New York: Harcourt, Brace & World, Inc., 1964. Chapters 11, 15–16.

Bliss, Perry, ed., *Marketing and the Behavioral Sciences,* rev. ed., Boston: Allyn and Bacon, Inc., 1968. Parts IV and V.

Boyd, Harper W., Jr., and Joseph W. Newman, eds., *Advertising Management: Selected Readings.* Homewood, Ill.: Richard D. Irwin, Inc., 1965. Part III.

Brink, Edward L., and William T. Kelley, *The Management of Promotion.* Englewood Cliffs, N.J.: Prentice-Hall, Inc., 1963. Chapters 10–12.

Crisp, Richard D., *Marketing Research,* New York: McGraw-Hill, Inc., 1957.

Hall, Edward T., *The Silent Language.* New York: Fawcett Publications, Inc., 1961.

Martineau, Pierre, "Social Classes and Spending Behavior," *Journal of Marketing,* October 1958.

Sandage, C. H., and Vernon Fryburger, *Advertising Theory and Practice,* 7th ed. Homewood, Ill.: Richard D. Irwin, Inc., 1968. Chapter 9.

Sherif, Muzafer and Carolyn Sherif, *Reference Groups.* New York: Harper & Row, Publishers, 1964.

Wolfe, Harry D., *Market Forecasting.* New York: Holt, Rinehart and Winston, Inc., 1966.

Zaltman, Gerald, *Marketing: Contributions from the Behavioral Sciences.* New York: Harcourt, Brace & World, Inc., 1965.

12 | Understanding Consumer Behavior

We are now ready to discuss some of the most intriguing questions in the entire field of persuasive communications—those having to do with consumer motivation. Among them are such questions as "What makes people buy?" "What makes people change their attitude toward a product?" "What makes people understand some advertising messages and not others?" In this and the following chapter we shall review some of the findings of behavioral scientists that have particular relevance to problems of promotion and examine some of the methods by which such information is collected.

WHAT MAKES PEOPLE BUY?

Not too many years ago a businessman assumed that he knew what the consumer wanted and what made him buy. The consumer would buy any good product that he really needed and could afford, and could be persuaded to buy others that he did not need but that satisfied certain inner cravings. The role of advertising was believed to be a very simple one. If advertising appealed to the right motives, people would buy the advertised product.

New and better methods of behavioral science research make the businessman suspect that his earlier ideas were only partly right. The consumer has often been shown to be a poor judge of his actual reasons

may be latent and may be stimulated by advertising, promotion, or even unplanned word-of-mouth communication. These forces are what we call motives—a term applied to cover the wide spectrum of wishes, desires, needs, and drives. According to Berelson and Steiner, a motive is "an inner state that energizes, activates or moves (hence 'motivation'), and that directs or channels behavior toward goals."[2]

Characteristics of Motives. Psychologists David Krech and Richard Crutchfield emphasize the dynamics of consumer motivation.

In any account of the behavior of people we start our description with reference to some kind of active, driving force: the individual seeks, the individual wants, the individual fears. In addition, we specify an object or condition toward which that force is directed: he seeks wealth, he wants peace, he fears illness. The study of the relationships between these two variables, the driving force and the object or condition toward which that driving force is directed, is the study of the dynamics of behavior, or motivation. And we shall find that the basic principles of dynamics accounting for the behavior of joining a church, going to war, choosing a mate, etc., are the same no matter how simple or complex the activity.[3]

Most social scientists agree that there is no such thing as a single motive for any conscious action we take. Consider some of our simplest actions—deciding to get up in the morning, or *not* to get up, wearing a coat, or *not* wearing a coat. Even these actions, simple as they may seem, are prompted by an interaction of several motives. Furthermore, motives can exist side by side or can block each other. For example, when you become excessively hungry or angry, the normal functioning of certain motives will be blocked out until the hunger or anger is satisfied.

Motives are not stable. What you feel like doing today may not appeal to you tomorrow. Circumstances may change, but it will more likely be your mood (for no easily understood reason). It is difficult to explain moods of depression or extreme happiness, but we know that when a person is exuberant even basic motives function differently from the way they do when he is depressed. When he is prosperous he reacts differently from when he is down on his luck. Only in a general sense is there any consistency of motives.

So much for the negative side of the picture. Obviously, advertising people cannot give up merely because the job is a difficult one. Let us see how advertising can cope with this problem.

Classification of Motives. A few years ago lists of motives were extremely popular, but the uncritical acceptance of such lists in some quarters led to a reappraisal of their role in motivation. It is now recognized by most communication researchers that such lists are useful only when they are related to communication objectives. They are much more relevant in some promotional strategies than in others. One aid in sorting them out for promotional purposes is to make use of certain classifications used by behavioral scientists. The following are some of the more useful classifications:

[2]Bernard Berelson and Gary A. Steiner, *Human Behavior: An Inventory of Scientific Findings* (New York: Harcourt, Brace & World, Inc., 1964), p. 240.
[3]David Krech and Richard Crutchfield, *Theory and Problems of Social Psychology* (New York: McGraw-Hill, Inc., 1948), p. 29.

Physiological versus Secondary Motives.   Most psychologists emphasize the difference between motives that are *physiological* or *basic* (stemming directly from man's physical needs and common to everyone) and those that are *secondary* or *acquired* (varying from one society to another).

The satisfaction of physiological motives is essential to a person's well-being. He cannot survive long without satisfying such physiological motives as hunger, thirst, sex, avoidance of pain, elimination, and so on. Consequently, they are also called *primary* motives.

As Berelson and Steiner point out, physiological motives are usually classified according to some such scheme as the following:

1. Positive or supply motives: These result from deficiency and produce seeking and consumption of needed substance (hunger, thirst).
2. Negative or avoidance motives: These result from the presence of harmful or potentially harmful stimulation and produce flight or avoidance (pain or fear).
3. Species-maintaining motives: These result from the nature of the reproductive system and produce mating, children, and nurturant behavior (sex).[4]

This classification is based on biological function rather than on any goal of the individual. Other lists emphasize the goal.

It is evident that all of these motives stem from innately determined physical needs. However, education and environment may have a great deal of influence on their importance and how they are satisfied. Some may be satisfied by a physical act, such as eating, but others may require some ritual that transcends biological function, such as a marriage ceremony or a religious rite. It should be mentioned that the name is perhaps misleading in that these are not always primary. Gratification is frequently postponed or renounced entirely in favor of some secondary or social motive. People often postpone food or sex as a result of various social influences.

Secondary motives are also known as acquired, learned, social, and psychogenic. These are even more difficult to classify than physiological motives, because they vary from one culture to another. In other words, an exhibitionistic attitude may be an important motive in one culture

[4]Berelson and Steiner, pp. 241–242.

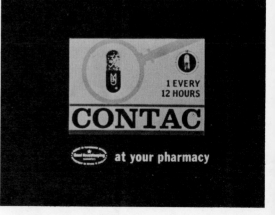

FIG. 12.2 *Ingenious use of humor in these television commercials to appeal to man's desire to avoid colds.* © MENLEY & JAMES LABORATORIES, LTD. 1968.

You think a dollar isn't what it used to be?

It'll still buy about 17 servings of Campbell's Vegetable Soup.

Less than 6¢ a serving and M'm! M'm! Good!

FIG. 12.3 *Effective appeal to secondary motives.* CLIENT: CAMPBELL'S SOUP COMPANY; AGENCY: BATTEN, BARTON, DURSTINE & OSBORN, INC.

but of little importance in another or even something to avoid. Consequently, the lists of secondary motives vary according to the purpose of the classifier. One psychologist reduces them to four types: security, recognition, response from others, and new experience. Most lists tend to be somewhat longer. One which is widely accepted lists twenty-eight secondary "needs":[5]

Acquisition	Inviolacy	Aggression
Conservance	Infavoidance	Abasement
Order	Defendance	Blamavoidance
Retention	Counteraction	Affiliation
Construction	Dominance	Rejection
Superiority	Deference	Nurturance
Achievement	Similance	Succorance
Recognition	Autonomy	Play
Exhibition	Contrarience	Cognizance
		Exposition

[5]See Berelson and Steiner, pp. 256–258, for discussion of this and other lists.

FIG. 12.4 *Television commercial which appeals to man's desire for popularity.* CLIENT: BRISTOL-MYERS PRODUCTS; AGENCY: OGILVY & MATHER.

There has been much discussion among behavioral scientists on the relation between physiological and secondary motives. They are understandably curious to know why people will strive so hard to acquire possessions or achieve situations that are not essential to their well-being and often actually harmful. Some persons have speculated that the secondary motives, important as they are, stem perhaps from the physiological motives.

George Horsley Smith makes a useful distinction among motives according to the levels of awareness at which they act.[6] At the first level are motives that the consumer is ready and willing to discuss (preference for a cake mix because it is more economical). At the second level are motives that people attempt to conceal and rarely discuss (desire to impress your neighbor with a bigger automobile). Pierre Martineau emphasizes the second level when he says, "Within every individual is that private conscious world where he spends 75 percent of his mental time but which he almost never reveals to anyone else."[7] At the third level are motives that are not discussed at all and that would, in fact, disturb the people involved if they realized they existed (some common colds may originate in the need for attention or in the loss of security). Psychologists agree that much of what we do is motivated by our subconscious.

Controllable versus Uncontrollable. The advertising man is interested primarily in the motives to which he can appeal. Many motives that influence people are so complex that advertising people can do little to cope with them. Martineau points out that some cigarette research reveals that masochistic tendencies (deliberate hurting of

[6]George Horsley Smith, *Motivation Research in Advertising and Marketing* (New York: McGraw-Hill, Inc., 1959), chap. 2.
[7]Pierre Martineau, *Motivation in Advertising* (New York: McGraw-Hill, Inc., 1957), p. 34.

oneself) are important motives in smoking. Whether this is true or false is not particularly important to the advertisers because there is little they can do about it. On the other hand, if taste is an important motive in buying cigarettes, we may well want to appeal to it in our advertising.

Rational versus Irrational. Advertisers once believed that most buying was a logical, rational process and that every advertisement should supply the "reason-why." There has been a rather consistent trend away from this in the last decade or so. We have seen some of our most successful advertisers emphasizing apparently rational appeals while really expecting the purchase to be made for irrational or emotional reasons. Martineau reports on a study of Camel cigarettes taken at the time its advertising was emphasizing the "mildness" of the product. Research indicated that few really believed Camels were mild. They were universally considered to be one of the strongest cigarettes.

FIG. 12.5 *Advertisement with a strong emotional tone.* COURTESY DE BEERS CONSOLIDATED MINES, LTD., AND N. W. AYER & SON.

At the same time, the message that the advertising actually communicated was that Camel was the brand for rugged masculinity, particularly directed at the mass-audience male.

Cadillac advertisements are good examples of combining irrational and rational appeals—offering the buyer a chance to rationalize a purchase he wants (emotionally) to make. The copywriters, according to the head of the agency which has long had the account, attempt to combine the dream and some rationality in each Cadillac ad. They utilize the symbols of success, but also provide the buyer with several practical reasons for buying the car. The owner can enjoy his dream, perhaps at the subconscious level, yet talk knowingly about safety of construction or high trade-in value.

Need versus Wants. A useful distinction can be made between what we need and what we want. Our needs are relatively easy to satisfy, but our wants can be stimulated by advertising. For example, our need for transportation can be satisfied just as well by a 1950 automobile in good running order as by the latest model. However, our wants lead us to trade in our old model and buy a new one. Our wants, directly or indirectly, shape all our behavior. Most acts involve the satisfaction of several wants at once, so that there is multiple motivation in most buying decisions. Psychologists have found that a buyer's initial purchase may depend on how well he thinks a certain product will satisfy his wants, and his loyalty to the brand will depend on how well he thinks the product really satisfies them.

Primary versus Selective. Marketers frequently distinguish between primary motives (which lead one to buy a generic product) and selective motives (which lead him to prefer one brand or type compared with another). For example, when you plan a campaign to sell automatic dishwashers as a type of product (as opposed to doing the dishes by hand), it is primary advertising. On the other hand, when your objective is to show that your brand is superior to your competition, it is selective.

LEARNING THEORIES

Many psychologists believe that we can better understand how people are motivated if we see how they learn to adopt objects and ideas. As pointed out earlier in the chapter, learning theories tend to be in line with the older ideas of behaviorism.

Learning theories maintain that in order to learn you must want something (be motivated), do something (respond), sense relevant cues, and be rewarded (have your drive reduced).[8] When you buy a product for which you have some drive, you satisfy that drive and are thus rewarded. The cue that signifies the reward may come in the form of an advertisement, a package, a sound on the radio, a sign indicating a price reduction, or any of various forms. Stimuli also serve as cues. Therefore some stimuli can serve both as drives and as cues. For exam-

[8]See Ernest E. Hilgard, *Theories of Learning,* 2d ed. (New York: Appleton-Century-Crofts, 1956); and Neal E. Miller and John Dollard, *Social Learning and Imitation* (New Haven, Conn.: Yale University Press, 1941; paperback, 1962), for explanations of learning theories.

ple, hunger as a drive motivates you to search out food. However, you may also have a hunger for a particular kind of food (for sweets or Italian food); then the kind of food you want causes you to respond by searching out candy or spaghetti.

Reward or reinforcement is a result of the satisfaction of a particular drive. When, for example, you find that a particular brand of product satisfies your drive, you will probably continue to make the same response each time you experience that particular drive. Thus the product becomes a *goal-object*. By the same token, you may learn that a particular brand does not satisfy your need as quickly; you will therefore probably avoid that product. On the basis of what you have learned, you may build up a hierarchy of responses. For example, you may consider two brands of soap almost equal in satisfying your drive; in this event you will be quite willing to substitute one for the other if the second happens to be slightly less expensive. On the other hand, you may have a strong preference for one on the basis of your past experience.

Learning is of two basic types: cognitive and affective. When you perceive or become aware of a stimulus (for example, a television commercial), cognitive learning is taking place. Affective learning, on the other hand, involves your liking a product or idea. Obviously this too is important in any persuasive communications such as advertising.

It should be apparent from this brief explanation of learning theories that they provide a rich basis for hypotheses concerning consumer behavior.

PSYCHOANALYSIS

Psychoanalysis involves so complex a body of theory that it is extremely dangerous to attempt to cover it in a few paragraphs. Yet it is so important in modern advertising—at least as a basis for hypotheses—that we cannot ignore it. Psychoanalysis comes from the clinic, not the advertising or even the social science laboratory. The Freudian sees a personality as the outcome of conflict. The superficial aspect is one of good adaptation, whereas a hidden aspect has a much less complete adjustment to the demands of real life. The consumer is seen as knowing himself only partly—and rather darkly at that. For some aspects of his own personality, the individual has ready opinions and definitions. Others can be evoked only by intensive interviewing. There are still other aspects that cannot be stated at all, but must be inferred by the observer.

How valuable is the psychoanalytic approach in understanding motivation? Psychologist John Dollard concludes:

For the moment we regard it [psychoanalysis] as a body of valuable hypotheses, intensely stimulating, and presenting a picture of man's nature which corresponds best to man as known to his secret self and to the artist. Freudian psychology does not pretend to be a test and therefore cannot be immediately accepted or rejected on the ground of method. It is steadily seeping into psychological thought and practice, and occupying the vacuum which has existed in place of a general theory of personality. We welcome it in our need as a brilliant innovation, but at the same time insist that it cannot be allowed the free circulation permitted to scientific ideas until it has passed scientific tests. Without doubt the adequate testing-out of Freud's work will take at least several generations.[9]

Such researchers as Ernest Dichter and Pierre Martineau have emphasized the role of man's secret self in motivating him to act.[10] In general the area of research known as "motivation research" stresses this phase of man's behavior.

CONSUMER PURCHASING PATTERNS

Let us next examine what people do. This field is obviously easier to observe and measure than the one we have been discussing. In this section we shall examine some of the areas of consumer purchasing that are of special interest to advertising and marketing executives.

Products and Services People Buy. In most studies of purchasing patterns one of the prime objectives is to find out what products and brands people are buying. If, for example, you manufacture toothpaste, you will want to know whether most people buy paste or powder, whether a sizable percentage use soda or salt as substitutes, what sizes they buy, and, of course, what are the relative standings of the various brands.

Until recent years automobile manufacturers made major model changes only once every three years. Then they experimented with a two-year cycle and found that more rapid changes stimulated sales substantially even when the changes caused an increase in the price. This inevitably led many to experiment with the idea of a major model change every year. Some manufacturers accepted the idea, some did not.

The acceptance by the public of "instant" food products, of frozen specialty foods, of aerosol containers for a variety of products, of antienzymes and faster acting drugs had an immediate and lasting effect on the marketing and advertising of many established products.

A certain food product suffered a declining sales trend, owing largely to the introduction and aggressive promotion of a new product in the same field. The new product had three demonstrable advantages and was rapidly accepted by the consumer. For seven years there was little change in the *total* market for the product; so the first brand suffered serious declines in its share of the market as well as its sales volume. Unfortunately, the maker did not know that his share was declining and took no corrective advertising or other marketing action.

Some researchers found that Drano, which clears clogged drains, also annihilates bacteria in kitchen sink drains. Before this new use was emphasized in advertising, consumer researchers found out that many women bought a special product to keep their sinks sanitary as well as sparkling. Consequently, when Drano entered this field the manufacturers knew there was a profitable market ready to be tapped.

[9]John Dollard, "The Motivation Problem Seen from the Viewpoint of Campus and Clinic," paper delivered at the Eastern Annual Conference, American Association of Advertising Agencies, October 19, 1955.
[10]See Ernest Dichter, *Handbook of Consumer Motivation* (New York: McGraw-Hill, Inc., 1964) for an extensive summary of buying attitudes and behavior based on psychoanalysis.

Most researchers agree that there is something called brand loyalty, but they have trouble agreeing on a definition or on its exact causes. In one study Tucker arbitrarily defined it as three successive choices of the same brand.[11] He concluded that "1. Some consumers will become brand loyal even when there is no discriminable difference between brands other than the brand itself. 2. The brand loyalty established under such conditions is not trivial although it may be based on what are apparently trivial and superficial differences." Kuehn found that

    a. The probability of a consumer's buying the same brand on two consecutive purchases of orange juice decreases exponentially with an increase in time between these purchases.

    b. Consumers buying frozen orange juice with greatest frequency have the highest probability of continuing to buy the same brand.

    c. The probability of a consumer's buying a particular brand on the fifth trial in a purchase sequence decreases exponentially with the recency of the last purchase of the brand.[12]

When People Buy. Usage during seasons of the year, days of the week, and even hours of the day, should be studied by the advertiser. Some products have pronounced seasonal patterns. The use of fuel oil is affected by temperature, and the more northerly the market the longer and more profitable is the season. Conversely, the sales of soft drinks improve as the weather becomes warmer. Sales of cold remedies hit their peak when colds are most prevalent, although latitude has little to do with them. They seem to become epidemic at the same time in all parts of the country. Seasonal patterns for colds are determined by natural phenomena. However, some seasonal patterns are man-made. Sales of sheets and pillowcases increase as a result of semiannual white sales, and furs sell in volume because of August fur sales.

Sometimes an advertiser can change seasonal buying habits to level out purchasing and production throughout the year. For example, at one time sales of ginger ale and cola drinks peaked enormously during the hot weather and the bulk of consumer advertising was run then. However, national surveys and an astute appraisal of the market convinced certain manufacturers that they could gain a much greater volume of business during the colder months if they went after it with vigorous consumer and dealer promotion. After examining research findings some soft-drink marketers instituted a policy of year-round advertising support. Today sales continue to be higher during the warmer months, but the increased volume of business during the colder months makes the year-round advertising investment profitable. However, there are also instances where management wrongly assessed the off-season potential, and had to give up its attempt. In general, if research indicates that sales volume will be slim during the off season, it is best to emphasize advertising during the peak season when sales come more easily.

[11]W. T. Tucker, "The Development of Brand Loyalty," *Journal of Marketing Research*, 1, no. 3 (August 1964), 32–35.

[12]A. A. Kuehn, "Consumer Brand Choice—a Learning Process," in R. E. Frank, A. A. Kuehn, and W. F. Massy, eds., *Quantitative Techniques in Marketing Analysis* (Homewood, Ill.: Richard D. Irwin, Inc., 1962), p. 397.

Similarly, usage patterns vary from one day of the week to another. Seafood, for example, is bought in quantity on Fridays, especially in areas where a high percentage of the population still eschews meat on that day.

How People Use the Product. One study of product usage disclosed that the leading brand of coffee in a large American city was Eight O'Clock. Another study in this same city indicated that Maxwell House was the leading brand. Both studies had included an adequate, carefully selected sample and were conducted at about the same time. Why the difference? One explanation was the difference in research methods. The first study utilized a purchase panel in which consumers recorded all purchases during a certain period of time. In the second study interviewers checked the pantry of each respondent household to find out what brands were present. The indication was, then, that one brand did have the largest number of purchases, but another brand was physically present in greater volume. The studies indicated that the first brand was used more frequently than the second, possibly because it was cheaper, possibly because it was not considered a prestige brand (the sort one would use on special occasions).

In another study it was found that the majority of American homes had Jell-O on their pantry shelves. The company decided to induce people who purchased it to use it more often. At that time it was mainly used as a dessert. As a result of the study a group of salad recipes was prepared, and a national campaign promoting use of Jell-O in salads was launched. This was in addition to the major campaign, which continued to promote Jell-O as a dessert.

Frequency of Purchase. It is extremely useful to know how often consumers repeat purchases of competing products. How much time ensues between the purchase of a can of one brand of peas and another can of the same brand? How loyal is the housewife to a brand? Does she buy a brand of cosmetics several times in succession and then switch to another brand to try it and finally return to the first brand? Manufacturers of soap keep a careful check on the frequency of purchase of various sizes of package. How often, they wonder, does the housewife buy the "large economy size," "the regular size," and so on?

Before the detergent "All" could be marketed it was necessary to focus on another product — automatic washing machines. "All" was designed to be used exclusively in such machines. Therefore, before national advertising could be launched, it was necessary to know how many housewives had automatic washing machines, how frequently the housewife used them, and whether she felt the need of a special detergent. On this basis it was possible to predict the frequency of purchase.

In two separate studies, Kuehn and Farley found that the frequency of purchases during a particular period is strongly associated with brand loyalty.[13] Farley found a significant correlation between the percentage of families switching favorite brands from the first half of

[13]See J. U. Farley, "Why Does Brand Loyalty Vary over Products?" *Journal of Marketing Research*, 1, no. 4 (November 1964), 9–14; and A. A. Kuehn, p. 397.

the year to the second half and the average number of purchases reported in a product class. Kuehn inferred from his data that frequent purchasers of orange juice rejected or accepted particular brands but that the very infrequent purchasers appeared to follow a random pattern of brand choice.

Buying Trends. Consumer buying trends can build or blight even a major business. Consider such short-lived fads as hula-hoops or coonskin caps. Consider then such fashion trends as the "chemise" for women and the "Ivy look" for men. Astute management will attempt to analyze buying patterns to determine whether they indicate basic trends or merely passing fads. A salt-free diet, for example, has received a great deal of publicity. It is inconceivable that a large part of the public would give up salt entirely; nevertheless, a marketer of salt would keep a wary eye on this trend and perhaps be prepared to add another product to his line that would not be affected by it.

The great increase in synthetic fibers has seriously affected the wool, cotton, and silk industries. A fabric manufacturer who decided to experiment with man-made fibers a few years ago is in a better position today than the one who thought it only a passing fancy. If you were in the food business you would be seriously interested in diet trends. There is, for example, the trend away from fatty foods on the theory that they may contribute to heart or circulatory troubles. A manufacturer of a high-calorie food will study the trend and find some way to work with it. In dealing with a trend the marketer must recognize it as early as possible and try to find out how long-lasting it may be. Consumer research is one of his best aids in analyzing fads, fashions, and other trends.

Anyone analyzing the various studies of consumer purchasing patterns will be struck by the contradictory nature of much of our research findings. Generalizations on buying behavior, as on consumer motivation or attitude change, are surprisingly sparse in spite of the plethora of studies in the area. In his review of research concerning buying behavior, Frederick May concluded that these contradictions are probably due to too much dependence on single surveys or panel studies (instead of the more rigorously scientific experimental approach) and to sampling errors.[14]

SUMMARY AND SUGGESTED READINGS

Because this and the following chapter are closely interrelated, a summary, readings list, and questions, designed to supplement both chapters, are given at the end of Chapter 13.

[14]Frederick E. May, "Buying Behavior: Some Research Findings," *Journal of Business*, 28, no. 4 (October 1965), 379–396.

13 | Influencing Opinions, Attitudes, and Beliefs

The relation between the opinions or attitudes of a person and his buying behavior has long been recognized by advertising people. Much of what we know today about opinion and attitude results from the work of advertising researchers who are trying to discover more about people's opinions and attitudes toward products, media, advertisements, and almost every aspect of advertising. However, much of what researchers have found out in areas not directly related to advertising — politics, occupations, foreign countries and God — has relevance to the problem of advertising communications. In this chapter an effort will be made to cover findings that have special application to advertising.

DEFINITION OF OPINIONS, ATTITUDES, AND BELIEFS

Behavioral scientists have never agreed on fixed meanings for opinion, attitude, and belief, but all three are accepted as referring to a person's preference for one side or another of something controversial — whether a brand of soap, a political party, a movie, or a department store.[1]

[1] Bernard Berelson and Gary A. Steiner, *Human Behavior: An Inventory of Scientific Findings* (New York: Harcourt, Brace & World, Inc., 1964), pp. 557–558.

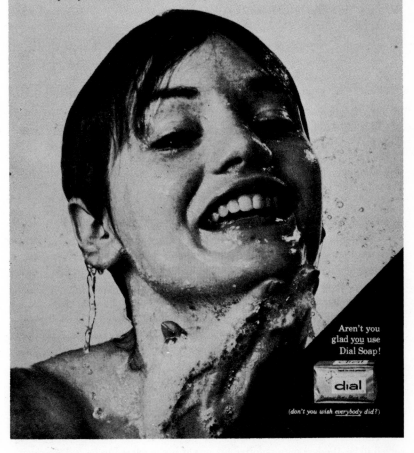

It's a pleasure

Dial and water. Helps you face the whole day without a worry.
Because Dial, with AT-7, removes skin bacteria that cause
perspiration odor. That's why people who like people use Dial.

Aren't you
glad you use
Dial Soap!

dial

(don't you wish everybody did?)

FIG. 13.1 *One of the
most successful soap
campaigns of recent
years, successful in part
because of its credibility.*
CLIENT: DIAL, ARMOUR
AND COMPANY; AGENCY:
FOOTE, CONE & BELDING.

Consequently, any time you make a judgment on something, we may
properly say you have formed an opinion, attitude, or belief.

The meanings of the three terms differ from one another according
to the intensity with which the judgments are held. Therefore any
judgments that are short-run we call *opinions*. Those that are more
enduring and inclusive we call *attitudes*. *Beliefs* refer to judgments that
have to do with the important issues in life. We have opinions about a
product we saw yesterday in a store, or a commercial we happened to
see on television last night. We might have attitudes toward the brand
of soap we normally use or toward the state of affairs in our nation's
capital. We probably have beliefs in advertising as an institution, the
value of hard work, and the tenets of our religion.

We expect opinions and attitudes to be consistent with beliefs, but
more subject to change by advertising or other forms of persuasion. We
thus find that *opinions* might be called "guesses," *attitudes,* "views" or

"convictions," and *beliefs*, "values." We find that when people sense some inconsistency between their attitudes and their beliefs, they undergo considerable strain but are usually able to work out a solution.

INFLUENCES ON OPINIONS, ATTITUDES, AND BELIEFS

Because opinions, attitudes, and beliefs are so closely related we shall discuss them together and in the interests of space refer to them as OAB's (as Berelson and Steiner, for example, have done).[2] The formation of OAB's is quite complex; thus we shall concentrate on factors that seem to have particular application to advertising: communication, reference and membership groups, family, and social class.

Communication. Every aspect of communication (for example, message, media, conditions of exposure) has some influence on a person's OAB's. Not only persuasive messages like advertising and public relations but those that are nonpersuasive are likely to influence OAB's. Because many of these messages are covered in other parts of this book there is no need to repeat them here. Let us, however, take special note at this point of two important aspects of communications: audience predisposition and credibility of source.

In general, people are more likely to respond to persuasive communications of any sort (advertising or otherwise) if they are in line with the person's predispositions. In other words, the advertisement is more likely to be effective if it tells people what they want to hear—or is consistent with their past beliefs. Communications are likely to convert neutral members of the audience toward an issue, an idea, or a product. There is therefore a great advantage in trying to influence people while a product is in the introductory stage and people's opinions and attitudes are flexible.

The source of the communication is also an important influence in changing a person's attitude. In summarizing a number of studies on this point, Berelson and Steiner say,

> The more trustworthy, credible, or prestigious the communicator is perceived to be, the less manipulative his intent is considered to be and the greater the immediate tendency to accept his conclusions.[3]

However, within reasonable limits, the credibility or prestige of the source has little influence on the actual transmission of *factual* information, although people are more apt to read an ad from a high-prestige source. As time passes, people tend to remember the content of a message but forget whether it came from a high-credibility or low-credibility source. The effect of a low-prestige source thus tends to increase over time, and the effect of a high-prestige source to decrease.

Reference Groups. Even more effective than attribution of a message to expert or prestigious opinion is to attribute it to a group. If a person likes or respects the group that advocates a particular idea, he will be strongly influenced to adopt that idea himself. Studies show that people forming new opinions or firming up their attitudes, wonder what

[2]Berelson and Steiner, chap. 14.
[3]Berelson and Steiner, p. 537.

a particular group would think of this new idea. We thus find that *reference groups* play an important role in the forming of OAB's.

Sherif and Sherif define a reference group as "the group with which the individual identifies or aspires to belong."[4] They point out that

underlying an individual's membership in informally organized groups through his own choosing, there is a motivational base in terms of this identity, his need for human company and mutual support, his felt need to act in concert with the fellow members for the effective attainment of his cherished goals.

There is general agreement on two important points concerning reference groups:

1. A person need not be an official member of the reference group or even have face-to-face contact with the group which influences his attitudes and behavior. He may well aspire to membership in some group and be strongly influenced by what he thinks are the norms of that group but never actually attain membership. In those cases where the person is a member, the group is often referred to as a "membership" group.
2. Different reference groups influence different attitudes and marketing decisions. We thus find that a person will be influenced by the norms and status structure of one group when deciding what food to buy but a different reference group when considering alternative fashion articles. A person may in fact have negative reference groups and avoid the adoption of attitudes or opinions that will associate him with that group.[5]

The effect of a reference group on a person's attitudes and on his behavior generally depends on two factors: the nature of the group and the nature of the OAB that is being influenced. For example, the more homogeneous the group, the more it will influence a person's habits. If you have lived in a tightly knit community for many years, it will exert much more influence on your OAB's than a newer community would, or one with a changing population. Similarly, if you are torn between two groups, one of which you are in close contact with, and one not so close, the former will have more influence over your OAB's.

Some OAB's are more influenced by reference groups than others are. For example, the more complex or ambiguous or unpredictable the consequences of the OAB, the more people rely on group ties as a basis for decision.[6] Studies have indicated that this is true of presidential elections, and it is probably also true of attitudes toward products. The more controversial or important the issue, the more closely a person tries to identify himself with a group. If you hold a radical political position or exercise radical buying behavior when you buy clothes, you will probably seek solidarity with like-minded persons.

Group influence is exerted through group norms. As Zaltman points out, "Norms establish a 'range of tolerable behavior' or frame of reference for the individual in his relations with other group members. Informal groups have implicit rules; formal groups have explicit ones." In clarifying norms, Sherif and Sherif say,

[4]Muzafer Sherif and Carolyn W. Sherif, *Reference Groups* (New York: Harper & Row, Publishers, 1964), p. 55.
[5]Gerald Zaltman, *Marketing: Contributions from the Behavioral Sciences* (New York: Harcourt, Brace & World, Inc., 1965), pp. 78–80, for a discussion of these points.
[6]Berelson and Steiner, pp. 568–569.

A *norm* for a given sphere of behavior defines what is expected, desirable, and even the ideal mode of behavior. But the expected mode of behavior is not usually a single action. The norm allows for variations and for alternative actions, within certain bounds. Behavior falling within these bounds is within the "latitude of acceptable behavior." Behaviors in the same sphere of activity which are outside the prevailing latitude of acceptance fall within the latitude of rejection, where again alternatives are graded as to how objectionable they are.[7]

Thus the latitude of acceptance and latitude of rejection in terms of a particular area of OAB's or of behavior constitute a scale of reference on the basis of which a person can rate alternative OAB's. Every situation has a different reference scale, and if the advertiser can discover the nature of this scale he can predict OAB's. For example, a preference for fast, flashy sports cars is within the latitude of acceptance in some reference groups but is quite unacceptable in others. Favorable and unfavorable attitudes for almost any product may be similarly positioned on the scale of acceptance.

Social Class. Berelson and Steiner point out the many social characteristics that exert strong influence on people's OAB's.[8] Among these are the following: whether they live in the city or the country; whether they live in one geographic region or another; whether they are white or colored; Protestant, Catholic, or Jewish; rich or poor; young or old; men or women; educated or uneducated.

In the United States, for example, attitudes toward buying behavior as well as toward political and racial issues differ widely between the South and most northern areas. Similarly, there is a marked difference in OAB's between rural and urban residents in any given part of the country.

The more strongly people identify themselves with a particular social class, the more sharply their OAB's are likely to stay within the boundaries of that class. For example, the upper class is generally more interested in public affairs and anything having to do with esthetic ideas. The lower classes, on the other hand, are less interested in these and less tolerant of deviant attitudes in the areas of politics and civil liberties. They are skeptical of motives and pessimistic of humanity's chances generally.

The relation between class and OAB's holds true whether we measure social class by income, source of income, occupation, education, inherited status, or some other criteria.

Age. In general, the older a person is, the more conservative are his OAB's. However, succeeding generations are better educated and more widely traveled. Consequently, today's young person is likely to be more tolerant of OAB's when he is sixty than were his parents at the same age, but less tolerant than when he was young.

Sex. Fairly pronounced differences between the OAB's of men and women are revealed by surveys. Berelson and Steiner say,

Social pressures and expectations everywhere lead men to take a more active political role than women, and everywhere women tend to be more

[7]Sherif and Sherif, p. 62.
[8]Berelson and Steiner, pp. 570–574.

religious and to take a more "conservative" political position than men, i.e., to follow the class leads and the religious lead more.[9]

Men appear to be more interested in theoretical and economic ideas and values; women, on the other hand, devote more attention to ideas of an esthetic or religious nature.

Family. The OAB's of children and young people tend to correspond with those of their parents in political, religious, ethical, and other areas. The OAB's also follow class differences in that upper-class children incline to more interest in politics and public affairs than their lower-class counterparts evidence.

The fact that parents occupy most of a child's time and also provide a stabilizing force makes their attitudes an important influence on those of the child. As children grow up and into new ways of life and new ideas, they tend to make certain shifts, but the idea of "rebellious

[9]Berelson and Steiner, p. 573.

It's the perfect day for...
a long, leisurely breakfast...
and a Long Distance visit with the folks.

What better day for family-time calling?
There's no need to wait till Sunday evening for lowest rates.
Now rates are lowest all day Sunday.
So call early, before or after church, and you'll agree,
Long Distance is the next best thing to being there.

FIG. 13.2 *A familiar situation — one with which many readers can easily identify.* COURTESY AT&T AND N. W. AYER & SON.

youth" does not seem to be borne out by the many studies. The best educated young people and those who are members of large minority groups seem to be most likely to deviate sharply from the attitudes and beliefs of their elders. There is also evidence that young people are more likely to differ from their parents on attitudes toward dating, hi-fi sets, popular music, and various other aspects of the youth culture than they are in such areas as politics, or underlying social values.

PERCEPTION AND INTERPRETATION

Most of us have had the experience of watching a play or reading a book and receiving an impression quite different from that of someone else seeing the same play or reading the same book. How, we may wonder, could two people be exposed to the same thing and yet differ so much in their impressions? The answer lies partly at least in the processes of perception and cognition. We are exposed to all sorts of sensory stimuli during each day, and we cannot possibly perceive all of them. Instead, we unconsciously *select* certain stimuli and organize and interpret them for ourselves.

Perception is a complex process, but we know that people are influenced by their own existing motives and predispositions. For example, they tend to see or hear communications that are favorable to their point of view and reject those that are unfavorable. Or they may, if they find something neutral or hostile to their point of view, misinterpret it so that it will agree with what they believe. A neutral message will be perceived by a Democrat as favoring the Democratic party's point of view, and by a Republican as favoring his party's viewpoint. Studies indicate that partisans see as "facts" a biased or unsubstantiated report that happens to agree with their own position. However, if a person sees a message conflicting with his own opinion, he will label it propagandistic or unfair. In fact, when a person sees or hears a message that he considers different from his own viewpoint, he will perceive it even further from his than it really is. Conversely, if his stand is fairly close to the point of view of the communication, he will tend to narrow the gap and perceive it as closer to his own view than it really is. The old adage, "People see what they want to see," is substantiated by research.

We have seen that a person's opinion on whether the source (person or organization) of a message is credible, his opinion on whether the group with which he identifies himself approves the message, and his opinion of the medium in which the message appears all influence the way he perceives the message. The more any communicator can find out about audience predispositions and audience motives, the more accurately he is likely to predict how his message will be perceived.

Nicosia makes a distinction between physical perception and cognitive (selective) perception.[10] After reviewing a wide variety of research evidence he concludes that the most important influences are personality, the message source, perception of the attributes of the

[10]Francesco M. Nicosia, *Consumer Decision Processes, Marketing and Advertising Implications* (Englewood Cliffs, N.J.: Prentice-Hall, Inc., 1966), pp. 165–167.

message, and motivated perception (that is; perceiving what he is motivated to perceive).

Subliminal Perception. Several critics of advertising have been concerned that advertising and public relations men might use subliminal (beneath the threshold or ·"limin" of awareness) methods of persuasion on unsuspecting audiences. Probably the most widely read of these is Vance Packard, who is afraid that these subliminal persuaders will "try to invade the privacy of our minds."[11]

We do know that some stimuli can be received without the receivers being conscious of seeing or hearing them. We thus say that the threshold of awareness may be higher than the threshold for effective perception. Various studies have demonstrated that people may make associations to words or drawings below the threshold of recognition.

There is no substantial evidence, however, that subliminal perception may be used to change people's attitudes or behavior. A well-known researcher, James Vicary, performed a series of experiments in late 1957 in Fort Lee, New Jersey, in an attempt to test the persuasive value of subliminal "advertising." He and some colleagues worked out an apparatus which consisted of an electric eye attached to a movie projector so that words like "Drink Coke" and "Eat Popcorn" were flashed on the screen so quickly that they were below the level of conscious awareness of the average individual. The preliminary findings indicated that people did indeed drink and eat more following the period when the message was flashed on the screen than when it was not. However, many tests both in the United States and foreign countries that attempted to replicate this experiment added nothing more than a welter of confusion. In Great Britain subliminal advertising was banned by law and in the United States the National Association of Broadcasters asked the broadcasting industry not to use it. It is not surprising that Berelson and Steiner conclude:

> There is no scientific evidence that subliminal stimulation can initiate subsequent action, to say nothing of commercially or politically significant action. And there is nothing to suggest that such action can be produced "against the subject's will," or more effectively than through normal, recognized messages.[12]

Cognitive Dissonance. Festinger's theory of cognitive dissonance helps to explain one aspect of OAB's familiar to most practicing advertising people—post-decision doubt.[13] When a person finds some discrepancy between the real world or an action he has taken and the world as indicated by his motives, he tries to rationalize or bring these into line. This is often impossible; so he attempts to reduce this discrepancy (or dissonance) by changing his perception of reality. For example, you might cancel your order or return merchandise in order to reduce the dissonance caused by a particular purchase you regret having made. The newer or more revolutionary the product you bought, the more special-

[11]Vance Packard, *The Hidden Persuaders* (New York: Pocket Books, Inc., 1957), chap. 23.
[12]Berelson and Steiner, p. 95.
[13]Leon Festinger, *A Theory of Cognitive Dissonance* (New York: Harper & Row, Publishers, 1957).

ized the item is, the more infrequently you purchase it, and the more expensive it is, the more likely you are to have some doubt about the wisdom of your purchase. For example, if you learn that a new automobile that you bought may be inferior in some ways to another that you considered, you begin to doubt the wisdom of your purchase, and you experience cognitive dissonance. What can you do to reduce this dissonance? You have several choices open to you:

1. You may look for information that will produce cognition in line with the action you took.
2. You may try to bolster your confidence in your decision or downgrade the alternatives.
3. You may look for ways of reversing the decision.
4. You may try to convince yourself that the decision was not a very important one after all.[14]

One classic study of cognitive dissonance involved comparison between smokers and nonsmokers who were exposed to material regarding the relation of smoking to cancer. Smokers tended to avoid reading any dissonance-creating material, such as articles indicating a positive correlation between smoking and cancer. When they were exposed to it, they were less likely to believe it than were nonsmokers.

It is possible therefore that a given advertisement may be perceived differently by different people according to their ideas of the product. A recently satisfied buyer will perceive it one way, a disgruntled buyer another, and an optimistic potential buyer still another. The advertising planner may find it necessary to have various campaigns aimed at the various groups, or he may be able to include in a single advertisement cues for each group.

Zaltman, in discussing the marketing implications of cognitive dissonance, points out that marketing managers should

1. Make sure that they do not oversell a particular product, particularly if it is a new product.
2. Attempt to show that many characteristics of the item chosen are approved by the relevant reference group and are consistent in many ways with the norms of that group.[15]

ADOPTION OF NEW IDEAS

In Chapter 3 we looked briefly at the use of opinion leaders as alternative communicators and the process of innovation or "diffusion process." Let us now consider this process in terms of its role in influencing attitudes. We noted that most authorities agree that new attitudes are adopted in five stages: (1) *awareness* (first exposure); (2) *interest* (goal-directed behavior); (3) *evaluation* (weighing the advantages and disadvantages of the innovation; (4) *trial* (a "dry run" of the idea); and (5) *adoption*.[16]

The evidence from the various studies of diffusion suggests that the consumer is looking for different types of help according to the stage of

[14]Festinger, p. 83, for amplification.
[15]Zaltman, p. 63.
[16]Everett M. Rogers, *The Diffusion of Innovations* (New York: The Free Press, 1962), for additional explanation of this process.

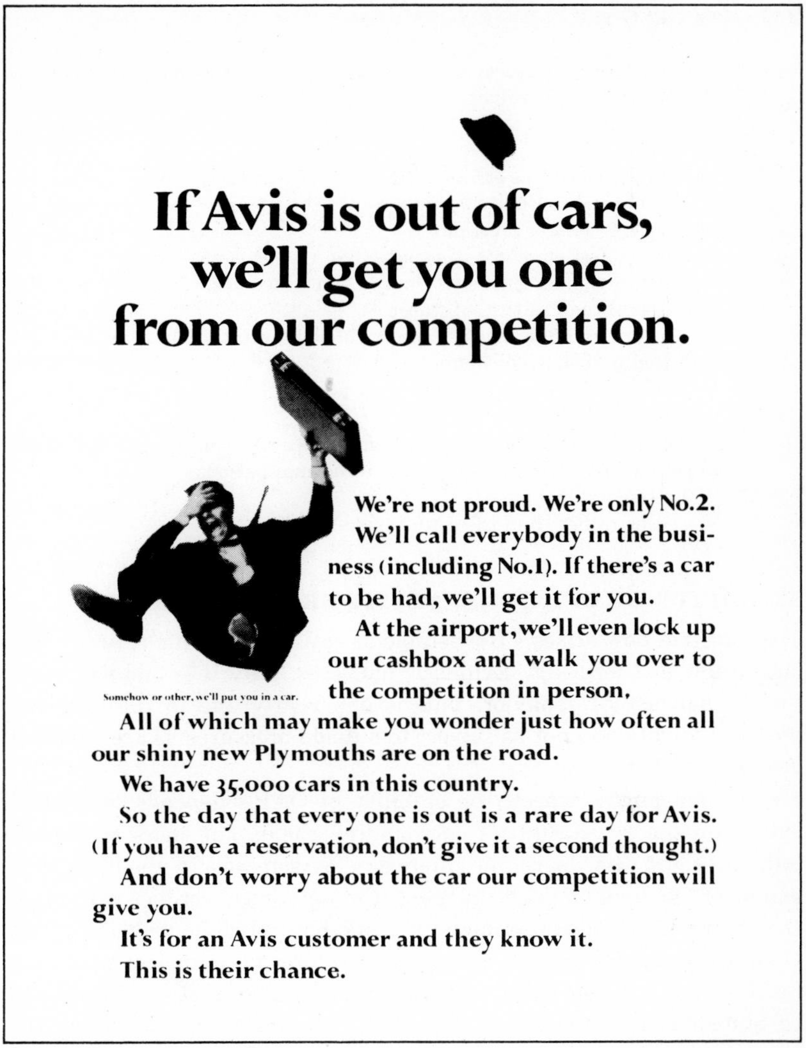

If Avis is out of cars, we'll get you one from our competition.

We're not proud. We're only No. 2. We'll call everybody in the business (including No. 1). If there's a car to be had, we'll get it for you.

At the airport, we'll even lock up our cashbox and walk you over to the competition in person.

Somehow or other, we'll put you in a car.

All of which may make you wonder just how often all our shiny new Plymouths are on the road.

We have 35,000 cars in this country.

So the day that every one is out is a rare day for Avis. (If you have a reservation, don't give it a second thought.)

And don't worry about the car our competition will give you.

It's for an Avis customer and they know it.

This is their chance.

FIG. 13.3 *Avis acts magnanimously and creates the impression of leadership in the car-leasing field.* © AVIS RENT-A-CAR SYSTEM, INC.; ADVERTISEMENT PREPARED BY DOYLE DANE BERNBACH INC.

the adoption process. For example, at the *interest* stage he can see that the product may provide some reward for him and he is seeking new information. At the *evaluation* stage he is searching for some rating scale by which he can compare the innovation with alternatives open to him.

We know also that innovations in OAB's or behavior tend to be developed in cities and then move to rural areas. Even ideas concerning agriculture seem to start in cities.

Among the problems people have in deciding whether to adopt an innovation is the way it fits in with their traditional values. If the innovation threatens these values there will be a good deal of resistance to the change. This has been a particular concern among emerging nations, because many of the nationals of these countries are reluctant to abandon traditional cultural values even though they realize that they are a barrier to economic development.

In summarizing a series of studies on innovation and social change Berelson and Steiner point out that changes are more likely to occur more frequently and readily as follows:

1. In the material aspects of the culture (e.g., technology) than in the non-material (e.g., values).
2. In the aspects close to the society's "cultural focus" than in those at the periphery.
3. In the less basic, less emotionally charged, less sacred, more instrumental or technical aspects (e.g., tool) than in the opposite (e.g., primary group relations, system of prestige).
4. In the simplest elements of society than in the complex ones.
5. In the nonsymbolic elements than in symbolic ones.
6. In the form than in the substance.
7. In matters arranged on a scale with narrow intervals than in those arranged in a sharp dichotomy.
8. In elements for which roughly equivalent substitutes are available or provided in the society.
9. In elements congenial to the given culture than in strange elements.
10. In periods of crisis and stress than in normal periods.
11. When the cultural base is large.
12. Via cities rather than the countryside.[17]

STABILITY OF OPINIONS, ATTITUDES, AND BELIEFS

The question now arises, "How stable or resistant to change are OAB's once they are formed?" Evidence indicates that they change more slowly than actual behavior. This is apparently due to the fact that they are private and not as subject to outside pressures as are modes of behavior.

As one might expect, the stability of OAB's depends to a great extent on the circumstances surrounding them. The more important influences are the degree of interest a person has in the OAB, the extent of his emotional involvement, the amount of conflict with other OAB's or with family or group norms, and how much he travels around.

For example, if you are particularly interested in or feel emotional involvement with an issue, you will probably take a strong stand and be quite resistant to change. You will also look for support from the mass media. A commitment in the form of purchase of a product becomes a barrier against your change of attitude or belief.

Much publicity has been given to "brainwashing" techniques whereby the beliefs of political or military captives are changed by constant indoctrination, interrogation, or the eliciting of confessions. However, the evidence suggests that such methods do not represent any new breakthrough in theory but have been used frequently throughout history.

It is certainly possible that a particular attitude may be acceptable to one reference group but be at variance (or at least seem to be) with the norms of another group. For example, a student who comes from a conservative home attends a liberal college. Or a housewife from an upper-class household may have certain lower-class tastes — pulp magazines, borax furniture. What does a person do to resolve this inconsistency? Some studies indicate that she is likely to go along with the norms of the group she likes the most. Sometimes people lose interest in the issue at stake or consciously try to forget it.

[17]Berelson and Steiner, pp. 615–616.

FIG. 13.4 *Mr. Clean, the first of a series of television crusaders against dirt.* COURTESY THE PROCTER & GAMBLE COMPANY.

Anncr, VO: Mr. Clean. He's mean. He hates dirt. You'll love him.

BEHAVIOR WITHOUT ATTITUDE CHANGE

There is danger that we may overestimate the influence of attitudes and beliefs on our behavior. Krugman points out that we may be underestimating the influence of advertising by looking too hard for attitude change as a result of advertising.[18]He suggests that there is danger in applying hypotheses from noncommercial communications to advertising; advertising may motivate people to action without changing their attitudes. This may result, he contends, because advertising a brand of soap evokes a lower degree of involvement than does a communication about the United Nations or the problems of racial equality. It is quite possible, as he suggests, that resistance to advertising communication is lower and that people can be taught to like the product more easily than we think. It is usually the lightly held opinion, not the deeply ingrained attitude or belief, that we are trying to influence through advertising.

METHODS OF OBTAINING DATA ON CONSUMER BEHAVIOR AND OAB'S

Information concerning behavior and OAB's, as in consumer groups, is really background research. It is used to study the market as a whole and to devise creative and media strategy and to decide how much money should be budgeted for a particular campaign. Although it may be used to work out alternative themes or concepts or even alternative advertisements, this researching can more properly be discussed in Chapter 32, "Measuring the Effectiveness of Advertising and Promotion." In practice, information about behavior and OAB's is obtained through a variety of methods, some direct, some indirect, some quantitative, some more qualitative. Many of the approaches are very complex. In discussing methods of conducting attitude research, Irving Crespi attributes the complexity of this research methodology to three causes:

1. Attitudes are an intangible quality.
2. We are not fully aware of how our behavior falls into certain consistent

[18]Herbert E. Krugman, "The Impact of Television Advertising: Learning without Involvement," *Public Opinion Quarterly,* Fall 1965, pp. 349–356.

patterns, the reasons behind their consistencies, and reasons why they vary.

3. The complexity of attitudes makes them difficult to interpret.[19]

We shall now discuss some of the more common methods of obtaining information about the consuming public.

We should note that usable information may come from both published and original studies. Studies may utilize either sample surveys or experimental design—sometimes both. In distinguishing between the two, Crespi says,

> In sample surveys, the research design is planned to measure the incidence of specified attitudes in a population and to determine the extent to which they are correlated with each other and with other characteristics in the population under study. Experimental studies are based on the deliberate manipulation of specified conditions in order to discover the extent to which variations in attitudes accompany this manipulation.[20]

Published Data. Many of the organizations that do consumer studies make all or part of their findings available to the public. This is true, for instance, of many of the consumer-buying behavior studies. The media, the trade associations, and nonprofit organizations like universities are usually willing to publish their findings. One must keep in mind, though, the danger of bias where the sponsor has a vested interest in the results of a particular study.

Question and Answer Techniques. Questions have long been used in consumer research, partly because they are easy to formulate and partly because the information is readily accessible. Nevertheless, one must not assume a perfect correlation between what people say and what they will do. The more common forms of the question technique are (1) direct questions, (2) open-ended questions, (3) comparisons, and (4) rating scales.

Direct Questions. A leading manufacturer of flat silver never puts a new pattern into production until it has been surveyed by a representative cross section of women. Kits consisting of the new pattern and several established patterns are shown to women who have been carefully selected as representative of the market. The respondents are asked to name their first, second, and third choices. If the new pattern stands well up in their preferences, it goes into production; if not, it is discarded. One company that is well known for its interest in people's opinions of their automobiles is General Motors. It regularly asks such questions as these:

Of course you want ALL these things—but which will influence you most when it comes to choosing your next car?

(Check 3 or 4 items)

Appearance?	Operating Economy?
Comfort?	Pickup?
Dependability?	Safety?
Ease of Control?	Smoothness?
First Cost?	Speed?

[19]Irving Crespi, *Attitude Research* (Chicago: American Marketing Association, 1965), pp. 20–21.
[20]Crespi, p. 21.

Suppose that you are a manufacturer wanting to find out people's attitudes toward electrical appliances and the companies that make them. You want to determine what degree of regard your several years of advertising has built with the public. Where would you rank in public esteem? You want to know how many electrical appliances the average home has and who made them. What are the consumers' opinions of your appliances versus competing ones? Are there weaknesses in competitive appliances and strengths in yours?

Open-ended Questions. In a study of attitudes toward three major corporations, two open-ended questions were asked: "What can you tell me about Company X?" and "What is your opinion of Company X?" Responses were coded on the basis of (1) over-all unfavorableness of comment and (2) a classification of the kinds of comments made. On the basis of these it was possible to rank the companies.

In general, open-ended questions are used to obtain the exact words of respondents concerning how they feel toward a product or message. However, they do have limitations. One is that people differ considerably in their ability to express themselves. Another is that they may avoid important issues or attitudes toward the product by talking around the real issue. Furthermore, the intentional ambiguity of the questions may encourage respondents to be equally ambiguous in their answers unless they are skillfully led.

Comparison Questions. Respondents may be asked to rate several food products on the basis of characteristics such as flavor, ease of preparation, and stability of texture. Such comparisons may be made either on the basis of "paired comparisons" (comparison of two brands at a time) or "multiple comparisons" (more than two at a time). In variations of this the respondent may be asked to designate the highest and lowest of the brands listed on the basis of a particular characteristic. It is not clear just how many competing brands or factors can be handled at a time, but the paired comparison produces more reliable results than the multiple comparison does, although obviously more information is obtained by the latter.

One of the most familiar of the comparison type of surveys is that in which respondents have to state their preference between two candidates for president. This same "forced choice" between two products sometimes occurs when a person is asked to make a choice between two brands.

Rating Scales. Respondents may be asked to place a brand somewhere on a rating scale ranging from "extremely favorable" at one end to "extremely unfavorable" at the other. This is a verbal scale. A variation is the pictorial scale where respondents are provided with a ladder or a thermometer and are asked to indicate their attitudes on the pictured object.

Numerical scales also are used in collecting information. The semantic differential, which is discussed in the next chapter, is widely used to measure brand and corporate images. Another scale (Stapel) consists of ten boxes, five white and five black, numbered from $+5$ to -5.

There is a danger that people will attribute an exactness to rating scales that will be misleading. Rating scales do not measure attitudes in the same sense that rulers, thermometers, or speedometers measure lengths, temperatures, or speeds. Social science researchers often find it useful to distinguish between ratio scales (those that measure for a single dimension from zero up), interval scales (which have no zero point but measure by intervals instead of along a continuum), and ordinal scales (which place items in rank order such as first, second, and so on).

Projective Tests. Projective tests are based on the concept of projection borrowed from Freudian psychology. Much of what we know, Freud pointed out, is repressed and hence cannot be produced in response to direct questioning. Projective tests are designed to outwit repression and to get the subject to express his true biases, feelings, and attitudes, by exposing him to ambiguous stimuli. The respondent selects certain aspects of the stimuli and projects his own personality. Crespi describes a case in point:

> In a study of consumer attitudes toward the styling of automobiles, the only questioning technique used was completely non-directive. Respondents were led to an automobile and asked to comment on its styling. No further cues were given. They were encouraged to talk for as long as they could on the car and its styling. All comments were recorded verbatim. Later they were analyzed in terms of what design features were mentioned. This produced a definitive profile of these aspects of the car's styling that were responded to spontaneously and thus were the ones that could be considered to be of greatest interest and importance to the respondent.[21]

One commonly used projective technique is the Rorschach test (devised by a Swiss psychiatrist), which exposes the subject to ink blots. Rorschach believed that patients' reactions to ambiguous blots might turn out to be a diagnostic aid. In another test respondents are shown a picture of people performing some action and are asked what these people are doing, or of people consuming some product and asked what it is. The respondent is shown a cartoon with blank balloons to indicate the speech of the characters and asked who they are and what they are saying as they examine the product. Other tests give respondents incomplete sentences to finish. Another common device is to ask respondents to talk about the attitudes of their neighbors or friends toward a particular subject.

In all of these there is danger that the answers may not be truly projective but merely reflect what the respondent thinks is characteristic of the neighbor or the people in the cartoons. The respondent may also avoid the issue by saying he has never thought about it and he doesn't think the people in the picture have either.

Group Discussions. In the early stages of a study of consumers, group discussions are often used. The group is used as a stimulus to generate a free-flowing discussion and to uncover basic ideas held by consumers when they think about a product or company. It is expected that the spontaneity of the discussion will cause people to bring forth ideas not obtainable in normal interviews. On the basis of such information it is possible to formulate more meaningful hypotheses and construct more valid questionnaires than would otherwise be possible.

[21]Crespi, p. 23.

Obviously, much of the value of group discussion depends on the skill of the leader. He must make sure that the discussion is not dominated by one or two persons and that norms that might stifle minority viewpoints are not put forth.

SUMMARY

In our attempt to analyze the complexities of man's behavior and his opinions, attitudes, and beliefs we have seen that much can be learned by styling his motives—the forces behind much of what he does and thinks, while taking into account their interrelation and their instability. The following dichotomies are useful in classifying motives: physiological–secondary, controllable–uncontrollable, rational–emotional, needs–wants, and primary–selective.

Among current theories that provide guidance in understanding man are the learning theories and psychoanalysis. We found many areas of consumer purchasing behavior of interest to advertising practitioners. Among these are what and when people buy, their product usages, and consumer trends.

Social scientists are giving increasingly more attention to understanding man's opinions, attitudes, and beliefs. Among the factors that seem to have special influence on OAB's are audience predispositions, sources of communication, reference groups, social class, age, sex, and family.

Much of what people believe seems to come from how they perceive and interpret the various stimuli that surround them. Subliminal perception, though possible, does not seem to have much application to advertising. On the other hand, the theory of cognitive dissonance provides guidance in the complex area of perception and cognition. Guidance also comes from the various studies of diffusion or the adoption of new ideas.

The stability of OAB's depends on influences such as the degree of interest a person has in the subject, his emotional involvement, and the amount of conflict with other OAB's or other norms.

Among the more useful methods of obtaining data on consumer behavior and OAB's are the following: question-and-answer techniques, projective techniques, group discussions, and the various studies of consumer behavior, particularly retail-store audits and consumer panels.

QUESTIONS FOR DISCUSSION

1. Discuss the concept of consumer motives in the decision-making process.
2. What is the relation in advertising between learning and persuasion?
3. Select current print advertisements that seem to appeal to the motives discussed in Chapter 12.
4. Select a current advertisement that attempts to reach consumers by emphasizing relevant reference groups who use or endorse the product.

5. What is meant by "audience predisposition"? How is this important in selective perception?
6. Why might advertising planners profit from a knowledge of the theory of cognitive dissonance?
7. What is the advantage of an open-end question in exploring consumers' OAB's?
8. Under what conditions might planners use indirect approaches, such as projective techniques, more satisfactorily than direct ones in the exploring of consumer attitudes?

SUGGESTED READINGS

Berelson, Bernard, and Gary A. Steiner, *Human Behavior: An Inventory of Scientific Findings*. New York: Harcourt, Brace & World, Inc., 1964.

Bliss, Perry, ed. *Marketing and the Behavioral Sciences: Selected Readings,* rev. ed. Boston: Allyn and Bacon, Inc., 1968.

Boyd, Harper W., Jr., and Joseph W. Newman, *Advertising Management: Selected Readings*. Homewood, Ill.: Richard D. Irwin, Inc., 1965.

Clark, Lincoln, ed., *Consumer Behavior*. New York: Harper & Row, Publishers, 1958.

Crespi, Irving, *Attitude Research*. Chicago: American Marketing Association, 1965.

Festinger, Leon, *A Theory of Cognitive Dissonance*. New York: Harper & Row, Publishers, 1957.

Green, Bert F., "Attitude Measurement," in Gardner Lindzey, ed., *Handbook of Social Psychology*. Reading, Mass.: Addison-Wesley Publishing Co., Inc., 1954.

Katz, Elihu, and Paul F. Lazarsfeld, *Personal Influence*. New York: The Free Press, 1955.

Rogers, Everett M., *The Diffusion of Innovations*. New York: The Free Press, 1962.

Sherif, Muzafer, and Carolyn W. Sherif, *Reference Groups*. New York: Harper & Row, Publishers, 1964.

Zaltman, Gerald, *Marketing: Contributions from the Behavioral Sciences*. New York: Harcourt, Brace & World, Inc., 1965.

14 | Brand and Corporate Images

To market a product or service successfully, you should find out as much as possible about what you are selling. You must learn not only the attitudes and opinions of people regarding your product or service, but find out how these are symbolized in a brand or corporate image. You must decide what are the product's strong points and capitalize on them in a promotion campaign. Most successful campaigns emphasize product strengths and minimize product weaknesses.

One of the first things to decide, as an aid in determining a pattern of search, is what kind of qualities you are looking for in analyzing your product. One useful approach is to consider product qualities as either *subjective* (depending on consumers' judgment or perception and not usually measurable by any commonly accepted standard) or *objective* (measurable by some commonly accepted standard). For example, a product's image is a subjective quality, its price an objective one. Data on subjective qualities must, of course, come from the consumers, whereas data on objective qualities may come from either the consumers or from technical research (often in the laboratory).

The purpose of this chapter is to explore in some detail the nature of brand and certain other images, the types of information one should look for in analyzing them, and some useful means of obtaining this information. Most of what we say about brand images as applied to product and services can be applied as appropriately to the analysis of corporate or retail store images.

SUBJECTIVE ANALYSIS OF PRODUCTS

Every product, service, or business establishment is a symbol. If an advertising expert can determine the true nature of a product's connotations he can use them to his advantage in an advertising campaign. An example of poor use is cited by researcher Burleigh Gardner, whose research firm did a study of certain beer advertising. One ad showed a well-known orchestra conductor having a glass of beer. He was dressed in tails, leaning against a grand piano and talking to women in evening gowns. "Apparently the idea of the ad was to impress beer drinkers with the high status of the brand and make them want to join the privileged ranks of users."[1] However, the research showed "a lot of negative and even hostile reactions." The respondents did not know the conductor, and so he had no meaning for them. They reacted negatively to the idea of imitating him. They felt the situation was incongruous because beer is not for formal occasions. Joseph Newman, however, cites a successful case of subjective analysis when he points out that coffee

has many meanings which enable it to contribute to emotional well-being. It symbolizes warmth, pleasure, leisure, luxury, intimacy, hospitality, sociability, belonging to a group, relaxation, adulthood, and an interest in homemaking. Research on the meanings of coffee and cultural trends led the Pan-American Coffee Bureau to promote coffee more as a part of gracious living, of the moving away from the earlier cultural restrictions on sensory pleasure and of the trend toward expression of personality by drinking different kinds of coffee and serving it in different ways.[2]

Brand Images. Product symbolism usually comes to focus in the brand image. As pointed out in an earlier chapter, the brand image means all those emotional and esthetic qualities that people associate with a brand. David Ogilvy calls it the "complex symbol" of the brand. He points out that most manufacturers make the mistake of wanting to be all things to all people and "end up with a brand which has no personality of any kind, a wishy-washy neuter."[3] The importance of the image is emphasized by Nicosia who says,

The purchase of a certain brand may be conceptualized as overt behavior deriving from the interaction between the consumer's attributes (e.g., his image of the brand) and the environment's attributes (e.g., a stimulus such as the brand's advertisement at the point of purchase.)[4]

[1]Burleigh Gardner "Symbols and Meaning in Advertising," *The Promise of Advertising*, C. H. Sandage, ed. (Homewood, Ill.: Richard D. Irwin, Inc., 1961).
[2]Joseph Newman,"Development of Better Marketing Concepts," *Effective Marketing Action*, David W. Ewing, ed. (New York: Harper & Row, Publishers, 1958).
[3]David Ogilvy "The Image and the Brand," in Harper W. Boyd and Joseph W. Newman, eds., *Advertising Management: Selected Readings* (Homewood, Ill.: Richard D. Irwin, Inc., 1965).
[4]Francesco M. Nicosia, *Consumer Decision Processes, Marketing and Advertising Implications* (Englewood Cliffs, N.J.: Prentice-Hall, Inc., 1966), p. 76.

FIG. 14.1 *Updated illustration from one of advertising's most successful image-building campaigns, the Hathaway shirt campaign.* PHOTOGRAPH COURTESY OF THE C. F. HATHAWAY COMPANY, WATERVILLE, MAINE.

Over the years brands such as Jell-O and Betty Crocker in food, Lucky Strike and Chesterfield in tobacco, and Mercedes-Benz and Cadillac in automobiles have conjured up strong images in the public mind. Hathaway shirts and Marlboro cigarettes are more recent examples of successful image building. Marlboro, for example, was, until recent years, a tipped cigarette with definite feminine appeal. Then a new agency set out to build an image of Marlboro as the cigarette for outdoor he-men "who came up the hard way." This purpose was accomplished in record time, because of some of the most rugged-looking men ever shown in advertising. Many early Marlboro men were actually executives of the agency who were selected because they looked like sportsmen or cowboys. They were shown with a tattoo. For television, Marlboro used the same general approach. Each of the rugged men told something of his he-man life and then explained why he chose Marlboro. More recently the Marlboro man has become international. (See Figure 10.4 for an example.)

The image concept, then, is an organizing concept. In exploring brand imagery we are really trying to find out what the brand means to the consumer. We are recognizing the fact that the consumer very often purchases the brand (and an assorted bundle of meanings and associations) rather than the product.

If we were to ask consumers directly why they prefer a certain automobile, we would be likely to hear "You can save on the gasoline," or "It will have a good trade-in value." They have difficulty verbalizing their real feelings toward their purchase. When we dig a bit further we may find some measure of what the car really means to them. Subjectively, the car may be regarded as a status symbol or an elixir of youth. In one experiment consumers were asked to describe their *writing* experience with three brands of ballpoint pens. One of these was a brand that stressed efficiency; the second emphasized general quality of competence; and the third focused on low price.[5] The interesting finding was that consumers described their experience in terms of the generalized brand image rather than in terms of objective qualities such as efficiency or price stressed by the manufacturer's advertising.

Another way of understanding brand imagery is as a means of self-fulfillment. A person's buying behavior depends partly on his image of himself. He buys a certain brand because he thinks of himself as a "Chesterfield smoker" or a "Chrysler man." The housewife envisions herself as a "Bisquick housewife." This attitude suggests one approach to product analysis: if we can discover what people see when they look in the product mirror, we have important clues for our advertising.

Most agencies soliciting the Rival canned dog food account emphasized the brand image. The agency that eventually landed the account emphasized that a pilot study of dog owners revealed "a lack of specificity in brand image." One of the principals maintained that many dog owners were worried because Rival was cheaper than some other dog foods—a poor "quality image." He felt that dog owners seemed to suffer from "gnawing nutritional anxiety" about the food they gave their dogs. He then suggested ways of improving the firm's brand image. Another agency soliciting the account expressed the relation between dog and housewife in the sentence—"A dog is nothing more than a four-year-old child with fur."[6]

Unique Selling Proposition. Many successful practitioners of advertising have noted the importance of looking for the differentiating qualities of the product or service. For example, Professor Neil Borden emphasized this in the early 1940s as one of the criteria to be used in determining how advertisable a product is—the more product differentiation possible, the more advertisable the product. Agency head Rosser Reeves says that all really successful campaigns are based on a prod-

[5]Irving S. White, "The Functions of Advertising in Our Culture," *Journal of Marketing,* July 1959.
[6]Spencer Klaw, "More Smooch in the Pooch," Editors of Fortune, *The Amazing Advertising Business* (New York: Simon and Schuster, Inc., 1957), for a detailed description of how an agency solicits accounts.

uct's U.S.P. (Unique Selling Proposition) and that the growth of the agency he heads is based to a great extent on its use of the "theory of U.S.P." More specifically, Reeves says that U.S.P. is divided into three parts:

1. Each advertisement must make a proposition to the consumer. Not just words, not just product puffery, not just show-window advertising. Each advertisement must say to each reader: "Buy this product and you will get this specific benefit."
2. The proposition must be one that the competition either cannot, or does not, offer. It must be unique either in the brand or the claim.
3. The proposition must be strong enough to move the mass millions, i.e., pull over new customers to your product.[7]

Inherent Drama. Another dimension of product symbolism is suggested by agency head Leo Burnett, who has emphasized the "inherent drama" of a product:

I have learned that this so-called inherent drama exists in almost every product and service.

In some cases, such as a new-type dome car or frozen soup, it is relatively easy to find. In other cases, such as a can of peas, a package of cereal, a bar of soap, a sack of flour, a tank of gasoline, a cigarette, or a piece of plumbing, you sometimes have to dig for it and for ways of interpreting it which will lay it before the reader or viewer with great simplicity and directness, still with engagement and interest and, of course, with great believability, without tricks or obvious borrowed interest.[8]

He offered as examples of "inherent drama" the placing of a piece of red meat against a red background to express the virility of meat, and symbolizing a cake as the highest achievement in the art of baking.

Leslie Beldo suggests we search for a "product's communicability" and recommends that the following five questions be asked:

1. Does the product concept fit an existing or developable pattern of consumer requirements among a sufficiently sizable segment of the population?
2. Is it a product of high or low inherent consumer interest?
3. Is the product concept unique, clear, believable, and appealing?
4. Does the product concept lend itself to unified product naming, packaging, and advertising?
5. Will the product concept communicate easily, or will its communication require intensive and extended effort?[9]

Corporate and Store Images. Like products, institutions have images, and many have spent a great deal of money trying to improve the "corporate image." Many executives feel that if the right psychological meanings are associated with their company, employees will want to work there and people will be favorably predisposed toward its product. Some retail authorities have urged supermarkets and department stores to develop store personalities so that the "prospective customer can consciously or unconsciously see a 'fit' between her own

[7]Rosser Reeves, *Reality in Advertising* (New York: Alfred A. Knopf, 1961), pp. 47–48.
[8]Leo Burnett, *Communications of an Advertising Man* (Chicago: Leo Burnett Company, Inc., 1961), p. 77.
[9]Leslie Beldo, "The CPP Model for New Product Evaluation," *The Executive Post Mark of Market Facts* (Chicago), October 1964.

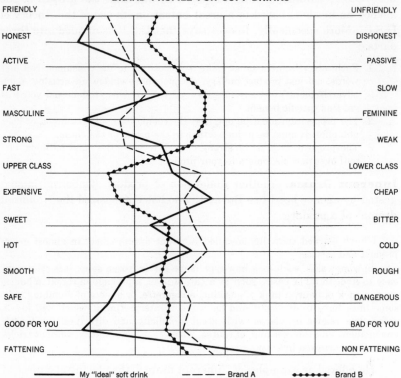

FIG. 14.2 *Points plotted for each scale represent the mean score of responses. Respondents were asked to rate each brand and their "ideal" brand on a seven-point scale for each pair of adjectival opposites. This is a common method for quantifying the brand image.*

self-image and the image of the store."[10] Unless she sees this "fit" she may refuse to patronize the store whether or not the price is favorable.

As corporations and retailing institutions diversify, their corporate image becomes diffuse and hard to define. Procter & Gamble, for example, makes products in such diverse fields as soap, food, paper, drugs, and dentifrices. Sears, Roebuck is not only a retailer but a major insurance and credit organization. Time, Incorporated owns magazines, broadcasting stations, and real estate and book publishing facilities.

As Martineau has pointed out, the corporate image is a much more complex concept than is generally realized. There are actually many corporate personalities and stockholders, employees, vendors, and customers who will all have different images of a particular company. The personality is the result of many different forces. Although the public relations expert is usually entrusted with studying and molding the corporate image, he can exert only limited influence through his press releases, his house organ, or his open house. Every activity of the company will add meaning to the corporate personality. There are both emotional and functional dimensions to the image of a business institution.

Methods of Measuring a Product's Subjective Qualities. A variety of techniques has been used to put this nebulous concept of image in specific or numerical terms. One popular approach is the use

[10]Pierre Martineau, "Sharper Focus for the Corporate Image," in Boyd and Newman, pp. 276–291.

of scaling techniques. For example, brand images are sometimes quantified by using the *semantic differential,* a technique utilizing a seven-point bipolar scale. Consumers are asked to mark on this scale their "feeling" toward a particular brand and toward an "ideal" brand of the same category. An example is shown in Figure 14.2. All rating scales require the respondent to place whatever is being tested (brand, firm, score, and the like) somewhere along a continuum ranging from one extreme to another on some characteristic. Several scales use verbal or pictorial representations to help the respondents. Others (for example, the semantic differential) rely on the respondent's ability to select scale positions only on the basis of position along a line and the distance between positions.

FIG. 14.3 *Range of movement for three independent variables — (relative competitive preference as measured by Schwerin, momentum or predisposition toward the brand, and television-advertising expenditures) — and one dependent variable, sales, during 67 brand measurement periods. Note the narrow range of movement for sales share as compared with the wide range for the other three variables.*
SOURCE: SCHWERIN RESEARCH CORPORATION.

The Schwerin Research Corporation has suggested that there is a measurable favorable (or unfavorable) predisposition to most brands. The firm recommends that this predisposition be called the brand's *momentum* (See Figure 14.3). The concept of momentum evolved from many years of experiments in which radio and television commercials for a variety of products were shown to theater audiences. In general, the effectiveness of commercials had been appraised through the years on the basis of "competitive preference" for the product advertised (comparison of the percentage of people who preferred the product *before* with the percentage of those who preferred it *after* exposure to the commercial). The results were usually compared with norms for the product field, but it became evident that allowance should also be made for the predisposition of consumers to the brand. It was therefore decided to quantify the difference between those who stated their preference for the brand before the television exposure and the brand's actual share of the market for that brand. For example, if 25 percent of the audience chose

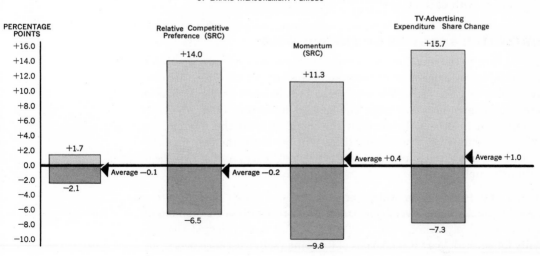

RANGE OF MOVEMENT
67 Brand Measurement Periods

the brand as their first choice in their prechoice questionnaire (for example, the attitude share of this audience) and the product's actual share of the market was 20 percent, it is assumed that the brand has a positive momentum of 5 percent *before* exposure to the advertising message. The momentum would, of course, be negative if the market share were greater than the attitude share.

Another method has been developed for evaluating the corporate image. It might be used also for a brand image. All words in *Webster's Collegiate Dictionary* and Roget's *International Thesaurus of English Words and Phrases* that can be used to describe a company are divided into synonym groups. The most representative word of each synonym group was then chosen and tested experimentally. On the basis of these experiments certain "trait" words were chosen ("friendly," "alert," "open-minded"). In developing a particular corporate image, interviewers ask a respondent to sort cards listing the traits on them, thus indicating his opinion of the company, its competitors, and the "ideal company" in the field.[11]

Another approach is to use either the direct or the indirect methods for studying consumers, which are outlined in Chapter 12. Carefully trained interviewers may conduct depth interviews to probe for beneath-the-surface clues to what consumers really think about your product. Regardless of which specific approach is taken in searching for a product's subjective qualities, it will be helpful to focus attention on the following:

1. What are the qualities that make the product *unique* (the associations, feelings and attitudes that, in the consumer's eye, distinguish it from competing brands)?
2. Which of these qualities give it *motivating power* (the qualities that satisfy some need or desire, either directly or indirectly, and ultimately cause the consumer to act)?
3. Which of these fit together best in a *coherent pattern* (qualities consonant with each other)?

OBJECTIVE ANALYSIS OF THE PRODUCT

Let us turn to the more objective aspects of product analysis—qualities measurable by some generally accepted standard (for example, 20 miles per gallon of gas). These are more important in some products than in others and appropriately more emphasized in certain types of advertising than in others. In general, the more rational the buying, the more important the physical qualities will be. Nevertheless, it is important to know these physical properties and whether they will bear primary emphasis in an advertising campaign.

What the Product Is Made of. The raw materials that go into a product are sometimes very important. Foam rubber in a cushion might be an effective talking point. Northern Tissue was promoted successfully for several years on the basis of its being "softer because it is made

[11]See John F. Bolger, Jr., "How to Evaluate Your Company Image," *Journal of Marketing*, October 1959.

of Fluff" (a bit of information obtained during a writer's visit to the paper mill).

The "raw materials" of a service may be its facilities, its conveniences, and the abilities and personalities of those who conduct the service. Meals served en route might influence people to travel by one carrier in preference to another. "We call at any hour of the day or night" would be a point worth emphasizing in talking about servicing oil burners.

How Well the Product Is Made. Good workmanship may be very important in promoting a product. Note in the Rolls-Royce advertisement (Figure 17.2) that "You adjust the shock absorbers to the changing road by flicking a switch on the new Rolls-Royce and Bentley."

How the Product Is Used. A product may have many uses, major and minor, varying from one market group to another. However, it will usually have one principal use. If the creative person is to plan effective advertising he must never lose sight of that major use. For example, a fountain pen may be striking in appearance because of its ultramodern design. Its color combinations may be unusually attractive. It may hold more ink, be easier to fill than other pens – or even write under water. But its primary function is to write under normal conditions. All the other features combined will never make the user happy if the ink does not flow freely. Sometimes, however, use may be subordinated to other considerations. No housewife will be happy with an ugly rug, even though it might wear for generations, be very simple to keep clean, and otherwise fulfill its function as a floor covering.

How it Does Competitively. Frequently advertising must convince consumers that the advertised product will offer greater advantages than competing products do. Certainly, if a product were provably best in the field, the adman's job would be simple. The fact is that there are many good products in most fields but few that are best by any universally accepted standard. A product that is very strong in certain points may be weak in others.

Research sometimes discloses that the manufacturer and the consuming public do not always agree on a product's greatest merit. A woman may buy a vacuum cleaner more for ease in changing attachments than for its cleaning power, although the latter may be emphasized by the maker.

The fact that what you are selling is first in its field may well be the basis for an effective promotional campaign. Note in Figure 14.4 how an advertising medium has used its leading position as the keynote of a trade paper advertisement.

How the Product is Packaged. There has been a decided increase during the past decade in the number of products packaged and in the utility and attractiveness of the packages. Sometimes – as with certain cosmetics – the package may cost more than the product itself. Most of the reasons for the growth of packaging are obvious. As self-service retailing has grown, manufacturers have tried to provide the consumer with an easy means of *identification*. In some products, such as fresh

HABITAT U.S.A.

Across the length and breadth of the United States, the winds of design are blowing in all directions. This free spirit of architectural and decorative self-expression is the substance of House Beautiful's April issue, Habitat U.S.A. Five remarkable houses in five states synthesize the spirited sweep of design, inside and out; from a lovingly restored early colonial in Easthampton to an avant-garde sculptured complex that houses pop, op and people in Beverly Hills. And proves that there is no single contemporary answer to the eternal question, "How to live?"

For Americans who seek beauty and self-expression each in their own way elsewhere, the April issue of House Beautiful is a wellspring of inspiration and information. We present landscape-lovers with a big colorful bouquet of flowering trees. We bow to collectors of Victoriana with a new American fabric collection of authentic reproductions from that long varied golden age. We explain the intricacies of collecting American art with the help of expert critic Emily Genauer. We look up and open their eyes to the possibilities of creative ceilings. We strike up the

band and tune them in to what's happening to the new sophisticated sound of the concert—a far cry from Sunday in the park.

Once again, House Beautiful takes the pulse of the times and gets to the heart of what matters. Each month we are the creative catalyst for Americans who believe in living beautifully, with flair and individuality. Call us for the inside story on our upcoming issues—full of ideas, vitality and journalistic firsts that make House Beautiful the best buy in the U.S.A. for over 4,250,000 readers. And for you.

House Beautiful
the home magazine of discovery

FIG. 14.4 *Image-building advertisement for a leading shelter magazine.*
ADVERTISEMENT FOR HOUSE BEAUTIFUL MAGAZINE REPRINTED BY PERMISSION.

fruits and vegetables, many of which are now packaged, the package may help to protect the product from spoilage or damage. Packages are also more convenient for the retailer who stocks the product and the consumer who stores it in pantry or refrigerator. The packagers themselves have developed many new packaging ideas to help the manufacturer sell his goods.

Suppose you are looking for objective qualities of a package to emphasize in an advertisement. What do you look for? Among the most promising possibilities are construction, design, size and shape, and closure.

In recent years we have seen many innovations in package construction, such as "squeeze-type" plastic packages in many product lines. Plastics, such as Saran, have been used to cover everything from liver sausage to refrigerated cookie dough. Soft drinks have been packaged in cans during the past decade, and beer has been sold in cans for a much longer time.

Package design includes shape, color, layout, use of illustration and copy, and general appeal of the package. Some of the best artistic talent in the country has been designing improved packages. Color is used more frequently to attract attention and to suggest certain qualities of the product. The clean-cut lines of modern design are evident in many packages.

The size of the package will depend on the product itself, but there has been a trend toward smaller, more compact packages. The size may also depend on the way in which the product can be used. Both Pepsi-Cola and Coca-Cola, after many years of marketing only one bottle size, now offer "family size" containers. Many ready-cooked cereals are marketed in one-serving sizes.

The closure has also come in for much attention in recent years. Ipana, for example, offers a closure that makes it possible to stand the tube of toothpaste on end. The Marlboro theme "Filter, Flavor, Flip-Top Box" has been used extensively in that advertiser's radio and television advertising. The closure, of course, may be influenced by the necessity of keeping the contents airtight.

How It Is Designed. The importance of good design has long been recognized in such products as automobiles. In recent years the attention of designers has been focused also on products such as typewriters and telephones, where the design's importance is not quite so obvious. More and more we find names like Raymond Loewy or Henry Dreyfuss mentioned in advertisements as the designers of certain products. *Fortune* has estimated that there are 180 important industrial design firms. These range from one-man or two-man studios to 200-man factories. Of the estimated $40,000,000 paid yearly to industrial designers approximately half goes to the twenty top firms. The growth of self-service has focused a great deal of attention on product design. High fees and increasing awareness of the importance of design have led several manufacturers to set up their own staffs, supplemented frequently by industrial design companies.

How Much It Costs. It is not often possible to quote retail prices in national advertisements, because prices vary from store to store and from one part of the country to another. The advertising planner, however, should always be aware of the prices of his product and of competing products. He can then make statements such as "Costs no more than other leading brands" or, if he believes it has a real price appeal, "Economical—less than 3¢ a serving." If the product is a little more expensive, he may emphasize that "you get all these extra features for only a little more than other leading brands."

Where It Is Sold. It is important that consumers know where to find the products they see advertised. They can assume that grocery products will be found in most grocery stores and that ovenware can be purchased in department, hardware, or food stores. The advertising planner should make sure he knows what kinds of outlets handle his product. He may want to emphasize that it is "available at all grocery stores" or, as Dial did when it wanted to establish prestige for this new brand, emphasize that it is sold only in "leading department stores."

Methods of Measuring Objective Qualities. Obviously, an *objective* quality will be easier to measure quantitatively than a *subjective* one. There are, by definition, accepted standards of measurement. However, we must not forget that the consumer, as well as the advertiser, is able to compare products on the same objective standards. He can readily check to see whether the uses or the prices are really as advertised. On the other hand, it is more difficult for him to check the validity of subjective claims. Although subjective evaluations must come from the consumer, objective evaluations may result from either technical product research or consumer product research.

Technical research is often directly related to certain subjective concepts. Lee Iacocca, group vice-president of the Ford Motor Company, points out that the idea for the 1965–1966 "Ford is quieter" campaign actually started several years earlier when, during an agency-client discussion, someone said that it would take Ford fifty years to overcome the "Tin Lizzie reputation for cheap, noisy bodies."[12] Someone else quipped that Ford should buy Rolls-Royce. When the first prototypes of the 1965 models were available it was evident, Iacocca says, that the car really had a lot of "quiet luxury." Both agency and client wanted to avoid clichés like "cloud smooth," "satin smooth," and the like. Then someone remembered the old Rolls-Royce idea. The agency rented a Rolls and a decibel meter and ran a brief test on Long Island with results that encouraged the company to compare Ford with Rolls. Two Rolls-Royces were purchased, a professional acoustical research firm was retained to supervise the testing, and the United States Auto Club was asked to observe the tests and certify the results. Even when the tests showed Ford was really quieter, company executives were afraid that people might think the campaign was ridiculous or untrue. Fortunately, they decided to go ahead. According to Iacocca, dealers got instantaneous reaction on the showroom floor, columnists picked up the story, comedians made jokes about it, and the company started to get mail—mostly favorable—from the public.

As researcher Richard Crisp points out, consumer-product research techniques, particularly when they involve objective qualities, have become relatively standardized. He suggests the following as "a distillation of the experience of many research practitioners, working on a wide variety of consumer products":

1. Test products only among qualified users.
2. Test no more than two products at a time.
3. Remove all identification from the products, except for identifying code letters or numbers.
4. Eliminate all variables in the packaging, color, etc., of the products being tested, unless those variables represent intrinsic features of the products being tested.
5. Have the product tested under normal usage conditions.
6. Remind test participants that a test is in progress.
7. Get reactions immediately after use.
8. Check early in the test for "bugs" in instructions or procedure.
9. Test your product against the market leader.
10. Let the test continue for a substantial period of time on continuing-use products.
11. Eliminate all irrelevant variables—be fair![13]

[12]Lee Iacocca, "The Four Freedoms of Advertising," speech before American Association of Advertising Agencies Eastern Annual Conference, New York, October 26, 1965.
[13]Richard Crisp, *Marketing Research* (New York: McGraw-Hill, Inc., 1957), pp. 563–569.

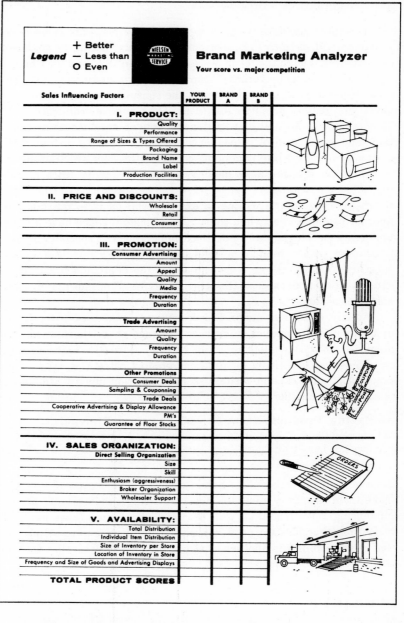

FIG. 14.5   *A brand score-sheet developed by the A. C. Nielsen Company.*
SOURCE: A. C. NIELSEN COMPANY.

A brand analyzer recommended by the A. C. Nielsen Company is illustrated in Figure 14.5.

ANALYZING PRODUCTS FROM THE MARKETING VIEWPOINT

Marketers frequently regard products in terms of how people buy them. We thus have *producer* and *consumer* goods. It is usually easy to determine whether what we are selling is used in the production of another product (producer good) or whether it is sold for ultimate consumption (consumer good). As we shall see later in this book, our advertising media tend to divide along these two lines, although there is some overlapping.

The three standard categories of consumer goods are *convenience*, *shopping*, and *specialty*. The distinctions here are not quite so sharply defined, even though the terms were conceived in 1924 and have become a part of marketing literature.[14] Briefly, the classic distinction holds that a convenience good is one for which the consumer expends a minimal effort. She readily accepts substitutes. Thus milk is ordinarily a convenience good. (To many practitioners "convenience" goods are those that offer some form of convenience to the consumer—instant coffee, cake mixes, and the like.) Shopping goods are those for which consumers feel there is a real gain to be made by comparing quality, price, or other important characteristics before buying. The specialty good is one for which the consumer is willing to exert special effort to purchase. We find, for example, that when consumers of instant coffee have a strong preference for it to regular coffee, the former becomes a specialty product. Consumers insist on their favorite brands and are reluctant to take substitutes. However, we try to minimize the effort and make it convenient for them to exercise this urge by having all brands readily available at most stores.

Agency executive Victor Bloede suggests that copywriters think in terms of four product categories—package goods, hard goods (appliances), soft goods (clothing), and services. Says Mr. Bloede: "There *are* differences in writing for different product categories. And, in my experience, some capable writers seem to function much better in one category than another."[15]

Analyzing Products from the Managerial Viewpoint. One of the big problems of marketing management is determining the relative amount of advertising versus other marketing elements to use in the marketing mix. Marketing managers have to analyze products on the basis of their advertisability. Some products have characteristics that make them especially adaptable for advertising; others do not. Factors influencing advertisability are discussed later in connection with budgeting; therefore we need not cover them here except to mention that advertisability is another aspect of product analysis that is sometimes overlooked.

SUMMARY

To plan a campaign effectively one should be thoroughly familiar with the product or service. It is usually helpful to analyze the product from both the subjective and the objective points of view. The former generally comes to focus in the brand image and includes the many emotional and esthetic associations the consumer has with the product. The latter are those for which there is a generally accepted standard of measurement (construction, quality, uses, competitive performance, packaging, product design, price, and distribution).

[14]For a discussion of these definitions, see Richard H. Holton, "The Distinction between Convenience Goods, Shopping Goods and Specialty Goods," *Journal of Marketing,* July 1958; David Luck, "On the Nature of Specialty Goods," and Richard H. Holton, "What Is Really Meant by 'Specialty' Goods?" both in *Journal of Marketing,* July 1959.

[15]Victor Bloede, "Four Major Product Categories," in Elbrun Rochford French, ed. *The Copywriter's Guide* (New York: Harper & Row, Publishers, 1959).

To collect data on a product's subjective qualities one must go to the consumers; data on objective qualities may be obtained from either consumers or through technical laboratory research.

A product analyst should take advantage of such time-tested marketing classifications as convenience, shopping, and specialty. Finally, he should consider the advertisability of products from the management point of view.

QUESTIONS FOR DISCUSSION

1. How would you define brand image? Why is the concept important in advertising?
2. Name a product whose subjective qualities are probably more important than its objective qualities in the final purchase decision. Name one in which the reverse is true.
3. Select two advertisements that seem to be building a brand or product image? Do they represent a sound use of psychological principles?
4. Which is likely to be more believable — psychological concepts used to help build a brand image, or performance data which are based on tests? Why?
5. Why is the semantic differential so often used to measure the dimensions of a brand's image?
6. Why should one analyze products from the marketing point of view?

SUGGESTED READINGS

Brink, Edward L., and William T. Kelley, *The Management of Promotion.* Englewood Cliffs, N.J.: Prentice-Hall, Inc., 1963. Chapter 9.

Burnett, Leo, *Communications of an Advertising Man.* Chicago: Leo Burnett Company, Inc., 1961.

Gardner, Burleigh B., "Symbols and Meanings in Advertising," in C. H. Sandage, ed., *The Promise of Advertising.* Homewood, Ill.: Richard D. Irwin, Inc., 1961.

Martineau, Pierre, "Sharper Focus for the Corporate Image," in Harper W. Boyd, Jr., and Joseph W. Newman, eds. *Advertising Management: Selected Readings.* Homewood, Ill.: Richard D. Irwin, Inc., 1965.

Ogilvy, David, "The Image and the Brand," in Harper W. Boyd, Jr., and Joseph W. Newman, eds. *Advertising Management: Selected Readings.* Homewood, Ill.: Richard D. Irwin, Inc., 1965.

Reeves, Rosser, *Reality in Advertising.* New York: Alfred A. Knopf, 1961.

Sandage, C. H., and Vernon Fryburger, *Advertising Theory and Practice,* 7th ed. Homewood, Ill.: Richard D. Irwin, Inc., 1967, Chapter 10.

Tannenbaum, Percy H., and Jack M. McCleod, "Public Images of Mass Media Institutions," in Wayne A. Danielson, ed., *Paul J. Deutschmann Memorial Papers in Mass Communications Research,* Cincinnati: Scripps-Howard Research, 1963.

Wright, John S., and Daniel S. Warner, *Advertising,* 2d ed. New York: McGraw-Hill, Inc., 1966, Chapter 4.

15 | Budgeting for Advertising and Promotion

Even the most seasoned and sophisticated businessman never feels quite sure whether he has appropriated the right amount for advertising or any other marketing function. One long-time advertising and marketing executive, Clarence E. Eldridge, goes so far as to claim that "the allocation of the budget and, even more important, the *amount* of the budget are determined more by guess work and instinct than by the application of scientific or even thoughtful analysis."[1] The advertising manager and the agency account executive will probably believe it is too low, and the controller will say it is too high. However, modern research has removed budgeting a long way from the days when advertising got what was left over after the company's other expenses had been met. This new objectivity produced in 1967 an expenditure that was the highest in history but less, as a percentage of our total national income, than advertising expenditures had been in the 1920s and 1930s.

ADVERTISING'S CHANGING ECONOMIC ENVIRONMENT

It was between the 1880s and 1920s that advertising came into its own.

[1]Clarence E. Eldridge, "The Budget: Its Marketing Role," *Marketing Insights*, April 10, 1967, p. 16.

It grew more rapidly than national income, reaching a peak of 4.5 percent of national income in 1921. This trend, as we pointed out in Chapter 1, was a result of such factors as growth in industrialization and the increased recognition of advertising as a valuable marketing tool.

In the boom year 1929, total advertising was approximately $3,426,000,000, or 3.9 percent of national income. During the lean years of the late 1930s it rose more slowly than national income, and so its percentage of national income declined. This trend continued to 1943, when advertising expenditure was $2,496,000,000, or 1.3 percent of income.

Compare these figures with what has happened since 1946. As Figure 1.5 indicates, United States expenditures increased every year from 1942 to 1957, dropping slightly in 1958. However, the $16,844,-000,000 spent in 1967 was still only approximately 3 percent of national income, well under the 4.5 percent spent in 1921.

We have seen, then, a generally rising level of expenditures since 1933. This reflects recognition of the role of advertising in marketing and communication, and the acceptance of advertising as an investment as important to corporate growth and health as the buying of new equipment. Finally, there has been some liberalization in the allowance of advertising as a tax deduction. We note, also, the long-range decline of advertising expenditure as a percent of national income, probably reflecting the increase in advertising's efficiency.

APPROACHES TO BUDGETING

The philosophy behind the individual businessman's budget is simple enough. He attempts to maximize his total profit by spending advertising dollars as long as each dollar spent adds to his total profit. If each dollar of advertising expenditure adds only a penny to his profit, the advertising money is still well spent. However, if he reaches a point where sales cost more than the profit on each unit sold, it is time to stop. The trick is to predict accurately how many additional sales advertising will bring and how much profit the company will make on each sale.

Hundreds of approaches are used by advertisers in determining how much to spend. Some advertisers use one method; others prefer the checks and balances of a combination of methods. There has been a decided change from simple methods like percentage of past sales to more sophisticated approaches, such as the "marketing program." It would not be practical to include in this volume all the possible approaches; however, the following classification includes most of those that are used today.

Percentage of Sales. Of the many approaches to budgeting developed over the years, the percentage of sales concept has been the most popular. However, it is not the most satisfactory or the most logical from the businessman's point of view. In its simplest form this approach is based on a fixed percentage of the previous year's sales (or the average of several of the past years). One advantage of this method is that expenditures are directly related to funds available—the more the company sold last year, the more it presumably has available for advertising this year. However, it would be more logical, under this reasoning, to allocate for advertising a straight percent of last year's profits. An important reason for the appeal of this system to advertisers—especially small ones—is its relative simplicity. Obviously, preparing the budget is a simple matter if you know last year's sales and have decided what percentage you will spend each year for advertising.

This procedure is illogical because it assumes that advertising is a result of sales rather than a cause. An important drawback is the inflexibility of the approach. It makes no allowance for the possibility that sales may decline because of too little advertising or that sales do not take advantage of a rising potential. There is a large variation in the productivity of advertising at different levels of operation; so it is entirely possible that the return on extra advertising expenditure may diminish, rather than increase, after a certain level of sales has been reached. There is always the haunting suspicion that a company that uses percentage of past sales may underspend when the potential is great and overspend when the potential is low.

Relating advertising appropriation to *anticipated* sales makes considerably more sense. Most major advertisers, whether or not they use this as a basic approach, make some attempt to study the relation between advertising and anticipated sales. This approach is more logical in that it is tied to the future rather than the past, and assumes that advertising precedes rather than follows sales. It also assumes that advertising is a major, though not the only, factor in producing sales. This approach depends heavily on the sales forecast; therefore provision should be made for a periodic review of the sales forecast and the amount budgeted, because economic and market conditions change.

Sometimes advertisers use a percentage of combined past and future sales. By referring to the past the budgeteer gives stability to the base, and the future offers him some chance to take advantage of market potential.

Unit of Sale. Unit of sale is, in many respects, a variation of the percentage-of-sales approach. Instead of dollar sales, the base is the physical volume of either past or future sales. A fixed amount of money is multiplied by the number of units of the product sold or to be sold. This approach is frequently used for durable goods of a high unit value, such as automobiles, refrigerators, and automatic washing machines. According to *Advertising Age,* per car advertising expenditures ranged in 1967 from a low of $24.98 per car (Pontiac) to a high of $61.84 (Lincoln–Continental) and beer advertising from 18 cents a barrel to $1.87. In instances where the approach is used for goods of small unit value, some unit such as the case, barrel, or carton is commonly used.

The unit-of-sale approach is also useful in association or cooperative advertising and where unit production is known fairly accurately in advance (as in the canning industry).

Objective. Some budgeteers call the objective method the "task" method; others call it the "research-objective." Presumably the advertiser starts with a thorough study of his market and product in order to set logical advertising objectives. The next step is a definition of objectives in such terms as units to be sold, profits to be attained and, distribution to be gained. The objectives can be set for one or several years. (Some large companies set their objectives five years ahead.)

After the objectives are set the advertiser must determine how much money will be necessary to achieve them. If the cost is greater than the money available, either the objectives must be scaled down or additional funds must be found.

The executive vice-president of A. C. Nielsen Company, J. O. Peckham, suggests that marketers of new products decide on the share of sales they want as their objective and then budget their advertising and sales promotion accordingly.[2] He maintains that even small companies can do very well if they have a demonstrably superior product and pick market segments not covered by the big companies. He recommends "sufficient advertising over the first two years to produce a share of advertising about one and one-half times the desired share of sales." He believes that about the same ratio of consumer promotion is appropriate.

One major advantage of the objective approach is its emphasis on building the budget from the ground up. Most other plans provide for first allocating the money and then setting the purposes for which the money is to be spent. The objective approach avoids inflexible reliance on either past or future sales, although in actual practice the budgeteer has to take both into consideration.

One of the principal dangers is that it may create a false feeling of objectivity. A. W. Frey points out that advertisers

who state that they use the method often have trouble in explaining just how they arrived at the amount of advertising necessary to reach the established objectives. They may even find it difficult to explain how they arrived at the objectives. The objectives themselves may be established with too little regard for their implications.[3]

Mathematical Approach. There has been much interest — especially since the advent of computers — in the use of mathematical approaches to budgeting. For example, Kuehn developed a model based on brand loyalty characteristics intended for use in a competitive market.[4] Friedman has applied game-theory logic to the problem of advertising budgeting.[5] The trouble is that each of these depends on information often not available to the average businessman and that neither is applicable to a wide variety of firms. Simon has suggested a simpler model that is, like most, designed to maximize profit by equating marginal revenue and marginal costs.[6] It requires information on (1)

[2]J. O. Peckham, "Guidelines for Marketing," *The Nielsen Researcher*, vol. 23, no. 2, 1965.
[3]A. W. Frey, *How Many Dollars for Advertising* (New York: The Ronald Press Company, 1955), p. 63.
[4]Alfred A. Kuehn, "Model for Budgeting Advertising," in Frank Bass, ed., *Mathematical Models and Methods in Marketing* (Homewood, Ill.: Richard D. Irwin, Inc., 1961).
[5]Laurence Friedman, "Game-Theory Models in the Allocation of Advertising Expenditures," in Frank Bass, ed., *Mathematical Models and Methods in Marketing* (Homewood, Ill.: Richard D. Irwin, Inc., 1961).
[6]Julian L. Simon, "A Simple Model for Determining Advertising Appropriations," *Journal of Marketing Research*, II (August 1965), 285–292.

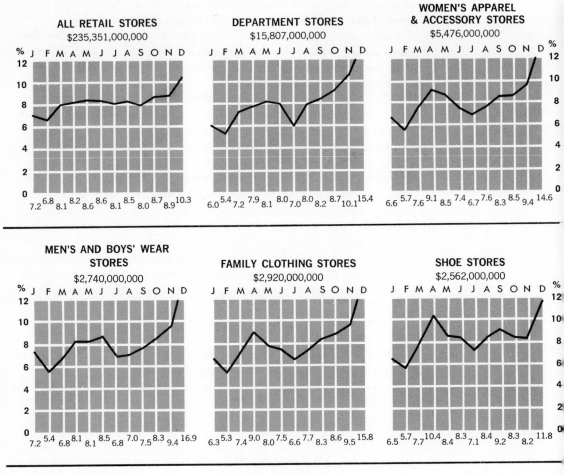

TOTAL RETAIL SALES BY TYPES OF STORES
PERCENT OF THE YEAR'S TOTAL SALES DONE EACH MONTH

ALL RETAIL STORES
$235,351,000,000

7.2 6.8 8.1 8.2 8.6 8.6 8.1 8.5 8.0 8.7 8.9 10.3

DEPARTMENT STORES
$15,807,000,000

6.0 5.4 7.2 7.9 8.1 8.0 7.0 8.0 8.2 8.7 10.1 15.4

WOMEN'S APPAREL & ACCESSORY STORES
$5,476,000,000

6.6 5.7 7.6 9.1 8.5 7.4 6.7 7.6 8.3 8.5 9.4 14.6

MEN'S AND BOYS' WEAR STORES
$2,740,000,000

7.2 5.4 6.8 8.1 8.1 8.5 6.8 7.0 7.5 8.3 9.4 16.9

FAMILY CLOTHING STORES
$2,920,000,000

6.3 5.3 7.4 9.0 8.0 7.5 6.6 7.7 8.3 8.6 9.5 15.8

SHOE STORES
$2,562,000,000

6.5 5.7 7.7 10.4 8.4 8.3 7.1 8.4 9.2 8.3 8.2 11.8

FURNITURE, HOME FURNISHINGS STORES
$6,997,000,000

7.0 6.6 7.6 7.6 8.3 8.3 8.2 8.9 8.6 9.0 9.4 10.5

HOUSEHOLD-APPLIANCE, TV, RADIO STORES
$3,817,000,000

7.6 6.9 7.4 6.8 7.8 8.2 7.8 8.4 8.3 8.8 9.5 12.5

VARIETY STORES
$4,457,000,000

5.6 5.9 7.3 8.1 7.9 7.9 7.2 8.2 7.9 8.1 9.0 16.9

FIG. 15.1 *Charts which show the percentage of a store's total sales for the year occurring in each month. Note the wide variation in seasonal pattern of sales from one store type to another.* SOURCE: BUREAU OF ADVERTISING, A.N.P.A.

TOTAL RETAIL SALES BY TYPES OF STORES
PERCENT OF THE YEAR'S TOTAL SALES DONE EACH MONTH

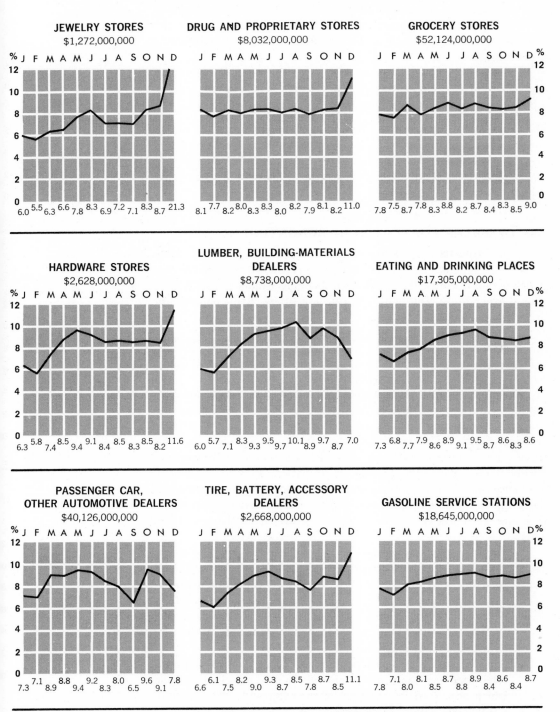

SOURCE: U.S. DEPARTMENT OF COMMERCE, 1962 SALES REPORTS
(Jewelry Stores—Retail Jewelers of America, Inc., 1959 Sales Reports.)
Dollar figures listed for each store type are 1962 sales totals except for jewelry stores.

the sales effect of advertising in the current period of different possible levels of advertising; (2) sales in the prior period; (3) the rate at which sales decline in the absence of advertising; and (4) the interest rate on the firm's capital. Unlike many of the others, this model works with absolute data that are likely to be available rather than with share-of-market data.

There is little doubt that we shall see in the years ahead a great many more attempts to formulate models that will help make appropriating promotion expenditures a more exact science.

The Arbitrary Approach. Illogical as it seems to call it an approach, some companies determine their appropriations in an arbitrary way. The whim of a top executive may determine the amount to be spent—or the advertising budget may consist of whatever funds happen to be available.

USE OF SALES FORECASTS IN BUDGETING

Sales forcasting techniques are especially useful in making budgets. The forecast tells where there is a sales opportunity in a particular area or demographic group. It is then up to the budget maker to work out a plan of expenditures that will take full advantage of this opportunity. Brink and Kelley say,

> All budgeting must start with the sales forecast. The forecast is often pulled together by the sales manager, or by a budgeting and forecasting committee, of which the sales manager will be a key member. In larger firms it may be worked out by an economist or sales analyst.[7]

An advertiser may invite trouble if he bases his appropriation too closely on the general sales outlook, either with it or counter to it. A wiser policy is to analyze the sales outlook for *his* firm and *his* products and appropriate the advertising money accordingly. One company that follows this "marketing-program" approach with considerable success is Bristol-Myers, makers of Ipana, Sal Hepatica, Bufferin, and other pharmaceutical and toilet items. Both the president of the company and the president of its major division have direct-advertising experience. Here are steps followed by the company in preparing the advertising budget:

1. Sales forecasts are worked out for each of the company's products. These forecasts are primarily the responsibility of the advertising brand managers for each product. The brand managers will normally make use of the company's market-research department, the sales departments, and the advertising agency involved. Competitors' marketing strength and advertising outlays are studied carefully.

2. Sales estimates for each product are given to a management committee for study and approval. In the principal division, which accounted for the bulk of the company's $23,000,000 to $24,000,000 dollars of advertising in 1958, the members of the management committee are the division president, sales vice-

[7]Edward L. Brink and William T. Kelley, *The Management of Promotion* (Englewood Cliffs, N.J.: Prentice-Hall, Inc., 1963), p. 225.

president, market-research vice-president, product-development vice-president, treasurer, and advertising vice-president.

3. Sales targets are turned over to the controller's office for estimates on all costs (other than advertising and merchandising) that can be expected in reaching the targets.

4. Final calculation of advertising outlay is made by the advertising vice-president. This calculation is based on two considerations: the percent of anticipated sales that seems appropriate and an earnings target previously agreed upon by division and corporate headquarters. According to the division's advertising vice-president, there tends to be "a sort of upward bias in fixing these percentages," because advertising is regarded as an investment in brand stability. In other words, if a product is doing well at an advertising investment of 10 percent of sales, there is an inclination to investigate the feasibility of investing 15 percent.

5. After six months the results are carefully assessed. If the division's profits are below the target figure, some dollars may be switched directly to advertising.

What should the businessman do when the sales outlook darkens? Should he increase his budget when selling becomes more difficult, or should he cut back? The evidence is inconclusive, but it does indicate that the businessman may, on occasion, profit from downturns if they cause his competitors to retrench. For example, Borden describes the experience of Philco during the depression of the 1930s:[8]

The Philco management was in a position to spend such increased amounts profitably because the low-price table models which it launched in 1930 enjoyed a large demand, not merely because they were low in cost in comparison with all models that had gone before, but also because they gave good broadcast reception and were convenient. In 1931 the company continued to push the sales of its table models, but it gave particular attention to the designing of higher-price radios in an effort to induce purchase by those who were still in the market for such models. Again in 1931 the company started intensive promotion on automobile radios, a new development. Aggressive selling was combined with skillful merchandising throughout this period to attain successful sales results. Thus is illustrated the generalization that increased advertising and selling effort in depressions must be accompanied by astute merchandising and pricing to produce profitable sales volume.

Printers' Ink has summarized five important studies of the relation of advertising to sales.[9] All five indicated that companies that kept promoting despite the ups and downs of the business cycle did the best in sales. McCann-Erickson studied expenditures and sales of 64 of the leading 100 advertisers between 1948 and 1957. Among these 64 companies, 16 showed steady growth, 28 showed slow growth, and 20 showed rapid growth. The companies reporting the greatest growth had increased advertising 197 percent and sales 113 percent.

[8]Neil H. Borden, *Economic Effects of Advertising* (Homewood, Ill.: Richard D. Irwin, Inc., 1942), pp. 729–730.
[9]"How Does Advertising Affect Sales and Company Growth in Recession and Boom?" *Printers' Ink*, August 29, 1958, pp. 25–34.

INFLUENCES ON THE ADVERTISING APPROPRIATION

In deciding which of the various approaches he will use, and in setting upper and lower limits on his spending, the astute advertiser will be influenced by such considerations as the following:

Newness of the Product. During the first year and a half that it sold Dial Soap—mostly in test markets—Armour and Company spent approximately $1,000,000 for advertising. During each of the next two years approximately $3,000,000 was spent. At the close of the fourth year the company realized its first profit on Dial—a modest $200,000; and it took two more years before cumulative profits were sufficient to cancel the losses of the first three years. And this, remember, is the story of a highly successful new product.[10]

Most businessmen concede that it takes substantially more advertising money to launch a new product than it does to keep an old one going. Consequently, few companies can expect to make a profit on a product or brand during its introductory period. Like other expenditures, advertising must come from capital rather than income. Advertisers should, however, set up some sort of profit timetable to indicate when the product is expected to show a profit. To do this the budgeteer must estimate various expense-to-volume relations that seem attainable.

Frequently the product is tested in various markets around the country to determine whether it is suitable for national distribution and whether changes should be made in the marketing plan. Sometimes the advertiser is so eager to beat the competition that he tries to attain national distribution before his competitors can catch up with him. For example, when DuBarry shampoo was introduced on the market, the campaign was quickly switched from local to national because the marketers felt the distinctive features were easily duplicative and that the company had to get a strong start on the competition if the product were to succeed.

Type of Product. As Table 15.1 shows clearly, there are significant variations from one product to another in the percentage of sales invested in advertising. The highest percentage is 14.19 percent of sales for perfumes, cosmetics, and other toilet preparations; the lowest is 0.10 percent for heavy construction. Why is the variation so great?

Certain product factors have a great deal to do with the percentage of sales devoted to advertising:[11]

Opportunity to Differentiate the Product. It is worth noting that products with a high percentage of sales invested in advertising are those that can be differentiated in some significant manner. With sugar, for example, very minor differences distinguish one brand from another, but with perfumes and cosmetics the differences may be significant and important to the consumer.

---

[10]Spencer Klaw, "How Armour Cleaned Up with Dial," *Fortune*, May 1955, p. 129.
[11]See Borden, pp. 424–435, for a more complete discussion of product factors that influence the advertisability of a product.

TABLE 15.1

PERCENT OF SALES INVESTED IN ADVERTISING
BY PRODUCT AND SERVICE CLASSIFICATION

INDUSTRY OR SERVICE	PERCENTAGE
Perfumes, cosmetics, and other toilet preparations	14.19
Drugs	11.05
Soaps, related products except perfumes and cosmetics	10.68
Malt liquors, malt	7.04
Bottled soft drinks, flavorings	6.39
Motion picture theaters	6.28
Tobacco manufacturers	6.06
Watches, clocks, and clockwork-operated devices	5.78
Real estate agents, brokers, and managers	5.53
Book publishing, publishing, and printing	3.18
Household appliances	2.67
Hotel and other lodging places	2.43
Advertising firms	2.31
Motion picture production	2.18
Periodicals	1.96
Radio and television sets	1.66
Dairy products	1.59
Banking, trust companies	1.40
Radio and television broadcasting	1.38
Furniture and fixtures	1.09
Insurance agents and brokers	1.08
Electric lighting equipment	0.96
Women's and children's clothing	0.84
Costume jewelry	0.82
Newspapers	0.72
Meat products	0.63
Sugar	0.34
Mining	0.17
All industrial and service groups	1.18

SOURCE: *Advertising Age,* September 18, 1967. Based on Internal Revenue Service data.

Presence of Hidden Qualities. If the basis for differentiating is hidden, the buyer is more likely to depend on advertising to guide him in his choice of brand. Note, for example, in Table 15.1 the percentage tobacco manufacturers invest in advertising. Cigarettes, once they are out of the pack, look and smell much the same — the primary differences are in qualities that are hidden.

Absence of Strong Price Competition. If products are sold largely on the basis of price, advertisers are reluctant to spend advertising money trying to create a preference for this brand. In cosmetics price is relatively unimportant, so there is sufficient margin available for promotion of the brand. People are willing to pay a higher price for a brand if they believe it will satisfy them more completely. However, where brand is relatively unimportant (fresh fruits or sugar, for example) people tend to buy the product that sells at the lowest price. Advertising works best in nonprice competition.

Opportunity for Strong Emotional Appeals. Cosmetics and perfumes are well adapted to sex appeal, medicines to health appeal, and both can profit from strong emotional appeals. On the other hand, products such as hardware and industrial products such as electrical machinery are bought on a more rational basis.

Favorable Primary Demand. If the product class in general is in good demand, it is easier to stimulate specific brand demand through advertising. For example, automatic dishwashers have been increasingly in demand in recent years; consequently, many manufacturers have been encouraged to advertise their own particular brand.

Ernest Sharpe and Donald Ward studied twelve factors mentioned in various references as those most likely to affect advertising expenditures by business firms.[12] Thirty-nine industries were chosen and ranked according to the percentage of sales devoted to advertising, as compiled from Internal Revenue Service data (see Figure 15.1 for examples). A group of ten experts then rated these industries on the basis of the twelve factors of "advertisability." Of the twelve, the following ten were found to be positively and significantly related to the level of advertising investment by industry: mass production, competition, luxury, profit margin, impersonal service, impersonal selling, emotional appeal, present market size, potential market size, and frequency of purchase. The highest correlation between percent and rating occurred for impersonal service.

Importance of the Retailer. Traditionally the management of the Lydia E. Pinkham Medicine Company appropriated 50 percent of its sales receipts for advertising.[13] The principal reason given for this unusually high percentage was the necessity of persuading consumers to ask for the brand by name. The company learned that the drug retailer would normally do little to promote the product but would have to stock it, if people asked for it by name. Therefore it was important that the consumer be impressed by the product strongly enough to ask for it. So in this product the margin for promotion to consumers was large; the margin for the retailer relatively small.

On the other hand, a manufacturer of automobiles must depend on his dealers to display and demonstrate the cars he sends them. Consequently, he has to be sure that sufficient retailer margin of profit is provided for this service. Impressive as the total automobile advertising outlay is, it is necessarily much less as a percentage of total sales than is the advertising expenditure for a product like Lydia Pinkham's Vegetable Compound.

Scope of the Market. If a manufacturer expects to cover a national or regional market rather than a local one, he will obviously have to spend more money. He may, of course, realize certain savings per person reached by using national mass media, but his total outlay will still be substantial.

[12]Ernest Sharpe and Donald Ward, "Determinants of the Level of Advertising Investment by Industries," unpublished paper. (University of Texas, 1964).
[13]Neil H. Borden and Martin V. Marshall, "Lydia E. Pinkham Medicine Company," in their *Advertising Management: Text and Cases* (Homewood, Ill.: Richard D. Irwin, Inc. 1959), pp. 186–193.

Competition. An unfortunate result of the publication of "average" advertising expenditures has been the blind use of them by some advertisers. Wiser advertisers use such data only as guides. Some, for example, use competitive advertising figures to assess the effectiveness of their competitors' advertising. Their competitors may be advertising too much or too little.

A study of competitive advertising may also provide some indication of the barrier that an advertiser has to penetrate. If competitive brands are heavily advertised, it is harder to make consumers conscious of one brand. On the other hand, an imaginative advertising theme or copy treatment or a unique selling proposition may do wonders in overcoming competitive advertising and in penetrating communication barriers.

Every advertiser must know what the competition is doing, and there are many fine reporting services that make it relatively easy to find out. On the other hand, there is seldom any reason to use these figures on a "follow-the-leader" basis. Every business is unique and requires individual study.

CONSIDERATIONS IN PREPARING THE RETAIL BUDGET

In Table 15.2 are listed the percentages of net sales spent for advertising by common types of retail stores. These figures are based on Internal Revenue Service data and include the small stores that do no advertising and the stores that take advertising seriously.

At one extreme, we have stores such as mail order retailers and jewelers, who spend a relatively high percentage of their net sales for advertising. At the other, we have a liquor store that spends only 0.43 percent of sales for advertising. Many of the factors that influence retail budgets are necessarily related to those that influence the advertising budgets of national advertisers. The following are the most important factors:

Age of the Store. In general a new store must invest more in advertising than an older, well-established one. During its first years the store must win the confidence of customers and make the store and its merchandise known in the community by advertising.

Location of the Store. A store located on the periphery of a main shopping area will need more advertising to attract people to its less convenient location. Often, however, these higher advertising investments are balanced by lower rent. One retail clothing chain — Robert Hall — has made this point a basic theme in its advertising. Sometimes stores in less convenient locations offer abundant parking space or freedom from crowds as an inducement.

Merchandising Policies. Promotional (bargain-appeal) stores depend heavily on rapid turnover at low price. Consequently, they need a higher advertising investment than do stores enjoying a steady business in regular-price merchandise. Also, a store that emphasizes fashion merchandise, which must be sold quickly, will need larger appropriations than stores that deal principally in staple goods.

Competition. If competition is keen in a community, a store manager must tell his story consistently and favorably to his customers and exert continuing efforts to attract new customers. A store manager will also profit from watching the success or failure of competitors' ads.

Type of Media Available. Communities vary widely in the number and quality of media and in the advertising rates that the media charge. Retailers in a one-newspaper town—a more and more common phenomenon these days—will not have to spend as much as those in a multinewspaper town. Often the multimedia town is one that draws business from a large geographic area. A retailer in a town with one strong and one weak newspaper will not have to spend as much as a retailer in a community where there are two strong papers.

PERCENTAGE OF SALES INVESTED IN ADVERTISING BY SELECTED RETAILERS		TABLE 15.2
TYPE OF RETAILER	PERCENTAGE	
Mail order houses	10.15	
Jewelry stores	3.80	
Furniture and house furnishings	3.01	
Department stores	2.93	
Apparel and accessories	2.26	
Variety stores	1.33	
Food stores	1.32	
Drugstores	1.27	
Eating and drinking places	1.24	
Automotive dealers and filling stations	0.91	
Building materials and hardware stores	0.76	
Liquor stores	0.43	
All retail stores	1.58	

SOURCE: *Advertising Age*, September 18, 1967. Based on Internal Revenue Service Data.

Scope of the Trading Area. The larger the store's trading area, the more money it will normally need for advertising. The dominant department and specialty stores in an area attract customers from the city's entire trading area and spend substantially more than the smaller stores that can capitalize on the drawing power of their big neighbors.

Type of Merchandise Handled. Variety stores depend on impulse buying of low-cost, high-turnover items for the bulk of their business. Consequently, advertising does not play as important a part in their marketing program as it does in the program of a furniture or jewelry store. In the latter two stores, buyers shop around for merchandise—in the pages of their newspapers as well as in the stores themselves.

WHAT SHOULD BE INCLUDED?

The advertising budget normally is combined with the budget of other departments to give the master budget. Almost all expenses will be included in someone's budget, but it is important to determine in advance just what sort of expenses will be charged to each department's budget. This determination is especially important in advertising, because it is easy to charge an expenditure to advertising when no other provision is made. Without some understanding of what is included in the budget, budgetary control is meaningless.

Figure 15.2 contains "black" and "gray" lists suggested by *Printers' Ink* and used by many advertisers as a guide in deciding what should be charged to advertising and what should go into some other account. Some items are obvious. For example, no one would question the inclusion of space and time charges in the advertising budget. These will, in fact, usually account for about 80 percent of the total budget. It is just as clear that contributions to local charities and the entertainment of customers should not be included—although they do occasionally creep in. Much of the trouble and confusion comes from in-between expenses that may or may not be classified as advertising. For example, samples and demonstrations usually help an advertising program, but they are

FIG. 15.2 *Useful list of questionable and acceptable charges for the advertising account.*
SOURCE: PRINTERS' INK.

WHITE LIST

(These charges belong in the advertising account)

SPACE:

(Paid advertising in all recognized mediums, including:)
Newspapers
Magazines
Business papers
Farm papers
Class journals
Car cards
Theater programs
Outdoor
Point of purchase
Novelties
Booklets
Directories
Direct advertising
Cartons and labels (for advertising purposes, such as in window displays)
Catalogs
Package inserts (when used as advertising and not just as direction sheets)
House magazines to dealers or consumers
Motion pictures (including talking pictures) when used for advertising
Slides
Export advertising
Dealer helps
Reprints of advertisements used in mail or for display
Radio
Television
All other printed and lithographed material used directly for advertising purposes

ADMINISTRATION:

Salaries of advertising department executives and employees
Office supplies and fixtures used solely by advertising department
Commissions and fees to advertising agencies, special writers or advisers
Expenses incurred by salesmen when on work for advertising department
Traveling expenses of department employees engaged in departmental business
(Note: In some companies these go into special "Administration" account)

MECHANICAL:

Art work
Typography
Engraving
Mats
Electros
Photographs
Radio & TV production
Package design (advertising aspects only)
Etc.

MISCELLANEOUS:

Transportation of advertising material (to include postage and other carrying charges)
Fees to window display installation services
Other miscellaneous expenses connected with items on the White List

BLACK LIST

(These charges do not belong in the advertising account although too frequently they are put there:)

Free goods
Picnic and bazaar programs
Charitable, religious and fraternal donations
Other expenses for good-will purposes
Cartons
Labels
Instruction sheets
Package manufacture
Press agentry
Stationery used outside advertising department
Price lists
Salesmen's calling cards
Motion pictures for sales use only
House magazines going to factory employees
Bonuses to trade
Special rebates
Membership in trade associations
Entertaining customers or prospects
Annual reports
Showrooms
Demonstration stores
Sales convention expenses
Salesmen's samples (including photographs used in lieu of samples)
Welfare activities among employees
Such recreational activities as baseball teams, etc.
Sales expenses at conventions
Cost of salesmen's automobiles
Special editions which approach advertisers on good-will basis

GRAY LIST

(These are borderline charges, sometimes belonging in the advertising accounts and sometimes in other accounts, depending on circumstances:)

Samples
Demonstrations
Fairs
Canvassing
Rent
Light
Heat
Depreciation of equipment used by advertising department
Telephone and other overhead expenses, apportioned to advertising department
House magazines going to salesmen
Advertising automobiles
Premiums
Membership in associations or other organizations devoted to advertising
Testing bureaus
Advertising portfolios for salesmen
Contributions to special advertising funds of trade associations
Display signs on the factory or office building
Salesmen's catalogs
Research and market investigations
Advertising allowances to trade for co-operative effort

not really forms of advertising—as least as we defined it earlier in this book.

There is no reason for all companies to use exactly the same classification of advertising expense, although comparisons with other advertisers or with industry-wide composites are more meaningful if the classification is standard. It is more important that every advertising and marketing operation be budgeted and that some attempt be made to control the application of the budget. A careful periodic check—ideally by a budget committee—should be made of all expenditures charged to advertising. If records are devised to show how much is appropriated for each item and how much is spent, effective control will be simple.

Brink and Kelley suggest that control of the budget can best be accomplished by "installing a good method of determining market potentials and of setting quotas . . . by which the sales manager can measure the amount of sales or business in his territories and the amount he can reasonably expect from each territory.[14] They further suggest that the modern marketing manager exercise control through sales-cost standards, using the following four steps: (1) segregate expenses into proper accounts; (2) allocate the expenses; (3) determine standard costs; and (4) compare allocated costs with standard costs. From forecast sales and all the various budgeted expenses a planner can determine how much profit he is likely to make during a given period.

WHO MAKES THE BUDGET?

Several studies of advertising department organization and functions indicate that a large number of executives participate in the approval, if not the actual building, of the budget. A study of 68 advertisers (mostly large companies) revealed that 47 company executives in one of the companies participated in "determining the size of their appropriation."[15] In other companies the president and advertising manager were named most often, followed in order by the executive vice-president, sales vice-president, sales manager, board of directors, general manager, product manager, and treasurer or comptroller.

Although the advertising manager of a firm is normally the most important figure in determining the budget, his semiautonomous status has tended to decrease somewhat with the growth of the marketing concept and the frequent incorporation of the advertising budget into the marketing budget. At the very least the typical advertising manager will have to defend his budget before his marketing bosses and often before a budget committee.

Usually the company's advertising agency is a major participant in budgeting decisions. Most commonly the account executive and the supervisor on the firm's account, the media director, and the research director will be involved. If the agency has a plans board or committee, the account executive will ordinarily have to defend his budget before this group.

[14]Brink and Kelley, p. 235
[15]Frey, pp. 6–7.

The decrease in importance of the advertising department per se and the emergence of the marketing department and the agency in budgeting are well illustrated by what has happened in certain automobile companies. In 1967 Chevrolet was the most heavily advertised product in the United States (approximately $75,000,000). Yet the Chevrolet Division of General Motors had an advertising department of only seven members at the time. (Ford had only eight.)

In retail stores, the budget is usually set up by the publicity or advertising manager and general management. At Gimbels (Milwaukee), a large department store, typical of many around the country, the tentative yearly advertising budget — the base for all other budgets — is made by the publicity director in conjunction with three assistants. They work with the merchandise managers to estimate what sales and advertising should be, month by month.

This same group sets up two six-month plans that include specific cost estimates of all major promotions in each period. The advertising manager meets with the merchandise-division managers at least once a week to review the current plan.

The monthly plan is based on the money each merchandise manager is given for the month. He, in turn, tells his buyers what they can spend. They check last year's sales, assess the sales potential for the items they want to advertise, and make up a checkerboard that indicates the breakdown of their sales allocation by selling days. These are checked by the divisional merchandise managers and are consolidated by the advertising manager into a master plan. He checks them against composites provided by the buying group to which Gimbels belongs and against the averages from the Controllers' Congress of the National Retail Merchants' Association.

SUMMARY

Although businessmen generally agree that advertising should be used as long as it adds to the company's profits, they utilize a variety of approaches in budgeting practice. Among the more common are percentage of sales, fixed amount per unit of sale, objective (task or marketing program), and mathematical. The most logical approaches are those based on an investigation of the sales potential and the assumption that advertising precedes rather than follows sales.

Regardless of the approach used, some business firms consistently spend a higher percentage of sales for advertising than others spend. Among the more important factors determining the amount to be spent are newness of the product advertised, the opportunity to differentiate the product, the presence of hidden qualities, amount of price competition, importance of the retailer, scope of the market, what competitors are doing, and sales outlook.

The most important item in the advertising budget is the amount spent for space and time in the various advertising media. All expenses should be scrutinized carefully to make sure that they really belong in the advertising budget. Then the budget should be controlled so that the actual expenditures work out as planned.

QUESTIONS FOR DISCUSSION

1. What is the relation between budgeting and the research methods discussed in Chapters 11–14?
2. What are the principal steps involved in making a budget? Which of these is likely to be the most troublesome?
3. How does the process of budgeting in the retail field differ from that used in general advertising?
4. What are the principal reasons for the substantial variations in percentage of sales devoted to advertising from one product class to another? From one type of retail store to another?
5. To what extent might computers be used to expedite the process of budgeting?
6. Why is the presence of hidden qualities a help in advertising a product?
7. What is the role of market forecasting in budgeting?

SUGGESTED READINGS

Barton, Roger, *Media in Advertising*. New York: McGraw-Hill, Inc., 1964. Chapter 1.

Borden, Neil H., *Economic Effects of Advertising*. Homewood, Ill.: Richard D. Irwin, Inc., 1942. Chapters 24–25.

Brink, Edward L., and William T. Kelley, *The Management of Promotion*. Englewood Cliffs, N.J.: Prentice-Hall, Inc., 1963. Chapters 11–13.

Dean, Joel, *Managerial Economics*. Englewood Cliffs, N.J.: Prentice-Hall, Inc., 1951. Chapter 6.

Frey, Albert W., *How Many Dollars for Advertising?* New York: The Ronald Press Company, 1955.

Friedman, Laurence, "Game-Theory Models in the Allocation of Advertising Expenditures," in Frank Bass, ed., *Mathematical Models and Methods in Marketing*. Homewood, Ill.: Richard D. Irwin, Inc., 1961.

Palda, Kristian S., *The Measurement of Cumulative Advertising Effects*. Englewood Cliffs, N.J.: Prentice-Hall, Inc., 1964.

Sandage, C. H., and Vernon Fryburger, *Advertising Theory and Practice*, 7th ed. Homewood, Ill.: Richard D. Irwin, Inc., 1967. Chapter 31.

Seligman, Daniel, "What's the Budget?", in Editors of Fortune, *The Amazing Advertising Business*. New York: Simon and Schuster, Inc., 1957.

Weinberg, Robert S., *An Analytical Approach to Advertising Expenditure Strategy*. New York: Association of National Advertisers, 1960.

Wolfe, Harry D., *Market Forecasting*. New York: Holt, Rinehart and Winston, Inc., 1966.

PART 3 | CREATING THE MESSAGE

16 | Communications Objectives and the Creative Mix

It should be clear from the last few chapters that effective campaigns are based on facts. Armed with the proper facts, a wise planner can work out his objectives (marketing and communication), and be on his way to writing the advertisement. But facts do not create the ad. In the next few chapters we shall explore the delicate—but very important—process of planning and putting together the message and set forth some principles that apply to its creation. In this chapter we shall examine the preliminary planning that should take place before the advertisement is constructed.

THE CREATIVE MAN'S POINT OF VIEW

There is a surprisingly persistent myth that the creative person waits for a Muse to perch on his shoulders and whisper impelling phrases in his ear. Then in a flurry of inspiration, a masterpiece of communication is born. Actually, few highly successful messages are "inspired." Instead, most are achieved by sweat and tears used intelligently. And although creative people by and large are of fairly high intelligence, there is no evidence that the most intelligent person is necessarily the most creative. As Gary Steiner points out after analyzing and editing papers presented by sixteen eminent scientists, scholars, and executives at a conference on creativity: "General intelligence seems to bear about the same relation to on-the-job creativity at the professional level as weight does to ability in football. You have to have a lot of it to be in the game at all; but among those on the team—all of whom have a great deal of weight to begin with—differences in performance are only slightly, if at all, related to weight."[1]

What makes a person creative? Why are some people more creative than others? These questions have long intrigued social scientists as well as businessmen. Steiner concluded on the basis of the papers described above that the creative individual tended to have the following characteristics:

Conceptual fluency (*able to produce a large number of ideas quickly*)

Originality (*generates unusual ideas*)

Separates source from content in evaluating information (*interested primarily in problem not status of originator*)

Suspends judgment and avoids early commitment (*spends more time in analysis and exploration*)

Less authoritarian (*more relativistic*)

Accepts own impulses (*undisciplined exploration*)

Independence of judgments (*less conformity*)

Rich, "bizarre" fantasy life (*superior reality orientation*)[2]

The evidence showed that management as well as individuals could do much to foster creativity within a particular organization. Among the most important factors influencing creativity were adequate compensation, channels for advancement, freedom in choice of problem and method of pursuit and good communication.[3]

David Ogilvy describes great creative people in particularly colorful terms:

Few of the great creators have bland personalities. They are cantankerous egotists, the kind of men who are unwelcome in the modern corporation. Consider Winston Churchill. He drank like a fish. He was capricious and willful. When opposed he sulked. He was rude to fools. He was wildly extravagant. He wept on the slightest provocation. His conversation was Rabelaisian. He bullied his subordinates. Yet Lord Alanbrooke, his Chief of Staff, could write: "I shall always look back on the years I worked with him as some of the most difficult and trying ones in my life. For all that I thank God that I was given the opportunity of working alongside of such a man, and of having my eyes opened to the fact that occasionally such supermen exist on the earth."[4]

The creative man in advertising is the trustee of large sums of money. Whether the expenditure returns a profit to the advertiser depends to a great extent upon how skillfully and thoughtfully each advertisement is planned and prepared. The job of the creative man is to fashion an idea that the advertiser wants to communicate into something thousands—perhaps millions—of people will read or listen to. These people are not waiting expectantly to hear what he has to say. They are

[1]Gary A. Steiner, "Introduction," in Gary A. Steiner, ed., *The Creative Organization* (Chicago: University of Chicago Press, 1965), p. 6.
[2]Steiner, pp. 7–18.
[3]Steiner, pp. 19–22.
[4]David Ogilvy, "The Creative Chief," in Steiner, p. 208.

not even anticipating the ad's arrival. In fact, they often wish it would go away, so they could get on with their favorite television program.

The neophyte is tempted to believe that readers and viewers take the advertising message as seriously as he does. If all advertisements announced a startling new model of automobile or pictured a sleek new cabin cruiser, this might be possible. However, most products are not so dramatic.

The creative man's attitude is basically one of humility. He is humble because he knows the difficulty of creating a really effective advertisement and how much his success depends on the efforts of other persons (researchers who provide the facts, media planners who put his ad in the right setting, merchandisers who make sure that the retailers follow through with promotion). With this humility comes a realization that he must think before he writes or visualizes the advertisement. This thinking frequently takes the form of an advertising plan — perhaps a plan for each ad; perhaps for several in a series.

PLACE OF CREATIVE EFFORT IN THE MARKETING PLAN

The logical place for starting to construct an advertising plan is the over-all marketing plan. Note in Table 16.1 how the objectives for the advertisements stem from the data collected. The relation between the advertisement and marketing plan becomes clearer if we borrow our terminology from the military and speak of creative strategy and creative tactics.

Creative strategy involves the substantive aspects of advertising — your choice of what to say. If both the marketing and communications objectives are clearly defined, they should outline what impressions your campaign is designed to convey to what audience. If we follow Colley's advice to define our "advertising goal" as a "specific communication task, to be accomplished among a defined audience to a given degree in a given period of time"[5] we have a good basis for formulating creative strategy. For example, Ohrbach's department store in New York City attempts in its newspaper advertisements to convey the impression that they can sell quality goods at substantial savings. This is a general campaign objective, and the creative strategy in individual ads is consistent with this general theme. In an Ohrbach's ad (see Figure 29.1 for an example) the store is saying, "If you buy your clothes at our store, people will think you bought them at the most expensive stores." Because the Campbell Soup Company occupies such a dominant position in the soup market, part of its basic marketing strategy consists in devising ways to increase the frequency with which any soup is served in the household. However, in individual ads the company wants to tell you about various new uses of soup or to induce you to try certain of them.

Creative tactics involve the carrying out of creative strategy. Once you have decided what a given advertisement's objectives are to be, you

[5]Russell H. Colley, *Defining Goals for Measured Advertising Results* (New York: Association of National Advertisers, 1961), p. 6.

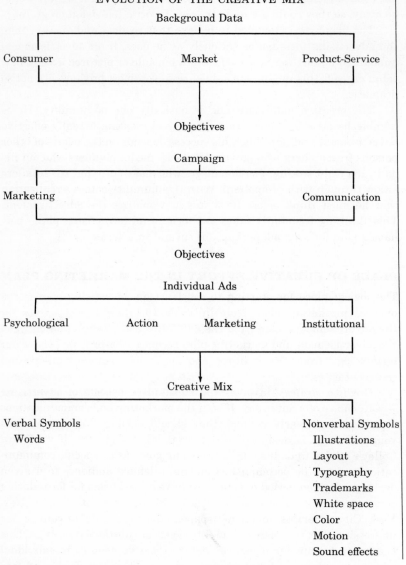

EVOLUTION OF THE CREATIVE MIX **TABLE 16.1**

Background Data

| Consumer | Market | Product-Service |

Objectives

Campaign

| Marketing | Communication |

Objectives

Individual Ads

| Psychological | Action | Marketing | Institutional |

Creative Mix

Verbal Symbols	Nonverbal Symbols
Words	Illustrations
	Layout
	Typography
	Trademarks
	White space
	Color
	Motion
	Sound effects

are ready to consider alternative ways of accomplishing these objectives—the various possible creative mixes. Note in Table 16.1 the relation between the objectives and the creative mix. The tactical tools of the creative man are verbal and nonverbal (visual) signs and symbols.

The advertisement in Figure 16.1 is an interesting illustration of how strategy and tactics were carefully planned. The universality and familiarity of Coca-Cola created this problem: how to make people aware and interested in a product they knew so well and that had not changed materially. It was decided to capitalize on this long-time familiarity with the idea that Coke had the taste "you never get tired of." It was felt that the copy, like the illustration, should reflect an image of effervescence and refreshment.

CREATIVE OBJECTIVES

In Chapters 3 and 4 the importance of objectives is emphasized. We considered objectives as marketing and communication targets. Now we shall concentrate largely on the creative strategy necessary to attain these objectives. Only by knowing our goal can we find out whether we have succeeded. This line of reasoning holds true for the creative phases of advertising just as it does for the planning of the campaign. In both planning and creating it is most important that we have a sharply defined target on which to focus our efforts.

In analyzing copy objectives it is helpful to make a distinction between *general* and *specific* objectives. A general objective is one we might expect *any* advertisement, regardless of product or market, to achieve (to arouse interest). However, a *specific* objective applies only to the advertisement or campaign that we are considering at a particular time. For example, the objective may be psychological (to convince women that they will be lovelier to look at if they use our cream twice a day) or action (to get women to send in a coupon for a free sample). Let us examine first some of the general objectives of advertisements, then some of the specific ones.

GENERAL OBJECTIVES

Sales versus Communication. Albert Lasker, while a fledgling advertising executive back in 1904, found out "what advertising is." According to his biographer, John Gunther, Lasker received the following note by messenger:

> I am in the saloon downstairs, and I can tell you what advertising is. I know that you don't know.[6]

Lasker received this brash stranger, John Kennedy, who turned out to be a Canadian Northwest mounted policeman. Lasker contended that advertising was "news," but Kennedy said he could tell him in three words what advertising really is—"Salesmanship in print." According to Gunther:

> All of Lasker's groping, his striving for terms of reference, his search for knowledge of the potentialities of the weapon he was handling, were crystalized by Kennedy's three simple words . . . . Now he knew what he was about, and today, half a century later, most of the art and practice of advertising is still based on those same three words.[7]

Many of today's admen would say Mr. Lasker was a little naïve to believe such oversimplification. Many of the older hands would argue that Lasker was, if not entirely correct, at least very close to the truth. The objective of every ad, they say, is to sell. They are right, in the sense that every advertisement is supposed ultimately to make or at least contribute to a sale. However, there are other marketing activities that contribute to the achievement of sales-volume objectives. Advertisements contribute in a specific way by communicating the desired

---

[6]John Gunther, *Taken at the Flood* (New York: Harper & Row, Publishers, 1960), pp. 57–58.
[7]Gunther; p. 58.

message effectively to the relevant market target, but advertisements cannot be expected to do the entire job of increasing sales. Not all ads are expected to influence sales volume in a measurable way. Not all ads are expected to create sales within the *immediate* future. Many of them make their contributions indirectly by creating an awareness of the product or brand and in helping to build an image in the minds of consumers.

Much of the problem of defining objectives can be resolved if we think in terms of short-range as compared with long-range copy objectives. On one hand, we can agree with those who emphasize communication in terms of the short-range accomplishments of a message we are creating. On the other, we can agree with those who emphasize sales if we are talking of longer range. Some, like researcher Charles Ramond, believe that the long-range objective is the wave of the future. In looking at advertising goals of the 1960s in terms of the advertising

Ice-cold Coca-Cola has the taste you never get tired of. It's always refreshing. That's why things go better with Coke after Coke after Coke.

FIG. 16.1 *Advertisement designed to dramatize the refreshing qualities of Coca-Cola. Note how heavily the visual is emphasized and how much more effective it is in color (see color plates).* THIS ADVERTISEMENT IS REPRODUCED THROUGH THE COURTESY OF THE COCA-COLA COMPANY, OWNER OF THE REGISTERED TRADE-MARKS "COCA-COLA" AND "COKE"; AGENCY: MCCANN-ERICKSON, INC.

man of 1999, he finds that "it seems strange to us in 1999 that such a book (as *Defining Advertising Goals for Measured Advertising Results*) was ever necessary. Yet until it was published few advertisers set communication goals for their campaigns, and fewer set goals in terms of sales and profits."[8]

Research executive Alfred Politz believes that the communication objectives of advertisements become clearer if we emphasize two primary functions: to persuade the consumer and to familiarize him with the product or brand. However, he also points out the following:

> But advertising copy is intended to perform a function *beyond* the mere development of familiarity with the brand name. Copy is intended to shape motives and desires, to build believability, and to provide a reason for selecting a particular brand over all others . . . . In the development of advertising, it is the copy function which demands the greatest skill, creativeness and intelligence.[9]

Let us look at some cases in point. In the advertisement shown in Figure 16.1 the primary emphasis is on selling the product advertised. On the other hand, the primary emphasis in the Berlitz advertisement in Figure 16.2 is on projecting an image of Berlitz as the one organization that can prepare you quickly and efficiently for speaking a foreign language. Note in both examples, however, that there is a secondary objective. An advertisement designed to sell, such as that in Figure 16.1, communicates an impression regarding the brand and the company that sells the brand. Nevertheless an advertisement that is primarily image-building may also try to make some immediate sales.

Mail order advertisements are somewhat simpler in that the emphasis is almost entirely on immediate sales and the words are chosen to spur action. For example, a Sears, Roebuck catalogue advertisement says: "Most luscious topping of all for your skirts and dashing sheaths . . . bulky Orlon. Just slip one on and cuddle into its softness, Here is the popular bulky look."

If you think of advertising and promotion as merely selling, you lose sight of the important differences between communicating on a person-to-person basis and communicating through the media as pointed out in Chapter 4.

Other Approaches to Defining Objectives. The advertising manager of Hunt Foods defined his company's approach to advertising planning in these words:

> The first step is to set up a procedure for developing written advertising strategies. Our procedure is this. The advertising department "quarterbacks" a presentation to the agency of product and market facts. I use the word "quarterback" here because in our company we have many specialists. Thus it is necessary to do considerable advance planning to bring together the right group. A typical presentation for a food product includes representatives from at least five different departments: advertising, market planning, market research, technical research, and the test kitchen. Following the presentation, the agency drafts the

[8]Charles K. Ramond, "How Advertising Became Respectable," *Journal of Marketing* 28 (October 1964), p. 2.
[9]Alfred Politz, "The Dilemma of Creative Advertising," in Harper W. Boyd, Jr., and Joseph W. Newman, eds., *Advertising Management: Selected Readings* (Homewood, Ill.: Richard D. Irwin, Inc., 1965), p. 322.

advertising platform. This is a concise, three- or four-page document summarizing pertinent facts and stating the communications goal and the strategy
for reaching it. No copy is written, and no layouts are made until agency and
client agree on the goal and strategy. This procedure promotes efficiency by
simplifying the agency's operating problems internally and externally. It
accelerates the advertising-approval process of creating effective advertising,
because it focuses copy and art talent on specific pre-agreed targets. It also accelerates the advertising-approval process by eliminating the common problem of
not being able to agree on an ad because of lack of agreement on what the ad is
supposed to accomplish.[10]

A useful way of classifying the general objectives of an advertisement (whether it is read on a printed page, heard on a radio, watched
on television, or glanced at through the window of a moving car) is in
terms of the five I's that follow: Idea, Immediate Impact, Interest,
Information, and Impulsion.

Wisely used, the five I's serve as a guide in preparing and evaluating advertisements. It must be pointed out, however, that the value of
this approach will depend on the judgment of the person using it. It is
not easy to appraise the worth of an idea in advance. What is impact
to one may be meaningless to another. Incessant interest can mean
uninterrupted dullness to certain sophisticated eyes. Enthusiastic
generalities are frequently confused with information. Impulsion can
vary widely in strength. Consequently, let us more closely appraise each
of these.

Idea. Every advertisement worthy of the name provides for its audience
an idea in some form. At best, it makes the product memorable, but
even a fair idea is far better than no idea at all.

You cannot expect technique, no matter how clever, to cover up the
absence of an idea. If you do so, you will find yourself in the position of
Churchy La Femme, the turtle in the Pogo comic strip, who excused an
abominable song he had written by mumbling that it might be a little
rough in spots but that he thought it would be pretty impressive if he
threw a chorus of a hundred katydids behind it.

Good ideas come from many sources. In the last four chapters we
have explored many of the most promising. How, then, do you know
when you have a good idea? Here is one helpful test: if the sales theme
of an advertisement can be summed up in a *single sentence*, the chances
are there is an idea in the ad. To illustrate this, let us examine two
pieces of copy about a fictitious shoe polish called Mumbo. Here is the
first one:

FOR A HANDSOME SHINE

Any person who cares about his appearance wants his shoes well polished.
Too, a good shoe polish preserves the leather, makes shoes wear longer. *Mumbo*
is an extra good polish because it is made of the finest ingredients. It gives a
high, lustrous shine that lasts and lasts. The next time you buy shoe polish, ask
for—and *get—Mumbo*, the shoe polish that's kind to your shoes.

Can you sum up the basic idea of this advertisement in one sentence? It
is virtually impossible. The copy has no central idea, no selling theme

[10]L. F. Ohliger, Jr., "How to Get the Most Out of an Agency without Really
Trying," speech before AAAA Western Region Annual Convention, Honolulu,
Hawaii, October 22, 1962.

FIG. 16.2 *Relevant use of a foreign language to achieve immediate impact with the reader.* AD PERMISSION OF THE BERLITZ SCHOOLS OF LANGUAGES OF AMERICA, INC., PREPARED BY GILBERT ADVERTISING AGENCY, INC., NEW YORK.

around which the advertisement is built. It is a lazy piece of copy, written without enough information about the product, the consumer, or the market.

Suppose, now, that the product is assigned to a more able writer. He wonders where that phrase comes from: ". . . a high, lustrous shine that lasts and lasts." A talk with the manufacturer reveals that the lasting quality of the shine is one of the major talking points of the polish. This writer tries polishing his own shoes with Mumbo. He looks up some information on buying habits and talks to dealers where the product is sold. Out of his investigation and his concentration comes the following idea:

SHINE YOUR SHOES EVERY OTHER DAY

Now you can have well-polished shoes every day without shining them every day. *Mumbo* gives you a shine that really lasts. Shine your shoes with it one day. Just whip a cloth over them the next. And the luster returns, bright as ever.

As a leather preservative, *Mumbo* is tops, too. And the shine it gives you has no equal for brilliance and lasting quality. How about changing *your* daily shine to every other day with *Mumbo*? Even better, get two tins—one tan, one black.

Now the picture has changed. The sales idea of this copy can be summed up in a single sentence: Cut your shoeshining work in half with Mumbo. Here are some other examples:

There are 293 words in one of the Listerine advertisements. The *idea* can be summed up in *eleven*, as follows: Listerine Antiseptic effectively combats germs that accompany colds and sore throats.

The central idea in a Pan-American Coffee Bureau's advertisement is this: It's a good idea to interrupt the routine of work periodically to enjoy a delicious beverage. This same idea is expressed in Coca-Cola's much-used phrase, "The Pause That Refreshes."

Each of the ideas summarized above provides something for the reader or viewer. Each provides a clear concept that can be grasped quickly and concretely by the audience and, even more important, is entirely relevant to the advertisement's objective.

Some ideas are better adapted to one medium than another. A good example is an ad that Westinghouse built around a sand test. This test was devised to show how clean clothes became when they were washed and rinsed in a Westinghouse washing machine. After showing this test for about a year and a half in various magazine advertisements, the agency and client decided to try it on television. According to the agency, this ad received one of the highest ratings ever recorded for a commercial. More important, the advertising department had evidence that the commercial was a vital factor in helping to increase Westinghouse washer sales at a substantially greater rate than the industry average.

Immediate Impact. One of the prime objectives of any advertising message is to get the attention of the prospective audience. Unless the ad makes enough impact to pull the audience into the message, it has lost its chance to communicate.

People seldom use judgment in deciding what advertisements they will look at or listen to. Caprice, vagary, impulse, inclination, curiosity, liking, immediate need—any of these may influence their choice. The prospective purchaser makes up his mind in one quick glance or after a few rapid syllables whether or not he will tarry a while or go on to what he considers greener pastures. In that instant an advertisement must either fasten attention or lose it. In less time than it takes to turn a page or a dial, the expensive sales message must engage a purchaser's interest. Impact is the "stopping power" of an advertisement. This is really the power to distract, to halt minds concerned with other things and give the audience greater concern for the advertising message that appears suddenly before them.

How then is one to know whether an advertisement will stop people or be ignored? First of all, impact is a relative quality. Few ads are designed to achieve impact on *everybody*. Instead, they are directed at a particular audience. In general we know from communications research that people are stopped by a communication either because they see in it some promise of reward or because it is easier to notice the communication than to ignore it. In a printed advertisement either the visual or the verbal elements signal a reward or make the ad difficult to ignore. In the broadcast media sound or motion may help get attention.

A few years ago an American Dairy Association advertisement appeared in a variety of media under a headline that later became a memorable slogan: "You Never Outgrow Your Need for Milk." This headline achieved impact, primarily, through the fact that it made the reward perfectly clear. Taking advantage of the almost universal belief that milk is a nearly perfect food, this statement reminded people of *all* ages that they needed its nourishment. It was difficult to ignore this ad in that it concerned a familiar product, yet talked about it in a fresh, interesting way.

Impact is a variable force. Most advertisements have some. A few advertisements have a great deal. The thing to test for is not presence but power. The question to ask is not "Does this advertisement have immediate impact?" but "Does it have *all* the immediate impact that can be put into it?" Will the first glance at a printed advertisement, the first phrase of a radio announcement, or the first flash of a television commercial make a profitable percentage of the audience want to linger and learn more? If the answer is "yes," the advertisement has immediate impact.

We shall be examining this question of impact in more detail in later chapters devoted to the two main devices for achieving impact — illustrations and headlines.

Interest. Ideally, every advertisement should arouse and hold a prospective customer's attention until he has absorbed the information it has to offer. Not just *some*, but *all* of it. Presumably, everything in an advertisement contributes in some way to the ad's specific objective; its persuasive value resides in the sum of its various parts.

Some products have inherent interest. A mink coat is more glamorous and interesting than a beaver coat. A Cadillac is more interesting than a Chevrolet. A cruise ship is more romantic than a transcontinental bus. However, two mink coats do not double the inherent drama. An electric refrigerator of one make might have little advantage over another of a different make. But if a mink coat and an electric refrigerator are both advertised in the same publication, the chances are that the luxurious fur will get more attention from women than the practical refrigerator, *if other things are equal.*

One of the functions of the advertisement is to make sure that other things are *not* equal. The ad writer must overcome the disadvantage of less inherent interest. He must make the refrigerator as interesting as the mink coat and more interesting than other refrigerators.

Here are three examples of copy which fulfilled unusually well the function of arousing reader interest. The first is an advertisement for the French Tourist Office under the intriguing heading, "Which woman deserved this Castle of Love ... the courtesan or the Queen?" The writer followed up this provocative headline with copy that started:
"One moonlight night a fantastic ball took place in this chateau. From the terrace you could see a ballet of nymphs in the garden and mer-

FIG. 16.3 *Effective use of visual and verbal elements to create interest in the advertising message.* CLIENT: SIMMONS COMPANY; AGENCY: YOUNG & RUBICAM, INC.

maids paddling in the moats. And glimmering in the night a new ballroom spanned the Cher. The Queen of France, Catherine de Medici, had just completed it . . . in bitter memory of the chateau's original owner . . . the other women in her husband's life. Catherine had always coveted this fairyland castle. But Henry II gave it to beautiful, blonde Diane de Poitiers, the woman he really loved. . . ." (Accompanying the copy is a striking picture of the Chateau of Chenonceaux with its arches and towers reflected in the Cher.)

The second is an advertisement for Simmons King-size Beautyrest (see Figure 16.3), an extension of the traditional double bed. The writer, emphasizing its attractive, comfortable roominess, stated, "End the battle for bed room with king-size Beautyrest."

The third is an advertisement for Port Charlotte, a sunny spot in Florida. The advertisement poses this question: "How can you afford to stay up North . . . when it costs so little to live in the sun?"

How, one may ask, do you ·judge whether an advertisement has interest? How do you provide the interest? As we shall see in Chapter 18, there are several possibilities, one of which is to compare advertisements to people.

Information. Creative people sometimes underestimate the informational function of advertising messages. Edgar Crane points out, "Not only is the human being so constructed that he can receive dozens of reports simultaneously from his environment, but he seems to require them for his mental well being."[11] Researcher George Gallup emphasizes the importance of advertising's informational function when he says, "We find an awful lot of advertisers seem to be afraid to tell people about their products. But the public is very much interested in products. They want to know all about these products they can buy."[12]

We must decide, then, what we mean by information. It has several dimensions.

First, information consists of facts presented in verbal form. We find, for example, the following in a retail advertisement for refrigerators:

You get adjustable height swing-out shelves with no center pole; refrigerator and freezer doors with offset hinges; foot pedal latch on freezer door; no-spill ice trays; heat resistant glass meat storer; automatic Frost-Away defrosting.

This is a logical, orderly presentation of factual data by means of words.

However, we should not confuse general statements with factual data. When an advertisement for a television set describes its pictures as "clear, sharp and excitingly real," it merely makes a claim that is true of any good television set. However, if it says, "clear, sharp pictures on the only tube guaranteed for three years," it gives information about a feature that is exclusive with that particular set. When an advertisement for DC–9 says, "More airlines have chosen the DC–9 than any other passenger plane," it provides information exclusive with that particular make of plane.

Second, we have factual information presented in visual form. In addition to telling Mrs. Jones how the dress is made, we include an illustration to show her how it looks. In advertising some products an illustration is essential.

Third, we have the information in its more subtle form. When you shake hands with a person his limp or vigorous handshake tells you something about him. You gain certain impressions of him from the way he is dressed. Similarly, people acquire information from an advertising· message about the product, service, or store involved. If, for example, there is a lot of white space in an advertisement (see Figure 4.5), a reader gains certain information (whether it is correct is irrelevant) about the product or store.[13]

In appraising the information function of a message, it pays to ask yourself two questions:

[11]Edgar Crane, *Marketing Communications*: *A Behavioral Approach to Men, Messages and Media* (New York: John Wiley & Sons, Inc., 1965), p. 366.
[12]"Gallup Tells. . .What Makes a Good Ad. . . on TV or in Print," *Printers' Ink*, November 6, 1953.
[13]See Edward Hall, *The Silent Language* (New York: Doubleday & Company, Inc., 1959), for elaboration of this point.

1. Does the advertisement contain sufficient information about the product and how it will reward the user?

2. Does the information seem to apply exclusively to this product or will consumers think it true of all similar products?

Impulsion. *Impulsion* should not be confused with *compulsion*. No advertisement can compel anyone to act. But it can impel him toward a purchase or a favorable image of the product. Thus, in judging an advertisement for impulsion, the question to ask is this: "Will this advertisement give the people we are trying to reach a keen desire to own the product?"

It is true that advertising is but one of many factors that influence sales. It is also true that advertising is much more important in some marketing mixes than in others. Therefore, its impelling function must be dovetailed with the other marketing and communication elements. However, advertising must contribute to impulsion—or the money spent for it is wasted.

As we noted earlier, motivation is complex and sometimes perverse. It ranges in intensity from zero to boiling point. It is possible, at times, to raise desire so high that some consumers feel they *have* to own a product or at least see and examine it at the earliest opportunity. Creative ability can almost alone send people into stores to purchase food products. But creative ability alone can seldom sell automobiles or high-fashion dresses.

An impulsion to act or feel as the ad directs generally comes from two basic forces:

1. A belief that what the advertisement says (either directly, or indirectly through symbols) is true.

2. A conviction that the product or service will satisfy one of the consumer's prime motivating forces (see Chapter 11).

The consumer need not be conscious of the action of these two forces. In fact, it is sometimes best (for advertisers) that he is not. Many people (particularly those with considerable education) rebel at the idea of having been driven to prefer a product because of advertising. They prefer to think that they have arrived at their decision more rationally.

SPECIFIC OBJECTIVES

The objectives that provide the best guidance for an ad writer are specific—those applying only to a particular advertisement or series of advertisements. Obviously, these provide a sharper, more clearly defined target toward which the writer can focus his efforts. When he is through, he can ask himself, "Does this ad fit this objective?"

The first step in outlining workable specific objectives is deciding what *kinds* of objectives we must have. Various copy experts have their favorites. However, the following four-part classification[14] seems to work well, because it offers a breadth of viewpoint while guiding the search.

[14]See S. Watson Dunn, *Advertising Copy and Communication* (New York: McGraw-Hill, Inc., 1956), chap. 5, for a more detailed discussion of specific copy objectives.

Psychological. We have emphasized that each member of the consuming public is a complex bundle of psychological drives, feelings, and attitudes. Every advertisement should be planned to make some psychological impression on the consumer. Some will call this the "ad's appeal," although this term oversimplifies the problem.

For example, one of the most consistent and successful of advertisers is Jell-O. Jell-O is a familiar product with a strong and generally favorable image, according to agency research. However, except for the introduction of a few new flavors, there have been no essential changes in the product since before World War II. Jell-O competes directly with other nationally advertised gelatin desserts and with several private brands offered at lower prices by grocery chains.

To the average consumer, Jell-O's actual superiority over other flavored gelatins is not easy to discern. Like all of them, it tastes good, costs little, is easy to prepare, versatile, and low in calories. The agency copy chief who has written and supervised much of the Jell-O copy says,

Over the years, Jell-O has been advertised in many different ways and in a wide variety of media. It has never taken itself too seriously in public or attempted to build the woman's problem of "What'll I serve for dessert today?" into a matter of earthshaking importance.

The most successful Jell-O advertising has taken its cue from the nature of the product itself. Although maintaining the impression of a delightful, helpful, and versatile old friend, the advertising has relied heavily on a constant flow of fresh, imaginative, and conspicuous ideas to keep this old favorite up-to-date and amusing.[15]

Thus is defined the communication objective. Consider how specific series carry this out. In one series ("Now's the Time for Jell-O"), the objective was to show how much happier children would be if they had a dish of Jell-O at the right time (and how much easier this would make life for the harried mother). One ad showed a child running away from home. The mother was in the background — in the kitchen. The child was coming out the door. Over his shoulder was a symbolic stick with a bundle of clothes tied to it, which immediately identified his purpose and intentions. The headline said, "Now's the Time for Jell-O." The text consisted of this sentence:

Just hold an irresistible bowlful of Jell-O gelatin dessert in front of his eyes, Mother — and your world traveler will gladly turn in his bundle and stick for a dessert spoon!

A less skillful writer might have said "and your youngster will quickly give up his idea about leaving home."

Every advertisement is supposed to make a psychological impression of some sort; every advertisement therefore has one or more psychological objectives. Some of the more common follow:

1. To convince consumers that this product will provide a certain reward more effectively than the competition.
2. To teach a new use for his product.
3. To convince consumers that they can avoid something distasteful with this product.

[15]Mary O'Meara, "The Creative Idea," in E. R. French, ed., *The Copywriter's Guide* (New York: Harper & Row, Publishers, 1959).

4. To associate the product with a desirable symbol.

5. To remind consumers of a slogan they already know.

6. To show how the product will satisfy some subconscious desire.

Action. Some advertisements are designed to induce action; others are not. The action, if any, will result from the psychological impression. The Jell-O ads, for example, are not expected to produce immediate action; but the grocery store ad (which may include Jell-O) is.

The following are some of the common types of action we might expect:

1. To induce consumers to purchase more frequently.

2. To cause consumers to buy at a different time—or different season of the year.

3. To cause consumers to substitute one product for another.

4. To induce consumers to sample a new product.

5. To obtain inquiries which will be followed up by personal calls.

Corporate (Institutional). Most advertisements are expected to make some contribution to a corporate or store image. If this is the main objective, we usually call it a corporate or institutional ad, if it is not, we call it a product ad. For either type, the following might be logical institutional objectives—primary or secondary:

1. To show how a firm contributes to the public welfare.

2. To indicate that the company is a pioneer in its field.

3. To show how friendly the firm is.

4. To indicate how happy (or skilled) its employees are.

Marketing. This is a sort of catchall classification, because it involves any marketing objectives not covered by the other three. That is to say, what *other* contribution is the ad supposed to make to the over-all marketing program? For example,

1. To stimulate primary demand for the product.

2. To stimulate the salesmen to work harder selling the product.

3. To encourage dealers to merchandise the firm's products at the retail level.

4. To obtain additional retail outlets.

We have been examining specific objectives here largely in terms of advertisements designed for consumer markets. As we shall see in later chapters, the objectives are different if we are considering copy directed at some specialized group. It is most important, however, that the objectives always be defined as carefully and specifically as possible. The chapters that follow will be concerned primarily with the tactics for carrying out these objectives—our creative mix.

SIGNS VERSUS SYMBOLS

We are now ready to consider the tools of the working creative person—signs and symbols. The salesman in the store can show you the product itself, so that you can see, hear, feel, and, if you like, even smell or taste it. The copywriter works with the next best thing—signs and symbols that are transmitted to audiences via the mass media. We all know that signs and symbols can be very effective, but sometimes, unfortunately, they can also be a waste of money.

ORIGIN OF SIGNS AND SYMBOLS

In the earliest civilizations crudely drawn pictures of animals and people were used to symbolize various ideas so that they could be communicated to others. We can assume that even the earliest people had certain grunts and grimaces and, later, sounds that helped them convey ideas. It was only a step from pictures and unrelated sounds to pictures and sounds representing objects and ideas.

Our progenitors found through experience that pictures alone were not adequate for all the material they had to communicate. How, for example, could you distinguish one man from another or a wolf from a dog? These early men did work out a sort of shorthand to take care of such nuances, but there had to be a clear understanding on the part of both communicator and audience about what each variation represented.

Eventually (around 3000 B.C.) the phonetic alphabet began to take form. For the first time, a small group of symbols could be used to represent a wide variety of sounds and ideas. Most Western languages today have less than thirty such symbols (or letters). In various combinations of these, any object or idea can be symbolized so as to be meaningful to other people. Letters are thus symbols of sounds, and the various combinations (words) are symbols of objects, thoughts, or impressions that are to be communicated.

Pictures, however, never lost their significance. During the Middle Ages, when writing skills were confined for the most part to the clergy, painting and sculpture were a primary means of communication. The range of emotions that people associated with the church, for example, was communicated most effectively through the visual elements.

During the early days of advertising, the copywriter was king, for advertisements were mostly copy. Words were the principal signs and symbols used by copywriters. Since 1945, there has been an upsurge of the visual in advertising. Many of today's display advertisements depend heavily on visual symbols. For example, Polaroid has run a memorable series of magazine advertisements without the traditional signature. Yet the dominant illustration is so different from most other advertisements in these media that the personality of the advertiser stands out immediately. What better way is there to symbolize the achievement of a camera manufacturer than by fine photographic reproduction? (See Figure 21.7.)

Signs in Advertising. At first glance, signs and symbols appear synonymous. Advertising people are called (both favorably and unfavorably) "symbol manipulators," when they are really manipulators of

ESTABLISHED 1818

Brooks Brothers,
CLOTHING
Men's Furnishings, Hats & Shoes

346 MADISON AVENUE, COR. 44TH ST., NEW YORK 17, N. Y.
111 BROADWAY, NEW YORK 6, N. Y.
BOSTON · CHICAGO · LOS ANGELES · SAN FRANCISCO

Peck *and* Peck

JAY THORPE

John Wanamaker

FIG. 16.4 *Signatures serve as signs, especially in retail advertisements. Here are a few well-known ones.*

both signs *and* symbols. They use both, knowingly or not, as they go about their job of providing ideas, impact, interest, information, and impulsion for their audiences.

Consider, for example, the following advertising headline:

General Electric Ranges 25% Off

The term "General Electric" is a word sign in this headline. In psychological terms we could describe it as a "pattern of stimulation which is not a given object but which produces in a receiving organism a disposition toward making some of the responses previously elicited by the object, and which would not have been made without the previous association of object and receiving organism."[16] In other words, the sign will probably produce a favorable reaction if your past experience with the company has been favorable. As you see each of the words in this headline, you connect them with your past experience. (For example, the Coca Cola signature in Figure 16.1.)

An advertisement, regardless of the medium in which it appears, is a collection of signs—verbal and nonverbal. These signs usually operate at a subconscious level and are not consciously associated with past and present impressions.

Certain signs are stronger than others and act as *cues*. Words like "sale" in an advertisement headline, or loud and unusual sounds in a radio or television commercial, stand out. In printed advertising the cues come from certain words or pictures, the size or blackness of the type or layout, the position on the page or in the medium, the relation to surrounding material, or from a familiar trademark or slogan. In radio or television they might come from the words or sounds, the type of motion used, the timing, the pitch, the articulation, the emphasis, and the relation to material going before and after.

Let us examine signs, then, from two viewpoints—that of the audience and that of the creative man. Schramm describes the audience reaction in this manner:

> Supposedly, the reader or listener chooses the cues which at the moment seem to have the greatest predictive value. That is, he punches the index button which seems to promise him the greatest reward. If he is in a hurry, he will punch fewer buttons; if he is distracted or diverted, he may miss a number of buttons he would otherwise punch. But in general he will punch a button, turn on his perceptive machine, and expect to collect a reward.[17]

Both verbal and nonverbal signs in advertisements point the way—like road or street signs. They tell the reader what the advertisement is about, whether it is something that interests him, and whether there is some reward in it for him. After he decides to read or hear or watch an advertising message, the signs tell him whether his decision was correct, and if he becomes disgusted, he will go on to something else.

The implications for the creative person are fairly obvious. As Zaltman points out, "All market communication proceeds by means of signs with which the producer tries to influence the behavior of customers who are buying significates."[18] Given his creative strategy, the advertising man should select the signs that will have immediate impact on the audience in terms of its experience and then arrange them in the best possible fashion.

Symbols. Although signs help point the way for the reader, symbols get down to the job of communicating. The elements of the advertisement (the words, the illustration, the logotype, and the like) all sym-

---

[16]Wilbur Schramm, "The Nature of News," in Wilbur Schramm, ed., *Mass Communications* (Urbana: University of Illinois Press, 1949), p. 301.

[17]Schramm, p. 303.

[18]Gerald Zaltman, *Contributions from the Behavioral Sciences* (New York: Harcourt, Brace & World, Inc., 1965), p. 104.

bolize various concepts. Each communicator depends upon a particular symbol system. The musician has one, the artist another, the choreographer another, and so on. For our purposes, however, it is best to classify them as either *verbal* (words) or *nonverbal* (everything else). These are the ingredients of our creative mix.

Terms such as "General Motors" or "General Mills" may be signs in that they tell the reader what the advertisement is about; at the same time, they symbolize certain ideas regarding these companies. These may or may not be favorable. Words may symbolize different meanings, according to the context in which they are used. Notice how the meaning of a word in a printed ad is changed if it is put in boldface or italics or in quotations. An announcer can change the symbolism of a word by the inflection of his voice, or, in television, even by his facial expression when he delivers the word.

Nonverbal symbols are even trickier to work with—especially for the writer who is accustomed to words. Many copywriters have difficulty in communicating to their friends in the art department the sort of illustration they have in mind for a particular ad. Unless the copywriter can draw, there is no satisfactory language he can use. Painters and musicians sometimes point out that you cannot translate the meanings of their creations into words. There must be communication, but the communication need not be symbolized by words. We can feel that the painting or the composition is beautiful or moving without being able to convey to someone else the exact definition of that feeling.

In advertising, symbols—as well as signs—must be kept under control. Although an advertisement may be an artistic composition, it is not art for its own sake. Rather, it is a creation that has been put together to accomplish some predetermined objective.

Every time a creative person uses symbols he is predicting. He thinks the person seeing or hearing an ad will respond in a certain way. He may know, from research, that the name "Wheaties" elicits certain responses. If he uses a word like "Puffies," he knows he will not get the same associations—perhaps no association at all.

A pounding headache is not easy to symbolize. The creator of a Bufferin advertisement decided to show a headache by combining a symbolic illustration with a realistic one. He used a photograph of the man's face in which it was clear he wasn't feeling well, and an animated sketch of a drum. The combination quickly and effectively told what was wrong with the man.

We have been talking here as though symbols had only one level of meaning, although actually they may operate at various levels. A good example is the pun—it plays on the double meaning of a word (see Figure 20.1). The word "copy," used as a noun, can, according to *Webster's New Collegiate Dictionary*, have any of four distinct meanings. In advertising, "copy" is used in still two other senses—as the complete advertisement prepared for a medium, and as the text or reading matter of an advertisement.

People frequently use words in other than their primary or surface meaning. If several people are asked to define certain words, their definitions will rarely be exactly the same. Ruesch and Kees described

FIG. 16.5 *Effective use of verbal symbols and white space.* CLIENT: PHILIP MORRIS, INC.; AGENCY: WELLS, RICH, GREENE, INC.

several interesting experiments that demonstrated this fact.[19] "Provocative" was defined as "stimulating," "annoying," "meaningful," "stirring," "exciting," "spiritual," "teasing," "alluring," "uncommon" and "argumentative." Pierre Martineau, in discussing words as symbols, says,

> When I say, "I'm going crazy," "My feet are killing me," or "I'm getting away with murder," I am just grasping at ways to express my feelings, my attitude more clearly, more adequately by using words completely out of their literal meaning. Everyone adjusts his behavior to the attitudes being expressed, not the surface meanings.[20]

Sidney J. Levy points out some of the broader implications of symbols in marketing:

[19]Jurgen Ruesch and Weldon Kees, *Non-verbal Communication* (Berkeley: University of California Press, 1956).
[20]Pierre Martineau, *Motivation in Advertising* (New York: McGraw-Hill, Inc., 1957), p. 100.

Earlier work has suggested the importance of symbols in the marketing world, particularly in regard to age, sex and social class. My present purpose is to reaffirm this importance. It is also to point attention to the fact that *marketers do not just sell isolated items that can be interpreted as symbols; rather, they sell pieces of a larger symbol—the consumer's life style.* Marketing is then a process of providing customers with parts of a potential mosaic from which they, as artists of their own life styles, can pick and choose to develop the composition that for the time may seem the best. The marketer who thinks about his products in this way will seek to understand their potential settings and relationships to other parts of consumer life styles, thereby to increase the number of ways he fits meaningfully into them.[21]

WHAT IS THE PROPER CREATIVE MIX?

Advertising and communication research have made it possible to set forth certain tentative guides for putting together the best creative mix to fulfill a certain objective. We are more concerned with the factors that determine when to use words and when to use pictures. The following are suggested as tentative guides in putting together the creative mix:

1. Where the appearance of a product is important in the ultimate purchase, the visual should be emphasized. A good example is the fashion advertisement. No words can recreate the exact design of a dress—the buyer wants to know just how it looks. Notice the emphasis given to the appearance of an automobile in most new-car magazine ads. The creators know that the car's attractiveness is important in the decision whether to purchase it.

2. The more important it is to make emotional associations with the product, the more we should emphasize the visual. Note how few words are used in perfume copy, where associations of glamour and romance are usually paramount. Many emotional associations are difficult to put in words. Some of the emotions we feel are never put into words—even to ourselves. This is not to say that words cannot be used to convey emotion—poets, for example, do so all the time. It is merely that the visual approach offers a richer and wider range of association. For instance, Green Giant, Aunt Jemima, and Elsie the Cow are visual symbols. The association they conjure up can best be communicated visually.

3. The more important the facts are in accomplishing the advertising objective, the more important the verbal will be. Consider the purchase of an expensive machine tool by a firm's purchasing agent: he will want facts and plenty of them. Most of the factual data he needs will be in verbal form—specifications, operation, and so forth. If you are buying a complicated product like a car or a refrigerator, there is certain factual information you will want. You find out how it looks from the visual symbols and how it works from the verbal. Here is information from a current Sears, Roebuck catalog:

Stereo Phonograph

Automatic 4-speed—plays Stereo and regular records. Exclusive balanced tone arm for less record wear. Dual-point synthetic sapphire needle with ceramic Stereo cartridge.

[21]Sidney J. Levy, "Symbolism and Life Style," in Harper W. Boyd, Jr., and Joseph W. Newman, p. 225.

It is obvious that such information can best be transmitted through words.

4. The more important narrative is in making the point of an advertisement, the more important words will be. Words are essential here to develop interest in the characters, the situation, and the outcome. Even in television — visual medium that it is — the words usually carry much of the burden of story impact.

5. The newer the product, the more likely you are to emphasize the copy. People naturally will have many questions in their minds. What does the product look like? How does it operate? What is the range of colors? Who is likely to use it? They may not verbalize these questions, but they are there all the same; and often they are questions that demand verbal answers. On the other hand, a question about the way it looks can best be answered by pictures. You will note that the introductory advertisement for the new model of an automobile will supply information on its horsepower, its wheelbase, and so forth. As the year goes on and consumers become familiar with the physical and performance characteristics of the car, the creative people are more likely to emphasize the visual. They do not feel it necessary to keep repeating the factual information. However, when you want to indicate symbolically the sort of people for whom your product is best suited you will ordinarily use a combination of verbal and nonverbal symbols.

6. Words are generally preferable for emphasizing action to be taken. Mail order advertising (advertising that impels the consumer to send an order through the mail) usually includes a great amount of copy. This copy is partly to provide information for the questions consumers have no opportunity to ask in person, and partly to outline the action. But this does not indicate that the visual symbols lack persuasion. We sometimes find that consumers develop a dislike for word claims, especially the more commonplace. Action then may be impelled more effectively by visual symbols. Usually, in advertising we use a mix of the two. The nonverbal symbol may operate as a message on its own to form important associations in image building. The verbal symbol also operates in the area of association, although its language is more circumscribed. For this reason, many creative people feel more at home with words because they know the rules. When these same people move into the world of the visual, they feel as though they are in a sort of never-never land.

We shall have more to say about the verbal versus the nonverbal as we move into our analysis of body copy, headlines, illustrations, and layout.

SUMMARY

The really astute creative man takes advantage of all the facts he can get and works out both creative strategy (what he intends to say) and creative tactics (how he will say it) for his advertisements. The strategy may well be determined by his marketing-communication plan.

The objectives of an advertisement can be considered as both general (those applying to every ad) and specific (those applying only to specific ads). Every ad is supposed to sell or to persuade. However, it is more meaningful to classify general objectives on the following basis: to leave the reader, viewer, or listener with a forceful idea regarding the product; to achieve immediate impact with the audience; to maintain interest among the audience; to furnish information of some sort to the reader; to supply an impulsion so strong it will give a large percentage of readers or viewers an irresistible urge to own the product.

An advertisement is a collection of signs and symbols. Any communicator uses both signs and symbols as a sort of shorthand for the object, the feeling, or the experience itself. Signs help attract and direct the audience; symbols tend to do more of the communicating.

Symbols are of two general types—verbal and nonverbal. One of the principal jobs of the creative person in advertising is to work out a mix of the two that will be most likely to accomplish the advertisement's purpose. In general, when appearance and emotional associations are important in a product's appeal, the visual will be emphasized. When factual data and direct or specific actions are more important, the stress will be on the verbal.

QUESTIONS FOR DISCUSSION

1. Why is it useful to define different types of objectives for advertisements?
2. Clip a current magazine or newspaper advertisement that appears to have as its primary objective each of the following: psychological, action, corporate, marketing.
3. Distinguish between signs and symbols. What are the problems one faces in using signs and symbols effectively?
4. Do you believe advertisements should provide more factual information? Cite examples to bolster your point of view.
5. What are the ingredients of the "creative mix"?
6. Distinguish between verbal and nonverbal symbols. Clip an advertisement that illustrates the effective use of each.

SUGGESTED READINGS

Berelson, Bernard, and Gary Steiner, *Human Behavior*. New York: Harcourt, Brace & World, Inc., 1964.

Boyd, Harper W., Jr., and Joseph W. Newman, *Advertising Management: Selected Readings*. Homewood, Ill.: Richard D. Irwin, Inc., 1965. Part IV.

Clark, George Timothy, *Copywriting: Theory and Technique*. New York: Harper & Row, Publishers, 1959. Chapter 2.

Colley, Russell H., *Defining Advertising Goals for Measured Advertising Results*. New York: Association of National Advertisers, 1961.

Crane, Edgar, *Marketing Communications: A Behavioral Approach to Men, Messages and Media*. New York: John Wiley & Sons, Inc., 1965. Chapters 14–15.

Dunn, S. Watson, *Advertising Copy and Communication*. New York: McGraw-Hill, Inc., 1956. Chapters 3–4.

Martineau, Pierre, *Motivation in Advertising*. New York: McGraw-Hill, Inc., 1957. Chapter 3.

Osgood, C. E., G. T. Suci, and P. H. Tannenbaum, *The Measurement of Meaning*. Urbana: University of Illinois Press, 1957.

Steiner, Gary, ed., *The Creative Organization*. Chicago: University of Chicago Press, 1965.

Wolfe, Harry D., *Measuring Advertising Results*. New York: National Industrial Conference Board, 1961.

Zaltman, Gerald, *Marketing: Contributions from the Behavioral Sciences*. New York: Harcourt, Brace & World, Inc., 1965.

17 | Verbal Communications: Headlines

Some advertising people maintain that an advertisement in print succeeds or fails largely on the strength of its headline. Dissenters point out, however, that this cannot be true because some advertisements do very well without any headline. To assess the relative merit of these arguments and to understand the place of the headline in advertising, we must examine the function of the headline.

It is important to remember that the headline is but one of the verbal elements of the advertisement, together with body text and identification marks (such as slogans and trade names). Sometimes it is the most important, sometimes it is not; but it is the verbal element that readers notice first. However, frequently in the process of creating an advertisement, the headline is written after the text has been completed.

HEADLINE FUNCTIONS

The prime function of the headline is to gain immediate impact. Sometimes the headline is expected to do this job alone — more often, it works hand in hand with the illustration or other visual elements. Notice the headline in Figure 17.1, which appeared in the *New York Times*:

100 GOOD ADVERTISING HEADLINES
— and why they were so profitable

100 GOOD ADVERTISING HEADLINES

—and why they were so profitable

An effective advertisement for a business audience with selective headline and small-type body copy arranged in columns.

FIG. 17.1   *An effective advertisement for a business audience. Note the selective headline.*

It is obviously the headline that is expected to stop the businessman reader of the *Times*. The promise of reward is in the headline.

A second function of headlines is the selection of the right prospects. Who but the businessman with advertising problems would be interested in whether headlines were effective or not?

A third function of most headlines (and subheads) is to lure readers into the text. In Figure 17.1 not only does the headline attract and select, but it invites the reader to step in and stay a while. Instead of telling the whole story, it tells just enough to arouse interest in the reward to follow. The headline is not expected to carry out the basic objective of the advertisement.

There is nothing in the rule book saying that you have to include a headline in every advertisement. If some other element can fulfill its functions more effectively, by all means consider omitting the head. You will probably find, however, that usually the headline is a very useful element.

ATTRACTING ATTENTION THROUGH HEADLINES

We have noted that the primary job of any headline is to attract the attention of potential consumers of the product or service. The subject of attention has been studied extensively through the years by psychological and advertising researchers, and their findings provide useful guidance for creative people.

We know, for example, that headline words act as signs, saying in effect, "Here, dear reader, is something meant just for you—please read on." Note the excellent use of headline signs in Figure 17.2, for example. "Rolls-Royce" and "Silver Shadow" have both *denotations* (meanings identifying a specific car) and even more important *connotations* (many associations) for anyone who has noticed automobiles and automobile advertising through the years. Who would expect, however, to defrost the rear windows merely "by flicking a switch"? Perhaps the most famous Rolls-Royce headline of all time is this one:

At 60 miles an hour the loudest noise in this new Rolls-Royce comes from the electric clock.

Note here how "60 miles an hour" and "electric clock" have been combined with the sign "Rolls-Royce" to pique the curiosity. In commenting on this advertisement, David Ogilvy, who considers this the best headline he has written through the years, said,

When I wrote that advertisement for Rolls-Royce, . . . I wrote 26 different headlines for it and then I got half a dozen other writers from the agency to go over them and pick out the best one. Then I wrote the copy (about 3,500 words) and then got all three or four other writers to go over it and cut out the dull and obscure parts and reduce it down.[1]

Berelson and Steiner point out that "people tend to see and hear communications that are favorable or congenial to their predispositions;

[1]"David Ogilvy Talks about How He Writes Copy," *Advertising Age*, March 13, 1965, p. 124.

The new Rolls-Royce Silver Shadow turns a trip to the library (or the hairdresser's or the supermarket or the post office) into a sinfully luxurious experience.

Read how this remarkable motorcar adapts itself to the daily round. Some wives say it's easier to drive than any car in the world. They're probably right.

The new Rolls-Royce is more than a motorcar. It is an experience. You begin to see why the moment you settle in the driver's seat.

The finest English leather surrounds you. Six to eight hides enrich every interior. The instrument panel and trim are faced with rare French walnut. Even the trunk is carpeted.

You reach down. A little knob lets you adjust your seat electrically *eight* ways. A hand lever lets you change the backrest angle independently.

You flip a switch. And a network of 1,300 invisible wires defrosts the rear window. Another switch sends the radio aerial up and down. Another lets you balance front and rear speakers.

Press a button on the dash and the gas tank flap opens. It locks automatically when it is shut.

Every Rolls-Royce Silver Shadow has an upper and lower ventilation system. You can warm your feet and cool your face at the same time. Air conditioning is standard equipment.

The new Rolls-Royce Silver Shadow has a monocoque construction. Chassis and body are built as a *single unit*—for a lower center of gravity and better road holding.

Step on the brake pedal and a sensing device balances braking front and rear for greater control. The Rolls-Royce has powerful disc brakes on *all four wheels*. It is the only car you can buy that has three completely separate hydraulic braking systems.

The new Rolls-Royce is only seventeen feet long. It's easy to get in and out of tight places. You can turn it full circle in only thirty-eight feet. Try that in the car you are now driving.

The Rolls-Royce Silver Shadow costs $20,600*. To find out for yourself what a sinfully luxurious experience it can be, see any dealer on the opposite page.

For more information about the car itself, write for the Rolls-Royce Owner's Manual.

This 142-page, hard-cover book is fully illustrated and costs $12.50. The man to write to is Mr. Norman Miller, Executive Vice President, Rolls-Royce Inc., Room 467N, 45 Rockefeller Plaza, New York, N.Y. 10020.   Copyright 1967 Rolls-Royce Inc.

Limited production. Silver Shadow Two-Door by H. J. Mulliner, Park Ward Limited, London coach builders. Hand crafted, specially styled. $31,800*. *Suggested retail price P.O.E., exclusive of local taxes, if any. Slightly higher in Alaska and Hawaii.

FIG. 17.2 *Excellent use of headline words as signs; proof that a headline need not be short to be effective.*
CLIENT: ROLLS-ROYCE, INC.; AGENCY: LAROCHE, MCCAFFREY AND MCCALL, INC.

they are more likely to see and hear congenial communications than neutral or hostile ones."[2] Consequently, if you can include a brand name, or an expression that people like in your headline, you are more likely to get their attention. If a person has recently bought a Ford, he will be favorably predisposed to a headline mentioning Ford, and he will read the copy to bolster his self-confidence and to justify his purchasing decision to his friends.

Although self-selection of material is mainly conscious and deliberate, it also operates nonconsciously. For example, it has been shown that people who say they are undecided on a particular issue still manage to expose themselves predominantly to the side favored by their predisposition.

The process of selection, as Zaltman points out, is not "a random affair. An individual's attitudes, opinions, beliefs and interests—in short, his predispositions at any particular time—are all important factors affecting the nature of his information-seeking and receiving experiences."[3]

John Caples, an agency executive who has tested headlines extensively, believes that certain headline words have a great ability to attract attention. Among those he considers most effective: Announcing, New, Now, At Last, Reduced, Free, How To, How, Why, Which, Who else, Wanted, This, and Advice.[4] He suggests that these be used (1) as a tool when you need a headline in a hurry, and (2) as a stimulus to spur your own imagination.

REWARDS IN HEADLINES

Another way to attract attention is to include in your headline a consumer reward—either direct or indirect. Because all of us as consumers are innately selfish, we look for some nice easy way to satisfy our drives. As they scan the advertisements in the mass media, consumers tend to select ads that promise some reward. Every ad has in it a host of signs that help the busy reader to predict which offer him a reward and which do not. Ideally, the signs in the headline (word signs) should flash a signal to the reader that there will be a reward if he reads on. Communication research shows conclusively that the headlines that show a promise of reward attract more attention, achieve more "impact," than those that do not.

Usually the reward has to do with the product; but, the ad may be so entertaining or so newsworthy that it offers its own reward.

Sometimes it takes only a single well-chosen word or two to suggest a reward. General Motors Fisher Body Division signaled a reward with one word: "Quiet." More often it takes several words (for example, Sears introduces a new tire with "This is Sears' new self-sealing tire. You could drive it with a dozen nails in it.")

[2]Bernard Berelson and Gary Steiner, *Human Behavior* (New York: Harcourt, Brace & World, Inc., 1964), p. 529.
[3]Gerald Zaltman, *Marketing: Contributions from the Behavioral Sciences* (New York: Harcourt, Brace & World, Inc., 1965), p. 56.
[4]John Caples, *Tested Advertising Methods*, rev. ed. (New York: Harper & Row, Publishers, 1961), Chap. 3.

The complexity of motivation has been dealt with in Chapters 11–13; therefore we need not review this subject here. Instead, let us assume that the creative planners have thoroughly explored the motivation involved in a particular ad, have decided what product rewards are to be emphasized, and have outlined them clearly in the objectives. The procedure, then, is to make sure that the headline contributes in every conceivable way to the communication of that reward. Furthermore, the headline should be made rewarding to read for its own sake if at all possible. Much of this chapter will be devoted to exploring ways of achieving these ends.

BASIC CLASSIFICATION OF HEADLINES

Headlines, like houses, animals, automobiles, and people, may be classified in a wide variety of ways. Direct, indirect, and combination, is one basic and quite useful classification.

The Direct Headline. Direct headlines are the more informative. However, the reader may have little incentive to read any more than the head. For example, a headline such as "Grade A Milk, 23¢ a Quart" offers complete information. There is nothing in this headline to arouse the curiosity or make readers feel they will find additional information in the text. Such a headline shuts off any desire to read further because it gives all the information needed to satisfy the readers' curiosity.

If you believe it is more important to make sure readers know what reward the product offers than to get them to read the copy, you have two choices. You can provide the information in a short statement set in large type with no accompanying text; or you can follow the statement with text, on the assumption that anyone who does read it is a plus that otherwise might be missed. The writer of an advertisement for the American Gas Association chose the former method. The complete copy consisted of a single statement, set boldly in a direct headline which said:

Only Gas gives you
tankful after tankful of hot water
3 TIMES FASTER

Here the product (gas) is mentioned first, followed by the reward it offers the user. Additional copy might be repetitious. However, if it were desirable to provide a fuller explanation, a slight change in the headline would give it curiosity value and cause readers to sample the text. Only one word would have to be changed:

WHY Gas gives you
tankful after tankful of hot water
3 TIMES FASTER

The word "why" promises an explanation in the text. Many readers might want to find out what it is. Whenever a direct headline is to be followed by text, the headline should include some curiosity-arousing elements. For example, Southern Pacific Railroad says "It's Fun to go to California on the SUNSET LIMITED." Many readers will wonder *why* it's fun. The headline states the reward directly and follows it with the name of the product.

Sometimes the illustration adds curiosity value to a direct headline. The following headline for Wall-Tex fabric wall coverings seems to need no further explanation:

This beautiful wall fabric is
pre-trimmed, easy to hang!

However, directly beneath the headline was a picture of the fabric being hung—and obviously by the man of the house, not by a professional paper hanger. Thus the illustration gives the headline curiosity value for people who want to save money by hanging their own paper and provides incentive to read further to find out whether the task is really within their capabilities.

An element of surprise in a direct headline can add curiosity value. For example, Church & Dwight's Baking Sodas (Cow Brand and Arm & Hammer) are well-known cooking products. One advertisement for these brands consisted of a direct headline, some text, and an illustra-

FIG. 17.3 *A slogan which serves double duty as a headline.* CLIENT: SCHLITZ BREWING CO., AGENCY: LEO BURNETT COMPANY, INC.

"When you're out of Schlitz, you're out of beer."

The Beer that made Milwaukee Famous

tion of the well-known package. Most readers would know at a glance what kind of product was advertised, but the headline said,

An economical dentifrice

Readers could readily agree it was economical, but were surprised to see it called a "dentifrice." This piqued the curiosity, in a relevant way, and told the reader he would find more about it in the text.

The *direct* headline can then really be double-barreled in that it usually makes a reader want to read the text. However, even if it fails to induce further reading, it leaves some residue of sales influence and may well dispose the reader favorably toward the product.

The Indirect Headline. It is generally best to use direct headlines if we want to attract the attention of a particular segment of the market. The direct headline tells a person whether the message is in line with his predispositions. However, there is a sizable minority of people "who read and listen to material against or indifferent to their prior positions — out of curiosity (e.g., no foreknowledge of what the content will be), lack of predispositional strength or importantly simple accessibility of materials."[5] These are the people who may be attracted by an indirect headline or illustration.

The writer of an Almaden wine advertisement used even more indirection in the headline "The promise of Paicines." The secret of the headline is revealed finally in the third paragraph of copy:

The promise of Paicines is that *only* Almaden grapes — their flavor carefully controlled by climate and soil (absolute essentials in fine wine production) — go into Almaden's finest varietal wines so that each and every bottle will have the same high quality.

An indirect headline that Shell Oil used effectively is

Invisible umbrella keeps off rust

The text explained that scientific research had evolved a new way to control rust. A direct headline could state the fact, but it could not explain the method. As the point of the advertisement was Shell's leadership in research, the complete story had to be read if the reader were to gain the desired impression.

Combination Headline. The combination headline seeks to combine the virtues of the direct and the indirect headline. Usually the idea is to tie a provocative thought to the specific name of a product. Thus the combination headline loses little in curiosity value but makes sure that readers know immediately what product has made them curious. A good example is Chevrolet's use of print advertising to emphasize its stepped-up power:

Chevrolet's special hill-flatteners

In the following headline the first line is indirect, the second direct:

Something we learned from the birds and bees . . . .
Sheaffer's SNORKEL Pen

[5]Berelson and Steiner, p. 531.

OTHER CLASSIFICATIONS OF HEADLINES

News Headlines. News headlines are the most effective of all because news is universally interesting. People like to know what is going on. The most important prerequisite of a news headline is that it provides the reader with something *new*. Copywriters sometimes believe naïvely that everyone is as interested in product news as they are, so they headline the ad this way:

> BIG NEWS for all car owners!

They later wonder why their advertisement had so little impact and aroused so little interest. The truth is that people are not necessarily intrigued by the word "news" alone. Genuine news interest does not have to be labeled as such.

What is news? Most editors would say news is anything of widespread interest (locally or nationally). Consider how much more effective it is to say "FBI Catches Local Counterfeiters" than "Big News from the Government." We know that people scan the headlines of advertisements for specific cues just as they do newspaper headlines.

Unlike a news story, advertising news need not be current. Readers will be interested in any product news as long as it promises some reward. Here are some better-than-average news headlines. Notice that the word "new" is not included in any of them:

This tough Du Pont plastic helps hold laminated safety glass together under impact

After 20 years of daily use, the only thing we had to fix on this Zippo lighter was the hinge

It's true! You can play beautiful music in 30 minutes without a lesson (Hammond Chord Organ)

Only seven hours to brush up on your French (Boeing jet travel)

Product news can cover a multitude of subjects. Almost any of the various lines of product investigation outlined in Chapter 14 might result in a newsworthy headline.

"How-to" Headlines. Before the book *How I Turned $1,000 into a Million in Real Estate—in My Spare Time*[6] was published, some publishers thought the title was too long. Had the author been influenced by the publishers and shortened the title the book might not have been a best seller. Every year the best-seller lists include books with the "how-to" approach. The secret is that these words offer a promise of power—and themselves have power to interest people and make them want to learn. They seem to address each reader personally. They help make a problem the reader's problem.

A "How-to" headline may be either direct or indirect. Here are some examples:

> How to fix *any* part of *any* car (*Motor Book*)
>
> How to tell which carpet is best for you (*Bigelow*)
>
> How to pick cottons that stay pretty (*Sanforized*)

[6]William Nickerson, *How I Turned $1,000 into a Million in Real Estate—in My Spare Time* (New York: Simon and Schuster, Inc., 1959).

In this type of headline the words "How to" can be implied as well as spelled out. It is important to show a spirit of helpfulness. For example, a Dan River headline says:

the prettier the sheet, the prettier you look

It tells each woman that here is a way to make herself look prettier — a logical, reason-why approach, but with strong romantic overtones.

Some headlines will say "How you can . . ." This is a way of making the headline seem more personal. Compare for example "How You Can Turn $1,000 into a Million in Real Estate — in Your Spare Time" to the book title actually used. Which is preferable? It depends on whether you want to aim the book at people who might actively consider going into real estate or at those who want some vicarious enjoyment from another man's experience. The latter are probably more numerous.

Question Headlines. Because curiosity is a natural, universal trait, there is a good chance that any question will stimulate an answer. When a writer frames a headline as a question, he expects to make his audience seek the answer in the text. A question headline will be provocative if it carries some interesting information or a stimulating idea. It is not too difficult to imagine the thinking of the writer of an advertisement for a General Electric Air Conditioner when he was searching for a headline to dramatize the comfort of air conditioning. After several tries he might well have come up with this:

Let a G. E. Room Air Conditioner
Keep you cool all summer long

He might then have decided that this headline did not really provide much incentive to continue reading. A reader might agree that the idea is good and then go blithely on to the next advertisement. So the writer decided to try a "How-to" headline and came up with this:

How to keep cool all summer long

But perhaps the writer felt that this headline did not set up any problem for the reader. It did not really dramatize the need. So he worked some more and wrote this:

Why swelter through another hot summer?
Let G. E. Air Conditioner keep you cool.

This is a better headline because of the reaction it is likely to provoke in the average reader. A good many will say, "That's right. Why *should* I?" Once he gains agreement with the point raised, the writer can expect considerable interest in the solution he offers.

Note the combination of curiosity and inquisitiveness in the question headline in Figure 17.4. The long headline fits well with the illustration and leads the reader naturally into the copy.

Here are some other good examples of effective, provocative question headlines:

Are you the same blonde he toasted last week? (*Clairol*)
Has your life insurance kept up with YOU? (*New England Mutual*)
Why a big breakfast for Betsy? (*General Mills*)

FIG. 17.4 *Effective use of a question headline.* CLIENT: BETTER VISION INSTITUTE; ADVERTISEMENT PREPARED BY DOYLE DANE BERNBACH INC.

These are all indirect headlines. However, questions may also be asked directly—for example:

> Why is it MORE FUN to go to California on the
> SUNSET LIMITED?

> Wouldn't you like to visit Hawaii?

The first headline holds much stronger invitation than the second. The second invites a "Yes, I would" answer and possibly nothing more.

Command Headlines. A command headline politely "orders" the reader to do something. As we have emphasized repeatedly, not all advertising is designed to get immediate action. It is, in fact, difficult to make a command headline as intriguing as some of the other types discussed here. For example, consider the headline:

> Save $15 every week

It becomes more interesting if we change it to a question:

Would you like to save $15 a week?

Interest is increased further if it is expressed as a "How-to" headline:

How to save $15 every week

Here is a combination of the two that appeared in a national magazine when a catalogue insert for Harry and David pears was included. The headline said,

> Tear it out!
> See how Harry and David make your Christmas Gift Huntin' the most excitin' ever

There are times when a command headline forcefully and concisely expresses a headline thought. How could you improve on the now much-used, admonitory command headline:

> Drive carefully—the Life You Save May Be Your Own

The command headline may be direct. An example is Scott's "Simplify your housework with 'many-use' Scott Towels." On the other hand, Dow Chemical uses an indirect form of the command head—"Don't include the mistakes of the past in your new home."

HEADLINE LENGTH

At a combined meeting of the Advertising Federation of America and the Advertising Association of the West, agency executive Whit Hobbs read this 70-word "headline" which he had written:

> I seem to spend my whole day picking up; picking up the laundry and the groceries and the mail; picking up Jim at the station and the children at school . . . and picking up after them all! Sometimes I feel like a squirrel in a cage . . . running in circles all day and never getting a chance to collect my thoughts and take a look at what's going on in the world.

Why 70 words? Mr. Hobbs says, "Because it took 70 words to say what I wanted to say."

In the midst of the many short automobile headlines this long one stands out:

> We believe we have just about every grunt, squeak, squeal, groan, whine, buzz, rap, rattle, beat, twang, clink, hiss, howl, rumble, roar, ruff, shudder, whistle and growl worked out of the solid Plymouth.

Western Union took 17 words to tell people on December 22 about its Candygram:

> This is about the only gift you can send *today* across the country in time for Christmas!

On the other hand one of the most effective advertisements of the past two decades had a headline consisting of one word. It was advertising the services of an advertising agency and showed a prizefighter receiving a blow on his chin from his opponent's glove. And the single word:

IMPACT

It should be obvious from these examples that there is no ideal length for a headline. It should use the words necessary to accomplish its job—no more, no less.

COMBINING HEADLINE AND ILLUSTRATION

In most advertisements a definite relation exists between headline and illustration, an interdependence that makes them work as a team. Sometimes the headline would be meaningless without the illustration. Sometimes each sharpens the other, or adds to its interest, or makes it more dramatic. Usually, then, the headline and the illustration are married. Obviously, however, it is impossible for the writer to combine his headline with the illustration unless he knows what the picture is to be.

Consider this headline for an RCA Victor Television set:

> Which of these beautiful RCA Victor Television
> sets "belongs" in your home?

The headline would have little or no meaning without the accompanying illustration of TV sets. The advertisement was a double-page spread in full color containing five separate illustrations, each showing a television set in a room of different decor.

The provocative headline and illustration of Figure 17.5 is an example of a near-perfect marriage of illustration and headline. Without the illustration the headline would have little meaning. Without the headline the picture merely portrays the Volkswagen.

Subheads. Many advertisements have only one headline. Some have several. Of several, one is usually the main headline, and the others subordinate. Subheads serve many purposes. For example, a writer who expresses a provocative thought in his main headline may want to expand upon that thought in a subhead directly following. The writer of an advertisement for Armstrong's floor covering used this interesting combination of main headline and following subhead:

> REBIRTH OF A HOUSE
> Good decorating ideas make
> Showplace out of drab dwelling

A writer may want to use a combination of indirect headline (to arouse curiosity) and direct subhead (to make a direct point). An interesting example is a Worthington Air Conditioning advertisement aimed at business executives:

> SUMMER HEAT WON'T SEND US LOOKING FOR NEW JOBS
> Worthington Packaged Air Conditioners make summer work pleasant, cut
> personnel turnover for large N.J. insurance general agents

Note that the subhead does not shut off interest, even though it is direct.

Westinghouse Electric uses main head, subhead, and picture (small boy turning knob on a television set) to very good effect. These are the main head and subheads:

ok Ma . . . . I'm tuning!

First from WESTINGHOUSE TV . . . a set with 7 special features for fam-
es with little kids

The writer of an advertisement for Bigelow Rugs and Carpets
thought of an unusually interesting combination of main headline and
subheads.

HAVE YOU ANY OF THESE DECORATING PROBLEMS?

See how beautifully

they can be solved

with Bigelow carpets

Notice how skillfully the main head directs attention to what is to
follow; it maintains interest and makes readers want to learn more.

FIG. 17.5 *Effective use
of understatement in a
headline. Note how well
the headline and the
illustration work together
to make the point.*
©VOLKSWAGEN OF
AMERICA, INC.;
ADVERTISEMENT PREPARED
BY DOYLE DANE
BERNBACH INC.

Following this subhead are four illustrations. Each depicted a decorating problem, and beneath each is a block of copy with its own subhead:

> Want to separate dining area from living room?
> Are you combining modern and traditional?
> Want to make a small room look bigger?
> Buying today for a home you'll have tomorrow?

Each head holds the reader's attention as the writer raises pertinent questions.

The headline, the illustration, and the subhead should be considered as a unit. The communication impact of the combination is the important consideration.

CHARACTERISTICS OF AN EFFECTIVE HEADLINE

Even experts often wonder, "Is this really an effective headline?" There is no universally applicable list of qualities that headlines should include, because every situation is different. The following, however, can serve as a sort of general check list. It includes many headline qualities that, according to our best research, increase effectiveness.

1. Headlines should be attention-impelling; make an immediate impact on the reader.

2. Headlines should have words or other cues that help select prospects from idle scanners.

3. If at all possible, some promise of reward should be included. Show how the product advertised will satisfy one or more consumer drives.

4. Words should be chosen carefully, for their sign value as well as their symbolic value. Clichés and other tired expressions should be avoided.

5. Headlines should be understandable at a glance. People will not spend time trying to figure out what you are saying.

6. Headlines should be specific and to the point, not general and applicable to any product or any situation.

7. Headlines should be coordinated with other elements of the advertisement.

WHAT ABOUT THE BROADCAST MEDIA?

From the preceding discussion one might gain the idea that headlines are found only in the print media. It is true that we usually associate them with such media as newspapers, magazines, and direct mail. However, they appear also in television—and to some extent even in radio.

Some television commercials—especially those used by local retailers—are little more than newspaper headlines written on a card and held before a television camera. However, even the most sophisticated writers for television frequently find it helpful to state a point in headline form ("Lasts Twice as Long") just before or after they have dramatized that same point. A common variation of the headline in television is the "crawl"—vertical or horizontal—in which the letters move slowly across the screen.

In general, television headlines are used for the following purposes:

1. To aid in putting over ideas that would take more demonstration time than you can allot.
2. To repeat a sales point.
3. To assist in establishing slogan or brand names.
4. To bring together or recapitulate ideas demonstrated throughout a commercial.
5. To reinforce the spoken word and the package signature by showing the product name written separately.

SUMMARY

The headline occupies a critical place in most print advertisements. Consequently, the writer should create it with extreme care, keeping in mind its functions of immediate impact, encouragement of further reading, and selection of the prospect. Words are signs that the writer can use to accomplish these ends.

Although what you say is more important than the form itself, it is helpful to have some basis for choosing the right headline. The three basic types are direct, indirect, and combination. If we classify them on the basis of purpose, we come up with these types (among others) —news, "how to," question, and command.

Headlines should work with the other elements of the creative mix (illustration, copy, and identifying marks) to achieve the advertisement's objective. Subheads can often be used to help the main headline accomplish its job, particularly in luring readers into the copy.

Although headlines are usually identified with the print media, they exist also in the broadcast media, though in a slightly different form.

QUESTIONS FOR DISCUSSION

1. What are the three basic types of headlines? Clip an example of each from a magazine or newspaper.
2. How can headlines best be coordinated with the other elements of the creative mix?
3. What are the characteristics of an effective headline? Evaluate two current ad headlines on the basis of this check list.
4. What is the function of rewards in headlines?
5. Why are some advertisements run without headlines? Under what conditions might this be a wise policy?

SUGGESTED READINGS

Bedell, Clyde, *How to Write Advertising That Sells*, 2d ed. New York: McGraw-Hill, Inc., 1952. Chapter 2.

Berelson, Bernard, and Gary A., Steiner, *Human Behavior*. New York: Harcourt, Brace & World, Inc., 1964. Chapter 13.

Caples, John, *Tested Advertising Methods*, rev. ed. New York: Harper & Row, Publishers, 1947. Chapters 2–5.

Dunn, S. Watson, *Advertising Copy and Communication*. New York: McGraw-Hill, Inc., 1956. Chapter 8.

Hepner, Harry W., *Creative Communications*. New York: McGraw-Hill, Inc., 1964.

Ogilvy, David, *Confessions of an Advertising Man*. New York: Atheneum Publishers, 1963. Chapter 6.

Sandage, C. H., and Vernon Fryburger, *Advertising Theory and Practice*, 7th ed. Homewood, Ill.: Richard D. Irwin, Inc., 1967. Chapter 15.

Wright, John, and Daniel Warner, *Advertising*. 2d. ed. New York: McGraw-Hill, Inc., 1966. Chapter 11.

18 | Verbal Communications: Copy

After all isn't ad-making
For print, radio and TV,
The best possible life for an adman,
The full life for you and for me?
Let others have gray suits and homburgs
We'll stick to black pencils and pads,
The life, core and heart of our business,
You're right—it's making the ads.

With this parody on Kipling, advertising executive Leo Burnett expressed before a convention of agency executives his deep affection for ad making, especially "writing the ads." Many other advertising leaders feel the same way and move with some reluctance from copywriting to executive positions, wondering whether they have really been promoted after all.

Although the copywriter's talent is only one of many that contribute to the production of a finished advertisement, it is generally true that the art director, the television director, the photographer, the artist, or the cameraman must accommodate their work to the copywriter's presentation of a campaign idea. It is in the copy itself that the advertising idea is most likely to come into full bloom.

APPROACH TO WRITING COPY

Before he starts to write the copy an experienced advertising writer has often decided on his objectives. For the printed ad, he has experimented with various headlines and illustrative ideas that show promise. When he has selected (at least tentatively) the best of the headlines and decided how the final ad will look, he is ready to write the text. For a television ad, visualization usually comes first.

The copy, regardless of medium, is basically an amplification of the headline theme or of the visualization. If your headline says, "Two new ways to get better heat, more comfort for your money," it is up to the body text to explain it. The function of the text is to whisk the reader along toward the advertisement's ultimate goal. It ordinarily does this by (1) arousing interest in the proposition, (2) providing believable information that is easy to understand and likely to whet desire to own the product, and (3) impelling the reader to see the product and to try it out, or at least to accept the image the writer has presented. We thus find the body copy taking over the last three of our five I's—*Interest, Information* and *Impulsion.*

The headline and illustration open the door and put the reader in a receptive mood for what the text has to say. Sometimes they do this by arousing curiosity, often by promising some reward. A highly successful advertisement headed "Do You Make These Mistakes in English?" has been run virtually unchanged for over forty years by the Sherwin Cody Institute. It promises to teach the reader better English in a direct, simple way. This is how the body text capitalizes on the headline:

> Many persons use such expressions as "Leave them lay there" and "Mary was invited as well as myself." Still others say "between you and I" instead of "between you and me." It is astonishing how often "who" is used for "whom" and how frequently we hear such glaring mispronunciations as "forMIDable," "aveNOO," and "incomPAREable." . . .

The firm experimented with a variation in the headline, "Maybe Youse Don't Talk Like This But . . ." According to the president of the company, this approach brought forth more inquiries but did not have the "staying power" of the old reliable approach.

In a magazine spread, Pan American Airways showed a happy couple exploring some unidentified ruins, with a fine headline below the photograph:

> Let someone else mow the lawn this summer.

There is a promise of reward here and the copy capitalizes on this promise:

> Europe wants you this very summer. Be a water baby. In a punt . . . gondola . . . or on the beach at St. Tropez. Be a steely-eyed gambler . . . Be an international golfer . . . Be a night person in London, Paris or Rome. Then sleep late in Zagreb, Corfu, or Positano. Do it all or do as you please, but please be there.

SEQUENCE OF IDEAS

Communication research verifies something alert college students have known for generations—the more effort it takes to read or listen to a message, the more likely the reader is to lose interest. We call this the least effort principle. One of the most obvious ways of minimizing reader effort is to express the ideas in proper, logical sequence. Much copy tends to follow this sequence: clarification of headline claim, proof of claim, other competitive advantages of the product, explanation of action or impression desired. Let us see how these work in a Canco advertisement.

Clarification of headline claim

A traffic cop on a busy corner couldn't feel more rushed than the mother who has to get children fed and off to school, and a husband off to work, all in the same short half-hour. That's when the convenience of the Canco disposable milk container means the most to you.

Proof of claim

This convenient, modern container is light and square-sided. It pours like a pitcher. It's easy for even small children to help themselves without spilling.

It's easy to open, too. Just a flip of the finger recloses it tightly, keeping out odors from other foods that sometimes give milk an unappetizing flavor.

Other competitive advantages

Not just at breakfast time. But all through the day, the Canco disposable milk container saves you work. Its compact shape makes it easy to store—actually increases storage space in crowded refrigerators. It's used once, and then discarded; there is no washing chore.

Action desired

Tell your grocer that you want *your* family's favorite brand of milk in the Canco disposable milk container. It will save you lots of work at busy mealtimes and all the rest of the day.

CLASSIFICATIONS OF COPY

Advertising people often divide body text into several classifications, such as "reason-why copy," "humorous copy," "descriptive copy," and so forth. From this, the neophyte might get the idea that the typical advertising writer sifts through the alternative types and picks one that suits his objective. In actual practice the writer is more likely to ask himself, "How can I make this copy interesting?" or "How can I make it believable?" than to ask himself "Which type of copy shall I use?" With certain standards in mind he begins to write. When the copy is finished it may be reason-why, human-interest, narrative or descriptive, or some other type.

Nevertheless, classifications are helpful, especially for a beginner. They help him organize his thinking and envision the possible forms in which a given idea may be expressed. He soon realizes that the classifications do not provide a formula. The classifications are seldom used in a pure form.

Reason-Why Copy. This is a heterogeneous classification. To some it means simply any factual interpretation of the product reward. Others say it is any copy that appeals to one's reason. The term was popularized by Claude Hopkins in the early part of this century. He believed advertising should give people reasons why they would benefit from a purchase. One of the first tests of his precept came when he and Albert Lasker started a campaign against home baking of beans (see Figure

2.3). Hopkins gave reasons why beans baked at home could never be digestible. He told how his company used only especially selected beans and soft water; how they were baked for hours at tremendous heat in steam ovens. He later applied the reason-why technique to soap, cereals, beer, and various medicinal products.[1]

Today any advertising copy that starts with a relevant reward or a factual statement about a product or institution and explains why it is true is called "reason-why." Travelers Insurance Company used this "reason-why" body text in an advertisement directed to businessmen:

Suppose a key man in your firm had just met with a bad accident. The doctor tells you that this man upon whom you depend for directing sales, for auditing your books or for performing some other vital function, will be laid up for months. You'd have to replace him, wouldn't you—and probably at a salary about equal to his?

Then you'd be faced with paying two salaries for one job—a circumstance forced on you because stopping the pay of an injured man would simply be out of the question.

You can prevent this kind of unproductive drain on your payroll by providing your key man with the protection of Travelers Business Accident Insurance.

This insurance provides medical expense coverage and a weekly income in case a key man is temporarily disabled. Should the disability prove permanent, *an income for life is guaranteed.* Why not make out a list of your key men now? Then get together with your Travelers agent or broker, and let him tell you how little it costs to apply this much needed protection to your business.

If you don't know the Travelers man in your community, write and we'll send you his name and address.

Note that a problem is posed here and a solution is implied. In another advertisement, aimed at the general public, the same company takes for granted that people realize the wisdom of having hospitalization insurance. It merely makes a statement and proceeds to explain why the statement is true:

See what all-inclusive benefits this economical Travelers Plan offers you and your family, under a single policy!

A WIDE RANGE OF COVERAGE

Each member of your family (you and your wife, up to the ages of 60, and all your children between the ages of 30 days and 18 years) may be covered for:

1. HOSPITALIZATION—daily room and board, up to 70 days of hospital care—a maximum of $1,050.
2. SURGICAL EXPENSES—up to $400.00
3. MISCELLANEOUS HOSPITAL EXPENSES (For X-rays, laboratory, anesthetics, operating room, et cetera, up to $150.00).
4. EMERGENCY TREATMENT—Costs of hospital out-patient service for accidental injuries, up to five times the amount of daily hospital benefit—a maximum of $75.00

MATERNITY BENEFITS INCLUDED

Your wife is covered for hospital expenses of childbirth or prenatal complications, up to ten times the amount of daily hospital benefit. What is more, these benefits are paid if pregnancy begins after her coverage has been in force thirty days even though the hospital confinement may commence before the coverage has been in force ten months.

[1]James Playsted Wood, *The Story of Advertising* (New York: The Ronald Press Company, 1958), pp. 290–291.

A TRULY WORLD-WIDE SERVICE

Insured members of your family may be treated in any hospital they choose — wherever they happen to be. Payment of benefits is made *direct to you*, the policy holder, unless you request that they be paid by the Travelers to the hospital or surgeon.

EVEN IF YOU ALREADY CARRY OTHER INSURANCE

This policy places no limitations on what you may carry in the way of other hospitalization coverage. Indeed, one of its purposes is to give holders of Group or other forms of Hospital Insurance the *extra* protection they may want or need.

Ask your Travelers agent or broker for full details of this economical, comprehensive plan for family protection. If you'd like the name and address of the Travelers man nearest you, just drop us a line.

Some might call the copy in Figure 18.1 "expository". Note, however, that the question headline and the subsequent answer promise something that demands a reasonable explanation. The headline refers to a competitor who does not exist. The copy shows the reason why in a breezy, regular-guy tone.

FIG. 18.1 *Believability is achieved through understatement in this reason-why copy. Note the deference paid to a former competitor, Uncle Sam.* CLIENT: OCCIDENTAL LIFE OF CALIFORNIA; ADVERTISEMENT PREPARED BY DOYLE DANE BERNBACH INC.

In broadcast commercials, the reason consumers should buy the advertised product is given orally or visually and subsequent copy is used to justify the claims.

Humorous Copy. Some advertisements are lightened by a touch of wit but do not depend entirely on humor for their impact. On the other hand, there are many that depend primarily on humor to get the point across. An interesting use of humor is illustrated in Figure 18.2

Humor is a popular device especially in the broadcast field. Kellogg has used a veteran vaudeville team, Homer & Jethro, with "cornfucius say" quips to sell its cornflakes on both radio and television. Another pair, Light and Hearty, have been used by Standard Rochester Brewing Company to promote its Topper beer.

Agency head Draper Daniels suggests four "rules" for the use of humor in advertising but cautions the reader that they are set down to "help you until you acquire the experience and judgment that will make them unnecessary."

Left to right, rear: Mr. Kenneth Dubler; Paul, age 2; Mrs. Kenneth Dubler; Nancy, 16; Karen, 19; Kevin, 15. Front: Sheilla, 9; Rachel, 11; Tony, 8; Betsy, 6; Carolyn, 5; Joey, 3.

Mrs. Dubler figures her 6-year-old Maytag Washer and Dryer are just getting broken in.

After all, her mother's Maytag is 39 years old, and still going strong.

Six years ago, Mrs. Kenneth Dubler of San Diego, Calif., decided it was high time to follow her mother's example.

She finally bought a Maytag Washer of her own. And a Dryer, too.

The 12 Dublers supply their Maytags with everything from permanent press slacks and dresses to diapers — four loads a day, seven days a week. The Maytags keep working merrily away, with just one small repair in six years.

You can get a New Generation Washer and Dryer, with a lot of new features Mrs. Dubler's Maytags don't have. Giant new washing capacity. Space-saving Dryer design. And a choice of decorator colors.

But one thing hasn't changed. When you have a lot of living to do, and laundry's the last thing you want to worry about, Maytag makes the Washer and Dryer you can depend on.

\\\\\\MAYTAG
® THE DEPENDABLE AUTOMATICS

FIG. 18.2 *Testimonial and a touch of humor add to the believability of the Maytag claim for worry-free long life.*
CLIENT: THE MAYTAG COMPANY; AGENCY: LEO BURNETT COMPANY, INC.

1. In most cases humor is better for selling a low-priced product than it is for selling a high-priced one.
2. Humor is an effective way to put new life and memorability into an old story.
3. Humor is effective in telling a simple story in a memorable manner.
4. Humor is effective in driving home the ridiculousness of an outmoded practice which militates against the use of a new product or method.[2]

Some products and situations (grave markers, serious illness, and so on) should not, of course, be used in humorous context.

Descriptive Copy. Copy that must describe a product or service and its features presents a real challenge to an advertising writer. At worst, it is insufferably dull. It is always a difficult kind of advertising to make interesting. Here is an example of dull writing, a composite of several actual automobile advertisements:

> Distinction speaks in many ways—but never more eloquently than when you drive the brilliant new Jupiter-Eight. This is far and away the finest Jupiter-Eight ever built—it's a bigger car, with more leg room, more hip room, more hat room. It has a longer wheelbase. It is completely new in every styling detail.
>
> The new Jupiter-Eight offers you unmatched performance and luxury in your choice of five distinguished models. Here yesterday's traditions of craftsmanship join tomorrow's advanced engineering to bring you everything you have desired in a car, and probably much you never dreamed possible.

Though a composite, it is fairly typical of the text in many automobile advertisements. Note that there is only one piece of specific information in the entire body text, the fact that it comes in five models. One might think that the writers who contributed to this composite were writing directly to the reader, for the word "you" is introduced here and there. The effect, though, is one of uninterrupted dullness, and there is little description specific enough to build a real image of the product.

Contrast the preceding copy with the fine descriptive copy in Figure 18.3, an advertisement that won the Arthur Kudner award for "excellence in writing institutional advertising."

Testimonial. Body text written in the form of a testimonial can carry unusual interest, conviction, and persuasion if used intelligently. However, the public often refuses to believe that movie stars wash their hair exclusively with a certain shampoo to make it lovelier, or even that they wash their own hair. Consumers grow even more skeptical when cinema celebrities or sports stars wax wildly ecstatic about a 79-cent ball point pen or a proprietary remedy.

We noted earlier that personal influence often flows horizontally rather than vertically and that people look somewhat more to people like themselves for guidance, and less to so-called opinion leaders. Therefore advertising people should make sure that the "authorities" they choose to deliver testimonials are really acceptable to the potential audiences as such. It is more important that the authorities be accepted as well qualified than as well known. The marketing manager must determine, as Zaltman points out, "which group exerts the greatest influence on the individual's behavior toward the product, service or idea

[2]Draper Daniels, "Humor in Advertising," Elbrun Rochford French, ed., *The Copywriter's Guide* (New York: Harper & Row, Publishers, 1959).

Henry VII, Elizabeth I and Mary Queen of Scots are buried in this chapel.

Tread softly past the long, long sleep of kings

THIS IS Henry VII's chapel in Westminster Abbey. These windows have filtered the sunlight of five centuries. They have also seen the crowning of twenty-two kings.

Three monarchs rest here now. Henry, Elizabeth and Mary. Such are their names in sleep. No titles. No trumpets. The banners hang battle-heavy and becalmed. But still the royal crown remains. *Honi soit qui mal y pense.*

When you go to Britain, make yourself this promise. Visit at least *one* of the thirty great cathedrals. Their famous names thunder! Durham and Armagh. Or they chime! Lincoln and Canterbury. And sometimes they *whisper.* Winchester, Norwich, Salisbury and Wells. Get a map and make your choice.

Each cathedral transcends the noblest single work of art. It is a pinnacle of faith and an act of centuries. It is an offering of human hands as close to Abraham as it is to Bach. Listen to the soaring choirs at evensong. And, if you can, go at Christmas or Easter.

You will rejoice that you did.

For free illustrated literature, see your travel agent or write Box 700, British Travel Association.
In New York—680 Fifth Ave.; In Los Angeles—612 So. Flower St.; In Chicago—39 So. LaSalle St.; In Canada—151 Bloor St. West, Toronto.

FIG. 18.3 *Excellent descriptive copy; winner of the Arthur Kudner award for "excellence in writing institutional advertising."* COURTESY BRITISH TRAVEL ASSOCIATION.

being promoted, and then he must attempt to define the qualities and traits of the opinion leaders and gatekeepers within this particular group."[3]

For example, a business executive who does a lot of traveling is qualified to speak about transportation from the passenger's point of view. The following text from a Pullman advertisement came unsolicited from such a person, the executive secretary of a national association:

Recently I had to go to St. Louis for a meeting. Instead of flying, as I have been doing for the past four years, I decided to take an overnight Pullman. It happened to be raining when I left. No matter. The train was exactly on time, and what's more, I didn't get drenched before boarding.

By the time I reached my roomette, my suitcase was there waiting for me. I hung my suit in the locker and changed into a pair of slacks. Then I settled back

[3]Gerald Zaltman, *Marketing: Contributions from the Behavioral Sciences* (New York: Harcourt, Brace & World, Inc., 1965) p. 82.

in that big, comfortable seat and managed to get more work done – in an hour – in the privacy of my roomette than I am able to accomplish in my own office in half a day.

I couldn't have slept better.

We arrived at the St. Louis station 30 seconds early. When I left the train, I was fortified with a good breakfast, an unwrinkled suit, shined shoes and a serene disposition. The cab ride to my engagement was a matter of seconds. What all this adds up to is that a journey I usually consider an ordeal turned out to be a pleasurable event. I am looking forward to many more trips by Pullman.

Note that the first paragraph established that the testifier is an air-minded executive who has been flying to St. Louis regularly for four years. Therefore he is qualified to make this comparison. The first competitive note is struck when he mentions that, although it was raining, he didn't get drenched before boarding the train. As this was an overnight trip, the implication is that the executive lost no working time from his office. In the privacy of his roomette, he got more work done than he could accomplish in his office in half a day. This is a statement with which any executive is likely to agree; he knows the value of an hour or two completely free from interruptions. In the text the testifier states simply that he couldn't have slept better. He then makes the point that he left the train fed, pressed, shined, and feeling good. The statement that "the cab ride to my engagement was a matter of seconds" is a subtle reminder that most airports are located a considerable distance from downtown.

In some testimonial ads the testifier is real, in some he is fictitious. Sometimes groups of people, real or fictitious, are used to add weight to the testimony.

Dialogue. Dialogue, when it is well written, is interesting, convincing, and persuasive. But it must be well written. The advertising writer who elects to use dialogue should have a touch of the playwright in him. Poor dialogue is dull. Unnatural dialogue is unconvincing. Too many writers fall into the error of believing that everything people say is interesting, regardless of what they say or how they say it. The following is an example of dull dialogue:

"Ann, I hear you've got a new Agitomatic washer. I've heard so much about its new counterbalanced, reciprocating agitator. Does it really get clothes cleaner?"

"I'll say it does, Mary. It *really* gets clothes cleaner. You see, the new type agitator, an exclusive Agitomatic feature, works on a new principle. Instead of merely whirling the clothes through a washing cycle, the eccentric cam gear assembly *flutters* them. This flutter action, which is offered by no other automatic washer, gently forces the water through the soiled clothes from nine different directions. You've never seen clothes so clean as those which come out of my new Agitomatic automatic washer."

These mechanical features would be dreary enough in reason-why text. Coming from two typical housewives, the words are unbelievable as well. No one will believe that housewives talk like mechanical engineers. The readers will either guffaw at the copy or ignore it.

Narrative. In narrative copy the story is the thing. Almost everyone likes to hear an interesting story. The story is one of the oldest forms of literature and is a reliable approach to communicating an advertising point. Among the common forms of narrative copy are the short story, picture-and-caption, and comic strip.

Unless there is a conflict, there is not much chance of interesting the reader or viewer in your story. Somebody must be troubled, doubtful, at least worried. And then, presto! The product or service advertised arrives on the scene. By using the product the principals solve their problems, and thus comes a happy ending. Finally, there is the suggestion that you, too, dear reader, may share in this solution. Without some involvement, the whole thing will lack empathy, and the reader or viewer will not think of the product as solving *his* problems, too.

An interesting narrative advertisement (to advertising people at least) is the one in Figure 18.4. It was of special interest to a limited number of people, and it had all the elements of a good story—a number of problems with solutions that were satisfactory to both the client and the agency.

FIG. 18.4 *Narrative copy used effectively in a campaign in business magazines aimed at advertising space buyers.* COURTESY THE BOSTON GLOBE.

Other Classifications. There are various other classifications of body text. We might classify it according to the media used. Certain media (such as television, radio, business magazines, direct mail) will be given special attention in later chapters because of the special problems involved. We might classify text according to its objectives. In a later chapter special attention will be devoted to public relations and institutional copy.

LENGTH OF BODY TEXT

Other variables being equal, short body text will attract more readers than long. Unfortunately, this probability leads some writers to work for brevity as an end in itself. Brevity is a hollow achievement if the writer neglects to include enough information to satisfy his readers' curiosity and enough persuasion to make them receive the image and want the product. The writer who divests his body text of these essentials leaves it clothed only in brevity—a flimsy garment. If he achieves greater reading attention than he would with longer copy he compounds the ineffectiveness. It is obvious that one person who is interested, convinced, and persuaded by longer copy is worth a thousand who read short body text without being so convinced and persuaded.

The copy should be just long enough to tell the story. Sometimes illustrations make long copy unnecessary. Sometimes the audience makes the difference. For example, direct-mail specialist Orville Reed[4] quotes this short—but effective—copy:

> Dear Bill:
> They're running.
> Yours,
> Joe

Most people would ignore such a letter. However, these words scribbled in stubby pencil, caused four businessmen to drive 250 miles, spend more than $100 in cash, and remain away from their businesses for two days. The letter to Bill came from an old friend who ran a boat livery on Lake Winapanco to tell him that the perch were coming in.

David Ogilvy warns writers not to shortchange the prospect in search of information:

> The consumer isn't a moron; she is your wife. You insult her intelligence when you assume that a mere slogan and a few vapid adjectives will persuade her to buy anything. She wants all the information you can give her . . .
> When I was a door-to-door salesman, I discovered that the more information I gave about my product, the more I sold . . .But most copywriters find it easier to write short, lazy advertisements. Collecting facts is hard work.[5]

A CHECK LIST FOR COPYWRITING

Most practicing writers are understandably suspicious of copywriting "formulas." They maintain that writing is basically a creative business

[4]Orville E. Reed, "Helpful Tips on Writing Better Sales Letters," in Elbrun Rochford French, ed., *The Copywriter's Guide* (New York: Harper & Row, Publishers, 1959).
[5]David Ogilvy, *Confessions of an Advertising Man* (New York: Atheneum Publishers, 1964), p. 96.

and that every communication situation is a little different. Yet they will admit that there are certain principles that distinguish effective copy from ineffective copy. Some of the more important principles are summarized here to serve as a useful check list for the neophyte.

Is the copy interesting? Former president George Gribbin of Young & Rubicam offers this advice for copywriters wondering how to evaluate an ad:

> I've never found a completely trustworthy set of guideposts. Nobody I know in this business ever has. Research and testing will tell you a lot, but they don't tell you quite enough . . . .
>
> Having found this out many years ago I drew up my own totally unscientific, hitherto undisclosed method of ad assessment. Undisclosed, that is, except at Young & Rubicam. They *have* to listen to me there. . .
>
> *I make it a point to compare ads to people.* I say to myself, would I like a man or woman to act the way this ad does? Would I choose this ad—if it were alive—for a friend? If the answer is yes, I figure the ad is on the right track. If the answer is no, I figure it's pretty likely something is wrong about the advertisement.[6]

Interest should begin in the first sentence of the first or "lead-in" paragraph. Advertising writers who want to perfect their ability to write interesting lead paragraphs might study *The Reader's Digest*, America's biggest-selling magazine. The writers in the *Digest* depend entirely on words to arouse interest in titles and text.

Here is the way two articles in one issue of *The Reader's Digest* began. The first promises new information on a subject of popular interest:

> Despite all the head-shaking and talk about the divorce rate, every sign points to the fact that marriage is better than it has ever been in our national history.

Another lead-in paragraph features a paradox, and paradoxes are usually interesting:

> Skimpy breakfasts may be one cause of the shocking number of overweight adults in the United States—a total set by Public Health authorities at fifteen million.

Although interest in advertised products or services may be less than that in divorce or overweight, the same techniques may be used to increase the interest of opening paragraphs in advertisements. For example, a Metropolitan Life Insurance Company advertisement about allergies had the headline "The strange case of the hidden rabbit and the allergic Prince." The lead paragraph promised the reader some interesting information on this intriguing topic:

> At the Pasteur Institute in Paris, the story is told about an Oriental prince who visited this famous medical center. Warned in advance that the Prince was allergic to rabbits, the tour was carefully planned to avoid all rooms in which the animals were kept.

Most readers will be so curious when they read this lead-in that they will want to read the rest of the body text.

[6]In a speech presented at the Eastern Annual Conference, American Association of Advertising Agencies, New York, October 27, 1958.

To most people the world's most fascinating subject is themselves. They choose ads—just as they choose friends—that show a genuine interest in them. They like to hear "you" rather than "I" or "we." They like copy that makes them feel important. Suppose you are writing copy for a product as prosaic as a household wall cleaner. The copy will evoke more response if it makes the housewife feel like a homemaker, not a drudge who spends all her time cleaning.

Image-provoking, fresh-sounding words are more interesting than tired or overworked words. Here is some copy for Zenith Shortwave Portable Radio that used both the "you" approach and image-provoking words:

Your passport to seventy-three countries now broadcasting in English and their native language. A single "trip abroad" for foreign language students!

The use of "passport" is good, imaginative writing—better than the more conventional "brings in" seventy-three countries. The addition of the thought that shortwave radio is a "trip abroad" is picturesque and appropriate. It reminds any reader who is interested in a foreign language that with this radio he can hear the language spoken by indigenous broadcasters in correct accent and idiom.

Is the Copy Specific? The specific word or phrase communicates a sharper image than the general one does. It is more effective communication to say "Mr. John Jones of Springfield, Missouri, gets 19.8 miles per gallon of gas on his new Viking V-8" than to say "You can enjoy more economical driving in this Viking V-8." It is more effective to say "Dermatophytosis, which is commonly known as Athlete's Foot, actually afflicts a large percentage of people who think they are healthy as can be" than to say "Free yourself of Athlete's Foot."

One of the reasons newspaper retail copy usually gets higher reading than general copy in the same paper is that one finds specific facts in retail copy. Retail ads tell where the product can be bought and how much it costs.

Sometimes space or time does not permit listing all the features of a product. In such a situation, specific copy can cover one feature and cover it fairly completely. Sometimes the audience determines how specific you can be. For example, if you are addressing an audience of chemical engineers you can use specific terminology you could not possibly use in text prepared for the general public.

Unlike the generalized claims usually found in tire advertisements, Goodyear is refreshingly specific with this copy:

These great mud and snow tires by Goodyear have been tested way up in Canada's Hudson Bay area. And they've proved their stuff where *you* drive —from driveway to superhighway.

In deep snow, in packed snow, in treacherous mud, those Suburbanites by Goodyear give you DYNAMIC TRACTION. You get extra grip under power from 3,728 biting edges on 260 massive tread cleats! Suburbanites *go.*

Is the Copy Simple? At an Association of National Advertisers convention, advertising manager Melvin Hattwick of Continental Oil reported on one of his company's "failure stories." The campaign was based on the idea "Break the Performance Barrier." Dealers, district sales managers, and agency personnel agreed that the idea was fine. It was topical because the papers were full of our aircraft's achievement in breaking the sound barrier. The company wisely decided to test the campaign in five markets. They found sales rose only slightly and that the theme did not register with people. Further research indicated that people did not understand the "performance barrier" analogy and did not try to figure it out.

Copy research indicates that ad readers and watchers do not like mental work. Common causes of unnecessary mental work might be too many ideas presented in one piece of copy or complicated thought patterns such as "just as this . . . so is this . . ."

Is the Copy Concise? Conciseness of copy is related to the simplicity of copy in that simplicity and conciseness often go together. However, any copy that gets to the point quickly is concise, and that is the kind people prefer. Time is valuable, and the copywriter has no license to waste it. Consider how concisely the ideas are stated in this Bufferin copy:

> It starts bringing relief from headaches and other painful cold miseries in minutes, actually acts *twice as fast* as aspirin!
> And you can take Bufferin right from the beginning to the end of a cold! For it's so safe and gentle you can use it continually.

Is the Copy Believable? As we noted in Chapters 12 and 13, believability is complex, particularly when persuasive messages are involved. Writers may add conviction to their copy in a number of ways. One is to use the soft-sell approach; avoid taking yourself too seriously. Avoid statements such as "Once you've used this amazing soap, you'll never be satisfied with any other brand."

Both Figures 18.1 and 18.5 are examples of advertisements that are believable because they do not take themselves too seriously. Examples from television are Figures 23.14 and 23.26. The tongue-in-cheek-approach is stronger when it is bolstered by evidence. For example, a fine American Express ad had no illustration but a large headline "We Hate Cash." This was followed by a subhead, "From now on, cash for travel is out," and the copy:

> Ever notice how a traveler will keep patting the pocket where his money is? Pickpockets notice it. Ever wonder how many travelers hide cash? (Ever hidden yours and forgotten where? Ghastly) Enough of this senseless fear! American Express answers the problem two ways.

Another ad in this series carried the headline "Cash is the curse of the traveling class."

Most of us like to think that we believe what is true and reject what is false. However, the evidence indicates that belief is bound up inextricably with feeling. We rarely change people's beliefs by facts alone. People accept facts and beliefs that are consistent with their feelings, rather than those that are logical. A Democrat is less likely than a Republican to believe a statement that reflects favorably on a Republican, and vice versa.

Research evidence indicates that people are more likely to believe copy that includes proof plus some sort of demonstration to back it up. If you tell them how your product is made, how it works, and how it is

The boys with the Friday night faces.

Every United stewardess knows a Friday night face when she sees one.

It's the tired face of a businessman who's put in a hard week and just wants to go home.

Maybe he wants to talk. Maybe he doesn't.

We'll feed him well. His favorite drink. Hors d'oeuvres. Sizzling steak. Or broiled lobster. Cornish hen, maybe.

A pillow for his tired back. Six channels of stereo and a movie to unkink the tensions.

Some people want to be fussed over. Some don't. Extra care is different for every passenger.

But they all get it.

That's why more businessmen fly United than any other airline.

They think the service is great.

We agree, but we think it's good business, too.

"Look! Charley's smiling."

Movies by Inflight Motion Pictures

FIG. 18.5 *High reader interest is achieved through a reverse promise, effective copy lead-in, and good coordination between headline and body copy.* CLIENT: UNITED AIR LINES; AGENCY: LEO BURNETT COMPANY, INC.

used, they are more apt to believe what you have to say than if you merely claim it is the best product.

A copywriter's feeling for believability will sometimes cause a client to change his marketing program. According to Martin Mayer, the Foote, Cone and Belding agency worked up what it considered a particularly persuasive campaign for Johnson's car polish based on what it could do for the finish of an automobile.[7] The creative staff feared, however, that no one would believe these claims made for a wax that sold at 69 cents a jar and that people would be wary about applying a cheap wax to their expensive automobiles. Tests were made at different prices. The higher-priced cans sold better. Johnson added some new and expensive ingredients to the polish and priced it at $1.69.

[7]Martin Mayer, *Madison Avenue, U.S.A.* (New York: Harper & Row, Publishers, 1958), p. 128.

We also know that the reputation of the advertiser and the brand has an important influence on believability. (Conversely, of course, advertising enhances or detracts from this reputation.) One excellent study of the influence of source credibility in propaganda is of interest in this respect. Researcher Hovland and Weiss summarized some of their findings:

1. No difference was found in the amount of factual information learned from the "high credibility" and "low credibility" sources, and none in the amount retained over a four week period.
2. Opinions were changed immediately after the communication in the direction advocated by the communicator to a significantly greater degree when the material was presented by a trustworthy source than when presented by an untrustworthy source.
3. There was a *decrease* after a time interval in the extent to which subjects agreed with the position advocated by the communication when the material was presented by trustworthy sources, but an increase when it was presented by untrustworthy sources.
4. Forgetting the name of the source is less rapid among individuals who initially agreed with the untrustworthy source than among those who disagreed with it.[8]

Is the Language Relevant? The focus of copy, as with all elements of the advertisement, is the objective. Words and statements that help to accomplish it should be included, and irrelevant ones thrown out. It is not always easy to practice this, but there are guides. For example, check the words and phrases to see whether there is not a better, fresher-sounding one to take the place of the one used. An ad in the highly successful Ford Mustang series carried no headline but merely an illustration of a sophisticated young male with girl friend beside his new Mustang and this copy:

Two weeks ago this man was a bashful school teacher in a small mid-western city. Add Mustang. Now he has three steady girls, is on first name terms with the best headwaiter in town, is society's darling. All the above came with his Mustang. So did bucket seats, full wheel covers, wall-to-wall carpeting, padded dash, vinyl upholstery, and more.
    Join the Mustangers.
    Enjoy a lot of *dolce vita* at a low, low price.

Taken literally, this is not believable. However, when presented in this tongue-in-cheek visual and verbal manner, it operates like poetry to set the right mood for building the car's image.

Studies by the Gallup-Robinson research organization indicate that extremely "ad-y" language tends to be a block to good communication. "Ad-y" words are those like "finest," "best by test," "wonderful," and "amazing efficiency." People tend to discount much of such language as irrelevant trade puffing.

It is easy enough to write copy like this:

Brown's bread is delicious in flavor, very rich in proteins, and also light and tender.

But how much better it is to use this copy:

[8]Carl I. Hovland and Walter Weiss, "The Influence of Source Credibility on Communication Effectiveness," Wilbur Schramm, ed., *The Process and Effects of Mass Communication* (Urbana: University of Illinois Press, 1954).

Brown's bread is as light and puffy as little popovers from your favorite baker, as rich and smooth textured as new creamed potatoes.

Copy usually has to be written and rewritten if it is to sparkle. Here are some other ways of making your language sparkle:

1. Use short rather than long words wherever possible, but do not discard the long word if it reflects your meaning more exactly.
2. Use dynamic verbs and adjectives. For example, consider this excellent copy that was written for Numaki Spread:

First, the livers of young chickens, impeccable in conduct, were mixed with herbs and spices.
To this aromatic spread we added water chestnuts, tiny trusting immigrants from the Orient.
The result: a spread so delicate, so tempting that lady guests mute their gabble as it passes.

3. Use the language your prospects might use in describing your product or service to their friends.

Is the Copy Persuasive? People cannot always be expected to react automatically the way you want them to. Successful copy usually states specifically what impression or action the ad expects of the reader or listener. This can vary from the oft-repeated "Don't delay, act today" to more imaginative uses of persuasion. In the fine Hathaway advertisement (Figure 14.1) the action close is in keeping with the soft-sell tone of the whole advertisement:

For store names, and free Dictionary of Shirts and Shirtings, write C. F. Hathaway, Waterville, Maine.

A General Electric Swivel-top Vacuum Cleaner advertisement aimed at women who might like their husbands to give them one for Christmas bore a text devoted to advising a woman how to hint to her husband in such a way that he would be sure to "catch on." After assuring her that he would if she followed directions, the final sentence said: "Yes, this holiday season will be one of the happiest (and cleanest) your family ever enjoyed." Almost every product advertises "make this the happiest Christmas," but the addition of the parenthetical words "and cleanest" made the persuasion here stand out.

SUMMARY

We can expect the body text in most advertisements to provide interest, information, and impulsion to act. Good copy starts out as an amplification of the headline, offers some proof of what the headline says, explains the product's competitive advantages, and makes clear what impression or action is desired.

The principal classifications of copy are reason-why, humorous, descriptive, testimonial, dialogue, and narrative. These are seldom used singly but serve as a method for organizing one's thinking in planning the copy.

In appraising a piece of copy he has created, a writer would do well to evaluate it on the basis of the following:

1. Is the copy interesting?
2. Is the copy specific?
3. Is the copy simple?
4. Is the copy concise?
5. Is the copy believable?
6. Is the language relevant?
7. Is the copy persuasive?

QUESTIONS FOR DISCUSSION

1. What is the proper relation between the headline and the body copy of an advertisement? Clip a current newspaper or magazine ad that is not consistent with this relation.
2. What are the principal types of copy? Find an example of each in current magazines or newspapers.
3. What is the main cause of ineffective copy?
4. What are some of the most effective methods of making copy interesting?
5. Why is copy eliminated in some advertisements?
6. Could copy written for print media be used effectively on radio or television?
7. How can copy be made more believable?

SUGGESTED READINGS

Barban, Arnold and C. H. Sandage, eds., *Readings in Advertising and Promotion Strategy*. Homewood, Ill.: Richard D. Irwin, Inc., 1968. Part III.

Burton, Philip Ward, and Bowman Kreer, *Advertising Copywriting*, 2d ed. Englewood Cliffs, N.J.: Prentice-Hall, Inc., 1962.

Caples, John, *Tested Advertising Methods*, rev. ed. New York: Harper & Row, Publishers, 1963.

Dunn, S. Watson, *Advertising Copy and Communication*. New York: McGraw-Hill, Inc., 1956. Chapters 9–10.

Editors of *Advertising Age*, *The Art of Writing Advertising*. Chicago: Advertising Publications, Inc., 1965.

Kleppner, Otto, *Advertising Procedure*, 5th ed. Englewood Cliffs, N.J.: Prentice-Hall, Inc., 1966.

Matthews, John E., *The Copywriter*. Glen Ellyn, Ill.: John E. Matthews, Ltd., 1964.

Schwab, Victor O., *How to Write a Good Advertisement*. New York: Harper & Row, Publishers, 1962.

Weir, Walter, *Truth in Advertising and Other Heresies*. New York: McGraw-Hill, Inc., 1963.

19

Slogans
and
Other Identifying
Symbols

Because the average marketer frequently depends on slogans or trademarks to identify his products, their importance in advertising is frequently overestimated. Slogans such as "The Pause that Refreshes" or trademarks like the bearded Smith Brothers are obvious and frequently repeated creations of advertising men, especially in television. Although identifying marks often are important in the success of a campaign, their creation occupies a relatively minor portion of the average advertising man's time.

In this chapter we will examine the communication function of slogans and other identification marks and summarize some of the principles involved in creating them.

SLOGANS

Purpose of a Slogan. On the basis of structure, slogans are similar to headlines. Many slogans have, in fact, evolved from headlines that proved unusually successful. However, the slogan's purposes are generally different from those of the headline. The following are the two most frequently occurring purposes:

1. To provide continuity for a campaign, perhaps for a year, perhaps for many years.

✳   2. To crystallize in a few memorable words the key idea or theme
one wants to associate with a product. Frequently, this is some
product reward.

Consider, for example, a slogan such as "Covers the Earth" (Sherwin-
Williams Paint). Everytime you see this slogan in an advertisement,
you feel somewhat as if you are seeing an old friend who stays the
same year after year. At the same time, it states concisely that this
paint is widely used and implies that it must be good (because so many
people use it).

An advertiser is most likely to use a slogan when he has some basic
idea or theme he wants to establish and continue for a long time. The
words in the slogan thus become signs, striking in the reader (or listener or viewer) an immediate spark of recognition. It thus predisposes
the reader to view favorably what is said about the product or the store.
"Here," he thinks, "is my old friend talking."

Types of Slogans. To be effective a slogan should be consistent with
the purpose of the advertisement. Therefore, if there is a drastic change
in the campaign's purpose or general advertising approach, it is usually
wise to change the slogan also. It will be useful if we classify slogans on
the basis of their specific purposes. Using this as our basis, we arrive at
two main types of slogans—those that emphasize a product (or institutional) reward and those that emphasize action to be taken.

Slogans That Emphasize Reward. Every product has some reward
to offer consumers, or it would not be on the market. This may well be
some hidden quality that differentiates a product from the competition's. The trick, then, is to find some way of dramatizing in memorable
words a particular product's advantage. Here are some slogans which
have succeeded admirably in dramatizing product reward.

Sometimes the reward is stated directly:

We try harder	Avis
A thinking man's filter, a smoking man's taste	Viceroy
Cleans your breath while it cleans your teeth	Colgate
Things go better with Coca Cola	Coca Cola

Sometimes the reward is stated more subtly:

Wonder where the yellow went	Pepsodent
When it rains, it pours	Morton Salt

Sometimes the institution (or store) is emphasized rather than the
product:

A business in millions, a profit in pennies	Ohrbach's
The instrument of the immortals	Steinway
You can be sure . . . if it's Westinghouse	Westinghouse
Progress is our most important product	General Electric
Has the strength of Gibraltar	Prudential

Slogans That Emphasize Action to Be Taken. The slogan might
urge very directly that you use the product. For example:

Be Specific—Go Union Pacific	Union Pacific
Always Buy Chesterfield	Chesterfield
✳ Come to where the flavor is	Marlboro

Some, however, urge you in a more subtle manner:

Give the Lady What She Wants	Marshall Field's
Don't be a Bulbsnatcher	General Electric
You're ahead in a Ford	Ford

It goes without saying than an individual slogan may be a combination of *both* reward and action ("Fresh Up with Seven-Up").

When to Use Slogans. Like any type of writing, sloganeering should be based on careful investigation. Aesop Glim says:

> Cues for copywriters . . . When you are bidden to create a slogan resist as hard as you dare. But if it's inevitable, don't try to create out of thin air. Go back over the old advertisements, ask the sales manager or the star salesman for copies of his most successful sales letters; study them all and see if the true slogan hasn't already written itself.[1]

Much of what we know about slogans comes from a field related to advertising in many ways—propaganda. Schramm has summarized the evidence on the slogan's place in propaganda: "Both research and practice present evidence of the importance of simplifying and using slogans and labels, but it should be remembered that more intelligent audiences may be repelled by slogan repetition and similar devices.[2] This confirms the findings of advertising researchers, that slogans are more effective with the poorly educated.

There is evidence, also, that slogans work best with products of the impulse type (soap, cigarettes), that are low in price and are bought without much thoughtful deliberation. Slogans are also used when advertisers believe that an idea should be strongly dramatized and used for a considerable length of time. Items of momentary or fleeting interest make poor material for slogans.

How to Write Effective Slogans. From the various studies of slogans, certain general rules for slogan writing seem to emerge:

1. Make the slogan easy to remember. "Does she or doesn't she?" is easier to remember than "You can't really tell whether she colors her hair."

2. Make it help differentiate the product. "The candy mint with the hole" (Life Savers) and "When it rains, it pours" (Morton's) help to emphasize qualities that differentiate these products from the competition.

3. Make it provoke curiosity, if possible. Respondents interviewed in a study of Pepsodent advertising had an unconscious compulsion to finish the sentence when they heard "You'll wonder where the yellow went." They wanted to add "when you brush your teeth with Pepsodent."

4. Make sure it highlights either a product reward or some action. In general, reward slogans are preferable.

5. Use rhythm, rhyme, and alliteration. Well used, any of these help consumers remember a slogan. "So round, so firm, so fully packed"

[1] Aesop Glim, *Copy, The Core of Advertising* (New York: McGraw-Hill, Inc., 1949), p. 209.
[2] Wilbur Schramm, *The Process and Effects of Mass Communication* (Urbana: University of Illinois Press, 1954), p. 213.

has a rhythmic sound to it. One of the most famous slogans of all time used rhyme to good effect—"Motorists wise, Simoniz." "Not a cough in a carload" used alliteration.

6. Make sure the slogan is not likely to confuse the consumer. If it is misleading, it is probably illegal as well as a poor slogan. Because the legal test of a slogan is the same as that for other identification marks, it is covered later in the chapter.

TRADEMARKS

What Is a Trademark? The Lanham Trade-Mark Act (1947), which regulates registration of identifying marks, states that "the term 'trade-mark' includes any word, name, symbol, or device or any combination thereof adopted and used by a manufacturer or merchant to identify his goods and distinguish them from those manufactured or sold by others." Under this concept (which is somewhat broader than common usage), we have (in addition to slogans) three main types of identification marks: (1) brand names, (2) corporate or store names, and (3) identifying symbols for brands or companies. Under the Lanham Act the mark need not be physically affixed to the product. It covers service marks (used to distinguish services rather than products), certification marks (used by persons other than the owner to certify geographical origin, grade, or quality), and collective marks (used to indicate membership in some organization).[3] In 1967 the total applications for trademark registration at the U.S. Patent Office totaled 27,982. Registrations were issued to 21,246 marks.

Growth in Importance. In the Middle Ages craftsmen were required to place a mark on the goods they made so that poor workmanship could be traced to the maker. The trademark thus started out as a method of policing. Gradually, however, sellers realized that certain trademarks enhanced the market value of the goods.[4] Certain producers and localities became famous for the high quality of their merchandise, and consumers came to prefer products of these areas over the competition. Because the literacy rate was low in the early days of trademarks, the earliest ones were frequently symbols rather than names or slogans.

In today's market, identifying marks are probably more important than ever. First of all, the buyer of most merchandise has no direct contact with today's typical mass producer and looks for some sign that indicates that a reliable firm made (or sold) the merchandise. Second, many products today have qualities that are so hidden by packaging or by the complexity of their structure that the purchaser cannot determine by its appearance whether the merchandise is of a high quality. He must therefore rely on the identifying mark of a firm he trusts. Third, the increase of self-service necessitates selling to the consumer *before* he goes into the market, especially with respect to packaged goods. Finally, mass communication makes it possible to capitalize on identifying

[3]See *Trademarks* (New York: American Association of Advertising Agencies, 1964), pp. 3–4.
[4]See Neil H. Borden, *Economic Effects of Advertising* (Homewood, Ill.: Richard D. Irwin, Inc., 1942), for a discussion of the growth and importance of trademarks.

FIG. 19.1 *In keeping with the internationalizing of this company the trademark is being changed gradually from U.S. Royal to UniRoyal.* CLIENT: UNIROYAL; ADVERTISEMENT PREPARED BY DOYLE DANE BERNBACH INC.

marks. These symbols can be communicated inexpensively to thousands, even millions, of people.

BRAND NAME

A brand name may come from almost any source. Sometimes, as in the much-publicized search for a name for Ajax's White Knight (Sir Galahad), thousands of names may be considered and rejected. In general, brand names are likely to come from one of the following—or a combination of these:

Company Name. In the gasoline field we find Gulf using the company name as a brand name, but Texas Company using the abbreviated form, "Texaco," and Standard Oil of California using "Calso."

Personal Name. In automobiles we have both "Ford and "Chrysler" named for individuals active in the industry. On the other hand,

"Lincoln" and "Pontiac" were named for people who lived long before automobiles were invented.

Coined Word. In 1899 N. W. Ayer coined "Uneeda Biscuit" for the products of the National Biscuit Company. We find "Vel" detergents in both powder and liquid form, and "Viv" in lipstick, and "Gleem" and "Ipana" in the dentifrice field. "Kodak" was created by George Eastman on the basis that, though meaningless, it is easy to pronounce.

Foreign Word. French words (*"vol de nuit"* and *"Bon Voyage"*) are common in the perfume field. "Tovarisch" is used for vodka, "Camaro" for automobiles.

Licensed Name. There has been some increase in recent years in the use of licensed names such as "Mickey Mouse," "Wyatt Earp," and "Duncan Hines." An advertiser who uses a licensed name capitalizes, of course, on the acceptance of that name, but he must pay a fee for using the name and must conform to certain licensing standards.

Commonly Used Word. Frequently, a good English word that has no relevance to the product advertised will be used. "Arrow" for shirts is a well-known example. It is completely meaningless when applied to wearing apparel, but it is easy to remember.

A desirable variation is the word that does not describe the product but suggests some desirable quality associated with it. Many successful brand names fall in this category. Consider for example, "Tide," "Whirlpool," and "Mum" all of which are suggestive rather than descriptive, or names of animals such as "Tiger" and "Mustang."

FIG. 19.2 *Retail store display which makes effective use of the advertising theme of the general advertiser.* COURTESY KRAFT FOODS, CHICAGO, ILLINOIS; AGENCY: J. WALTER THOMPSON COMPANY.

CORPORATE OR STORE NAME

The firm name is usually less important than the brand name. Certainly, more people know "Anacin" than "American Home Products" and "Camel" than "R.J. Reynolds." Yet the firm's name may have a definite plus value. "Made by General Motors" adds prestige to an otherwise new and unknown product. Some companies (such as H.J. Heinz) use the firm name throughout the entire product line, although the trend is against this practice. Ford Motor Company, for example, used to get along nicely with a Model T and then a Model A, but now it has added Custom, Fairlane, Ranch Wagon, and Country Sedan to its line, not to mention such separate brands as Thunderbird and Torino.

Retailers are equally anxious to protect their firm names. Kroger's uses its name on many products it sells. Mainly, however, retailers are anxious to build and protect patronage for their stores. Suppose, for example, your name was Macy and you wanted to start a department store in New York. Naturally, the management of the famous store at Herald Square would be disturbed unless you devised some way of making it quite clear to consumers that yours was not the well-known store of the same name.

IDENTIFYING SYMBOLS

Visual symbols have long been used to identify goods and services. According to Wood, the first trademark registration by the U.S. Patent Office was granted in 1870 to the Averill Chemical Paint Company.[5] The trademark was described thus in the application:

> In the foreground, on a rock, with the word chemistry upon it is an eagle holding in his mouth a paintpot or canister, with a brush and a ribbon or streamer, on which are the words, Economical, Durable, Beautiful. Below the feet of the bird is represented water upon which is a steamer and other vessels. In the background is a bridge or viaduct, with a train of railroad cars upon it. Further in the background are seen buildings and manufactories.

Since then, we have seen many variations of the patriotic motif, plus Indian heads, diamonds, squares, circles, ovals, and innumerable variations of both animals and people.

A few trade characters used today are more than a century old, having been nurtured by careful advertising treatment. The German maid bearing a glass of water and a cup of chocolate has been used by Walter Baker & Company in advertising since 1825. The Victor dog, used first by the Gramophone Co., Ltd., in London, has appeared in United States advertising since 1901. The Dutch Boy (who was really an Irish boy, Michael Brady) has been used in conjunction with National Lead Company's paint for many years.

Other designs and trade characters that have remained unchanged from one generation to the next are The Prudential rock and Kleenex's Little Lulu. Some companies such as soap manufacturers occasionally redesign their packages, to suggest that theirs is a very modern product, embodying up-to-date discoveries but retain their trademark symbols.

[5]James Playsted Wood, *The Story of Advertising* (New York: The Ronald Press Co., 1958), pp. 260–261.

FIG. 19.3 *Large sign used at service stations to dramatize the change of the company's name from Cities Service to Citgo.* COURTESY CITIES SERVICE OIL COMPANY.

The Campbell Soup Kids were first used in the early part of this century (see Figure 12.3). They were dropped, during the 1940s and revived in the 1950s in magazines and on television.

Executives of the Cities Service Company (diversified oil firm) decided to change the company's name and signature in the middle 1960s. Research had indicated that consumers thought the name "Cities Service" too much like that of a public utility and that although the old green signature was pleasant, it was not sharp and dominant enough to compete effectively. The new name "Citgo" was suggested by the company's research firm after it "had screened 80,600 variations." The first syllable comes from the parent company, and the "GO" is to suggest strength and the power of a company in motion. The name plus the new bold red instead of the old green was, according to the company, "geared to a modern America—one with high-speed toll roads and freeways and consequently a need for clarity and sharp visibility—an aggresive name instead of a long, drawn-out restive one."[6]

[6]Wally Perry, "CITGO Zooms . . . with Name Change," *Torch*, January 1966, pp. 40–41.

USE OF IDENTIFICATION MARKS ON TELEVISION

Television has made it possible to capitalize on identifying symbols and trade characters as never before. For example, it is possible to have a variety of animated trade characters—bears, birds, dogs, and caricatures—to demonstrate products. Newport cigarettes have spent much time and money building consumer identification of the trade symbol—a formalized version of a sailing vessel's spinnaker. It appears on the package and is on each cigarette. In one series of commercials a variety of dance routines were built around the symbol.

HOW TO DEVISE EFFECTIVE IDENTIFICATION MARKS

Although brand names, firm names, and symbols differ in format, their purpose is similar enough to make certain generalizations. First, we shall consider these from the legal standpoint.

Avoid Any Identification Mark or Slogan That will Confuse the Consumer. The legal test of identification marks is simple and intensely practical. The mark should not confuse or deceive the normal purchaser. Legal rights are measured by the possibility of confusion in the consumer's mind. It is therefore necessary to consider the methods by which the products are marketed or distributed, the care with which they are selected, and the type of individual who is likely to purchase the article.

Courts generally use the common-sense principle that consumers do not usually have an opportunity to make side-by-side comparisons between products bearing similar marks or names; so the fallibility of the human memory is a consideration. If there is uncertainty, the law is likely to give benefit of doubt to the first user. It is therefore important that you search carefully to check whether any identifying marks already used are similar to one you anticipate using. A mark should not be confusingly similar to an existing one in sound, appearance, or generally accepted meaning. It will not do simply to alter the spelling; obviously some people may only hear the name and never see it at all. You may think the name should be pronounced quite differently from an existing one, but the consumer may pronounce it the way it looks, not necessarily the way you propose.

Foreign languages are no refuge. If there is a "Black Cat" perfume, you had better not expect to market one called "Chat Noir."

If a brand name or symbol is known in only one field, you may be able to use it in a different one. On the other hand, if it is very widely known, it may be barred from use in a great many fields. For example, the maker of Rolls-Royce automobiles was able to get a court order prohibiting the use of Rolls-Royce as a brand name for radio tubes. The Patent Office turned down Kodak as a trade-name for cigarette lighters. A somewhat less distinctive name, however, such as Blue Ribbon, might be used for various brands.

The United States Shoe Company made and sold Red Cross shoes for many years before it was stopped on the basis that this name might imply sponsorship by the American National Red Cross. The name was changed to Gold Cross with this accompanying statement. "The same fine footwear known as *Red Cross* shoes for over 50 years." The company continued its fight and finally won the right to use *Red Cross*, provided it used the disclaimer, "This product has no connection whatever with the American National Red Cross."

Avoid Names That Describe the Product or One of Its Characteristics. Suppose you were marketing a toothpaste whose chemical composition gave it a green color. The word "green" would not then be a proper choice for a part of its brand name, because anyone who makes a similar product has the right to use the word. As the AAAA points out:

> Do not be too concerned about relevance. A trademark becomes accepted as a symbol and eventually the public reads no meaning into it except that of brand identification. What, for instance, could be less pertinent than FRIGIDAIRE kitchen range, HOTPOINT refrigerator, CHOCK FULL O'NUTS coffee? Actually the more apt a trademark is, the harder it may be to protect it.[7]

The Name Should Not Be a Family One. A name like Jones, for example, makes a poor brand name for a product. Another Jones might want to use his name in the same business and might even have a prior claim. The name "Amilar" seems safe enough, but Du Pont ran into trouble when it filed this name with the patent office for a new product it had developed. A Mr. Amilar who sold fish nets under his surname objected to Du Pont's use of his name. Du Pont conducted another search and came up with the name "Dacron" polyester fiber for this product.

The Trademark Should Not Name or Symbolize a Geographical Spot. Either the name "New York" or a pictorial version of the Manhattan skyline would be a poor choice for trademarks. "Newcastle" would be a poor choice as a name for a new brand of coal.

So far, we have been examining trademarks principally from the legal standpoint. Now let us consider certain other suggestions.

Any Trademark Shoud be Easy to Pronounce or Identify. This helps to make it truly a symbol of the product the consumer is looking for. With the increased importance of the broadcast media, it is especially important that the name be easy for the announcer to pronounce and for the listener to catch.

The Name Should Be Free of Unpleasant Connotations. Questionable connotations are worth checking thoroughly, because what is acceptable in one part of the country may be questionable in another. Certain expressions that can be used in polite company in the United States are considered in bad taste in Great Britain.

The Mark or Name Should Be Adaptable to All Media. Even though it is used first in only one medium (magazines, for example), the possibilities of dramatizing the name on television, pronouncing it on the radio or showing it in big colorful display on outdoor media should be kept in mind. If the brand name is really successful, the chances are that many media will be used.

The Mark Should Be International. As companies expand into the rapidly growing international market, they often wish that their

[7]*Trademarks*, p. 11.

identification mark were not so closely identified with the United States. For example, the U. S. Rubber Company decided in the middle 1960s to adapt its name to the company's diverse businesses around the world. The name chosen was Uniroyal. During phase one of the introductory campaign a cartoon series featured the question "What is a Uniroyal?" The second series of advertisements showed the company's product diversification. Each ad included a number of U. S. Rubber products with copy pointing out that "these are all products of Uniroyal." The company makes 33,000 products in 1,200 categories.

OBTAINING AND RETAINING PROTECTION

The big problem in using any identifying mark is how to avoid conflict with earlier users. Although there is no complete directory of all the brand names, slogans, symbols, and other identifying marks, trademark lawyers have access to various sources of information, including Patent Office records and trade directory listings. Reports and opinions can be obtained indicating whether a proposed trademark will be considered confusingly similar to one already in use.

It is highly advisable that an identification symbol of any kind be registered. If the mark meets the legal requirements for registration, you can be reasonably sure that you have succeeded in creating a distinctive one that will stand up in court if necessary. In other words, if a trademark is registered, it is considered that everyone has legal knowledge of the trademark, whether or not he has bothered to check. There can be no innocent infringement if the trademark is registered.

An ever-present danger is that the marketer may find that his brand name has become so successful that it has come to represent a whole class of products and appears in the dictionary as a generic name. Aspirin, zipper, linoleum, and escalator are examples of names that became generic. The American Thermos Company said in its catalog in 1910 that "Thermos is a household word." More than fifty years later it found it had indeed made the name a household word and that the courts would consequently offer it no protection from competitors. On the other hand, General Motors successfully defended its right to exclusive use of Frigidaire, and Minnesota Mining and Manufacturing held on to Scotch Tape.

SUMMARY

The many types of identification marks discussed in this chapter consume a relatively small part of the advertising practitioner's total creative effort but are important symbols of the product in the mind of the average consumer. We should not expect too much of them, but we should put them together with care so that they will work effectively and not involve lengthy litigation.

Most slogans emphasize some product reward, some action to be taken, or a combination of the two. They should be easy to remember, distinctive, dramatic, and, if possible, rhythmic or alliterative.

Other important forms of identification marks are brand names, firm names, and identifying symbols or characters usually called collectively "trademarks." The most important of these for most advertisers is the brand name.

There are various tests for trademarks of all sorts—both commonsense and legal. Legally, it is important that your mark not be confusing, descriptive, or a family or geographical name. It should also be easy to pronounce, free of unpleasant connotations, and adaptable to all media (particularly to television, if it is a product for mass consumption).

QUESTIONS FOR DISCUSSION

1. How would you define a trademark? a brand name? a trade name? Give an example of each.
2. How can a slogan be considered an identification mark?
3. What are the main characteristics of an effective slogan? On the basis of these characteristics, evaluate three slogans currently used in advertising.
4. What is meant by federal registration of a trademark? What are the principal legal pitfalls in determining the proper trademark or trade name for a new product?
5. How does a trademark differ from a copyright? Why do you suppose the two are handled by different agencies of the United States government?
6. To what extent is it possible to protect a trademark internationally?

SUGGESTED READINGS

American Association of Advertising Agencies, *Trademarks*. New York: The American Association of Advertising Agencies, 1964.

Barksdale, Hiram C., *The Use of Survey Research Findings as Legal Evidence*. New London, Conn.: Printers' Ink Books, 1957.

Digges, I. W., *The Modern Law of Advertising and Marketing*. New York: Funk & Wagnalls Company, 1948.

Frey, A. W., *Advertising*. New York: The Ronald Press Company, 1953. Chapter 4.

Howard, Marshall C., *Legal Aspects of Marketing*. New York: McGraw-Hill, Inc., 1964.

Simon, Morton J., *The Law of Advertising*. New York: W. W. Norton & Company, Inc., 1956.

United States Trademark Association, *Trademarks in Advertising and Selling*. New York: United States Trademark Association, 1968.

Wood, James Playsted, *The Story of Advertising*. New York: The Ronald Press Company, 1958. Chapter 17.

20 | Visual Communications: Illustrations and Color

In the last two chapters we have been investigating the problem of verbal communication and exploring some of the ways to use words effectively. In this and the next two chapters we shall examine methods of communicating without words.

Traveling in Europe, a person discovers how well he can communicate without words if necessary. Instead of a road sign that says "No Passing Zone," European countries use a picture showing the silhouette of a car in black. Trying to pass it is another car in red with an X drawn through it. Instead of the words "Men at Work," the sign pictures a man with a shovel.

Martineau points out that "visual symbols are highly significant carriers of meaning in any advertisement. But in the enormous increase of advertising exposure that the consumer is being confronted with, the visual symbols are increasingly important in their own right. The visual symbols communicate much faster, much more directly than any long involved argument in words. There is no work called for, no mental effort."[1]

[1]Pierre Martineau, "The Illusion of Communcation," in Harper W. Boyd, Jr., and Joseph W. Newman, eds., *Advertising Management: Selected Readings* (Homewood, Ill.: Richard D. Irwin, Inc., 1965).

WHAT IS VISUALIZATION?

Visualization is used in two different senses, both of which are important in the creation of effective advertisements. We talk of "visualizing" an idea, in considering the complete advertisement (the headline, the illustration, the body text, and the like). We also put an idea into visual form by using illustrations, layouts, signatures, and other nonverbal elements. The first concept has been considered at some length in Chapter 16; we shall therefore concentrate here and in the following chapter on the second concept.

Man put ideas in visual form long before he invented words. Many great artists were relatively illiterate men. They invented shapes, colors, and textures that somehow, they felt, symbolized what they wanted to communicate. Few of them were able to intellectualize or verbalize their artistic creations.

Visualization deals with the language of vision, which is only one step removed from fact, and therefore closer to reality than written language is. However, as agency creative director Fred Ludekens points out, "Good pictures must be good copy." He recommends that "a competent visualizer, as well as a writer . . . has a knowledge of marketing, merchandising, research, media and, of course, printing, engraving, typography, color, drawing, painting, and photography."[2]

In this chapter we discuss two of the main tools of the visualizer: illustrations and color. In the next two chapters we shall continue our examination of advertising's visual elements: layout, printing, engraving, and typography. We have already dealt with one of the visual elements, trademarks and trade characters, in our analysis of identification marks.

Visualization is sometimes confused with layout. The layout of an advertisement is the arrangement of the various elements in a given space; visualization is the broad conception of the elements with which the layout artist works. The visualizer considers alternative means of expressing an idea visually; the layout artist considers alternative ways of arranging the visual and verbal elements in a given space. Visualization, therefore, precedes layout.

The basic purpose of visualization is to communicate. Only elements that carry forward the advertising message should be included — all others should be discarded. The more clearly defined the communication objective, the easier it is to decide which elements should be included.

FUNCTIONS OF ADVERTISING ILLUSTRATIONS

We expect the illustrations in an advertisement to contribute to its effectiveness in one or more of the following ways: (1) communicate a relevant idea quickly and effectively; (2) attract the attention of the desired audience; (3) interest the audience in the headlines and copy; (4) to communicate an idea that might be impossible or even offensive

[2]Fred Ludekens, "Good Advertising Picture Must Be Good Copy," *Advertising Age,* November 11, 1957, p. 110.

to say in words; and (5) help make the advertisement more believable. Let us see how each of these works in the case of illustrations—usually the most important visual element in the advertisement.

Communicating an Advertising Idea. A roll or a large square of linoleum that clearly showed the pattern would not make a very interesting picture. But when an advertisement for Armstrong Cork Company shows one of its patterns laid in an attractive kitchen, the illustration communicates something to the reader or viewer. It tells how the linoleum might look in the viewer's kitchen. It may help her to realize the variety of patterns available. It may help her to build a specific image of the product: "What types of people have this kind of linoleum in their kitchens? What would my friends think of this?"

A Ray-O-Vac flashlight battery advertisement told the warm, human story of a puppy lost at night in a rainstorm. The illustration showed the finding of the puppy with the aid of a flashlight. It illustrated the advisability of having a flashlight and batteries ready for all emergencies.

The best illustrations usually have a simplicity that makes it easy for the reader to get the point. In a simple picture, chosen with singleness of purpose, the reader can get the point almost as soon as his eye falls on the page. Some advertising professionals use a "hide-the-copy" test to check the illustration's power of communication (that is, does the illustration tell the story with the copy blocked out?).

Attracting Attention. Some pictures attract attention because they seem to say to the reader, "Here's a reward you'll be interested in." A woman sees an advertisement and says to herself, "That beautiful girl in the illustration—that could be me." The ad may promise a way to save a few minutes each day, or a way to become more popular, or a method of satisfying some of many other drives. There is a suggestion, overt or implied, that here is a solution to one of your problems.

Some illustrations attract attention because of the "least-effort principle" (it is less effort to look at them than to ignore them). Art consultant Andy Armstrong calls this principle "surprise" and describes it thus:

> Imagine your reader, his guard up, sliding along through the magazine. He is braced psychologically against all advertising. Suddenly, you confront him in his reluctant progress with a break in the terrain—a cliff he didn't know was there. He stops short on the edge; he loses his balance; he topples forward. Meeting nothing to push against, he falls into your ad like Alice down the rabbit hole. He has come upon something real and possible, something simple, grasped at once—*but he has never seen it before.* That's what throws him, and he lands with *you.*[3]

Selecting the Desired Audience. An unusual picture of an orangutan would attract high readership. People would be curious, but it might be difficult to make the ape relevant to the product advertised—unless you're selling trips to Borneo.

[3]Andrew F. H. Armstrong, "Graphic Impact in Advertising," in Elbrun Rochford French, ed., *The Copywriter's Guide* (New York: Harper & Row, Publishers, 1959).

If you are selling baby foods, it is generally a good idea to have an illustration of a baby somewhere in the advertisement. But if you are selling machine tools, what is the use of having an illustration of a baby that attracts young mothers to your advertisement? Bathing beauties and cocker spaniels are fine for attracting general readership, but they do not select prospects.

To make a picture selective you must make sure it has a relation either to the product or to the copy. This relation should be immediately clear to the reader or at some time soon during his reading of the copy.

Interesting Readers in the Headline and Text. The most interesting picture is the one the reader can identify with himself or his own problems. In this sense, interest, selection, and attention getting go hand in hand. But the picture must intrigue, as well as interest, the reader. It must tell just enough to whet the reader's desire to find out the details of the product, the situation, or the image you are trying to communicate. If the illustration tells too much, the reader can say, "Why wade through that copy?" On the other hand, if it is irrelevant or tells too little, the reader will be derailed before he gets to the copy.

Making the Message Believable. An illustration that is out of key with reality starts any message off on the wrong foot. Women do not ordinarily clean house in high heels or smile happily as they do the dishes; yet some advertising illustrations show them doing these things. If the picture is consistent with a woman's experience, she will believe it and will tend to accept the verbal part of the advertisement.

KINDS OF ILLUSTRATIONS

Illustrations might be classified as realistic or symbolic. If we want to tell people how attractive Paris is in the springtime, we might use a realistic illustration of flowers in bloom along the Champs Élysées, or we might use abstract art to symbolize the same idea. Sometimes we have to resort to symbolism. How, for example, would you represent a concept such as "truth" except by visual symbols?

The manager of the Gourmet Foods Division of General Foods tells of his troubles in visualizing the abstract concept "out of this world" when this new food line was introduced:

We tried many approaches [to the problem of illustration]. I remember some experiments I had seen in the studio of Larry Beall Smith, well-known American illustrator. These experiments were with a reverse technique on glass developed by Degas, called monoprint because only one print can be made. The medium is oil, and the result light and airy.

The floating ingredients and utensils over floating shadows say exactly what we meant to say: This is food so good, it is out of this world.

Illustrations are commonly classified on the basis of the subject matter. Because this is an extremely useful classification, it will be covered in some detail in this chapter. Some of the common alternatives are

1. The product itself
2. Part of the product (to illustrate some feature)
3. Product ready for use

4. Product in use
5. Product being tested
6. Differentiating features of the product
7. Consumer reward as a result of using the product
8. Effect of *not* using the product
9. Testimonial for the product

Which is best? Like many other solutions to problems in advertising, it all depends on what you are trying to do. Some interesting evidence on six of these types comes from an extensive study made by H. J. Rudolph. Table 20.1 summarizes his findings. Note, however, that this study considers only attention and readership of the copy.[4]

Type of Picture	Index of Attention*	Percentage of Observers Who Read Some of Copy
Result of use	96.9	80.0
Product	101.7	77.7
Irrelevant	102.8	88.9
Product in use	106.4	78.7
Testimonial	110.5	88.1
Result of nonuse	122.7	88.6

RELATION OF TYPE OF ILLUSTRATION TO ATTENTION AND READERSHIP   **TABLE 20.1**

*Based on an average of 100 for all illustrations, adjusted for size and color of advertisement.

The Product Itself. Some advertising people underestimate the public's interest in products. "Pictures of products," they say, "are among the poorest read of all advertising illustrations." They are right to the extent that, of a given 1,000 or so advertisements, those that have illustrations of products alone will have a lower percentage of people *noting* the advertisement than those that have other types of illustrations.

There is more, however, to communicating than attracting attention, important as that is. Consider the advertisement in Figure 20.1. It would be difficult to find an illustration with more genuine appeal to the television fan than this one. Nevertheless, the illustration is selective in that it is directed at people who want a portable that will give them excellent performance under any circumstances. This enthusiastic group will give the ad high reading traffic.

It is especially important to show the product if it is to be ordered by mail. It is also helpful where a basic part of the product's appeal is appearance or style, such as clothing or automobiles. For packaged goods, a picture of the product makes it easier to identify in the super-

[4]H. J. Rudolph, *Attention and Interest Factors in Advertising* (New York: Funk & Wagnalls Company, 1947), pp. 66–89.

PLATE 1   *Effective use of color in a business magazine*
advertisement. COURTESY OF TIME, INCORPORATED.

PLATE 2

Color photography highlights the freshness of Coca-Cola and aids product identification.
AGENCY: MCCANN-ERICKSON, INC. THIS ADVERTISEMENT IS REPRODUCED THROUGH THE
COURTESY OF THE COCA-COLA COMPANY, OWNER OF THE REGISTERED TRADE-MARKS
"COCA-COLA" AND "COKE."

PLATE 3

The Hunt's Catsup Story:

Striking use of color to emphasize freshness and to heighten appetite appeal. AGENCY: YOUNG & RUBICAM, INC.; CLIENT: HUNT-WESSON FOODS, FULLERTON, CALIFORNIA.

The end of the plain plane.

PLATE 4

ROP newspaper color is used effectively to glamorize a service to the public.
AGENCY: WELLS, RICH, GREENE, INC.; CLIENT: BRANIFF INTERNATIONAL.

1. (MUSIC UNDER) ANNCR:
The first time you use . . .

2. new Simoniz Non-Scuff
Floor Wax . . .

5. (MUSIC)

6. (TELEPHONE RINGS)

9. fast as ordinary floor wax.
It just doesn't look that way.

10. (MUSIC) Because new
Simoniz Non-Scuff is made . . .

13. so bright . . .

14. it still looks wet.

3. it may fool you.

4. (MUSIC)

7. (TELEPHONE RINGS)
Dry? Sure it's dry.

8. New Simoniz
Non-Scuff dries just as . . .

11. with tough, crystal-clear
acrylics . . .

12. it dries . . .

15. (MUSIC OUT)

Color storyboard for Simoniz Non-Scuff Floor Wax. Note how color is used effectively to emphasize the brightness of the floor after waxing and to heighten viewer involvement.
AGENCY: J. WALTER THOMPSON COMPANY;
CLIENT: SIMONIZ COMPANY

PLATE 5

PLATE 6

Eight packages which make effective use of color to attract attention and to suggest product qualities.

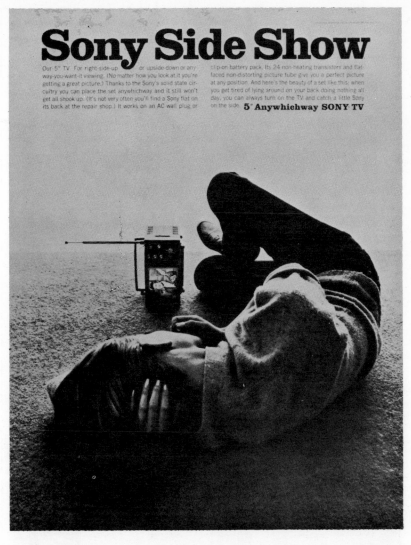

Sony Side Show

Our 5" TV. For right-side-up or upside-down or any way-you-want-it viewing. (No matter how you look at it you're getting a great picture.) Thanks to the Sony's solid state circuitry you can place the set anywhichway and it still won't get all shook up. (It's not very often you'll find a Sony flat on its back at the repair shop.) It works on an AC wall plug or clip-on battery pack. Its 24 non-heating transistors and flat-faced non-distorting picture tube give you a perfect picture at any position. And here's the beauty of a set like this: when you get tired of lying around on your back doing nothing all day, you can always turn on the TV and catch a little Sony on the side. **5" Anywhichway SONY TV**

FIG. 20.1 *Effective visualization of the versatility of this portable television set.* CLIENT: © SONY CORP. OF AMERICA; ADVERTISEMENT PREPARED BY DOYLE DANE BERNBACH INC.

market or drugstore. The illustration of the product may be combined with the signature to achieve maximum impact of the brand name.

Part of the Product. Sometimes it is advisable to emphasize a part of the product rather than the whole. Through close-up photography, for example, you can emphasize some outstanding product feature. A full-color, half-page advertisement for Saran seat covers used the front seat of an automobile as its main illustration. The picture showed the complete product, how attractive it was, and how well it fitted the seat. But across the top and down one side of the advertisement were ten smaller illustrations. They were pictures in full color, showing swatches of ten different designs in which seat covers were made. Here, part of the product was illustrated to convey additional information, to show readers different patterns and color combinations.

In many products the real selling point lies in some feature that becomes lost in a total picture. How much more effective the illustration is, therefore, if it focuses attention without distraction on just that one feature.

When the zipper on his trousers breaks, he doesn't look to see who made the zipper. He wants to know who made the pants. That's you, Charlie. And everytime he thinks of you from now on he'll get fire in his eyes and frost on his heart.

Therefore it may interest you to know that Talon makes the least-breakable zipper in the world. The Talon Zephyr.* A beautifully engineered little thing made with flexible nylon coils instead of breakable metal teeth. The Talon Zephyr lasts through more than 10,000

zips up and down. Or about 9 years when worn every day by our merciless testing machine. Get some Talon Zephyrs, Charlie. They can't hurt your reputation. They can only help.

FIG. 20.2 *The picture in this trade advertisement (directed at garment makers) tells most of the story—that the pants manufacturer, not the zipper company, will be blamed if the zipper breaks.* CLIENT: TALON, INC.; AGENCY: DELEHANTY, KURNIT & GELLER, INC.

The Product Ready for Use. By itself, one piano may merely look like a piano. However, when we place a lamp and some beautiful furniture near the piano we know what kind of home it belongs in. If we place a sheet of Beethoven's "Moonlight Sonata" on the music rack, we help build one type of image, but if we put the latest rock and roll music there, we create a different image. Then, too, we can bring people into our scene. Their manner of dress, their age, and their general appearance all make some contribution to the product image.

Illustrations of products ready for use are often found in food advertisements. The point is to show, not what the product is, but what can be done with it. A picture of a bottle of Kraft Safflower Oil does not make a very intriguing illustration. However, a four-color photograph of a plate of butterfly shrimp, freshly fried in Kraft oil and ready to serve, makes a provocative and mouth-watering illustration. Note how appetizing the oranges appear in Figure 12.1 and how strong an appeal to the senses is made by the fine photography and the headline "Open up an orange and have some sunshine."

Product in Use. A product that is rather dull when shown alone may become quite interesting when it is shown in use. A good example is clothing, which is much more appealing to the reader when it is worn by models than when it is shown hanging on a rack. A picture of a person enjoying a cool bottle of soda pop communicates more quickly and dramatically than one in which the bottle alone is shown.

Showing the product in use brings a dull product to life and reminds readers of how they can benefit from it. It helps translate product purchase into consumer reward. At the same time, however, the product-in-use illustration has its drawbacks. Perhaps the main one is the competition it faces. The product-in-use illustration is used so often that visual

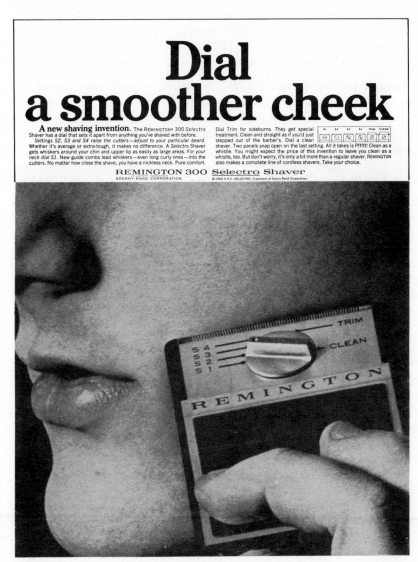

FIG. 20.3 *Good illustration of product in use.* CLIENT: SPERRY RAND CORPORATION; AGENCY: YOUNG & RUBICAM, INC.

clichés have been built up. There is little surprise in a picture that shows the smiling housewife opening the refrigerator door and pointing to the ample space inside, or in the illustration of the happy driver behind the wheel of his new V – 8.

On the other hand, the Remington illustration in Figure 20.3 is not hackneyed; it launches this new product in a striking setting.

Product Being Tested. An astute creative man often will think up tests to dramatize the consumer rewards of a product. Sometimes he merely capitalizes on tests that are a routine operation at a manufacturer's plant. In either case, tests often make interesting and impressive illustrative material.

Johnson's Wax wanted to show that a car polished with Car-Plate looked just as good as a car with a professional polishing with paste wax. To show this visually, first an automobile was cleaned, and then half was waxed with paste wax and the other half with Car-Plate. The car was photographed three months after the two sides had been waxed. The headline asked, "Even after 3 months – can you pick the Car-Plate wax side from the $20.00 professional job?" A caption assured the reader that the photo was unretouched.

Differentiating Features of a Product. Almost every brand has some characteristic that differentiates it from competitors. If this can be illustrated, it is easier to build brand preference. If the differentiating feature is outstanding, it will probably be the subject of the main illustration, and the whole advertisement will be built around it.

For example, when Singer invented its slant-needle sewing machine, it broke a tradition of one hundred years. Instead of being vertical, the needle now slanted toward the operator; it was easier to see and to feed. Good judgment dictated that this innovation should be the subject matter of the main illustration in each advertisement that introduced the new sewing machine. The obvious question in women's minds would be, "What does this new slant-needle look like?" An illustration could satisfy this curiosity fairly quickly.

Figure 4.2 was used to depict the advantages of Clairol Great Day, compared with other hair rinses. This is a truly dramatic way of showing Clairol's versatility in that it involves participation by the reader. The good visual is backed with excellent copy.

Consumer Reward from Using Product. All products offer the consumer some type of reward – otherwise, why should he bother to buy it? Sometimes the result is immediate and visually dramatic. A good example is shown in Figure 20.4. The humorous mood adds a new touch to this successful campaign.

The Stauffer Home Reducing Plan ran a double-page advertisement with twenty-one illustrations and the headline "America's 10 Happiest Women." This ad included ten case histories of overweight women – a "before" picture of each when she was overweight and an "after" picture after undergoing the Stauffer treatment. In addition to these twenty pictures, there was one small picture illustrating the plan and more than 1,000 *words* of text. In spite of all this, the advertisement was clear and the point was made quickly. The use of twenty pictures

FIG. 20.4 *Effective differentiation of the product.* CLIENT: POLK MILLER PRODUCTS CORPORATION, A SUBSIDIARY OF A. H. ROBINS, RICHMOND, VIRGINIA; AGENCY; N. W. AYER & SON.

strengthened the advertising impact immeasurably—one pair of "before and after" pictures might seem to represent a special situation but ten of them make the plan's merits seem universally applicable.

Effect of Not Using a Product. Advertisers of patent medicine and insurance often find such warning illustrations useful. The illustration of the man suffering a pounding headache, the homeless family after a fire, the man who has had an automobile wreck—these have become almost stereotyped. (It is not easy to find fresh, arresting ways of emphasizing the penalties of not using a product.)

Testimonials. The conventional way to illustrate a testimonial advertisement is with a photograph of the testifier. The headline will quote "the noted pitcher of the New York Yankees . . ." and the illustration will picture him (usually smiling).

As in all forms of advertising, one can usually gain by departing from the conventional. Freshness, originality, and ingenuity are as

FIG. 20.5 *An interesting variation of the conventional testimonial advertisement to make the point that the railroad's cars are washed twice a week.* CLIENT: BURLINGTON LINES; AGENCY: TATHAM-LAIRD & KUDNER, INC.

effective in the testimonial advertisement as in any other. A case in point is the illustration in Figure 20.5.

SOME ILLUSTRATIVE TECHNIQUES

We have been discussing the subject matter of the illustration. Let us now examine some of the techniques by which these various subjects may be illustrated. There are two basic illustrative techniques available to the advertiser—photographs and artwork.

Photographs. We are accustomed to seeing photographs of news events; so it is appropriate that the announcement of a new product or product improvement be accompanied by a photograph. We associate realism and authenticity with photographs. An actual photograph goes a long way toward adding the stamp of authenticity to a testimonial or a product test. The illustration in the Sony advertisement (Figure 20.1) would not be convincing in any technique other than a photograph. Naturally, Polaroid and Eastman use photographs to demonstrate their wares.

Photographs are used extensively in industrial and trade publications, so that the technicians who read them will learn what the products look like and how they will perform.

Ogilvy is outspoken in his preference for photographs:

Over and over again research has shown that *photographs* sell more than *drawings*. They attract more readers. They deliver more appetite appeal. They are better remembered. They pull more coupons. And they sell more merchandise. Photographs represent reality, whereas drawings represent fantasy, which is less believable.

When we took over the "Come to Britain" advertising, we substituted photographs for the drawings which the previous agency had been using. Readership tripled, and in the subsequent ten years U. S. tourist expenditures in Britain have tripled.[5]

See Figure 18.3 for an example of the "Come to Britain" series.

Artwork. Original artwork is often used to create a desired mood. If some product feature is to be exaggerated or if a mood of warmth or coolness or sophistication is sought, a skillful artist is engaged. In the Massachusetts Mutual Insurance Company's advertisements, paintings by Norman Rockwell have been used effectively to create a feeling of warmth and friendliness and to imply that the company is interested in such homely virtues.

Cartoons. One of the most popular types of artwork in both print and television is the cartoon. In the cartoon world it seems perfectly natural that bears should talk and that Snow White should have seven dwarfs for friends. The cartoons in *The New Yorker* represent a quality of humor every advertising writer should try for; they have a freshness found in only a few of the best advertising cartoons. It is useful to make a distinction between "humorous" and "gag" cartoons. The humorous illustration may be whimsical, amusing, or merely lighthearted. The illustration in Figure 20.6 is a good example.

On the other hand, the illustration in Figure 20.7 is unmistakably a gag. We don't really expect people to saw holes in their TV sets, but the absurdity is presented in such good humor that it represents memorable communication. It illustrates a continuing Nicholson File theme, "A Nicholson File for every purpose."

Both kinds of cartoons can be used effectively for portraying most of the subject types discussed in the preceding section. A cartoon sometimes allows you to say something in a memorable manner. However, do not

[5]David Ogilvy, *Confessions of an Advertising Man* (New York: Atheneum Publishers, 1964), p. 146.

FIG. 20.6 *Effective use of humor and animation on televeision to tell people about Mountain Dew. This commercial was produced in color.* CLIENT: COPYRIGHT © PEPSICO, INC., 1968; AGENCY: OGILVY & MATHER INTERNATIONAL.

be misled by the obvious appeal of the cartoon. Use this simple test: "Would an editor accept this for editorial use and pay money for it?"

Diagrams. The diagram is another useful form of artwork, especially in illustrating complicated products. For example, if a writer were creating an advertisement for a prefabricated house, he would probably want to use an illustration of the finished house to show how attractive it is, but he would increase interest and information if he included a floor plan.

COLOR

The first newspaper color was run in 1891 in the *Milwaukee Journal*, but the first advertisement in full color on regular newsprint did not appear until 1937. By 1968 color had become an important visual device in almost every medium. NBC had 96 percent of its prime time in color during the 1965 – 1966 season when newspaper r.o.p. color was accounting for 80,000,000 of newspaper volume. Two developments,

FIG. 20.7 *"Gag" visualization of a product reward.*

Hi–Fi and SpectaColor, introduced in 1958 and 1962, accounted for close to 11,000,000. In mass-circulation magazines color linage passed black and white for the first time in 1965. Some media, such as point-of-purchase, outdoor, and car cards are printed almost 100 percent in color.

Reasons for Use of Color. Thomas B. Stanley lists seven reasons why advertisers use color:[6]

1. Attracting attention to the advertisement
2. Representing objects, scenes, and people with complete fidelity
3. Emphasizing some special part of the message or of the product
4. Suggesting abstract qualities appropriate to the selling appeal
5. Creating a pleasant first impression for the advertisement
6. Creating prestige for the product, service, or advertiser
7. Fastening visual impressions in one's memory

A list prepared by the Magazine Advertising Bureau includes most of these reasons. It is apparent that color is used by advertisers to (1) attract attention, (2) achieve literal communication, and (3) achieve symbolic communication. See Plates 1–8, in the four-color section following this chapter.

Attention. The ability of color to attract attention has been extensively researched through the years. Summaries of a few of the more recent and more extensive studies follow.

1. In 1967 Daniel Starch reported on a study of 25,081 advertisements in seven product categories in national magazines. Comparisons were made on the basis of the number of people who "noted" or saw the advertisement. Results showed

	HALF PAGE	FULL PAGE	TWO PAGES
Black and white	100	100	100
Two color	102	92	
Four color	187	152	149

2. An extensive study of advertisements (on the basis of readership) that appeared in *Wallace's Farmer* and *Iowa Homestead* indicated that the addition of color to an advertisement did little to increase male readership. Women's readership was more variable. In approximately half of the advertisements color increased female readership; in the rest it did not.
3. Two comprehensive readership studies, of the *Milwaukee Journal* and the *Houston Post*, indicated that newspaper color advertisements attracted a higher percentage of readers than did identical ads printed in black and white. The color rates were higher, but the cost differential was not as great as the differential in readership.
4. Several studies indicate that warm colors (yellows, reds) are better attention-getters than the cool ones (blues, greens). Some scattered evidence shows that yellow may have some

[6]Thomas B. Stanley, *The Technique of Advertising Production*, 2d ed., (New York: Prentice-Hall, Inc., 1954), p. 59.

edge on the other colors in attention-getting, although that depends substantially on its visibility.

Literal Communication. The value of color is obvious for products such as citrus fruits, baked ham and almost any food product. Color tells you more graphically than any words just how appetizing these products really are. For a car or a dress, color can show you how the product really looks. And if consumers have seen a product's trademark or package in color they are more likely to recognize it in the supermarket.

Symbolic Communication. Almost all authorities agree that different colors symbolize certain feelings, but that this is a complex area of communication in which good empirical evidence is sketchy. They are fairly certain that colors are either cool or warm. Note Plate II. The makers of a mentholated cigarette would be ill-advised to use bright reds to symbolize cool refreshment. Cool colors seem to have a sedative effect; warm colors appear to stimulate.

The symbolic connotation of a color depends on the situation in which it is used. Green is associated with relaxation and vacations as well as coolness. It is popular when associated with vacations but not nearly so well liked when associated with foods. Gold and silver suggest luxury when properly used; yellow suggests fire. Preferences seem to vary by social groups. The higher social classes prefer delicate hues; and lower social groups like the bright, pure hues.

There is little doubt that the trend to color in both print and television will continue. However, advertisers are more wary than they were in the early post-World War II years. Some have shifted to color and then reverted to black and white. Color authority Faber Birren makes the point that often it is not how much color is used but how well it is used that counts. Too much color can hurt the communication power of an advertisement. Color must be used wisely and well to do its job of communication properly.

SUMMARY

Visualization includes the whole field of nonverbal communication. In this chapter we have analyzed two of the most important tools of the visualizer—illustrations and color.

The most important visual element in most advertisements is the illustration. Primary purposes of illustrations are (1) to communicate, (2) to attract attention, (3) to select prospects for the product advertised, (4) to interest readers in the body text, and (5) to convince readers that the advertisement is true.

If we classified illustrations by subject matter, we should have to include the following: the product itself, part of the product, the product ready for use, the product in use, a special feature of the product, a consumer reward from using the product, the effect of not using the product, and testimonials for the product.

Among the more important illustrative techniques available to the advertising illustrator are photographs and original artwork. On special occasions cartoons and diagrams may help the advertiser communicate more effectively.

Color has become increasingly important in both print and television. The extra cost of color is usually justified on the basis of one or more of the following: attention value, more exact communication of a product's qualities or rewards, and symbolic communication. (Of the three, there is considerable evidence for the first factor, much less for the other two.)

Visualization works best when it works with the words in carrying out the ad's objective. It is, after all, the advertisement's total communication power that counts.

QUESTIONS FOR DISCUSSION

1. Of the five reasons for using illustrations, which is usually the most important? Why?
2. How does the visualizer know which type of illustration he will use in a particular advertisement? Select current examples of three types from print media.
3. What are the special problems of preparing visualization for small-space advertisements?
4. Under what conditions is the extra cost for color justified? Is it possible that a black-and-white advertisement could have greater attention-getting power than a color advertisement? If so, under what conditions?
5. What is the best way to coordinate the visual and verbal elements of an advertisement?
6. Under what conditions can one use photographs more effectively than artwork? Under what conditions is the reverse true? Clip ads from current newspapers or magazines that show an effective use of each method.

SUGGESTED READINGS

The readings for Chapters 20 and 21 appear at the end of Chapter 21.

21 | Visual Communications: Layout and Reproduction

The advertising layout performs a mechanical and a symbolic function. It is a plan indicating where the component parts (headlines, text, illustrations) are to be placed. It serves as a blueprint for the advertisement. It permits the artist to experiment with alternative arrangements until he arrives at one that pleases him. It permits the copywriter to see how his advertisement will look when it is completed. It is an important guide to lettering men, typographers, and other production people. It helps those involved in production to estimate costs. These are the *mechanical* functions of a layout.

The layout also possesses a *psychological* or *symbolic* function. A very formal layout makes the advertiser seem stable, conservative, and solid. A retail layout with crowded elements gives the impression that the store caters strongly to bargain hunters; conversely, a layout with a considerable amount of white space projects an image of exclusiveness.

A layout is sometimes known by other names. In certain Madison Avenue circles it may be called a "preliminary sketch." In the television field, layouts are "storyboards" (See Figure 22.1a, b, c, d.) that consist of a series of pictures or frames. In package design, direct mail, and point of sale, the word "dummy" is frequently used instead of layout.

354

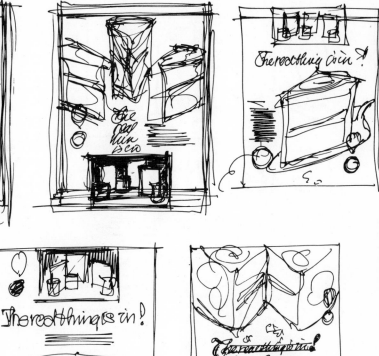

FIG. 21.1 (a) *Five thumbnail sketches prepared for possible use in a magazine advertisement for Pillsbury Cake Mix.* COURTESY THE PILLSBURY COMPANY AND LEO BURNETT CO., INC.

HOW THE LAYOUT IS PREPARED

The layout artist obviously works within certain space limitations. If he is using post cards his advertisement must fit the confines of the cards. If he is working with outdoor posters he is limited by the standard poster size. In newspapers and magazines he is confined to certain shapes and sizes for his arrangements.

Ideally, before he begins his layout the artist should have in hand all the elements that he expects to include in the advertisement. If at all possible, he should have the headlines, subheadlines, and body text. With these before him he can estimate how much space he can devote to type and how much to illustration and other visual elements. The subject matter of the illustration should be agreed on in advance.

Thumbnail Sketch (Miniature Rough). Most artists begin by making several small sketches of possible layouts. Ordinarily these rough sketches are one eighth to one fourth of the size of the final product. A thumbnail sketch offers the artist an opportunity to try out a variety of ideas; later he can select the most promising ones and blow them up to actual size. Where format remains much the same from one advertisement to the next, there is little need for making thumbnail sketches.

Rough Layout. Unlike the thumbnail, the rough layout will be the exact size of the final advertisement. For example, if the advertisement

FIG. 21.1 (b) *Rough layout for one of the most promising of the sketches shown in 21.1 (a).*
COURTESY THE PILLSBURY COMPANY AND LEO BURNETT CO., INC.

is to occupy a full page in *The Saturday Evening Post*, the artist will draw his rectangle 9 3/8 inches wide and 12 1/8 inches deep. This is the size of the *type* page, not the size of the entire page. All standard pages in the *Post* have a border of white around them. The dimensions of the type page are those beyond which neither text nor illustrations may extend; but by paying an extra 15 percent an advertiser may purchase the entire page, which is called a "bleed page."

The rough layout stage is an experimental one, but it is very important. When we get to the finished or comprehensive stage, the layout is more difficult to change. Art director Stephen Baker says,

The vital thing to keep in mind is: a layout is never an end in itself. It won't be mounted in a gilded frame. It will never be exhibited in a museum. In fact it won't appear "as is" in public anywhere—not in a publication, not on a television screen.[1]

[1]Stephen Baker, *Advertising Layout and Art Direction* (New York: McGraw-Hill, Inc., 1959), p. 15.

356

FIG. 21.1 (c) *Semi-finished layout for the Pillsbury advertisement.*
COURTESY THE PILLSBURY COMPANY AND LEO BURNETT CO., INC.

Some artists make many roughs; some, but a few. Although these layouts may look rough to the uninitiated, they enable an experienced advertising man to visualize fairly satisfactorily what the final advertisement will look like. The pictures may be hastily drawn sketches. The headlines may be crudely lettered in. The body text may be indicated by rough pencil lines.

Finished Layout. When a selection has been made among alternative roughs, the "finished layout" can be made. The layout artist may do this layout himself, or he may have it done under his direction. The illustration, the lettering, and the logotype will be drawn the way they are to appear in the final advertisement. The text will be indicated by lines neatly ruled in blocks of varying lengths to imitate paragraphs. A finished layout, then, is almost a facsimile of the finished advertisement.

Comprehensive. When the finished layout is carried one step further, a "comprehensive" layout is constructed. This is an exact facsimile of the finished advertisement. If, for example, the illustration is to be a painting, the artist may be asked to make a sketch for the com-

FIG. 21.1 (d) *Comprehensive, which shows the advertisement as it is to appear in several national magazines.* COURTESY THE PILLSBURY COMPANY AND LEO BURNETT CO., INC.

prehensive layout. The type will be set and a proof of it pasted down on the layout. The comprehensive is constructed to represent the advertisement exactly.

Dummy. A multipaged layout (that is, for a brochure) having the same number of pages as the final job is often called a "dummy." At a later stage, proofs of the type and illustration are pasted into place to help guide printers and other production personnel.

LAYOUT SIZES AND SHAPES

Obviously, the size and shape of given space will influence an artist's layout decisions. However, the media buyer, rather than the artist, is usually responsible for final decisions on size and shape. These considerations are discussed in detail in Chapters 24 and 25.

QUALITIES OF EFFECTIVE LAYOUTS

Like copywriting, layout cannot be done by formula. There are, however, certain qualities that tend to distinguish the more effective layouts from the ineffective ones. Some of the more important are discussed in this section.

Composition. Composition has been analyzed and discussed for centuries. Although professionals often disagree among themselves on specifics, they seem to have an instinctive appreciation of good composition and an aversion to bad composition. With practice, however, even a layman will be able to make fairly sophisticated judgments about the composition of an advertisement. His critical faculties will develop more rapidly if he is guided by the following rules:

1. Ideally, the picture should occupy slightly more than one half of the entire space. If there is only one illustration, it should occupy the allotted space. If there are several, the total area of all of them combined should occupy that amount of space. According to Gallup-Robinson data, it is especially important in beauty, style, and appetite-appeal advertisements. The report shows a 32 percent playback (unaided recall) of a beauty theme where an illustration covers 50 percent or more of the page, 21 percent if it is less than 50 percent of the page. Recall was also higher where the advertisement was in color and when photos were used instead of drawings or paintings.

2. As a general rule, it is best to place the headline directly above the body text. The text that has a headline gets higher reading than a text without a headline. If a layout indicates that the main head should go above the illustration, it may be well to put a subhead directly above the copy.

FIG. 21.2 *An effective layout which ran in several architectural publications. Instead of calling on an art studio for the illustration the agency had architect Albert M. Francik do it—for more "authenticity, believability."* COURTESY THE CECO CORPORATION.

3. Unless the name of the product is prominently displayed in the headline or shown in the illustration, the logotype should be emphasized and put in a prominent setting. Size, contrast, or isolation may be used to emphasize a logotype or illustration of the package.

4. Repetition of the same motifs helps to unify an advertising layout. A natural affinity between masses or overlapping helps to keep an ad from falling apart. Note in Figure 21.3 how effectively repetition is used.

5. Borders are useful to keep readers from wandering away from you, especially in newspaper advertisements.

6. Typographical consistency reassures the reader that he is looking at one ad, not several.

Balance. The word "balance" is often misused in reference to advertising layout. Some believe that it connotes absolute symmetry. Actually, flawless equilibrium can be boring to the human eye because

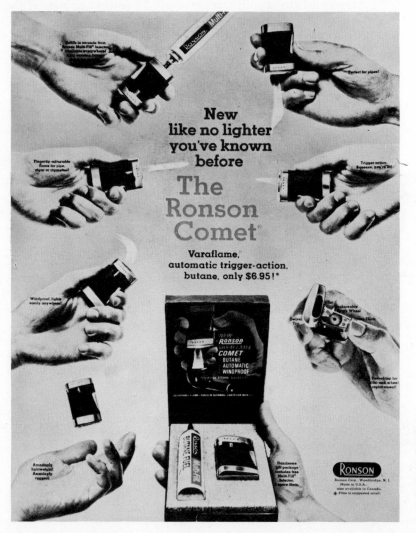

FIG. 21.3 *An example of a formally-balanced layout. Note how the interesting composition avoids monotony.* COURTESY RONSON CORPORATION.

there is nothing unexpected about it. Symmetrical balance is *formal* balance and is used most where dignity or stability is dominant. Note in Figure 21.3 how the somewhat formal balance, with the addition of interesting composition and good movement, strikes the eye and directs attention to the product. *Informal* balance usually generates more excitement and is used in the majority of print advertisements. Good examples of informal balance are Figures 20.1 and 21.2.

An advertisement is balanced when it *looks* balanced. The optical center of the advertisement is at a point about five eighths of the way up the page. A way to test this is to take a sheet of blank paper and point to its center. You will find that you normally point above the actual geometric center.

If one side of the ad seems too light we can add "weight" in several ways. One is to darken that side. Another way is to move elements from the light side away from the center and make them heavier.

Movement. Every advertisement should move naturally from one element to the next. The reader is likely to start off somewhere above and to the left of center and then roam around the page. However, his eye movement can be controlled by skillful manipulation of the elements, in the same way a policeman routes traffic. Some of the more common devices follow.

1. Gaze motion. Studies show that eyes direct other eyes. There is a natural tendency to follow the gaze of people or animals in illustrations.

2. Size. Most people are attracted by the largest and most dominant matter on the page.

3. Pointing devices such as hands, arrows, rectangles, or lines of type.

4. Cartoons or pictures and captions. The reader must start at the beginning and follow the sequence if he is to get the point.

5. Gutters of white space. These are areas between dark masses of type or illustrative material. The contrast between these and the dark background directs eye movement.

Proportion. The ancient Greeks knew that two areas were more pleasing to the eye if one were slightly larger than the other. It is more appealing to have masses of space in such proportions as three to five or two to three. These are less monotonous than equal masses. Note the use of space in Figure 21.2.

Contrast. One way to emphasize an element in a headline is by contrast. Dark masses stand out against a light background as does almost any illustration that is surrounded by a sea of white space. Both Figures 21.4 and 21.6 provide interesting examples of the uses of contrast. Well-devised contrast emphasizes what you want emphasized by making it stand out.

Simplicity. Simplicity sounds deceptively easy to achieve. The temptation to overload an advertisement is so great that many ads become far too complex. Some advertisers believe they are getting more for their money by adding elements, but the opposite is often true.

Vodka comes in loud and clear with Sprite.

Sprite. The soft drink with a message: tingling tartness. Switched on. Exuberant. Noisy. Not sweet. Not anything you've heard before. Or tasted. Get a carton of Sprite and hear how it turns vodka on. Then taste!

FIG. 21.4 *Effective use of contrast in a layout.* CLIENT: SPRITE, REPRINTED WITH THE PERMISSION OF COCA-COLA USA. "SPRITE" IS A REGISTERED TRADEMARK OF THE COCA-COLA COMPANY.

A layout is simplified when you keep down the number of different type faces and make sure the illustrations are harmonious. You should avoid decorations that seem "cute" but add little. A good test is to ask yourself if each element helps communicate your message. If it doesn't, eliminate the element.

Clarity of Presentation. It is up to the layout artist to make sure that the visual and verbal elements work together to carry forth the advertising objective. Note in Figures 21.2 and 21.5 how skillfully the two have been blended. The reader can hardly fail to gain a unified impression from these advertisements. It is more difficult if the artist has to juggle a large number of elements (as he often does in retail advertisements). However, even a casual scanning of retail ads indicates that some artists handle this juggling much better than others do.

Judicious Use of White Space. There is sometimes a difference of opinion between artists and copywriters on how much white space should be included in an advertisement. The artist often prefers a great deal of white space to make the layout look clean and attractive. Copy-writers, however, sometimes fight to use as much space as possible for their copy. Actually, white space can sometimes communicate as effec-tively as the text of illustrations. If you want to tell people that you have a prestige product or that your store is one for the "carriage trade" it is more logical to use plenty of white space so that the layout will convey this impression. (See Figure 21.7.) On the other hand, a bargain basement that overused white space would make the store look too ex-pensive, and the advertisement might drive away potential customers.

SMALL-SPACE LAYOUTS

Small-space layouts present special problems. However, look over a newspaper or magazine page filled with small advertisements, and see

FIG. 21.5 *Simplicity in the layout and the illustration. Effective blending of copy and layout to make the point.* COURTESY LENTHÉRIC, INC.

"*Aren't you wearing Tweed (   )?*"

AVAILABLE IN PERFUME / COLOGNE / MIST / SHEER TWEED BODY BOUQUET / SOAP / BATH POWDER   LENTHÉRIC   LONDON • PARIS • NEW YORK

It's like opening a present.

Polaroid
Color Pack
Cameras
start at
under 60.

FIG. 21.6 *Judicious use of white space to communicate the advertising message. Note how the headline and the camera are emphasized.* CLIENT: POLAROID CORP.; ADVERTISEMENT PREPARED BY DOYLE DANE BERNBACH INC.

how some stand out and some are lost in the shuffle. Simplicity is always important, but in small-space advertising it is essential. Gray tones that are subtly pleasing in a large ad will be lost in a small one. Simple boldness is achieved by using masses of black and white, because color is seldom available for small advertisements. A single focal idea and simple display type are essential in the small advertisement. (See Figure 21.2.) If the idea is complex and explanation is needed, it is better to use a larger advertisement, even though you may not be able to run it as frequently.

REPRODUCTION

The best creative efforts of advertising people may never fulfill their promise if they are not properly reproduced in the media. In this section we shall examine the production of printed advertising, often called production for the graphic arts. In Chapter 22 we shall consider some of the problems involved in the production of advertising messages for television and radio.

We can approach the graphic arts in two ways. On the one hand, we regard them as an invisible *window* through which the reader sees the message of the creative man. The clearer and less obtrusive the

N-M's bright ones love pedal extremity chromatics. (wouldn't you like to be in their shoes?)

Oh, wearing shoes will be fun this year! Matching a jumper, zinging green shoes against orange tights – humdrum shoes are finally out! Hurry, hurry to N-M for just-your-size from our Alexis collection. (What a shoo-in for the bright ones!) Teeny size 6 to Teen size 8: the collection priced from 9.00 to 12.00. Children's Shoes. fifth floor. Downtown; NorthPark.

Neiman-Marcus

window, the more visible is the message. A second approach is to view the graphic arts as a *stage*, dramatically lighted and interestingly furnished, on which we see the ideas of the writer played out. The professional graphic arts expert will usually try to fuse the two. He wants to make the message interesting to look at, easy to read, and perfectly comprehensible.

Whether you are working with mass media, such as newspapers or magazines, or with more selective media, such as folders or booklets, your problems probably will fall into three major categories:

1. Typography
2. Photoengraving
3. Printing of the completed advertisement

PROCEDURE FOR THE PRODUCTION OF AN ADVERTISEMENT

When the typewritten text, the layout, and the finished artwork have all been approved, the advertisement is ready for mechanical production. Let us review briefly the necessary steps in the production of the typical printed ad.

The type face must be chosen. The choice of a suitable type face is vital to the over-all effort to achieve the objectives of the ad. After selection of the type face, sizes must be selected and cast (measured) to fit into the space allotted to the text in the layout. The layout (or a tracing of it), the typewritten text, and specification for size and face of type to use are sent to the compositor. (In retail advertising the newspaper production department is likely to serve as the compositor.) When he has set the text in type, the compositor will pull what are known as "type proofs" and return them to the person who gave him the order.

Next, the exact size of each piece of artwork to be engraved must be determined. The engraver is then given the artwork, together with instructions for screen, type of engraving desired, and the time schedule. When the engravings are made, the engraver pulls proofs of them and returns them for approval.

The engraver's goal is to reproduce as faithfully as possible the photographs, paintings, or drawings. Some colors are difficult to reproduce with modern printing inks and high-speed presses. Some black-and-white photographs or drawings lack enough contrast for good reproduction. It is usually wise to discuss any piece of finished artwork with the engraver before the engraving is made; he may be able to suggest changes that will make better engraving possible.

Completed engravings are sent to the compositor. He locks them, together with the type, into a form, using the layout as a guide. All elements of the advertisement have now been assembled in printable form. The compositor pulls proofs of the complete advertisement and submits them for approval to the one who gave him the order. If any type corrections or revisions are needed, a proof is returned to the compositor with the corrections indicated. Then a final corrected proof is submitted for approval (in general advertising, to the client or agency).

Finally an electrotype (a metal impression) is made of the complete advertisement and shipped to the publication. Some magazines (for example, the *Saturday Evening Post*) do not accept electrotypes of engravings; original plates must be furnished. However, the typical retail newspaper advertisement is reproduced by stereotyping, a process which is described later in this chapter.

TYPOGRAPHY

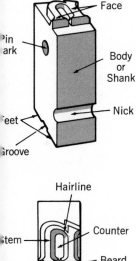

FIG. 21.8 *A slug of type from two different vantage points.*

Many centuries before Gutenberg invented printing from movable type, the Chinese were printing from wood blocks, one block carved for each page. Gutenberg's contribution was the invention of typesetting. Although originated over 500 years ago, his methods are still used. Setting type is the first step in most printing jobs. Today most type is set by machine. Hand setting is usually reserved for headline and display copy and for very small and special jobs. Obviously it is cheaper to set the type by means of one of our modern metal or photo typesetting machines than by hand.

It takes years to learn typography thoroughly, but certain fundamentals are not too complex. In this section we shall examine some of the characteristics of various type faces, the methods by which type is set, and "rules" for selecting type and fitting type to a given space.

What is Type? The word "type" is both singular and plural. As a singular noun it means a rectangular block (or slug) of metal that has a letter or character in relief on its upper face. As a plural noun it means any number of these blocks collectively. Type also means the image of these letters and characters printed on paper.

Groups of Type Faces. Some of the type faces that are common today had their origin hundreds of years ago, but new faces are designed almost every year. The hundreds of type faces available today fall into certain easy-to-use classifications. A basic design such as Caslon or Bodoni is available in various sizes and in condensed and extended forms. These variations are usually called a type *family.* A somewhat broader classification is the type *group* (for example, Old Style, Transitional, Modern, Egyptian, and Script).

Abstract. Abstract (or block) is a heterogeneous classification that includes several type families. There are two main styles of abstract type—sans serif and square serif. They are used quite often in headlines and not so frequently in body text. The line below is set in an abstract face:

A B C D E F G H I J K L M N O P Q R S T U V W X Y Z a b c

Old Style. By far the largest group of type faces is the Roman. There are many different Roman styles, but all contain heavy stem strokes as well as lighter strokes. The faces have serifs, or small hairlines, at the end of each stroke.

Most Americans learn to read from the Roman types used in schoolbooks, and the majority of today's advertising body text is printed in Roman faces. The contrast of heavy and light strokes and the variation in letter design make for easy reading.

Roman is usually divided into four main classifications: *Old Style*, *Transitional*, *Modern*, and *Egyptian*. The Old Style used today was developed during the Renaissance when European designers devised freehand versions of the various letters used by the ancient Romans. Typical Old Style faces are the types of Garamond, Caslon, and Jenson.

10 pt. Garamond ————————————————————

A   B   C   D   E   F   G   H   I   J   K   L   M   N   O   P   Q   R

S   T   U   V   W   X   Y   Z   a   b   c   d   e   f   g   h   i   j   k

l   m   n   o   p   q   r   s   t   u   v   w   x   y   z   1   2   3   4   5

Transitional. The types of Baskerville and Bulmer bridge the gap between Old Style and Modern; that is, they are straighter than the Old Style yet maintain a sharper contrast between thick and thin strokes than do the Modern faces.

10 pt. Baskerville ————————————————————

A   B   C   D   E   F   G   H   I   J   K   L   M   N   O   P   Q

R   S   T   U   V   W   X   Y   Z   a   b   c   d   e   f   g   h   i   j

k   l   m   n   o   p   q   r   s   t   u   v   w   x   y   z   1   2   3

Modern. In their search for new type designs, some eighteenth-century designers decided to make changes in the old styles. The chief characteristic of the modern Roman types that evolved is mechanical precision. Note that there is a much greater contrast between the thin and thick strokes of the letters and a sharper definition of the horizontal serifs than in the Old Style. A popular Modern face is Bodoni.

10 pt. Bodoni ————————————————————

A   B   C   D   E   F   G   H   I   J   K   L   M   N   O   P   Q

R   S   T   U   V   W   X   Y   Z   a   b   c   d   e   f   g   h   i   j

k   l   m   n   o   p   q   r   s   t   u   v   w   x   y   z   1   2   3

Egyptian. Of more recent design, these types have little contrast between thick and thin strokes, and have square serifs. Typical examples are Fortune, Clarendon, and Consort.

10 pt. Clarendon ————————————————————

A   B   C   D   E   F   G   H   I   J   K   L   M   N   O   P

Q   R   S   T   U   V   W   X   Y   Z   a   b   c   d   e   f

g   h   i   j   k   l   m   n   o   p   q   r   s   t   u   v   w   x

y   z   1   2   3   4   5   6   7   8   9   0 $ fi   fl   ff

Script. Script (or cursive) type is an imitation of handwriting. It tends to link the letters and give the impression of a flowing hand. Like italics, script is difficult to read in mass and is used principally to convey the impression of exclusiveness or airiness. It is often used in fashion advertising and for headlines or signatures.

10 pt. Mistral _____

A B C D E F G H I J K L M N O P Q
R S T U V W X Y Z a b c d e f g h i
j k l m n o p q r s t u v w x y z 1

Italic. The *italic* type was introduced by a Venetian printer named Manutius and named by him in honor of Italy. It imitates the slanting script of Italian handwriting. In most type faces italic is a sloped version of the standard face. Italics are often used for subheads or in body text to lend emphasis to a word or statement.

Garamond Ital

Ink-smudged hands with calloused, nimble fingers, they gave the wo

Alt No. 2 Ital

Ink-smudged hands with calloused, nimble fingers, they gave the world

Bodoni Ital

Ink-smudged hands with calloused, nimble fingers, they gave th

Baskerville Ital

Ink-smudged hands with calloused, nimble fingers, they gave

Fortune Bold Ital

Ink-smudged hands with calloused, nimble fing

Methods of Typesetting. There are five principal methods by which type may be set: by hand, by monotype, linotype, Ludlow, and photocomposition.

Handsetting. When type is set by hand the compositor picks the letters individually from the case, sets them in order in a three-sided metal box called a stick to form words, and arranges the words into sentences and paragraphs. The lines are then put into a form which is locked to hold them together. After the type has been used, the form is unlocked and the letters are returned to their proper boxes in the type case. Handsetting is obviously slow, but it does permit a flexibility not present in the more highly mechanized methods. In handsetting the compositor can space the letters more carefully and can make all necessary adjustments in the composition.

Monotype. Monotype is a mechanical method of setting letters one at a time. A monotype is really a combination of two machines. One machine produces perforations on a ribbon, much as a card puncher prepares cards for the tabulating machine. The keyboard that controls the punching is operated by compressed air. After the ribbon is perforated, it goes to the caster, which casts and assembles the type, one letter at a time. Because the letters are not molded together, it is easy to change a single letter and to adjust for proper spacing between words. Monotype is used for tables, compositions of irregular width, and for certain fine bookwork.

Linotype. The invention of the linotype made it possible to set type much more quickly than by hand or even by monotype. The linotype keyboard looks like that of a typewriter, but the inner workings of the former machine are vastly more complicated. When letters and words of text are spelled out on the keyboard, a metal bar (or slug) is formed with a complete line of type molded on its printing edge that bears the letters and words designated by the operator. Thus the entire body text is set, one line at a time. When the slugs have been used, they are put back in the melting pot in the machine where they are melted, ready to be recast.

It should be kept in mind that with linotype a change or correction is somewhat more complicated than with the other methods, in that the whole line must be reset. Also, any irregularly shaped type areas may be difficult to set by linotype.

Monotype composition tends to be a little more expensive than linotype on simple material, but may be less expensive on more complicated or tabular work.

Ludlow. This method is widely used for setting headlines and display type. The type matrices (brass molds for each letter) are set by hand in a frame, and the line is then molded. It is, in effect, a method of handsetting in which the final molding is accomplished by a machine.

Photocomposition. A photocomposition machine consists of a letter keyboard that operates an electric camera and a film printing device. The copy is set in the desired face, size, and line width, and produced in film form. From the film a print is made similar to a metal-type proof. The print is then pasted in position in the mechanical.

"Rules" for Proper Use of Type. With practice almost any advertising neophyte can train himself to distinguish an appropriate type face from an inappropriate one, and a readable face from one that is not readable. Below are several rules or principles that may be helpful.

Legibility. There is a decided difference in the legibility of copy set in different methods and in different types. Certain types, such as Roman, tend to be more legible than others, but any can be misused. Here are a few general suggestions regarding type usage:

1. Solid lines of capital letters or italics are difficult to read, but both can be used effectively for emphasis.
2. The background has a decided influence on legibility. (Black type on a white background is much more legible than the same type on a dark background.)
3. Leading (insertion of white space) between lines of type increases legibility.
4. Short paragraphs and sentences are more readable than long ones.
5. Sizes below 8-point and above 12-point are not ordinarily good for body text in the print media.

6. Lines should not be too long (or too short). In general, about forty characters per line is advisable.
7. Spacing between words should be watched. Words should not be isolated by white space or placed so close together that it is difficult to tell where one ends and the other begins.
8. Readability is improved by allowing greater space between paragraphs than between lines within the paragraph.

Appropriateness. The type face you choose should be appropriate to the objective and mood of your copy. Appropriateness comes both from the type design and the way it is used. For example, Bodoni faces have a crisp mechanical look that fits well with modern designs and layouts. So do the sans-serifs. Either, however, may be so crowded in a layout that it loses its modern appearance.

A study of the esthetic qualities of type faces was made by Professor James Brinton, using the semantic differential to measure verbal associations.[2] Twenty pairs of polar adjectives were used (for instance, imperfect-perfect, hard-soft, old-new, expensive-cheap), and both professionals and laymen were asked to rate selected type faces on the seven-point bipolar scale. Differences were found between the qualities ascribed by professionals and those mentioned by the laymen. For example, the professionals saw Cheltenham Bold as imperfect, hard, constrained, old, ugly, old-fashioned, and cheap. Laymen did not mention these qualities but, instead, viewed it as active, plain, strong, dark, simple, masculine, usual, rugged, and honest. Brinton recommends further studies in this field, to lead to an eventual cataloguing of a large number of type faces.

You may well wonder whose opinion is right—the professional's or the layman's. Brinton suggests that whenever the two agree the more sensitive judgment of the professional is probably better; but whenever there is actual disagreement it might be advisable to follow the preference of the layman.

Emphasis. In any visual communication it is possible to achieve emphasis through contrast. A large type face in the midst of smaller faces or italics amid Roman will stand out; so will an unusual type face or one located in a sea of white space. The typographer should not attempt too much emphasis, which usually ends up as no emphasis. The type face should not call attention to itself—always to the message.

Harmony. Type should always harmonize with the other elements of the advertisement. It should harmonize with the message to be conveyed, the layout, the illustrations, and the other type. For example, if the layout is tall, the type selected should have prevailingly perpendicular lines.

Frequently a single type family provides all the contrast needed for a single advertisement. By using boldface, condensed, italic, and different sizes, a surprising amount of variety can be achieved. There should always be some kinship among the type faces used.

---

[2]"Measurement of Aesthetic Qualities of Type Faces," report presented at the Advertising Research session, Association for Education in Journalism convention, August 28, 1958.

SPECIFYING TYPE

In order to specify type it is necessary to identify it by size and by face (for example, 14-point Bodoni Bold). Its size is measured in *points*; the face indicates the style or name of the type (Bodoni and so forth).

Point System. Points measure the depth (or height) of the type. There are 72 points to the inch. The point system measures the over-all size of the piece of type metal from which the letter is printed—not the size of the individual letter. Thus 12-point type is not quite 1/6 of an inch in height, but six lines of 12-point type (set solid) would take up about an inch of depth on the printing surface. Type is not specified by width, as this depends on the type design.

The smallest type you ordinarily see is 6-point (in classified advertising copy). Sizes range up to 144 points. Most body text in ads is 14-point size or less. Anything above 14-point is considered headline type.

Pica. The width of a line is measured in picas (a pica is one sixth of an inch); thus a line of body text 3 inches wide would measure 18 picas, 3 1/2 inches would be 21 picas, et cetera.

Upper and Lower Case. The layman distinguishes between capital and small letters. The printer calls the capitals "upper case" and the small ones "lower case." The terms come from the position of the two cases holding the capital and small letters when the compositor is setting type by hand.

Type may be set in all caps, in caps and small caps, or in caps and lower case. Examples of each follow:

All caps | REPRODUCING THE ADVERTISEMENT
Caps and small caps | REPRODUCING THE ADVERTISEMENT
Caps and lower case | Reproducing the Advertisement

In both the upper-case and the lower-case alphabet of every type face there are certain letters sufficiently different in design from the same letters in any other type face to make identification possible. Some difficulty may be encountered, however, in recognizing the type face when a small size is used, because the characteristics that are obvious in the large size are then less apparent.

Because there is a great variation in the design of lower-case letters, it is often difficult to estimate size. In the lower-case alphabet, there are seven ascending letters (b, d, f, h, k, l, and t) and five descending letters (g, j, p, q, and y). The remaining letters have neither ascenders nor descenders. In some faces the ascenders and descenders are long and the letter size is small. In others the letter size is larger and the ascenders and descenders are proportionately shorter. Thus the lower-case letters of one type face set in 10-point may appear smaller than those of another set in 9-point.

Leading. Type set as it is cast (without special provision for spacing between lines) is said to be set *solid.* Some space is provided by the way type is cast. However, it is possible to increase the space between the lines by inserting thin strips of metal called *leads* and pronounced "Leds." You can have 1-point leads if you want only a small amount of space added, 2-point leads if you want a little more, and so on.

Agate Line. The agate line is the standard unit of measuring (and ordering) space in most publications. It is always 1/14 of a column inch, regardless of whether there are printed lines within that space.

COPYFITTING

It is easier than it appears to estimate how many words of text will fill a given space or how much space your written text will take.

One approach is to use your typewriter for measuring. You count the characters in the typewritten copy and compare the total with the type selected. Typewritten copy has 12 characters an inch if it is elite, 10 if it is pica. Therefore, if you have 20 lines of elite typewriting with an average width of 6 inches, you will have 1,440 characters.

The next step under this system is to find out how many characters per line the type you choose will take. For example, if you have 20 pica lines and are using 12-point type, you will have 45 characters per line. Divide 1,440 by 45 and you have 32 lines of type. Now you have the two dimensions of your space—20 picas or 3 1/3 inches *wide*, and 32 times 12 points or 384 points (5 1/3 inches) *deep.*

Another method is to use Table 21.1. Count the number of words and divide by the number of words per square inch. For example, if you have written 210 words and you intend to use 10-point type solid, you will find that it will take 10 square inches (210 divided by 21).

TABLE 21.1

COPYFITTING TABLE

NUMBER OF LINES, WORDS PER SQUARE INCH

	Point Size of Type								
	6	8	10	12	14	18	24	30	36
No. lines per inch:									
Solid	12	9	7+	6	5+	4	3	2+	2
Leaded									
2 points	9	7+	6	5+	4+	3+	2+	2	1+
Approx. no. words per sq. inch:									
Solid	47	32	21	14	11	7	4	4	2
Leaded									
2 points	34	23	16	11	7	5	3+	3+	1+

PHOTOENGRAVING

Anyone who has ever snapped a shutter knows that his camera takes a negative picture, which becomes a photograph only when printed on sensitized paper. Every photoengraving also begins as a photograph. However, a negative of the art work is printed (in reverse) on sensitized zinc or copper, instead of on paper. There are four principal kinds of photoengravings; line cuts, halftones, Ben Day engravings, and color plates.

Line Cuts. Line cuts go by a variety of names (zinc etchings, line etchings, line engravings, line plates, and others). Pen-and-ink drawings are usually reproduced by line cuts, whereas photographs are typically reproduced by halftones. The illustration in Figure 20.7 is a line cut.

Line cuts are required only for letterpress, because offset and other processes have other ways of reproducing solid areas. They are made by photoengravers by means of a photomechanical process. The design is transferred photographically to a sensitized zinc or copper plate. Acid etches away all of the plate except the parts not protected by the design (the printing surface). Thus the etching leaves lines that follow the design. The unetched lines constitute the printing surface, which is then mounted on a wooden block so that it will be type-high.

A rubber name stamp is a kind of line cut. So are woodcuts and linoleum blocks.

Halftones. Unlike the line cut, the halftone can be engraved to produce the many shades of gray between white and black. The entire surface of the halftone is broken up by a series of minute dots. The size of each dot determines the amount of ink it will carry, and therefore the shade of gray that it will give to the paper. The dots are put on the negative by photographing the art work through what is known as a "halftone screen." This screen is placed in the camera between the lens and the negative holder. When the image on the negative is printed on the sensitized metal, the pattern of dots becomes part of the picture. During the etching process, the acid eats away the metal between the dots, leaving them standing as tiny blunt cones. These cones are the only part of the halftone that prints. Small dots produce a gray effect, larger ones (with less white space) produce a much darker effect.

A halftone is identified by its screen. It may be a 50-screen halftone, a 100-screen halftone, and so on. These numbers refer to the number of dots there are in each linear inch. A 50-screen halftone has 50 dots per inch; a 133-screen halftone has 133 dots per inch. The more dots there are per inch, the better the paper needed to print the halftone, and the sharper the reproduction.

Newspapers are printed at extremely high speeds. A single press in a modern metropolitan newspaper plant prints 850 copies per minute. Newsprint is comparatively poor paper, with a poor printing surface. Consequently, screens used for printing on newsprint or other rough-surfaced papers are 50, 55, 60, and 65.

A typical magazine press runs at about half the speed of the newspaper press. It produces about 425 impressions per minute in four colors on a 20-page signature (a sheet folded ready for stitching in the magazine). It prints on a paper of finer quality than that for newsprint. *Life*, for example, specifies 110-line screen for black and white and for black and one color; 120-line for red, blue and black; and 133-line screen for yellow.

When the mechanical etching of a plate is completed, the halftone is turned over to a "finisher." He continues the etching by hand until all the fine tonal values of the original art work are brought out in the finished engraving. There are a number of types of halftones. Those in general use are the following:

Silhouette Halftone. A silhouette halftone has no background. To achieve this effect, the finisher outlines all of the subject to be printed

with a fine cutting tool. Then all the screen of the background is removed, by either cutting it or etching it away.

Vignette Halftone. A vignette halftone has a background that fades
off into the white paper. This effect is also accomplished by the finisher.

Highlight Halftone. This kind of halftone is used particularly for
the reproduction of wash or pencil drawings where areas of pure white
are wanted in the illustration. To get these areas the dots are etched
until they disappear and will not print.

Combination Halftone. Figure 21.3 is a combination halftone. The
hands and lighters are reproduced from photographs. The headline was
reproduced from type proofs. The effect is achieved by stripping together a line negative (without dots) and a halftone negative (with
dots). Stripping is a hand operation that is performed in the negative
room.

Ben Day. A Ben Day engraving is often drawn in simple pen-and-ink
outline. Then a wash in light-blue water color (which does not photograph on a black-and-white negative) is applied to parts of the drawing
where a Ben Day pattern or tint is to be laid. Various tones may be
designated. Tints of the different tonal values are then laid on the
metal plate and etched to produce the textures shown. Today, however,
the Ben Day process has been replaced by the use of tinted screens and
tint sheets, both of which are applied to the section to be tinted by the
engraver.

Four-Color Engravings. One of the wonders of modern printing is
that a magazine or newspaper press can reproduce with fidelity all the
colors that an artist can mix on his palette or a camera can see through
its lens; it can accomplish this by using only *four* different colors of
ink — the three primary colors (red, blue, and yellow) and black.

The work to be reproduced is photographed through color filters
that shut off all except the color desired. For example, one filter shuts off
all colors other than red, and reproduces every light ray of red to be
blended in the final picture. Thus, four halftone negatives are required
to make a set of four color plates; one for yellow, one for red, one for
blue, and one for black. The filters through which the illustration is
photographed are pieces of gelatin placed in the lens; they allow only
the rays of light of a certain color to reach the negative. The filters used
in photographing a piece of full-color art work are the following:

Violet or blue filter for the yellow plate.
Green filter for the red plate.
Orange or red filter for the blue plate.
Yellow filter for the black plate.

When these filters are used, all degrees of one color are collected on
each negative; all degrees of yellow on the yellow negative, and the
like. These values are transferred to each plate when each negative is
printed (in reverse) on the sensitized metal. The black plate is known as
a "general plate" that is used for depth of color and as an aid to the
photoengraver in approaching the true color values of the original art
work.

The negatives are developed, stripped, printed on metal, etched, and finished in much the same way that halftones are, but they require considerably more time for "staging in" and re-etching by the color finisher to achieve true color reproduction when color proofs of the plates are pulled.

The engraver returns to the person who gave him the order not only a complete set of color proofs but also a set of what is known as "progressives." There are usually seven proofs in a set of progressives: (1) a proof of the yellow plate; (2) a proof of the red plate; (3) a proof of the yellow and red plates printed together; (4) a proof of the blue plate; (5) a proof of the red, yellow, and blue plates printed together; (6) a proof of the black plate; and (7) a proof of the yellow, red, blue, and black plates printed together. These proofs show printing values and the progression or rotation in which the various plates are printed.

PRINTING THE ADVERTISEMENT

Anyone who has his own rubber name stamp demonstrates the principle of printing every time he presses the stamp into an ink pad and then onto a piece of paper. He is transferring an inked image from one surface to another. Printing, or the transference of the image onto paper, is the final step in reproducing any advertisement.

Although there are numerous variations, there are really only three basic mechanical methods of printing: (1) letterpress, (2) gravure, and (3) lithography.

Letterpress. A rubber stamp works on the same principles as *letterpress* or *relief* printing. There, too, the printing surface is raised above the rest of the pad.

The raised effect in letterpress is accomplished by etching the metal plate with acid. All parts of the plate that are to print are protected by an acid resistant so that they are not affected. The acid eats away the remainder of the plate, and this etched-away part is the nonprinting area.

Letterpress is used for virtually all newspapers and a great many magazines and books. Therefore most printed advertisements are printed by letterpress, although an increasing number of publications are being printed by offset lithography.

Gravure. Gravure (or intaglio) is the opposite of the letterpress method. As Figure 21.9 indicates, the printing surface (again, the lower semicircle) is depressed instead of raised. The ink lies *between* the raised surfaces rather than on top of them. The design is incised or etched into the plate below the general level of the metal. The surface of the plate is inked and then wiped clean, leaving ink only in the depressions. When printing takes place, the hollows below the surface give up their ink and transfer the design that is on the plate to the paper. The rest of the plate, having been cleaned, has no ink to give up. The newspaper rotogravure section is reproduced by this method. The picture is photographically printed on copper cylinders in which the image to be reproduced is depressed. When paper is pressed against this copper cylinder, the ink is transferred to paper and the image is then reproduced.

LETTERPRESS
Ink Carried on a Raised
Surface

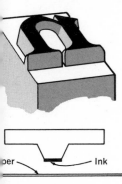

per ———— Ink

LITHOGRAPHY
Ink Carried on a Flat
Surface

per ———— Ink

GRAVURE
Ink Carried in Depressed
Areas

per ———— Ink

FIG. 21.9 *Illustration
of the three basic
mechanical methods of
printing.* COURTESY
LITHOGRAPHIC TECHNICAL
FOUNDATION.

The principal advantage of gravure is the pleasing reproduction of illustrative and tonal effects even on cheap paper. Because the cost of preparation of fine-line screens is high, gravure is used mainly for large runs. Its reproduction of type tends to be a little fuzzy.

Lithography. Figure 21.9 illustrates the principle of lithography. Note that the printing surface is smooth; it has no ridges or depressions. This smooth plate is attached to a cylinder which, as it revolves, comes into contact with a roller that dampens the blank areas of the plate. The design, which is covered with a greasy substance, repels the water. Consequently, the nonprinting areas are dampened. Ink, being oily, will not adhere to a damp surface, but will to the dry surface. As a result, when the printing surface comes into contact with paper, the image is transferred.

When the plate prints directly on the paper, the process is known as *direct* lithography. Colored posters, display cards, and many labels are printed by this method. However, when the plate deposits its design on an intermediate rubber roller, which in turn acts as the printing surface, the process is known as *offset lithography.* Offset gives a somewhat richer effect than you get from direct lithography and is used for considerable book work and folders, especially for long runs. (This book, for example, was printed by offset.) The offset process is used to a great extent in promotion and direct mail. Very often proofs from a letterpress run are photographically reproduced by offset for these purposes.

Silk Screen or Serigraphy. One of the oldest and simplest methods of reproducing material is *silk screen.* It is a process of Chinese and Japanese origin in which semiliquid ink or pigment is pressed through a fine mesh silk screen or bolting cloth for a given design on a surface. Ordinarily, one stencil is used for each color, and it can be used on surfaces of any size or texture. It is frequently used for small runs of display or car cards. Recently, high-speed machinery has made silk screening practical for some long-run work.

DUPLICATING THE ORIGINAL

Once the type and engravings have been converted to metal, it is possible to make duplicate copies at a small percentage of the original cost. Three common forms of duplicate plates are (1) electrotypes, (2) matrices, and (3) stereotypes.

Electrotypes. Electrotypes are metal duplicates of pages of type with or without illustrations. They can be made from type forms, line etchings, halftones, or any combination of these. If an electrotype is to be made of a complete advertisement, the form in which the type and engravings are locked up together is used. The first step is to make a mold of the complete advertisement. The four types of materials generally used are these:

Wax Mold. A wax mold consists of a thin lead or copper base which supports a wax compound about 1/8 inch thick.

Tenaplate Mold. A tenaplate mold consists of a sheet of aluminum foil supporting a special molding composition.

Lead Mold. A lead mold is a thin sheet of soft, pure lead.

Vinylite Mold. A vinylite mold consists of a thin, flexible sheet of vinyl plastic. It is an all-purpose molding medium and can be used for molding type forms as well as pattern plates and original cuts.

With any of these materials, an impression is made of the matter to be duplicated. Then metal is electrolytically deposited on the mold until a metal shell is formed to a desired thickness. If a copper shell is to be made, copper is deposited electrolytically on the mold to a thickness of .01 of an inch. If nickel is to be used, it is deposited on the mold electrolytically to a thickness of .001 – .002 of an inch and is reinforced with a deposit of copper to a desired thickness. When the desired thickness is achieved, the shell is removed from the mold and cast or "backed up" with molten metal.

After this shell is cast or "backed up" with metal, the plate is "finished"; that is, it is shaved to any desired thickness and either beveled, blocked, or curved. A beveled plate is one trimmed close to the edge of the subject matter. A blocked plate is one mounted on wood to type-high thickness (.918 of an inch). A curved plate is one that is curved mechanically to fit any specified printing press cylinder.

Matrices and Stereotypes. One of the cheapest and oldest forms of duplication is *stereotyping*. The mold used is a matrix or mat. The matrix is made from layers of soft paper or similar material. It is dampened and then forced, under great pressure, into the interstices of type, line plates, or coarse-screen halftones. When the mat is removed from the form, it preserves the raised portion of type and engravings as depressions on its surface. Once the mat has dried, molten metal may be poured over it. The result is a casting (stereotype) of the original form, though the hollows are not quite so deep as the original or as those you would obtain on an electrotype. The stereotype is a money saver because the process is so simple.

You cannot print directly from a mat, because it is only a mold with indentations where the letters and illustrations are. However, it is flexible; it can therefore be curved and a corresponding metal stereotype cast from it to fit on the cylinders of a rotary press. This is what is done on metropolitan newspapers.

SUMMARY

A layout for a printed advertisement is both a plan indicating where the various elements are to be placed and a visual symbol to present a product, corporate, or store image. A layout normally starts with a thumbnail sketch, which can be made quickly to check alternative arrangements. Then come the rough layout, made in the actual size of the finished advertisement, and the finished layout, which is almost a facsimile of the finished advertisement.

There is no layout formula, but the neophyte should try for good composition, balance, movement, proportion, contrast, simplicity, clarity of presentation, and the judicious use of white space in his advertising layout. Simplicity is important especially in the small-space layout.

The mechanical elements of the printed advertisement act as an invisible window and as a stage for the message. Problems fall into three major categories—typography, photoengraving, and the printing of the completed advertisement.

Mysterious though typography seems, certain fundamentals are within the grasp of any beginner. Among these are the characteristics of the various type faces, "rules" of type selection, methods by which type is set, specifying type, and fitting type to a space. It is especially important that the type chosen and the way it is used be readable and appropriate to the advertising message.

The principal types of photoengravings with which the advertising man works are line cuts, halftones, Ben Day engravings, and color process plates.

The advertisement is finally reproduced by one of three basic printing methods: letterpress (printing surface is raised), gravure (printing surface is depressed), and lithography (printing and non-printing surfaces on the same plane). We also have silk screen.

After the original copy of the advertisement is set in metal, duplicates may be made through either electrotyping or stereotyping, or copies for promotional purposes may be produced by the offset process.

QUESTIONS FOR DISCUSSION

1. To what extent should the layout be used to get attention in a print advertisement? What is the danger inherent in emphasizing attention getting in a layout?
2. What is the function of a thumbnail sketch? of a rough layout?
3. What are the main criteria of good layouts? Select examples illustrating the effective use of each from current newspapers and magazines.
4. Under what conditions would you prefer line cuts to halftones? offset to letterpress?
5. Explain the function of stereotyping. Of electrotyping.
6. Describe the process of setting type.
7. Select current examples of the various type families discussed in this chapter. What is the value of knowing one type face from another?

SUGGESTED READINGS

Arnold, Edmund C., *Ink on Paper: A Handbook of the Graphic Arts.* New York: Harper & Row, Publishers, 1963.

ATA Advertising Production Handbook, 3d ed. New York: Advertising Typographers Association of America, Inc., 1963.

Baker, Stephen, *Advertising Layout and Art Direction.* New York: McGraw-Hill, Inc., 1963.

———, *Visual Persuasion.* New York: McGraw-Hill, Inc., 1961.

Berrien, Edith Heal, *Visual Thinking in Advertising.* New York: Holt, Rinehart and Winston, Inc., 1963.

Birren, Faber, *Color: A Survey in Words and Pictures.* Hyde Park, N. Y.: University Books, Inc., 1963.

Burns, Aaron, *Typography*. New York: Reinhold Publishing Corporation, 1963.

Dair, Carl, *Design with Type*. Toronto: University of Toronto Press, 1967.

Dunn, S. Watson, *Advertising Copy and Communication*. New York: McGraw-Hill, Inc., 1956. Chapter 7.

Gottschall, Edward, and Arthur Hawkins, eds., *Trends in Visual Advertising*. New York: Art Direction Book Co., 1959–1964.

Hymes, David, *Production in Advertising and the Graphic Arts*. New York: Holt, Rinehart and Winston, Inc., 1963.

Nelson, Roy Paul, *The Design of Advertising*. Dubuque, Iowa: William C. Brown Company, Publishers, 1967.

Ogilvy, David, *Confessions of an Advertising Man*. New York: Atheneum Publishers, 1964. Chapter 7.

Pinney, Roy, *Advertising Photography: A Visual Communication Book*. New York: Hastings House Publishers, Inc., 1962.

Rosen, Ben, *Type and Typography: The Designer's Type Book*. New York: Reinhold Publishing Corporation, 1963.

Stanley, Thomas Blaine, *The Technique of Advertising Production*, 2d ed. Englewood Cliffs, N.J.: Prentice-Hall, Inc., 1954.

Stone, Bernard, and Arthur Eckstein, *Preparing Art for Printing*. New York: Reinhold Publishing Corporation, 1965.

Turnbull, Arthur T., and Russel N. Baird, *The Graphics of Communication*. New York: Holt, Rinehart and Winston, Inc., 1964.

22 | Writing for Television and Radio

In the early days of radio many people thought that the copywriters had to adapt printed ads to the new medium; when television arrived it was believed that the writer must adapt radio copy to television. He was looked on as a technician rather than a creator. Research, however, has proved that each medium has its own form — that radio is not just print with sound nor television merely radio with pictures.

By the late 1960s television had become the dominant advertising medium for most mass-consumed packaged goods, and print, the supplementary medium. Television accounted for more than $2,500,000,000 of the total advertising bill. Radio had come back from the slump it suffered when television came on the scene, but it had drastically changed.

HOW THE BROADCAST MEDIA ARE DIFFERENT

Most of the previously outlined principles that govern creative efforts apply equally well to writing for radio and television. In these media it is just as important as in print to define your objective specifically, to keep the advertisement simple, and so forth. Also, the five I's — idea, impact, interest, information, and impulsion — are just as important here as they are in any commercial communication. This chapter will concentrate on the differences and special applications of basic principles, and not review the basics themselves.

Structure of Commercials

Time-Orientation. Broadcast messages are delivered in terms of time, printed messages in terms of space. Into a segment of time the radio writer pours a variety of sounds to communicate his message, whereas the television writer manipulates sounds plus picture plus motion.

Simplicity of Structure. Partly because of the time orientation and partly because of audience reaction, almost all broadcast commercials are simple. Veteran writer Louis Redmond[1] says, in discussing television commercials:

> To be effective, a commercial is virtually forced, by the nature of the medium, to be simple and to be repetitive. It might be said that a good TV commercial is *essentially a continuous restatement of a single point, using a variety of means to drive the point home.* Its typical structure might be represented as follows:
>
> State — Restate — Demonstrate — Recapitulate

Emphasis on Showmanship. Many of the creative people who have been most successful in the broadcast media are show business experts. Sound effects, jingles, jokes, animated cartoons, and unusual camera angles are used to make the product message attention-compelling and entertaining. Program producers are occasionally engaged to create television commercials. Even small agencies find this a practical step. For example, a small agency in Memphis had the problem of dramatizing a local sausage brand. They called in an outside producer who created an ingenious combination of live action and animation in eye-catching geometrics in the manner of Piet Mondrian. The result was both artistic and highly successful in terms of sales.

The Broadcast Audience

Control over the Speed of the Message. In the print media, readers can start at any point in the ad they like — the signature, the headline, or the illustration. They can review points that interest them. They can skim the ad or read the copy in detail. On the other hand, the advertiser has control in the case of television and radio. The listener or viewer must take the material as provided by the copywriter.

Personal Nature of Broadcast Media. Television and radio come into your living room, bedroom, or kitchen, or — with radio — into your automobile. Broadcast personalities thus are humanized to an extent impossible in the print media.

High Memory Value. Simple play on words, such as "There's less toil with Lestoil," or institutional slogans like "Better Things for Better Living through Chemistry" or melodic jingles usually gain better audience recall in broadcast media than in print.

Half-listening or Half-viewing. Because people seldom sit down pri-

[1]Louis Redmond, "Writing the TV Film Commercial," in Elbrun Rochford French, ed., *The Copywriter's Guide* (New York: Harper & Row, Publishers, 1959).

ily to listen to the radio, most of the thirteen hours a week the average person spends at the radio is actually half-listening. Even with
television, people may be doing something else at the time they are supposedly watching the screen.

Response to Key Words and Sounds. Key words or sounds are even
more important in the broadcast media than in print. For example, if
the opening words of a radio commercial about accident insurance are
only descriptive, chances are that a lot of listeners will not stay with
it but if the commercial begins with the wail of a siren, the audience
may be brought to attention.

RADIO COMMERCIALS

Although fewer dollars are spent on radio than on television, we shall
discuss radio writing first because it is ordinarily less complex than
television writing. (Many of our most successful television writers got
their start in radio.) Radio is a unique medium in one important respect—it is nonvisual. Sound alone must accomplish the communication
job. Once a mass medium for millions, it is more likely these days to
talk to smaller audiences of thousands. We shall examine some of the
types of commercials in modern radio and then discuss certain principles of writing effective commercials.

Types of Radio Commercials. In addressing the American Association of Advertising Agencies, President Kevin Sweeney of the Radio
Advertising Bureau listed four "schools of thought about the radio sales
message": (1) the say-it-with-music, or jingle school; (2) the one-minute
program or narrative-with-jokes school; (3) the straight commercial
—the mimeo-machine-is-an-agency's-best-friend school; and (4) the
personality commercial-let-the-personality-play-with-it school.

Jingles. The jingle is usually a catchy tune—perhaps original, perhaps based on a popular song of today or yesterday. It is one of the oldest
forms of advertising, although its real popularity came when it was
adapted to radio. In the early 1800s this commercial was used by a land
developer to attract people to the Midwest:

> Move your family westward; bring all your girls and boys,
> And rise to wealth and honor in the state of Illinois.

This one was used in the 1960s and was set to calypso music:

> Charley the horse was none too spry.
> His rider, Joe, was mighty dry,
> When lo, beneath the burning sky
> They heard the famous Ballantine cry.

Jingles need not be musical but usually they rhyme:

> 'Twas the night before Sunday
> And all through the house
> Mother searched for the Pall Malls—
> And so did her spouse.

Narrative. The narrative commercial obviously has a story to tell.
Because the time (usually 60 seconds or less) is quite short for plot

development, many commercials depend on humor. It is essential that the point of the story be relevant to the product reward you are trying to emphasize.

SAILOR: Columbus—we can't turn back without an order from you.
COLUMBUS: I'm not talking while the flavor lasts.
SAILOR: What are you chewing?
COLUMBUS: Beech-Nut gum.
SAILOR: We could be in for a long voyage.

Straight. This type of commercial is delivered by one person and is much like straight-line copy in the print media. No special devices are used to disguise the message. It is simple to produce and adaptable to almost any product or situation. It may start with something such as "I want to tell you about . . ." and end with "Try it." Or it may emphasize humor. In a commercial for General Motors Guardian Maintenance Service, Stan Freberg, who wrote the commercial, plays an off-beat garage man who has invented a way to bring car owners back for servicing. He says,

You see these golf balls? I peel 'em down to the long rubber band here, see . . . and put the ball in this metal box bolted to my work bench. Then out of that little hole I feel the end of the rubber band and I tie it to the rear bumper of the car when it leaves. Well, the ball starts unwinding in the box and when it's time for Guardian Maintenance, the car snaps back.

Personality. Certain personalities such as Don McNeil and Arthur Godfrey have done well with the personality commercial. There is danger, however, that the personality will get in the way of the message or that the copy will not be suited to the style of the personality. Here is an effective commercial written for Henry Morgan, long a well-known wit on radio and television:

HENRY: And now—the "Romance of Bubbles Hoffman." The story asks, "Can a woman over 35 find curliban?" As you remember, Helen is in the kitchen making a drink for Marvin, the hi-fi repair man who has come to fix her tweeter. "Irving," she says—she's terribly nearsighted—"please pass me that bottle of Hoffman pale dry ginger ale. It's by far the best ginger ale for mixing party drinks."
Meanwhile Edna, unbeknownst to George, has sent out for a case of Hoffman steady sparkle club soda for his party. She likes Hoffman pale dry ginger ale, too, but ever since Horace has been back from the hospital she had a case in the house. Well, what will happen now? Will Rocco *demand* the return of his motorcycle? To keep this thrilling drama on the air, buy Hoffman mixers. They keep your spirits up.

Writing Effective Radio Commercials. One leading research firm, Daniel Yankelovich, made a large-scale study of radio's impact, with special emphasis on what makes some radio commercials more effective than others in stimulating buying interest. Eight key elements were isolated, four of which the writer should strive for, four of which he should avoid:[2]

Four elements to strive for:

1. Make the content meaningful and informative about the product.
2. Stimulate a wide range of positive associations with the product.

[2] *The Yankelovich Report* (New York: ABC Radio Network, 1965).

3. Match the preconception that listeners already had toward the product.
4. Make the listener feel that he could see himself in the situation depicted.

Four elements to avoid:

1. Offense or alienation of the listener.
2. Suspicion and disbelief.
3. Confusion that distracts from the message.
4. Boredom and dullness.

Here are a few "rules" for writing effective radio commercials, regardless of the type:

1. *Make it sound the way people talk.* Monologues and conversation must sound natural. If they do not, the listening public soon loses interest in what is said. Consider the following commercial:

> ANNOUNCER: As the sun sinks in fiery splendor behind the purpling hills these days, a chill creeps in with the lengthening shadows that makes a Busco Electric Room Heater a welcome addition to any home. The wise wife and mother who owns one plugs it into a convenient outlet at sundown and with her family assembled, basks in comfortable relaxation. For what better purpose could one make the modest investment of only $21.75? — an investment that pays dividends of comfort throughout many years to come — an investment to be made today at your favorite store.

Here is a more conversational version:

> ANNOUNCER: You know what's going to happen when the sun sets tonight? It's going to get *chilly*. Not cold enough to start your furnace but cool enough so a spot of warmth will feel *mighty good* to you and your family. Here's a swell way to keep warm. Buy yourself a Busco Electric Room Heater. It floods an average size room with comfortable warmth in next to nothing flat. And it only costs $21.75. A Busco Electric Room Heater will keep you warm tonight — and on chilly nights for years to come. Remember that name — Busco.

2. *Spell out the product name.* If the name is at all confusing, spell it out at least once. Three times is usually better.
3. *Use short words and sentences.* These add a conversational lilt to the copy and give it better emphasis. "Fine" car has more punch than "excellent" or "exceptional" car.
4. *Supply the visual if needed.* If your product has a green label and it's the only one that has, get the package identification by saying so. You can say or sing "look for the green label."
5. *Repeat basic ideas.* Repetition is the heart of today's radio. Repetition per se does not become boring to today's half-listener. If possible, repeat with variations.
6. *Keep in mind how people listen.* Try to disengage their attention from washing the dishes or reading the newspaper long enough to get your message. Note this commercial for Levy's cinnamon raisin bread:

LITTLE BOY'S VOICE: I want Wevy's cimmumum waisin bwead.

HIS MOTHER'S VOICE: Not bwead—bread, not cimmumum—cinnamon, not Wevy's—Levy's.
MOTHER: All together now—
BOY: I want Wevy's cimmumum waisin bwead.

7. *Use sound in all its many dimensions.* Sound cannot show the audience how a new car looks, but it can dramatize a point of difference. Here is how Pall Mall makes sound easy to remember, "Particular people take particular pleasure in the good taste of Pall Mall."

TELEVISION COMMERCIALS

In the early days of television the emphasis was on copy. Later it was realized that pictures were as important as words. Now, copywriters are rated on the basis of their ability to create images as sharp and convincing as the words that accompany the images.

Rosser Reeves uses this parable to point up the central problem of the commercial writer:

You ring the doorbell. An unholy commotion busts loose inside, then the door opens six inches, and there, grimly, stands your prospect . . . The baby in her arms is pelting her with strained prunes. Little Johnny is clobbering little Suzy with an educational toy. The cocker spaniel is trying to squirm out the door with the lamb chops. The water is running over the sink and the telephone is ringing. You have exactly three and a half seconds to be fascinating before she slams the door in your face. What are you going to say? Answer that and you've got yourself the core of a good commercial.[3]

Television versus Radio Commercials. Radio is, of course, written for the ear, television for the eye and the ear. What is the difference in practice? This difference is perhaps best illustrated by the following Humble Oil (Enco) commercial for radio and a version that ran on television at the same time:

VOICE 1: Did you say a *tiger*?
VOICE 2: Yes, sir!
VOICE 1: In my gasoline tank?
VOICE 2: That's right, sir! You asked for ENCO/ESSO EXTRA Gasoline?
VOICE 1: Well, yes, but . . .
VOICE 2: Then there's a tiger in your tank!
VOICE 1: I find that hard to believe!
VOICE 2: Just remove the gas cap, sir.
SOUND: TIGER ROAR.
VOICE 1: I'll be darned!
MUSIC: TIGER RAG. ESTABLISH & FADE FOR:
REX: Let your ENCO/ESSO/HUMBLE dealer uncage a *tiger* for *you*! Just ask him to fill the tank with the Humble Company's *New* Power-formula ENCO/ESSO EXTRA gasoline! Talk about high octane! You'll take off like a cat! Talk about smooth performance . . . *New* Power-formula ENCO/ESSO EXTRA keeps your engine purring smooth, because it keeps it running *clean* . . . actually cleans the carburetor . . . helps restore lost power! *Today* . . . stop at the ENCO/ESSO/ HUMBLE Sign and . . . put a tiger in your tank!
MUSIC BUTTON.
REX: Happy Motoring!

[3]Rosser Reeves, quoted in French, p. 211.

Here is part of the television version. Note the use of "Tiger Rag" in both to tie them together.

VIDEO	AUDIO
1. CAMERA CARD: ART OF TIGER. (CU ON TIGER'S HEAD)	MUSIC: "TIGER RAG." ESTABLISH & UNDER FOR
2. PULL BACK TO SHOW TIGER WITH FLAG.	REX — VOICE OVER Whether he's flagging a winning race car across the finish line . . .
3. CUT TO TIGER PUSHING CAR.	Or giving *you* that extra push you need for lively starts . . .
4. MOVE IN ON TIGER'S HEAD.	. . . you can be sure of getting the best out of your car, when you ride with a *tiger* in your tank!
5. DISS TO REX BESIDE TIGER — DRESSED ENCO EXTRA PUMP.	SNEAK MUSIC OUT. REX — ON CAMERA Why? Because the tiger, High-Energy ENCO EXTRA Gasoline, boosts power *three ways.*
6. SUPER: "CLEANING POWER."	First . . *cleaning power*! ENCO EXTRA *cleans up* fouled carburetors . . . keeps engines starting fast . . . idling smooth

Kinds of Television Commercials. Some television experts divide commercials into three simple categories — live, film, and tape. Some classify them on the basis of time (10-second, 20-second). Some use the presentation format (straight announcer, demonstration). Some talk of commercials in terms of production techniques. This confusion testifies to the dynamic nature of modern television. It would be unfortunate if writers become too closely wedded to strict categories at this stage. However, some typology is helpful in organizing one's thinking. We shall examine some of the common formats and then some of the most common techniques used in connection with each.

Straight Announcement. As the name implies, this format consists primarily of someone (usually an announcer) delivering a sales talk directly to the camera, ordinarily pointing at or holding up the product while he talks. If the presenter is attractive and if his talk is well written, this can be quite effective — especially if it is combined with demonstration. There is a certain appeal in having an interesting personality talk to you, even through the screen. For example, one of the Lipton's Tea commercials started this way:

VIDEO	AUDIO
STAR IS SEATED AT TABLE, HOLDING UP PIECE OF PAPER . . .	STAR: I have here before me the latest masterpiece by the poet laureate of the advertising agency, Henry Wadsworth Pekoe. A few thousand words on the virtues of Lipton's Tea. It can all be condensed into just three or four. Take . . .

The economy of the straight announcement is obvious. One salesman and a simple set can do all the work. On the other hand, if the sales talk is too long, it may be a poor investment.

Demonstration. Demonstration is so important that it should be considered for every commercial. In many commercials, demonstration of the product or service is the dominant theme. Because people are interested in what products will do for them, demonstration is usually good communication. Here is an excellent demonstration for Dial Soap:

VIDEO	AUDIO
0 FT. FADE IN	2 FT. SILENT PULL-UP
PICTURE ON BLACKBOARD OF MAN WITH SOUR FACE. ART GILMORE WALKS INTO SCENE FROM FRAME LEFT.	People who like people . . . Oh! Oh! Wrong guy.
8 FT.—CUT TO PICTURE ON BLACKBOARD OF MAN WITH HAPPY FACE. ART GILMORE WALKS INTO SCENE FROM FRAME LEFT.	People who like people . . .
PAN WITH ART AS HE WALKS TO PICTURE OF DIAL BAR ON BLACKBOARD.	like Dial Soap. Because perspiration odor never comes between friends who use Dial.
ON CUE WORD "COMES" FAST PAN TO PICTURE ON BLACKBOARD OF HAPPY BOY AND GIRL. ART WALKS INTO SCENE FROM FRAME LEFT.	

VIDEO	AUDIO
PAN WITH ART AS HE WALKS TO OUTLINE OF DIAL BAR ON BLACKBOARD WITH LEGEND AT-7.	And here's the reason . . . the AT-7 in Dial removes the cause of odor like nothing else can.
32 FT.—5 FRAMES—CUT TO OUTLINE FIGURE OF MAN ON BLACKBOARD. UPPER PORTION OF BODY IS CHALKED IN. ART WALKS INTO SCENE FROM FRAME LEFT. ON CUE "BEST" ART BEGINS TO ERASE CHALK LEAVING RESIDUE ON MAN'S BODY.	And here's the cause . . . the bacteria that cover your skin. Most soaps— even the best of them—leave thousands
44 FT.—8 FRAMES—CUT TO INSERT OUTLINE MAN AS IN PREVIOUS SCENE. HAND ENTERS SCENE AND FINGERS MAKE A SWIPING MARK IN CHALK.	of these trouble-makers . . . . . . like this
47 FT.—2 FRAMES—CUT BACK TO ART STILL AT BLACKBOARD. ON CUE "AT-7" HE BEGINS TO ERASE CHALK RESIDUE TILL BOARD IS CLEAN	But Dial's AT-7 gets off more than 95%!
62 FT.—5 FRAMES—TO CUT BACK TO ART AND PAN WITH HIM TO OUTLINE PICTURE OF BATHTUB WITH SHOWER. TITLE "MILLIONS" IS ON BATHTUB.	People who use Dial . . . (And you can count them in millions)
PAN WITH ART AS HE CROSSES TO PICTURE OF FLOWER ON BLACKBOARD. FACE OF CLOCK IS IN THE FLOWER. ON CUE WORD "ODOR" ART DRAWS HANDS ON CLOCK.	don't have to do another thing—to keep themselves free from odor every minute of the day. Aren't you glad you use Dial? (Don't you wish everybody did?)

78 FT.—ON CUE WORD "USE" CUT TO IN-
SERT CLOSE-UP DIAL BAR.

82 FT.—5 FRAMES—ON CUE WORD "DID"   Dial . . . the soap for people who
CUT BACK TO ART AND PAN WITH HIM AS
HE WALKS TO OUTLINE OF A NUMBER OF   like people. . . .
HAPPY FACES ON BLACKBOARD.

FADE OUT.

90 FT. . . .

Often demonstration commercials are filmed or taped because the
best of products occasionally fail to operate correctly—for example, the
refrigerator door will not open. The demonstrator should be someone
who might be expected to use the product under the circumstances shown
or to demonstrate it in a store. It is most important that the point of the
demonstration be as clear and dramatic as it is in the Dial commercial.

Testimonial. In the testimonial commercial someone whose word
carries "authority" recommends the product. Frequently it is a sports
star, a movie personality, or someone else well known to the public.
Sometimes just an ordinary looking housewife may provide the most convincing testimonial that the food preparation or the appliance will work.
In a series of tests Schwerin Research found that a little girl was a more
effective testifier for a cake mix than a prominent chef. The firm concluded that the chef was possibly too expert for the advertiser's purpose:
to show how easy it was to get good results. If the little girl could get
good results, obviously any housewife could also.

Dramatization. In a dramatized commercial the point is presented
through a story. The theme is often presented as a contrast ("before
using the product" versus "after"), or it shows that satisfaction is
achieved (from using the product). If the situation is interesting and the

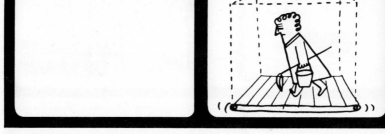

FIG. 22.1 (a)
*Storyboard for one of
television's most
successful commercials.*
CLIENT: GENERAL FOODS;
AGENCY: YOUNG &
RUBICAM, INC.

WE OPEN ON A GRIM LITTLE   WOMAN'S VOICE: FLAT, WEARY
STEINBERG HOUSEWIFE WITH   MONOTONE:
MOP AND BUCKET...ON TREAD-   Busy day! Busy, busy,
MILL, INSIDE HER SQUARE   busy, busy...
HOUSE...INDICATED BY DOT-   SWEPT UNDER BY RISING
TED LINE.   MARCH, PLAYED ON HORN,
                                  BASS DRUM, AND CYMBALS.
                                  STEADILY IT PLAYS, TO
                                  MATCH THE ENDLESS TREAD-
                                  MILL...STEADILY...AND
                                  BUILDING TOWARD THE LAST.

A TELEPHONE SNAPS IN AND
RINGS...AND IN CONTRAST TO
ITS PIERCING, FRANTIC TONE
...WOMAN'S VOICE:
Too busy....

A HAND SNAPS IN AND KNOCKS
ON DOOR. WOMAN'S VOICE:
Too busy....
THE DOOR SLAMS.

A BABY SNAPS IN...AND
CRIES. WOMAN'S VOICE:
Oh, Herbert!

POTS AND PANS RATTLE: BUT
THE POTS AND PANS (CYM-
BALS) INSIST AND BUILD...

OUTLINE OF BOX DRAWS IN.

DISSOLVE TO CU OF WOMAN'S
HANDS PUTTING PUDDING IN
BOWL. ANNOUNCER:
Just add to milk

FIG. 22.1 (b)   CLIENT:
GENERAL FOODS; AGENCY:
YOUNG & RUBICAM, INC.

characters are attractive, the dramatization may be very effective. An
excellent dramatized commercial done in animation is shown in storyboard form in Figure 22.1a through 22.1d.

Dramatization is particularly well adapted to television because the
story can be told with the use of both sound and picture. Though the

WOMAN'S HANDS BEGIN TO
BEAT. ANNOUNCER:
and beat! In minutes...
this terrific new busy-day
dessert is...

CUT TO SINGLE FINISHED
PUDDING. ANNOUNCER: (OVER)
ready to eat! Creamy...
nourishing...sooh deli-
cious! And so quick...

DISSOLVE TO ANIMATION
AGAIN. NOW HAPPY WOMAN
HOLDS BOX OF PUDDING AS
SHE PASSES LITTLE GIRL
CARRYING DISHES FROM
TABLE. ANNOUNCER:
you can make it just be-
fore dessert time...while
the children are clearing
the table!

ANIMATION MOVES TO LITTLE
BOY WITH BOWL AND BEATER.
LITTLE GIRL ADDS PUDDING
...HE STARTS TO WHIP IT
UP. ANNOUNCER:
Or let the children make
it themselves...It's that
easy!

FIG. 22.1 (c) CLIENT:
GENERAL FOODS; AGENCY:
YOUNG & RUBICAM, INC.

BLACK LINES BEGIN TO
SWIRL. WOMAN'S VOICE:
Dinner time...oooh, DINNER
TIME! Too late to make
dessert!

SCREEN IS FILLED WITH
BLACK LINES.

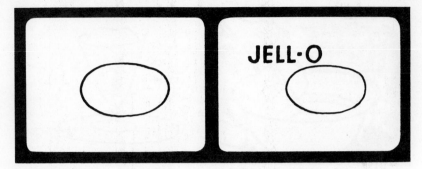

SCREEN CLEARS AND OVAL
OUTLINE DRAWS IN. AN-
NOUNCER: (OVER)
Wait! It's not too late to
make dessert! Never too
late anymore! Because
now...

"JELL-O" SNAPS IN. AN-
NOUNCER:
The Jell-O Family of fa-
mous desserts brings
you...

"NEW INSTANT PUDDING"
SNAPS IN. ANNOUNCER:
new Jell-O Instant Pud-
ding...

"NO COOKING" SNAPS IN.
ANNOUNCER:
That needs NO COOKING!

DISSOLVE TO SINGLE LIVE
BIG PACKAGE. ANNOUNCER:
New Jell-O Instant Pud-
dings are at your grocer's
now!

CUT TO 3 PACKAGES...WITH
SUPER "NEW BUSY-DAY DES-
SERT." ANNOUNCER:
Stock up...with the ter-
rific new busy-day dessert
...New Jell-O Instant Pud-
dings!

FIG. 22.1 (d) CLIENT:
GENERAL FOODS; AGENCY:
YOUNG & RUBICAM, INC.

audience knows the ending will be happy and the product will come out on top, there is a basic interest in dramatic situations and an innate curiosity in most audiences that help to hold attention.

Documentary. Occasionally a dramatized commercial will be handled in documentary form. This is particularly true in commercials that have institutional objectives. Sometimes the story is that of research behind a firm's leadership or the development of a new product. One Du Pont commercial was built around the development of "Mylar." It began this way:

FADE IN:
(MUSIC: IN AND UNDER)
1. Our camera is shooting directly through a film of "Mylar" which is fastened in a frame that can be removed. The background can fade into shadow. All we see clearly is a boy about sixteen in a baseball uniform. He winds up elaborately and pitches the ball right at the camera. It strikes the "Mylar" and bounces off.

ANNOUNCER (O.S.)

Strike one!

CUT TO:

2. Medium shot of commentator in office in which "Mylar" frame is fastened in wall. Commentator is beside frame.

COMMENTATOR

Now, why didn't that ball smash the camera lens?
Here's why. . . .

Dialogue. Any commercial in which two or more people are talking could be called a dialogue commercial. In practice, the dialogue is usually part of some other type of commercial (dramatization, testimonial, documentary). It is an obvious method of stimulating interest. However, in writing any dialogue it is most important that the lines given the actors be within the possible experience of the characters involved and therefore credible.

Harry Wayne McMahan describes five techniques available for television film and tape commercials: cartoon, live action, stop motion, puppets, and photo animation.[4] To this we might add such live techniques as camera card or film with live voice over.

Cartoon. Says McMahan, in describing the cartoon:

In television commercials, the animated cartoon often has the highest viewer interest, the longest life, and lowest cost-per-showing. Yet it remains the most misused and abused technique in the business . . .

From a psychological standpoint, the cartoon is primitive, childlike in imagination. The cartoon is not *you*, it is someone else. When it becomes too rational and tries to depict actual people in normal activities, it becomes unbelievable.[5]

Notice in the Jell-O storyboard how skillfully the cartoon material is combined with live action so that it will never become so unreal that the housewife will fail to identify herself with the reward. This commercial won the gold medal in the New York Art Directors' competition and was considered by *Advertising Age's* "Eye and Ear Man" as "one of

[4]Harry Wayne McMahan, *The Television Commercial* (New York: Hastings House Publishers, Inc., 1957), chaps. 7–12.
[5]McMahan, pp. 87–88.

the best TV commercials yet written." It is rare that a clear-cut sales success can be ascribed to any one advertisement or any one campaign, because of the influence of other marketing variables. On this occasion, however, Jell-O instant pudding was introduced by these commercials and these commercials alone, and within a few weeks the advertiser had sold far more of his product than was originally expected. It was observed that the pudding sold out as fast in areas without any special pricing to help the introduction as it did in areas where a special two for one deal was offered.

The following commercial is entirely cartoon. Note how skillfully it blends dramatization and humor to make its point.

VIDEO	AUDIO
HAND HOLDS "ON THE AIR" SIGN.	($1\frac{1}{2}$ SECOND SILENCE)
MR. OOPS RUNS BEHIND SIGN.	Ah—
SIGN IS REMOVED. MR. OOPS STANDING BESIDE STACK OF DIRTY DISHES.	Fellow dishwashers . . . Are you beset by a . . .
ELECTRICIAN MOVES INTO SCENE WITH A SPOTLIGHT.	tired and listless . . .
ELECTRICIAN FIDDLES WITH LIGHT TO THE ANNOYANCE OF MR. OOPS.	tired and listless . . .
OOPS INDICATES DISHPAN.	*Detergent* that lets dishwater get flat
CU OF DISHPAN AS SUDS START TO GET "TIRED" AND END UP "GREASY."	and ugh—greasy?
CU TO MR. OOPS PUSHING DISHPAN OFF-CAMERA. IN SO DOING HE HITS SPOTLIGHT STAND.	Well, then may I suggest—
SPOTLIGHT STARTS TO WOBBLE.	new Liquid Chiffon? It puts dishwashing in a
SPOTLIGHT FALLS ON MR. OOPS AND THE LIGHT GOES OUT.	new *light* . . . (SOUND: CRASH)
MR. OOPS DIMLY SILHOUETTED IN DARKNESS.	Heh—Heh . . .
MR. OOPS GETS TO HIS FEET TO CONTINUE HIS MESSAGE.	Little dark—heh—heh . . .
HOLDS UP CHIFFON CAN.	This *extra-rich*—
CU OF CHIFFON CAN STILL IN SILHOUETTE. OOPS STRIKES A MATCH TO LIGHT UP THE CHIFFON LABEL.	Liquid Chiffon . . .
ADDS CHIFFON TO ANOTHER DISHPAN OF DISHES. SUDS RISE TO COVER STACK OF DISHES.	Actually absorbs the grease in dishwater.
OOPS ADDS UTENSILS TO PILE OF SUDS.	It stays sudsy and keeps on cleaning dishes—long after other detergents stop.
OOPS HOLDS UP PAN AND A GLASS.	That's why your *last* pan is as bright as your *first* glass!
LIGHTS COME ON BRIGHTLY.	Oooooooo . . . Well not *that* bright . . . but brighter than ever before!

VIDEO	AUDIO
OOPS HOLDS UP CAN OF LIQUID CHIFFON	Yet, *on your* . . .
ANIMATED HAND REACHES OUT FROM CAN AND PATS OOPS ON THE HEAD. HE BLUSHES.	*hands, Chiffon* is gentle as its name . . .
LS OF OOPS. ELECTRICIAN WALKS BY WITH SPOTLIGHT. OOPS IS STANDING IN LOOP OF CORD FROM SPOTLIGHT.	*Oh my*, but you'll be so happy with this . . .
AS CORD TIGHTENS AROUND OOPS ANKLES HE IS PULLED OFF OF HIS FEET AND TO-WARDS DOORWAY AT SCREEN LEFT.	*exceptional extra ordinary energetic hard-working hand-smoothing* . . .
OOPS HANGS ON TO DOOR JAMB, HOLDING UP CAN OF CHIFFON.	*extra-rich* . . .
CORD CONTINUES TO PULL OOPS OFF SCREEN. AS HE LETS GO OF DOOR THE CAN OF CHIFFON ZOOMS UP TO FULL SCREEN.	NEW LIQUID CHIFFON!

Live Action. Live action brings the viewer into a world of reality. He should be able to identify the characters and the situation with everyday life. In a Kitchens of Sara Lee commercial curtains open and this scene takes place:

VIDEO	AUDIO
OPEN ON SHEER DRAPERIES GENTLY BLOWING CAMERA MOVES IN	SOUND: LIGHT, AIRY MUSIC, SOFT HARP GLISSANDO ANNCR: When you're looking for something *extra* special *extra* delicious
CURTAINS PART AS CAMERA APPROACHES	for your family and guests you want THE "NEW" SARA LEE ALL BUTTER
CAMERA IN FOR CLOSE-UP OF CAKE	CINNAMON NUT COFFEE CAKE

Stop Motion. Stop motion is an ingenious technique in that it can make products march, walk, dance, and do tricks. The product is set up and photographed for the first frame of film, then moved to its next position, photographed again, and so on. The result is that twenty-four successive photographs, when projected, give the illusion of movement of one second's duration.

Puppets. The three common types of puppets used in television commercials are string puppets (*Howdy Doody*), hand puppets (*Kukla and Ollie*), and stop-motion puppets (*Mr. Aristocrat Tomato* for H. J. Heinz).

Photo Animation. This is a low-budget technique that can, if carefully used, be most effective. The commercial is photographed on a stand, like the cartoon, using stills, sketches, and titles. Its effectiveness depends on the ingenuity of the script writer in creating interesting tricks with products, boxes, bottles, and so forth, that will present his ideas effectively.

Writing Effective Television Commercials. The writing of television commercials is relatively new and the cost of failure is so high that advertisers and agencies have spent millions of dollars in research to find out which commercials are the most effective—and why. Here are some principles that have emerged from this research:

Visualize the Message. In *My Fair Lady* Eliza sings, "Don't talk of love—*show* me" to her verbose suitor. This, says Louis Redmond, is a "canon for all TV commercial writers to follow. The eyes are the royal road to the brain . . . In television you must show what you are telling, and tell what you are showing."[6] You should always make sure that the video and audio portions work together, but don't waste words describing what is obvious in the video. Mr. Redmond stresses the importance of using many close-ups and saving the most important picture idea for the most important point—a visual epigram.

Schwerin tests show that advertisers should "employ the video but make certain that the audio reinforces it." Too many words can hurt the commercial's impact. Schwerin's studies indicated that those 60-second commercials with 101–110 words are most effective and those with 170 or more words least effective.

Demonstrate. Whether you are demonstrating the product performing its normal function, a side-by-side comparison with a competing product, or something totally unexpected (for example, an electric razor shaving a peach), it is most important that the demonstration be plausible. A demonstration should never appear to be a camera trick. Note how convincingly and naturally the demonstration is tied into the Jell-O "busy day commercial." And a Betty Crocker cake mix commercial opened with this demonstration:

VIDEO	AUDIO
OPEN ON TIGHT SHOT LIVE ANGEL FOOD CAKE AND BETTY CROCKER PACKAGE. SAMPLER EDGE IS IN BACKGROUND.	WOMAN'S (VOICE OVER) (SOFT STORY TELLING QUALITY) With time-savers like Betty Crocker Cake Mixes in the kitchen—life is so much simpler and easier—
TILT UP TO REVEAL SAMPLER. MOVE IN TIGHT SHOT SAMPLER AND MOTTO.	than it was in days like this. (SOUND: MUSIC BOX TINKLE)

Du Pont and its agency wanted to demonstrate how the firm's antifreeze, Zerex, can work even under the most difficult circumstances. It was decided to show a car working perfectly even though embedded

[6]Redmond, p. 211.

in a block of ice. A man chipped his way to the car door, then drove away in the car. However, in filming this action, it was found that ice was too bulky and cloudy, and it was difficult to show the silhouette of the car through the block of ice. For filming the commercial, Lucite was the answer. A metal block was built around the car to shape the Lucite mold. The metal was removed and the Lucite was treated with a resin and crinkled celophane which gave it a translucent look.

Simplify. It is always wise to simplify — especially in television. The viewer, after all, is often not paying close attention to the commercial — to the backgrounds, the scenes, or to what is said. In general, television is less tolerant of complex wording than is print media. The simple declarative sentence is usually preferable to the rhetorical one, and often a sentence fragment or a simple, everyday word will make the meaning perfectly clear. In the interest of simplicity every element not relevant to the objective should be dropped.

Use Action Where Possible. The eye comprehends very quickly, but it easily travels away. However, motion on the screen makes it difficult for the viewer to leave the commercial. According to Agnew and O'Brien, "A picture should be simple enough to grasp in five seconds; so, as a rule of thumb, a picture should not be kept static any longer than that."[7]

Don't Use Entertainment for Its Own Sake. Entertainment, in a commercial at least, should be a means to an end. It is simply a vehicle to help you get your point across in a painless way. Schlitz has successfully run a series of entertaining television commercials featuring Sid Raymond. The purpose of this series is to provide the framework for the reward concept. The commercials stress the consumer use of Schlitz as a reward for a good day's work. All of the Sid Raymond commercials attempt to identify the brand with the friendly and engaging personality of Sid. In one of the most successful of these Sid has a mysterious visitor to his tavern who shows him the "Gusto Gun," a little cannon whose cannonballs turn mysteriously to glasses of foamy, Schlitz beer. Fantasy is used here both to entertain and to drive home the advertising point.

Adapt the Commercial to the Program. This applies, of course, mainly to program commercials or participations in a show. It is natural to have "Gunsmoke's" Matt Dillon (James Arness) say a few kind words for L & M Cigarettes after each dramatic episode. It might not be so acceptable for him to step out of character while the criminal hunt is on to tell you what brand he smokes. In general, it is wise to keep the commercial sufficiently compatible with the show so that the viewer is not jarred too abruptly, but different enough so that it registers some commercial message.

Above All, Make Commercials Believable. Achievement of believability is one of the oldest "principles" of *any* type of writing, and it has special application to television. Falseness of any sort — in language, in idea, in the settings — is more easily discernible in television than in any other medium. The television commercial starts out with an initial disadvantage (people are more likely to believe something in print), but

[7]Clark M. Agnew and Neil O'Brien, *Television Advertising* (New York: McGraw-Hill, Inc., 1958), p. 98.

carefully chosen language, settings, and scenes can do much to create believability. In a Lava Soap commercial believability is achieved by concentrating on strong working hands that get really dirty. The problem for this prosaic product was to make the soap interesting and the message believable. The solution decided on was to show close-ups of the hands of rugged, virile men who worked at unusual jobs such as wrestling the parts of an oil rig into place or driving a 20-ton bulldozer.

Coordination of Commercial Elements. Ideally, television communication uses all three of its dimensions—sound, picture, and motion. As noted earlier, good communication starts with a plan and usually comes to focus (particularly in filmed commercials) as a *storyboard*. Walt Disney is usually credited with establishing the storyboard in film making. Instead of roughing out each of the twenty-four frames shown per second, he found that it required relatively few drawings to show the progress of the story and indicate the action required at each step.

Agnew and O'Brien note four purposes that storyboards serve: (1) visualization of the story to be told; (2) immediate revelation of any weakness in script or concept; (3) provision of information for cost estimates; and (4) service as the shooting script.[8]

Note in the storyboard in Figures 22.1a–22.1d how the animated cartoon opening builds up the consumer reward. Notice that only twenty frames have been used to show the entire action in this 60-second commercial.

COLOR COMMERCIALS

We have already noted that color is making strong headway in all media. By 1967 more than 80 percent of the commercials coming out of the big agencies were in color. Shows in color generally have higher ratings—though not necessarily because of the color. A Crossley study showed that color commercials were 34 percent better remembered than black and white, and 69 percent more persuasive in their ability to make the viewer want to buy the product. Rememberance of sales points was 59 percent higher for color than for black and white in similar commercials.

The following illustrations, Figures 22.2(a)–22.2(f), record the principal details of the production of ten television commercials made for the television broadcasts of *"The Magnificent Yankee"* and *"Lamp at Midnight"* for the Hallmark Hall of Fame. The agency that developed the commercials is Foote, Cone & Belding. The subjects were valentines, Mother's Day messages, everyday greeting cards, and gift wraps and ribbons.

Gordon Webber, television vice-president of Benton and Bowles, warned advertisers that color commercials would cost from 20 to 30 percent more than black and white. He suggested the following nine guidelines for the proper use of color:

1. Color film is less flexible than black and white in its exposure, its development, and its printing.

[8]Agnew and O'Brien, p. 139.

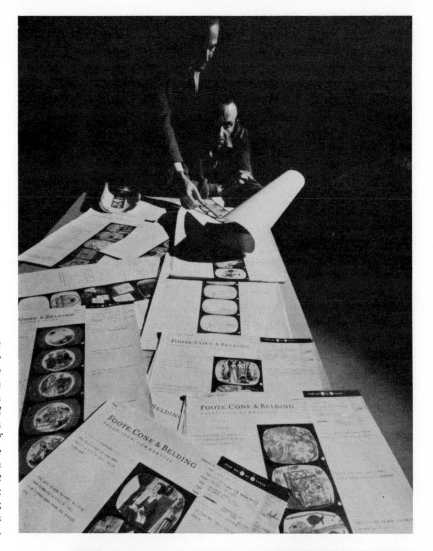

FIG. 22.2 (a) *The art director and copy director review picture possibilities for Hallmark color television commercials to be used in connection with two "Hallmark Hall of Fame" telecasts. Note the color television storyboards in front of them.* CLIENT: HALLMARK CARDS; AGENCY: FOOTE, CONE & BELDING.

FIG. 22.2 (b) *The copy supervisor at the agency and three of her writers select the specific products to be featured in these commericals. Sometimes they will consider as many as 1000 items before choosing the dozen or so Hallmark items that seem to be most expressive and are clearly demonstrable of the whole line.* CLIENT: HALLMARK CARDS; AGENCY: FOOTE, CONE & BELDING.

FIG. 22.2 (c) *Costumes
for the cast are fitted in
the wardrobe department.
Some have been designed
especially for these
Hallmark commercials.
More than 300 models
were tested for the
51 roles in this series of
commercials.* CLIENT:
HALLMARK CARDS;
AGENCY: FOOTE, CONE &
BELDING.

FIG. 22.2 (d)
*Construction of sets
for the commercials
includes the carefully
textured exterior of a
contemporary brick house
and the high arched
stone entrance to a
medieval castle. In
close-up scenes their
appearance must be solid
and authentic.* CLIENT:
HALLMARK CARDS;
AGENCY: FOOTE, CONE &
BELDING.

FIG. 22.2 (e) *The
last step is the recording
of the announcer's
voice and the music,
which will be
synchronized with video
tape and become the
sound track. Last-minute
cuts and revisions are
given the announcer by
the agency copy director
and the advertiser's
own representative,
both of whom began work
on these nine minutes
of broadcasting months
ago.* CLIENT: HALLMARK
CARDS; AGENCY: FOOTE,
CONE & BELDING.

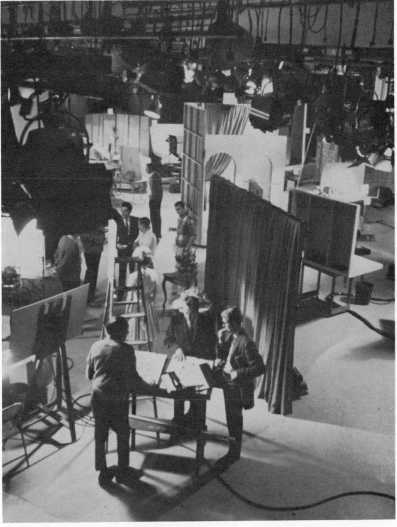

FIG. 22.2 (f) *In this way two complete commercials may be taped by the four cameras in a single day by the agency personnel for Hallmark. Thus, weeks of work are compressed into minutes.* CLIENT: HALLMARK; AGENCY: FOOTE, CONE & BELDING.

2. It takes longer to produce an acceptable color print of a commercial—from two to three weeks longer.

3. Don't use color unless there is a reason—preferably an advertising reason.

4. Full, well-lighted scenes are generally better than sharply contrasting highlights and shadow lighting.

5. Quality printing from 16 mm. reduction prints and especially 16 mm. contact prints from 35 mm. originals increases print density and contrast.

6. Use color balance that will produce a good monochrome as well as a good color print.

7. Strive for consistency in background and lighting.

8. Do some experimental color shooting of packages before full production for color correction.

9. You can screen test in color simply and fast by using 16 mm. Kodachrome 2 reversal stock.[9]

[9]Gordon Webber, "The Color Revolution," talk before the Eastern Annual Conference, American Association of Advertising Agencies, October 27, 1965.

Color may be used for almost any type of commercial. On one hand, we find it used in a documentary manner to show how the Chrysler Marsh Amphibian goes through the Everglades. On the other, we find it used in an impressionistic, semi-abstract manner to suggest Beech-Nut "Five Mint Gum." It is especially adaptable to animation. Schwerin tests indicate that it can pay off particularly "if there is a need to put across the idea of two or more varieties of the product or the contrasting results of using or not using it."[10] Schwerin warns, however, that when the treatment is documentary, it is sometimes preferable to stay away from color—"a truth that TV may well be advised to borrow from the Italian movie makers."

According to Schwerin two danger signals are already evident:

1. Using as much color as possible, changing scenes frequently and getting a jumpy effect.
2. Making the presenter (a beautiful girl, for example) so colorful that the product is lost.

Some have suggested that color television is indeed a new medium of communications and that it involves use of a new language. For example, T. Joseph Scanlon found some support in experiments for three hypotheses which he had formulated: "that color changes the emotional impact of television; that color alters the importance of the spoken word; that color makes viewers more participants and less observers. In short, that color is a new language."[11]

SUMMARY

General communication principles apply to *both* the print and the broadcast media. However, television and radio are different from the print media in that they are time-oriented, somewhat simpler in structure, emphasize showmanship and entertainment more, are more personal, achieve a high degree of recollection for simple ideas and have to depend on a less attentive audience.

The main types of radio commercials are jingles, narrative, straight, and personality. For commercials, modern radio tends to be a spot announcement medium. Effective commercials are distinguished from ineffective ones in the following ways: most sound quite conversational (unless they are jingles), they use short words and sentences, indicate the visual when needed, are strong on repetition, and use sound in all its many dimensions.

New as television is, already distinguishable types of commercials and certain principles of effective television writing have emerged. The common types of commercials are straight announcement, demonstration, testimonial, dramatization, documentary, dialogue, and reminder. If we classify them by technique we find the main ones are cartoon, live action, stop motion, puppets, and photo animation.

The more effective commercials work on a visual basis, they demonstrate, they simplify the message, they use action, they use enter-

[10]*SRC Bulletin*, 14, no. 4 (April 1966).
[11]T. Joseph Scanlon, "Color Television: New Language?" *Journalism Quarterly*, Summer 1967.

tainment as a device rather than an end in itself, they fit the mood of the program, and, above all, they are believable.

The great new field of color commercials, if wisely used, provides a potential for increasing the effectiveness of the medium.

QUESTIONS FOR DISCUSSION

1. How does broadcast time orientation influence the content of radio and television commercials?
2. What purposes does a jingle serve? How do you account for its continued popularity?
3. What are the principal types of television commercials? Find an example of each on your local television station and appraise its effectiveness.
4. Which commercials have impressed you most with their communication effectiveness? Why?
5. How has the trend toward the "magazine" concept and cosponsorship, or multiple sponsorship, of television commercials influenced the writing of commercials?
6. For what types of products is the color commercial likely to be most effective?

SUGGESTED READINGS

Agnew, Clark M., and Neil O'Brien, *Television Advertising.* New York: McGraw-Hill, Inc., 1958. Chapters 5–8.

Bellaire, Arthur, *TV Advertising: A Handbook of Modern Practice.* New York: Harper & Row, Publishers, 1959. Chapters 6–13.

Chester, Giraud, Garnett R. Garrison and Edgar E. Willis. *Television and Radio.* 3rd edition. New York: Appleton-Century-Crofts, 1963.

Coleman, Howard W., ed., *Color Television—The Business of Colorcasting.* New York: Hastings House Publishers, 1968.

Dunn, S. Watson, *Advertising Copy and Communication.* New York: McGraw-Hill, Inc., 1956. Chapters 15–16.

French, Elbrun Rochford, ed., *The Copywriter's Guide.* New York: Harper & Row, Publishers, 1959. Chapters 15–19.

McMahan, Harry Wayne, *The Television Commercial.* New York: Hastings House Publishers, Inc., 1957. Chapters 7–12.

Ogilvy, David, *Confessions of an Advertising Man.* New York: Atheneum Publishers, 1963. Chapter 8.

Ross, Wallace A., ed., *Best TV Commercials of the Year.* New York: Hastings House Publishers, Inc., 1967.

Seehafer, Gene F., and Jack W. Laemmar, *Successful Television and Radio Advertising.* New York: McGraw-Hill, Inc., 1959. Chapter 9.

Steiner, Gary A., *The People Look at Television.* New York: Alfred A. Knopf, 1963.

23 | Creative Case Histories

Some advertising and promotion campaigns are effective in part but not in their entirety. Some have tremendous attention-getting power but do not hold the reader's or viewer's interest and therefore do not project the basic advertising idea. Others are interesting, but the audience does not really believe what is said. Some contain information but create little or no impulse to act. In this chapter are summarized some outstanding advertising campaigns of recent years. They are Chase Manhattan's "You Have a Friend at Chase Manhattan," Green Giant Food's "Jolly Green Giant," Yellow Pages' "Let Your Fingers Do the Walking," American Oil Company's "Keeping a Promise," Curad's "The Ouchless Bandage," and Goodyear's, "When There's No Man Around, Goodyear Should Be." These were selected by a committee of top advertising agency executives to represent various categories of creative problems successfully handled. Each was based on a good idea successfully executed in a series of advertisements.

CHASE MANHATTAN BANK[1]

Chase Manhattan was known as a great commercial bank. It com-

[1]Based on a presentation by Donald E. Booth, vice-president and creative director, Ted Bates & Company, before the American Association of Advertising Agencies, Eastern Annual Conference, New York.

Your savings earn interest right up to the day you withdraw. Listen!

WOM: If I take five hundred dollars out in the middle of this interest period, will I lose interest on it?

SHIPLEY: Not at Chase Manhattan.

With many other savings accounts,

you'd lose the interest earned since the interest period started.

you have a friend at Chase Manhattan... the bank that serves New York, the nation and the world.

FIG. 23.1 (Above)   *One of the early "You have a friend at Chase Manhattan" commercials.* CLIENT: CHASE MANHATTAN BANK; AGENCY: TED BATES & COMPANY.

FIG. 23.2 (Below) *This "You have a friend..." attempts to identify the bank with its market—New Yorkers.* CLIENT: CHASE MANHATTAN BANK; AGENCY: TED BATES & COMPANY.

manded the public's respect, but in 1960 respect was not enough because the big source of deposit money was drying up. Corporations were switching their deposits from banks into nonbank investments.

After research and creating, the third leg of the tripod was media. Chase had used every medium but painted rocks. Bates media philosophy is to put all your eggs in one medium. They wanted massive frequency at the lowest cost per thousand—spot television. Note Figure 23.1 to see how it was used.

Bill Shipley's straightforward announcement worked. People began to change their minds about Chase. The next campaign identified Chase with its market—New Yorkers. (See Figure 23.2.)

If you need money for any worthwhile purpose

check Chase first. Save on interest at a full service bank. Remember,

you have a friend at Chase Manhattan.

By the time these spots were retired, New Yorkers knew they had a friend at Chase Manhattan. The theme recall was great. But how about recall of bank services? As can be seen in Figure 23.3, "You have a friend . . ." went from 8 percent in 1960 to 17 percent, 29 percent, 37 percent, 43 percent, and 45 percent. By 1965 it was 58 percent. Instead of the vague cluttered impression the public had had of the bank, the agency and advertiser were getting a strong theme recall and a significant recall of the advertised bank service. In three years the "friend" theme gave Chase a 25 percent awareness rating. (See Figure 23.4.) This is especially interesting in view of the fact that a major competitor was outspending Chase Manhattan 4 to 1 in advertising.

Subsequent commercials were designed not only to keep the friend theme going but also to emphasize individual bank services. A current example is shown in Figure 23.5. In this commercial there was no loss in theme recall—the "home mortgage" theme got 57 percent recall, and the specific USP (Unique Selling Proposition)—"No prepayment penalty"—got a 52 percent recall. That is like getting a 300 percent return on your investment.

FIG. 23.3
CLIENT: CHASE
MANHATTAN BANK;
AGENCY: TED BATES &
COMPANY.

DETAILED ANALYSIS OF CHASE MANHATTAN COPY RECALL

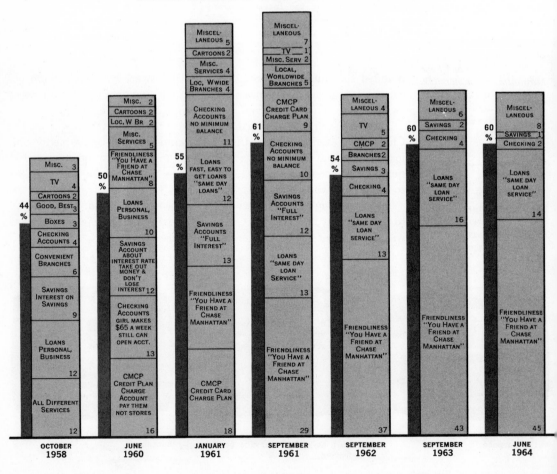

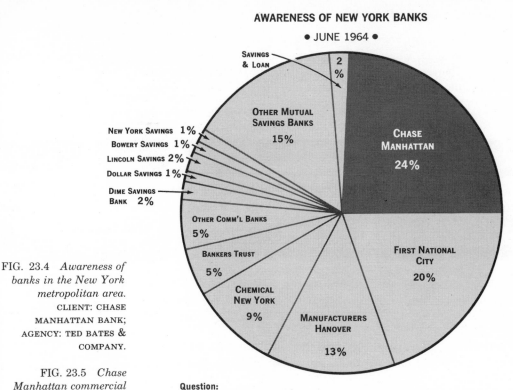

AWARENESS OF NEW YORK BANKS

• JUNE 1964 •

SAVINGS & LOAN — 2%

OTHER MUTUAL SAVINGS BANKS 15%

CHASE MANHATTAN 24%

NEW YORK SAVINGS 1%
BOWERY SAVINGS 1%
LINCOLN SAVINGS 2%
DOLLAR SAVINGS 1%

DIME SAVINGS BANK 2%

OTHER COMM'L BANKS 5%

BANKERS TRUST 5%

CHEMICAL NEW YORK 9%

MANUFACTURERS HANOVER 13%

FIRST NATIONAL CITY 20%

FIG. 23.4 *Awareness of banks in the New York metropolitan area.* CLIENT: CHASE MANHATTAN BANK; AGENCY: TED BATES & COMPANY.

FIG. 23.5 *Chase Manhattan commercial which emphasizes individual services of the bank.* CLIENT: CHASE MANHATTAN BANK; AGENCY: TED BATES & COMPANY.

Question:
"Would you name a bank which does business in the New York Area? Just tell me the name of the first one that comes to mind?"

My new mortgage is with Chase Manhattan Bank.

No pre-payment penalties on a Chase Home Martgage. Oh, here dear.

Any time I want to pay up my Chase Martgage

and at no extra cost.

You know they really mean it.

when they say...you have a friend at Chase Manhattan.

The big idea, "You have a friend at Chase Manhattan," changed the public mind about Chase. It changed the viewpoint and attitudes of every bank employee from guards to bank officers. It also changed the advertising philosophy of the entire banking industry. Most important, it brought in billions of dollars in new business.

(Chorus) In the valley of the Jolly...(ho! ho! ho!)...Green Giant!

(Chorus) Good things from the garden...garden in the valley...

...valley of the Jolly...(ho! ho!)...Green Giant!

GREEN GIANT FOODS[2]

In Jolly Green Giant ads, canned vegetables and frozen vegetables have followed very different formats. In Figure 23.6 is an ad for Green Giant Brand Baby Peas (canned). On the other hand, frozen corn utilizes the sort of approach shown in Figure 23.7. The first format is one you might call the "basic" one. The formula embodied there is this:

FIG. 23.6   *Typical commercial for canned Green Giant baby peas.* CLIENT: GREEN GIANT; AGENCY: LEO BURNETT COMPANY, INC.

Try to create a strong television personality for the brand and sell the individual items for their specific appeals within the framework.

Try Green Giant Niblets Corn frozen in Butter Sauce, and you'll say...

GNOME: Ho, ho! That's the ol' goin' in there Giant baby!

...from the Green Giant. Ho, ho!

Although the idea is not new and depends on execution, it has some obvious merits in operation:

1. It can make a 22-cent can of corn or a 19-cent can of peas into good television.
2. It's efficient because a commercial for any *one* item is a commercial for all the others too.

FIG. 23.7   *Commercial for Green Giant frozen corn. Note the difference in approach.* CLIENT: GREEN GIANT; AGENCY: LEO BURNETT COMPANY, INC.

[2]Based on a presentation by Robert Noel, vice-president, Leo Burnett Company, before the American Association of Advertising Agencies, Eastern Annual Conference, New York.

3. It provides a consistent look from one commercial to the next—and from one year to the next. (The Giant has run essentially the same commercial for five years.)

4. For the writer it has a special appeal: once he has worked out the first format, he has written the campaign.

5. In this format he is forced to deal with irreducible minimums —nothing extraneous—and he says them over and over. There is automatic discipline.

Here is how the campaign was built. First, it was decided to portray an almost magical giant in an almost magical place as shown in these sketches. This would be a valley, and as one can tell from the feet, the Valley of the Jolly Green Giant.

FIG. 23.8 *Original sketch for the "Valley of the Jolly Green Giant."* CLIENT: GREEN GIANT; AGENCY: LEO BURNETT COMPANY, INC.

Next, the railroad station was drawn like this.

FIG. 23.9 *Original sketch of the railroad station in the "Valley."* CLIENT: GREEN GIANT; AGENCY: LEO BURNETT COMPANY, INC.

And a train to go with it.

FIG. 23.10 *The Giant's helpers.* CLIENT: GREEN GIANT; AGENCY: LEO BURNETT COMPANY, INC.

The giant would need helpers—farm helpers like this.

FIG. 23.11 *Close-up of a helper.* CLIENT: GREEN GIANT; AGENCY: LEO BURNETT COMPANY, INC.

And an engineer for the train who looked like this.

FIG. 23.12 *Engineer for the train that covers the "Valley."* CLIENT: GREEN GIANT; AGENCY: LEO BURNETT COMPANY, INC.

The creative group wrote a song that started:

"Good things from the garden . . ." and ended ". . . in the Valley of the Jolly Green Giant."

It was decided that the song was not "Gianty" enough; so they added some "HO HO HO."

"In the Valley of the Jolly (HO HO HO) Green Giant."

As the format evolved, the group found that an opening "setup" line was needed for the song. So they cut off the last line and stuck it up front.

At first they tried the Giant on the tube. He was bad "live" and bad in animation. He looked "monsterish" no matter what was done. They even built an articulated skeleton covered with a green rubber skin. For $35,000 it looked like an out-take from "The Beast from 50 Fathoms." They also discovered that the man who made the puppet owned the skeleton; so the company owned only the skin. However, the experience was not a total loss because the creative group learned something. They learned that the best approach was to build a miniature *valley* instead. (See Figure 23.13.) Those hills are styrofoam covered with fake

FIG. 23.13 *The model "Valley" and the Green Giant.* CLIENT: GREEN GIANT; AGENCY: LEO BURNETT COMPANY, INC.

grass. The corn is crepe paper. The sky is painted, and this time the Giant is real. He does not move much because if he did he would surely squash somebody. The model valley was built on the floor of the Swift-Chaplin studios in Hollywood. They shot the Giant in the set going "HO HO HO" with his hands on his hips. They shot him laughing and pointing and bending over to pick something up or put something down. But he doesn't walk—not ever.

Everything was shot in both color and black and white, in daylight and in moonlight. They then put the set in storage and haven't taken it out since. The Giant remains obscure, legendary, and romantic—and most of all, imaginary.

These commercials purvey a sort of bucolic charm. Although they are unabashed "corn," they work and they sell—and they "wear like iron." A current example is shown in Figure 23.14.

FIG. 23.14 *Successful "Valley of the Jolly Green Giant" commercial for Niblets Corn.* CLIENT: GREEN GIANT; AGENCY: LEO BURNETT COMPANY, INC.

To keep his Niblets Corn crisper, the Giant gives you just as much corn but almost no water.

Then it's vacuum-packed. (Sound: pffffft!)

Niblets Brand Corn is the Giant's own special kind grown to be sweeter. For the crispest, freshest tasting corn,...

(Anncr VO) You'll really cheer about the Green Giant's new... Young Broccoli Spears frozen in Butter Sauce.

(Anncr VO) The Giant takes only tender young broccoli spears... and freezes them fresh in a flavor-tight cooking pouch.

That way all the garden fresh flavor stays in the broccoli.

FIG. 23.15 *A different format is used for the frozen vegetables to separate them from the canned. Humor, rather than charm, is emphasized for this more sophisticated audience.* CLIENT: GREEN GIANT; AGENCY: LEO BURNETT COMPANY, INC.

For frozen vegetables a different format was used. It plays against the other format like counterpoint. The frozen products need separation from the canned because the market requirements are different. These are new and more expensive products, and their audience is more sophisticated. Consequently, a straight cartoon animation was used. It was played for humor, rather than charm. There is no lyric. Every commercial contains a live demonstration of the new boil-in-bag product form. An example is shown in Figure 23.15.

As far as television is concerned, the creative people are convinced that more and more of the credit must be given to the phrase "HO HO HO" as a device. It's an easy thing to pick up, and it gives the Giant instant identification.

Here is a smattering of the current magazine advertising.

He is still a good magazine giant, as these ads indicate.

While this advertising was running, corporate sales rose from $69,000,000 in 1962 to about $130,000,000 in 1965. Slightly more than $30,000,000 of this was new vegetable business.

FIG. 23.16 (a) and 23.16 (b) *Current magazine advertisements featuring the Giant.* CLIENT: GREEN GIANT; AGENCY: LEO BURNETT COMPANY, INC.

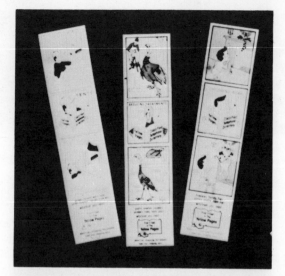

FIG. 23.17 *Typical cartoon advertisements used for Yellow Pages in the early 1960s.* CLIENT: BELL SYSTEM; AGENCY: CUNNINGHAM & WALSH INC.

Find it Fast...
Wolley Segap says...
Smart Shoppers look...
Molley Segap says...
Why are Yellow Pages Yellow?
Look with Luke...
9 out of 10 people look...
9½ out of 10 people look...

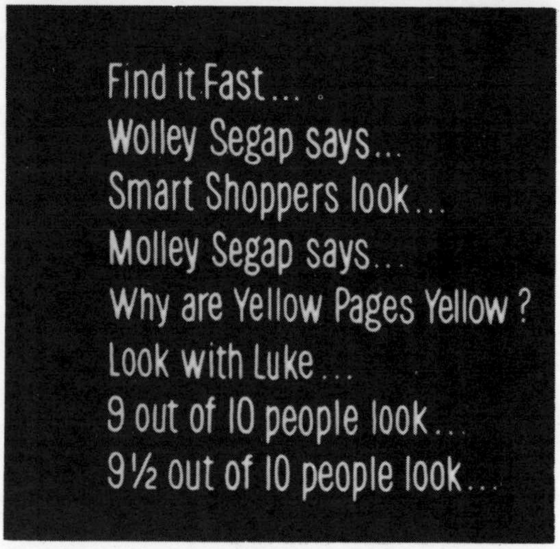

FIG. 23.18 *Sampling of Yellow Pages advertising used in the early 1960s across the United States.* CLIENT: BELL SYSTEM; AGENCY: CUNNINGHAM & WALSH INC.

YELLOW PAGES[3]

AT&T comprises 21 Bell Telephone companies serving 48 states and Canada. Each is autonomous. Each retains its own advertising agency to promote its own services in its area. AT&T retains Cunningham & Walsh to promote the use of Yellow Pages nationally. For some years, a cartoon campaign appeared in national magazines, and it was extremely effective (high Starch ratings and so forth). (See Figure 23.17.) The individual companies were welcome to pick up the national theme, and some did. But most of the advertising of the 21 companies differed from state to state because independent approvers—with independent minds—okayed independent ideas. In Figure 23.18 is a sampling of the Yellow Pages advertising you would have encountered in the early 1960s if you had traveled across the United States.

[3]Based on a presentation by Anthony C. Chevins, executive vice-president, Cunningham & Walsh, before the American Association of Advertising Agencies, Eastern Annual Conference, New York.

Another factor complicated the situation. In seeking to gain recognition as a national advertising medium, the Bell System introduced National Yellow Pages Service, a service designed to simplify the placement of Yellow Pages advertising for large national and regional advertisers and their advertising agencies. They were selling the concept of "one contact, one contract, one monthly bill."

Meanwhile the companies were continuing to advertise independently on a regional basis with 21 different themes. It did not make sense somehow to advertise regionally when what was needed was a national program. The problem was to convince all 21 Bell companies and their advertising agencies that not only national but local interests would best be served by a single unified promotion for Yellow Pages.

To solve this problem the agency searched for a single, simple selling idea . . . a powerful, memorable sales message to present all the benefits of the product in a way that would work locally and nationally and that could be repeated in all media — from matchbook covers to network television.

As a start, everybody in art and copy was called together for an indoctrination meeting to develop fresh new ideas. Everyone who was then working on the Yellow Pages account or anyone who had worked on it previously was excluded. This was not for punitive reasons. The firm wanted a fresh approach.

After presenting the necessary background information to this group and outlining the problem, the creative head sent them all back to their offices, hoping that some great ideas would spring forth. The program produced a multitude of ideas — good, fair, and terrible. The creative leaders sifted them through and killed almost all. However, four survived. One crazy idea about fingers seemed somewhat intriguing. (See Figure 23.19). The next few days were spent developing copy and layout approaches for these ideas. Then, two ads from each campaign were selected for extensive pretesting, not only with the

FIG. 23.19   *The glimmer of a new idea about "Walking Fingers."*
CLIENT: BELL SYSTEM;
AGENCY: CUNNINGHAM &
WALSH INC.

consumers but also with retail merchants who were Yellow Page advertisers. More then 1,000 interviews were conducted.

One idea survived the stringent pretesting. It was created by an art director, improved on by a copywriter, and almost killed by a committee. In its simplest form, this was the selling idea — the umbrella that was developed for Yellow Pages:

"Let your fingers do the walking through the Yellow Pages." (Figure 23.20.)

Next, the agency had to find out whether it was superior to (or at least as good as) any theme that the 21 companies were then using. So, with the use of an outside research organization, more pretesting was conducted to determine the relative effectiveness of these commercial messages. Results were convincingly in favor of the "Walking Fingers." All 21 Bell companies were called together. It was then up to the client, AT&T, to face and sell these 21 independent companies. Never before had so many Bell companies given on-the-spot approval to a recommendation from headquarters. Nineteen of the 21 companies soon approved the plan and adopted the "Walking Fingers" theme in their own advertising and promotional efforts. The other two came aboard later.

Cunningham & Walsh prepared and provided an advertising program that showed how well the theme worked in magazine ads, television, newspaper, outdoor, and car and bus cards, as well as internal company promotional materials. It soon became obvious that this idea was so easily grasped and so simple that it worked everywhere. (See examples in Figures 23.21 and Figure 23.22.) The agency sent out advertising press kits to all of the Bell companies, who enthusiastically went to town with this theme. They incorporated the "Walking Fingers" theme into virtually every advertising and sales promotion medium available to them.

How successful has this theme been? Right after introduction, and periodically since then, the agency has conducted research to measure penetration and awareness of the "Walking Fingers" line. Using a national projectable sample of adult Americans, they asked respondents to complete the following phrase:

"Let your fingers do the walking through the _____."

FIG. 23.21 *"Walking Fingers" theme used in various media.* CLIENT: BELL SYSTEM; AGENCY: CUNNINGHAM & WALSH INC.

FIG. 23.22 *"Walking Fingers" television commercial.* CLIENT: BELL SYSTEM; AGENCY: CUNNINGHAM & WALSH INC.

After only 8 weeks of advertising this new line, they found that 30 percent of the United States population could complete it correctly, and after one full year, 55.5 percent could. In three years, 70 percent could complete it. R. H. Bruskin Associates, in studying awareness and recognition of advertising slogans, trademarks, and symbols, confirmed the fact that "Walking Fingers" is in the top 10 percent of advertising theme-awareness figures. Starch Readership scores were equally sensational. Frequently they have been first or second in a given issue of a magazine. The client and agency have received several awards and extensive publicity in various publications.

ANNCR: (VO) Yes, let your fingers do the walking thru the Yellow Pages. You'll find everything you want right at your finger-tips...

This way, you're ready to call or see the firm that has exactly what you're looking for.

JINGLE: Let your fingers do the walking through the Yellow Pages. (MUSICAL EFFECT)

FIG. 23.23 *Other advertisers pick up the "Walking Fingers" theme.* CLIENT: BELL SYSTEM; AGENCY: CUNNINGHAM & WALSH INC.

Several advertisers have used the theme in their own advertising—for example, Chrysler and Mercury featured it in their advertising and promotional efforts. (See Figure 23.23.) Acceptance and recognition were shown also through use of the line by cartoonists and comedians. For instance, Phyllis Diller remarked at The Royal Box of the Hotel Americana in New York City, "If anyone has an ambition to succeed Richard Burton as Elizabeth Taylor's next, just let your fingers do the walking through the Yellow Pages."

AMERICAN OIL COMPANY[4]

Gasoline is a common and familiar product. You don't see it or feel it, yet you use it every day. When your gauge approaches "empty," you subconsciously curse the upcoming forced purchase. When the gauge again says "full," you are suffused by a momentary sense of comfort and security. Of all the products in the broad spectrum of marketable items, gasoline is probably the most impersonal. Yet gasoline, through the great regional, national, and international petroleum marketers, has well over $150,000,000 of sounds and words and pictures spent on it each year, and reaches the busy eyes and crowded ears of motorists across America. However, although the advertising budgets of petroleum marketers are sizable, expenditures in this product category generally represent less than one cent of the marketing dollar.

Thus in gasoline we have a major force in advertising of a product that by nature has a relatively low consumer interest and a small percentage of the marketing dollar. Add to this the realism of the marketplace and the fact that one gas station is not very different from the competitor's across the street. Even gasolines themselves are not very different from one another. There are degrees of difference in

[4]Based on a presentation by William T. Raidt, executive vice-president, D'Arcy Advertising Company, before the Central Region Annual Meeting, Chicago, American Association of Advertising Agencies.

octane ratings, additives, mileage and performance claims. But by and large there is no pronounced difference that gives one marketer a great product advantage over another. Probably the single exception to this rule would be Certified Lead-Free Amoco Gasoline—an exclusive product of American Oil, but marketed only in the East and South.

Though gasoline is admittedly a low-interest item, and the consumer is bombarded by a myriad of product claims and confronted by the profusion of service stations, there is still consumer loyalty. Each year the large and substantial companies serve more people, serve them better, and many increase their hardcore following. It is the contention of American Oil and its agency that nothing sells gasoline better than the quality and attitude of service on the part of the neighborhood service station dealer. He is the key to success or failure in petroleum marketing, although advertising plays a vital and important role. The principal objectives of the advertising are (1) to build consumer confidence in the product; (2) to stimulate and reinforce the dealer's desire to serve customers with more and better products and services; (3) to surround the dealer with an image of stability, industry, and expertise, and in doing so reflect well over the network of dealers and the company. Basic to the communications program for the American Oil Company are two areas: the product's image and the dealer's image.

American Oil is the marketing wing of Standard Oil Company (Indiana). American Oil markets petroleum products and accessory items through more than 22,000 stations coast to coast. In the Midwest these are marketed under the name Standard Oil Division of the American Oil Company and in the East, South, and Far West as the American Oil Company.

First let us consider the product and its image. In 1962 the American Oil Company, in search of a meaningful consumer plus, began promoting the company's Final/Filter, which is the exclusive property of the American Oil Company. Here was an opportunity to offer the consumer something different—an opportunity to enhance American Oil's reputation as an innovator. It is an uncontested fact, according to the company, that all gasolines in transport and storage pick up harmful particles of rust, dirt, and other contaminants that can get into the tank and the fuel system and cause harm to an engine. The American Final/Filter at the end of the pump hose blocks, traps, screens, and

FIG. 23.24 *One of the introductory spot announcements featuring the Final/Filter.* CLIENT: STANDARD OIL OF INDIANA; AGENCY: D'ARCY ADVERTISING COMPANY.

MAN: Final filter?
ATTEND: Yep. And this is the filter element.
MAN: Well, what's it do?

ATTEND: It filters our gasoline just as it goes into your tank.

It looks like you Standard Dealers have come up with a gasoline improvement a fellow can actually see.

The American Final Filter.

At your Standard Oil Dealers.

Standard Oil Division, American Oil.

cleans out these harmful particles so that people get clean gasoline just as it enters the tank. In Figure 23.24 is shown parts of the storyboard for one of the original introductory television spot announcements featuring the Final/Filter.

FIG. 23.25 *An attempt to dramatize the product reward for the Final/Filter.* CLIENT: STANDARD OIL OF INDIANA; AGENCY: D'ARCY ADVERTISING COMPANY.

Twice yearly the agency takes benchmark consumer readings to determine progress in four important areas — recognition, identification, comprehension, and conviction. Several years' readings indicated increasingly higher degrees of recognition, identification, and comprehension for the Final/Filter. But there was some indication that reinforcement was needed in the area of conviction. In Figure 23.25 is shown an example of the way the agency attacked this problem and attempted to dispel the idea that the American Final/Filter was merely a merchandising "gimmick." The result was an 11 percent increase in consumer conviction — even better than the target objective. In Figure 23.26 are shown parts of a color commercial for the Final/Filter.

This television campaign is supported with radio spots such as this one-minute commercial:

ANNCR: The going's great with Filtered American Brand Gasoline.

VOCAL: TAKE A LOOK

TAKE A GOOD LOOK

SOMETHING'S HAPPENED TO GASOLINE

A BENEFIT YOU CAN SEE!

FIG. 23.26 *A color commercial for the Final/Filter.* CLIENT: STANDARD OIL OF INDIANA; AGENCY: D'ARCY ADVERTISING COMPANY.

ANNCR: Many people think it's quite worthwile to go just a little bit out of their way

to buy gasoline.

You expect more from Standard... And you get it. (Music)

SEE THE FINAL/FILTER

THE BRIGHT RED FINAL/FILTER

THE AMERICAN FINAL/FILTER

AT STANDARD OIL DEALERS.

MUSIC: BRIDGE

ANNCR: Only American Gasolines are filtered one last time—just as they go in your tank . . . to protect complex fuel systems . . . and precision carburetors. So—

VOCAL: TAKE A LOOK

TAKE A GOOD LOOK

DRIVE IN TODAY . . .

AND LOOK FOR THE FINAL/FILTER

THE BRIGHT RED FINAL/FILTER

THE AMERICAN FINAL/FILTER

AT STANDARD OIL DEALERS.

MUSIC: EXTENDED CHORD

ANNCR: Find out why millions say—
ANNCR: You *expect* more from Standard . . . and you *get* it!
Standard Oil Division American Oil Company.

FIG. 23.27 *A Standard Oil commercial which attempts to build the image of the dealer. Note the absence of dialogue.* CLIENT: STANDARD OIL OF INDIANA; AGENCY: D'ARCY ADVERTISING COMPANY.

As was mentioned earlier, the second problem (after the product and its image) was the dealer and his image. In Figure 23.27 is an example of a television spot addressed to this problem. Note that although the emphasis is on the dealer, an effort is also made to promote the Final/Filter.

The latest campaign is directed to what the client and agency consider the prime target audience—that segment of the motoring public identified as High Mileage Drivers. He has these qualifications:

(Music)

(Music)

(Music)

1. Drives 15,000 miles per year or more.
2. High incidence of two-car or more ownership.
3. White collar worker.
4. Lives in suburbs.
5. Higher than average income.
6. Uses his car to and from work.

He is important because he uses seven times more automobile products than the low-mileage driver. He spends seven and one-half more time in his car. One important medium for reaching him is television. And on radio he is addressed like this:

MUSIC: INTRO RHYTHM

ANNCR: Saturday night at the country club . . . and there's Mister Shugert . . . over there, with the fresh carnation in his lapel.
Busy man . . . tennis this afternoon . . . dancing tonight.

MUSIC: UP

ANNCR: He's a High Mileage Driver . . . and a Standard Oil Customer. Mr. "S" figures his Standard Oil Dealer knows as much about cars as *he* knows about real estate. One good dealer, even with the best equipment and experience, doesn't make an oil company great . . . but 20,000 good ones do.
You *expect* more from Standard . . . And you *get* it.
Standard Oil Division . . . American Oil Company.

One television spot announcement used an "a capella" background and featured the American Final/Filter through the make-believe world of children.

The promotion of the American Final/Filter does not stop with mass-consumer media. It is heavily and consistently supported at the service-station level. Heavy use is made of point-of-purchase driveway and pump-island displays featuring these same themes.

In summary, the strategy in approaching the modern motorist is to feature the benefits of the American Final/Filter, to sell the dealer as a substantial, dependable community friend, and to talk primarily to the High Mileage Driver.

CURAD[5]

About four years ago some of the creative people walked into a tough meeting with the rest of the account group. The creative people were acting smug—not because they were naturally smug, but because they had found a solution to a problem that had stumped a lot of people for a long, long time. Complacently they laid a piece of scratch paper on the conference table. On the paper in a careless copywriter's lazy lettering was the one word "Ouchless."

The history of the "ouchless" bandage goes back many years. At the close of the Korean war, the Kendall Company developed a superior dressing for wounds. They laminated a thin plastic film to a soft absor-

[5]Based on a presentation by Robert Bassindale, vice-president and associate copy director, Tatham-Laird & Kudner, before the American Association of Advertising Agencies, Central Region Annual Meeting, Chicago.

bent pad and perforated it. Moisture drained through the plastic into the absorbent pad but did not drain back into a wound. These remarkable pads (named Telfa) would not stick to the wound. The wound stayed dry.

One of the people who worked on the account in the early days went to hospitals to see the initial trial runs. A busload of school children, seriously burned in a smashup, were unable to resist screaming when doctors and nurses merely reached toward their dressings. The pain of removing an ordinary pad from burns or other serious wounds can be excruciating. The new Telfa pads were applied to the youngsters' burns. The children still cried out when nurses reached out to remove the dressings for the first time. But then a miracle seemed to happen. The pads did not stick, and there was no pain. It was one of the most dramatic new-product orientations any advertising man ever went through.

It was not hard to write professional advertising for such a product. Doctors and nurses needed little hard sell to get interested.

The Kendall Company made the obvious decision to extend these remarkable Telfa Pads to their consumer product—the Curad bandage. However, mothers do not perform much surgery in backyards these days, and there are not many patients with third-degree burns, who are being treated in ranch houses. Consumer bandages, dominated by Johnson & Johnson's Band-Aid, had built their volume on playground cuts and scratches, boils, shaving nicks, and an occasional freak mishap such as a dowager stepping on a martini toothpick while climbing out of her swimming pool.

It quickly became apparent that it was not going to be easy to fit this remarkable product development meaningfully into the life and times of the split-level trap. Little Johnny was not running around complaining about his Band-Aids sticking to his little lacerations. In fact, people were more concerned over how securely the adhesive part of the bandage *did* stick than they were over whether the pad part of the bandage *did not* stick. For many consumers the color and shape of the bandage seemed more important than how well it performed its function.

The client had a consumer benefit but no widespread consumer problem. The previous agency had written much fine copy explaining how Curad would not stick to a wound. Names such as the "mercy" bandage were tried, but nothing seemed to emerge as a sharply focused, memorable, meaningful story. Every time somebody tried to write an advertisement or commercial about Curad it seemed to come out like a giant molehill—too technical and medical for the suburban first-aid kit—too gruesome for the backyard.

The creative group had to find some way to put the story into sharp, memorable focus and at the same time to give it the right emotional tone. That's why they felt just a little bit smug when they came up with "ouchless." It seemed to solve all the communication and emotional problems in one word.

The main visual elements seemed to fall into place naturally. The creative people simply lettered the word "ouchless" under a Curad bandage and pulled the bandage off. To dramatize the competitive advantage they lettered "ouch" under an ordinary bandage and let the

 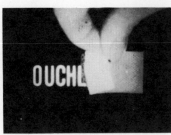 

ANNCR: Until recently, there
was an "Ouch"! in every
adhesive bandage.

ANNCR: Then came Curad.
Curad, the first ouchless!
bandage...

Curad has everything the other
bandage has except the "ouch"!
It's ouchless!

letters stick when that bandage was pulled off. It proved to be a natural
for television—first with a simple but hard-hitting tabletop approach
(see Figure 23.28) and then with a warm, whimsical involvement with
children (see Figure 23.29). The magic word "ouchless" was finally put
on the package.

You may wonder, as someone has asked, "If ouchless is a word
that's worth ten thousand pictures. . . , how many Nielsen share points
is it worth?" Certain marketing categories are dominated by smart,
well-entrenched brands to such an extent that a competitor measures
the success of his advertising—not on the basis of what it helps him do
to the dominant brand but on the basis of what it prevents the dominant brand from doing to him. "Ouchless" has not turned the bandage
market upside down. You cannot prove its success by looking at small
shifts in Nielsen shares, but it is selling more bandages. It has set up a
tough counterattack against a carniverous competitor. It has established "ouchless" as an important consumer benefit. Attitude studies
show a significant increase in the percentage of people who think it is
important that a bandage not stick to a wound. It has produced a good
increase in brand awareness for Curad—no small achievement considering that, for most people, Band-Aid had come to be the generic term
for bandage.

One other question inevitably arises. Is it wise to build advertising
around a benefit that does not solve a widespread or significant problem? Has anyone else gone anywhere on such a tack? Consider that 10

FIG. 23.28 *Commercial
using the direct,
hard-hitting approach.*
CLIENT: CURAD; AGENCY:
TATHAM-LAIRD & KUDNER,
INC.

FIG. 23.29 *Commercial
for Curad using the
warm, whimsical
approach.* CLIENT: CURAD;
AGENCY: TATHAM-LAIRD &
KUDNER, INC.

CHILD SINGING: My
mommy put a Curad on,
Curad's ouchless!

Curad, it's ouchless!

Mommy put a Curad Bandage on.

years ago nobody went around complaining that the front wheels of his car were too close together. Few who tipped over in a car suspected that narrow-track wheels were to blame. Weight and center of gravity and a lot of other engineering and design elements play major roles in determining the stability of an automobile. But when Pontiac announced wide-track wheels, a rather tired automobile scene began to swing.

A word *can* be worth 10,000 pictures. That's "ouchless."

GOODYEAR[6]

About three years ago several persons sat around an office on Madison Avenue and listened to an idea. Then they looked at it. The room got very quiet after the projector was turned off. Then one voice said, "I like it." From that moment on, other people at Young & Rubicam recognized that the Go-Go-Goodyear campaign was something really big.

Goodyear has for 51 years been the world's leading automobile-tire manufacturer. As such, the company produces an amazingly complex line of tires—original equipment, snow tires, ice tires, inner tires, high-performance tires, and so on, in widely varying price ranges. The tire in itself is a low-interest product. Only when its particular excellences are delineated and translated into meaningful benefits does anyone take real notice of it.

The long-range objective of the Goodyear campaign was to (1) invest all Goodyear automobile-tire advertising with the look and sound of corporate leadership and (2) present the specific attributes and superiorities of each individual tire line. The immediate assignment was a new TV campaign for Goodyear snow tires.

The copy platform was something like this: Goodyear snow tires will take you through deep snow better than other tires will because (1) they are made with Tufsyn and (2) they have 3,700 gripping edges. The basic approach the Goodyear group settled on to implement this copy strategy was this—problem and solution, snow and go.

The problem in execution was how to tell this story most dramatically and believably, most memorably and convincingly on television—and simultaneously to invest it with a corporate identity that could be extended into future advertising for other tire lines. That was when the big idea (for the campaign) happened. A few months earlier the creative head, Hanley Norins, had seen a film technique that he could not get out of his mind. It was a movie trailer for *La Dolce Vita* that told the story entirely with graphics and music, and that communicated simply, brilliantly, completely through film alone without a single word being uttered.

Why not, he said, exploit the dimensions of television totally; why not use the communication power and the impact of film to a degree far beyond any yet attained in television commercials? Why not mate it with music that moved with the story and lent it aural life? And the group—a writer, an art director, a producer—agreed and caught fire.

[6]Based on a presentation by Dermott F. McCarthy, senior vice-president and creative director, Young & Rubicam, Inc., before the American Association of Advertising Agencies, Eastern Annual Conference, New York.

To keep the idea as pure as it had been conceived, they imposed a severe discipline on themselves; no dialogue. If they could not speak a single word about their product, their problem and its solution—why then they would *have* to tell the story entirely in visuals and music.

During the next five days they reviewed 15,000 feet of stock snow footage (they were working in Southern California) and old Goodyear commercials. About this time a copywriter came up with the epitomized expression of the total message, "When snow says no . . . Go-Go-Goodyear." And a composer in Hollywood caught the infection and overnight wrote and scored music to a commercial film in an utterly new way. And the client had faith in the idea and backed his belief with hard cash for a prototype commercial. In Figure 23.30 is one of the first commercials that evolved from the five-day prototype prepared earlier. Still not a word—but it says an awful lot.

The next assignment was to develop a campaign for Tufsyn—a Goodyear ingredient and process that endows tires with extra toughness and longer life. In these spots oral dialogue was introduced for the first time because in that particular instance it was felt that the message benefited from it. Yet the simplicity and purity essential to the idea are retained. "Go-Go-Goodyear" is definitely adaptable, as you can see in Figure 23.31. There you can see the evolution designed to accom-

FIG. 23.30   *One of the first commercials that evolved from a five-day session reviewing stock snow footage in preparation for the snow-tire campaign. No dialogue was used.* CLIENT: GOODYEAR TIRES; AGENCY: YOUNG & RUBICAM COMPANY, INC.

FIG. 23.31   *The "Go-Go Goodyear" theme is extended to another Goodyear product —Double Eagle with Lifeguard Safety Spare. It attempts to dramatize to men the inconvenience and danger that tires vulnerable to blowout could visit on their families.* CLIENT: GOODYEAR TIRES; AGENCY: YOUNG & RUBICAM COMPANY, INC.

modate the changed copy strategy. The Goodyear Double Eagle with Lifeguard Safety Spare eliminates the possibility and the fear of blowouts and punctures. The strategy is to talk to men by dramatizing the inconvenience and danger that tires vulnerable to blowout or puncture could visit on their families. The execution relies on a short drama in an environment calculated to convey a mood of imminent peril. It uses dialogue sparingly yet effectively. The quick cuts are gone. It is simple, still pure, still definitely "Go-Go-Goodyear."

QUESTIONS FOR DISCUSSION

1. What similarities in approach do you note in the campaigns analyzed in this chapter?
2. To what extent do the campaigns included here carry out the principles discussed in the five preceding chapters?
3. What changes would you have made in these campaigns?
4. Compile three generalizations that appear to emerge from these case histories.
5. Which of these campaigns was the best planned? Which was most effective, in general? Why?

PART 4 | **MEDIA OF ADVERTISING AND PROMOTION**

24

A Broad Look
at
Media Strategy

Before it can be effective an advertisement needs an audience. It cannot communicate unless someone has a chance to read it, hear it, or view it. Product messages may, of course, reach audiences through face-to-face discourse as well as through the mass media. However, advertising is usually aimed at large audiences and consequently must depend primarily on the mass media. Most advertising planners devote a good deal of their time and effort to the complex business of formulating the best possible "media mix."

Fortunately, there is more factual information available on media than on any other phase of advertising. Data on circulation, audiences, rates, cost per thousand, among others, are readily available. Frequently the medium salesman supplies special data on brand usage, motivations of audiences to buy, or personal buying habits. But in spite of all the data available, buying media is still a highly subjective operation. There are two reasons for this situation: (1) the almost infinite number of different mixes available in a given situation and (2) the fact that the ingredients of the mix are really not as susceptible to comparison as they seem at first.

Consider, for example, the number of alternative ingredients. There were in mid-1968 in the United States approximately 1,830 daily

Whether they prefer their paintings to be "pop", "op", or Grandma Moses, it's the art of living that really turns on the readers of American Home. And it's at home where their living begins. BRI* tells us, for example, that they are "heaviest users" in more product categories than any other mass circulation magazine in the home and woman's service field. In fact, American Home is literally tops among heaviest users of almost everything from soup to nuts, including aluminum foil, floor wax, orange juice, tea, coffee, wine, dog and cat food—and you name it. Small wonder. American Home talks the active, adventuresome language of the active, responsible young homemakers who make up the cream of the market for every type of quality product used in the home. American Home talks to prospects, not just people.

*Brand Rating Index, 1966

AMERICAN
HOME
for active young homemakers

A Curtis Publication

FIG. 24.1 *An image-building advertisement for a leading home magazine.* COURTESY AMERICAN HOME MAGAZINE — A CURTIS PUBLICATION.

newspapers, 9,000 weekly newspapers, 660 commercial television stations, 6,000 AM and FM radio stations, 600 consumer or farm magazines, 310,000 billboards, and several million car cards in public transit vehicles. Each of these can be used in an almost infinite variety of ways.

Then, too, the alternatives are not easily comparable. It can be shown that one magazine has a cost per thousand of $4.50 and another, of $8.00. But does this mean you should buy the first? Not necessarily, because the readers of the second magazine may be wealthier, more interested in the publication, or in an area of better distribution for your product. Consequently, there is always a large subjective element involved in evaluating the data.

In this chapter we shall examine over-all media strategy. In the succeeding chapters we shall see how the specific types of media (newspapers, magazines, and so on) fit into this strategy.

TABLE 24.1

Use of Major Media by 125 Leading National
Advertisers (1967)

Medium	Total National	125 Leaders	Other National Advertisers
	(In millions of dollars)	(In percentages)	
Newspapers	874.9	35.42	64.58
General magazines	1,135.3	46.03	53.97
Network television	1,500.3	84.41	15.59
Spot television	1,194.0	65.46	34.54
Network radio	72.8	61.87	38.13
Spot radio	287.6	63.64	36.36
Business publications	760.0	14.83	85.17
Outdoor	141.3	36.92	63.08

Source: *Advertising Age*, August 26, 1968.

MEDIA TRENDS SINCE WORLD WAR II

Media strategy has been very much influenced by certain changes in media during the years since World War II. Following are some of the most important changes that have taken place.

The Rise of Television. The most obvious and most significant factor in the media picture has been the rapid growth of television. The number of television homes has grown from about 8,000 in 1946 to 58,000,000 in 1969. Revenue grew from $57,800,000 in 1947 to $2,923,000,000 in 1967. Within these few years television has become the dominant medium for many nationally advertised package goods and is a major part of the media mix of most important national manufacturers (distillers are a notable exception because alcoholic beverage advertising is not accepted on television).

Increase in Complexity of Media. Since World War II major changes have occurred in all types of media. We find, for example, that network radio has declined in importance, but that much of the slack has been taken up by the independent local stations, whose number has more than tripled since World War II. Although newspaper circulations are up, the number of dailies and weeklies has been declining. In the magazine field such once-important publications as *Collier's* and *Woman's Home Companion* have disappeared and new ones such as *Sports Illustrated* and many specialized magazines have appeared. These problems will be discussed in more detail in the chapters dealing with each of the media.

Technological Developments. In the electronic media, Videotape, glass-panel screens, color television, and transistorized radios are among the important developments. In the print-media field, improvements in inks, paper, reproduction processes, and r.o.p. (run-of-paper) color are among important developments since 1946. The media have become so advanced and all pervasive that Marshall McLuhan has advanced the widely quoted idea that "the medium is the message."[1] He

[1]See H. Marshall McLuhan, *Understanding Media* (New York: McGraw-Hill, Inc., 1964), and *The Medium Is the Massage* (New York: Random House, Inc., 1967).

maintains that we have overemphasized the importance of content of the message and overlooked the power of the medium through which the message is transmitted.

Increase in Total Advertising Volume. Total volume more than tripled between 1946 and 1967. During this period advertising has increased faster than the total national income or gross national product (although it does not represent as large a percentage of national income as it did in the 1920s). This means that media buyers have had increasingly larger dollar budgets to allocate among the media.

Changes in Buying and Selling Methods. Media are bought and sold in much more complex ways than they were a few years ago. For example, television can be bought as a single minute in one show one time or a combination of minutes in any number of shows on any network. This compares with the days when it was common to buy a half hour or an hour every week for 52 weeks on a given network. In the magazine field the situation has changed also. For example, until 1961 an advertisement in *Life* appeared in every copy of a certain issue. In 1968 you could buy an advertisement in any of 26 geographical areas or in any of several major metropolitan areas.

Growth of the Marketing Concept. As Chapter 3 pointed out, the average businessman puts more emphasis on marketing (compared with production) than he did before the 1940s. He realizes that he has the machinery and the labor to produce as much as the market will buy. His orientation is more toward the consumer, less toward the machine that makes his product.

Changes in the American Market. The American market has undergone basic changes since 1946. Among the most important changes in demographic groupings have been those in geographic concentrations in population, age distribution, size of families, suburbanization, educational level, number of working wives, and income distribution. Social classes have also undergone changes. Market changes are reflected quickly in reading, listening, and viewing patterns.

THE MEDIA PLAN

Because media strategy is part of marketing strategy, it follows that the media plan is a part of the marketing plan. At the Eastern Annual Conference of the American Association of Advertising Agencies, two teams of media experts worked out the media strategy for a hypothetical tomato concentrate—a powder concentrate "which can do just about anything one could expect of a tomato except reassemble itself into a fresh slice on a lettuce leaf." A teaspoon of this hypothetical powder dissolved in water will make a glass of delicious tomato juice and it can be used anywhere else tomatoes might be used. One team was composed of Anne Wright of J. Walter Thompson Company and Lewis H. Happ of Geyer Advertising. The first part of their presentation provides an interesting example of how marketing and media objectives are tied together. In the following pages the presentation is quoted, just as it was delivered.

TABLE 24.2

UNITED STATES MEDIA PROFILE

(IN MILLIONS OF DOLLARS AND PERCENTAGES OF TOTAL EXPENDITURES, 1950–1967)

Medium	1950		1960		1962		1964		1966		1967		PERCENTAGE OF CHANGE '67 vs. '66
Newspapers	$2,075.6	36.3%	$3,702.8	31.0%	$3,681.4	29.5%	$4,148.0	29.2%	$4,895.0	29.4%	$4,900.0	29.1%	+0.1
Magazines*	536.1	9.3	975.3	8.1	1,007.0	8.0	1,140.2	8.0	1,324.5	7.9	1,313.8	7.7	−0.8
Television	170.8	2.9	1,605.0	13.4	1,897.0	15.2	2,289.0	16.1	2,824.0	16.9	2,923.0	17.4	+3.5
Radio	605.4	10.6	668.0	5.5	796.0	6.3	846.4	5.9	1,010.0	6.1	1,027.0	6.1	+1.7
Direct mail	803.2	14.0	1,830.2	15.3	1,933.0	15.5	2,184.0	15.3	2,461.0	14.8	2,478.0	14.7	+0.7
Outdoor	142.5	2.4	203.2	1.7	170.5	1.3	174.6	1.2	177.7	1.1	188.8	1.1	+6.2
Business papers	251.1	4.3	609.3	5.1	597.2	4.8	622.5	4.3	711.5	4.3	712.0	4.2	+0.1
Transit†							30.2	0.2	33.6	0.2	36.8	0.2	+9.5
Miscellaneous	1,125.6	19.7	2,337.8	19.5	2,358.7	18.9	2,750.3	19.3	3,232.7	19.4	3,264.6	19.4	+1.0
Grand total	5,710.0		11,931.7		12,440.8		14,185.2		16,670.0		16,844.0		
Newspapers													
National	533.4	25.6	836.1	22.5	781.6	21.2	848.0	20.4	975.0	19.9	940.0	19.1	−3.6
Local	1,542.2	74.3	2,866.7	77.4	2,899.8	78.7	3,300.0	79.5	3,920.0	80.0	3,960.0	80.8	+1.0
Magazines													
Weeklies	261.1	33.1	525.3	33.1	519.0	32.3	583.0	33.0	658.2	32.3	651.6	32.6	−1.0
Women's	129.4	16.4	183.8	11.6	199.8	12.4	230.9	13.0	280.0	13.7	282.0	14.1	+0.7
Monthlies	87.5	11.1	200.0	12.6	223.2	13.9	260.3	14.7	316.2	15.5	312.4	15.6	−1.2
Farm-national	36.9	4.6	31.7	2.0	31.0	1.9	33.5	1.9	36.6	1.7	35.0	1.7	−4.4
Farm-regional	21.2	2.6	34.5	2.1	34.0	2.1	32.5	1.8	33.5	1.6	32.8	1.6	−2.1
Business papers	251.1	31.8	609.3	38.4	597.2	37.2	622.5	35.3	711.5	4.9	712.0	35.7	+0.1
Radio													
Network	196.3	32.4	43.0	6.4	45.8	5.7	59.1	6.9	63.6	6.2	64.2	6.2	+1.0
Spot	135.8	22.4	210.0	31.4	288.8	36.2	250.6	29.6	300.2	29.7	297.2	28.9	−1.0
Local	273.3	45.1	415.0	62.1	461.4	57.9	536.7	63.4	646.2	63.9	665.6	64.8	+3.0
Television													
Network	85.0	49.7	805.0	50.1	975.5	51.4	1,132.0	49.4	1,393.0	49.3	1,476.0	50.4	+6.0
Spot	30.8	18.0	520.0	32.3	611.0	32.2	779.8	34.0	960.0	33.9	947.0	32.3	−1.4
Local	55.0	32.3	280.0	17.4	310.5	16.3	377.2	16.4	471.0	16.6	500.0	17.1	+6.1

*Includes farm national and regional.

†Prior to 1963 transit was included under miscellaneous.

SOURCE: Compiled from various issues of Printer's Ink (Marketing/Communications) based on McCann-Erickson estimates.

Media Strategy for a New Food Beverage. There are actually three phases in the development of any new product:

1. The introductory phase
2. The national development phase
3. The competitive phase

Marketing Objectives

In this presentation, we are concerned with the first two of these. Our broad marketing objectives are therefore:

a. to introduce and maintain distribution of the product on a region-by-region basis, while full production is being attained, with the goal of having national distribution within a one-year period. We have assumed that test marketing has been completed and that production of the product will grow slowly, calling for a gradual regional introduction.
b. to establish the brand nationally before competitive products can get a foothold—in other words, to pre-empt the market for the brand as effectively as possible while it has the field to itself. We estimate we may have a lead period of about one year in which to gain this entrenched position before the final or competitive stage begins.

Some of the factors which must be considered in preparing a campaign of this type are (1) the size and effectiveness of the sales force; (2) the established distribution pattern of other products put out by the same company; (3) size of the total market; (4) expected share of that market for the product under discussion; and (5) a payout plan.

We have had to make some assumptions. We have assumed that the sales force is large and well-organized and that this product is one of an already established food company. Also, we have assumed that any televison purchase we make must stand on its own, although it is more than likely that other programs are used by the corporation and that in actual practice, commercials would be placed within the structure of the corporate buy.

One very important consideration in developing Phase 1 (the regional introduction) is the relationship between national and introductory advertising weight.

It is desirable to maintain a close relationship between the advertising exposure given the product during the first year regional introductions and the second year consolidation and to ensure that advertising-to-sales ratio will not be too far out of line during the introductory period.

One way of achieving this relationship is to start with an ideal national plan based on the given budget, determine the number of advertising impressions it will deliver in each region, and then set up schedules in comparable local media that will approximate this effort. With the regional campaigns worked out to match the ultimate weight of the national effort, we can determine through experience whether or not the final plan will be adequate to maintain a solid market position for the product.

Under this method, the *dollars* will be proportionately greater during the introduction because of the difference between local and national rate structures, but this extra expenditure must be undertaken to be sure the product receives as much consumer exposure during the regional phase as it can expect to receive later on.

The first step for this assignment, therefore, was to design media strategy and a tactical plan which would be used when nation-wide distribution is completed.

Media Objectives

Based on the outline of the problem, the specific objectives of the media plan are

. . . to reach large families with special emphasis on the housewife, who is usually the chief purchasing agent.

. . . to concentrate the greatest weight of advertising in urban areas where prepared foods traditionally have greater sales and where new ideas normally gain quicker acceptance.

. . . to provide advertising continuity and a fairly consistent level of impressions throughout the year except for extra weight during the announcement period.

. . . to deliver advertising impressions over the entire country in direct relation to food store sales.

. . . to use media which will help to strengthen the copy strategy which will put major emphasis on convenience, ease of preparation, taste, and economy.

. . . to attain the greatest possible frequency of advertising impressions consistent with the need for broad coverage and the demands of the copy plan.

Since, as we have pointed out, the regional strategy normally stems from the national plan, we will outline first the campaign that is proposed for Phase 2 when full national distribution is attained.

National Announcement Period – January–February

Figure 24.2 shows how we have divided the $4,000,000 appropriation by media.

The schedule for this appropriation is broken down in our planning into two periods:

. . . national announcement period in January–February.

. . . the sustaining period to run from March through end of year.

General Types of Media Judgments. It should be apparent from this presentation that after one has worked out his marketing and media objectives, he has four types of media judgments to make:

1. General type of medium (newspapers, magazines, and the like)

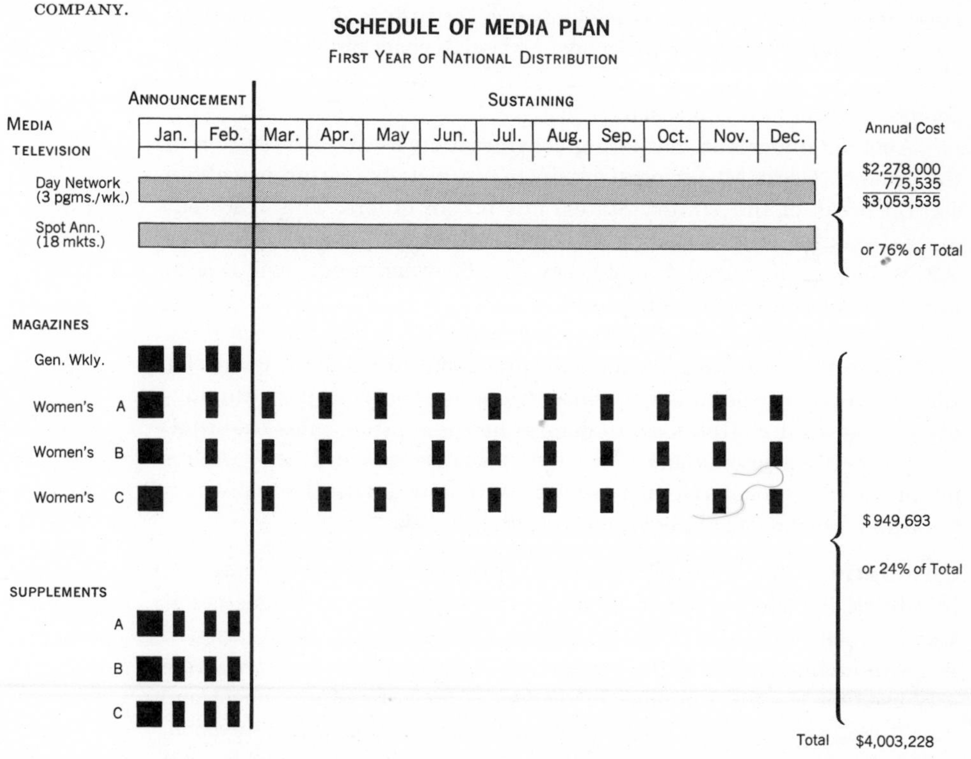

FIG. 24.2 *Allocation of first year's advertising appropriation for hypothetical tomato concentrate. Note the two periods – announcement and sustaining.* SOURCE: J. WALTER THOMPSON COMPANY.

SCHEDULE OF MEDIA PLAN

FIRST YEAR OF NATIONAL DISTRIBUTION

2. Class of medium (women's, general, clear channel, and the like)
3. Individual vehicle within each class (*Woman's Day, New York Times*, WABC-TV, and the like)
4. Effective use of each medium and combination of media.

In the next two sections we shall examine the two major types of factors one must evaluate in making these judgments—*quantitative* factors and *qualitative* factors.

QUANTITATIVE FACTORS

Quantitative factors are those considerations which can be expressed in numerical form. Although the media planner need not be a mathematician, he works with quantitative concepts and has to make decisions based on them. Nowhere in the advertising business has computerized knowledge intruded so sharply as in the area of media selection.

Market Considerations. "Markets make media" is almost a truism. All media buyers think they are covering potential markets when they buy space or time, but they often do not know with certainty where their markets are. The tools of the market analyst were discussed in Chapter 11—they are important aids in planning the media mix just as in creative strategy. Note the careful definition of marketing objectives in the plan for our hypothetical tomato concentrate—in terms of both markets and action.

The more the media analyst knows about the market the better his purchase is likely to be. It is easy enough for him to discover that he sells some of his product to those over sixty-five years old and those who live on farms. But how much does he sell? Are these markets important enough for him to try to reach?

Another important marketing consideration is the distribution of the product. Oscar Mayer meat products are distributed intensively in certain areas of the United States, but not in others. This rules out magazines as media (although regional editions might work) because that would entail a great deal of waste. On the other hand, various local media might be used efficiently.

In certain situations distribution is national, but thinly scattered over the country. An advertiser may find some areas more fertile for sales than others and prefer to concentrate his efforts on those. Buying-power indexes are often used to determine the relative sales potential.

As we have noted, market considerations are qualitative as well as quantitative. The behavioral scientists have joined with the marketers to fathom psychological needs, desires, and the like.

Circulation. The word "circulation" is a frequent cause of confusion in advertising circles. When applied to newspapers and magazines it usually refers to *copies* of the magazine, although some people use the word interchangeably with "readership." (Readership is more properly used for the total number of readers of an issue of a publication.)

"Circulation" is also used sometimes in connection with television, radio, outdoor, and car cards. The term becomes misleading because it implies figures that can be compared with one another and with news-paper and magazine circulation. Such is not true; instead, each medium has its own definition of "circulation." Consequently, most media experts tend to restrict "circulation" to magazines and newspapers, using "audiences" or "coverage" in referring to other media.

Circulation data show an advertiser whether a particular publica-tion covers his potential market. If his product is sold in small towns, he will not be eager to buy space in a newspaper that is sold mainly in a metropolitan area. An advertiser selling his product in the eastern United States only would not be inclined to buy space in a magazine with a large national circulation.

Circulation data are used also as a qualitative measure. For exam-ple, some publications temporarily boost their circulation through group offers, subscription associations, or the offer of premiums to new subscribers. All such methods are brought to light in the auditing of circulation.

The *Audit Bureau of Circulations* is the oldest and largest organi-zation that audits circulation. The A.B.C. was established in 1914 and is sponsored by advertisers, agencies, and publishers, all of whom are anxious to protect themselves against unreliable figures. Only publica-tions with 70 percent or more paid circulation (that is, paid at not less than half the established basic price of the unit) are eligible for A.B.C. membership and audit. The A.B.C.'s most important service is to pro-vide a reliable standard for reporting the quantity, quality, and dis-tribution of circulation. Buyers of space are understandably skeptical of circulation figures not audited by the A.B.C. or some other auditing organization. Consequently, the majority of the large-circulation maga-zines and most daily newspapers are members.

The *Business Publications Audit of Circulations* audits the circula-tion of certain publications that distribute their copies to selected groups and are not therefore eligible for membership in the A.B.C. These are usually called "controlled-circulation" publications, and copies are sent (usually free) to business or professional people who are likely to be interested in the editorial material.

Verified Audit Circulation verifies the validity of circulation figures by a statistical sampling procedure which determines the accuracy of circulation lists, receipt of the publication, and qualification of recipients.

Circulation data for most publications with the source indicated are available in the *Standard Rate & Data Service*, the primary source of information for most media buyers.

Audience. The term "audience" focuses attention *directly* on the number of people who are contacted by an individual vehicle. Where circulation emphasizes *copies*, audience (or readership) emphasizes *people*. Audience data are compiled by the publication or by a buyer interested in more complete information on audience coverage.

Among the common questions investigated by audience studies are these: How many readers does the publication have per copy? What is the total number of readers reached? (According to studies by W. R. Sim-mons, more than 33,000,000 Americans eighteen years of age or above see any given issue of *Life*.) How is the audience distributed by demographic or social variables? What is the overlapping among audiences of different media?

Communications Effectiveness. In recent years media researchers have made a substantial start toward providing data far beyond the mere exposure of audiences to a medium. Such data make it possible to compare the communication effectiveness of one magazine with another or even to compare a magazine with a television program. Communication yardsticks used in media comparisons are likely to take one or more of the following forms:

> Exposure to the message.
> Perception of the advertising idea.
> Awareness of the advertising idea.
> Change of attitude toward the product.
> Sales.

Naturally advertisers would prefer to compare one medium with another on the basis of the ability of each to produce sales. Such studies are being conducted, but they are complicated and costly, particularly when they are controlled experiments in the field. It is much easier, however, to study the effectiveness of a given message in changing peoples' attitudes if the message is placed in one medium and then compared with its effect in another.

Cost Comparisons. Advertisers always wonder whether they might be able to make the same impact more cheaply with a different media mix. It is almost impossible to make any realistic cost comparisons from one *type* of medium to another, because there are no standards for comparison. How, for example, can you compare an agate line with a minute of TV time? However, certain yardsticks are commonly used *within* media types:

> Milline rates (for newspapers)
> Cost-per-page-per-thousand copies (for magazines)
> Cost-per-commercial-minute-per-thousand (for television and radio)

Given the rate and appropriate audience figures, you can usually work out comparisons to fit your own problem. (One advertising agency, concerned with the farm market, compares magazines on the basis of "cost per thousand hogs.") Or you may compare newspapers on the basis of milline rates for the trading area only (tru-line).

(Cost comparisons will be discussed in more detail in connection with individual types of media.)

QUALITATIVE FACTORS

In spite of all the data available there is still a subjective element in media decisions. Suppose that you are considering two magazines, *Banking* and *Life*. The former has a cost per page per thousand of $18.54, and *Life*, a cost of only $5.26. On such a quantitative basis *Life* is the better buy. Suppose further that you are interested primarily in bankers, not in a mass audience. Then it would cost around $600 per thousand to reach them in *Life*, compared with $18.54 per thousand in *Banking*. But more important than the quantitative factors are qualitative ones such as how seriously each magazine is read.

Groups of Qualitative Factors. Brown, Lessler and Weilbacher divide qualitative factors into three groups: (1) "pure" qualitative factors such as prestige; (2) more specific factors such as enjoyment; and (3) those that are relatively easy to measure, such as time spent.[2] This threefold classification is useful for organizing one's thinking in this nebulous qualitative area.

Many media emphasize the "pure" qualitative factors in promoting their space and time. Some claim more prestige, some claim more influence, and at least one claims more "togetherness." A glance through the trade advertisements in *Media/scope* or *Advertising Age* will indicate how much these factors are emphasized. Buyers and sellers agree that these qualities are important—the trick is to put them in usable terms. For example, in discussing the prestige of a magazine, do we mean the editorial prestige, the advertising prestige, or some other type of prestige? Both the sellers and buyers in the media field use research, direct ("Which of these media do you prefer?") and indirect (use of the semantic differential, depth interviewing, and so on) in an attempt to pin down some of the vague qualitative concepts.

Here, for example, are some findings from a study that used the direct approach in soliciting opinions from the consuming public about the various media.[3] In the first column we have the characteristics in which newspapers came out on top, and in the second, those in which television took first place.

Newspaper Firsts	*Television Firsts*
most helpful	most pleasure
practical	deepest impact
honest	most fun
dependable	best relaxation
best informed	friendliest
best advertising	
means the most	
most educational	
hardest to be without	

The more specific qualitative factors are, of course, somewhat easier to measure. However, we still run into definition troubles (for example, what does it mean when the *Ladies' Home Journal* states, "The reader enjoys the ads—gets direct and vicarious satisfaction from studying them . . ."?).

There are, however, certain qualitative factors that are relatively simple to measure. We can, for example, compare media on the basis of the time people spend with them. In one such study media were compared

[2]Lyndon O. Brown, Richard S. Lessler, and William M. Weilbacher, *Advertising Media* (New York: The Ronald Press Company, 1957), pp. 219–225.
[3]Wesley I. Nunn, advertising manager, Standard Oil Company (Ind.), in a talk, "A Case History in Media Selection," delivered at the advertising seminar, University of Wisconsin, February 9, 1957.

on the basis of the number of hours per day which a given sample of homes spent with each.

Creative Considerations. Creative people sometimes feel a particular message "belongs" in a certain medium. Martin Mayer reports:

> An advertiser selling a high-quality liqueur or an imported sports car wants people who consider themselves sophisticates and advertises in *The New Yorker*; a man selling a home ice-cream-maker wants people who do not consider themselves sophisticates, and advertises in the *American Legion Magazine*, in *Grit*, in *Farm Journal*, all of which go primarily to rural and semi-rural America.[4]

One useful way to differentiate media for creative purposes is suggested by Wilbur Schramm:[5]

Space-Time. Printed materials, still pictures, and art objects are space organized. Radio and television are time media. The space media are preferable for complicated concepts, for masses of detail, for criticalness, discrimination, and selectivity on the part of the audience. On the other hand, time-organized media offer advantages for rote learning of simple material (such as slogans) and for encouraging suggestibility in an audience.

Participation. Television permits more participation on the part of the audience than magazines do. The nonmediated channels (for instance, conversation) permit the greatest amount. In general, the more social participation, the more we have a sense of involvement, a group bond, a circulation pattern of influence (feedback), and decision making.

Speed or Timeliness. Timeliness is greatest in television and radio, somewhat less in newspapers, and still less in magazines and direct mail. The more timely the medium, the more it lends itself to giving news about products and what they will do for consumers. The less timely media are better adapted to more lasting and reflective messages.

Permanence. Magazines are more permanent than most other media. The least permanent are the time-organized media. The more permanent media are better adapted to organized and reasoned persuasion; the less permanent are better adapted to straight persuasion.

Content Analysis. The content of a medium is a reasonable guide to the type of people who comprise its audience. This is obvious if we compare women's magazines with those of a general nature. It is not so obvious in the case of one woman's magazine as compared with another (for example, one may carry more editorial content about food, another more about fashions). Some radio stations emphasize folk music or sports events, others classical music. Editorial matter may emphasize a subject compatible with the advertiser's product, or it may provide prestige for the advertiser's message.

Content of the media is usually analyzed on the basis of the topics covered (for example, percentage of foreign news or sports news) or the way it is presented (such as themes or characters presented in daytime television dramas). Both give the media analyst some clues to the type

---

[4]Martin Mayer, *Madison Avenue, U.S.A.* (New York: Harper & Row, Publishers, 1958), p. 173.
[5]Wilbur Schramm, *The Process and Effects of Mass Communication* (Urbana: University of Illinois Press, 1954), pp. 87–90.

of person in the audience and the frame of mind in which that person approaches the medium. Although a woman might read both *Life* and *True Story*, her frame of reference is not the same for each.

Mechanical Considerations. Mechanical considerations such as quality of color, the availability of fine screen reproduction or Videotape, may cause a media buyer to include a particular medium on the advertising schedule, or to use it in a certain way. These considerations will be discussed with each of the media.

PROBLEMS OF MEDIA USAGE

After you have decided on types, classes, and vehicles, you must determine *how* these will be used. This involves a variety of decisions culminating in the advertising schedule, which shows which ads will appear on what days (and what time of day in the case of the broadcast media). For example, if you are using television, you will have to decide among spot announcements, spot programs, special network shows, alternate sponsorships, and the lot. If you are using newspapers, you may use black and white or color and a variety of insertion sizes. In general, problems of media usage fall within four major categories: continuity, coverage, frequency, and size.

Continuity describes the general pattern of message deliveries over a given period of time. For example, you can schedule advertisements at about the same frequency the year round, or you can concentrate them in a particular season.

Coverage refers to the number of persons or households reached. If we use more than one medium, we thus have duplicated coverage. With successive issues of a newspaper or magazine we reach some of the same people again and again; consequently, we may be concerned with "cumulative coverage."

Frequency involves the number of times the advertising messages are delivered during a given period of time. The greater the frequency, the more likely the audience is to see or hear your message.

Size can be measured in either space or time. In general, the larger the space or time segment you buy, the greater the impact. The greater size, however, costs more. You are always plagued by budget limitations that prevent you from achieving as much as you want of all four categories. You may well decide to sacrifice continuity for frequency of impression for a new product. Brown, Lessler and Weilbacher suggest the following approach:

> It is necessary to define, individually, an optimum dispersion program for each brand or product. In defining this program the degree to which simple coverage (the number of people reached in a given period of time) is sufficient to accomplish an advertising objective must be considered. In defining this program, the average number of impressions required to catalyze action (effective frequency) must also be appraised. The need for regularity of impression (continuity) must likewise be considered.[6]

Look, for example, at the media plan for our hypothetical tomato product (Figure 24.2). Note that during the announcement period of the

[6]Brown, Lessler, and Weilbacher, p. 342.

campaign heavy network television is used together with a very strong print advertising program. The objective is to create excitement about the product in the maximum number of homes, to establish familiarity with the package, and to induce sampling. Sufficient coverage is then provided to sustain the initial impact. Note, however, that the frequency need not be as great as in the first stages.

It should be plain that these problems of media usage do not lend themselves to any offhand solution. They are complex, and many choices confront the media buyer faced with making up a schedule. In the chapters that follow, problems of media usage are discussed in terms of the individual media.

MODELS, COMPUTERS AND MEDIA STRATEGY

Media planning has been somewhat glamorized in recent years by the addition of computers to the media departments of several large agencies and to the planning operations of some of the larger corporations. For example, Batten, Barton, Durstine & Osborn developed a *media model* applying the mathematical technique of linear programming to the problems of media evaluation and selection. The model is intended "to help media planners select and schedule media purchases so as to accumulate the largest audience of prospects to whom advertising messages can be transmitted with desired frequency over specified periods of time."[7] An important part of the procedure is the setting of goals in terms of gross impressions, reach or coverage, average frequency of exposure, and frequency distribution of the number of occasions members of the target audience are to be exposed to various media vehicles. Computers are used to facilitate the linear programming computations to select the combination of media that will best satisfy the various goals.

Another approach is the High Assay Media Model developed by Young & Rubicam.[8] This model is based on simulating the communications and behavior process of the target consumer. The model is fed data in the following three categories: consumer-product behavior, consumer-media behavior, and consumer-advertising behavior. The decision system uses the computer to find out the lowest-cost medium per prospect, adjusting for the effect of purchases. It attempts also to determine whether optimum prospect exposure has been reached. The approach differs from linear programming in that an attempt is made to simulate the effects of specific media schedules, whereas linear programming—given certain media goals—is designed to choose the best or close-to-best schedule from a large number of possible advertising vehicles.

It is easy to overdramatize the contributions of computers to media programming and research. After all, the computer can only process

[7]See Harry Deane Wolfe, James K. Brown, G. Clark Thompson, and Stephen H. Greenberg, *Evaluating Media* (New York: National Industrial Conference Board, 1966), p. 115. This book describes in some detail five generalized media models currently in use.
[8]William T. Moran, "Practical Media Decisions and the Computer," in Harper W. Boyd, Jr., and Joseph W. Newman, eds., *Advertising Management: Selected Readings* (Homewood, Ill.: Richard D. Irwin, Inc., 1965).

information someone has collected and quantified. If you want to study such qualitative factors as the image of the media, these factors must be expressed in numerical terms before they can be introduced into the computer. The NICB study points out that "to a large extent the use of computers has been aimed at manipulating large quantities of data efficiently rather than developing new techniques of analysis." The report further states:

> Several large advertising agencies employ computers for media research; but here again, part of the computer's function is to expedite the routine work of their media departments. One of these agencies states that its computer has helped it handle the three billion facts and figures a year that it collects and utilizes in planning advertising campaigns for clients.[9]

Joseph St. George points out also that computers enable the advertising man to concentrate his attention on key areas where evaluation and judgment are needed rather than on the tedious drudgery of statistical comparisons.[10]

Brown suggests that perhaps media planners have been overly concerned with linear programming and simulation and have overlooked the possibilities of incremental analysis, because it too can take full advantage of a properly programmed digital computer.[11]

SUMMARY

The media bring the communicator and the audience together. In practice, the buying of media is highly complex. It is based on careful formulation of media objectives and an evaluation of both quantitative evidence (which is fairly plentiful) and qualitative evidence (which is not). Certain trends, such as the rise of television, changes in the older media and technological and marketing developments, have made the business of working out the media mix a complex one.

In skeleton form the plan is based on marketing (and communication) objectives. Decisions must be made about what types and classes of media and what media vehicles will be used and what coverage and frequency will be needed. These decisions are partly based on quantitative evidence, partly on qualitative evidence, and partly on educated hunches.

Among the more important quantitative variables are the markets to be reached, circulations and audiences of the media, and comparative costs. Among the qualitative factors are "pure" ones such as prestige; not quite so pure ones such as enjoyment or time spent; and certain creative considerations (such as the ability of the message to provide the right climate for what is to be said, comparative content, and mechanical facilities).

The final step in the preparation of the media plan is deciding how the chosen media will be used. In general, media usage problems center upon continuity, coverage, frequency, and size.

[9]Wolfe *et.al.*, p. 106.
[10]Joseph St. George, "How Practical Is the Media Model?" in Boyd and Newman, pp. 455–458.
[11]Douglas B. Brown, "A Practical Procedure for Media Selection," *Journal of Marketing Research,* August 1967.

QUESTIONS FOR DISCUSSION

1. To what extent is media strategy related to creative strategy?
2. What are the main ingredients of the "media mix"? What are the principal factors influencing the mix?
3. What influence have computers had on media strategy?
4. To what extent is it possible to compare one medium with another on the basis of cost?
5. What types of media research are needed to make media strategy more valuable?
6. How do you balance coverage, frequency, and continuity in working out a media plan?
7. What is the value of applying the heavy-user concept to media planning and strategy?

SUGGESTED READINGS

Barban, Arnold and Sandage, C. H., eds., *Readings in Advertising and Promotion Strategy.* Homewood, Ill.: Richard D. Irwin, Inc., 1968, *Part IV.*

Barton, Roger, *Media in Advertising.* New York: McGraw-Hill, Inc., 1964.

Bogart, Leo, ed., *Psychology in Media Strategy.* Chicago: American Marketing Association, 1968.

Brown, Lyndon O., Richard S. Lessler, and William M. Weilbacher, *Advertising Media.* New York: The Ronald Press Company, 1957.

Gaw, Walter A., *Advertising Methods and Media.* Belmont, Calif.: Wadsworth Publishing Company, Inc., 1961.

Langhoff, Peter, ed., *Models, Measurement and Marketing.* Englewood Cliffs, N.J., Prentice-Hall, Inc., 1965.

McLuhan, H. Marshall, *Understanding Media.* New York: McGraw-Hill, Inc., 1964.

Mayer, Martin, *Madison Avenue, U.S.A.* New York: Harper & Row, Publishers, Inc., 1958. Chapter 9.

Moran, William T., "Practical Media Decisions and the Computer," in Harper W. Boyd, Jr., and Joseph W. Newman, eds., *Advertising Management: Selected Readings.* Homewood, Ill.: Richard D. Irwin, Inc., 1965.

St. George, Joseph, "How Practical Is the Media Model?" in Harper W. Boyd, Jr., and Joseph W. Newman, eds., *Advertising Management: Selected Readings.* Homewood, Ill.: Richard D. Irwin, Inc., 1965.

Wedding, Nugent, and Richard S. Lessler, *Advertising Management.* New York: The Ronald Press Company, 1962.

Wolfe, Harry Deane, James K. Brown, G. Clark Thompson, and Stephen H. Greenberg, *Evaluating Media.* New York: National Industrial Conference Board, 1966.

25 | The Print Media

Approximately half of the total advertising expenditures is accounted for by the three principal print media—newspapers, magazines, and direct mail. In subsequent chapters the other major types of media —broadcast, outdoor and display, and sales promotion media—will be covered.

NEWSPAPERS

If you were rating media on the basis of total dollars spent, you would put newspapers in first place by a huge margin. Daily and Sunday newspapers account for approximately 30 percent of total advertising expenditures, three fourths of which comes directly or indirectly from retailers. (In "cooperative advertising programs" the manufacturer pays part or all of the bill for advertising that features his merchandise but is run over the retailer's signature.)

The first regularly published newspaper in the colonies, the *Boston Newsletter*, had a circulation of approximately 300 copies a week and continued publication until 1776. The first regularly published *daily* paper did not appear until 1783. During the nineteenth century the newspaper became truly a mass medium. Benjamin Day established the

New York Sun in 1833, the first major paper to sell for a penny. Day put publishing on a businesslike basis. Later in the century, publishers such as Joseph Pulitzer, James Gordon Bennett, and Horace Greeley made newspapers a dynamic force in American social and political life.

Newspapers are usually classified according to frequency of publication. Thus we have two primary groups—daily and weekly. Table 25.1 indicates the number, circulation, and rates of three standard classifications of daily newspapers. According to the *N. W. Ayer Directory of Periodicals*, there were, in addition, 8,958 weeklies and 363 semiweeklies in the United States in 1968. The rate concepts included in this table are discussed later in the chapter.

AGGREGATE CIRCULATION AND RATES OF
UNITED STATES NEWSPAPERS (1968)
                                                                                                TABLE 25.1

CLASSIFICATION	TOTAL NO. OF PAPERS	COMBINED CIRCULATION	AGGREGATE LINE RATE	COST PER MILLION CIRCULATION
Morning	121	11,407,015	$43.956	$3.85
Evening	1,212	25,565,983	181.184	7.09
All-day	197	23,105,446	88.656	3.84

SOURCE: *Standard Rate & Data Service, Inc., Newspaper Rates and Data,* April 12, 1968.

The paper with the largest circulation, the *New York Daily News*, sold more than 2,000,000 copies a day; the smallest daily may have a circulation of only a few thousand. Most daily papers serve local areas. (The *Wall Street Journal*, with a national circulation in excess of 850,000, is a notable exception.) By 1968, the combined daily circulation of all United States newspapers was approximately 61,400,000, a new high.

Daily newspapers are often categorized on the basis of the size of the market area. Thus advertisers may decide to take the "first 10 markets," "first 50" and so on (see Table 25.5). A 10-year analysis of the growth of daily newspapers indicates that the highest rate of growth (as measured by newsprint consumption) in recent years has been in cities of less than 100,000 and the lowest rate in cities with more than a million population, although it should be kept in mind that smaller papers have a smaller base for comparison.[1] If we take circulation as our standard of growth, we again find the smaller areas (particularly when they are in suburban areas of large cities) growing more rapidly than the large metropolitan daily.

Usually, the weekly or community newspaper is published in a small, homogeneous community. This may be a small town in Montana or a suburban area near New York City. The publisher of a weekly newspaper frequently depends heavily on job printing for his revenue.

Newspapers may also be classified according to paid circulation or controlled circulation. The shopping-newspaper, or "shopper," for example, is normally distributed free and therefore its circulation is controlled. It is usually distributed to certain parts of a town or to

[1]See Jon Udell, *The Growth of the American Daily Newspaper.* Madison: University of Wisconsin, 1965.

selected types of homes. The majority of newspapers, however, are not distributed free.

Newspapers may also be distinguished on the basis of the audience they attract. Thus, in addition to the general-interest newspapers we have many that cater to special groups (Negro or Chinese, foreign language, labor, trade). These papers are like magazines in many ways, although their format is similar to that of other newspapers.

Size is another criterion for classifying newspapers. We have two basic sizes—the tabloid (usually 5 columns wide and about 200 agate lines in depth) and the standard size (usually 8 columns wide and approximately 300 agate lines in depth).

Other bases for classification include frequency of publication (daily, weekly), type of audience (general, foreign), and color (black and white, r.o.p.—run-of-paper color).

WHY RETAIL AND GENERAL ADVERTISERS BUY NEWS-PAPER SPACE

There are two distinct types of newspaper advertisers—retail and general. Some characteristics of the newspaper appeal to both types; others appeal to only one. As we pointed out in Chapter 1, retail (or local) advertisers sell products and services to the ultimate consumer, whereas the general (or national) advertiser sells to the distributors and is usually more interested in promoting his brand than a particular store.

The newspaper is the major advertising medium for most retailers. According to *Marketing/Communications* (see Table 24.2), more than 60 percent of all retail advertising expenditures in 1967 went to newspapers. It is easy to understand the attraction that newspapers have for retailers when we consider how well their characteristics fit retail communication needs (for example, their circulation distribution in the trading area, their day-after-day appearance, their use as shopping guides by consumers, and their prestige).

Until the middle of the 1940s the newspaper was the leading medium for general or national advertisers. Since 1955, television has been the leader—in direct expenditures, at least. Actually, it is almost impossible to estimate how many dollars of general advertising are diverted through retailers' hands as cooperative advertising and thus show up in retail classifications (see Chapter 29). However, newspapers have fared much better in the face of competition from television than many predicted in the mid-1940s. Their flexibility for use in test campaigns and in filling in gaps in national schedules has kept them in high esteem among space buyers who represent general advertisers.

In this section an attempt will be made to assess the various advantages and limitations that might be of importance to either retail or national advertisers.

Advantages

Flexibility. Newspapers offer the general advertiser more territorial flexibility than other media do. Whether he uses them for basic coverage or to fill in gaps left by network television, he is able to advertise heavily in one area and lightly in another. The market may be fertile in Kokomo, Indiana, but not in Kankakee, Illinois. One area may be having a heat wave while another is having moderate temperatures. With newspapers you can place your advertising where the potential market looks best.

Territorial flexibility has special appeal to general advertisers who want to test a new product. They can advertise it in certain test areas and save the time, the trouble, and the expense of a national campaign. Also, the mass coverage most newspapers provide, the chance to put the new product ad in a news context, and the opportunity of getting fairly immediate action all enhance the desirability of newspapers for introducing new products.

Retail advertisers, operating within a trading area, are not so concerned with territorial flexibility. They are, however, like their counterparts in the general field, interested in the newspaper's *time* flexibility (that is, the advertisement may be changed up to a few hours before the paper goes to press). Changes in the weather or in merchandise available for sale, or myriad other unforeseen circumstances may make last-minute revisions desirable.

The rise of r.o.p. (run of paper) color offers advertisers still more flexibility in their use of newspapers. (More than 1,000 daily papers provided at least one color in 1968.)

Community Prestige. Both retail and general advertisers like to associate themselves with the prestige most local papers enjoy in a community. One of the best indications of how people feel toward their newspaper is their behavior when they are without it. Several studies have been made in United States cities that have been deprived of their daily paper. All have indicated the deep impact a newspaper has on a community. For example, a study made for the Bureau of Applied Social Research of Columbia University attempted "to go beyond the general protestations of the newspaper's indispensability and seek out certain basic reader-gratifications which the newspaper supplied." In reporting the findings, Bernard Berelson says:

. . . we have noted certain typical uses of the modern newspaper—both "rational" (like the provision of news and information) and "non-rational" (like the provision of social contacts and, indiscreetly, social prestige). In addition, however, we have hypothesized that reading has value per se in our society, value in which the newspaper shares as the most convenient supplier of reading matter. In addition, the newspaper is missed because it serves as a (non-"rational") source of security in a disturbing world, and finally, because the reading of the newspaper has become a ceremonial or ritualistic or near compulsive act for many people.[2]

Intense Coverage. In many areas you can reach more than 90 percent of the homes through a single newspaper. In most areas all except a few homes (mostly those low on the economic scale) take some paper. A quick glance through almost any newspaper will show you that it includes news of interest to all groups of the population—the sports fans, the women, and the businessmen. It is, however, possible to select

[2]Bernard Berelson, "What Missing the Newspaper Means," in Wilbur Schramm, ed., *The Process and Effects of Mass Communication* (Urbana: University of Illinois Press, 1954).

customers of a particular group by placing your advertisement in a special-interest section (perhaps sports pages for men).

Reader Controls Exposure. Because the reader can scan, skip, or plod through the paper, he need not suffer the boredom, bewilderment, and resentment he might undergo in the time media.

This point is of special importance to retailers who depend on newspaper advertisements to provide shopping information for readers. Through newspapers they can tell consumers what the merchandise looks like, how much it costs, and where they can get it. The reader can take as much or as little time as he or she wants in reading the ad and can refer to it later if he likes.

Dealer-National Advertiser Coordination. Both the general advertiser and the dealer can profit from the fact that their advertisements can complement each other. The advertiser of a new biscuit mix advertises the advantages of this mix over competing products. The local food chains tie in with these ads and tell you where you can get the mix and how much it costs a box. Sometimes the space cost is shared by the dealer and the manufacturer (cooperative advertising). Many newspapers have special staffs to help dealers and manufacturers coordinate their advertising. (See, for example, the organization of the *Milwaukee Journal* in Figure 9.7.)

Services Offered by Newspapers. For the general advertiser many newspapers make available merchandising services. They can help him broaden his distribution in local stores, convince local retailers that they should promote his product, and assist the manufacturer's representative to analyze the local market. Many papers send out newsletters to drugstores and grocery stores, notifying proprietors that certain brands will be advertised by their makers in the newspaper during the coming week. Many offer extensive research facilities (such as readership studies and consumer surveys). Some newspapers prefer to emphasize the space rather than the extra services, and some buyers complain about the cost of these services. They maintain they would prefer to have lower line rates.

For the retailer the services are important but in somewhat different ways. The small store is probably impressed by the free copy and art service he gets from the paper, although some of the larger stores might use the research facilities of the paper.

Limitations

Short Life. There is nothing quite so stale as a newspaper a few days old. The chances that advertising will have any impact beyond the day of publication are therefore very low. On the other hand, potential buyers know that each day's production is a fresh one.

Hasty Reading. Most studies indicate that the average reader spends between twenty and thirty minutes on the paper. This means the ad has to make its impression quickly or not at all.

Poor Reproduction. Even though reproduction has improved substantially in the last decade, the newspaper still rates well below magazines in this respect. If appearance is important in the sale of a product, the product is likely to suffer when its picture is reproduced in the newspaper. Note how often an automobile manufacturer will emphasize the beauty of the car in his magazine ads, but stress mechanical superiority or economy in his newspaper advertising.

WHAT KINDS OF ADVERTISERS USE NEWSPAPERS?

In Table 25.2 we have the dollar volume spent in newspapers by product classification for two years. Note the dominant position here of two classifications—automotive and groceries.

LEADING NEWSPAPER ADVERTISERS (1966–1967)   **TABLE 25.2**
(In dollars)

ADVERTISER	1967	1966
General Motors	46,039,401	58,848,332
Ford Motor Co.	24,191,929	26,619,940
National Dairy Products	15,997,362	12,932,138
Chrysler Corp.	13,539,645	17,111,923
Distillers Corp.-Seagrams	12,730,497	13,988,861
Radio Corp. of America	10,856,245	8,682,265
General Foods Corp.	6,686,779	5,747,286
Goodyear Tire & Rubber Co.	6,446,847	5,870,113
National Distillers	5,636,222	6,498,774
Hiram Walker-Gooderham	5,598,483	4,729,449

SOURCE: Bureau of Advertising, American Newspaper Publishers Association, compiled by Media Records Inc.

In the retail field, department stores are the dominant classification. They contribute slightly less than one third of all retail lineage.

CIRCULATION AND READERSHIP PATTERNS

Circulation patterns vary somewhat by type of paper. In general, the circulation of a morning paper will be dispersed over a larger geographical area than will an evening paper in the same city. More morning newspapers will be mailed out on rural routes, and more evening papers will be picked off the newsstand during the day. However, in many larger cities there is a higher proportion of morning papers than of evening papers distributed at the newsstands.

People who read the paper are usually a cross section of the people who live in the trading area served by each newspaper. In itself, a newspaper is not a selective medium. It is read by men and women at all educational and income levels. Yet, although it is read by both men and women, a newspaper is not a dual-appeal medium in the strictest sense of the word. Research shows that the first page of a daily newspaper is read thoroughly by both sexes. The second and third pages receive a reasonably high percentage of dual readership, but after that dual readership is more difficult to obtain except on the picture page and comics page. Afternoon papers generally have higher readership among women than morning papers.

The wide audience appeal of newspapers is evident in Table 25.3. Note that in more than 86 percent of United States households at least one newspaper is read.

Studies of newspaper reading show the high male readership of sports material. A preponderance of women turn to the society and women's pages. Thus in a daily newspaper it is possible to have an advertisement that is assured of wide exposure to one sex but will exclude much of the other. It is therefore evident that although the newspaper itself is not a selective medium, certain positions in it can be selective. It also is possible to get exposure to a sizable dual audience with an advertisement on page two or three. These are often considered special positions available only at a premium price.

TABLE 25.3

AVERAGE DAY READERSHIP OF NEWSPAPERS BY
HOUSEHOLDS AND INDIVIDUALS
(In percentages)

	HOUSEHOLDS	ADULTS (21 & OVER)			TEEN-AGERS (15 – 20)
		Total	Male	Female	
Total U.S.	100	100	100	100	100
Daily newspapers					
Total readers	86.4	79.7	80.5	79.0	71.5
Primary*	80.4	72.0	74.2	70.1	62.4
Secondary†	6.0	7.7	6.3	8.9	9.1
Readers per newspaper	–	2.0	1.0	1.0	0.2
Sunday newspapers					
Total readers	72.7	65.7	64.8	66.6	60.4
Primary*	68.8	50.3	53.5	47.6	44.3
Secondary†	3.9	15.4	11.3	19.0	16.1
Readers per newspaper	–	1.9	0.9	1.0	0.2

*Readers in households where newspaper is purchased.
†All other readers.
Table reads: In 86.4 percent of all United States households, at least one newspaper is read on the average weekday.
SOURCE: A national study of newspaper reading (Bureau of Advertising).

TYPES OF ADVERTISING

McClure and Fulton suggest the following[3] as a workable outline for types of newspaper advertising:

Display advertising	general (national)
	regional
	retail (local)
	retail
	local service
	farm auction
	political
	miscellaneous
Classified advertising	classified
	classified display

[3]Leslie McClure and D. C. Fulton, *Advertising in the Printed Media* (New York: Crowell–Collier and Macmillan, Inc., 1964), Chaps. 5–7.

Classified advertising	business and professional cards
	farm auction
	political
Public notices	legal
	public treasurers' reports
	other public reports
	public notices by private citizens
	and organizations
	financial reports
Readers	paid reading notices

The first two of these classifications, display and classified, are far more important than the other two in terms of total dollar volume. If you are a retailer selling dresses or a manufacturer selling air conditioners, you will be interested mainly in display advertising. In fact, display advertising accounts for about 82 percent of the advertising revenue of the average medium-sized newspaper.

FIG. 25.1 *Advertisement from a trade paper emphasizing the newspaper's services to media buyers.* COURTESY THE PHILADELPHIA INQUIRER.

Display advertising has strong attention value because of the illustrations, the arrangement of headlines and body text, the white space, color, or other visual devices. Much classified however, is published without conspicuous display. As the name implies, classified advertisements are arranged under subheads according to the product advertised or the want the advertisement is supposed to satisfy. If you were selling your house or your car, you would use the classified advertising. Classified display allows more flexibility of arrangement than regular classified in that borders, larger type, white space, photos, and occasionally color may be used. Some newspapers have the advertising of real estate agents and builders handled under classified display, others under retail. In some newspaper markets, classified is growing faster than retail.

Public notice and legal advertising is material required by law to be published in newspapers. Reader advertising is advertising printed in an editorial format so that it looks, at first glance, like a news story. Most newspapers require that such copy be labeled as advertising.

The ratio of advertising to editorial content, as measured by Media Records, has reversed since 1941, when advertising represented 40 percent of the total. By the 1960s advertising was about 60 percent and editorial content 40 percent.

NEWSPAPER SIZES AND SHAPES

The space unit for newspapers is the *agate line* or the *column inch*. An agate line is 1/14 inch in depth and one column wide, regardless of the width of the column. The *Chicago Tribune*, for example, is an 8-column newspaper with each column 310 lines deep. The total number of lines on the page is therefore 2,480. On the other hand, the *New York Daily News* is a tabloid-size paper with 200 agate lines to the column and 1,000 lines to the page.

Rates for general advertisers are usually quoted in lines, and retail rates in either lines or inches. A column inch is a space 1 inch deep and one column wide. It is easy to convert lines to inches by dividing by 14. Thus, the 2,480 lines per page in the *Chicago Tribune* equal 177 2/14 inches.

Fractional page units are more common in newspapers than in magazines. One sixth, one eighth, one twelfth, and one twenty-fourth of a page are standard units of newspaper advertising space. Because a newspaper page normally includes more advertisements than does a magazine page, each ad has to fight for visibility. Most papers will permit you to use layouts in which one part of the advertisement is deeper than another (for example, part may be 4 columns wide and 15 inches deep, and part of it 3 columns wide and 8 inches deep). However, many papers require that the advertisement be as many inches deep as it is columns wide.

RATE STRUCTURE

R.O.P. versus Premium Positions. The basic line rate applies to an advertisement placed "r.o.p." (run-of-paper), which means that it can

FIG. 25.2 *(a) and (b)
Typical pages from
Standard Rate & Data
Service—Newspapers.*
SOURCE: STANDARD RATE
& DATA SERVICE, INC.

appear on any page, in any position in a column, or even buried in among other ads. If the advertiser wants to make sure that he has his ad next to reading matter, he can usually order specific pages or positions at an extra charge. For example, if he is using the *Los Angeles Times* and wants to make sure his advertisement is placed at the very top of the page and next to reading matter along one of its vertical sides (full position), he will have to pay 33.3 percent more. If he wants to make sure it is next to reading matter or if he wants a special page, but is not particular about being at the top, he will have to pay an extra 15 percent. These charges are at the "publisher's option," and apply only if the advertiser asks for this specified position. Frequently, of course, he can obtain these positions without extra charge.

Retail versus General Rates. Most newspapers charge more per agate line for general than for retail space. This is a sore point among the general advertisers and their agencies, because retail rates (with discounts) sometimes cost less than half of those for general advertising.

Newspaper publishers and business managers defend this differential on several bases. In general, their experiments with lowering general rates to the same level as retail have resulted in only small increases in total linage from general advertisers. Newspaper executives maintain that the demand for general advertising is inelastic (will not expand as the price lowers or contract as the price increases), compared to that for retail advertising. They also point to the agency commission granted on general but not usually on retail rates, the payment to the national representatives for their services (for example, selling agencies and their clients on the local newspapers), the merchandising services furnished general advertisers, and the fact that the general advertiser is less likely than his retail counterpart to be a year-round user of advertising. Some newspaper executives point also to the higher readership of the retail advertisements, maintaining that these add more to the newspaper's attractiveness and reader appeal.

However, the general advertisers and their agencies do not generally accept these as valid reasons for the huge differential that often exists. They point to the fact that most papers maintain a large and costly staff to service the advertising of the local retail advertiser (usually at no extra charge to him). They hint also that the newspaper managements may be somewhat more sensitive to protests from the retailers, who are, after all, their friends and neighbors, than from the more distant general advertiser. There is some evidence that newspaper publishers are making efforts to narrow the differential and are rechecking to find out whether they had perhaps overestimated the inelasticity of demand for space by general advertisers. Studies by Simon and Ferguson indicate that the retail-general rate differential is narrowing.[4] Simon found that newspaper executives do indeed find retail advertising demand more elastic than general. Ferguson devised a joint product hypothesis based partially on the idea that retail advertising contributes to circulation growth but general does not.

Sliding Scale. Newspaper rates may either be *flat* (the same, regardless of how much you use) or *open* (subject to various discounts). When the newspapers feel the price is elastic, they may set up a schedule of discounts (or a sliding scale) to encourage businesses to advertise more, or more often. These discounts are most frequently used at the retail level, but certain newspapers offer them to general advertisers as well.

[4]See James M. Ferguson, *The Advertising Rate Structure in the Daily Newspaper Industry* (Englewood Cliffs, N.J.: Prentice-Hall, Inc., 1963), and Julian Simon, unpublished manuscript, "The Cause of the Newspaper Rate Differential: A Subjective Demand Curve Analysis."

Here, for example, is the scale of rates for general advertising in the *New York Times*:

GENERAL CONTRACTS (Rate per line, in dollars)		TABLE 25.4
	DAILY	SUNDAY
Open	2.90	3.55
2,500 lines	2.73	3.39
5,000 lines	2.70	3.36
10,000 lines	2.69	3.35
15,000 lines	2.68	3.33
25,000 lines	2.67	3.32
50,000 lines	2.65	3.29
75,000 lines	2.63	3.27
100,000 lines	2.60	3.23

SOURCE: *Standard Rate and Data Service,* Newspaper Rates and Data, April 12, 1968.

Some newspapers offer a schedule of frequency discounts so that advertisers will be encouraged to advertise regularly throughout the year. Some papers offer *earned rates*, used when an advertiser has no contract but receives the lowest applicable rate (under any combination of frequency and quantity) for his advertising during a specified time—usually a month. *No-change rates* often are offered to daily advertisers who will use the same copy day after day, or weekly advertisers who will use the same copy week after week.

One study of the elasticity of demand indicates that buyers often fail to take advantage of discounts:

> The evidence presented here lends small support to the contention of space buyers that they would have increased their budgets if the price had been right. Instead, they seem to have bought more on a nonprice than price basis. It is, of course, true that this study is limited in scope in that only two variables (linage and space usage) are studied in a complex situation influenced by such factors as the competition of alternative media, the change in price levels generally, the increase of such inducements as r.o.p. color and preprinting, etc.
>
> The data suggest that buyers were not discouraged by the price increases studied. In fact, one can carry the analysis a bit further and speculate that the publishers, beset by rising costs, have been too hesitant about increasing their prices. This point is especially significant when one considers that a major part of the increase in total costs was due to newsprint cost—a cost which increased directly with the pages and number of copies printed.[5]

RATE COMPARISONS

The rates charged per line or per inch are often a poor guide to the actual cost of the space. Common sense should tell any buyer that a newspaper with a large circulation would naturally charge more than the newspaper with a small circulation. Consequently, it is necessary to reduce rates to some sort of common denominator if we are to compare them realistically. The yardstick most frequently used is the *milline*

[5]Robert Kahan and S. Watson Dunn, "Elasticity of Demand for National Advertising in Newspapers" (Madison: University of Wisconsin, 1964).

rate (cost per line of space per million circulation). Individual millines, however, often vary substantially from the aggregates. Here, for example, are the milline rates of two large-city dailies, *Chicago Daily News* (open line rate $1.70) and *St. Louis Post-Dispatch* (line rate, $1.15):

$$\text{Chicago Daily News} \quad \frac{\$1.70 \times 1,000,000}{466,392} = \$3.58$$

$$\text{St. Louis Post-Dispatch} \quad \frac{\$1.15 \times 1,000,000}{370,392} = \$3.14$$

After comparing millines, the buyer is in a position to decide whether the higher milline rate is justified. He will find, in general, that the smaller the newspaper's circulation, the higher its milline rate will be.

Circulation is commonly used by the newspaper management in setting the rate in the first place. However, Brown, Lessler, and Weilbacher comment:

> When compared to other available measurements of media audiences, the use of circulation in setting of media prices must be considered a relatively crude standard. The advertiser, in reviewing the price scales set by a particular medium, should not be satisfied with price relationships which are based only on circulation as a measure of audience size. He should consider media pricing from the stand-point of audience size at various levels; the gross potential audience, the net potential audience, and in the case of the broadcast media, the program delivery.[6]

Run-of-paper color will, of course, cost more than black-and-white space of the same size. Most newspapers will not sell color for advertisements smaller than 1,000 agate lines. Color surcharges vary a good deal from paper to paper, but they average from 19 percent for a full page to 37 percent for 1,000 lines if black and one color are used. If full color (black and three colors) is used, surcharges average from 34 percent for a full page to 70 percent for 1,000 lines.

HOW NEWSPAPER SPACE IS BOUGHT

Marketing Considerations. Although newspapers collectively offer both the widest and the most concentrated national coverage, their cost makes it difficult to use them on a truly national basis. If a buyer wanted to use a combination of all daily and all weekly newspapers, the cost per agate line would be more than $600. This means that the cost of a 100-line advertisement would be in excess of $60,000. If he wanted a 100-line ad a week for a year his bill would be in excess of $3,000,000. He would be getting substantial frequency, but a 100-line advertisement would not be very impressive in size.

One can see that the media buyer who thinks that newspapers should be the sole medium to support a product nationally is in trouble unless he has an unusually large advertising budget to invest. Because of the cost factor, all newspapers or even all the newspapers in any classification are rarely purchased. Sometimes an extensive newspaper list will be used for a single advertisement, such as the announcement

[6]Lyndon O. Brown, Richard S. Lessler, and William M. Weilbacher, *Advertising Media* (New York: The Ronald Press Company, 1957), p. 232.

CIRCULATION/COSTS UNITED STATES NEWSPAPERS (1967)   **TABLE 25.5**

Markets	Total Circulation	Line Rate	300 Lines	1,000 Lines	Full Page
			(In dollars)		
Top 10	15,039,776	47.45	14,235.00	45,172.70	94,209.91
Top 20	20,967,809	65.15	19,545.00	62,260.70	134,040.69
Top 30	24,988,843	77.37	23,211.00	74,155.20	162,589.20
Top 50	30,002,316	94.47	28,341.00	91,213.20	203,244.54

of a new car or a special offer of some kind. But when a sustained effort is to be made, newspaper advertising is usually planned in flights and often in selected areas and in selected markets (see Table 25.5). For example, during a calendar year it might be planned to have three flights, each of eight weeks' duration. These might be spaced uniformly throughout the year, or they might be planned to appear during a product's three best selling seasons. They might perhaps be planned to put extra sales effort into certain territories.

Suppose a media buyer decides that a flight of eight weeks' newspaper advertising is desirable in all cities of more than 25,000 population. The aggregate rate for all daily newspapers in these (approximately 600) cities is high, but there are ways in which the expenditures can be kept within reasonable limits. The first thing the media buyer can do is divide the cities (or metropolitan areas) into population groups:

Group 1—All cities of 1,000,000 population or more.

Group 2—All cities between 500,000 and 999,999.

Group 3—All cities between 100,000 and 499,999.

Group 4—All cities between 50,000 and 99,999.

Group 5—All cities under 50,000.

In general, we find smaller papers in the smaller cities. They have fewer pages and less advertising. Thus, as the size of the city decreases, the chances of exposure of an individual advertisement increase. Smaller space can be used, which will be as effective as larger space in the larger newspapers. The buyer thus progressively reduces the size of the advertisements, without necessarily reducing the number of insertions. This progressive reduction in size and, therefore, in cost provides the desired coverage in the approximately 600 cities with a population of more than 50,000. If you used a 1,000-line advertisement in the Group I cities, you might cut the size to 800 lines in the Group 2, 600 lines in the Group 3, and so on.

Primary versus Supplementary Usage. Newspapers may be used as primary or supplementary media in the media mix. When they are used exclusively, it is usually on less than a national basis. However, they are often used as the major, but not exclusive, medium—on both a national and a regional basis. For example, they are commonly used to high-spot a campaign and are thus confined to approximately

100 markets that have more than 100,000 in population. The media buyer might then support this primary effort with advertising in magazines or spot television. When they are used as supplementary media, newspapers can put pressure on a weak sales area or support magazines in certain areas where the coverage is weak. Newspapers are often chosen to fill in the spots not covered by network television.

Color Preprint. One of the most rapidly growing areas of newspaper advertising is color preprinting. In 1968, of the daily newspapers 93 percent were offering it as compared with 89 percent who offered r.o.p. color. In its simpler form, "Hi-Fi" color advertisements are preprinted on a roll like wallpaper, and the rolls are fed into the presses. In SpectaColor, which was introduced in 1962, the register is insured by electronic controls that cut the roll at the point where it is in register with the newspaper page.

Color preprints provide the general advertiser with many of the advantages of magazine color while allowing each of his retailers to place his imprinted copy next to the general advertiser's four-color advertisement on the same page. Costs (including space and inserts) were estimated by one leading agency at from $15 to $16 for a full page in four color to from $12 to $13 for a half page in four color.

NEWSPAPER SUPPLEMENTS

A supplement is a part of most Sunday papers. There are two types — the syndicated national supplement and the locally edited supplement. Each of the syndicated supplements is compiled, edited, and printed by a central organization. It is then sold to newspapers at a fixed cost per thousand. Magazine supplements often compare favorably with leading national magazines in quality of editorial matter. Linage in all the Sunday newspapers that distribute one of the syndicated supplements is usually sold at a group rate. *This Week*, for example, is distributed by Sunday newspapers all over the United States, and the cost of advertising space in it is a group rate for all these newspapers. Comic supplements are usually sold on a national or group basis.

Magazine supplements offer four-color printing at rates surprisingly close to that of black and white. They are printed on paper that is heavier and better finished than newsprint. Therefore, reproduction, both in black and white and in color, is superior to anything that can be offered in the regular columns. The same mechanical advantages are found in the locally edited supplements. Advertising can be bought separately in each of them, but for greater convenience to media buyers and to compete successfully with the syndicated supplements, a number of them have been formed into cooperative selling groups (to illustrate, the Metropolitan Sunday Magazine Group).

SOURCES OF INFORMATION

Standard Rate and Data Service. SRDS lists rates, circulations, mechanical requirements, issuance and closing dates, copy regulations, and market data for newspapers, as well as other media.

Media Records, Inc. This organization measures and reports the advertising linage carried by 401 daily and Sunday newspapers in 128 cities. Linage data are reported by individual general advertisers, by retail-store classification and department.

Bureau of Advertising, American Newspaper Publishers Association. This ANPA body acts as the promotional arm of the newspaper industry. It conducts research, collects case histories, and stands ready to provide information useful to its member newspapers. For instance, in 1967 an official of the Bureau of Advertising pointed out that in the near future newspapers were likely to start facsimile copy sending and receiving, electronic copy scanning, electrostatic printing, demographic studies of newspaper circulation.[7]

MAGAZINES

Although magazines rank fourth among the media in total dollar revenue, more manufacturers advertise in magazines than in any other mass medium. This is not surprising when we consider some of the special advantages magazines offer. Most products appeal to some groups and not to others. Few but "hi-fi" enthusiasts want stereophonic phonograph records and diamond needles; few but fishermen need spinning rods and reels; only farmers want hybrid seed corn. Special-

[7]A. W. S. Thomson, *What's New in Newspapers* (New York: American Association of Advertising Agencies, 1967).

**TOTAL RETENTIONS OF THE AVERAGE AD
DURING THE FIRST SIX WEEKS OF THE LIFE OF THE ISSUE**

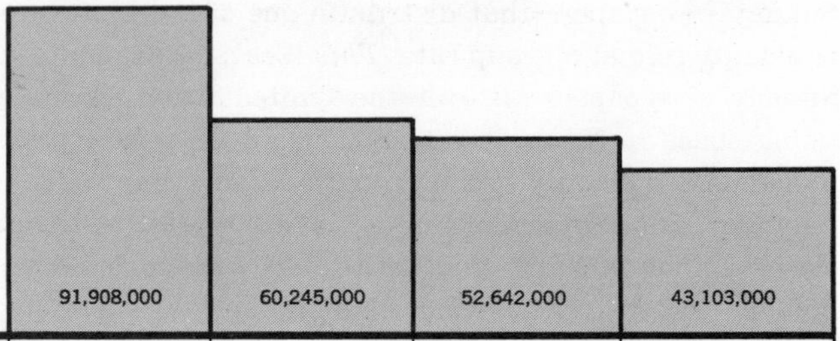

	THIS WEEK & PARADE	POST & LIFE	LIFE & LOOK	POST & LOOK
TOTAL OF THE SIX WEEKS	91,908,000	60,245,000	52,642,000	43,103,000
FIRST WEEK TOTAL	47,468,000	14,587,000	12,330,000	9,393,000
SECOND WEEK TOTAL	22,361,000	13,670,000	11,343,000	14,938,000
THIRD WEEK TOTAL	22,079,000	13,010,000	14,667,000	8,216,000
FOURTH, FIFTH & SIXTH WEEK TOTAL		18,978,000	14,302,000	10,556,000
READER BASES:	(THIS WEEK = 800) (PARADE = 819)	(POST = 686) (LIFE = 826)	(LIFE = 826) (LOOK = 850)	(POST = 686) (LOOK = 850)

FIG. 25.3 *Newspaper supplements and general magazines are compared on the basis of the number remembering certain advertisements.* SOURCE: W. R. SIMMONS & ASSOCIATES RESEARCH, INC.

interest magazines offer to the manufacturers of such products a unique opportunity to reach a select audience. Magazines thus make it possible for companies with small budgets to make a substantial impact on the limited market at which they aim.

Although several periodicals existed during the 1700s in the United States, the magazine did not really become an important literary and advertising force until late in the nineteenth century. The Postal Act of 1879 granted second-class mailing privileges to magazines and made possible low-cost national distribution through the mails. By the end of the nineteenth century magazines had taken on their present character and had become major advertising media. Yet magazines have continued to change in character.

During the twentieth century American magazines have shifted more to factual material and have emphasized fiction somewhat less.[8] During the 1950s and 1960s more emphasis has been placed on reaching special audiences not served adequately by the other mass media. Thus a new magazine like *Playboy* has achieved a circulation in excess of 4,000,000 within a few years, exceeding all the national news magazines. The magazine with the highest circulation, *Reader's Digest*, has a monthly circulation of more than 16,000,000 and reaches a total audience of more than 37,000,000 persons eighteen years of age or more.

TYPES OF MAGAZINES

Standard Rate & Data Service classifies magazines according to frequency of publication and the audience to which they are directed. On the basis of frequency, weeklies and monthlies are the most important types. We find, in addition, a smattering of semi-monthlies, bimonthlies, and quarterlies. But monthly magazines outnumber all other types.

On the basis of the audience served, we have three principal types of magazines:

1. *Consumer magazines.* These are edited for people who buy products for their own consumption.
2. *Farm magazines.* These circulate to farmers and their families. Although there is some overlapping with the "consumer" classification, the farm audience is a fairly distinct one.
3. *Business magazines.* These are published for business readers. They fall into three sub-groups: (1) trade papers—addressed to retailers, wholesalers, and other distributors; (2) industrial magazines—addressed to businessmen engaged in all phases of manufacturing; and (3) professional magazines—directed at physicians, lawyers, architects, and other professional people.

One might also make a geographical distinction between national and regional magazines (there are few strictly local magazines).

Consumer Magazines. In the *Standard Rate & Data* listing, consumer magazines are divided into forty-nine subclassifications, from

[8]See Theodore Peterson, *Magazines in the Twentieth Century*, 2d ed. (Urbana.: University of Illinois Press, 1964).

"almanacs and directories" at one end of the alphabetical listing to "youth" magazines at the other. Magazines such as *Life* and *Look* and *Saturday Evening Post* are considered "general" magazines. Martin Mayer describes this coverage graphically when he looks at it from the media buyer's point of view.

> To the media buyer, the magazine market appears as a great set of eccentric and overlapping circles. The three great circles of *Life*, the *Post*, and *Look* fill nearly two-thirds of the households in America—five-sixths of the households with more than $7,000 annual income—during any given month. Partly inside each of these circles, and covering small sections of the market which the mass-circulation magazines do not reach, are the magazines aimed at major categories of the population—men or women, urban or rural, upper income or lower income. And dotted mostly inside, a little outside, and all around the bigger circles are the specialist magazines, for hobbyists, limited age groups, limited interest categories.[9]

Consumer magazines might be distinguished also on the basis of their distribution. Among the "women's service magazines" we have both "circulation distributed" magazines and "store distributed" magazines. *Ladies' Home Journal* is an example of the former, and *Woman's Day* (distributed through food stores) is an example of the latter classification.

Farm Magazines. Farm magazines may be general or specialized, nationwide, or regional. If you want to reach all types of farmers, you might use *Successful Farming*. However, if you are trying to reach a more specialized group, you might buy space in *Turkey World* or *Hoard's Dairyman*. To reach Wisconsin farmers you might use the *Wisconsin Agriculturist*.

Business Publications. In the thick *Standard Rate & Data* book for business magazines, 2,400 business publications are listed and described. This includes such general business publications as *Fortune* and *Harvard Business Review*, which SRDS covers also in its consumer magazine edition. Although trade magazines (or papers) are edited primarily for retailers and wholesalers, many of them are read also by the sales personnel of manufacturers. Some, such as *Women's Wear Daily*, try for fairly broad coverage. Some, such as *Florist's Review*, are more specialized.

Industrial magazines may cover the field in either of two ways —*horizontally* or *vertically*. The horizontal publication is aimed at a specific function or activity within many industries, while the vertical one attempts to do a complete job of covering one industry. *Sales Management*'s coverage is horizontal because it is edited for sales managers and their staffs, regardless of their type of business. On the other hand, *Iron Age* and *Railway Age* attempt to cover the whole industries.

It is important, also, in the field of business publications, to distinguish between controlled- and paid-circulation business magazines. A publisher of a controlled-circulation magazine concentrates on a specialized business audience and limits his coverage to this one group tailoring the editorial material to its needs. He usually sends the maga-

FIG. 25.4 *Typical pages from Standard Rate & Data Service—Consumer Magazines—from Class 9A Civic (Male) and Class 51 (Youth).* SOURCE: STANDARD RATE & DATA SERVICE, INC.

zine free to this select group in order to get high coverage, depending entirely on the advertising revenue for support. Some controlled-circulation magazines are sold in bulk, to such firms as utilities, which then distribute them free to special classes of customers (such as *Food Service*, for owners of eating establishments).

WHY ADVERTISERS BUY MAGAZINE SPACE

Advantages

Selectivity. Unless the market you are trying to reach is a very small one, there is probably at least one magazine edited primarily for it. As soon as any group starts to grow, someone sees the chance of making a profit by publishing a magazine especially for this new market. This is a happy situation for most businesses, because few of them are trying to talk to everybody. Even the biggest companies are more interested in certain audiences than others, and they need channels to reach them. The small company may make a considerable impact in the limited market at which it must aim if it is able to reach it cheaply and intensively.

You will note, however, that sometimes an advertiser of a specialized product, such as grass seed or outboard motors, will use general magazines like *Life* or *Look*. He is probably aware of the fact that much of the circulation is wasted, but he may have other media objectives in mind. He may be trying to win new users. Or he may have found that the total market reached here is greater than any of the specialized magazines, in spite of the waste. Or he may want to impress his dealers with his firm's success and to get them to feature his brand "as advertised in *Life*."

The selectivity of magazines can be translated into a low cost-per-thousand for reaching desired audiences. If most members of your audience are real prospects, you can divide *total* circulation into page cost, but if only half the circulation are prospects, only half the circulation can logically be used in your calculations. If you can manage with half or quarter pages, your cost-per-thousand drops even further.

Reproduction. Most magazines are printed on good paper stock and can provide excellent reproduction in black and white or in color. (A study of leading magazines indicated that 45 percent of magazine advertising appeared in color in 1965).

In recent years magazines have widened the variety of mechanical features offered to advertisers. Some magazines offer special attention-attracting inks. Some offer gate folds and odd-sized pages that are likely to attract attention.

Long Life. Magazines are kept around the home longer than other media and are often used for reference. Alfred Politz made a study for the *Reader's Digest* of the "reading days" of several leading general magazines. He was attempting to measure "the superficiality or the intensity of [readers'] contact with the medium."[10] He used an unusually large sample (14,515 completed interviews) and asked those inter-

[10]*A Study of Seven Publications* (Pleasantville, N.Y.: Reader's Digest Association, Inc., 1956).

viewed to reconstruct their actions of the day before. The interviewers discovered that the average person picked up a monthly magazine on four different days or more (5.3 reading days for the *Reader's Digest*) and picked up a weekly or bi-weekly on fewer than two days (1.3 days for *Life*, 1.5 for *Look*).

Possible Prestige. Many magazines claim that advertising in their publication lends prestige to the product (*Good Housekeeping*, for example, claims in a trade ad that "40,930,000 women are influenced in their purchases by our Guaranty Seal"). It is difficult to prove just how much prestige magazines in general provide. Many studies indicate, however, that copies of such prestigious magazines as the *Fortune*, the *National Geographic*, and the *New Yorker* enjoy an exceptionally long and active life, a good part of it spent in doctor's and businessmen's reception rooms. There is little doubt, however, that many advertisers buy space in such magazines for prestige purposes. On the other hand, magazines such as *Modern Romances* probably do little to add prestige to a product, although they may be quite useful for other purposes. Readers per copy are much lower than for the more prestigious magazines.

Services Offered. Some magazines offer many extra services. *Life* pioneered in merchandising services shortly before World War II by sending sales trainees around the country to tell retailers about *Life*, and how much *Life* valued the retailer. They pushed the idea of featuring products bearing the tag "as advertised in *Life*." The promotion was successful. The *Saturday Evening Post* supplies tags bearing "A *Post* Recognized Value" for use by advertisers.

Another service that appeals to many advertisers is the opportunity of testing one's advertisements through a split run. In split-run testing, two or more versions of the copy for an advertisement are printed in alternate copies of a given press run. In each test advertisement some offer is made to spur replies. The assumption is that the version that prompts the most replies is superior. The split run is often used to test advertisements on a small-scale basis to see which is the best action producer; the winner is then used in large space in a national campaign. According to *Standard Rate & Data Service*, eighty consumer magazines offered alternate copy split runs in 1968.

Limitations

Lack of Flexibility. Magazines are not as flexible as newspapers or spot radio and television in either area or time. Most magazines are so widely distributed that it is not possible to fit copy to local conditions. However, many publishers try to overcome this problem by offering regional editions.

The nature of magazine publishing makes it impossible to make last-minute changes in advertising. Most magazines are printed in great quantities, sometimes by several printers, and the forms must be closed several weeks before the publication date. In 1948 one advertiser (a business service) was so convinced that Dewey would win the presidential election that he placed a full-page ad in *Time* to be published a few days after the election, headed by this question in boldface: "What

Will Dewey Do?" The ad urged readers to subscribe to the business service and find out "what to expect from the new administration."

WHAT KINDS OF ADVERTISERS USE MAGAZINES?

Almost all general advertisers use some form of magazine advertising. (The distribution pattern obviously does not make magazines attractive to most retail stores for advertising purposes.) Table 25.6 shows the amount spent by leading magazine advertisers in each of the three types of magazines.

Note that all the automobile companies depend heavily on magazines as a means of communication. Fine reproduction shows their products off to good advantage, and they can achieve mass coverage at fairly low cost-per-thousand.

LEADING GENERAL MAGAZINE ADVERTISERS IN 1967   **TABLE 25.6**

ADVERTISER	GENERAL MAGAZINES
General Motors Corp.	$40,864,013
Ford Motor Co.	22,585,111
Bristol-Myers Co.	21,645,557
Distillers Corp. Seagrams, Ltd.	21,180,386
American Tobacco Co.	15,447,134
Procter & Gamble Co.	15,111,177
American Telephone and Telegraph	12,762,909
Chrysler Corp.	12,428,320

Sources: Publishers Information Bureau, Inc.

CIRCULATION AND READERSHIP PATTERNS

To match coverage with potential markets most buyers of magazine space depend on both circulation and audience (readership) data. Consider, first, some of the circulation data from A.B.C. Some buyers consider newsstand sales as one criterion of the quality of a medium's circulation in that purchases at a newsstand are completely voluntary. On the other hand many media analysts watch carefully the trends in subscription sales of various magazines, especially the rate at which subscribers renew their subscriptions.

From circulation data you can compare magazines also on the basis of how the subscriptions were produced (by mail, by catalog, by field selling staff), duration of subscription, percentage sold in combination, percentage in arrears, percentage sold at regular price, and percentage with special offers.

During recent years the general circulation trend has been up, but single copy sales have decreased. Circulation of the more selective magazines has been increasing at the most rapid rate of all magazines.

Distribution of magazines pretty well follows distribution of the population. For example, 58 percent of the population lives in twelve states, and 62 percent of all magazine circulation is in these same twelve states — New York, Pennsylvania, California, Illinois, Ohio,

Michigan, Texas, Massachusetts, New Jersey, Indiana, Missouri, and Wisconsin. Even more important to advertisers is the fact that more than 62 percent of total United States retail sales is made in these states.

Many surveys are made to show the comparative audiences of various magazines. In Figure 25.3 you can see one which was made by W. R. Simmons & Associates for *This Week* and *Parade*. Note that the retention of the "average ad" during the first six weeks is used as the criterion for audience comparison.

Media analysts are often confused by the fact that a particular magazine seems to have audiences of different sizes, according to which researcher made the study. In Table 25.7 you can see how studies made by three highly regarded research firms (Alfred Politz, W. R. Simmons, and SRDS-Data) differ about audience size. These studies were based on

TABLE 25.7

HOW THREE RESEARCH FIRMS FIGURE TOTAL AUDIENCES OF PUBLICATIONS*

(In Thousands)

	POLITZ	SIMMONS	SRDS-DATA
American Home		9,698	8,287
Better Homes & Gardens	19,200	17,408	21,451
Business Week		3,423	
Family Circle	15,550	12,435	16,536
Good Housekeeping	15,080	14,200	17,013
Holiday		3,905	4,477
House Beautiful		3,724	5,572
House and Garden		4,700	6,731
Ladies' Home Journal	14,770	13,871	15,972
Life	29,550	31,859	33,693
Look	28,110	29,303	27,800
McCall's	21,750	16,598	20,221
Newsweek		9,807	10,932
Parade		21,464	
Playboy		7,754	
Reader's Digest	35,770	37,395	35,930
Redbook	9,600	8,232	11,148
The Saturday Evening Post	23,370	22,893	19,795
Seventeen			5,105
This Week Magazine		24,924	
Time		13,630	13,456
True		6,147	7,163
True Story		6,622	
TV Guide		22,953	26,895
U.S. News & World Report		6,442	7,773
Woman's Day	13,310	10,957	15,543

*This table lists total adult audiences (age eighteen and over) for periodicals as given by Alfred Politz Media Studies; W. R. Simmons & Associates Research; and SRDS-Data, Inc. Blank spaces opposite a researcher's name indicate that the company did not measure the audience of that publication.

SOURCE: *Advertising Age*, August 16, 1965, p. 66.

much the same definition of audience and thus can be compared. However, it should be noted that much of the difficulty in analyzing magazine claims as to the audiences they reach stems from differences in the concept of "audience." Both researchers and media specialists have long urged that the industry adopt a general standard for "audience" as they have for "net paid circulation," and that there be a standard auditing organization for checking claims similar to Audit Bureau of Circulations and Business Publications Audit.

On the other hand, a *Better Homes and Gardens* study, also made by Politz, examined, among other things, people's "venturesomeness"—a psychological willingness to try new products. Politz reported that of 123,800,000 persons more than ten years of age in the United States, 40,100,000 could be called "venturesome," and of these, some 17,400,000 read at least one issue of *Better Homes and Gardens* during the course of a year.

In *The Readers of the Saturday Evening Post* (still another Politz study), the *Post* focused attention on "exposure days." According to this study, the average issue of the *Saturday Evening Post* has 20,621,000 readers, 41,783,000 exposure days (that is, the average reader sees it for 2.0 days), and 29,456,000 "exposure days per advertising page" (total number of reader-days on which the average advertising page in the average issue is fully opened).

MAGAZINE SIZES AND SHAPES

The largest regular unit of space in a magazine is the double-page spread. This usually consists of two pages that face each other. In magazines that are saddle-stitched (pages are held together by staples, which are pushed through the magazine when it is open), it may be the center spread. For example, the *Saturday Evening Post* and *Life* are saddle-stitched. In order to stitch a magazine in this way, one sheet of paper must be laid on top of another until the complete magazine is assembled (each sheet consists of four printed pages, two on the front and two on the back); thus, the only two pages that are printed opposite each other *on the same sheet of paper* are the two found in the exact center. Any other two pages will have a space of white between them (gutter), running from the top to the bottom of the magazine. In designing a spread, the artist attempts to "jump" or "bridge" the gutter by making sure that no headline words run through the gutter and that all body text is on one side or the other.

Other shapes of advertisements may be made by full, half, and quarter pages. The full page is, of course, a common size in all magazines. A few advertisers like the full page plus either a half or a quarter page facing it. These ads may be designed as a complete unit or as two separate facing advertisements.

Most magazines offer "bleed" pages, which permit the dark or colored background of the advertising to extend to the edge of the page (or to "bleed" off the page). The printing space is a little greater than on ordinary pages, and the artist has more leeway in expressing an idea.

Layout artists and media buyers often wonder what size is most efficient. Shall a given amount of money be used to buy a large number of smaller advertisements or a smaller number of larger advertisements? Much depends on the purpose of the campaign outlined by the marketing plan. Some guidance is available through general studies. An analysis by Dr. Daniel Starch of 12,000,000 inquiries indicates that large advertisements bring in more inquiries than smaller ads do, but *not* in proportion to the larger space. If we assume that returns from one-page advertisements equal 100, the average half-page advertisement brings returns equal to approximately 60, and a quarter page produces returns equal to approximately 33. Or, to put it another way, doubling the space does not double the number of readers attracted. If a half-page advertisement attracts 60 of 100 readers, doubling the size could not possibly double the readers. Instead, the extra half page would, if efficiently used, attract 60 percent of the remaining 40, or 24 additional readers, resulting in a score of 84 for the full-page advertisement.

RATE STRUCTURE

Although magazine space is quoted in agate lines as well as in larger segments, it is actually sold primarily on the basis of pages, half pages, quarter pages, and so forth. If the space buyer consults Standard Rate & Data for consumer magazines, he will find the following scale for black and white space in the *Saturday Evening Post*:

1 page	$26,780
1/2 page (vertical)	14,350
1/2 page (horizontal)	14,820
1/4 page	7,490
1 column	7,490
1/8 page	3,770
Agate line	45.57

These are standard space units in the *Post*. Other publications may have different sizes of space listed as standard units. Each page of the *Post* is 4 columns wide. A 3-column magazine (such as *Time*) sells 2/3 and 1/3 pages instead of halves and quarters.

If you want the fourth (back) *Post* cover, you will have to pay $51,100; for the second or third (inside) cover, $39,000.

The *Saturday Evening Post*, like many magazines, charges an extra 15 percent for bleed pages, whether full- or half-page. Some periodicals, however, make no extra charge for bleed, and some charge only 10 percent.

The rates quoted so far have been for single insertions. Most publishers offer discounts to encourage you to buy more space or to advertise more frequently. These practices may be combined, however, in a single-rate schedule. Thus, your discounts increase as you use more space — but they increase even faster if you spread this throughout the year.

One study of the rate structure of 24 leading consumer magazines and the elasticity of demand for space indicated that discount schedules influenced selection of the magazine medium *as a whole* but that discounts were not important in the choice of any particular magazine.[11]

[11]See Robert S. Kahan and S. Watson Dunn, *Pricing and Demand for Magazine Advertising Space* (Madison: University of Wisconsin, 1965).

RATE COMPARISONS

Every media buyer knows that no magazine page is exactly the same as another; so he usually keeps an eye on the cost-per-thousand circulation. Here are the cost-per-thousand rates for a black-and-white page in several leading magazines:

	(Cost per thousand)	
	CIRCULATION	AUDIENCE
The Reader's Digest	$2.71	1.10
The New Yorker	8.39	1.20
Business Week	11.55	2.15

Note how much lower the cost-per-thousand is for reaching *Reader's Digest* readers than it is for audiences of the other two magazines. The differential here may be due to the much larger circulation of *Reader's Digest*, the fact that it is a monthly, and the fact that its audience has a lower average income than the audience of the *New Yorker* or *Business Week* has. It generally costs more to reach a selective audience.

Another method of comparing rates is use of "maximal and minimal." These words represent the highest rate you would pay (without discounts) and the lowest rate (with all possible discounts) for one agate line of space per million circulation (that is, maximum and minimum milline rates).

DIRECT MAIL

When a company enters business, its first advertising communications are on a person-to-person basis. Later, as it grows, it sends letters or cards through the mail to prospective customers. Finally, if it continues to prosper, the company branches out into using mass media with the preselected audience these media provide. Nevertheless, the firm probably continues to use direct mail.

Although direct mail is not truly a mass medium, it is an important one. It would be hard to find a business firm that did not at some time use direct-mail advertising. Since 1947, direct mail has ranked second or third among the media in dollars spent, according to McCann-Erickson estimates.

Effective direct-mail advertising is based on an efficient postal system. Like many other forms of advertising, direct mail owes a debt to Benjamin Franklin, who, in 1775, was the first head of the post office in this country. The big growth of the postal service and of direct-mail advertising came in the nineteenth century. Penny postage after 1850 encouraged use of the mails for delivery of advertising material. After the Civil War not only notices and circulars but almanacs became very popular. Toward the end of the century catalogues started to appear —the forerunners of our big modern general mail order catalogue. These catalogues profited from the improvement in printing in the twentieth century that made it possible to visualize fairly satisfactorily the products that were being sold.

The first Montgomery Ward catalogue consisted of one hundred pages. It was distributed in 1872.[12] Like the catalogues of the then mail order king E. C. Allen, it offered several hundred articles for sale in a periodical whose main objective was to sell mail order merchandise, although it included some editorial material. The catalogue brought to the thriving rural and small-town communities information about items the people wanted and could not buy at the few general stores. It is little wonder that catalogue sellers prospered, even though the copy in many of these early advertisements was high-pressure by today's standards and the printing was not very good.

The growth of direct mail in the twentieth century has been helped by the expansion of the mail order houses, the dispersal of population around the country, and the ingenuity of the direct-mail professionals in devising new techniques for communicating effectively.

TYPES OF DIRECT MAIL

Problems of Definition. Three terms—direct mail, direct advertising, and mail order advertising—often cause confusion.

Direct advertising is any form of advertising that is issued direct to definite, specific prospects usually through the mails, by salesmen, by dealers, or other means. This advertising is usually reproduced in quantity. It may be used to sell, to educate, or to build a long-range brand or corporate image.

Direct mail is any direct advertising that is sent through the mail. We thus distinguish it from nonmailed direct advertising. A brochure sent to a prospect by mail is direct mail. However, if this same brochure is distributed by a house-to-house canvasser or handed to the prospect by a salesperson, it is direct advertising, but *not* direct mail.

Mail order advertising includes any method of selling in which the product is promoted through advertising and ordered by the customer through the mail. No personal salesmanship is involved. Consequently, the term "mail order" does not, like direct mail, refer to an advertising medium, but to the use of any of the media that might be appropriate—especially direct mail, newspapers, and magazines. Letters may go either first or third class.

Specialized Forms. "Direct mail" is a catchall phrase that includes anything from post cards to catalogues containing hundreds of pages. The letters of application you send to prospective employers are direct mail. These are forms you can prepare for yourself. However, if you take a communication problem to one of the specialized direct-mail houses, you find that varieties of the forms are almost infinite—limited mainly by your ability to pay. The following are among the more common forms:

Sales Letters. This is the most frequently used form of direct mail—normally the first form any business firm will use. They may be individually typed, multigraphed, or reproduced by some other dupli-

---

[12]See George Clarke, *Copywriting: Theory and Technique* (New York: Harper & Row, Publishers, 1959), pp. 322–325, for additional background.

cating process. The salutation may be filled in or replaced by a caption across the top.

Post Cards. Cards may be sent either third or first class. If you pay first-class postage you may include an individually written message. However, if you want the lower third-class rate you must stick to printed matter only, with either a hand-signed or stenciled signature. Reply cards are often used to encourage a direct reply from the receiver of a mailing piece. These are usually attached to a folder or booklet or fastened by a seal to another card. The advertiser pays the postage on these when they are returned. He must first secure a permit from his postmaster and print its number on the card.

Leaflets. A leaflet is usually a single printed sheet. It is often used in conjunction with a letter to explain an offer or idea more fully. It is normally folded once or twice.

Folders. Folders are larger than leaflets and are usually printed on heavier stock. The larger size holds more of the sales story and permits use of more in the way of visual material. Folders can often be handled economically as self-mailers with the name and address stenciled on an open area of the cover.

Broadsides. A broadside, as the term implies, is even larger than a folder. It should be so large that its size helps to impress the receiver with the importance of the offer. Some broadsides are sent to dealers for display in the store as posters or point-of-sale promotion pieces. Others are designed for the ultimate reader. However, when folded, a broadside should be suitable for the mailbag.

Booklets. A leaflet that contains several pages is more properly called a booklet. If the sales story is complicated and considerable information is needed, a leaflet is not enough—it is better to use a booklet. Information about product manufacture and various models available are often included in a booklet. Most automobile companies produce such booklets. Gasoline companies produce booklets that deal with safe driving or how to take care of your new car.

Catalogues. Like a booklet, a catalogue has many pages. However its main function is to serve as a reference book. Most consumers are familiar with the big catalogues of the general mail order houses. These are buying guides, designed to be used over a period of time. In the more specialized fields catalogues are more technical, but their purpose is essentially the same. An advertisement in *Oil and Gas Journal* may invite readers to send for a catalogue that shows drilling equipment or different types of spudders; or a mailing may be sent to small retailers with a reply card enclosed inviting them to send for free catalogues. In either event, the ultimate sale will probably be made by a salesman who can tell the prospect how the machine or equipment will fit his particular needs. The expense involved in preparing a catalogue makes it uneconomical to send it to any except real prospects for the product.

House Organs. A house organ is a publication issued periodically by a business organization. Although they are commonly thought of as "company magazines" or "company newspapers," thousands of them are put out by schools, governmental units, welfare agencies, and military units. Cutlip and Center estimate that 10,000 such publications are

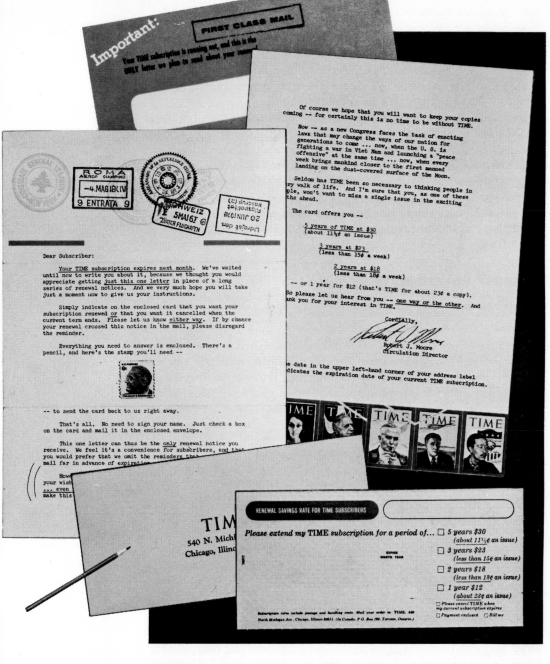

FIG. 25.5 *A highly successful direct-mail solicitation used by Time, Inc.* COURTESY TIME, INC.

issued on a regular basis in the United States.[13] According to the International Council of Industrial Editors, publications sponsored by business and industry reach a circulation in excess of 300,000,000 an issue. To reach employees, customers, shareholders, dealers, and other audiences, industry is currently investing approximately $500,000,000 a year.

Some house organs are "internal" in that their circulation is for employees or organization members. Some are "external" in that they

[13]Scott M. Cutlip and Allen H. Center, *Effective Public Relations,* 3d ed. (Englewood Cliffs, N.J.: Prentice-Hall, Inc., 1964), p. 153.

go to dealers, customers, and others. Some serve both inside and outside audiences. There is little uniformity of format among house publications. Some are printed on slick paper, some are on newsprint, some are made by letterpress, some by offset, some even by mimeograph. A few, such as *Arizona Highways*, have a paid circulation.

In some companies the house organ is published by the advertising department, but in many it is considered a duty of the public relations department. It also has implications as far as industrial relations and sales are concerned. The content is usually of two types—that which the editors think readers will enjoy and information the editor thinks that the readers should have.

Other Forms. Among the other forms of direct mail are charts, research bulletins, printed novelties of all kinds, calendars, blotters, and business cards.

WHY USE DIRECT MAIL?

Advantages

Selectivity. Probably the outstanding advantage of direct-mail advertising is its extreme selectivity. You seldom find a mass medium whose coverage will correspond exactly with the audience you are trying to reach; so you work out a "mix." In the case of direct mail, theoretically at least, you build any circulation you want. Whether you are trying for a small audience or one of millions, whether you want high or low income, white or blue collar, you can work out your own coverage pattern.

Intensive Coverage. Suppose you want to reach all your dealers once every few days for several weeks. Through direct mail you can make the coverage as intensive as you like.

Speed. Because direct mail can be moved out quickly, it can take advantage of timely or seasonal appeals. For example, you can have a mailing all ready to go when the first snow arrives, and within a few days you can reach all the people on your list.

Flexibility of Format. The previous section discussed some of the possible formats you can use. Unlike the mass media, where you are bound by certain physical rules, there are none—except, of course, your budget—in direct mail.

Complete Information. If the product or the situation demands it, direct mail can furnish a great deal of information. Long copy, illustrations, diagrams, or any other device that will provide useful stimulus to the sale can be included.

Personal. Each mailing piece can be as individualized as you see fit to make it. Many of the sales letters and cards are highly personalized; the catalogues and folders are less so.

Limitations

High Cost per Reader. Even the cheapest mailing piece has a high cost per reader. When the audience is highly selective, the high cost can be justified, because there may be much less waste circulation than in the alternative way of reaching your audience—the mass media.

Difficulty of Maintaining Effective Mailing List. Much of the success of any direct-mail campaign depends on the quality of the mailing list.

Customer Resistance. Ordinarily there is no editorial or entertainment material to soften the impact of the advertising message. Consequently, direct-mail advertising must evoke its own attention, arouse its own interest in what is said.

TYPES OF USERS

Manufacturers. Both manufacturers and retailers use direct mail. The manufacturer may be trying to reach his distributors, certain industrial users, or ultimate consumers. He is a little more likely to emphasize direct mail with the first two audiences than with the third.

Although most companies use some direct mail, there is a wide variation in the importance that different users give it in the media mix. Among the types of industries that spend heavily (usually more than 30 percent of the media budget) are these: agricultural equipment, auto equipment, house furnishings, confections, and office equipment. On the other hand, the following industries devote only a small percentage of their media budget to direct mail: proprietary medicines, food, beverages, and textiles.

Note, first, that the heavy users have a more selective, more clearly defined market than the second group, which tends toward a mass market (agricultural-equipment and office-equipment users, for example, are primarily businessmen rather than consumers); second, that the products in the first group are bought on a more rational basis than those in the second. Consequently, longer copy and more information are needed to stimulate purchase by this second group. Finally, note that the products in the first group are more expensive. This means, among other things, that there is somewhat less price competition among the various firms and that a higher advertising cost per unit may not be too serious—if it helps convince the prospect of better quality or provides more information for purchasing.

Retailers. According to the National Retail Merchants' Association, the average retailer spends between 5 and 6 percent of his media dollar for direct-mail advertising. An individual store often has lists to which it may send special mailings, perhaps one to the sporting goods prospect, one to the bookstore customer. Some stores keep as many as thirty or forty separate lists. The monthly statement is, of course, an easy way to send envelope stuffers (leaflets, and folders, for example) to the store's customers.

THE MAILING LIST

It is obvious that your entire direct-mail campaign will fail unless the people addressed are really prospects. Once you have defined your "audience mix" you can put together your own mailing list to match it. This list is likely to come from one of the following sources: a broker (by rental), a professional list house (by purchase), or a periodical (rental or trade). One list house advertises the following lists:

200,000 new births each month

20,000 new firms, corporations with names of owners, incorporators

200,000 northern guests in southern and west coast hotels

12,000 women heads of Protestant fund-raising organizations

112,000 members of golf and country clubs

22,000 high-income farmers

30,000 buyers of arthritic remedies

78,000 buyers of sex information books

50,000 home sewers' supplies buyers

65,000 agencies who replied to opportunity ads

24,000 wealthy men residing in New York City

25,000 buyers of fishing waders

20,000 race track system players

10,000 social registrites in 13 southern cities

10,000 millionaires

Of course, you can often build your own list more satisfactorily —and more cheaply—than you can buy one. Some of the common sources you might consult are the following:

Company records and personnel

Company billings

Business directories

Yellow pages of your telephone directory

Clipping bureaus (you could easily get births, deaths, and new businesses from these)

City directories

Property tax lists

Building permits

Automobile registrations

Government directories

Once the list is built you have to check it constantly for such things as misspellings, duplication, and accuracy of addresses. People are also constantly moving, getting divorced, having babies, and dying. Business firms go in and out of business and merge. Anyone who uses lists must watch for changes so that lists can be kept up to date.

Preparation of Direct Mail. Traditionally the advertiser has taken on the job of planning, manufacturing, and mailing his direct-mail pieces, and he has left his agency free to concentrate on the mass, commissionable media such as television or newspapers. In the 1960s, however, several large agencies became seriously interested in direct mail and some set up or bought subsidiaries that concentrated in this medium. Many of the larger mailing houses providing lists also handle printing and mailing, and allow the agency a commission on all these charges.

According to Kleppner, the direct mail planner, whoever he might be, should go through the following steps:[14]

[14]Otto Kleppner, *Advertising Procedure*, 5th ed. (Englewood Cliffs, N.J.: Prentice-Hall, Inc., 1966), p. 308.

1. Decide general format.
2. Decide what printing process is to be used.
3. Select paper.
4. Get printing estimates.
5. Get proofs.
6. Get delivery.
7. Arrange for addressing and mailing.

Many of these steps involve technical knowledge, and it is essential that the planner draw on the knowledge of a specialist. For example, paper comes in a wide variety of finishes, weights, and sizes, and only an expert will be able to predict which is best for a particular job.

As Kleppner points out, it is wise to have the mailing checked by the post office for size, weight, postage, and general mailability. You may, for example, not be up to date on postal rate increases and be underestimating the total costs of the mailing.

In the future we are likely to see much greater use of the computer in direct mail. *Grey Matter* points out that it could be used to "compile a central *master list* of all United States mail order buyers."[15] The computer's selective memory can produce direct-mail letters that repeat the name of the recipient several times in the body copy, as well as mentioning his neighborhood or his car. *Grey Matter* sees, in fact, the emergence of a "new breed of *direct response advertising specialists*. They are young, computer-oriented, research-minded marketing professionals, either working through their own direct mail marketing organizations or increasingly through newly founded direct mail subsidiaries of advertising agencies."

SUMMARY

With 30 percent of all advertising dollars going to them, the newspapers are in an entrenched position in the advertising field. The two major types of papers are the dailies and the weeklies.

The newspaper's strength among retail and general advertisers is based on its flexibility, its acceptance in a community, its intense coverage, the fact that readers can scan, skip, or concentrate on it as they like, coordination between dealer and national advertiser, and the services — usually free — offered buyers.

The largest users of general (or national) advertising are the makers of automotive and grocery products, and the largest users in the retail field are the department stores. Newspaper space may be bought by the agate line or by the column inch. If you want special or full position or color, you will have to pay extra. Most advertising sold to general advertisers is sold on a flat rate that is substantially higher than the open rate charged retailers.

Rates are most frequently compared on a milline basis, although special yardsticks to fit an individual need can easily be devised. An important part of the newspaper business is the Sunday supplement, which is part newspaper and part magazine, offering advertisers some of the advantages of both.

[15]*Grey Matter*, September 1967.

The term "magazines" covers a multitude of publications in three main fields—consumer, farm, and business. Of these, consumer magazines account for the greatest dollar expenditures, business magazines for the largest number of magazines.

The main advantages of magazine advertising are its selectivity, high quality of reproduction, long life, and services offered. Against this must be weighed its lack of flexibility.

The largest single type of user of magazine advertising is the automobile company.

Magazines have been studied extensively both on a circulation and a readership basis. Circulation studies often focus attention on the quality of the circulation. As a result of the readership studies, it is possible to delineate certain patterns of magazine usage by age, income, and other demographic factors. Unfortunately, the audience studies are highly competitive and are often contradictory.

Rates are most frequently based on circulation and comparisons made on a cost-per-thousand basis. However, it is usual to find that magazines (in all fields) that cater to a high-income class or to a highly selective class charge more per thousand than others.

Almost every business firm uses at times some form of direct mail.

Among the most common forms of direct mail are sales letters (not always designed to achieve direct sales), post cards, leaflets, folders, broadsides, booklets, catalogues, and house organs.

The principal advantages of direct mail are its selectivity, intensive coverage, speed, flexibility, long copy, and personal approach. Its main limitations are the high cost per reader, the problems of maintaining a mailing list, and possible customer resistance.

Heavy users of direct mail tend to be distinguished from light users by the selectivity of the market, the amount of copy needed, and the cost per unit.

QUESTIONS FOR DISCUSSION

1. How do you explain the fact that newspapers account for more advertising dollars than any other advertising medium does?
2. What is meant by magazine types? On what basis does the publisher or editor of a magazine decide which audience he is trying to reach?
3. Make a list of all the newspapers, magazines, and direct-mail literature you have seen during the past week. What is the approximate percentage of time you have devoted to each?
4. On what basis are newspaper and magazine rates established? To what extent do they follow pricing policies you have learned in your economics or marketing courses?
5. What is the primary function of newspaper supplements? Why are they sometimes classified as magazines instead of newspapers?
6. How is cost per inquiry computed? Is it possible to compare costs per inquiry for newspapers, magazines, and direct mail?
7. Under what conditions will an advertiser devote the major portion of his budget to newspapers? to magazines? to direct mail?

SUGGESTED READINGS

Barton, Roger, *Media in Advertising.* New York: McGraw-Hill, Inc., 1964.

Brown, Lyndon O., Richard S. Lessler, and William M. Weilbacher, *Advertising Media.* New York: The Ronald Press Company, 1957.

Buckley, Earle A., *How to Increase Sales with Letters.* New York: McGraw-Hill, Inc., 1961.

Gaw, Walter A., *Advertising Methods and Media.* San Francisco: Wadsworth Publishing Company, Inc., 1961.

Hodgson, Richard S., *Direct Mail and Mail Order Handbook.* Chicago: Dartnell Corporation, 1964.

Kleppner, Otto, *Advertising Procedure*, 5th ed. Englewood Cliffs, N.J.: Prentice-Hall, Inc., 1966. Chapters 11–12, 18.

McClure, Leslie W., and Paul C. Fulton, *Advertising in the Printed Media.* New York: Crowell–Collier and Macmillan Company, 1964.

Peterson, Theodore, *Magazines in the Twentieth Century*, 2d ed. Urbana: University of Illinois Press, 1964.

Udell, Jon, *The Growth of the American Daily Newspaper.* Madison.: University of Wisconsin, 1965.

Wood, J. P., *Magazines in the United States.* New York: The Ronald Press Company, 1956.

Yeck, John D., and John T. Maguire, *Planning and Creating Better Direct Mail.* New York: McGraw-Hill, Inc., 1961.

26 | The Broadcast Media

Television and radio have much in common as media of communication and will be covered together in this chapter. They are both, unlike the media we discussed in the last chapter, *time-* rather than *space*-oriented. Both market this time in segments ranging from a few seconds to an hour or more. Both have the same three general classes of time to sell—network, national spot (time bought by a general advertiser in one or more markets), and local. Both use the same methods of measuring their audiences. In many cities the same communications company will operate both radio and television stations. In either event, both use the public airwaves and can operate only under a license from the Federal Communications Commission.

TELEVISION

For some advertisers television seems to be the ideal medium. However, certain others became disenchanted with television after the glamour of the early years wore off and sales failed to reflect any serious impact. The purpose of this chapter is to analyze the present status of television and to assess its present usefulness in the media program.

Television has grown faster than any advertising medium in history. The growth in television households is shown graphically in

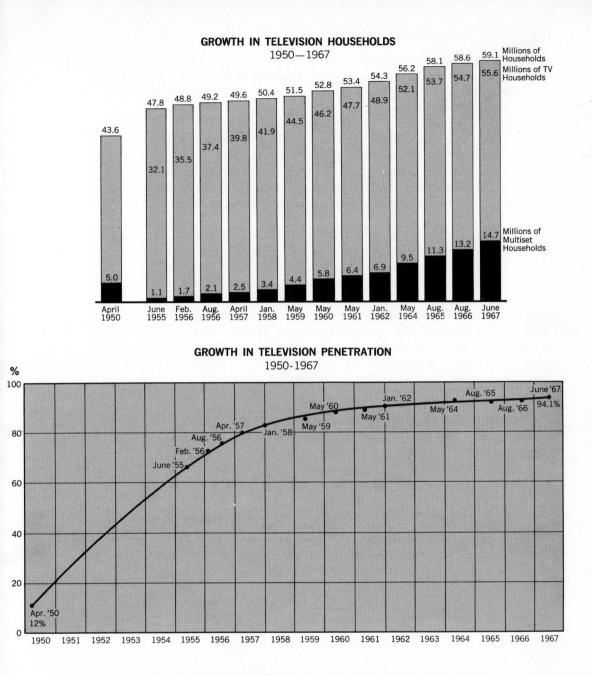

GROWTH IN TELEVISION HOUSEHOLDS
1950—1967

GROWTH IN TELEVISION PENETRATION
1950-1967

FIG. 26.1 *Two indications of the growth of television in the United States. Note the sharp rise in percent of homes with television in the 1950s and the rise in multi-set households in* ~~*the 1960*~~ ... ISING ~~...~~ UNDATION, INC., 1967.

Figure 26.1 In 1968, 94 percent of the homes in the country had at least one television set, and 35 percent had two or more sets. More than 20 percent had color television.

Within twenty years, total estimated expenditures rose from nothing to more than $2,900,000,000. Because all except 500 million of this sum is spent by national (general) advertisers, television is the leading medium for national advertisers.

The increase in television stations has been almost as spectacular. The first commercial station began operation in New York City in 1941. By 1954 the number had risen to 402, and by 1968 there were 565 VHF (very high frequency) stations and 175 UHF (ultra high frequency) on the air. Until 1952 all stations licensed were VHF; after 1952 some of the new stations were licensed to operate on channels 14 through 83, or the UHF band. As a group, the VHF stations have been much more profitable than the UHF, partly because they were established fairly early in the major markets, partly because they have been favored by the networks. In addition, there were over 1,800 community antenna TV stations in 1968, with more than 2,500,000 subscribers.

All three networks reported record billings in 1967 with the largest, Columbia Broadcasting System, reporting net sales of $594,617,000. Net sales in the three networks were 6.3 percent above those of the year 1966.

Television has grown extremely fast, but, in spite of its newness, we have a surprising amount of information on how to use it effectively. It did not have to go through the evolution typical of the other media. Instead, television very quickly developed into a major advertising medium. Consequently, any mistakes made were costly. In the early days of newspapers, magazines, and radio, an advertising campaign could be tried and thrown away if it did not work. In television, the cost of even very modest efforts is so great that the advertiser has to know what he is doing. From this expensive search for answers many significant findings have emerged within a relatively few years.

TYPES OF TELEVISION ADVERTISING

Television advertising is usually designated as network, national spot, or local. Figure 26.2 shows the growth of these three classifications. Note that in 1967 network expenditures accounted for approximately 8 percent of total advertising expenditures, with national spot 8 percent and local 3 percent.

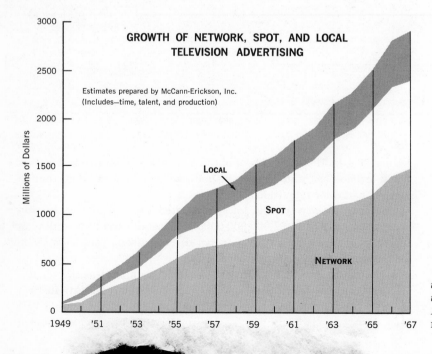

FIG. 26.2 *Trend in network, spot and local television advertising in the United States 1949 = 100.* SOURCE: MCCANN-ERICKSON, INC.

Networks. There are three national television networks—Columbia Broadcasting System, National Broadcasting Company, and American Broadcasting Company. (Each of them also operates a radio network.)

Network telecasting involves tying together stations by means of either a microwave relay or a coaxial cable. Under the first system, relay stations are spaced from 25 to 50 miles apart. These stations beam both the sound and video messages from one on to the next. The coaxial cable is a special type of underground cable (used also for long-distance telephone calls) that is capable of carrying both audio and video messages.

The main advantages of network broadcasting (compared with national spot) are (1) wide and simultaneous coverage through a single telecast, (2) low cost-per-thousand coverage of the country, and (3) the prestige of using first-rate talent.

National Spot. In broadcasting circles the word "spot" is used in both a geographical and a time sense. "National spot" advertising is any non-network broadcasting paid for by a general advertiser. A spot telecast, whether live, filmed, or taped, thus originates in the studio of the station from which it is telecast. It may be a program of an hour or longer; it may be only a short announcement. The term "spot" is also used in a time sense (for example, a "spot announcement," which may be paid for by either a general or a local advertiser).

The big advantage of national spot advertising is its flexibility. An advertiser can buy on a market-by-market basis and put the pressure on where it is more likely to pay off. Differences in sales potential, in dealers, or in some local condition may make it advisable to advertise in one area and not in another. Through national spot, you can introduce a new product, one area at a time. Also, it is often advisable to vary the programs or the times from one area to another, depending on local conditions.

Local. Local advertising is primarily advertising by retailers. Sometimes it consists of programs developed locally and sponsored by one or more local firms. Often "local" means that a local firm has bought a syndicated film series, which it has decided to sponsor in its own particular market. Considerable local television advertising consists of spot announcements, of various types and lengths, that are paid for by the local advertiser. As in newspapers, a great deal of the advertising classified as local is cooperative advertising placed by the retailer and paid for, at least partially, by the manufacturer.

WHY ADVERTISERS USE TELEVISION

Anyone faced with making up a media program has to decide whether to include television in a particular schedule. If the decision is affirmative, he must then tackle the vast number of additional decisions involved in using it correctly. In this section we shall consider some of the advantages and limitations that serve as a guide in making these decisions; then we shall investigate some of the problems involved in using this medium. It must be kept in mind that we are discussing two types of users—general and retail—and three different types of television —network, spot, and local.

Advantages

Impact. Used wisely, television has almost unbelievable impact. Witness the rapid rise of Lestoil from obscurity to leadership in its field, almost entirely through the use of spot television. Who can prove that the same time and money put into another medium might not have produced as well? The president of the company, having tried and abandoned newspapers, thinks that no other medium could have had this impact.

The fact is that television brings into the viewer's living room a combination of moving picture and the speaking voice. It is thus almost the equivalent of a door-to-door sales staff who can make visits at less than one cent a call. And when the person presenting the sales pitch is a great salesman (such as Dean Martin or Johnny Carson), the advertising can be very effective indeed.

Mass Coverage. Theoretically, you can reach almost everyone with a combination of newspapers, or even of magazines. However, television reaches with considerable impact a large number of persons not effectively reached by the print media, in addition to the many who are also reached by print. It is well known that a large number of theoretically literate Americans (some say from 30 to 50 percent) find reading so arduous that they do very little of it. On the other hand, these people are willing to spend several hours a day watching television programs.

Repetition. Repetition helps to explain the success of such campaigns as those of Winston and Mr. Clean, and of local advertisers such as Polk's in Chicago. That you are constantly delivering your sales message helps make people feel that they know you — whether or not they like you. Television makes it possible to repeat your message as often as you can afford.

Flexibility. There are few directions in which a television advertiser cannot move. Whether he wants to demonstrate his product, create a mood, use abstract symbols, make a blockbusting announcement of his product, or try it out in certain areas — he can usually find some combination of television presentations that will communicate the desired impression. A retail store can change its commercials from dresses to coats if a spring day turns chilly, or it can capitalize on a sudden snowstorm by changing from footballs to sleds.

Prestige. Not all television has prestige, but some of it has a great deal. There is little doubt, for example, that Hallmark has improved its prestige through its "Hall of Fame" dramatic presentations or that Bell Telephone has gained prestige through its programs. Some national advertisers buy because they can buy a section of an outstanding program or one with a name they can merchandise to their dealers. Through Ed Sullivan, Kodak has gained prestige with dealers, especially when he visits them or they have a chance to meet him at a sales get-together.

Limitations

Control in Hands of Telecaster. Like any time medium, television depends on the control of the communicator. If he goes too fast or too slowly, or otherwise fails to predict audience reaction, he may lose

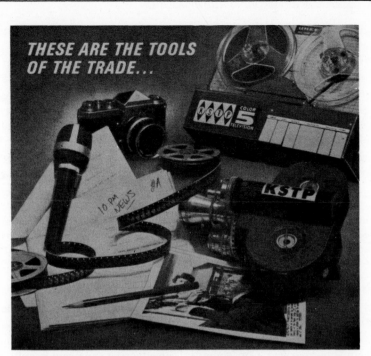

THESE ARE THE TOOLS OF THE TRADE...

... for KSTP-TV's award-winning Photo-News Department. Their expert use by a specially trained, completely equipped staff of reporters, writers, editors, photographers and technicians first made KSTP-TV news a habit for the majority of viewers. Now it's a tradition in the Northwest market.

For twenty years, KSTP-TV has pioneered in all phases of the television industry. It was NBC's first TV affiliate and, of course, the first television station in the Twin Cities. KSTP-TV was first with maximum power, first with color (in 1954), first with *total* color (in 1960) and the first and only station in the nation with a high-speed color film developer.

As a result, an entire generation of viewers has learned to depend on KSTP-TV to deliver *all* the news *first* — and in the clear, concise manner that today's news demands.

Represented Nationally by Edward Petry & Co.

KSTP TOTAL COLOR TELEVISION · CHANNEL 5 **NBC**
100,000 WATTS · MINNEAPOLIS. SAINT PAUL
HUBBARD BROADCASTING, INC. KSTP·AM·FM·TV/ KOB·AM·FM·TV/W·GTO·AM

FIG. 26.3 *Television station sells both itself and its medium.* COURTESY PROMOTION DEPARTMENT, KSTP-TV, MINNEAPOLIS-ST. PAUL; COURTESY: EDWARD PETRY & CO.

effectiveness. It is true that film or videotape lessens this limitation. There are, however, certain times of the day when housewives are not free to watch television or when they may only half-watch it while they go about their household chores.

Costs. Although some network shows reach viewers for a surprisingly low cost-per-thousand, there are certain minimum cost considerations that can sometimes price the medium-sized advertiser out of the television field. In addition to the charges for air time, the advertisers incur heavy costs for artwork and art material, for talent, music, sound effects, licenses and fees, direction, supervision, scripting, camera, rehearsal, and so forth. The production of a one-minute film commercial is a costly affair, which becomes less expensive only if it can be used many times and can reach a sizable audience.

Mortality Rate. The sheer impact of television causes both programs and commercials to wear out at a rate unparalleled in other media. Public tastes in entertainers, program formats, and commercial approaches are ephemeral and require constant checking.

Distrust of Personal Selling. The printed word carries a stamp of authenticity that broadcasts can never attain. People tend to believe something if they see it in print.

Lack of Selectivity. Mass coverage can be a handicap as well as an advantage. As the last chapter pointed out, many advertisers need a special audience.

Fortune quotes the agency for Cadillac and Pontiac as avoiding television because of, in the words of the agency,

. . . television's lack of selectivity. In television you must entertain them all. Now, that's well and good when you're selling a 30-cent product. But when you are attempting to sell a product that costs from $3,000 to $5,000, a product that is the second-largest purchase a man makes, next to his home, then you must have selectivity.[1]

KINDS OF USERS

It is apparent from Table 26.1 that package goods (such as drugs and food) constitute a substantial portion of television expenditures. These are widely distributed mass-consumption products sold, for the most part, in supermarkets. Consequently, the advertisers depend heavily on the mass media to reach a mass audience and presell them on the brand. Television also is well suited for demonstrating how these products can be used — products that are sold on an emotional rather than a rational basis.

TOP TEN UNITED STATES TELEVISION ADVERTISERS (1967)   **TABLE 26.1**

(In dollars)

ADVERTISER	TOTAL TV	NETWORK	SPOT
Procter & Gamble	192,052,300	113,173,600	78,878,700
General Foods	93,812,000	50,707,000	43,105,000
Bristol-Myers	74,278,800	52,455,900	21,822,900
Colgate-Palmolive Co.	71,087,800	37,771,600	33,316,200
American Home Products Corp.	57,834,400	45,244,600	12,589,800
R. J. Reynolds Tobacco Co.	57,230,300	48,084,600	9,145,700
Lever Brothers Co.	55,969,400	31,280,300	24,689,100
American Tobacco Co.	49,869,700	31,021,400	18,848,300
Gillette Co.	43,068,600	32,888,200	10,180,400
General Mills	42,571,400	28,385,600	14,185,800

HOW TELEVISION IS USED

Like any medium, television may be used in a wide variety of ways. However, the choices available to the television advertiser are probably more numerous and more complicated technically than in the other media. For example, the time buyer for a general advertiser has to decide among regularly scheduled network shows, special network

[1]Richard Austin Smith, "TV: The Light That Failed," *Fortune*, December 1958.

shows, alternate sponsorship, participating sponsorship, spot announcements, spot programming, and the various other classes of time.
Even the retail advertiser in a one-station market has to decide among
announcements and programs, kinds of program sponsorship, and
classes of time. It would be far beyond the scope of this book to explore
the possibilities in detail. The various copy treatments have already
been considered in Chapter 22, and the pros and cons of network and
spot programming have been discussed earlier in this chapter. Let us
look briefly at two additional problems involved in television usage
—the choice between programs and spot announcements, and the
choice of stations.

Programs versus Spot Announcements. When you sponsor a
program you gain at least two important advantages. The first is sponsor prestige if the program is a popular one and your firm sponsors all
or a major portion of the show. The public may then identify your
product or your firm with the program. The second is the control you
have over the placement and content of your commercials. For example,
you may wish to integrate your commercials into the show. Or you may
want to concentrate them on two or three strategic positions. You are,
of course, limited in the amount of total program time you may use for
commercials (10 percent of the total time at night and 15 percent in the
daytime).

The spot announcement provides much greater flexibility. You can,
if you like, spread your available money over a wide variety of time
slots or market areas. Or you can concentrate your energy and money
in a saturation campaign. You may want to introduce a new product
with a strong spot-announcement campaign, then later switch to a less
concentrated campaign or a program that will sustain interest week
after week.

If an advertiser is the sole sponsor of a program he will obviously
capitalize more on the program's prestige than if he shares sponsorship.
Many advertisers, however, are not willing to sacrifice flexibility by
committing themselves to sole sponsorship. They prefer to share sponsorship with other (noncompeting) advertisers. Consequently, you may
find your favorite network television show sponsored one week by a
cigarette company and the next week by a soap company. Often by
participating in sponsorship an advertiser can save enough money to
use spot announcements in addition to his program sponsorship. With
the high cost of today's television it is difficult for even the big advertiser to buy heavily in both program and spot campaigns.

There has been a definite trend away from program sponsorship in
television and toward programming by networks or stations and selling
of spot announcements only. This shift is often called the "magazine
concept," in that the TV advertiser, like a magazine advertiser, buys
and prepares only the advertising portion of the communication content, not the editorial matter. In many other countries with commercial
television this is the only choice available to the advertiser on television. Some critics (many in the advertising industry are included)
advocate complete control of programming by the station or networks.
Others suggest that the advertisers have the option of choosing.

Agency head John Cunningham has said,

> I believe that the editorial function on TV will some day be separated from the advertising—as it is in the public prints . . . .
>
> The advertiser will buy a block of commercials—let's say of 20 in a 13-week cycle. In fairness to all advertisers, these must be rotated on various kinds of shows of various ratings—so each advertiser will get about the same average rating. The commercial will have to stand on its selling feet.
>
> This will accomplish many good things. It will end blind devotion to rating. It will soften the monopolies on good prime time by a few large-spending advertisers. It will cut down a lot of imitation and mediocrity in programming. It will relieve sponsors' concern for the content of the program.

To an extent not generally realized, this concept had already taken over by the late 1960s. Agency media head Thomas Wright said,

> We used to buy television in segments, such as a half hour every week for 52 weeks. Now it can be bought as a single minute in one show one time or a combination of minutes in any number of shows on any network.

Another possibility is a system under which four different companies sponsor a program, one every 4 weeks. Instead of selling a weekly show to four different advertisers, the network sells each a cycle of 13 weeks to be used on an every-fourth-week basis. Four advertisers would then sponsor—not one program—but four different programs which would be broadcast in the same time slot. Perhaps commercials would not wear out so quickly if they were seen only once every four weeks.

Station Selection. Even when you buy network time you have some choice in stations—beyond the basic network buy, that is. The only advertiser who does not have to worry about station selection is the retailer in a one-station market.

In general, the agency time buyer will decide on the market before he selects the station. If the market is desirable, he looks over the available stations. Similarly, the retailer evaluates the stations that cover his market.

Stations are almost always evaluated on a coverage basis. In determining this, you are likely to depend partly on such mechanical factors as power, frequency, antenna height, type (UHF or VHF), and partly on evidence from research. For example, the research methods discussed later in this chapter are used in appraising stations as well as programs. Data from the Nielsen Coverage and Nielsen Station Service indicate frequency of viewing by area and by station. Many buyers will be influenced by the network affiliation of a station and by the extra merchandising it offers buyers. And, of course, you will consider the cost data of the stations.

MEASURING BROADCAST AUDIENCES

Early Measurement Efforts. Television research methods evolved from the study of radio audiences. Several organizations have been established primarily to measure television audiences, but the methods are the same as those used for radio. It is interesting to note that radio was a medium for almost 20 years before research became an important part of the business, whereas extensive television research was begun while the medium itself was still in its infancy.

In the early days of radio great stress was laid on listener mail as an indication of audience size and distribution. Later, it was determined that more accurate measurements could be obtained if interviewers asked people about their listening habits or telephoned them to find out what they were listening to at a given moment.

Broad-scale public-opinion-type surveys are still used. Among the most common are penetration studies, used to estimate the extent of ownership and the distribution of sets; coverage surveys, used to measure the geographical area in which people view or listen to a particular station; and program popularity studies, designed to measure preference or viewing of programs or types of programs.

Modern Broadcast Rating Services. Four techniques are used today to measure broadcast audiences.

Mechanical Recorder Method. An electronic measurement device, the Audimeter, was developed by the A. C. Nielsen Company to measure objectively the tuning of television sets. Attached to a set is a small metal box that automatically records on magnetic tape, minute by minute, the wavelength (or channel) to which the set is tuned. The tapes are sent to Nielsen from the 1,200 carefully selected panel members every week. Then the tapes are matched against known rosters of stations and programs to arrive at national ratings for programs.

The Nielsen Audimeter service has two outstanding advantages: (1) it is objective and thus free from memory lapse or vanity, and (2) it can provide highly comparable ratings week after week (with considerable side data) because it uses the same panel. Its main disadvantages are (1) the cost, (2) the lack of information on audience composition (how many or what type of viewers watched the show), and (3) the fact the sample tends to become dated and has too many substitutions.

Telephone Coincidental. This is one of the oldest methods. It was widely used in radio before television became a major medium. An interviewer calls a household chosen at random and asks the person who answers what program he is watching at the moment. The great advantage of the coincidental is its rapid reporting of ratings (usually the next morning). The main disadvantage is its lack of complete coverage — only the cities, only the daytime and evening hours, and only the homes with listed telephones are covered.

Trendex, Inc., largest of the coincidental organizations, reports on 27 major cities. In alternate interviews it collects information on sex and age of viewers.

Diary Method. Preselected homes are given diaries in which each person is asked to write down the programs watched. The diary sits on top of or near the television set, and everybody is supposed to write down what he is watching when he tunes in the set. The main advantages of the diary method are (1) its cheapness and (2) the completeness of the information it provides (continuous information because of its fixed sample and the breakdowns of viewing by age, sex, and so forth, of viewers). An important limitation is the impossibility of getting everyone in the sample to fill out the diary (or even to return it).

American Research Bureau uses TV diaries placed in telephone homes in 105 cities on which reports are issued. Videodex reports

AMERICAN RESEARCH BUREAU TV AUDIENCE ESTIMATES

PROGRAM SEGMENTS
CHICAGO AVERAGE QUARTER HOUR ESTIMATES

SPOT BUYING GUIDE
DECEMBER 1967 MONDAY

TOTAL SURVEY AREA, IN THOUSANDS (Average Quarter Hour)

TIME AND PROGRAM	STATION	METRO Rating	METRO Share	TV Households	Adults 18+	WOMEN Total	WOMEN 18-49	WOMEN 18-34	HSWV Total	HSWV Under 50	MEN Total	MEN 18-49	MEN 18-34	TEENS Total 12-17	TEENS Girls 12-17	CHILD Total 2-11	CHILD 2-5
6.15 PM																	
=NEWS/EDITORL	WBBM	13	29	293.8*	407.5	223.2	78.1	23.1	197.9	67.4	184.3	73.4	23.5	18.6	7.0	16.0	9.0
=HUNT-BRINK	WMAQ	12	27	291.0*	401.0	196.6	91.8	36.8	196.6	87.8	193.8	86.4	41.2	19.4	9.0	19.5	5.6
=TRUTH-CONSEQ	WBKB	6	13	146.6*	224.1	124.8	78.2	31.9	106.7	69.3	99.3	51.4	25.5	39.6	20.2	39.8	9.6
=FLINTSTONES	WGN	15	33	381.5	210.3	120.5	108.8	64.4	106.7	98.9	99.3	73.8	43.9	161.9	72.4	544.8	208.6
SPAN SERIAL	WCIU	-1		3.5*	5.1	3.4	1.7	1.7	1.7	1.1	1.7						
TRAILS WEST	WCIU	-1			1.8						1.8	1.8	1.8				
MCHLES NAVY	WFLD	-1		1.8*	1.8						1.8	1.8	1.8				
HUT AND TOTALS		45		1118.2*	1249.8	679.1	358.6	157.9	609.6	323.4	570.7	286.8	135.9	239.5	108.6	620.1	232.8
6.30 PM																	
=GUNSMOKE	WBBM	18	36	434.6*	652.0	334.9	150.8	70.8	282.2	121.3	317.1	135.5	45.0	68.6	23.6	101.7	40.0
=THE MONKEES	WMAQ	14	20	343.1	172.3	101.4	80.9	45.3	73.9	57.5	70.9	54.9	33.0	235.6	132.5	353.9	33.7
=COWBY AFRICA	WBKB	10	20	241.3*	337.2	185.4	102.5	48.1	162.7	99.3	151.8	59.0	59.0	67.7	30.3	90.4	31.8
=LUCY-DANNY	WGN	10	18	225.3	240.6	152.2	110.3	66.0	128.1	99.9	88.4	48.8	26.7	65.3	32.4	167.6	65.1
RACING/MARKT	WCIU	-1		2.0*	3.1	1.1	1.1		1.1	1.1	2.0	9.0	3.8	5.0		1.1	1.1
MCHLES NAVY	WFLD	-1	2	14.1*	18.2	9.2	9.2	5.7	9.1	9.2	9.0	9.0				6.7	1.7
HUT AND TOTALS		50		1260.4	1423.4	784.2	454.8	235.9	657.2	378.3	639.2	342.1	167.5	442.2	218.8	741.4	233.4
7.00 PM																	
=GUNSMOKE	WBBM	17	33	427.3*	652.1	334.4	154.8	67.7	280.6	124.2	317.7	142.0	48.0	68.3	22.1	119.0	36.0
=MAN-UNCLE	WMAQ	17	22	404.8	484.6	268.9	199.1	102.3	217.2	150.0	215.7	145.2	78.0	173.7	83.1	220.3	78.3
=COWBY AFRICA	WBKB	11	22	247.5*	338.2	189.7	108.6	50.2	165.4	105.4	148.5	95.5	15.5	67.3	30.3	146.2	41.2
=LUCY-DANNY	WGN	7	14	177.5	193.1	124.9	90.3	59.4	101.6	69.8	68.2	38.5	15.5	42.4	25.0	144.3	49.8
TELE-BINGO	WCIU	-1									9.0						
=DIVORCE CRT	WFLD	-1	2	11.1*	16.5	8.9	7.1	1.8	7.1	5.3	7.6	5.5	5.2	1.8	1.8	6.7	.9
HUT AND TOTALS		51		1268.2*	1684.5	926.8	559.9	281.4	771.9	454.7	757.7	426.7	196.7	353.5	162.3	629.8	205.3
7.30 PM																	
=LUCY SHOW	WBBM	19	36	447.9*	616.4	377.1	193.6	67.2	323.1	171.4	238.7	100.2	34.3	66.1	36.0	195.9	52.5
=MAN-UNCLE	WMAQ	16	30	399.4	498.6	278.1	204.4	115.5	228.3	158.3	230.5	139.7	74.2	165.4	82.1	196.3	68.3
=RAT PATROL	WBKB	14	8	324.7*	422.4	197.6	131.5	69.3	161.0	107.6	224.8	98.1	27.0	98.1	40.3	92.6	39.7
=F TROOP	WGN	4		102.7	111.6	56.6	42.0	27.1	44.6	33.5	55.0	41.6	18.8	27.0	13.0	91.4	23.6
LIND INTERVW	WCIU	-1		3.7*	5.5	1.8	1.8		1.8		3.7						
ADULT-MOVIE	WFLD	-1	2	12.7*	21.4	8.9	5.2	5.2	7.2	3.5	12.5	10.7	5.2	1.8	1.8	3.3	
HUT AND TOTALS		53		1291.1*	1675.9	920.7	576.7	280.3	766.0	474.3	755.2	446.8	212.2	356.6	171.4	629.5	184.1
8.00 PM																	
=ANDY GRIFFITH	WBBM	22	37	537.5*	676.1	419.9	231.8	100.3	360.7	201.4	256.2	129.0	40.2	121.7	60.8	287.1	79.6
=DANNY THOMAS	WMAQ	17	29	401.8*	576.4	357.1	198.2	82.1	301.1	165.1	219.3	123.4	54.4	113.8	68.7	170.8	59.0
=CAROL B.	WBKB	14					163.0	83.6	202.7	140.0	215.6	140.4	60.3	80.1	33.3	91.2	22.2
I SPY	WGN						100.5	57.2					41.7	21.1	9.8		
=BIG VALLEY		18	28	387.7*	545.5	292.0	230.1		88.0	66.6	99.3	72.4		3.5			
MON NT MOVIE	WGN	6	9	441.6*	681.0	387.3					10.7	5.4	1.7			3.3	
WRESTLN CHMP	WCIU	-1	2	137.2*	232.3	129.3	100.5				7.0	5.2		5.2			
ADULT-MOVIE	WFLD	-1		12.6*	14.0	7.0	5.2		2.1	3.5	10.7	7.0	5.2				
HUT AND TOTALS		65		1545.3*	2339.9	1346.2	873.3	401.5	1153.0	740.4	993.7	622.5	296.0	402.2	181.5	213.7	46.1
9.30 PM																	
=CAROL BURNET	WBBM	24	37	554.9*	856.8	533.4	317.7	129.3	471.9	269.6	323.4	178.4	59.0	127.0	64.3	94.8	15.8
I SPY	WMAQ	17	28	395.0*	560.8	299.4	226.3	109.9	246.5	190.9	261.4	193.1	104.1	147.9	76.8	54.0	11.6
=BIG VALLEY	WBKB	18	26	423.1*	654.4	363.0	223.4	59.0	312.0	190.9	291.4	172.5	80.2	100.7	32.4	42.0	11.4
MON NT MOVIE	WGN	6	9	135.2*	233.2	129.0	105.2	59.0	98.6	78.7	104.2	76.9	45.6	12.2	6.1	18.3	5.5
WRESTLN CHMP	WCIU	1	2	12.3*	20.7						10.7	10.7	10.7				
=NEWSCOPE	WFLD	-1		11.7*	16.5	11.3	5.2	5.2	9.6	3.5	5.2	5.2	5.2	5.3		3.3	
HUT AND TOTALS		65		1532.2*	2332.4	1336.1	877.8	412.8	1139.5	741.5	996.3	631.5	295.8	393.1	179.6	214.2	44.3
10.00 PM																	
=BIG NEWS	WBBM	19	32	443.0*	663.9	358.9	193.1	66.7	326.9	176.7	305.0	146.5	53.2	35.7	12.7	5.0	
NIGHT REPORT	WMAQ	24	40	567.7*	877.4	473.6	288.6	120.3	421.5	217.5	403.8	271.4	113.6	20.5	1.7	5.3	
NEWSNIGHT	WBKB	8	13	200.7*	303.4	181.4	114.2	51.5	149.7	94.7	121.9	83.1	32.5	31.8	9.2		
=NEWS	WGN	8	13	199.8*	298.1	167.1	118.3	53.3	143.5	101.0	131.0	76.0	18.6	6.5			
=TRAV-PIERROT	WFLD	-1		8.5*	15.0	6.6	3.6	1.8	6.7	3.7	8.4	3.6	1.8			10.3	3.5
HUT AND TOTALS		60		1419.7*	2157.8	1187.6	717.8	293.6	1057.3	647.6	970.2	580.6	219.7	94.5			3.5

TOTAL SURVEY AREA, IN THOUSANDS (Spot Buying Guide — Metro Time Periods)

TIME AND PROGRAM	STATION	METRO RATING	Metro Time	TV HOUSEHOLDS	WOMEN Total	WOMEN 18-49	WOMEN 18-34	HSWV Total	HSWV Under 50	MEN Total	MEN 18-49	TOTAL CHILD 2-11
=NEWS/EDITORL	WBBM	13	6.00–6.30	296.8*	226.2	79.0	24.0	199.9	67.4	185.5	73.4	16.9
=HUNT-BRINK	WMAQ	12		289.5*	205.8	91.0	36.8	195.1	86.9	193.1	86.4	19.5
=TRUTH-CONSEQ	WBKB	6		147.2*	119.5	77.9	32.5	106.4	69.0	100.2	52.3	39.2
=FLINTSTONES	WGN	15		377.2	119.6	107.9	64.4	105.9	98.1	100.2	73.8	540.3
	WCIU	-1		3.5*	3.4	1.7	1.7	1.7				
	WFLD	-1		1.8*						1.8	1.8	
=GUNSMOKE	WBBM	15	6.15–6.45	362.2*	315.6	114.4	46.9	239.5	94.3	249.3	102.9	58.8
=THE MONKEES	WMAQ	13		315.6	153.5	86.3	41.5	134.4	72.5	131.2	70.1	184.8
=COWBY AFRICA	WBKB	8		193.4*	155.1	90.4	40.0	134.7	84.3	125.0	72.7	75.1
=LUCY-DANNY	WGN	12		303.8	137.6	110.8	65.2	118.6	95.6	91.5	63.7	358.7
	WCIU	-1		2.8*	2.7	1.9	2.8	1.9	1.9	1.9	1.1	1.1
	WFLD	-1		8.0*	4.5	4.5		4.6	4.6	5.4	5.4	3.3
=GUNSMOKE	WBBM	18	6.45–7.15	432.5*	334.6	152.3	68.8	281.4	122.3	318.8	140.3	107.9
=MAN-UNCLE	WMAQ	16		376.0	187.1	140.7	73.5	147.0	104.4	149.9	101.2	288.6
=COWBY AFRICA	WBKB	11		244.1*	187.3	98.6	62.7	163.9	101.6	149.9	101.2	126.8
=LUCY-DANNY	WGN	8		201.1	136.4	98.6	62.7	113.2	78.2	74.9	40.7	153.5
	WCIU	-1		.9*								
=DIVORCE CRT	WFLD	-1		12.6*	9.1	8.2	3.8	8.2	7.3	8.3	7.2	3.3
=LUCY SHOW	WBBM	18	7.15–7.45	440.0*	358.6	174.6	67.8	303.6	148.2	278.1	121.0	160.0
=MAN-UNCLE	WMAQ	17		401.9	272.4	201.1	106.7	222.1	153.5	216.6	149.3	209.3
=RAT PATROL	WBKB	12		285.5*	193.9	120.9	59.8	163.4	107.3	189.5	116.1	145.9
=F TROOP	WGN	6		139.1	91.5	66.5	43.2	73.5	52.1	62.5	40.5	115.8
	WCIU	-1		1.8*	.9			.9		1.8		
ADULT-MOVIE	WFLD	-1		11.9*	9.0	6.2		7.2	4.4	10.1	8.1	1.7
=ANDY GRIFFITH	WBBM	20	7.45–8.15	489.1*	396.2	212.2	83.2	340.0	185.9	246.9	114.1	241.1
=DANNY THOMAS	WMAQ	17		397.7*	314.4	200.2	96.7	261.1	160.2	218.9	139.1	181.9
=CAROL B.	WBKB	14	8.15		216.9	147.3	77.8	181.9	123.8	228.8	141.6	
I SPY	WGN	19		375.0*	410.9	263.0					74.5	17.4
=BIG VALLEY			9.15–9.45	446.2*	125.3	98.1		125.3		7.1	2.6	
MON NT MOVIE	WGN	-1		134.9*	98.1			1.1	3.5	8.0	8.0	3.3
WRESTLN CHMP	WCIU	-1		7.2*				4.4				
ADULT-MOVIE	WFLD	-1		7.2*								
=CAROL BURNET	WBBM	24	9.15–9.45	557.7*	532.2	317.0	129.1	472.3	269.7	327.5	180.3	94.9
I SPY	WMAQ	17		392.3*	297.5	223.2	107.5	244.6	187.8	258.0	189.7	54.0
=BIG VALLEY	WBKB	18		431.8*	374.2	228.8	109.9	323.3	204.2	292.4	171.6	43.0
MON NT MOVIE	WGN	6		134.7*	127.7	101.4	57.2	98.1	75.7	103.0	75.7	18.3
WRESTLN CHMP	WCIU	1		12.5*	1.1	1.1		1.1		10.1	5.4	.9
=NEWSCOPE	WFLD	-1		9.4*	9.2	5.2	5.2	7.5	3.5	6.1	6.1	3.3
=BIG NEWS	WBBM	19	9.45–10.15	499.0*	446.2	255.4	98.0	399.4	223.2	314.3	162.5	49.9
NIGHT REPORT	WMAQ	22		482.1*	385.8	257.4	114.8	337.9	212.0	332.8	232.5	29.7
NEWSNIGHT	WBKB	13		311.9*	272.2	168.8	80.7	231.2	146.7	206.7	127.8	21.0
=NEWS	WGN	7		168.5*	149.1	112.8	56.6	122.1	90.9	118.1	77.0	9.1
=TRAV-PIERROT	WFLD	-1		10.1*	8.9	4.4		8.1	3.6	6.8	4.4	1.7

STANDARD FOOTNOTE SYMBOLS IN ARB REPORTS: *=COLOR TELECAST. ==COLOR TELECAST. ‡=TECHNICAL DIFFICULTY—SEE PAGE 2. +=PARENT/SATELLITE RELATIONSHIP. AT LEAST 55.0% OF TOTAL PERSONS VIEWING ARE 21+.

TIME: 7:00 7:15 7:30 7:45 8:00 8:15 8:30 8:45 9:00 9:15 9:30 9:45 10:00 10:15 10:30 10:45 11:00

Eve.—Fri. Dec. 29, 1967

WEEK 1

ABC TV

TOTAL AUDIENCE (Households (000) & %)

	7:00	8:45	9:45	10:15	11:00
	11,140 / 19.9		11,090 / 19.8	12,940 / 23.1	

— Off to See the Wizard "ZEBRA IN THE KITCHEN" PART 2 (Sustainer) → | Hondo (Co-sponsor) | Guns of Will Sonnett (Co-sponsor) | Judd, for the Defense (Co-sponsor) →

AVERAGE AUDIENCE (Households (000) & %)
SHARE OF AUDIENCE %
AVG. AUD. BY ¼ HR. %

Program	8:00	9:00	9:45	10:30	10:45	11:00
Hondo		14.0* / 23.5* / 14.1				
			16.6* / 28.6* / 16.5			
Guns of Will Sonnett				19.3* / 35.8* / 19.4	20.5	20.1* / 39.5* / 19.8

CBS TV

TOTAL AUDIENCE (Households (000) & %): 15,960 / 28.5 (8:45)

Gomer Pyle USMC (Co-sponsor) | CBS Friday Night Movies B "PORTRAIT OF A MOBSTER" (9:00–11:00 PM) (Co-sponsor)

AVERAGE AUDIENCE / SHARE / ¼ HR:
Wild, Wild West (Co-sponsor): 10,020 / 17.9 / 31.7 / 16.7 ... 18.1
Gomer Pyle USMC: 14,730 / 26.3 / 44.1 / 25.9

Movie: 14.0* ... 18.1* / 31.2* / 17.6 ... 19.5* / 34.5* / 19.4 ... 20.2* / 37.5* / 20.2 ... 19.8* / 38.9* / 19.3

NBC TV

TOTAL AUDIENCE: 11,310 / 20.2 (7:45); 11,480 / 20.5 (8:45); 4,870 / 8.7 (9:45)

Tarzan (Co-sponsor) | Star Trek (Co-sponsor) | Accidental Family (Co-sponsor) | Bell Telephone Hour (Bell Telephone System)

Tarzan: 8,960 / 16.0 / 28.4 / 15.5 ... 15.6* / 28.1* / 15.7 ... 16.1
Star Trek: 8,850 / 15.8 / 26.9 / 15.2 ... 15.0* / 25.2* / 14.9 ... 16.5* / 28.4* / 16.4 ... 16.6
Accidental Family: 5,940 / 10.6 / 17.0 / 9.6 ... 19.6 ... 9.6
Bell Telephone Hour: 3,020 / 5.4 / 10.3 / 5.3 ... 5.9* / 10.9* / 6.6 ... 4.7 ... 4.9* / 9.6* / 5.0

Eve.—Fri. Jan. 5, 1968

WEEK 2

ABC TV

TOTAL AUDIENCE: 11,030 / 19.7 (7:45); 12,540 / 22.4 (8:45); 15,510 / 27.7 (9:45); 16,070 / 28.7 (10:15)

— Off to See the Wizard "MIKE & THE MERMAID" (Co-sponsor) → | Operation: Entertainment (Co-sponsor) | Guns of Will Sonnett (Co-sponsor) | Judd, for the Defense (Co-sponsor) →

AVERAGE AUDIENCE / SHARE / ¼ HR:
8,740 / 15.6 / 25.3 / 14.0 ... 16.8* / 26.5* / 17.2 ... 16.3
9,460 / 16.9 / 25.9 / 13.6 ... 14.0* / 21.4* / 14.4 ... 19.7* / 30.3* / 20.0
14,390 / 25.7 / 41.3 / 25.3 ... 19.5* ...
23.3 / 23.0* / 42.1 / 22.7 ... 23.8 ... 23.7* / 44.7* / 23.6

CBS TV

TOTAL AUDIENCE: 14,670 / 26.2 (7:45); 16,580 / 29.6 (8:45); 16,460 / 29.4 (9:00)

Wild, Wild West (Co-sponsor) | Gomer Pyle USMC (Co-sponsor) | CBS Friday Night Movies ® "THE MUSIC MAN" PART 2 (9:00–10:40 PM) (Co-sponsor) | "The Legend of Jimmy Blue Eyes"

11,820 / 21.1 / 34.3 / 20.2 ... 22.0* / 34.7* / 22.4
15,340 / 27.4 / 42.0 / 26.7 ... 18.2* / 27.9* / 18.3 ... 18.0 / 30.3 / 17.9 ... 17.6* / 27.1* / 17.2 ... 19.6 ... 19.2* / 30.9* / 18.8 ... 19.8* / 34.2* / 20.1 ... 17.1 ... 15.3* / 28.9* / 13.6

NBC TV

TOTAL AUDIENCE: 11,590 / 20.7 (7:45); 14,060 / 25.1 (8:45); 8,230 / 14.7 (10:15)

Tarzan (Co-sponsor) | Star Trek (Co-sponsor) | Accidental Family (Sustainer) | Actuality Specials "TOMORROW'S WORLD, BEYOND THE SKY" (ECAP)

9,800 / 17.5 / 28.4 / 17.1 ... 17.3* / 28.9* / 17.5
10,920 / 19.5 / 29.9 / 18.1 ... 18.2* / 27.9* / 18.3 ... 20.9* / 32.2* / 20.7
5,380 / 9.6 / 17.3 / 10.4 ... 9.7* / 16.8* / 9.1 ... 9.4 ... 9.5* / 17.9* / 9.6

TV HOUSEHOLDS USING TV	7:15	7:45	8:15	8:45	9:15	9:45	10:15	10:45	11:00
WK 1	55.3 / 58.4	56.7 / 59.9	55.2 / 59.2	56.3 / 62.9	57.9 / 63.9	59.4 / 64.5	57.6 / 65.1	56.6 / 62.8	56.4 / 61.5	54.7 / 58.1	53.0 / 57.6	51.9 / 54.6	49.8 / 51.4

(See Def. 1)

U.S. TV Households: 56,000,000.   * Half-hour ratings (for immediately preceding and subject quarter-hours).   † For Sponsorship Detail, See Program Index.   (OP) Other Programs: See Pages 72–77   R Repeat.   B Originated in Black & White.

FIG. 26.4 (a) and (b) Typical pages from American Research Bureau and Nielsen audience estimates. SOURCES: AMERICAN RESEARCH BUREAU AND A. C. NIELSEN COMPANY.

regularly on TV viewing in 28 cities. The Nielsen Television Index is based in part on a diary (placed through direct canvassing). Diaries cover both radio listening and TV viewing and are placed at all sets within a home. Media Stat uses the diary to measure radio listening.

Roster Recall Method. This method involves personal interviewers who ring doorbells and ask the person who answers what shows he saw or heard the day before. Each interviewer carries a roster of programs shown the day before and lets the householder look at the roster while answering. At the end of the interview, the interviewer asks questions about age, education, and so forth.

The advantage of this method—used mainly by The Pulse, Inc.—is that it is relatively inexpensive considering the large block of time covered and the detailed audience information it provides. The main limitation is the danger that the lengthy roster may discourage careful response, because people may exaggerate the amount of listening or point to prestige programs.

How Audience Research Data Are Used. Broadcast ratings have been the target of both satire and extensive serious criticism. Congressional investigations have been suggested. All the hullabaloo must seem strange to people who take for granted the right of communicators to collect as much information as possible. The trouble comes in the misuse of the research data. A salesman who is promoting a moderately successful program can usually find some audience-measurement rating to indicate that his program is outstandingly successful; his competitor, through other research, may "prove" that the rating is untrue and that the one *he* offers is superior.

In general, buyers of television time are most interested in the following types of audience data: *program rating* (percentage of homes in the sample tuned in to the program); *sets-in-use* (percentage of homes in the sample where the set was turned on); *share of audience* (percentage of sets-in-use tuned in to a particular program); *total audience* (total number of homes reached by some portion of the program as projected from the sample); and *audience composition* (distribution of the audience by demographic factors).

Although television research is more accurate than many critics both in and out of the industry believe, it is still subject to sampling error. It means little when one program receives a rating of 27.8 and another one of 27.2. For all practical purposes the programs can be considered to have the same number of viewers, because the difference is insignificant. On the other hand, if one program receives a rating of 34.4 and another one of 20.0, the first is most probably attracting a significantly larger audience than the latter.

There are still significant gaps in audience data. There is too little information on viewing by individuals; most services concentrate on what happens in the home, rather than on individual action and preference. Many of our best data are concerned with network shows on a nationwide basis and are of limited use in buying stations, time, and programs in specific markets.

Even the buyers of media often concentrate too strongly on the program ratings (some regard them as types of batting averages) and lose sight of the wealth of extra data which help to clarify them and make them meaningful in a given marketing situation.

Many agencies buy spot television time on the basis of "gross rating points." This is the sum of the ratings for the individual spot announcements or programs. For example, if a person purchases 10 television spot announcements, each of which averages a 15 rating, he has purchased 150 gross rating points. A rating point means an audience of 1 percent of the coverage base; hence 150 gross rating points means 1.5 messages per average home. One large national agency, for example, listed the "cost of 100 gross rating points weekly" for groups of television markets in the United States in its 1967–1968 "Media Rate & Audience Guide." These ranged from a $46,000 low (for 55 percent coverage in the first 25 markets with a daytime 60-second commercial) to $157,000 (for a 60-second commercial in fringe night-time in the first 100 United States markets).

AUDIENCE TRENDS

From the wealth of audience data have come many indications of how people are using television:

1. The heaviest viewing (and listening, in radio) comes from the middle cultural (middle-income, high-school educated) classes. There are two reasons for this. First, most programs are directed toward this large group. Second, people with above-average education and income have a diversity of interests and are less likely to depend on home entertainment. People at the lower ends of the economic and educational scales do not emphasize the home and the family quite so much as do those in the middle.

2. The average number of hours of television viewing stays remarkably constant year after year. Some people believed that viewing would drop after the novelty of television wore off. Instead, A. C. Nielsen figures show a slight increase in viewing between 1950 and 1967, with women in 1967 spending 28.7 hours a week viewing television, men 21.0 hours, and children under twelve, 21.8 hours.

3. Viewing stays about the same in total hours, regardless of the size of the city. Big-city people, however, stay up a little later than small-town or rural residents.

4. Viewing varies according to the time of day and period of the year. The audience rises steadily through the morning and remains fairly level until late afternoon. The number of homes that will have the set tuned in between 7:00 and 10:00 P.M. is roughly twice the number of those using the set during the morning hours. Peak set usage (68.7 percent of the United States homes) occurs during the winter months between 8:30 and 9:00. Set usage is highest from January to March, lowest during the summer months, when it will average 20 to 30 percent less than during the winter. During all periods of the day and all seasons of the year, viewing tends to be higher

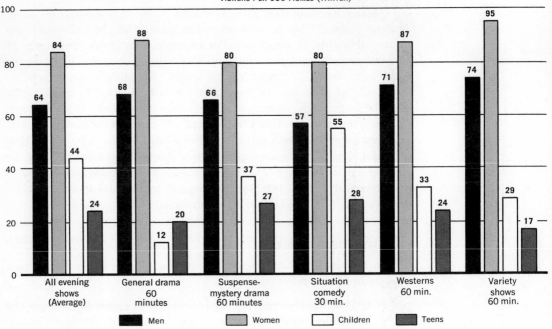

NIGHTTIME TELEVISION AUDIENCE BY PROGRAM TYPES

Viewers Per 100 Homes (Winter)

FIG. 26.5   source: a. c.
nielsen company.

among women than among men. During the 5:00 to 7:00 P.M. period it is relatively high among children.

5. Television viewing is about the same in areas where only two television shows can be seen as it is in areas where three or even seven programs are available. If people want to watch television, they check what is available, and even if they don't like the programs, they will nevertheless watch something.

6. Television viewing by children is heaviest among the duller and less emotionally secure. This is substantiated by large-scale studies in both the United States and in Britain.[2]

7. Individual television programs vary substantially in their appeal to demographic groups. For example, early in the 1968-1969 season "Here Come the Brides" and "Mayberry R.F.D." were the top favorites among teen-agers (according to Nielsen). However, "Here Come the Brides" was not even in the top ten in terms of total U.S. families reached. Among children 6-11 "Gomer Pyle" was the top favorite, although it, too, did not make the top ten for all-family viewing.

8. Steiner found that people's opinions of television are a poor guide to their viewing habits.[3] People who complained about the lack of informational programs and those who had no complaints watched practically the same fare.

[2]See Bernard Berelson and Gary Steiner, *Human Behavior: An Inventory of Scientific Findings* (New York: Harcourt, Brace & World, Inc., 1964), pp. 535–536, for summaries of these.
[3]Gary A. Steiner, *The People Look at Television: A Study of Audience Attitudes* (New York: Alfred A. Knopf, 1963).

RATE STRUCTURE

The standard units of time in television and radio and the cost ratios of each are the following:

TIME IN MINUTES	PERCENTAGE OF HOURLY COST
60	100
45	80
30	60
15	40
10	33 1/3
5	26 2/3 (20 for radio)

Although there are exceptions, most stations use the hourly rate and apply these standard percentages in setting the rates for other time units. Thus, if the hourly rate is $200, the half-hour rate would be 60 percent, or $120. Units of one minute or less are "announcements." These may be placed between shows or in participating programs.

Networks and individual stations divide their time into certain classifications. Commonly, they are AA, A, B, C, and D. These are based primarily on sets in use during the various hours. Here is part of the rate schedule for an hour (one time) of WABC–TV in New York (1968):

CLASS	1 HOUR (one time)
AAA	$10,000
AA	7,500
A	6,000
B	3,500
C	2,500
D	2,000

Because not all stations classify their time the same way, one has to be careful in making station-by-station cost comparisons for a particular time segment. Class AA time is normally the time during evening hours when viewing is at its height, although the exact times included may vary from station to station (see Figure 26.6).

When issuing a contract for a unit of television time, a media buyer wants to know, as nearly as possible, how long his rate will be in effect. The rates of television stations are subject to change at any time. Under certain circumstances, however, it is possible to protect the rate in effect at the time of purchase for a period; for example, time ordered prior to an effective date of increase often receives rate protection for 6 months.

Television rates are subject to a variety of discounts. For the most part, these are variations of the quantity and frequency discounts. We have already noted that the rate per minute is less when a person buys a full hour than when he buys a fractional part of an hour. This is really a quantity discount. Frequency discounts are usually in cycles based on 13 (13, 26 times, and so on).

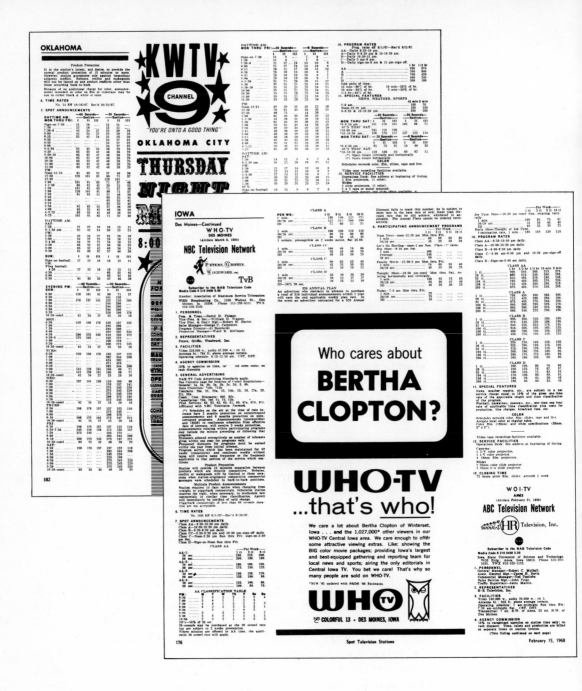

FIG. 26.6 *Typical pages from Standard Rate & Data Service—Spot Television.* SOURCE: STANDARD RATE & DATA SERVICE, INC.

The cost of a half-hour sponsored show or participating sponsorship in prime (evening) time on a major network was in the range of $114,000 to $144,000 in 1968. The variations are accounted for by talent, discounts, contiguity, and similar factors. Average cost per minute on a scatter (non-sponsored) show ranged in 1968 from $34,000–46,000 in winter to $18,000–28,000 in summer.

Rates for network time are in essence based on the sum of the stations making up the network. There are certain discounts available, depending on how many stations are bought, the number of weeks contracted for, and annual volume of business. Like newspapers (and radio), many stations have both general and retail rates. According to a survey made by Batten, Barton, Durstine and Osborn, 63 percent of the television stations have separate local and national rates, national being higher. Answers on how much higher ranged from 11 percent to 39 percent to "varies from day to day."

In addition to time costs, the buyer must consider at least two other types of costs: (1) talent and (2) production and incidental costs. Talent costs can normally be figured by the television production department of the agency. The most important production cost is the use of studio facilities and remote equipment. If the purchase is a package deal, these incidental costs will be included.

COST COMPARISONS

It sounds deceptively easy to make comparisons between times or between programs or stations. The usual yardstick is the cost-per-thousand. The difficulty is that this concept is often muddied by lack of clear definitions. Cost-per-thousand is usually figured by (1) dividing the gross rate of the time period by the potential set circulation, or (2) dividing the total cost per program to the advertiser by the program audience as projected from the sample reported on by a rating service.

For example, if a person pays $200,000 for a program that delivers an audience of 20,000,000 homes, he says his cost is $10 per thousand for that program. However, whether he uses the gross rate for a time period or the total cost for a program, he has to make sure that the audience figures he is using for comparisons are really comparable. It is dangerous to compare cost-per-thousand on the basis of one rating method with cost-per-thousand on a different basis. The cost-per-thousand (or a common variation, the cost-per-commercial-minute) is a useful guide only if it is applied with extreme care.

RADIO

When commercial television came onto the scene at the close of World War II, there were some who thought radio was finished as a major advertising medium. Experience has proved these prophets much too rash. Radio has had its troubles and has undergone basic changes, but it is a major and a healthy medium.

After radio became established as an advertising medium in the early 1920s, expenditures rose through the 1920s and 1930s and the 1940s. By 1952 the expenditures had risen to $624,000,000. Then expenditures started to drop off and did not look up again until 1956. By 1958 expenditures had passed the previous high.

In terms of total potential audience, radio can be considered the number one medium. By 1968, 98 percent of the nation's homes had at least one usable radio. According to the Radio Advertising Bureau, there were at the beginning of 1968 approximately 262,700,000 working radio sets in the United States. This total included 64,500,000 automobile radios, however, and an estimated 10,000,000 in public listening places. Table 26.2 shows the distribution of listening by age and time of day.

COMPOSITION OF RADIO AUDIENCES
(In percentages)

TABLE 26.2

| | TRAFFIC TIME | | DAYTIME | | NIGHTTIME |
	Morning 6:30–9A.M.	Afternoon 4P.M.–6P.M.	Morning 9A.M.–noon	Afternoon Noon–4P.M.	8P.M.–1A.M.
Total Listeners	52.231	36.465	23.730	29.887	20.339
Men	42	44	36	41	39
18–34	15	18	11	13	18
35–49	13	13	10	13	11
50+	14	13	15	15	10
Women	44	39	58	46	37
18–34	13	14	17	14	13
35–49	16	12	20	17	9
50+	15	13	21	15	15
Teens	14	17	6	13	24

SOURCE: *Ogilvy & Mather Pocket Guide to Media, 1967.*

In terms of stations also, radio's post-World War II growth is worth special notice. The number of AM stations more than tripled between 1945 and 1960. In 1969 there were more than 4,000 AM and 2,000 FM stations on the air.

TYPES OF RADIO ADVERTISING

As in television, radio advertisers are normally classified into network, national spot, and local advertisers. The terms are used in the same sense as in television, so we need not redefine them here. However, the relative importance of these three classifications is quite different in radio. Notice, in Table 25.1, how important local radio is compared with the other two classifications—approximately twice the expenditure for national spot and nearly eight times that for network. This is a reversal from the early days of radio, when network was the most important type. For example, in 1935 network radio accounted for $62,600,000 of the total $112,600,000 spent for radio—well over half. The decline of network radio has taken place since 1949, when network television came into its own, although total radio expenditures kept rising until 1952.

We can also classify our radio advertising as *live*, *taped*, or *transcribed*. In the days when network radio was king, many programs were broadcast live. As radio has shifted more and more to the local level, there has been a decided increase in recorded shows, with little but the news and on-the-spot broadcasts coming in live. Through recorded material that is used repeatedly, the advertiser can keep down costs for each commercial and make sure that the quality is up to par.

TYPES OF RADIO STATIONS

We can also classify radio advertising on the basis of the stations that carry it (method of transmission, power, and range). Station classification is important in radio time buying because so much advertising

—even by nation-wide advertisers—is placed on a market-by-market basis.

Method of Transmission. The majority of radio stations transmit their message through amplitude modulation (AM); the other method is frequency modulation (FM), which came into widespread use in the 1940s. One difference between the two is the distance covered. FM waves go in a straight line and are not usually received effectively more than 75 miles from the transmitter. On the other hand, AM radio can be heard far beyond the horizon because a ceiling of electrical particles high above the earth (the Kennelly-Heaviside layer) bounces them back to earth, particularly at night. At night you can often hear stations located hundreds of miles away from your receiver. If the radio signal reaches your set directly, it is called a *ground* wave; if it is reflected back by the Kennelly-Heaviside layer, it is called a *sky* wave.

Power and Range. The coverage of an AM station is influenced by its power, by the height of its transmitter, and by its frequency. The estimated daytime range of a 250-watt station is approximately 15 miles, compared with more than 100 miles for a 50,000-watt station. Obviously, a higher transmitter will add to the area (and the quality) of reception of a station. Frequency is measured in kilocycles, with the lower frequencies offering greater coverage than the higher, other variables being equal.

Broadcast channels are divided into *local*, *regional*, and *clear*. The local channel covers only a small area, usually around a small city, and has from 100 to 250 watts of power. Consequently, several local stations around the country may operate on the same frequency. Often these stations will be restricted to daytime operation or will be required to cut down their power at sundown, because signals travel farther after dark.

A regional channel is usually operated with from 1,000 to 5,000 watts of power. It is expected to cover more territory than the local station and must be farther away from other stations that operate on the same frequency.

The clear-channel station is usually located in one of the larger cities and can operate with 50,000 watts. Each clear channel in the United States is reserved for one clear-channel station, with perhaps a distant regional station allowed to use the same frequency.

WHY ADVERTISERS USE RADIO

Advantages

Immediacy. Surveys show that listeners expect to find the latest news on radio. In a study of radio listening for the Henry I. Christal stations, Alfred Politz asked people, "Suppose you were at home and heard a sudden rumor that war had broken out. What would you do to find out if the rumor were true?" Over half the people interviewed said they would turn on the radio.

Low Cost. Most cost-per-thousand studies show radio delivering audiences at an extremely low cost.

If spot television is reasonably priced . . . spot radio is the discount house of the media business. Six one-minute announcements a week at 12:00 noon will cost an advertiser $903, after all discounts, on Philadelphia's WCAU-TV; for the same money he can buy 25 minute spots on WCAU radio. A four-to-one ratio is common in the television/radio comparison . . . The realization of this big numerical difference—plus the realization which dawned suddenly on many advertisers, that people still listen to radio—has produced a continuing boom in radio time.[4]

One survey by a large national advertising agency showed radio's cost-per-thousand listeners as 95 cents (other media ranged from $1.05 to $10.79).

Flexibility. Any communication that can be adapted to sound can be used on radio. Whether your message involves speaking, music, or some other type of sound, whether it takes 3 seconds or 3 minutes, you can use radio. As we saw in Chapter 22, advertisers have in recent years devised some ingenious ways of communicating through radio. Also, an advertiser can change his message or the tone of his message or even the entire commercial up to the time it goes on the air. He can, if he likes, reach his listeners several times a day, picking the times when he is most likely to reach potential consumers of his product.

Consider the flexibility of radio as far as geography is concerned. Suppose you want your message heard in Denver but not necessarily in Dubuque, in San Antonio but not San Francisco. You can pick areas where dealers need the most support or where you think the potential is greatest.

Audience Selection. Unlike television, radio provides a practical, low-cost vehicle for reaching a specialized audience. If you want to reach hi-fi fans or young housewives or any particular group, there are sure to be a variety of stations around the country and program segments that make a special appeal to that group. Like magazines, some radio stations concentrate on special market segments (for example, Negroes); others try for mass markets.

Mobility. Radio is extremely mobile. It follows the housewife from room to room, goes to the beach, rides in the car. There are few places it cannot go. It can even follow workers to their places of business.

Limitations.

Audience Fragmentation. There are few parts of the country where the listener is limited to fewer than ten stations. Radio must fight for its audiences.

Transient Quality. Radio, like any time medium, is gone quickly. The message is not available for reference or for rereading.

Lack of Research Data. Although there are several audience survey methods in common use, there is not the concerted attempt to find information that there is in television. The local advertiser is not so willing to sponsor research as is the national advertiser; therefore a great deal more money is being spent these days on television research, where the general advertiser has his big stake.

[4]Martin Mayer, *Madison Avenue, U.S.A.* (New York: Harper & Row, Publishers, 1958), pp. 166–167.

HOW RADIO IS USED

Today's radio time buyer has many choices. Radio's extreme flexibility makes it possible for him to use a saturation campaign if he thinks it advisable, or he can buy into the strong specialized appeal of a particular station or personality. He may decide to buy local sponsorship of a network or transcribed show (possibly local sponsorship of news commentary). Because of the great increase in stations, even the retail advertiser has, in his own market area, many possibilities from which he may choose. We have already considered some of the differences among stations and their coverage. We shall be looking at some of the programming and audience trends later in this chapter. Let us now consider briefly the problem of "saturation" campaigns, because so much of today's radio is used on a saturation basis.

It is difficult to tell just how many radio spots can be used effectively in a given situation. Daniel Denenholz of the Katz Agency (radio-television representatives) recommends a minimum of 24 spots per week per station, or 120 every week in a five-station market.[5] Media director Jim McCaffrey thinks 600 spots a week is too many, that 200 spots is the minimum for a larger market. Grey Advertising says, on the value of reaching a particular market through radio,

> ". . . one type of segmentation is a station's specialization by type of music ranging from the most popular record to show music through concert music over to symphonic . . . The significance for advertisers of this program specialization is that each station type tends to attract its own demographic slice of the market."[6]

USERS OF RADIO

The Radio Advertising Bureau reports that automotive and food products receive the highest dollar expenditure of any product categories (see Table 26.3). Gasoline and lubricants and tobacco products follow. Note that the order of products is somewhat different in network radio. The largest spender in network radio in 1967 was General Motors, with $5,675,000; P. Lorillard was second, with $2,506,000. In spot radio General Motors was first, with expenditures of $19,339,000, and Ford second, with $12,756,000.

In the retail field, the largest users of radio are the automobile dealers. Next in order come food retailers, department stores, and home furnishings stores. (In a study of retailers' use of advertising made in the middle 1940s, department stores were not even among the top ten users.) In general, the larger the store's gross, the more hours it uses a week (stores with from $2,000,000 to $5,000,000 gross average 1-1/2 hours a week; those with from $20,000,000 to $50,000,000, more than 3 hours a week).

PROGRAMMING TRENDS

As television changed listening habits, radio programming content changed also. Radio tried to offer types of programs not found on tele-

[5]Mayer, p. 167.
[6]Grey Matter, June 1967.

TABLE 26.3   RADIO EXPENDITURES BY PRODUCT CATEGORIES (1966)

	Spot Radio		Network Radio	
	Gross Expenditure (Time and Talent)	Percentage of Total	Gross Expenditure (Time and Talent)	Percentage of Total
Automotive	$57,000,000	20.7	$10,100,000	16.2
Foods	37,000,000	13.4	13,800,000	22.2
Beer, ale, wine	33,000,000	12.0	900,000	1.4
Cigarettes, cigars, tobacco	29,500,000	10.7	7,500,000	12.1
Soft drinks	26,000,000	9.4	300,000	0.5
Gas and oil	22,000,000	8.0	3,700,000	6.0
Consumer services	17,500,000	6.4	6,300,000	10.1
Travel and shipping	15,000,000	5.4	1,100,000	1.8
Drugs and Proprietaries	12,500,000	4.5	6,000,000	9.7
Cosmetics and toiletries	8,000,000	2.9	6,200,000	10.0
Apparel	4,700,000	1.7	500,000	0.8
Soaps, cleansers, and detergents	4,500,000	1.6	2,400,000	3.9
Agricultural	4,000,000	1.5	*	*
Paint, hardware, and building	2,500,000	1.0	1,100,000	1.8
Confections	2,300,000	0.8	2,200,000	3.5

*No expenditure reported
Source: Radio Advertising Bureau.

vision and avoided competing in areas where television had a distinct advantage (for example, variety shows). The percentage of sponsored news programs has risen sharply since 1948. One station gave away a portable radio each week to the listener who telephoned in the best news tip. Another station had its employees carry tape recorders to and from work to pick up unusual on-the-spot reports.

Evening musical programs declined for several years, then started to come back in the late 1950s, as did the dramatic shows. Quiz and audience-participation shows have held their own, both in the daytime and the evening. Children's programs, however, have declined substantially in relative importance.

An interesting innovation in network radio was National Broadcasting Company's "Monitor" program—a continuous week-end programming arrangement inaugurated in 1955. "Monitor" sought to break away from the conventional segmented schedule of earlier days, at the same time maintaining the network's prominent position in the local affiliate station's broadcast time. This system has proved generally attractive to advertisers. It was an early application of the "magazine concept" in that NBC provided everything except the commercials.

AUDIENCE TRENDS

The methods of collecting audience information are much the same for radio and for television; consequently, they need not be covered in detail. However, certain new developments of the middle and late 1960s are worthy of note. For example, the Radio Advertising Bureau and the

National Association of Broadcasters sponsored the All-Radio Methodology Study (ARMS) in an attempt to measure the relative accuracy of eleven different research techniques commonly used in radio-audience measurement. A second study was the Cumulative Radio Audience Method (CRAM), which was designed to overcome the "cooperation bias" usually found in surveys (the bias represented by the fact that heavy listeners are more likely to cooperate than light listeners). This was done by tracking down the noncooperators and then building these groups back in at the weight they should have in the final figures.

Perhaps the most ambitious radio-audience research project to date has been RADAR (Radio's All-Dimension Audience Research). During 1967 and 1968 Brand Rating Research Corporation surveyed a national sample of 17,500 homes to collect audience data on a quarter-hour basis by program and demographic groups and to find out product and brand usage of these listeners.

1. There are now more than 4 radios per American family. Of these, 188,000,000 are household and personal radios, and 64,500,000 auto receivers.
2. During the average week 140,000,000 Americans 12 years or older (95 percent of the total) listen to radio. On the average day, 3 of 4 adults listen to radio.
3. Radio angles sharply toward the middle-income ($5,000 to $10,000) segment of the United States population. (In this group are 53 percent of all radio listeners.)
4. Millions of people on the move can be more readily reached by radio than by other media.
5. Network radio often reaches people in areas of low population density where television reception is poor.
6. Radio can often reach demographic groups not easily reached by other media. For example, radio reaches 99 per cent of all teen-agers.
7. Radio has the capacity to reach 75 percent of all persons eighteen years of age and older during one or more half hours a day.

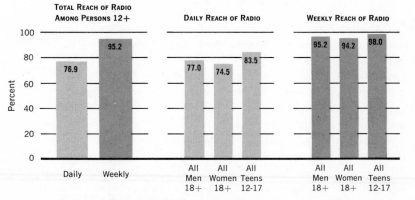

FIG. 26.7 *Percentage of U.S. Population reached by radio.* SOURCE: RADIO ADVERTISING BUREAU, INC.

RADIO'S AUDIENCE DIMENSIONS

Source: Published by Radio Advertising Bureau from RADAR study (Radio's All Dimension Audience Research) conducted by Brand Rating Research Corp. for ABC, NBC, CBS and MBS Radio networks 1967.

8. Radio offers seasonal listening peaks. In the summer, when television viewing declines, it may reach a larger audience than television does.

9. FM radio, through its emphasis on quality programming, has attracted audiences who are not heavy users of AM radio or TV.

10. Several studies have shown that the cream of radio's audience was skimmed off by TV at a relatively early stage. The first people to acquire television were those who had previously been the heaviest radio listeners. However, as these people become used to television and their viewing becomes more selective, they again listen more to the radio. Surprisingly, radio listening and television viewing frequently increase at the same time in the newer television homes.

11. Audiences look to radio for news and music. The music and news format which has become so popular in radio programming seems to be based solidly on listeners' tastes.

RATE STRUCTURE

Present radio rate structures reflect the changes in audiences resulting from the rise of television. Before television it was common to find radio's evening time priced substantially higher than morning or afternoon time, just as it is in the typical television rate schedule today. However, today's radio buyer will find that many stations either have a one-class policy (all times of the day priced the same per unit of time sold) or charge more for morning than for evening time.

Here are some radio station rates for one 60-second announcement, one time:

STATION	CLASS AA	CLASS A	CLASS B
		(In dollars)	
WLS (Chicago—ABC)	103.00	*	*
WNEW (New York)	225.00	175.00	135.00
WKOW (Madison)	16.00	12.00	*
KPEN (FM) (San Francisco)	35.00	32.00	23.00

*Class not used.

SOURCE: *SRDS Spot Radio.* Jan. 1, 1968.

Another change comes from the fact that a time buyer these days is purchasing station popularity rather than sets-in-use, as he formerly did. He may buy a particular personality or a particular program format and by rotating announcements build a particular image in the minds of local listeners—an image measurable with some accuracy.

Rate levels in radio are influenced also by the structure of the audience at a particular time. It is generally believed that teen-age girls make up a large part of the radio audience. A study at Ohio State University based on 2,168 interviews with girls fourteen years of age or more and women indicated that the relative importance of the teen-age audience may be overestimated. For example, between 4 and 6 P.M. there were "65 teen-age listeners per 1,000 homes as against 245 women in the 31-45 age group."

Some stations have been able to reduce rates by bringing in automatic equipment to cut operating expenses. Stations can rent equipment that will enable them to beam recorded music, punctuated by
taped commercials for up to 36 hours at a time. The lower operating
costs can be passed on in lower rates, which help to bring in an increased volume of advertising.

SUMMARY

Both television and radio must be classed as new advertising media.
Within a little more than 20 years, television has become the leading
medium for national advertisers, although it is exceeded by newspapers
in the total expenditure. By 1968 an estimated 94 percent of American
homes had at least one television set and 98 percent had at least one
radio.

The principal types of advertisers in television and radio are network, national spot, and local. In television, network advertising accounts for the largest portion of expenditures, but in radio, local advertising is most important. We can also make a meaningful distinction
between AM and FM transmission in radio, and VHF and UHF transmission in television.

Television and radio both have the advantages of a very personal
approach and of extreme flexibility. Both may, if carefully used, deliver
audiences at a low cost-per-thousand. Radio can be very selective,
whereas television is usually a mass medium. Both have the innate
limitations of the time media—a transient quality and control in the
hands of the broadcaster rather than the audience. The huge initial cost
for even a modest television campaign often limits television advertising to the large national advertiser.

In general, makers of widely distributed, mass consumption products are the heaviest users of both media. Retail stores are more important users of radio than of television, with the large stores using radio
more than the small ones do.

Research data are fairly plentiful in the broadcast field. In both
television and radio there are four basic methods of finding out who is
listening: mechanical recorder, telephone coincidental, diary and roster
recall. Each has both advantages and limitations, and many advertisers
use data from several sources.

The basic unit of time in both television and radio is the hour.
Other time units are usually sold as fractional parts of the hour. Rates
are usually compared on a cost-per-thousand basis, but such comparisons should be made with extreme care.

QUESTIONS FOR DISCUSSION

1. What are the advantages of spot compared with network television?
2. For what types of products is television best adapted? Does the
   addition of color to television make it more widely adaptable as a
   medium?
3. On what basis are the rates for radio and television set?
4. How do you account for the difference in program ratings of the

same program when the research method is changed? Why do you think the Nielsen services have been more widely used than those of the other audience-research services?

5. What is the "magazine concept"? What is its significance in television and radio advertising?

6. What is community antenna television? Why has it grown in popularity?

7. Why is research used less widely in radio than in television?

SUGGESTED READINGS

Agnew, Clark M., and Neil O'Brien, *Television Advertising.* New York: McGraw-Hill, Inc., 1958.

Bellaire, Arthur, *TV Advertising: A Handbook of Modern Practice.* New York: Harper & Row, Publishers, 1959.

Bogart, Leo, *The Age of Television,* 2d ed. New York: Frederick Ungar Publishing Co., Inc., 1958.

Chester, Giraud, Garnett R. Garrison, and Edgar E. Willis, *Television and Radio,* 3d ed. New York: Appleton-Century-Crofts, 1963.

Mayer, Martin, *Madison Avenue, U.S.A.* New York: Harper & Row, Publishers, 1958.

Minow, Newton N., *Equal Time: The Private Broadcaster and the Public Interest,* Laurence Laurent, ed. New York: Atheneum Publishers, 1964.

Roe, Yale, *Television Station Management.* New York: Hastings House, Publishers, Inc., 1964.

Seehafer, Gene, and Jack W. Laemmar, *Successful Television and Radio Advertising.* New York: McGraw-Hill, Inc., 1959.

Steiner, Gary A., *The People Look at Television: A Study of Audience Attitudes.* New York: Alfred A. Knopf, 1963.

Zetl, Herbert, *Television Production Handbook.* Belmont, Calif.: Wadsworth Publishing Company, 1961.

27 | Other Advertising Media

The media we have analyzed so far account for approximately 80 percent of the total United States advertising expenditure. The rest is spent in a wide variety of media, many of which are of considerable importance in the communication mix. Most are entirely advertising media — not a combination of editorial and advertising as in newspapers or the broadcast media. This chapter will cover four of the most important of these media — outdoor, transportation, point-of-purchase, directory and specialty advertising.

OUTDOOR ADVERTISING

Today's outdoor poster is really a distant cousin of our first advertising medium — a sign identifying a place of business. Signs were followed in the nineteenth century by circus and show posters, which were widely used to publicize show business. In 1967 outdoor advertising expenditures totaled approximately $188,000,000, two thirds of it placed by general advertisers. In certain foreign countries, where the number of media is limited or where the rate of literacy is low, outdoor advertising is among the most important of all media.

Kinds of Outdoor Advertising. There are three major types of outdoor advertising — posters, painted bulletins or displays, and electric

509

FIG. 27.1 *Prize-winning electric spectacular in Tokyo.*

spectaculars. According to Outdoor Advertising Incorporated, the national sales representative for the outdoor industry, in 1966 there were approximately 307,000 outdoor panels in the United States.

Posters. There are four sizes of paper posters in common use in the United States at the present time: the 24-sheet, the 30-sheet, the 3-sheet, and the 1-sheet. The 24-sheet is by far the most common and is what many people call the "billboard." It consists of 10 or 12 sheets of paper on which the advertisement has been printed, usually by lithography. When these sheets are posted in proper sequence on a poster panel, they form a complete poster 8 feet 10 inches high and 19 feet 8 inches long. The conventional poster structure is 12 feet high and 25 feet long, leaving a margin of white space (blanking) around the poster.

The 30-sheet poster is a "wide-screen" version of the standard 24-sheet poster providing approximately 25 percent more space.

A 3-sheet poster consists of three separate sheets on which an advertisement is printed. Together these three sheets form a poster 6 feet 10 inches high and 3 feet 5 inches wide. These sheets are sometimes used close to the sidewalk to reach pedestrian traffic. They are often placed at the point of purchase (for example, side walls or entrances of grocery or drug stores). As the name implies, the 1-sheet is a single sheet, 46 inches high and 30 inches wide. It is often used on the platforms of subway or elevated trains, or around railroad stations.

Painted Bulletins. Painted advertising is more custom-made than the poster. Each advertisement can be painted to order from a design furnished by the advertiser or his agency.

Two kinds of painted space are marketable — bulletins and walls. The bulletin is somewhat similar in structure to a poster panel — but longer. The standard painted bulletin is 15 feet 6 inches high and 55 feet long. Some are three-dimensional with an embellished cut-out, usually to emphasize the product or some feature of it. The wall is, as the name implies, the blank space on the side of a building. It is obviously impossible to standardize painted walls because the shape and the area vary according to the size and shape of the building where space is available. Locations for both are generally sought where vehicular traffic is heavy and where visibility is good.

Spectaculars. Spectaculars are the large illuminated, often animated, signs one finds on Broadway's "Great White Way" or Chicago's Michigan Avenue. They are custom-made to fit special high-traffic locations.

Why Advertisers Use Outdoor Media. Certain advertisers, such as the makers of gasoline or tires, like outdoor advertising because it reaches potential customers close to the point where the products are on sale. Communication must be quick and simple in outdoor advertising. This quality has both virtue and limitation. The simplicity of the message makes it easy to comprehend. The advertiser hopes, through his color, art, and short copy, to generate a quick feeling or association that will contribute to his brand image. At the same time, some messages are too complicated to be told in the few seconds a driver devotes to a sign as he speeds along the street or highway.

Repetition is another quality that appeals to many advertisers. If your product or service is advertised at a busy crossroads, audiences will see the ad again and again. Well used, repetition can build reputation. However, it can also beget familiarity which, in turn, can breed contempt, indignation, indifference, confidence, expectation, or desire — depending on what is repeated. Mechanical action, by itself, cannot and will not produce the mental stimulation needed to induce people to buy advertised products. Ideas motivate people.

Retention of an idea is essential in order to induce action. The more often the idea is repeated, the more likely it is to be retained. Even though the audience is limited to a specific area, the sheer weight of constant repetition is likely to produce results.

On the other hand, outdoor advertising has certain built-in limitations. One obvious limitation is brevity. How much can you tell consumers about your product on a 24-sheet poster? There is no chance for the housewife to browse leisurely as she does with the newspaper or magazine or to see the product demonstrated as she does on television.

Another limitation is the public's fear that outdoor advertisers are despoiling the landscape. This feeling came to focus in the "Highway Beautification Act of 1965," when Congress regulated the placement of outdoor advertising near interstate highways. Among other things, this act calls for a penalty of 10 percent of the Federal-aid highway funds usually provided for a state in the case of failure to effect control of outdoor advertising within 660 feet of the nearest edge of the highway. In areas zoned commercial or industrial, provision is made for the placement of signs closer than 600 feet.

Barton emphasizes the value of repetition in outdoor posters and cites studies by Starch and others that make this point.[1]

General Motors for several years has been the leading national user of outdoor advertising. The other automobile companies are also substantial users. Gasoline and tire manufacturers are important users. Many of the largest users of outdoor advertising come from the beverage industry.

How Outdoor Advertising Is Bought. The basic insertion unit for both 24-sheet and 30-sheet posters is the showing. A "100 showing" means that a specified number of poster panels are so distributed that virtually every mobile person in the community passes one or more of them on his way to work, while shopping or out driving for recreation.

In buying a showing you buy exposure of your message to the public. You have your choice of showings, which vary by intensity on a numerical basis—25, 50, 75, 100, 125, 150 and so on. For example, the No. 100 showing provides enough posters to reach approximately 93 percent of the population, an average of 21 or 22 times during a 30-day period, and the No. 50 showing enough to reach 85 percent 10 or 11 times. A No. 100 showing in the top 10 markets (population 29,800,100) consists of 1,510 panels, 469 of which are illuminated in locations where there is heavy night traffic. In Cedar Rapids, Iowa, a smaller city, a 100 showing consists of 14 posters in all.

Another approach offered by the seller of outdoor space is the "bottling-up" strategy. All the major traffic arteries leading into a city are covered by posters within a certain radius (perhaps 30 miles) so that it would be difficult for the driver to proceed into the city without exposure to one of the posters. Another approach is to locate posters every 20 miles on the important roads of an area. This is a method of covering a large area of many small adjoining communities.

It is also possible to work out special coverage patterns. For example, a food manufacturer might want his poster close to supermarkets, and an oil company might prefer locations near service stations.

With 3-sheets, coverage can be tailored to specific needs (such as posters near all drugstores), or market coverage can be bought at railway, bus, subway, and elevated stations.

Painted displays and spectaculars are bought on an individual basis, usually for 1-, 2-, or 3-year periods. On an illuminated bulletin, the original design is painted, and twice during the year it can be repainted with entirely new copy. On unilluminated locations, one extra painting is usually provided without extra cost. In many cities cutout displays can be rotated every 30, 60, or 90 days among certain choice locations. Display units may also be rotated between cities.

[1] Roger Barton, *Media in Advertising* (New York: McGraw-Hill, Inc., 1964), pp. 305–306.

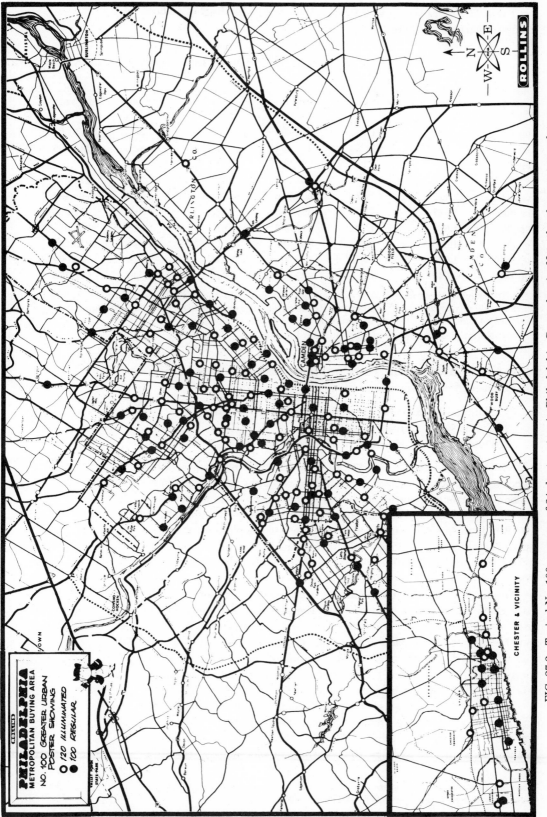

FIG. 27.2 Typical No. 100 coverage of 24-sheet posters in Philadelphia, Pennsylvania. Note the placement near heavy traffic artieries. COURTESY ROLLINS INC.

Table 27.1 gives the rates for a No. 100 and 50 showing of 24-sheet posters in various markets.

CUMULATIVE SUMMARY OF OUTDOOR IN 100 LARGEST MARKETS   **TABLE 2**

	100 Showing			50 Showing		
MARKETS	UNILLUMINATED PANELS	ILLUMINATED PANELS	MONTHLY COST	UNILLUMINATED PANELS	ILLUMINATED PANELS	MONTHLY COST
Top 10	469	1,041	$144,404	251	537	$ 75,501
Top 20	784	1,623	219,664	411	838	114,805
Top 30	1,042	2,158	282,762	543	1,113	147,917
Top 40	1,296	2,530	334,340	676	1,312	175,337
Top 50	1,419	2,871	368,786	743	1,497	194,198
Top 60	1,567	3,079	394,755	822	1,614	208,900
Top 70	1,668	3,264	414,953	877	1,715	220,087
Top 80	1,818	3,499	442,482	957	1,846	235,289
Top 90	1,934	3,652	460,526	1,018	1,928	245,007
Top 100	2,040	3,838	485,889	1,077	2,026	258,775

A No. 100 showing is considered to be exposed to 93 percent of the population on an average of 21–22 times in a 30-day period. A No. 50 showing is considered to be exposed to 85 percent of the population on an average of 10–11 times in a 30-day period.

SOURCE: National Outdoor Advertising Bureau, Inc., 1968.

Sources of Information. There are three basic sources of information for the outdoor advertising industry:

1. National Outdoor Advertising Bureau, Inc. (NOAB)
2. Traffic Audit Bureau (TAB)
3. Outdoor Advertising Incorporated (OAI)

NOAB is owned and supported by more than 200 major advertising agencies. It collects all the data that buyers might need to evaluate outdoor advertising. Consequently, if a media buyer's agency is a member of NOAB, he can obtain almost any needed information. NOAB bills the agencies and handles payment to the plant operators. It issues contracts and provides field inspection to make sure they are carried out. Agencies that are not members of NOAB place their orders directly with the plant operators (local outdoor firm).

The TAB is a nonprofit auditing organization sponsored by the Association of National Advertisers, the American Association of Advertising Agencies, the Outdoor Advertising Association of America, and the counterpart of each in Canada. Its primary purpose is to provide information and to audit (through counts of automobile and pedestrian traffic) the circulation of various outdoor poster and paint plants. It is the principal research arm of the outdoor industry.

The Advertising Research Foundation has recommended that the outdoor industry provide "market-by-market estimates . . . . . on a periodic basis, perhaps annually."[2] Says the ARF, "By estimating potential exposures to average 100 showings in each market, the stud-

[2]*Recommended Research Program for Institute of Outdoor Advertising* (New York: Advertising Research Foundation, 1967).

ies would provide outdoor buyers with an essential tool in selecting markets. As is the case for other media, persons would be the basic unit of analysis."

The OAI is the sales representative of the outdoor industry. Although plants often have their own sales staffs, the OAI makes sales presentations to agencies and advertisers and prepares promotional material for the entire industry.

TRANSPORTATION ADVERTISING

Transportation advertising is like outdoor advertising in that audiences encounter it away from home. It is the advertising inside the many public carriers—streetcars, buses, suburban railway coaches, and subways and elevated trains. It is available also on the outside of streetcars and buses, taxis, and Railway Express delivery trucks, at railway, subway, and elevated stations, and at many bus stations.

The typical or standard *inside* space fits a card 11 inches high and 28 inches wide, although widths of 14, 42, 56, and the long, lean 85 inches are sold in some markets. These cards are placed along each side of the carrier above the windows. In some cities, card spaces that are larger and different in shape are at each end of the car and in the middle. The middle card usually hangs from the ceiling and faces both ways. Ends and center are premium positions and carry higher rates.

Outside space units are normally available at transportation terminals and on the outside of public carriers. Standard outdoor space sizes are 21 by 44 inches and 21 by 27 inches.

During the 1950s the king-size poster (2-1/2 by 12 feet) became popular and was standardized by the National Association of Transportation Advertisers. These posters are printed on ordinary poster paper and shipped to the transportation advertising operator, who then mounts them on rigid panels and slips them into stainless steel frames carried on the exterior of buses.

FIG. 27.3 *Typical advertisement of a major transit advertiser.*
COURTESY WM. WRIGLEY JR. COMPANY.

Posters on trucks come in two sizes—2-sheet (46 by 60 inches) and 4-sheet (46 by 120 inches).

Of the several kinds of transit advertising, the most frequently used is the 11-by-28-inch inside card. This space may be purchased as

"full," "half," or "quarter" showing. "Full" showing or "run" provides one card in every car or other unit of transportation, "half" showing, half the cars, and so on. Occasionally an advertiser buys double service or two cards in every car. The contract for any size run is usually for a year. Contracts for shorter periods are acceptable but generally at a higher cost. Thus, full showing might cost an advertiser $150,000 a month for national coverage if the contract were signed for an entire year; however, less than 12 months would cost an additional 5 percent per month, and less than 6 months an additional 10 percent. Outside displays are more commonly sold on a unit basis. Like a 24-sheet poster, the car card is often replaced by a new advertisement at the end of the month (the cost of changing cards is included in the rate).

One way of saving production costs is to print the card on both sides. When the time comes to change the card, it can be reversed in the rack. Paper and shipping costs are thus cut in half.

Transportation advertising can be bought by the advertiser or agency direct from the local transportation company or from a national sales representative of the local operator. For example, in late 1967 an advertiser or agency could buy the first ten United States markets with full coverage for $91,000 a month, and he would receive 33,900 transit cards.

Why Advertisers Use Transportation Advertising. Car cards can reach large numbers of consumers very cheaply and with great frequency. Almost every city in the United States with a population of 25,000 or more supports a public transportation system. Each month there are approximately 1,000,000,000 riders on the public transit vehicles in these cities. Approximately from two thirds to three fourths of all men and more than three fourths of all women use the public transportation systems in the larger cities during the average month.

Studies made by Alfred Politz and by the Advertising Research Foundation indicated that the average 11-by-28-inch car card had been seen by 25 percent of the audience after 30 days of exposure. However, as with the other media, the inherent interest of the product and the skill with which the advertisement is executed are important influences on total readership.

This large audience is reached at a low cost-per-thousand—low, that is, if we consider aggregate audiences where people are counted once each time they ride the transportation system. According to Barton, transportation advertising delivers readers at a cost of 3 to 9 cents a thousand with the national average being 4 1/2 cents.[3] The low cost results largely because advertising is essentially a by-product of the transit industry. Consequently, many of the basic production and distribution costs common in other media are not applicable in transportation advertising.

Like outdoor advertising, transportation advertising offers color so that the advertiser can show the package or label as it appears in the store or can show the product reward more effectively. Unlike outdoor advertising, it provides an opportunity to use considerable body text if

[3]Barton, p. 310.

desired. Alcoholic beverages, financial institutions, media and food were the leading categories of transit advertisers in 1967, according to estimates of the Transit Advertising Measurement Bureau.

POINT-OF-PURCHASE DISPLAYS

The potential communication value of display space in retail stores can hardly be overestimated. However, in practice this space is often misused. Personal selling is generally declining in importance; therefore good display is more essential today than it was in the 1940s or 1950s. It is difficult to estimate the total expenditure for point-of-purchase displays, but the official spokesman for the industry, the Point-of-Purchase Advertising Institute, estimates the total in excess of $400,000,000.

The trend toward self-service means that advertisers must depend more and more on good displays to remind people of the advertising

FIG. 27.4 *Effective point-of-purchase display.* REPRODUCED BY PERMISSION OF SHULTON, INC., CLIFTON, NEW JERSEY.

they have seen and of the merits of the product. Barton believes also that television has increased the need for point-of-purchase advertising:

> The efficacy of self-service retailing has been strengthened by the demonstrative powers of television. Viewers see a product demonstrated and may well be convinced of its desirability. They go to the market and do not need another demonstration or sales talk by store personnel. All they need is to be reminded of what they have seen in television advertising. This is, therefore, another area where point-of-purchase advertising is effective.[4]

Studies by Du Pont (long-time researchers in the point-of-purchase advertising field) indicate that six of ten purchases in supermarkets are unplanned. In general, drug purchases there are more likely to be unplanned than purchases of other items are.

Because the retailer is the final link in the chain of communication with the consumer, retail display can be extremely effective if the material is well planned. For the manufacturer the problem is twofold: first, to design a display that will meet the needs of the retailer; and, second, to get the retailer to take advantage of it. The retailer's biggest problem is to decide what he will use of the mass of material he receives—he cannot possibly use it all without making his store a jungle. The retailer himself, of course, designs a large amount of the display material he uses.

Types of Point-of-Purchase Advertising. Any kind of display that can be used either in a dealer's window or inside his store can properly be called point-of-purchase advertising. The following list was prepared by the Point-of-Purchase Advertising Institute:

TYPES OF DISPLAY

Deep etched glass sign	Card with motion
Transparent plastic self-sticking sign	Mechanical book
	Mechanical mannequin
Decalcomania	Steady lighted unit
Mobile	Flashing lighted unit
Plaque	Moving letters
Fabric banner	Diorama
Illusion and projector units	Related item unit
Adhesive shelf tape	Backbar menu sign
Molded ceramic figurine	Indoor electric sign
Wall clock	Large itinerant units
Shelf topper	Mirror units
Enameled sign	Fluorescent units
Super basket units	Self-adhesive footprints
Cash register displays	Changing scene units
Heat rotor	Sound display
Change tray	Blowup of product
Rubber mats	Plastic reproduction of product
Shadow box	Molded plastic sign
Over-the-wire banner	Floor cutout
Easel-back card	Window cutout
Tuck-in shelf card	Checkout unit
Ad reprint holder	Light-cord hanger
3-D board units	Self-adhesive strip for gondola molding
Turntables	
Departments	Window streamer
Demonstration stand	Self-selector units

[4]Barton, p. 317.

Merchandise floor stand
Display carton
Jumble basket
Metal or wood racks

Wallboards
Exhibition type units
Wall posters
Display shipping cartons[5]

Obviously, these can be used in combination. For example, it is logical to have the product or a blowup of it as the basis of a display, and to use an easel-back card, a turntable, and a related item unit in conjunction with the product display.

Helene Curtis, a large cosmetics company, spends a large portion of its budget on point-of-purchase, most of it on prepack floor stands and counter displays. Revlon, one of its big competitors, has a policy of

[5]See *Printers' Ink Advertisers' Guide to Marketing for 1959*, p. 312.

FIG. 27.5 *German counter display for a brand well-known around the world.*

shipping counter and window displays with each merchandise delivery. All Revlon displays (copy and art) are approved by top management.

Some displays are permanent and some are not. There has been a trend in recent years toward the more permanent display, usually made of wood, metal, or plastic. However, temporary displays—disposable, timely, and therefore popular in the high-turnover grocery field—are still the industry's volume item. Light and motion are increasingly popular as advertisers look for new and different ways to attract attention. In the semipermanent field, wire is becoming increasingly popular.

Why Use Point-of-Purchase Advertising? Basically, advertisers spend money on display in order to take advantage of their preselling in the print and broadcast media. It is used as a direct action follow-through for the mass advertising. This may consist of reminding audiences of a campaign theme or product reward. Display may emphasize uses of a product or certain details that differentiate it from the competition. If the product is a very well-known one, perhaps the name itself should be emphasized.

Point-of-purchase advertising is also used to build brand and corporate images. It may help to associate a scientific background with a product. Occasionally it may help the product to appear luxurious or antique—or very modern. It may associate the product with fun or fashion or an exotic background. The displays for Gillette Blue Blades, like Gillette's mass advertising, associate the product with sports activities and participants.

Display may help secure a better location in a store by raising the product closer to eye level or by increasing the amount of shelf space devoted to the product. It may help move the product nearer some choice location such as the check-out counter.

Occasionally, the point-of-purchase display actually dispenses the product. It may dispense it from a bin or a counter top. It can also be used to dispense coupons or instructional literature. Consider the advertising impact of the Coca-Cola vending machines.

Both general advertisers and retailers are attracted by the cheapness of point-of-purchase advertising. Circulation is very high past many choice window and interior locations. For an inexpensive display piece, like a window strip, the cost-per-thousand viewers is very low. Obviously, it would be higher for a more elaborate display.

How Point-of-Purchase Advertising Is Used. The Association of National Advertisers has been working with the Point-of-Purchase Advertising Institute to find out how industry uses point-of-purchase. Findings to date indicate the following:

> The degree of emphasis placed on point-of-purchase varied widely from one company to the next. For example, the distilled beverage industry uses a great deal (average of 26 percent of the advertising budget), while textiles use less than 1 percent of the advertising budget.

In general, companies marketing impulse products devoted the largest amount of money to point-of-purchase. They were, of course, interested in stimulating a preference for their products, and the actual appropriation was most often based on that.

FIG. 27.6 *Italian point-
of-purchase
advertisement.*

The advertising manager initiated most of the planning. In the larger companies the sales managers and sales promotion managers took an active part in the planning. In most industries advertising agencies were seldom mentioned as initiating point-of-purchase plans. Garment, food, and electrical appliance industries were exceptions.

Point-of-purchase material was normally planned about 24 weeks in advance. It was designed 18 weeks ahead of time, tested for 15 weeks, produced 10 weeks, and distributed 4 weeks before the breaking date. The larger the company, the further in advance the planning.

Most companies had regular pretesting of point-of-purchase promotions and materials. Most used their own sales force; some worked through agencies or supplying firms; few used research firms. The big users also postchecked their point-of-purchase advertising.

Most delivered materials through their own sales force or shipped separately to jobbers or wholesalers.

Of the 138 companies reporting on one survey, 61 percent reported that no part of the point-of-purchase expense was borne by either wholesaler or distributor.

The policy of paying dealers for display space appeared to be most prevalent in the drug field but was common in many others. Retailers receive much more display material than they can possibly use, so they are faced with two alternatives—to use the material that will be most helpful or to use that for which they are paid. Obviously, the first of these is the best for both the manufacturer and the retailer, but many persons succumb to the lure of immediate cash.

Costs of Point-of-Purchase. Point-of-purchase is not a measured medium; it is therefore difficult to provide exact estimates of cost-per-thousand impressions. However, the Point-of-Purchase Advertising Institute has developed a slide-rule calculator that enables the advertiser to estimate the indoor cost-per-thousand exposures.[6] First it developed a so-called *exposure factor* for outlets like supermarkets and variety stores. In determining exposure factors, the count of actual transactions (one or more items purchased in one sale) was averaged for the various types of outlets and various types of areas (downtown, suburban, and so on). The total of checkouts per day was divided by 1,000 to obtain an exposure factor (that is, 1.420 means 1,420 exposures per day for a particular type of store). Barton gives as an example an advertiser who buys 10,000 point-of-purchase units for use in drugstores. He pays $4 for each of them. The total program costs $40,000. His average unit stays up for 18 shopping days. The calculator estimates that he gets 89,000,000 real exposures for each program and that the cost per thousand real-point-of-purchase exposures is 45 cents.

SPECIALTY ADVERTISING

The terms "specialty advertising" or "advertising specialties" are catchall classifications that include a variety of items carrying the advertisers' name and address and frequently a short sales message. The specialty is usually inexpensive and is presented to a preselected audience. It differs from premiums or contests, which are essentially methods of promoting sales, and not media of communication. The donor hopes that if the calendar or letter opener or some other specialty is a useful one, the recipient will be reminded of the donor many times a year and will feel kindly toward him and his product. Gaw says,

In summary, the advertising specialty, unlike the premium, the prize or high-priced business gift, usually carries the donor's name frequently combined with a slogan, trademark, or other advertising. It is always given without cost or obligation, and although its monetary value rarely exceeds $10 it does possess value—intrinsic, sentimental or otherwise—to those to whom it is presented.[7]

Perhaps the most important advantage of the advertising specialty is its long life. Every time you look at a firm's calendar or use a pencil with its name imprinted, you are reminded of its name and perhaps of

[6]Barton, pp. 319–320.
[7]Walter A. Gaw, *Specialty Advertising* (Chicago: Specialty Advertising Association, 1964), p. 11.

FIG. 27.7 *French outdoor sign for motor oil, placed near the point of sale.*

some slogan attached to it. Another advantage of the specialty is that the advertiser can preselect his audience. Like direct mail, it can be directed to either a large fairly heterogeneous audience or to a very small select one. There is thus little waste circulation. A further advantage is its extreme flexibility. The advertiser can choose a fairly expensive item if the audience justifies it, or sometimes he can get by with a very inexpensive one. According to Gaw, there are some 10,000 items from which the user of specialty advertising may choose.[8] Obviously, the advertiser can find a suitable specialty for almost any audience or any particular advertising need. The major limitations of specialty advertising are its high cost per prospect reached and the brevity in copy. Like direct mail the selectivity makes it expensive. The brevity in copy means that it is more useful as a reminder than as basic advertising.

There are, according to Gaw, at least three criteria to be kept in mind in the choice of an advertising specialty: (1) it should be of good quality; (2) it should be familiar to the audience and easy to use; and (3) it should be useful.

The Westinghouse Electric Corporation's Air Conditioning Division wanted to impress on building owners in New York City that they might lose tenants if they did not install air conditioning. General Electric developed an air conditioner especially designed for low-cost installation in older buildings. In order to soften resistance to straight sales calls, it was decided to use an attention-getter — a toy moving van — to symbolize the problem of having tenants move out because air conditioning was

[8]Gaw, p. 19.

not provided. It was reasoned that the toy could later be given as a present to a child. Furthermore, it was not expensive—$2.55 per van —and it could be delivered with the salesman's calling card to a selected list of New York building owners and managers. After the van was delivered, the sales representative called to make an appointment.

The Clark Equipment Company, a large producer of earthmoving and automotive equipment, wanted to develop more customers among certain large common carriers and private fleets. The agency decided to use a "Clark Cookout," which involved six mailings of specialty items for backyard barbecues. Each item was associated with the advantages of the Clark product. Thus a chef's hat arrived to remind the recipient that "Clark's salesmen wear many hats—equipment specialist, financial expert, etc." Barbecue tools were "just the right Equipment for the job."

Calendars account for approximately one third of the advertising specialty volume. We find the Ford Motor Company distributing more than 3,000,000 Norman Rockwell–illustrated calendars, and the neighborhood retailer or service station sending a few hundred to his best customers. One study indicated that 75 percent of all calendars distributed are kept by recipients, and many individual firms report a much higher percentage. Calendars may be classified on the basis of where they are to be used (wall, desk, pocket) or on the basis of their format (art, utility, 12-sheets, weekly, daily, and the like). In the art calendar the picture is the dominant element. The 12-sheet calendar, one sheet for each month, is a common form, but some advertisers make it a practice to send out 3-month calendars to relate the calendars to the seasons when their salesmen are calling on the audience.

DIRECTORIES

Although most people associate directory advertising with the yellow pages in the back of the telephone book, there are an estimated 4,000 classified directories of various sorts published annually in the United States.

The directory gives the advertiser an opportunity to call special attention to his product or service at the time the prospective customer is in the mood to buy. This is particularly well adapted to the needs of certain types of advertisers. For example, if your furnace stops working on a cold wintry day, you want help as soon as possible; you will probably look in the yellow pages for the name of a furnace expert. If you are interested in shopping for an automobile or a home appliance, you may, through calls to various stores, find out which stores have what you want and what the prices are. (See Figures 23.17–23.23.)

The messages are usually of the reminder type and often tie in with other advertising on television or in the newspapers. General advertisers commonly use telephone or city-directory advertising to list the names of their local dealers. This lessens brand switching at the local level after interest has been aroused by a persuasive message in another medium.

Circulation and rate information for yellow-page advertising is shown in Table 27.2. The three-space units shown there are those commonly used by yellow-page advertisers.

FIG. 27.8 *Yellow page advertising emblems used around the world.* CLIENT: BELL SYSTEM; AGENCY: CUNNINGHAM & WALSH INC.

Perhaps the best-known directory in the industrial market is the *Thomas Register of American Manufacturers*. We find also many directories that cover a particular industry (for example, papermaking) and others that cover a particular type of function in many industries (sales managers, for instance).

TABLE 27.2   YELLOW PAGES COSTS AND COVERAGE

METROPOLITAN MARKETS	CENTRAL CITY DIRECTORIES	TOTAL DIRECTORY COVERAGE
10 Largest Markets: Number of Directories	17	233
Trade Mark	$4,100	$20,000
Bold-Face Listing	700	5,000
One Quarter Column	7,500	34,000
50 Largest Markets: Number of Directories	76	590
Trade Mark	$14,500	$45,600
Bold-Face Listing	2,900	11,700
One Quarter Column	25,600	75,600
100 Largest Markets: Number of Directories	143	864
Trade Mark	$23,000	$63,000
Bold-Face Listing	4,800	17,000
One Quarter Column	41,500	104,000

SOURCE: *Pinpointing Your Market,* National Yellow Pages Service, 1967.

SUMMARY

In this chapter we have considered certain media that are not as important in terms of dollars as those in the preceding chapters, but are still important ingredients of the media mix. Outdoor advertising, which can trace its lineage to our first medium (signs), comes in three forms: posters, painted bulletins, and spectaculars. The main advantages are its nearness to the point of sale, its simplicity, and its repetition. Its brevity and its stimulation of public ill-will are disadvantages. The 24-sheet poster is the most important form of outdoor advertising.

Transportation advertising includes the ads inside and outside the public carriers and at stations where people wait for them. Its main advantages are that it can reach great numbers of people cheaply and with great frequency and can provide color and copy to communicate product information.

Point-of-purchase displays can provide the final link between advertiser and consumer and help build a favorable image in his mind, provide necessary information leading to the sale at a relatively cheap rate, and move the product closer to the consumer.

Although specialty and directory advertising do not provide much in the way of product information, they can both be quite effective in backing up campaigns in other media by reminding the prospect of the product or service at a particularly opportune time.

QUESTIONS FOR DISCUSSION

1. Under what conditions might an advertiser use outdoor advertising as his primary medium?
2. What are the three principal types of outdoor advertising? Describe the most important advantages of each.
3. What is the nature of the criticism directed at outdoor advertising? Do you agree with this criticism? What has the industry done to counteract it?
4. What are the main advantages of transit advertising? For what kinds of products is it most useful?
5. Would you classify point-of-purchase as a medium of advertising or of sales promotion? Why?
6. Look in your local telephone directory at some of the examples of directory advertising. What are the characteristics of the most effective ads? For which types of advertiser is this medium best suited?

SUGGESTED READINGS

Association of National Advertisers, *Essentials of Outdoor Advertising.* New York: Association of National Advertisers, 1958.

Barton, Roger, *Advertising Media.* New York: McGraw-Hill, Inc., 1964.

Gaw, Walter A., *Advertising Methods and Media.* San Francisco: Wadsworth Publishing Company, Inc., 1961.

Kirkpatrick, C. A., *Advertising: Mass Communication in Marketing.* Boston: Houghton Mifflin Company, 1959. Chapters 15–17.

Lackey, James B., Jr., *Transportation Advertising.* Cambridge, Mass.: Harvard University Press, 1950.

Sandage, C. H., and Vernon Fryburger, *Advertising Theory and Practice,* 7th ed. Homewood, Ill.: Richard D. Irwin, Inc., 1967. Chapter 23.

Wright, John, and Daniel Warner, *Advertising,* 2d ed. New York: McGraw-Hill, Inc., 1966. Chapters 9–10.

28 | Media of Sales Promotion

Like many of our terms in the marketing-communications field, "sales promotion" is a fuzzy term that means different things to different persons. Some say that it is synonymous with "promotion" and includes "the coordination of all seller-initiated efforts to set up channels of information and persuasion to facilitate the sale of a good or service."[1] As such it encompasses advertising, personal selling, and public relations.

The editor of *Advertising & Sales Promotion* calls it "the supplementary selling activity which coordinates personal selling and advertising into an effective persuasive force."[2] Others distinguish it from advertising by claiming that "sales promotion moves the product toward the buyer, while advertising moves the buyer toward the product."

The American Marketing Association, although recognizing that some find "sales promotion" all encompassing, recommended that the term be applied only to "those marketing activities, other than personal selling, advertising and publicity that stimulate consumer purchasing

[1]Edward L. Brink and William T. Kelley, *The Mangement of Promotion* (Englewood Cliffs, N.J.: Prentice-Hall, Inc., 1963), p. 7.
[2]*Studies in Sales Promotion* (Chicago: Advertising & Sales Promotion, 1964), p. 1.

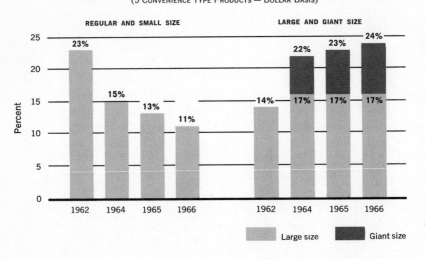

COMPOSITE SHARES — BY PACKAGE SIZE

(5 Convenience Type Products — Dollar Basis)

FIG. 28.1 *Share of market gained by various package sizes. Note the difference in popularity of the regular and small sizes as compared with the large and giant sizes of these products. While the large and giant sizes have increased their share, the small and regular size had decreased to slightly less than half their original share by 1966.* SOURCE: A. C. NIELSEN COMPANY.

and dealer effectiveness."[3] Frey makes a useful distinction between sales promotion and advertising on the basis of the media.[4] He believes that messages carried in media owned and controlled primarily by people other than the advertiser should be labeled advertising. On the other hand, when the tools, devices, and other properties are controlled by the company itself, we can properly call these the media of sales promotion. This is the general distinction made in this book, although some media such as direct mail could fall into either category. In this chapter we shall cover as media of promotion: packages and package inserts, trade fairs and exhibitions, sampling, premiums, coupons, cents-off deals, contests and trading stamps. Displays, which some would classify as promotion, were covered in the preceding chapter.

PACKAGES AND PACKAGE INSERTS

According to a study by Arthur D. Little, Inc., packaging is a $20,000,-000,000-a-year industry, and its value to the consumer is increasing, primarily because of the rise of supermarkets.[5] However, the packaging is not growing as fast as the gross national product, according to this report, in spite of the fact that "it reduces a product's cost, reduces the risk of purchase, increases the consumer's choice and stimulates consumer demand."

Packages communicate and promote the product while serving as containers. As consumers browse in supermarkets or department stores they gain certain impressions and information from the packages they see. A good package promotes the sale of a product, a poorly conceived one does not. Even after the sale is made, the package keeps up its

[3]Ralph S. Alexander, *Marketing Definitions: A Glossary of Marketing Terms* (Chicago: American Marketing Association, 1960), p. 20.
[4]Albert W. Frey, *The Role of Sales Promotion* (Hanover, N.H.: The Amos Tuck School of Business Administration, 1957), p. 8.
[5]"Packaging Lags behind Economy But Its Benefits to Consumer Grow Little," *Advertising Age*, April 11, 1966, p. 112.

promotional job. Package designer Walter Margulies points out that a cigarette package, for example, has to work very hard because it is taken out twenty times and placed on view before friends, business associates, intimates, and perfect strangers. Hence the design must "give consideration to what the user thinks others would regard as prestigious. Indeed cigarettes are a classic example of those so-called 'irrational products' in which fancy, whim and mystique all operate in place of rational choice."[6] On the other hand, a cake mix on a pantry shelf stays out of the public eye, and it does not have to work quite so hard.

As a communication tool, packages communicate both nonverbally and verbally. A bakery that put a green wrapping on its bread as a symbol of freshness discovered too late that green conveyed the impression of mold to consumers. On the other hand, the flip-top box of Marlboro helped symbolize the new look of these cigarettes and thus contributed to the brand's sales success. Carter Products' entry into the toiletry field was helped by the fact that it marketed its shaving cream Rise in an aerosol package.

The package can promote the sale of the product most successfully if it suggests some desirable qualities of the product and some product reward. The product should have real eye appeal as it stands on the shelf with competitive brands. How is this accomplished? One method is to flatter the product by using the best possible colors for contrast and background. Another is to use package size or shape to suggest desirable qualities of the product. The brand name or identifying insignia should be easy to recognize at a distance. The general appearance of the package might well suggest the integrity of the manufacturer or the many years during which the product has been marketed. The packages often have to be adapted to regional differences. For some reason, the buyers of margarine in eleven Western states prefer an oblong package to the square package familiar to the rest of the United States.

Some manufacturers have found that suggesting through gift packaging that the product is a gift item helps to promote the sale of the product. Candy, fruit, liquor, and perfume, among other merchandise, have profited from this practice. Other manufacturers promote sales by providing a package that has re-use value. Thus we find candy in glass tumblers and breakfast cereals in forms that can be used as cut-out toys.

Some products are distributed in more than one package. The advertiser should then consider both packages as advertising media and make both work to carry forward his sales message. The inside package should give the same message and impression that the consumer received when he bought the product. Sometimes manufacturers use multiple-unit packaging. A number of units are combined in one package in the hope that consumers will be encouraged to take several items instead of one. The familiar soft drink six-pack is an example.

Verbal communication is also very important. Packages are often examined in great detail—especially by the housewife in the self-

[6]Walter Margulies, "Shelf Appeal vs. Self-Appeal—Two Different Jobs for the Package," *Advertising Age*, February 28, 1966, p. 76.

service store vacillating between buying or not buying the particular product. She may be looking for information, or she may be looking for a way of rationalizing her purchase. Consequently, it is important that the wording on the package be as concise and accurate as possible. It should identify the major uses quickly and show how the product is prepared for use.

However, the copy does not have to be strictly utilitarian. It can also emphasize and dramatize some of the rewards the purchaser may enjoy.

Package Inserts. When it is well used, the package insert can be extremely effective in promoting the product. The buyer of the product is obviously a good prospect for additional sales messages. As Sandage and Fryburger point out, the package insert is often misused by marketers. They suggest the following for improving the use of inserts:

1. Printing in legible type.
2. Emphasizing one copy theme.
3. Changing the sales message occasionally.

FIG. 28.2 *Attractive cart for a special Jell-O promotion which may be used by grocers for other displays later.* CLIENT: GENERAL FOODS; AGENCY: YOUNG & RUBICAM, INC.

4. Making greater use of pictures and briefer copy.
5. Judicious folding (fold so that an interesting picture or headline appears on the front and unfolding is easy and logical).
6. Printing on substantial paper and, if possible, on a form that encourages keeping.[7]

TRADE SHOWS AND EXHIBITS

Trade shows and exhibits provide excellent opportunities for a marketer to promote his products or services through display and demonstration. Customers are able to examine the product in its natural setting and make comparison with competing products. Exhibitors can enlarge their dealer contacts and distribute literature and samples. They can thus do an important educational job for the advertiser if they are handled well.

Trade shows are particularly useful in promoting new products or innovations in existing products or services. They are especially important in fields where innovations, many of which are quite technical, are coming along at a rapid rate. At the 1968 convention of the National Association of Broadcasters in Chicago, more than 400 exhibitors crowded four large hotel exhibition halls for the purpose of exhibiting and demonstrating the many new developments in broadcasting. Radio and television executives from all over the United States come to this annual convention.

A great deal of professional skill is required for the effective design of exhibits.

SAMPLING

Sampling is often an effective medium for promoting a product — particularly a new one. When Procter & Gamble introduced its new detergent, Top Job, it distributed millions of samples throughout the country. In many colleges students are employed by tobacco companies to give away samples of their product to fellow students. When you walk through a supermarket you may be offered a sample of a new cheese spread or coffee. Doctors receive many samples of both new and old drugs from representatives of pharmaceutical houses.

A sample of a product is given in the hope that it will help sell the product. Normally, sampling is coordinated with such matters as advertising, pricing, and point-of-purchase display. Ideally, the consumer would see or hear the advertising messages promoting the product, then receive a sample so that he could try it out immediately to test the manufacturer's claims.

In addition to store demonstrations, consumer sampling is ordinarily carried out through delivery to the consumer at her home. Occasionally the person giving the sample will tell the housewife something about the purpose of the sampling when she receives the product. However, it is simpler to have crews go through a neighborhood and leave the sample, with a written sales message, on the housewife's

[7]C. H. Sandage and Vernon Fryburger, *Advertising Theory and Practice*, 7th ed. (Homewood, Ill.: Richard D. Irwin, Inc., 1967), pp. 543–544.

doorstep or in her mailbox. Another form of direct delivery is through the mail, either as a result of a coupon or on a blanket mailing basis.

In an industrial or professional market the detail man or salesman is an ideal means of distributing samples. He can explain the product and perhaps demonstrate it.

Effective as sampling is, when properly used, it does bring up certain problems. One of these is cost. Not only is the sample itself costly to produce, but also the sampler must pay for getting it into the hands of the consumer. A related problem is deciding on the size and form of the sample. The consumer should be given enough of the product to enable her to give it a fair trial but not enough to keep her so well supplied that she will be out of the market for a long time. If the size is similar to that which she might buy in the supermarket, she will not feel inclined to replenish it very soon, and the retailers will object to losing sales they might otherwise get. Sampling is often tied in with couponing, where consumers clip coupons from newspapers, magazines, or direct mail. Sometimes potential customers are urged in a car card to help themselves to coupons attached to the cards. In any event, the sampling campaign should be coordinated as much as possible with other elements of the marketing mix.

PREMIUMS

According to the Premium Advertising Association of America, premiums constitute an industry of something between $2,000,000,000 and $3,000,000,000 a year. One of almost every seven premium users spends more than $100,000 a year.[8] When you buy a box of breakfast cereal you are likely to find that the box tops can be exchanged for a toy space ship. Or you may buy potato chips and find that for a few cents more you can have a package of flower seed.

The objective of the premium is to give the customer a reason for buying the product now. The premium she gets may be free, or it may be self-liquidating (the customer pays enough to cover the marketer's out-of-pocket costs), but it always should appear to be an irresistible bargain. In general, self-liquidating premiums represent about 15 percent of the total spent for all premiums. One large agency with several accounts offering premiums kept track of offers and returns in the period 1954–1961. Offers of self-liquidating premiums by clients were in excess of $3,000,000,000, and the average number of returns was 1.3 percent. The most successful adult premiums were bowl covers, rose bushes, tablecloths, and an apron and towel set. Among children the most popular were puppets, submarines, and frogmen. The agency found low price was not as great an inducement as many think; the attractiveness of the premium was the important thing. They have found it is just as easy to get adults to send for premiums as it is children.

Premiums are distributed by mail, by retailers, in the package (factory pack), or attached to the product. Frequently the premium attached to the product will have some relation to the product itself (for example, a cleaning sponge worked well as a premium packed with

[8]Roger Barton, *Advertising Media* (New York: McGraw-Hill, Inc., 1964), p. 348.

Procter & Gamble's Joy). The premiums are sometimes designed to create long-term sales. For example, a service station might give as a premium a piece of chinaware for the purchase of five gallons of gasoline. Once the housewife has one of these she has a vested interest in continuing to patronize the station to complete her set.

One of the big problems is to decide on the attractiveness of the premium, because it has much to do with the success of the promotion. The premium should be a recognizable bargain and if possible have some dramatic appeal. Another problem is to make sure that the appeal is to nonusers, because the manufacturer gains little if only regular customers take advantage of the offer. A final problem is that of communication. It is important for the manufacturer to make sure that the offer is clearly stated on the label and that the chance of ambiguity or misunderstanding is minimal.

Premiums are used for retailers and industrial buyers as well as for consumers. For example, a premium might be given to a grocery store operator if he buys a certain number of cases of your product.

COUPONS

Coupons used as a sales promotion device are, in effect, offering consumers a reduction in price. When Procter & Gamble or Lever Brothers wants to stimulate sales of a soap brand, the company may send out millions of coupons through the mail. The consumers take these to the retail store where they can buy the item at the regular price less the amount specified on the coupon. The retailer is reimbursed for the amount of the coupons, which are somewhat like "accounts receivable" to him.

The growth of couponing is shown dramatically by Figure 28.3, compiled by the A. C. Nielsen Company, which handles coupon redemption for many leading manufacturers. It is estimated that approximately 10,000,000,000 coupons are issued annually in the United States and that about 1,000,000,000 of these are redeemed for a total cash value of somewhere between $75,000,000 and $100,000,000.

There are two types of coupons that are approved by the Grocery Manufacturers Association. They are the punch card coupon, which can be handled by electronic data processing, and the dollar-bill-size coupon.

INCREASE IN COUPON PROMOTIONS*

FIG. 28.3 *Four-year trend in coupon redemption.*
SOURCE: A. C. NIELSEN COMPANY.

1961   1962   1963   1964

*Based on coupon redemptions of 15 typical Nielsen Clearing House Clients

TRADE AND CONSUMER DEALS

(10 Brands on the Market 10 Years or More)

C = COUPONS   D = CONSUMER DEALS   T = TRADE DEALS

Brand	1st 6 mos.	2nd 6 mos.	3rd 6 mos.	4th 6 mos.
B*	T	CT	D	T
C	T	T	CT	CT
D	T	CT	DT	DT
E	CT	CT	CT	T
F	CT	C	CT	T
H*	DT	CDT	CDT	CDT
M*	DT	CDT	CDT	CDT
R	CT	CT	CT	CT
V	CT	CT	CDT	DT
EE	—	T	T	T

*We're also known to have used house-to-house sampling

FIG. 28.4 *Use of consumer and trade promotion by ten leading brands during the first six months of new product promotion.* SOURCE: A. C. NIELSEN COMPANY.

One of the prime objectives of coupons is to attract consumers to the store by offering them a reduced price for a limited time. Coupons tell the consumer that she is getting a bargain and that she should act right away to take advantage of it. They are directed also to the retailer. A. C. Nielsen, Jr., points out that they are designed "not only to attract customers but to provide an incentive to stores to stock the product." He points out too:

Coupons also have the particular advantage of providing an effective sales incentive to consumers without disturbing the store manager's current inventory; there is no need to stock special-deal merchandise, which creates inventory and pricing problems.[9]

Retailers sometimes object to the nuisance of handling coupons because of the extra clerical work and the slowing up of sales transactions. They normally receive compensation for handling the coupons, although they may be processed by a coupon redemption service. Some retailers also claim that coupons merely cause switching of brands. There is some danger of misredemption where the customer is given credit for the face value of the coupon even though the product was not purchased. This is illegal but difficult to control.

A study by one large agency revealed the following:

1. Couponing's major contribution is usually the achievement of product trial in the rising stage of a brand's life cycle.
2. When so used for a product that will win repeat purchases after an initial sampling, it can pay off handsomely over the long term.
3. There are differences between types of consumers who will and will not be prone to use coupons.
4. Selectivity can make couponing more efficient.
5. Misredemption, while a serious problem, can be minimized by eliminating particularly bad markets or areas.
6. The retailer's attitude is improving toward couponing generally and on the specific point of legitimate redemption.[10]

[9]A. C. Nielsen, Jr., "The Challenge of the Marketing Explosion," speech at AAAA annual meeting, East Central Region, Pittsburgh, November 17, 1965.
[10]"Couponing Grows, Gives Boost to New Products, Repeat Purchases, Kenyon & Eckhardt Study Shows," *Advertising Age*, February 12, 1962.

CENTS-OFF PROMOTIONS

As the name implies, cents-off promotions are designed to attract consumers through price appeal. By offering a price reduction for a limited time only, the manufacturer gives a reason for buying now but avoids regular price reductions. If the person likes the brand advertised she will probably continue to buy it even after the price goes up again. However, the cents-off or other price promotion cannot help an inferior product. In fact, if the cents-off deal is run too often, consumers may become suspicious of its quality and refuse to buy it at the regular price. It should be used only as a special stimulus to sales.

Variations of price promotions are those that offer two for the price of one or at least less than you would regularly pay. For example, cake-mix manufacturers have introduced new products in this way. You may be able to buy a box of the old product and the new product bundled together for only slightly more than it would cost you to buy the old product alone.

CONTESTS

FIG. 28.5 *Promotion for "Let's Go to the Races" by Big Bear Super Markets.* COURTESY BIG BEAR SUPER MARKETS

In Chapter 7 some of the legal problems of contest promotions were discussed. We are concerned here with contests as a means of helping advertising and other promotion to sell the product. Like premiums, contests are devised to attract people who might not otherwise buy the product.

In general, contests can be divided into those that emphasize skill and those that are based somewhat on chance but are not lotteries in

the legal sense. The contest of skill might involve writing the last line of a jingle about the product or writing 25 words on "Why I like . . . ." In recent years the contest based on chance or the "sweepstakes" has gained considerably in popularity. The names or numbers of all entrants are pooled and the winner is selected at random. The increased popularity is due partly to some relaxation in the interpretation of *what is* a lottery in some of the states and partly to the increased cost of attracting contest entries. One manufacturer found that the cost per entry received in a contest increased from 16 cents in the late 1930s to 66 cents in the early 1960s. Also, the sweepstakes is successful in getting large numbers of people (often in the millions in large national contests) involved in the contest. If each entry requires the purchase of the sponsor's product, a substantial sales increase will result. It is thus well adapted to the needs of a marketer of low-price, mass-appeal products. On the other hand, if the appeal is more specialized, a contest in which skill is emphasized may be more appropriate.

One of the most successful contest promotions in the late 1960's was the supermarket "Let's Go to the Races" game. It combined in-store distribution of racing slips with special films of horse races which, when televised, produced the winners. One chain reported a sales increase of 20 percent and another a 66 percent increase in customer count during this promotion.[11] An example is shown in Figure 28.5.

One expert on games cites seven criteria necessary for a successful promotional game:[12]

1. *Simplicity.* If your number wins, the prize is a specified amount of money. There are no confusing place or show prizes.
2. *Fun.* A combination of excitement, suspense, and action, plus the chance to win cash, produces the desired effect.
3. *Suspense.* Participants must wait a short time to see if they have won.
4. *Minimum frustration.* No long period of time is required before the winners are determined. Publication of the names of local winners regenerates hope for the losers.
5. *Continuity.* The game can be continued or rerun more than once.
6. *Low cost.* For chains, "Let's Go to the Races" is usually pegged at approximately 1 percent of sales. This is less than stamps, which generally run near the 2 percent level.
7. *Appeal to both sexes.* While most efforts are designed for women, getting the men involved has to be a plus.

TRADING STAMPS

A major form of sales promotion in the retail field is the trading stamp. According to the Trading Stamp Institute, approximately 80 percent of the homes in the United States save trading stamps, some avidly, some on a very casual basis.

Retailers normally pay 2 or 3 percent of their sales if they decide to give trading stamps to their customers. Among the largest users are food stores and gasoline dealers. In some states customers may redeem stamps for merchandise only, in some for cash only, and in some they may take their choice of redemption.

[11]*Promotion News*, Ogilvy & Mather, Inc., January 1967.
[12]*Promotion News*, January 1967.

Retailers may buy stamps from any of 300 different stamp companies, although the leading four have been estimated to do about 90 percent of the business in the United States. Those who use stamps believe that they help call attention to their store or service establishment, that they make customers more loyal, and that they help to offset price appeals of competing stores since they offer something in addition to the merchandise or service.

The principal disadvantage of stamps to the store is the cost. This may have to be taken from the advertising budget or it may cause the retailer to increase his prices. However, he hopes that the stamps will bring in sufficient new business that the reduction in fixed costs will more than offset the additional cost of the stamps.

SUMMARY

We have seen that there are many forms of sales promotion media which can, if wisely used, make the advertising much more profitable. Packages are used to promote the product as well as to communicate material about it. Packages can communicate both verbally and nonverbally to a prospective consumer. Through suggesting other uses for the product or for the package, they can help to promote its sale. Package inserts provide extra promotional impact on the person who has already purchased the product.

Trade shows and exhibits help to promote a product or service through display and demonstration of its ability to satisfy wants.

Sampling, premiums, coupons, contests, and cents-off deals are all promotional media geared to stimulating immediate action. A good sample provides just enough of the product to whet the prospect's desire and urge him to get more of it, but not enough to satisfy him for any length of time. Premiums are designed to get action through providing a good substantial money-saving reason for prospects to buy now: customers receive something extra they want free or at low cost in addition to the product itself. Coupons and cents-off deals stimulate action by offering a reduction in price—but for a limited time only. Their purpose is also to get retailer cooperation. Contests, though dangerous from the legal standpoint, can be an effective way of persuading large numbers of persons to try your product—either to get their name in the sweepstakes or to gain them entry in a test of skill.

QUESTIONS FOR DISCUSSION

1. Why should packages be considered a medium of sales promotion?
2. For what types of products is sampling best suited?
3. How do you explain the great waves of popularity, then waves of relative calm, in the field of contest promotion?
4. What are some of the legal pitfalls in contest promotions?
5. Under what conditions might you prefer to use a premium rather than a sample in the introduction of a new product?
6. What is the proper role of the retailer, compared with that of the manufacturer in the use of sales promotion devices or media?

SUGGESTED READINGS

Aspley, J. C., *Sales Promotion Handbook*, 4th ed. Chicago: The Dartnell Corp., 1965.

Barton, Roger, *Advertising Media*. New York: McGraw-Hill, Inc., 1964. Chapter 10.

Brink, Edward L., and William T. Kelley, *The Management of Promotion*. Englewood Cliffs, N.J.: Prentice-Hall, Inc., 1963.

Gross, Alfred, *Sales Promotion: Principles and Methods for Intensifying Marketing Efforts*, 2d ed. New York: The Ronald Press Company, 1961.

Robinson, Patrick J., and David J. Luck, *Promotional Decision Making: Practice and Theory*. New York: McGraw-Hill, Inc., 1964.

Turner, Howard M., Jr., *Sales Promotion That Gets Results*. New York: McGraw-Hill, Inc., 1959.

Wright, John S., and Daniel S. Warner, *Advertising*, 2d ed. New York: McGraw-Hill, Inc., 1966. Chapter 18.

29

Retail Advertising and Promotion

Most of the principles we have discussed in the previous chapters apply equally to general and retail advertising. However, retail advertising deserves special emphasis here, because it represents an annual expenditure of more than $6,600,000,000 (roughly 40 percent of the total). Unfortunately, much of this retail advertising is not well planned and executed, because the people responsible for it often have other duties — especially in the smaller stores. Stores do not usually have the help of an agency, yet the advertising campaigns of some of our large department stores (and also of some of the small specialty shops) are excellent and are prepared by skilled specialists. We frequently have, in retail advertising, the confusion and controversial problem of cooperative advertising (cooperation between the retailer and the manufacturer). The purpose of this chapter is to explore some of the more important problems peculiar to retail advertising and promotion — not to cover the entire field.

"Retail advertising" is a term covering all advertising by stores that sell goods directly to the consuming public. It includes, also, advertising by establishments that sell services to the public, such as beauty shops, gasoline stations, and banks. In this chapter the emphasis will be placed on retail *merchandise* advertising, because it is the most important form and gives the best picture of retailing.

RETAIL VERSUS GENERAL ADVERTISING

When you walk into a store, the chances are that you are in a buying frame of mind. You may be in search of a specific product, or you may just be looking around to see if anything appeals to you. Even if you are merely satisfying your curiosity, you have become a potential customer. The store that persuades you to enter its portals has already succeeded in one retail advertising objective—building store traffic. The volume of a store's traffic has an important effect on its total sales.

If a store handled a wide variety of desirable and fairly priced merchandise and if it were the only store of its kind in a particular locality, it would have no problem creating store traffic. However, virtually every store has competitors—other stores that sell similar merchandise and are anxious to attract customers. Therefore one of the primary promotional aims of a store is to persuade people that they should shop in that store. The department store may seek a mass market; the specialty store, as the name implies, seeks a more specialized audience.

The general (or national) advertiser is eager to build a favorable image of his product and to persuade consumers to ask for his product rather than for competing brands. The general advertiser is willing to leave the choice of store up to the consumer. The store management, therefore, must promote the belief that the nationally advertised product—which is identical in all stores—can be purchased more advantageously in this particular store. To persuade successfully, a store must add something of its own to the nationally advertised product. It must promise the public something other stores do not offer or do not offer so well. For example, it may advertise larger selections of merchandise, or easier credit, or generous parking space in order to enhance the store image.

Some stores have exclusive distribution for a particular brand within their trading area. Some meet competition by maintaining their own brands—brands not handled by any competing stores. Thus only at Sears, Roebuck and Company can you buy Kenmore appliances, and only at A & P stores can you buy Ann Page products.

The national advertiser would like dealers to give special emphasis and attention to his brand. But when a dealer invests his inventory money in several competing brands, he is committed to all of them. His stock of items of each brand represents working capital that is tied up until the stock is sold. Merchandise helps to pay expenses only when it is sold. If a dealer devoted so much attention to one brand that another did not sell readily and had to be moved at bargain prices, he would reduce his combined profit from both brands. Consequently, a dealer is more interested in selling *all* his merchandise than in putting extra effort behind any one brand. And if he is a reputable merchant, he is proud of all his competitive brands, just as each manufacturer is proud of his own brand. For example, a men's store might carry Hickey-Freeman suits as its top line. It might also handle two or three other nationally advertised lines that are priced lower than the Hickey-Freeman line. Such a store would normally stress the superiority of its top line, and its salesmen would be prepared to explain that Hickey-Freeman suits are more expensive because they are worth more than the lower-priced brands. At the same time, its advertising and its salesmen would emphasize the economy of the lower-priced brands to men who did not want to buy an expensive suit. The store improves its appeal by having several price lines ready to offer consumers. Its advertising will stress all of these, not one.

In this section we have stressed the differences between retail and general advertising. In many respects their objectives coincide, and they work together (as in cooperative advertising, a subject we shall explore later in this chapter).

ADVERTISING AND THE RETAILER'S MARKETING MIX

It was pointed out in Chapter 15 that the relative importance of advertising varies widely from one type of store to another, and even among stores of the same type. Department and specialty stores spend substantially more of each sales dollar than do food or variety stores (see Table 15.2). In all types of stores, however, the expenditures for personal selling are proportionately greater (account for a higher percentage of total expenses) than those for advertising.

The retailer's marketing program will make much more sense if it is carefully planned. Unfortunately, however, the frenzied pace of much retailing, the pressure of making immediate decisions, and, to some extent, tradition, tempt a good many retailers to forego planning. In general, the large store is more likely than the small one to follow the steps outlined in Chapter 3 — analysis of background material, definition of objectives, and working out of the marketing mix.

Innovation and experimentation do pay off in the retail field. Consider the case of the supermarket in the 1930s, and, more recently, the discount house. Certain retailers realized that service was being overemphasized and price appeal underestimated. Certain manufacturers and retailers were attempting to avoid price competition. Consequently, innovators dispensed with some of the services that people normally got with their purchases, cut their percentage of markup, and offered items to consumers at a substantial saving. They usually found that they had to use considerable advertising as part of their marketing mix. Later, however, many of the discount operators found it necessary to add services. The point is that the retailer who keeps his eyes open to new trends and is willing to change his marketing mix from time to time is likely to be the most successful.

Influences on the Marketing Mix. In deciding on the ingredients in his mix, the retailer should be guided by his store objectives, the attitudes and habits of potential customers, the attitude of the trade generally, characteristics of the products to be sold, and the activities of the competition. These factors are easier to analyze in the retailer's marketing program if we look at them in terms of store types. We could, of course, classify stores on the basis of the type of merchandise they carry, such as appliance, furniture, food, or drug. A more useful classification for working out the mix is that of promotion policy — promotional, semipromotional, and nonpromotional.

Promotional Stores. The typical promotional store receives only a small part of its business from regular customers. It depends heavily on consumers who come into the store in response to advertised promotions. The promotional store emphasizes its low price, and customers are used to waiting for reduced-price promotions which, in some promotional stores, are almost continuous.

Most cities have several promotional stores, especially in the men's and women's wear field, and the jewelry field. These stores sacrifice dignity to hard selling and price reminders. Some promotional stores,

FIG. 29.1 *An excellent advertisement for a promotional store.* © 1958 BY OHRBACH'S INC.; ADVERTISEMENT PREPARED BY DOYLE DANE BERNBACH INC.

FIG. 29.2 *Typical promotional store advertisement.* COURTESY S. KLEIN.

however, manage to give their advertising copy a considerable amount of individuality. For example, Ohrbach's uses an institutional approach with striking, large layouts and copy dramatizing the theme, "A business in millions, a profit in pennies" (see Figure 29.1).

The promotional store spends a higher percentage of its marketing dollar on advertising than do the less promotional stores. The high advertising cost is necessary because there is so little drop-in business; the store, therefore, has to shout its wares in large newspaper advertisements or strong ads in other media. The management hopes to keep total marketing expenses low by cutting down on services and increasing its stock turnover. (See Figure 29.2.)

Semipromotional Stores. Many of the large department and specialty stores fall within the classification of semipromotional. This type of store advertises regularly but devotes less of its sales dollar to advertising than does the promotional store. Its advertising usually emphasizes service, fashion, and variety of selection. Its prices tend to be higher than those of the promotional store.

The advertisement in Figure 29.3 is typical of the advertising done by the semipromotional store. Note that while price is mentioned, the dominant theme is the reward offered by the merchandise.

Most semipromotional stores depend on regularly scheduled sales events (August fur sale, after-Christmas clearance) rather than on a barrage of special "sales" in rapid succession.

Nonpromotional Stores. In the last classification is the "carriage-trade" store. It usually has a loyal patronage that depends on it for the latest fashions or the finest merchandise. It is usually expensive, so it lists prices, if at all, only for information—never for basic appeal. Note how well the advertisements in Figures 29.4 and 29.5 reflect the

FIG. 29.3 *Advertisement for a semipromotional store.* COURTESY WALLACHS MEN'S STORES, GREATER NEW YORK.

"Primavera"... coatdress by EMERIC PARTOS.
A spring zephyr of dyed black Russian broadtail
lamb with back-buckled satin belt.
Made to your order in our workrooms.

ON THE PLAZA • NEW YORK
BERGDORF GOODMAN
5TH AVENUE AT 58TH STREET

FIG. 29.4 *Advertisement designed more to enhance the image of this nonpromotional store than to gain immediate sales.* COURTESY BERGDORF GOODMAN.

nonpromotional character of the store. Bergdorf Goodman's clientele is composed largely of upper-bracket families. The advertisement does not mention the cost of the coat. Even in New York one would hardly expect a rush of customers to buy it. It is quite possible that this advertisement alone would not sell enough to pay for itself. However, it makes a worth-while contribution to the nonpromotional image — and that is well worth the money. The ad glorifies the coat, but it also stands as a symbol of the character and the quality of merchandise carried by Bergdorf Goodman.

The nonpromotional store is ordinarily a regular advertiser, but it depends more on long-range, prestige-building copy than do other types of stores. It is likely to spend a higher percentage of sales dollar for rent, window and store display, personal selling, and service of all kinds

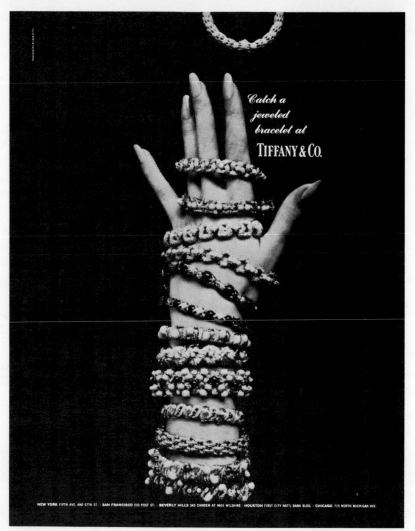

FIG. 29.5 *Good use of small space by a well-known nonpromotional store.* COURTESY TIFFANY & COMPANY.

than do other types of stores. On the other hand, its expenditure for advertising is usually lower than that of semipromotional and promotional stores.

RETAIL ADVERTISING AND THE COMMUNICATION MIX

The manager of the average retail store must address his local audience in a dual role. On one hand, his store is the purchasing agent for the people of his community. They look to his store as *their* representative, to bring them the goods that will best satisfy their wants. He buys for them what he thinks they would buy if they were dealing directly with the many suppliers.

On the other hand, he is the local representative for many manufacturers, each of whom expects him to conduct aggressive promotions for their particular brands.

This dual role epitomizes the communication problem of the retailer. He must build confidence both in his store as an institution and in specific merchandise that he has available. However, the image-building function (building a specific image of the store) and the action-stimulating function (getting immediate sales) are not really so separate as they might seem at first glance. Martineau says,

> For all of the retailer's remarks that his advertising is measured strictly in terms of immediate sales, that he has no intention of wasting his expenditures in high-sounding institutional advertising which convinces nobody, it is perfectly clear that every ad he runs is an institutional ad. Whether he realizes it or not, all of his advertising is creating an image of his store. One of the most important functions in the housewife's role is to know the stores. She learns to single out certain cues in the advertising which will tell her about the store's status, its sense of styling, its policies on returns and credit, its general atmosphere, its customer body, even its physical qualities; and then she decides intuitively whether this is where she fits in. Far more than by any explicit claims about the store by the store, her intuitive judgments are formulated by the nonrational symbols: the type, the whiteness or fullness of the ad, the general tone, the sophistication of the art—in other words by the totality of the advertising style.[1]

The Tiffany advertisement in Figure 29.5 is a good case in point. Tiffany's, a long-time leader in the jewelry field, has used advertising astutely as part of its communication mix. The store management believes the store should be an advertising leader, too. But how can a store with a relatively small advertising budget achieve such dominance? First, Tiffany's believes in leadership through position in the newspaper. It buys what some consider the most preferred of all spots in New York City newspapers—full position at the top of the two righthand columns on page three. Second, Tiffany's appreciates the importance of frequency. In spite of its small budget—by New York standards—its advertising appears virtually every week of the year, on a schedule that ranges from once a week to four times a week, depending on the season. Third, Tiffany's has developed an art style that supplies cues to readers, helps them know just what kind of a store it is and whether it is the right kind of store for their needs. The art style provides a helpful nonrational symbol. Fourth, Tiffany's makes sure the store's traditional image is reinforced in each advertisement. It attempts to keep up the symbolic value of the Tiffany name on any gift box. Note that the cost of each item is given despite the high price.

The astute modern retail communicator uses his mix of channels wisely. He provides, in his promotions and his advertisements, something for housewives to talk about when they get together for coffee or a bridge party. He uses all channels. He uses windows, store interiors, fixtures, displays, and special events, such as fashion shows and travel bazaars, to add to the total store image.

Retail Media. The retailer can use any of the local media but not such media as national magazines and network television. In practice, the most important medium, by far, is the newspaper. In Table 29.1 the estimated expenditures by local advertisers in the various media are shown.

Newspapers account for roughly 61 percent of local ad expenditures. Note the dominance of the newspaper in the retailer's media picture. This is not too surprising when we consider the major role the

[1] Pierre Martineau, *Motivation in Advertising* (New York: McGraw-Hill, Inc., 1957), p. 175.

ESTIMATED EXPENDITURES FOR LOCAL ADVERTISING IN 1967 | **TABLE 29.1**

(Millions of dollars)

Newspapers	$3,960
Radio	665
Television	500
Outdoor	64
Miscellaneous	1,368

SOURCE: *Marketing/Communications,* March, 1968.

newspaper plays in helping shoppers make shopping decisions. A study was made in Madison, Wisconsin, of purchasers of television sets and furniture. Table 29.2 summarizes the opinions of the purchasers when they were asked to recall which source they used in making their purchase decision.

SOURCES OF INFORMATION RESPONDENTS RECALLED USING | **TABLE 29.2**

(Unaided and Aided recall)

SOURCE OF INFORMATION	PERCENTAGE OF ALL RESPONDENTS (Base—174)	PERCENTAGE OF TELEVISION PURCHASERS (Base—92)	PERCENTAGE OF FURNITURE PURCHASERS (Base—82)
Newspaper advertising	55.7	54.4	57.3
Friends or acquaintances	51.7	67.4	34.2
Magazine advertising	20.7	21.4	19.6
Telephoning a store	17.2	19.5	14.6
Catalogues	15.5	14.2	17.0
Television advertising	14.4	19.6	8.5
Consumer rating magazines	10.3	18.5	1.2
Radio advertising	9.8	10.9	8.5
Yellow pages	8.0	3.3	4.9
Mail advertising	4.6	10.9	6.1

SOURCE: Jon G. Udell and Bruce LeGrande, "Consumer Behavior in the Market Place," *Journal of Retailing,* Fall 1964, p. 37.

The housewife depends on the newspaper for many shopping cues. Consider how she scans the retail ads as an aid in selecting her clothes. Although she may be interested only in a cheap everyday wash dress, she is probably interested both in objective qualities such as fabric, color, and washability and also in subjective ones such as "Would I feel comfortable with my friends if I wore a dress like this?" One sociologist says that clothing is the woman's equivalent of heraldry—a colorful way of telling the world about herself as a person. (Another sociologist says that shopping itself is the woman's equivalent of a man's hunting trip—a spree where she can let herself go.)

In the newspaper the housewife can find essential information that she can read at her own speed, reread it, and even cut it out to refer to when she likes. Also, there is an authority to the printed word that the broadcast media find difficult to approach. The average local newspaper, being the prime source of noncommercial news in a community, has even more prestige and authority than almost all other print media. An interesting study made in 1959 by Social Research for the Bureau of Advertising, ANPA, indicated that the printed word's prestige is highest among middle-class households.

One other characteristic of newspapers with special appeal to retailers is their flexibility. They may be used day after day or in any pattern the advertiser wishes. This medium is not, of course, as flexible as the broadcast media, but changes may be made in the advertisement itself up to a few hours before press time.

Most newspapers provide information that will help the store managements to use newspapers effectively. Many do research and provide free copy and layout service. Most newspapers provide free use of the syndicated mat services to which they subscribe. Most offer planning guides to help retailers spend their money during the months when potential sales are greatest.

During the 1950s the broadcast media increased their acceptance among retailers. For example, between 1955 and 1967 retail radio expenditures increased from $326,400,000 to $665,600,000, and television from $224,700,000 to $500,000,000 while newspapers increased from $2,344,000,000 to $3,960,000,000. The advent of department stores into radio advertising and the huge increase in radio usage by automobile dealers helped account for much of radio's growth.

Both radio and television have been wooing the retailer in recent years. Like the newspapers, both offer planning guides and copy service to help the retailers use these media wisely. The Television Bureau of Advertising, for example, has prepared a 31-page manual, "Selling Your Customers with Television," to guide the uninitiated in a medium that often seems strange to them.

Most retailers use one or more of such media as outdoor advertising, transportation advertising, handbills, and such specialties as calendars, blotters, and letter openers. Most, of course, use displays as primary means of communication. Attractively decorated windows and interiors help to supplement advertising in the mass media.

Many neighborhood stores have too small a market area to use the established media effectively. Some find direct mail, dodgers, and handbills effective methods of reaching neighborhood audiences; however, the neighborhood newspaper, where available, is more effective.

THE RETAIL ADVERTISEMENT

The retail advertisement is more likely than the general one to have a ready-made audience. People get in the habit of reading the advertisements of certain local stores. They tend to look on an established store as an old friend. This friendly status is reflected in the personal nature of good retail advertisements. Wisely used, the ad is the voice of someone you know. Unfortunately, many retail ad writers miss the opportunity to take advantage of this personal feeling and end up creating advertisements that are mainly lists of facts.

Another special characteristic of the retail advertisement is its strong emphasis on identification. Most good stores achieve identification through the character of their layouts, the originality of their artwork, the distinction of the type faces they use, and the manner in which the type is set. Quick and positive identification is helped greatly by a prominent signature. The all-important logotype gives immediate identification, partly because it names the store, partly because of its design. Each store's signature should be distinguishable from those of other stores. It should lend character to the store and serve as a sort of trademark.

Retail advertising tends to be more direct and urgent than general advertising. Much of it tries to achieve immediate action. The copywriter hopes to get the reader interested in buying the merchandise whereas the general advertiser is more likely to confine his efforts to building a favorable brand image. Every store manager has to keep his stock moving. For example, a gross volume of $100,000 may mean that a store has maintained an average inventory of $50,000 and has turned it over twice during the year; it may mean that the manager has kept an average of only $10,000 inventory and has turned his inventory over ten times during the year. The latter example obviously shows more profitable operation.

And, finally, retail advertising is likely to include considerable factual data. Whether the store is talking about bargains or regular price lines, and whether it is a promotional or a nonpromotional store, it should tell consumers how much the merchandise costs and why it is a good buy. Most retail advertising is packed with solid factual information—not only about prices but about such things as sizes, colors, weight, or thread count. The ad should tell the consumer where in the store he can expect to find the merchandise.

One of the basic reasons for the high readership of retail advertising is that the housewife looks to it for information. She develops an awareness of current economics and a sense of trends and styles from the items featured. There is, however, considerable evidence that retailers are not taking full advantage of this potential. Martineau says,

> . . . inasmuch as the same woman will not only accept but actually look for the advertising in women's service magazines and home magazines, which sets out to be purely informative, I would think that the retailer could do much more open and extended informational advertising. For instance, from a study we [the *Chicago Tribune*] did to explore some of the motives underlying the do-it-yourself trend in home improvement, it was easy to see an enormously powerful area of satisfaction which this activity provided. It offers an outlet for creative expression . . . . Home improvement is a perfectly acceptable manifestation of status striving.[2]

COOPERATIVE ADVERTISING

Let us turn now to a more controversial side of retail advertising—the use of cooperative advertising. The name "cooperative" comes from the fact that the cost is shared by the manufacturer and the retailer. (Some prefer to call it "vertical cooperative advertising" to distinguish this advertising from cooperation by firms that normally compete.) This advertising is controversial because manufacturers in many fields

[2] Martineau, p. 183.

complain about its abuses and ask themselves whether they should use this type of advertising. Although many retailers favor it, some are quite critical. The media generally favor cooperative advertising.

Exact estimates of how much advertising money is handled on a cooperative basis are hard to come by, but *Grey Matter* estimates it at one out of every six United States dollars spent on advertising.[3] It reports also that the number of companies using it is increasing and that the general attitude toward it is becoming more realistic. For example, a study made by the Association of National Advertisers showed that in 1956, 23 percent of the advertisers paid 100 percent of the cooperative costs but that by 1966 only 8 percent did. Meanwhile the number of programs in which costs were shared 50-50 grew. The trend, according to this report, is toward programs like that of Pittsburgh Plate Glass, where the company pays 25 percent of advertising costs and 15 percent of production costs.

Cooperative advertising will be analyzed here from the standpoints of the three principal types of institutions involved — manufacturers, retailers, and advertising media.

The Manufacturer. In deciding whether he should use cooperative or not the manufacturer must evaluate the advantages and disadvantages in the light of his own advertising objectives. Although trade paper articles often focus attention on the abuses, there are many distinct advantages.

Advantages. The basic advantage of cooperative advertising is that it permits the manufacturer to buy more advertising space or time for less money. If he advertised in the *Chicago Daily News* or the *Houston Chronicle*, he would pay general rates. If he runs the advertisement over the local dealer's signature he will probably pay only local rates. If local rates are, let us say, half the general rates (as they often are when discounts are taken out) he can get twice as much advertising space for each dollar spent.

Another advantage of cooperative advertising to the manufacturer is that it localizes his advertising. The manufacturer's cooperative ad tells the consumer where to buy the product and takes advantage of varying local conditions. The dealer is closer to the local situation than the manufacturer or his agency.

Cooperative advertising almost inevitably means more advertising, because more dealers will advertise if cooperative money is available, and nonadvertisers will be encouraged to start advertising.

Properly executed, a cooperative program can improve dealer relations. It lets the dealer fit the advertising to his needs. He can select the media more intelligently than someone in a distant city. He knows which night of the week the stores are open and which days are favored for shopping.

Since cooperative advertising is really partly general and partly retail, it represents a synchronization of the two. Consequently, it is most important that the copy approach and the layout serve the objectives of both.

[3]*Grey Matter*, 37, no. 3 (March 1966)

Some manufacturers use cooperative advertising to "buy" distribution. They use it to recruit new outlets, to meet competition. The manufacturer depends on the retailer to carry his products—and to sell them—but many retailers refuse to carry products that are not supported by cooperative money. Sometimes dealers carry several brands of a product but display and promote only the one with the cooperative fund behind it.

Because cooperative allowances are normally keyed to dealer sales (that is, the greater the sales volume, the more money the dealer is allowed), the system provides an automatic control of advertising expenditures so that they go to the most deserving dealers.

Disadvantages. The most important disadvantage of cooperative advertising to the manufacturer is the relative lack of control he has over the advertising, compared with placing his own advertisements. The larger dealers seldom use the mats he sends. Or his ad may become lost in a mass of products advertised by the local store. Inferior layouts, inept copy, and puerile art that would make any alert manufacturer or agency shudder are bound to crop up in some of the cooperative ads.

Also, a cooperative program may reduce needed funds for advertising in national media. If more money is needed for the program, the advertiser may decide that the money must come from the national budget.

Some of the problems of control are staggering. The more effective the control, the more likely dealers are to complain. When cooperative is confined to particular media, certain dealers complain. When a mat or a certain type of copy or layout is required, there will be complaints. When a dealer spends beyond his allowance, disagreement between dealer and manufacturer may result.

Although the manufacturer can improve dealer relations through cooperative ads, the reverse can happen. Once dealers are used to having the money, they take it for granted, and it is very difficult to take it away or to use it as an effective stimulant to advertising.

The legal difficulties represent one of the major disadvantages of cooperative advertising. Every manufacturer involved in these programs has to worry about action by the Federal Trade Commission. Some of the distributors ask for special deals. If the manufacturer goes along with them, he violates the Robinson-Patman Act. If he refuses to go along, the dealer becomes angry and may threaten to take his business elsewhere. Sometimes the cooperative program is used as a price discount disguised as an advertising allowance. If the money is not really used for advertising, the manufacturer may find himself in legal trouble.

Sometimes dealers will schedule ads for second-rate papers or poor days of the week in order to qualify for frequency discounts.

Manufacturers sometimes find that they are being double billed. Under this practice, two bills are prepared by the medium—a high one for submission by the retailer to the manufacturer to collect the cooperative money and a lower one for actual payment to the medium. How prevalent is double billing? The media claim it is not common. Yet merchandising expert E. B. Weiss says:

. . . the completely indefensible practice of double billing is routine in some newspaper offices. Before more modern refinements of this routine of covering up the rate the retailer pays had been developed, double billing billed more manufacturers out of more co-op dollars than any other single procedure. And double billing was not and is not possible without the connivance of the newspaper — although it is true that in a few instances retailers were found to have printed local newspaper billheads without the knowledge of the paper.[4]

Retailers. When we speak of retailers' use of cooperative advertising we are talking mainly about the large retailers. According to Weiss, in many industries as much as 80 percent of the cooperative advertising dollar of manufacturers is paid to a small group of giant retailers. The manufacturers make a special effort to get the support of these big retailers. Often it is not possible for the small retailers to qualify for cooperative money. A survey of food and appliance retailers in Madison, Wisconsin, indicated concern on the part of certain medium-size and small retailers that they were being left out of cooperative programs.

The main advantage of cooperative advertising to retailers is the chance to do more advertising than they would do otherwise. Money from the outside helps them do what they know they should do anyway — advertise regularly. Some of them look on it as a gift, and to some, as the cooperative arrangement works, it is; but in either situation it is a welcome addition to the advertising budget.

[4] E. B. Weiss, "Media Are Encouraging Retailers to Become Space, Time Brokers," *Advertising Age*, June 29, 1959.

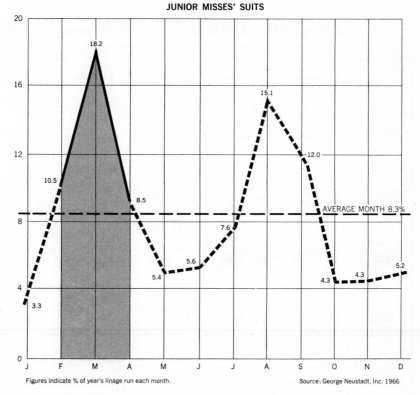

FIG. 29.6 *Guide for promotion of junior misses' suits, prepared for local retailers by the Retail Department, Bureau of Advertising, ANPA. Note the wide variations in percentage of the year's linage from month to month.* SOURCE OF ORIGINAL DATA: GEORGE NEUSTADT, INC.

JUNIOR MISSES' SUITS

AVERAGE MONTH 8.3%

Figures indicate % of year's linage run each month.

Source: George Neustadt, Inc. 1966

Yet, the blessing is not without its disadvantages. Some large retailers chafe at the restrictions that go along with cooperative money. Although they realize the need for controls, they think they can decide better than the manufacturer what copy and media they should use. They think that the manufacturer should allow them more flexibility in their use of the cooperative allowance.

Some retailers object to being used by the manufacturer as a means of avoiding national advertising rates. They feel that a more open approach to cooperation between the manufacturer and the retailer should be possible. There is evidence that many retailers suspect that someone else is getting a better deal than they are. Small retailers observe that the large retailers can sometimes successfully manage to ignore the controls in a cooperative contract, and they suspect that they may be losing out on other deals that the big retailers are enjoying.

Media. In an extensive study made of cooperative advertising in Pennsylvania, a check of sixty-six newspapers led to the conclusion that "newspaper advertising managers have an even more aggressive attitude than retailers toward co-op. Most of them try to get all they can and over 80 percent encourage local merchants to pressure manufacturers for co-op funds."

For the most part, both the individual media and the associations have strongly supported co-op. Many of the media associations compile lists of current cooperative agreements and send them on to their members so the local sales force can remind the local dealer about the cooperative money he should be spending in the local paper or broad-

FIG. 29.7 *Newspaper advertising work sheet prepared for use by the retailer in planning his month's advertising.* PREPARED BY THE BUREAU OF ADVERTISING, ANPA.

Newspaper Advertising Work Sheet—April 1968

Plan Your April Advertising Now—To Make It More Effective and To Save You Time During the Month

SUNDAY	MONDAY	TUESDAY	WEDNESDAY	THURSDAY	FRIDAY	SATURDAY
	1967 Sales $____ 1968 Sales $____ Weather____ **1**	1967 Sales $____ 1968 Sales $____ Weather____ **2**	1967 Sales $____ 1968 Sales $____ Weather____ **3**	1967 Sales $____ 1968 Sales $____ Weather____ **4**	1967 Sales $____ 1968 Sales $____ Weather____ **5**	1967 Sales $____ 1968 Sales $____ Weather____ **6**
1967 Sales $____ 1968 Sales $____ Weather____ **7**	1967 Sales $____ 1968 Sales $____ Weather____ **8**	1967 Sales $____ 1968 Sales $____ Weather____ **9**	1967 Sales $____ 1968 Sales $____ Weather____ **10**	1967 Sales $____ 1968 Sales $____ Weather____ **11**	1967 Sales $____ 1968 Sales $____ Weather____ **12** GOOD FRIDAY	1967 Sales $____ 1968 Sales $____ Weather____ **13** PASSOVER (First Day)
1967 Sales $____ 1968 Sales $____ Weather____ **14** EASTER SUNDAY	1967 Sales $____ 1968 Sales $____ Weather____ **15** EASTER MONDAY (Canada)	1967 Sales $____ 1968 Sales $____ Weather____ **16**	1967 Sales $____ 1968 Sales $____ Weather____ **17**	1967 Sales $____ 1968 Sales $____ Weather____ **18**	1967 Sales $____ 1968 Sales $____ Weather____ **19**	1967 Sales $____ 1968 Sales $____ Weather____ **20**
1967 Sales $____ 1968 Sales $____ Weather____ **21**	1967 Sales $____ 1968 Sales $____ Weather____ **22**	1967 Sales $____ 1968 Sales $____ Weather____ **23**	1967 Sales $____ 1968 Sales $____ Weather____ **24**	1967 Sales $____ 1968 Sales $____ Weather____ **25**	1967 Sales $____ 1968 Sales $____ Weather____ **26**	1967 Sales $____ 1968 Sales $____ Weather____ **27**
1967 Sales $____ 1968 Sales $____ Weather____ **28**	1967 Sales $____ 1968 Sales $____ Weather____ **29**	1967 Sales $____ 1968 Sales $____ Weather____ **30**				

APRIL 1967

Sun.	Mon.	Tues.	Wed.	Thur.	Fri.	Sat.
						1
2	3	4	5	6	7	8
9	10	11	12	13	14	15
16	17	18	19	20	21	22
23	24	25	26	27	28	29
30						

25 SELLING DAYS

APRIL 1968

Sun.	Mon.	Tues.	Wed.	Thur.	Fri.	Sat.
	1	2	3	4	5	6
7	8	9	10	11	12	13
14	15	16	17	18	19	20
21	22	23	24	25	26	27
28	29	30				

26 SELLING DAYS

	Fair Days	Cloudy Days	Rainy Days	Aver. Temp.
1967 Weather				
1968 Weather				

casting station. Media managers look upon cooperative advertising as a rich source of revenue.

There have been a few voices raised inquiring whether the local media were not losing some valuable linage from the manufacturers —but these do not appear to be representative of the media attitudes generally.

The television and radio sales managers object to the exclusion of their media from some cooperative contracts. Obviously, the problem of control is even greater in the broadcast media, where not even a tear sheet can be submitted and local rates usually are not available in printed form.

SUMMARY

Retail advertising is an important part of the total advertising picture, representing roughly 40 percent of the total volume. This includes all the advertising done by institutions selling goods or services directly to the public and much advertising that is really a cooperative arrangement between the retailer and the manufacturer.

Stores that use advertising most successfully evaluate it in terms of both the marketing and the communication mix. The promotional store uses the highest percentage of sales for advertising, the nonpromotional store the lowest.

The newspaper is by far the most important of the retail media, but radio and television are increasing their share of the retailers' media dollar. Retail advertising is a little different from that of the manufacturer, and the wise retailer will know these differences and adapt his advertisements to his own needs.

Many manufacturers are giving their cooperative programs careful study. Although they realize the advantages to be gained, many are concerned about the abuses and the legal problems. For the most part, retailers and media executives favor co-op, although some warnings have been sounded here too.

QUESTIONS FOR DISCUSSION

1. Why has the newspaper traditionally been the major medium of retailers? Is it likely that any other medium will become dominant in the retail field in the near future?
2. What are the advantages and disadvantages of cooperative advertising to the manufacturer? to the retailer?
3. Does the retailer have to be as knowledgeable as the manufacturer concerning sales promotion? Why?
4. What are the principal differences between retail and general advertising copy in newspapers? in direct mail?
5. What means might a store use to build a favorable image?

SUGGESTED READINGS

Bedell, Clyde, *How to Write Advertising That Sells,* 2d ed. New York: McGraw-Hill, Inc., 1952. Chapters 4–9.

Burton, Philip W., *Retail Advertising for the Small Store*. Englewood Cliffs, N.J.: Prentice-Hall, Inc., 1951.

Dunn, S. Watson, *Advertising Copy and Communication*. New York: McGraw-Hill, Inc., 1956. Chapter 12.

Edwards, Charles M., Jr., and Russell A. Brown, *Retail Advertising and Sales Promotion*, rev. ed. Englewood Cliffs, N.J.: Prentice-Hall, Inc., 1959.

Martineau, Pierre, *Motivation in Advertising*. New York: McGraw-Hill, Inc., 1957. Chapter 15.

Rosenblum, M. L., *How to Design Effective Store Advertising*. New York: National Retail Merchants Association, 1961.

Sandage, C. H., and Vernon Fryburger, *Advertising Theory and Practice*, 7th ed. Homewood, Ill.: Richard D. Irwin, Inc., 1967. Chapter 30.

30 | Public Relations

The emphasis in this book so far has been on the promotion of goods and services. In this chapter we want to examine an increasingly important aspect of modern communication — the promotion of ideas rather than products, and the creation of favorable attitudes toward the company or organization.

There is no completely satisfactory term to cover this type of communication. At various times it is referred to as "institutional," "idea," "nonproduct," and "public relations" advertising. Occasionally, in a derogatory way it is termed "propaganda." Much of the difficulty in labeling stems from the fact that it covers such a wide variety of objectives, audiences, and communication tools. It includes, for instance, advertising in which a given company announces what its management thinks about a proposed piece of legislation. During strikes, both management and labor use advertising to explain to the public their points of view. This kind of advertising includes the efforts of trade associations to build good will for their members, or to fight some idea they consider dangerous. Political candidates are increasing their use of advertising; so are such noncommerical institutions as churches and schools.

In this chapter we shall use the term "public relations" advertising, because this term, better than most, puts the emphasis where it belongs—on the communication objectives. It was pointed out in Chapter I that public relations involves the use of a variety of tools to build good relations between an organization or individual and certain important sections of the public. Kenneth Henry points out, however, that the answers to "What is PR?" could fill a good many books. He found after a comprehensive review of public relations books published since 1963 that the most satisfactory definition was one by Paul Burton: "Corporate public relations is a function of management which helps a company establish and maintain a good name for itself and its products or services through professional communications techniques." He found that three dominant ideas emerged strongly from a plethora of public relations books:

> (1) It is argued that U.S. business has become urgently aware of its social responsibilities and that it sees PR as playing a key role in deciding and executing those actions of the corporation most appropriate to the "public interest"; (2) It is claimed that the corporate PR manager of the future must be a trained behavioral scientist; and (3) it is predicted that effective PR programs will be increasingly based on and judged by responsible continuous research.[1]

Among the major tools of the public relations man is advertising. We thus find the public relations and the advertising staff of a firm working together on an advertisement that urges everyone to drive carefully—an advertisement designed to improve the public's image of the firm, as well as to make some contribution to the public interest.

WHY USE PUBLIC RELATIONS ADVERTISING?

An organization may turn to public relations advertising for a variety of reasons. The company or group may feel it is getting a "bad press" in nonadvertising columns. Common examples are a strike at the company or an unpopular cause supported by the company. Sometimes the organization (or individual) feels strongly about a certain issue and is afraid the public is apathetic. At other times the advertiser merely hopes to add a helping hand to a generally accepted cause (for example, "Support your Community Chest") and to create good will for the firm. Again, the firm's management may be upset about a piece of pending legislation and hopes to inspire a flood of protest letters to legislators that will turn the tide. In all these situations the advertiser is dealing in the realm of public issues and trying to sway public opinion. He is taking advantage of his freedom to speak out as he sees fit, unencumbered by the restrictions of editors.

The objectives of public relations advertising fall into two general categories—image building and action inducing. Many companies find in their research that the public holds a distorted image; they then turn to advertising (as well as other communication tools) to help correct it. Producing action is, of course, related to image building. An organization may urge you to call city hall, but it knows that you are not likely to do much unless you feel kindly toward the sponsor of the advertisement. The classic type of action-producing advertisement is the political advertisement, in which the vote represents the action to be taken.

[1]Kenneth Henry, "Perspective on Public Relations," *Harvard Business Review*, July–August 1967.

SOME OF THE PROBLEMS

The problems involved in public relations advertising are too numerous and too complex to be discussed in detail here. Fortunately, much that we have said in other chapters about planning, research, motivation, and creative strategy applies here, just as it does in more commercial communication. Let us therefore concentrate our attention on some of the differences.

First, public relations advertising involves dangers unknown in product advertising. If you advertise your breakfast cereal as an aid to health, some people will still prefer one of the competing brands. However, they will bear you no ill will, and some will probably come over to your brand as time goes along. Suppose, though, that you advertise your support of free trade, or your opposition to it. Either way, you are bound to have a certain reaction from people who disagree, perhaps violently, with your point of view.

Second, issues involved in public relations advertising are more complex than those involved in the purchase of a product. In discussing motivation in Chapter 10 we noted how complex even our simplest actions and feelings can be. However, there is frequently one dominant reward offered by a particular product, and the advertising can concentrate on this point. Issues such as free trade, inflation, whether you should go to church, and many others covered in public relations advertising are extremely complex, and it is extremely difficult to distill them into a few sentences of copy.

Third, it is difficult to chart any cause and effect between a particular campaign and the formation of particular opinions or attitudes. Consider, for example, the case of the political candidate who is trying to decide how much advertising to use. We noted in Chapter 6 that advertising was an important tool of today's political campaign but that it probably influences results only in close elections. The skillful use of the media by John Kennedy both for advertising and other persuasive communications may well have influenced the results of the close election of 1960. On the other hand, no serious analyst could claim that any public relations advertising, no matter how good, could have reversed the outcome of the one-sided presidential election of 1964.

Fourth, there seems to be both mistrust and misunderstanding of public relations advertising on the part of business executives. One public relations specialist claims that advertising is the most misunderstood of the public relations tools, mainly because even the practitioners do not understand how it really works or how to sell it even when they do understand it.[2]

ORGANIZING FOR PUBLIC RELATIONS

According to the Public Relations Society of America there are approximately 60,000 persons employed in public relations and the amount of money spent on the field is around $1,500,000,000 annually. Most of these people work for individual business firms, for advertising or

[2]See W. H. Depperman, "PR Advertising Is a Misunderstood Tool," *Advertising & Sales Promotion*, April 1966.

public relations agencies, for industry-wide organizations or nonprofit organizations such as education or government units.

The individual business firm has many public relations problems. Some firms concentrate primarily on fending off attacks from competitors or critics, but more and more they are taking positive attitudes in looking to new areas where they can assume a role of social responsibility. A case in point is the gift of money by some companies to universities, and the efforts to encourage their employees to donate also. They believe such actions represent enlightened self-interest because they build a favorable corporate image among faculty members, present and prospective employees, and the public at large.

The largest United States company, General Motors, is an interesting example of a corporate public relations organization. It has a large public relations department headed by a vice-president, public relations departments in its various divisions, and a public relations counsel. Advertising is an important part of its public relations program, because it enhances the image of the corporation with the consuming public, governmental organizations, lawmakers, stockholders, and union groups.

Advertising agencies are sharply divided on whether they should provide public relations help for their clients. The most common arrangement is to have a public relations division within the agency. Several agencies, however, have established entirely or partly owned public relations subsidiaries (an example, Infoplan at Interpublic). A number of agencies maintain working relations with outside public relations firms, both for the agency's public relations and that of clients. Even where agencies have a public relations department, organizations vary widely from one agency to another and even from account to account within the agency. Some provide everything from production of clients' house organs to operation of test kitchens and open houses. Others confine their activities to getting favorable publicity for the client's product. Some public relations counselors maintain that public relations can best be performed by a firm that devotes its entire time and energy to this one function.

The world's largest agency, J. Walter Thompson, has had a public relations department since 1934, and by 1967 had 137 persons on the departmental payroll. They worked out of six offices and handled 45 accounts generating revenue of about $2,000,000 a year.[3] According to the agency, its department is one of the five largest in the United States. As the department head explains, the staff members "are advertising and marketing people first. They're recruited from media, so they know how to write for media. But we never lose sight of what the advertising and marketing goals are."

William Safire of General Electric argues that public relations men can make their greatest contribution if they avoid compartmentalization. He maintains that what is needed is not public relations specialists, advertising specialists, and the like, but "communications generalists" who can deal on a cohesive basis with all of a firm's "relations problems."[4]

[3]"PR Arm Helps JWT Service Ad Clients," *Advertising Age,* June 12, 1967.
[4]See William L. Safire, *The Relations Explosion* (New York: Crowell–Collier and Macmillan, Inc., 1963).

REQUISITES OF AN EFFECTIVE PUBLIC RELATIONS CAMPAIGN

In general, public relations is for companies that conscientiously try to live up to the modern concept of social, as well as economic, responsibilities. Any business that chooses to disregard this concept should probably leave public relations alone, for it is not a means of manipulating public opinion at will. Instead, public relations, like kindness, must begin in the heart. Unless a public relations program is backed by good intentions, it has little chance of success. Today few business policies are set without appraisal of their ultimate effect on the firm's public relations. Some critics are disturbed at the hesitancy of today's businessman to take a stand that might antagonize some of the public—but at the same time it is a far cry from William Henry Vanderbilt's saying, "The public be damned."

According to Cutlip and Center, there are four basic steps in any successful public relations program:

1. Research-Listening. This means probing the opinions, attitudes, and reactions of persons concerned with the acts and policies of an organization and evaluating the inflow. This task also requires determination of the facts regarding the organization.

2. Planning-Decision Making. This means bringing these attitudes, opinions, ideas, and reactions to bear on the policies and programs of an organization. This will enable it to chart a course in the mutual interests of all concerned.

3. Communication. This means explaining and dramatizing the chosen course to all those who may be affected and whose support is essential.

4. Evaluation. This means evaluating the results of the program and the effectiveness of techniques used.[5]

THE PUBLIC RELATIONS ADVERTISEMENT

The public relations advertisement could include almost anything that would help advance the objective. The trick is to determine just what you can do and to define it as specifically as possible. The following, for example, are objectives common to many company public relations programs:

To indicate a corporation's public-spiritedness
To improve a company's labor relations
To convince consumers that the company is a pioneer
To attract employees to a company

The following television commercial is an excellent example of a well-executed public relations advertisement. It is designed to convince consumers that Du Pont does indeed have a chemical treasure house where they are trying to discover ways of saving human life. It thus lends respect and warmth to a cold, impersonal corporation.

DU PONT CHEMICAL TREASURE HOUSE

FADE IN:

1. MEDIUM LONG SHOT A SOLID "OAK" DOOR. DOLLY IN. THE DOOR OPENS BY ITSELF, AND OUR "EYE"—THE CAMERA—GOES RIGHT THROUGH. THIS IS THE DU PONT SAMPLE ROOM. WE SEE ROW UPON ROW OF VARIOUS SHAPED BOTTLES AND JARS. VARIOUS DEGREES OF LIGHT MAY PLAY ON THE BOTTLES FOR DRAMATIC EFFECT. WE DOLLY IN TO ONE SHELF.

(MUSIC: GOES UNDER)

[5]Scott M. Cutlip and Allen H. Center, *Effective Public Relations*, 3d ed. (Englewood Cliffs, N.J.: Prentice-Hall, Inc., 1964), p. 108.

Food...

INTERNATIONAL HARVESTER

Food for a hungry world: that is a challenge of particular importance to International Harvester, the world's principal manufacturer of farm tractors and equipment.

As a constructive force on the local scene in some 144 different countries, the company helps to produce more food at lower cost for increasing numbers of people. Its McCormick International equipment is engineered to meet specific farming problems in many individual countries, to make possible the most *efficient* food production.

At the same time, International construction and earthmoving equipment is helping to clear new land, develop irrigation facilities and build new roads from farms to markets. International trucks deliver a large share of the world's food to hungry populations everywhere.

Thus International Harvester helps to meet a basic need of mankind—food.

INTERNATIONAL HARVESTER

Supplying world markets from factories in England, France, Germany, Sweden, South Africa, Argentina, Australia, Philippines, Brazil, Mexico, Canada and the U.S.A.

International Harvester Export Company, 180 N. Michigan Avenue, Chicago 1, Illinois, U.S.A.

FIG. 30.1 *Institutional advertisement designed to build a favorable image for the advertiser.* CLIENT: INTERNATIONAL HARVESTER EXPORT COMPANY; AGENCY: MCCANN-ERICKSON, INC.

COMMENTATOR

This is a remarkable room. Known simply as the "Sample Room" at Du Pont's Jackson Laboratory, it contains a wealth of stored-up chemicals that have served their purpose and then been put away. But experience has shown that one day they may be used again—perhaps to provide some startling new benefit to mankind.

(MUSIC: STRINGS UNDER)

(BEGIN TO MOVE IN TO XCU OF ONE BOTTLE CLEARLY MARKED: "Para-amino-benzene-sulfonamide")

COMMENTATOR (CONT'D)

For example, let us tell you the story of one in particular—*this* one.

(MUSIC: HITS HARD AND GOES UNDER)

DISSOLVE TO:

2. DR. PERRIN H. LONG OF THE JOHNS HOPKINS HOSPITAL. HE IS IN HIS OFFICE (OBVIOUSLY A DOCTOR'S OFFICE) DICTATING TO HIS SECRETARY. HE IS TALKING ON PHONE.

COMMENTATOR

It began in 1936 in Dr. Perrin Long's office in the Johns Hopkins Hospital.

DR. LONG (INTO PHONE)

Okay, Bob, thanks.
(HANGS UP PHONE AND TURNS HIS ATTENTION TO HIS SECRETARY)
Now — where was I?

SECRETARY

(READING WHAT HE'S DICTATED) The Du Pont Company, Wilmington, Delaware. Dear Sirs: I would like to obtain some Para-aminobenzene-sulfonamide for experiments on hemolytic streptococcal infections in mice . . .
(LOOKING UP AT DR. LONG)
That's as far as you went, Doctor Long.
(MOVE IN FOR CU OF DR. LONG)

DR. LONG

All right. We have evidence that it may be valuable in the treatment of these infections in man. Do you have any of this product on hand?

DISSOLVE TO:

3. LAB ASSISTANT DIGGING THROUGH FILES.

COMMENTATOR

At the Du Pont Company, a check was made to locate the chemical. And, on a card dated 1929 . . .

(LAB ASSISTANT PULLS OUT CARD AND SMILES)
(MUSIC: SWELLS UP A BIT — UNDER)

COMMENTATOR (CONT'D)

they found it!

(LAB ASSISTANT TURNS, WALKS OUT OF SCENE WITH CARD)

COMMENTATOR (CONT'D)

It had been developed for use in dye research. Later other dyes proved better . . .

DISSOLVE TO:

4. INSERT: TIGHT SHOT OF SHELF. HAND PICKS "SULFA" BOTTLE FROM SHELF, MOVES OUT OF SCENE.

COMMENTATOR

. . . and since there were no other known uses for it, the left-over chemical was stored here until it was shipped to Doctor Long.

(MUSIC: IN AND UNDER)

DISSOLVE TO:

5. CLOSEUP OF DR. LONG AND OTHER MAN EXAMINING CHART IN TYPICAL BIOLOGICAL LAB SETTING. HE TURNS FROM EXAMINING CHART AND THOUGHTFULLY PICKS UP JAR THAT IS EMPTY.

COMMENTATOR

The experiments on streptococcal infections in mice proved so successful Doctor Long decided to extend them to humans. But all of the chemical Du Pont had sent him was gone. He wired for more . . .

DISSOLVE TO:

6. LAB ASSISTANT AND ANOTHER MAN — A DU PONT EXECUTIVE IN OFFICE.

LAB ASSISTANT

Sorry, there's not another gram in the sample room.

EXECUTIVE

But Doctor Long needs a pound of it—so let's make it for him.

LAB ASSISTANT

(PROTESTING) But we'll have to hold up on other work . . .

EXECUTIVE

That's right . . . but this may save human lives. Let's make up what he wants, hmm?

(MUSIC: STINGS DRAMATICALLY)

SLOW DISSOLVE TO:

7. DR. LONG WITH ANOTHER DOCTOR IN HIS OFFICE. THEY ARE LOOKING OVER MEDICAL CHARTS.

DR. LONG

(EXCITED) The results have been amazing! It works wonders in peritonitis, blood-poisoning, scarlet fever, and abscessed ears.

(HANDS CHART TO OTHER DOCTOR)

(OTHER DOCTOR LOOKS AT CHART AND NODS HIS HEAD)

(MUSIC: IN AND UNDER)

COMMENTATOR

This new wonder drug—attacked and killed infections and diseases that had ravaged mankind for centuries.

WIPE TO:

8. INT. OF SAMPLE ROOM. CAMERA TIGHT ON SHELF CONTAINING "SULFA" BOTTLE.

COMMENTATOR

You know it today by its shortened name—

(WIPE ON AND SUPER OVER LABEL ON BOTTLE)

9. ONE WORD—SULFANILAMIDE

COMMENTATOR

Sulfanilamide!

(MUSIC: STINGS HARD—UNDER)

DISSOLVE OUT:

10. WORD—SULFANILAMIDE—CAMERA PANS AWAY FROM BOTTLE AND BACKS OUT OF ROOM.

COMMENTATOR

Eventually the manufacturer of Sulfanilamide was taken over by pharmaceutical firms. But this incident once more pointed up the logic of Du Pont's policy of preserving the results of its research.

(SAMPLE ROOM DOOR CLOSES SLOWLY)

COMMENTATOR (CONT'D)

For who knows what unforeseen benefit may be sealed away *today* to join *tomorrow's* . . .

11. DU PONT OVAL AND PLEDGE

COMMENTATOR

Better things for better living . . . through chemistry!

(MUSIC: TO CLIMAX)

One of the most successful writers of institutional copy is Louis Redmond, who has won wide recognition for John Hancock Mutual Life Insurance Company advertisements. He offers three "conjectures" based on his experience:

First, use a subject matter, if possible, about which your readers already have strong and favorable emotions. It is difficult, for example, for one to write a really bad advertisement about Lincoln if he writes sincerely.

Second, develop your message (again, if possible) in terms of concrete subject matter rather than through an abstract statement of purposes and attitudes.

Third, remind yourself frequently that advertising is not a *form* of writing, but only a *function*. Most of us suffer a little from over-professionalism, and tend to write ads that sound like ads, and occasionally run the danger of parodying ourselves.[6]

The problem of believability is always a thorny one in any public relations advertising. In discussing the "Free Enterprise" campaign of certain manufacturers and the Advertising Council, *Fortune* editor William H. Whyte, Jr., pointed out that the campaign was psychologically unsound, abstract, defensive, and negative. "Most important," he said, "in a great many of its aspects, it represents a shocking lack of faith in the American people, and in some cases downright contempt." Whyte felt that the whole campaign was unbelievable.

People form their judgments not just by what a company says but by a subtle (some say intuitive) process compounding their feelings. If a firm neglects to answer a customer's letter, he receives an unfavorable impression of the company that is difficult to erase through any advertising campaign.

What about Publicity? Although publicity is not advertising and is only one part of public relations, it is worthy of mention here. Broadly speaking, publicity can be divided into two categories: publicity for a company and publicity for a product.

Company publicity involves any activity of the business that is of interest to the general public. Editors and newscasters are happy to tell about local businesses in their news columns and over the air if the companies have something to say that is genuinely newsworthy. If a company were to build a new plant in a state where there had been none before, the facts about it—its size, location, number of employees—would be of state-wide interest. The quarterly earnings of a large corporation have nationwide interest. If a store in a small city were to install the first moving stairway in town, the event would be a newsworthy one.

Some products can be made a continuing source of news. An ingredient food product can be used in a never-ending variety of recipes of interest to many food editors. New products are news. So are research improvements that will benefit the consumer. With some products it is difficult to come up with continuous publicity. The introduction of a new model car is big news, but between model change-overs it takes ingenuity to find newsworthy events that will be of interest to the general reader and the editor.

[6]Louis Redmond, "Writing a Public Interest Campaign," in William D. Patterson, ed. *America: Miracle at Work* (Englewood Cliffs, N.J.: Prentice-Hall, Inc., 1953).

INDUSTRY-WIDE ORGANIZATIONS

Sometimes competing firms find it advisable to pool their promotional efforts. This practice is often called "horizontal cooperative advertising." The dairy industry combines efforts through the American Dairy Association; the railroads, through the Association of American Railroads. Industry-wide campaigns are usually conducted for one of two purposes—to stimulate primary demand for the product or to handle some public relations problem of interest to the industry as a whole. For example, the American Meat Institute, the Cling Peach Advisory Board, the California Raisin Advisory Board, and the American Petroleum Institute, among others, conduct campaigns to increase the demand for the products of their industries.

These groups have many public relations problems that they can often attack more effectively if they pool their efforts. For example, the Association of American Railroads, representing an industry that is chafing under regulation, sets up an interview situation in one of its

The Magazine Advantage...

L IKE YOU, this man is a magazine reader.
He has a good grip on the future. He has every advantage in facing it—for himself and his youngster. He's financially prepared—he does a very good job on a very good job.
He's personally prepared—he is far better educated than most—he'll see that his son is, too. (Fact: magazine readers are 65% above the average in attaining a college education.)
Like yours, this magazine reader's education never stops. He, for example, reads this magazine regularly . . . keeping ahead of the present, up with the future. Its editorial and advertising pages are his personal guide to the good life he leads—as a person, as a parent and a provider.

MAGAZINE READERS
Read Much More Into Their Lives
MAGAZINE ADVERTISING BUREAU OF MAGAZINE PUBLISHERS ASSOCIATION

FIG. 30.2 *Cooperative advertising by the magazine publishers designed to build the image of magazines and in the longer run to sell more space in magazines.* SOURCE: MAGAZINE ADVERTISING BUREAU OF MPA.

How your appestat* and sugar can control weight.

Your "appestat" is a kind of hunger switch in your brain.

When it's turned up, you're hungry. And you may overeat.

Sugar turns your appestat down—helps you eat less.

Read how.

In these days of artificial sweeteners and fad diets, you may have some trouble thinking of ordinary sugar as a key to weight control. But that's exactly what sugar can be to you when you understand how your appestat and sugar work together.

When your *blood sugar level* is low, your appestat is turned way up, and you're hungry. You're apt to eat more than you need, before your blood sugar level can rise again.

So what you do is this: when you're very hungry, take a little sugar—in coffee, a soft drink, ice cream, pastry, or candy. Sugar raises your blood sugar level faster than any other food. (Artificial sweeteners have no effect on blood sugar level.) And then your hunger switches off. As a result, you can eat less and feel better when you keep sugar in your diet.

The calories in sugar burn up fast and they give you energy to go on. And sugar tastes good, too. Do you need any more reasons to stay with sugar?

Only 18 calories per teaspoon— and it's all energy.

*"A neural center in the hypothalamus believed to regulate appetite."— Webster's Third New International Dictionary.

SUGAR INFORMATION, INC.
P.O. Box 2664, Grand Central Station, New York, N.Y. 10017

FIG. 30.3 *Excellent horizontal cooperative advertisement of Sugar Information, Inc., representing the sugar producers.* CLIENT: SUGAR INFORMATION, INC.; AGENCY: LEO BURNETT COMPANY, INC.

advertisements. The statement in the headline is quoted from the reply of the man being interviewed.

"Competition gives better value
— we got a good buy on our TV set!"

INQUIRING REPORTER: What do you folks think of the proposal in Congress that would give regulated forms of transportation more freedom to price their services in competition with each other—and with unregulated trucks and barges too?

HUSBAND: Well, we've just bought a new TV set at a very good price. . . .

The purpose of this ad, of course, was to reach congressmen and to get the consuming public to write their congressmen urging them to vote for the bill freeing railroads from certain restrictions and allowing them to compete more freely with other forms of transportation. Other industry-wide campaigns are aimed at erasing some erroneous impression. Sugar Information, Inc., has advertised extensively in an attempt to combat the idea that sugar is fattening. The American Meat Institute has run a series of specific and imaginative ads providing information on meat prices.

Horizontal cooperative advertising has great appeal to many advertising people, and it seems logical for an entire industry to pool its efforts for some common objective. In practice it is not quite so easy. Borden and Marshall point out some of the dangers:

> Too often the advertising programs of associations have employed as their principal copy appeal an abstract idea that is not likely to induce the consumer to action. For example, years ago the retail jewelers carried on a rather extensive campaign trying to induce people to "buy gifts that last." It is questionable whether such an abstraction is likely to be effective. Certainly it lacks the force of an appeal centered on specific merchandise, the possession or use of which can be made to appear desirable.[7]

THE ADVERTISING COUNCIL

One of the most interesting experiments in industry-wide public relations advertising has been conducted by the advertising industry itself through the Advertising Council. During World War II the advertising industry, disturbed by the mounting public criticism of advertising, organized the War Advertising Council, which represented a conviction on the part of a number of leaders in the industry that well-planned, well-executed advertisements could sell ideas as effectively as they could sell products and services.

The results were generally gratifying both to the people who started the Council and to the government officials who worked with them in planning the campaigns. In 1942 an Act of Congress created the United States Cadet Nurse Corps with a quota of 65,000 women for 1944. The Council moved in with "a creative task force" to plan a campaign based on the idea, "Nursing is a proud profession." Within one year after the campaign started, 237,000 women applied for training in nursing. Within two years, 446,000 women had applied and the Cadet Nurse Corps had more applications than it could handle.

The Council was nearly disbanded at the close of World War II, but some of the executives came to its rescue and saw that it continued as the Advertising Council. As it exists today, the Advertising Council may plan and execute an advertising campaign designed to solve or help solve any of the country's serious problems. Its organization is shown graphically in Figure 30.4. Note that all campaigns that are proposed (except those strictly in the public interest as clearly established by an Act of Congress) must be approved by a three-fourths vote of the Council's Public Policy Committee.

A board of directors representing industry, advertising agencies, and media supervises the Council's operation and plans its policies. Its main support comes from the American Association of Advertising Agencies, Association of National Advertisers, Bureau of Advertising of the ANPA, Magazine Publishers Association, American Business Press, National Association of Broadcasters, and the Outdoor Advertising Association of America.

[7]Neil H. Borden and Martin V. Marshall, *Advertising Management: Text and Cases*, rev. ed. (Homewood, Ill.: Richard D. Irwin, Inc., 1959), p. 45.

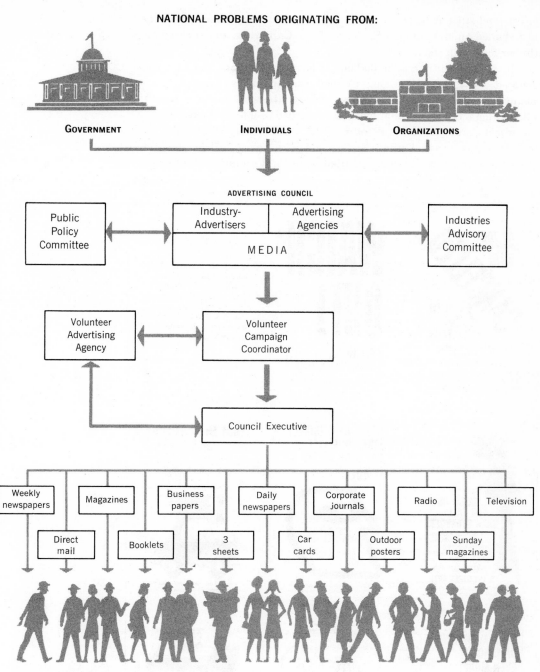

NATIONAL PROBLEMS ORIGINATING FROM:

GOVERNMENT · INDIVIDUALS · ORGANIZATIONS

ADVERTISING COUNCIL

Public Policy Committee · Industry-Advertisers · Advertising Agencies · MEDIA · Industries Advisory Committee

Volunteer Advertising Agency · Volunteer Campaign Coordinator

Council Executive

Weekly newspapers · Magazines · Business papers · Daily newspapers · Corporate journals · Radio · Television

Direct mail · Booklets · 3 sheets · Car cards · Outdoor posters · Sunday magazines

FIG. 30.4 *Organization of the Advertising Council.* SOURCE: THE ADVERTISING COUNCIL, INC.

Typical advertisements prepared by the Council are shown in Figures 30.5 and 30.6. Because these campaigns are recent, it is too early to assess results. In these campaigns, as in most, it is difficult to determine which of the results came from the Advertising Council campaign and which from other factors. However, the Forest Service estimates that the fire-prevention campaign with its lovable star Smokey has prevented a million fires and saved 272,000,000 acres of forest land since it began in 1942, shortly after a Japanese submarine had shelled an oil field near Santa Barbara, California, and endangered timber forests in the area.

In 1967 more than $250,000,000 of advertising space and time was donated for such Advertising Council campaigns as Keep America Beautiful ("Don't grown-ups know? Every litter bit hurts"), mental retardation ("Over 2 million mentally retarded people hold jobs. What's the world coming to? It's getting better"), traffic safety (Watch out for the other guy"), and United Nations ("You're having a beer and the guy next to you starts in on the United Nations. It's a hangout for spies,

FIG. 30.5 *Small-space advertisements prepared for use by advertisers and media—the Advertising Council's "Drive Defensively" campaign.* COURTESY, THE ADVERTISING COUNCIL.

FIG. 30.6
Advertisement featuring the Advertising Council's most famous spokesman, Smokey Bear. COURTESY, THE ADVERTISING COUNCIL.

he says. A tool for the Russians. And we pay the bills. What do you say?"). By 1966 it had moved into the controversial area of race relations with advertisements bearing headlines such as "There is something to be said on both sides. Are you ready to listen?"

SUMMARY

Advertising can be a very important tool of the corporation or an industry's public relations program. It cannot, however, convince the public that a certain firm or industry is something it is not. However, it may capitalize on good deeds and communicate them to the public.

The public relations campaign should be carefully researched and planned. A special effort should be made to make it as believable as possible, because credibility is a common area of difficulty.

Publicity, like advertising, can be used as part of the public relations program. However, your success in getting a specific item accepted by an editor will be determined primarily by its news value.

Industries, like companies, have public relations problems and can often use advertising to help alleviate them. One of the more successful examples of industry-wide cooperation is the Advertising Council.

QUESTIONS FOR DISCUSSION

1. How should the promotion man coordinate advertising and public relations in his company's communications program?
2. What kind of research might be helpful in planning a public relations program?
3. What is the difference between publicity and public relations? Outline the function of each in a company's promotional program.

4. What are the principal contributions of the Advertising Council? Why was it continued after the end of World War II?
5. Do you think your school should engage in a public relations program? If so, to what extent should it use advertising?
6. Why do many government organizations have a public relations department?

SUGGESTED READINGS

Canfield, Bertrand R., *Public Relations Principles, Cases and Problems*, 4th ed. Homewood, Ill.: Richard D. Irwin, Inc., 1964.

Cutlip, Scott M., and Allen H. Center, *Effective Public Relations*, 3d ed. Englewood Cliffs, N.J.: Prentice-Hall, Inc., 1964.

Lesly, Philip, *Public Relations Handbook*, 2d ed. Englewood Cliffs, N.J.: Prentice-Hall, Inc., 1962.

Robinson, Edward J., *Communication and Public Relations*. Columbus, Ohio: Charles E. Merrill Books, Inc., 1966.

Safire, William L., *The Relations Explosion*. New York: Crowell – Collier and Macmillan, Inc., 1963.

Sandage, C. H., and Vernon Fryburger, *Advertising Theory and Practice,* 7th ed. Homewood, Ill.: Richard D. Irwin, Inc., 1967. Chapter 6.

Schoenfeld, Clarence A., *Publicity Media and Methods*. New York: Crowell–Collier and Macmillan, Inc., 1963.

31 | International Advertising and Promotion

During the years since World War II business enterprises—in the United States and other well-developed countries—have moved rapidly into the profitable markets in other countries. Not only the manufacturers but the communications media, the advertising agencies, and the research firms have moved abroad in force. Although much of what we have covered earlier obviously applies internationally as well as domestically, there are so many special aspects of this growing field that this book would not be complete without some coverage of its nature and growth.

It is true, of course, that certain industries, agencies, and media have long had thriving international operations. In the industrial field, for example, General Motors, I.B.M., and Singer, to mention only a few, have had strong foreign operations for many years. And such agencies as J. Walter Thompson and McCann-Erickson have long offered clients a full service in many foreign countries. A few of the American magazines (particularly *Reader's Digest* and Time, Inc.) have had international editions with substantial circulation and advertising revenue for many years. In the 1950s and 1960s a great many American companies established foreign subsidiaries for the first time. American agencies and market research organizations bought or established foreign offices,

TABLE 31.1   SUMMARY OF APPLIANCE AND AUTOMOBILE OWNERSHIP
(In percentages)

	E.E.C.*		France		W. Germany		Italy		Netherlands		Belgium		Luxembourg		Great Britain	
	Total	RD	Total	RD	Total	RD	Total	RD	Total	RD	Total	RD	Total	RD	Total	RD
Household has one or more																
Radio	79	87	72	78	90	96	70	90	85	89	79	77	92	92	76	79
Transistor radio	17	32	30	41	12	25	11	31	16	22	18	36	23	40	32	43
Electric vacuum cleaner	42	64	37	57	66	84	7	28	95	97	40	72	60	90	72	78
Electric iron	81	90	84	92	87	92	66	79	96	98	83	88	93	100	91	94
Electric or gas refrigerator	40	62	41	61	52	70	30	61	23	40	21	51	57	81	30	42
Washing machine without dryer	18	24	12	13	24	31	4	15	58	46	43	40	47	35	31	28
Washing machine with dryer	12	21	20	32	12	17	4	11	11	16	9	21	27	34	14	19
Electric floor polisher	5	12	5	11	5	8	5	17	4	11	5	22	7	15	2	3
Portable typewriter	9	20	7	14	13	29	7	17	10	23	7	20	13	42	8	17
Office typewriter (in the home)	5	11	3	4	8	19	3	10	5	15	4	8	5	10	3	7
Television set	34	44	27	35	41	48	29	53	50	43	37	44	21	27	82	80
Electric coffee percolator	2	4	5	9	–		2	3	3	2	6	2	11	19	4	7
Electric dishwashing machine	–	–	–	–	–	1	–	–	1	–	–	–	–	2	–	1
Electric food mixer	21	42	24	39	23	46	14	40	22	40	31	56	39	66	5	7
Electric toaster	9	23	4	7	15	44	3	12	18	39	12	31	17	50	14	23
Pressure cooker	14	28	30	44	13	27	2	7	9	15	10	17	7	13	16	20
Sewing machine hand or foot powered	48	51	42	47	50	51	51	61	55	50	34	34	47	52	34	35
Electric sewing machine	11	19	14	21	10	18	5	9	24	36	13	27	15	34	12	20
Tape recorder	5	11	2	4	8	15	3	12	9	12	3	8	6	16	9	12
Movie camera	2	4	3	7	1	1	1	6	3	9	2	9	5	11	2	3
Record player	28	46	30	45	29	47	23	46	39	57	19	34	25	39	39	49
Knitting machine	2	4	3	6	3	5	1	1	3	3	1	–	3	2	2	2
Camping tent	4	8	6	10	4	8	–	2	8	19	2	7	3	11	5	5
Trailer	–	1	–	1	–	2	–	–	1	2	–	–	1	–	1	1
Automobile	28	50	40	57	26	42	20	51	26	49	30	51	48	71	35	45
Motor scooter	5	5	2	2	2	4	14	10	3	6	2	3	6	3	3	5
Motor bicycle	5	3	3	3	3	1	10	8	3	1	3	–	3	2	5	5
Full-size bicycle	44	43	43	39	43	45	40	37	78	76	44	30	36	42	32	26
Moped (bicycle with built-in motor)	15	16	33	31	10	5	2	4	32	25	11	7	3	3	2	1

*This table reads: 79 percent of E.E.C. People and 87 percent of Digest Readers in the E.E.C. have one or more radios in their household.
SOURCE: *Reader's Digest*

and the membership in organizations such as the International Advertising Association boomed.

Total advertising expenditures in 52 leading countries has been estimated by the International Advertising Association at approximately \$23,000,000,000 in 1964. Advertising volume during the five years 1960–1964 increased slightly less rapidly than income. However, if we look only at 18 still-developing countries, we find that advertising volume was up 50 percent and income 35 percent. The highest rate of advertising investment, according to this study, was in Australia, where advertising expenditures were 2.03 percent of national income. Next in order were United States and Canada. Table 31.2 summarizes estimated advertising expenditures for several of the leading nations as estimated by *Advertising Age*.

TABLE 31.2

ADVERTISING EXPENDITURES AROUND THE WORLD

COUNTRY	Total Advertising Expenditures (in millions of U.S. dollars)			Tot. Adv. Exp. per Capita	Tot. Adv. Exp. as a % of GNP
	1965	1966	1967		
United States	15,600	16,800	17,300	$87.86	2.3
West Germany	1,596	1,772	1,854	31.05	1.5
Great Britain	1,559	1,572	1,550	28.18	1.4
Japan	956	1,064	1,276	12.90	1.3
France	680	756	831	16.82	.8
Canada	733	821	830	41.29	1.5
Italy	450	540	500	9.61	.8
Sweden	117	368	387	49.61	1.8
Australia	296	311	342	29.48	1.3
Switzerland	170	310	380	63.33	2.5
Netherlands	210	235	270	21.60	1.3
Spain	N.A.	267	257	8.05	1.0
Mexico	140	185	205	4.64	0.9

SOURCES: Total Advertising Expenditures: *Advertising Age*, June 26, 1967, p. 82. *Advertising Age*, June 17, 1968, p. 82. Population Figures: Mid-1966: *Advertising Age*, June 17, 1968, p. 88. Gross National Product: 1966 *Advertising Age*, June 17, 1968, p. 88.

WHAT IS INTERNATIONAL ADVERTISING?

The term "international advertising" causes confusion in some quarters. To certain persons there is a basic contradiction in the term itself. For example, SCM Corporation recently disbanded its international division and turned responsibility for international marketing over to its domestic marketing department. The company preferred to make no distinction between selling a product in the United States and selling it in another country.[1] The idea of distinguishing between domestic and international sales seems a bit out of date to companies where foreign sales are just as important as domestic ones. Consequently, we hear some people speak of *global*, *multinational*, or *transnational* (rather than international) advertising and marketing.

To other persons, international advertising is that which is carried in such international media as *Time International* or any of the many foreign editions of *Reader's Digest*. This viewpoint, however, seriously understates the true scope of advertising activities that cut across national boundaries. It has been suggested that "cross-cultural" is a better term than "international," because markets are often better defined by cultural or demographic variables than by political boundaries.

There is general agreement, however, that certain problems that are not present in domestic advertising arise when a firm or agency is advertising in more than one country. Consequently, we shall include here as "international" all advertising and promotion that are designed to persuade or communicate to consumers in more than one country, and we shall concentrate in this chapter on some of the advertising

[1]John Fayerweather, *International Marketing* (Englewood Cliffs, N.J.: Prentice-Hall, Inc., 1965), p. 1.

problems peculiar to the international field. Thus we find it covers Procter & Gamble advertising for Ivory soap in Italy and India and Volkswagen advertising in the United States. It includes some not-so-obvious occasions where the products advertised are made under license by a government corporation (such as Coca Cola in Egypt), or when they are imported into a Communist country and sold or promoted by a state corporation (for example, Maidenform brassieres in Russia). Some of the goods promoted internationally are sold through export divisions, some through wholly — or partially — owned subsidiaries in a foreign country, some through distributors, and some through licensees.

WHY THE INCREASE IN INTERNATIONAL ADVERTISING?

The growth in international advertising appears to be due to a variety of factors. The most important are the following.

Increase in Foreign Living Standards. Developments in the United States have demonstrated that improvements in living standards make markets. As people become more prosperous, they consume more and produce more. Arno Johnson, vice-president and senior economist for J. Walter Thompson, points out, "In most of the nations where freedom of initiative is allowed, there is today growing evidence of rapidly increasing productivity and rising levels of education of the masses of population."[2]

FIG. 31.1 *English and Chinese versions of a successful Lufthansa advertisement.*

[2]See Arno Johnson, "Dynamic Trends in World Markets," in S. Watson Dunn, ed. *International Handbook of Advertising* (New York: McGraw-Hill, Inc., 1964), p. 23.

During the decade from 1955 to 1965 United States industry almost trebled its investments in western Europe. This represented both new capital and reinvested profits of United States companies operating in the area. Similarly, the underdeveloped countries of Asia and the Latin-American countries have experienced substantial growth and present substantial markets. Consider, for instance, Brazil with a 24 percent increase in national income between 1967 and 1968 and approximately one seventh of the world's population.

Trade Agreements. During the years since World War II several significant moves have been made toward international unification. These have been in the direction of lowering tariffs between the nations involved, eliminating quotas, and stimulating competition. As any American marketer knows, these advances are among the important ingredients of a healthy mass market.

Agreements in western Europe have undoubtedly attracted the greatest interest. Among the important treaties were the Brussels Treaty of 1948; the Organization for European Economic Cooperation in 1948; the Benelux customs agreement of 1948; the Council of Europe in 1949; and, most of all, the European Economic Community (European Common Market) established by the Treaty of Rome in 1957;[3] followed by the European Free Trade Association established in 1958.

Among the innovations of the ECM Agreement were the eventual elimination of tariffs between the six countries involved (France, West Germany, Italy, Belgium, Netherlands, and Luxembourg), free movement of goods between these countries, removal of restrictions on the movement of capital and labor across national boundaries, establishment of a social fund to assist families of any workers whose well-being might be injured by the increased commercial competition that the treaty encourages, and the establishment of two investment funds — one to channel constructive capital into backward areas of the ECM and the other to do the same for underdeveloped regions of the overseas territories of the six countries involved.

Such agreements as these also present dangers to American marketers. They could result in tariff walls against United States goods. However, indications so far seem to be that they increase the prosperity of the area and thus improve its potential as a market — just as a more prosperous United States is a better market for foreign goods. Also, the consolidating of countries for marketing purposes makes it possible for American companies and agencies operating in the area to consolidate foreign marketing operations for greater efficiency.

Higher Profits. Some American companies marketing in foreign countries have enjoyed profits substantially higher than those they make at home. Tradition, the slower growth of competitors, and the liberal tax laws in certain countries have made it possible for firms to realize profits per dollar sometimes two or three times those made at home. In 1961 United States companies were making a 30 percent higher rate of profit in their foreign operations than at home; by 1965 the rate, however, had slipped to 10 percent higher for foreign subsidi-

[3]See Bertil Liander, *The European Economic Community* (New York: McGraw-Hill, Inc., 1964).

aries and affiliates. These profits, of course, must be balanced against the inconvenience of operating in a foreign country, the difficulty of getting raw materials, and the vagaries of local governments. In view of this profitability it is not surprising that American investments abroad have gone up two-and-one-half times between 1945 and 1967. *Fortune* estimated direct United States investments abroad in 1967 at $54,000,000,000. These were divided as follows:[4]

Canada	31.0%
Western Europe	29.7
Latin America	21.1
Africa	3.8
Middle East	3.1
Japan	1.5
Other	9.8

Sales of United States products in foreign markets have increased at approximately the same rate as investments.

TECHNIQUES OF INTERNATIONAL ADVERTISING

In general, the techniques that work well in the United States work also in foreign countries. However, there are differences worth noting — differences that have caused even experienced advertisers serious trouble. Among the most important areas the international marketers should watch are those of the marketing mix, advertising creation, research, and media selection.

The Marketing Mix. Most companies who move into foreign markets wonder to what extent they will be able to use the same marketing mix that they used in the home market. One study of the marketing programs of 30 large United States manufacturers revealed the following pattern of expenditures:

TABLE 31.3

COMPARISON OF UNITED STATES AND
FOREIGN ADVERTISING EXPENDITURE
(As percent of sales)

Type of Product	Number of Companies	Spend Higher Percent Than in U.S.	Spend About Same Percentage	Spend Lower Percentage
Cosmetics, soaps, and drugs	11	3	4	4
Food and food products	7	2	2	3
Beverages	2	—	1	1
Automotive	3	—	—	3
Miscellaneous	7	—	2	5
Total	30	5	9	16

SOURCE: S. Watson Dunn, "The Case Study Approach in Cross-Cultural Research," in *Journal of Marketing Research*, 3 (February 1966), p. 27.

[4]Walter Guzzardi, Jr., "Why the Climate Is Changing for U.S. Investment," *Fortune*, September 15, 1967.

Mylène Demongeot a choisi LUX - le savon de beauté des stars - pour garder son teint lisse et éclatant.

Peau satinée avec la mousse reposante de LUX

C'est un petit miracle quotidien : la mousse légère et délicatement parfumée de LUX, si douce sur votre peau, si tendre pour votre teint, transforme votre toilette de chaque jour en une merveilleuse "mise en beauté". Après, vous êtes reposée, détendue, toute lisse de la tête aux pieds. Vous vous sentez plus belle... et vous avez raison !

FIG. 31.2 *A campaign used with little change in every market where Lux is sold. This is the French version of this famous campaign.*

There was little apparent relation here, between the type of product and the amount of money spent in the United States compared with the type of product and the money spent in foreign markets. The heavy users in the United States were generally the heavy users in foreign markets.

One large United States corporation marketed two major food products in France and finished with two quite different promotional mixes. The first was a high-quality biscuit product promoted through advertising, which met with some, but far from satisfactory, success. The company tried to build consumer loyalty for the brand as it had in the United States but found it impossible. They experimented then with various mixes and decided to drop media advertising completely. Instead, they concentrated on contests, color films, and regional meetings where the retailers were wined and dined. During the same period the company introduced a second biscuit that had been highly successful in the United States. The company decided to use advertising here but to

design each advertisement specifically for the French market and to drop a seal identifying the package as American. This campaign also was successful.[5]

Fayerweather offers two guides that a marketer might use in determining how much emphasis to put on promotional expenditures when he enters a market:

First, there is a progression in the structural aspects of marketing that causes the differences in the *over-all level of expenditures*. In primitive societies, goods are produced to meet a limited group of known needs, producers and consumers are close and the quality of products is easily known and judged. . . .

Second, we have the question of notable *deviations* from the general pattern such as those for France and Germany. These would appear to be due to national attitudes toward advertising, attributable to various causes. The aversion to promotion that exists to a degree in the United States is quite strong in many countries. In Europe, the feelings are of the traditional old-line business character. "A good product will sell itself."[6]

FIG. 31.3 *French advertisement for a famous international brand. This advertisement was created by the French agency; it represents a distinct departure from the advertising used concurrently by Frigidaire in the United States.*

[5]S. Watson Dunn, "The Case Study Approach in Cross-Cultural Research," in *Journal of Marketing Research*, 3 (February 1966), 30.
[6]Fayerweather, pp. 83–84.

Arthur C. Nielsen, Jr., warns that persons who open foreign markets sometimes erringly pursue the same marketing policies that they use in the United States because they see similarities in overseas markets. He points out 15 major errors that are made:

1. Failure to adapt the product to the market.

2. Failure to gauge the underlying differences in custom, religion, etc.

3. Failure to exploit markets in the proper sequence (and to avoid countries where excessive facilities already exist).

4. Failure to enter potentially profitable markets due to personal repugnance to political institutions.

5. Failure to build a strong management of nationals.

6. Failure to appreciate differences in the connotation of words (especially important in labeling, ad copy, etc.).

7. Failure to understand differences in rules for advertising (such as which claims can be made, and which cannot).

8. Failure to achieve a domestic personality or image (through advertising and public relations).

9. Failure to understand and weigh correctly the relative importance of retailers and other intermediaries in the distribution of the product.

10. Failure to grasp the consumer's attitude on the relationship between price and quality.

11. Failure to appraise properly the degree of acceptance of the competitive system (controls and price fixing are accepted in some countries).

FIG. 31.4 *Advertisement for Vicks VapoRub which was run throughout the Middle East.*

12. Failure to pay due attention to the various pertinent government regulations.

13. Failure to insulate the business from arbitrary acts of government (such as building a local plant to avoid high tariffs).

14. Failure to invest funds for the long pull (by not plowing back profits for advertising and sales promotion, for example).

15. Failure to provide for an adequate flow of information to and from the parent company.[7]

Sometimes the creative person preparing material for the international market will be told that every foreign market is different and that he will run into a variety of problems, including cultural taboos, if he tries to use the American approach abroad. Then again he will be told that everything from hair spray to tourism can be sold throughout the world with much the same illustrations, copy, and advertising approach.[8] Findings on this question from the series of case studies referred to earlier indicated

> . . . that U. S. international marketing executives tend to take a pragmatic approach both to the problem of budgeting for foreign advertising and to the problem of deciding on the extent to which a given U. S. campaign is transferable to a particular foreign area. This situation results, at least in part, from their wariness to tie themselves to hard-and-fast guidelines in such a dynamic, relatively uncharted area. The campaigns that have been most successful are those where marketers have managed to work out a balance between complete internationalization and complete localization. One method of allowing for this needed flexibility has been to employ a "prototype" campaign (a basic plan with art and copy which may or may not be used in a given country), although not all users have experienced satisfactory results with such campaigns.
>
> The criteria which are used to determine transferability tend to fall within three general categories: market or economic, cultural or psychological, and media. The first of these seems to be the most widely used, apparently because more data are available and because it fits more readily into the marketing man's frame of reference.[9]

Experiments in France and the Middle East in which variations of successful American advertisements were tested under field conditions indicated that advertising (at least successful advertising) was perhaps more transferable than is generally realized.[10]

Motivation researcher Ernest Dichter contends that "In most countries I have visited, I find that human desires are pretty much alike. The big difference lies in the level of achievement, in its many different forms."[11] He believes that "growth and progress" are the real goals of people regardless of where they live.

[7]Arthur C. Nielsen, Jr., "Do's and Don't's in Selling Abroad," in Dunn, *International Handbook of Advertising*, pp. 15–20.

[8]Erik Elinder, "How International Can Advertising Be?" and Claude Marcus, "France," in Dunn, *International Handbook of Advertising*, p. 31, for defense of these two points of view.

[9]Dunn, "The Case Study Approach," p. 31.

[10]Evangeline S. Lorimor, "Effects of Source and Certain Other Factors on Cross-Cultural Persuasive Communication" (unpublished Ph.D. thesis, University of Wisconsin) contains a description of this study.

[11]Ernest Dichter, "The World Customer," in Harper W. Boyd, Jr., and Joseph W. Newman, eds., *Advertising Management: Selected Readings* (Homewood, Ill.: Richard D. Irwin, Inc., 1965), p. 257.

FIG. 31.5 *Example of British magazine advertisement. Note the differences in usage of the English language.*

Research. Until the 1950s advertisers had scant market and media information on which to base their promotional decisions. However, the available information has increased because of postwar expansion of American research organizations and the growth of research in foreign countries. For instance, A. C. Nielsen Company added offices in 10 countries between 1939 and 1959. The *Reader's Digest* in 1963 sponsored a major marketing survey of the European Common Market and Great Britain. Findings were based on 12,500 personal interviews incorporating 140 marketing items and numerous attitude and opinion questions. These were related to readership of the *Reader's Digest* (see Table 31.1).

In spite of the progress, however, executives of American corporations still have surprisingly little research evidence on which to base their decisions. Even companies that are avid testers in the United States do surprisingly little research when they operate in foreign markets. The following seem to be the principal reasons for the slow growth of research by United States corporations:[12]

1. The expense of good research.
2. Skepticism regarding the quality of foreign research personnel and their organizations.
3. Difficulty of communicating with local researchers' respondents.
4. Doubt as to the validity of U. S. testing techniques (either in the U.S. or in a foreign market).
5. Lack of research by the U.S. firm's competition in most markets.

Media Strategy. Almost everyone who delves even lightly into the problems of international advertising is struck by how greatly media availabilities differ from one country to the next. Certain American advertisers, for example, who depend heavily on the broadcast media are understandably frustrated when they go into markets where such media

[12]S. Watson Dunn, "Cross-Cultural Research by U. S. Corporations," *Journalism Quarterly*, 42, no. 3 (Summer 1965), 456–457.

FIG. 31.6 *Example of a Swedish magazine advertisement.*

are not available — or if available only on a limited basis with long waits to get on the air. In several countries cinema advertising — a relatively minor medium in the United States — is important and provides an outlet for some of the best creative minds in the country. In England, if you want to reach the whole country with a print advertising campaign, the obvious choice would be the national newspapers. On the other hand, if you wanted to concentrate on special groups, you would be likely to choose magazines. However, in Italy the situation is almost the reverse. Newspapers are primarily local media and are read much more by men than by women. To achieve more general readership of the whole country, you would use a combination of magazines which cover the whole country and are read by both sexes.

The relatively low degree of literacy in some countries makes print media a poor buy and radio and cinema particularly attractive. Consequently, in countries where income is lowest and economy in scheduling is very necessary, you are forced to use expensive media to reach the poorest classes. Colin McIver points out that before the advent of television it was virtually impossible to reach the working class Italian housewife through advertising.[13] Those who could read did not, and they did not travel enough to see transportation advertising or posters. Poster campaigns within the villages were expensive and difficult to administer. Point-of-sale material was restricted by the smallness of the shops. Cinema advertising was a possible alternative, but it was quite expensive.

Such common yardsticks as milline rates and cost-per-thousand are of only limited benefit in many countries. We are used to thinking of rates as based on costs of production and on demand in a free market. However, in many countries rates are either set or heavily influenced by the government, by monopolies, and by density of population. Advertising rates are firm in some countries; in others they are merely a point from which one starts to bargain.

The trend in most countries is toward more emphasis on television. In western Europe, for example, some governments have found it too expensive to support a national television system entirely with public tax funds. The logical alternative is to make it commercial. As Carson points out, the increased availability of media and the rise in the standard of living have made substantial changes in media buying.[14] We find also an increase in the availability of information in developed countries. Most of the western European countries now have at least one auditing organization and many have a cooperatively supported research organ somewhat similar to the Advertising Research Foundation in the United States. There is also a trend toward international media like those of Time, Incorporated, and McGraw-Hill. The international media are often good for reaching upper-class, well-educated people — often the best market for a foreign product anyway. In time the satellites orbiting the earth may expand availabilities in the international field. Wilbur Schramm points out that

[13]Colin McIver, "Formulating Media Strategy for Foreign Markets," in Dunn, *International Handbook*, pp. 133–139.
[14]David Carson, *International Marketing: A Comparative Systems Approach* (New York: John Wiley & Sons, Inc., 1967), pp. 416–417.

FIG. 31.7 *Advertisement which was run in English-language publications in Southeast Asia.*

The first use of these new instruments which is likely to be important to developing countries is an expansion of facilities. Perhaps the first effect of communication satellites in most of the developing countries is likely to be felt by news agencies and news media. Such satellites will make it possible to circulate more news and to extend live coverage of widely important news. It may be that satellites will help fill in some of the areas where radio coverage is still scant.[15]

Schramm points out, however, that there are many problems (such as overlapping of signals, copyrights, performers' rights, selection of a language for broadcast, assignment of channels) which must still be worked out. However, there is no reason to think that advertising messages will be barred from these satellites. Eurovision, which links several European countries for simultaneous televising of certain events, is an impressive start in international television.

ORGANIZING FOR INTERNATIONAL ADVERTISING

The organizations involved in international advertising are much the same — on the surface at least — as those in the domestic picture. As in the United States, the important institutions are advertisers, agencies, and media. There are some differences worth noting in both agencies and media, although advertisers are organized much as they are in the United States.

For one thing, a significant portion of overseas advertising is carried on by foreign branches of American agencies. The largest of these is J. Walter Thompson, which has had branches outside the United States since 1899, when it opened a one-man office in London.[16] In 1967 it handled $227,000,000 of billing outside the United States — which represents approximately 38 percent of the agency's total billings. In 1967 Thompson had 7,164 employees, 4,544 of these in the 40 offices abroad.

Agency organizations vary from one country to the next. In some countries (France and the communist countries for example) at least some agencies are owned and operated by the government. In many countries agencies and media have joint ownership — a practice that would be considered highly suspect in the United States because of possible conflict of interest.

Suppose, for example, that you are running a large United States agency and wanted to expand, as many have in recent years, into foreign markets. One alternative is to establish a new branch in London or Buenos Aires or Tokyo. Another is to find an agency already established in each market and purchase an interest in it. Another alternative is to set up joint agencies in one or more foreign countries. These are separate entities controlled by the domestic agency and a foreign agency. The domestic agency does not serve local accounts but maintains direct control over its clients' advertising in the local market and taps the local talents of the joint agency involved.

[15]Wilbur Schramm, *Mass Media and National Development* (Stanford, Calif.: Stanford University Press, 1964), p. 294.
[16]"The J. Walter Thompson Company, Including Its International Operations," *Advertising Age*, December 7, 1964.

A growing method is the agency network system. There are now in Europe several networks of agencies that have formed integrated groups to offer local services, talents, and ideas on an organized exchange basis.

Another alternative for the agency is to work through affiliate agencies abroad. The method seems to work fairly well where the United States agency has an international department set up with good media files and some specialized personnel to keep tab on the operations.

A final alternative for the agency is to work with another agency that specializes in international accounts. Usually the international agency operates through the use of associate agencies throughout the world instead of maintaining its own branches. It functions much as the international department of a domestic agency.

Miracle found in his study of international advertising management that the following four conditions seemed to govern what kind of international organization evolved in a particular agency:

1. Agencies whose primary motive for expansion abroad is to serve existing clients tend to avoid direct investment except when there is no alternative, preferring instead to depend on associate agencies.
2. Large agencies with a well-diversified list of consumer accounts tend to favor wholly or partially owned branches.
3. Very large agencies tend to favor wholly owned branches.
4. Agencies that have been slow in establishing their capability to serve clients abroad have engaged a number of associate foreign agencies on a temporary basis.[17]

An interesting case history of an American agency that moved successfully overseas is recounted by Harold Burson.[18] This is a case where the agency was not large and was not pressured by clients to go abroad. Instead, the agency executives felt that, for an agency like theirs — Marsteller — to go abroad was the logical avenue of growth. However, George Theophilopoulos, principal in a Greek agency, warns Americans that expansion abroad is becoming riskier all the time.[19]

Like the agencies, internationally minded companies and media have been strikingly divided on just how their international advertising and promotion operation can best be organized. Companies like International Business Machines and National Cash Register have worked toward an international identity by emphasizing IBM and NCR rather than their American-sounding names. Although some large companies like International Harvester have been selling abroad for more than a century, the major expansion has come since World War II.

There are of course, many differences in the way international advertising operations are organized, based primarily on differences in products, markets, and management philosophy. There are, however, certain similarities too. Miracle found that

. . . generally large corporations heavily committed to business abroad are tending to evolve away from a domestically oriented organizational structure.

[17]Gordon Miracle, *Management of International Advertising* (Ann Arbor: University of Michigan, 1966), pp. 84–85.
[18]Harold Burson, "An American Agency Goes Overseas — A Case History," *Occasional Papers in Advertising*, September 1967.
[19]George Theophilopoulos, "The Problems of American Agencies Entering Foreign Markets," *Occasional Papers in Advertising*, September 1967.

Many companies are finding that a domestic company with an international division which is set apart from other divisions is becoming inadequate to serve their best over-all interests.[20]

According to a study made by the National Industrial Conference Board, companies around the world tend to follow one of five patterns: (1) functional organization—with foreign operations integrated into the functional units; (2) functional organization—but with foreign operations assembled into one separate over-all international unit; (3) product organization—with foreign operations integrated into product divisions or product groups; (4) product organization—with foreign operations reporting directly to top management or assembled as a separate international unit; and (5) regional organization—with total operations grouped into components under regional structure. NICB reports several case histories of each type of organization.[21]

The problem of home-office control is sometimes complicated by the fact that the advertising manager of the subsidiary, licensee, or distributor is strongly nationalistic and wants to be on his own.

SUMMARY

During the 1950s and 1960s there was a decided increase in all three types of international advertising: that by American companies in foreign countries; by foreign firms in their own and other foreign countries; and by foreign firms in the United States. Among the principal reasons for this growth seem to be (1) the increase in foreign living standards, (2) trade agreements, (3) the potentially higher profits from foreign operations, and (4) hedging against possible recession in domestic operations.

The techniques used in foreign advertising are not far different from those in the United States in that the basics are really international. There are differences, however. Research is important in both the United States and foreign markets, but research data are not as plentiful in foreign countries. The creative efforts and the use of media have to be adapted to the cultural and marketing characteristics of each particular market. This may require considerably more information. To do this well, agencies, advertisers, and media may find it necessary to work harder to get information—particularly as the foreign competition becomes more skillful.

Agencies, advertisers, and media are experimenting with a variety of organizational patterns in their efforts to cope with the needs of international advertising and promotion.

QUESTIONS FOR DISCUSSION

1. What are the principal reasons for the growth of international advertising and promotion since World War II? What are the prospects for growth during the next ten years?
2. Why do some people prefer the term "multinational" to "international" to describe advertising in more than one country?

[20]Miracle, p. 82.
[21]Harold Stieglitz, *Organization Structures of International Companies* (New York: National Industrial Conference Board, 1965), pp. 6–7.

3. Why is television not available as an advertising medium in many countries of the world? Do you think it should be noncommercial in the United States?

4. What guidelines might an advertiser use in deciding whether to use in a foreign market a campaign that had proved successful in the United States?

5. To what extent can advertising be used to raise the standard of living in some of the underdeveloped countries of the world? Should the governments of such countries encourage or discourage advertising?

6. Why do socialist as well as capitalist countries allow advertising of goods and services?

7. Is it generally more advisable for an American agency desiring to expand into foreign markets to buy stock in an existing agency in these markets or to start a new agency?

SUGGESTED READINGS

Barton, Roger, *Advertising Media.* New York: McGraw-Hill, Inc., 1965. Chapter 11.

Carson, David, *International Marketing: A Comparative Systems Approach.* New York: John Wiley & Sons, Inc., 1967.

Dunn, S. Watson, ed. *International Handbook of Advertising.* New York: McGraw-Hill, Inc., 1964.

Fayerweather, John, *International Marketing.* Englewood Cliffs, N.J.: Prentice-Hall, Inc., 1965.

Hess, John M., and Philip R. Cateora, *International Marketing.* Homewood, Ill.: Richard D. Irwin, Inc., 1966.

Liander, Bertil, *Marketing Development in the European Economic Community.* New York: McGraw-Hill, Inc., 1964.

Miracle, Gordon, *Management of International Advertising.* Ann Arbor: University of Michigan Press, 1966.

Sargent, Hugh W., ed. *Occasional Papers in Advertising.* Urbana: University of Illinois Press, 1967.

Stanley, Alexander, *Handbook of International Marketing.* New York: McGraw-Hill, Inc., 1964.

Stieglitz, Harold, *Organization Structures of International Companies.* New York: National Industrial Conference Board, 1965.

32 | Measuring the Effectiveness of Advertising and Promotion

Advertising men are fond of quoting a statement attributed to that successful nineteenth-century merchant, John Wanamaker, "I know half the money I spend on advertising is wasted; but I can never find out which half." In their attempt to find out which of their advertising is wasted and which is successful, advertising agencies, advertisers, and media are spending many millions of dollars each year. Specifically, they are trying to discover whether a particular ad or series of ads accomplished what was expected of it. This is the "feedback" to the communicator to tell him how many persons received his message and how they interpreted what was said.

In previous chapters we have emphasized the necessity of building the advertising and marketing plan from a solid basis of facts. From the facts and your interpretation of what they mean you formulate your objectives and work out your mixes. Copy testing (the term commonly applied to all tests of ads, parts of ads, or campaigns) takes place when it is too late. The same is true for testing media. Yet the experienced communicator is attentive to test findings and modifies his mix in the light of what he finds out from his audience.

TO TEST OR NOT TO TEST

Although copy and media testing were practically unknown in advertising until the 1920s, it is today a major part of the research efforts of most large and medium-sized advertisers and agencies. Behind this growth lie three major factors: growth in the scale of advertising expenditures, the general trend toward factual bases for decisions in business, and the generally accepted fact that there are important differences in the effectiveness of individual advertisements and media. The first two of these have been dealt with in previous chapters. Let us look briefly at the third factor.

Everyone knows that some advertisements are more effective than others. However, the extremes in effectiveness between advertisements that cost the same amount of money did not become apparent until we had adequate measuring sticks. The studies of Starch, Gallup, and Robinson, the Advertising Research Foundation, and practically everyone who has tested large numbers of ads—regardless of the yardstick used—testify to wide variation in effectiveness. Through research, each agency and advertiser hopes to find out whether his ads have the high or low ratings.

Unfortunately, the experts who plan and put together the ads can not always be good judges of the advertisements' ultimate effectiveness. Mayer points out that businessmen probably know less than ever before about the efficiency of their sales promotion efforts.[1] The early advertisers for the most part were mail order advertisers, and they could calculate the effectiveness of their advertising by using the most valuable check of all—actual sales. However, the optimism of advertising pioneers like Claude Hopkins turned out to be unfounded when it was discovered that general consumer advertising and advertising designed for mail order sales were different in a great many ways.

Counter to forces encouraging the growth of copy testing are others that inhibit its growth. Four of the most important negative forces are the following:

First, there is the almost insurmountable task of isolating the effects of advertising from those of the many other variables that produce a sale. A sale seldom is made in such a rarefied atmosphere that the advertising researcher can point to the ad and say, "This ad produced that sale." The interweaving of the variables discourages many from even trying to unravel them. Many, however, do not give up but instead concentrate their efforts on certain measurable factors —such as readership, recall, consumer opinion, belief or disbelief, attention, comprehension, registration of message, and change in attitude. They are assuming, of course, that what they measure has a positive relation to ultimate sales.

Second, good research is expensive and time consuming. Some large agencies budget several hundred thousand dollars a year for copy testing, an expense not usually passed on directly to the client. Even more discouraging to advertising people is the delay in getting results. They want quick answers to their questions.

[1]Martin Mayer, *The Intelligent Man's Guide to Sales Measures of Advertising* (New York: Advertising Research Foundation, 1965), pp. 1–2.

Third, certain creative people have objected both publicly and privately to copy testing as it is practiced today. (This statement does not mean that all creative persons feel this way, because many are enthusiastic boosters of copy testing.) They have expressed concern about the rush of certain writers and account people to ape the "best read" or "highest rated" ads. They fear that creative people are taking research findings too literally. Then, too, some creative people mistakenly suspect that copy testers are trying to interfere with their creative efforts. They believe that consumers are so complex and unpredictable that no method of research can measure accurately the effect of an individual ad. By and large, these fears are not well founded. Few copy testers claim the omniscience about which creative people sometimes complain. Few of them attempt to write the ads. They know as well as the creative people that this is a complex business, but they also believe current methods of research are better than no research at all.

Fourth, advertising people are understandably confused by the apparent disagreement among the researchers themselves regarding the validity of the different methods of measuring audience response. The disagreements are sometimes decidedly heated and occasionally are aired on public forums. However, these disagreements often turn out to be about details (methods of field interviewing, sampling) rather than about basic approach.

WHAT SHOULD BE TESTED?

Every marketing man would like to find out whether each element in his campaign actually paid off. This kind of detailed testing is not practicable. The time consumed, the expense, and the uncertainty involved in most testing mean that the marketer must concentrate on the particularly important problems that he feels he can measure with some exactness. Most of these have to do with the message or with the media.

In the case of message research, the tester may wonder as to the degree "what is said" is important in the ultimate effectiveness of the message and to what extent "how it is said," is important. This dilemma has led researchers to put more and more emphasis on completed advertising alternatives (campaigns or sets of advertisements) and somewhat less on the testing of individual advertising components. Advertisers are becoming increasingly concerned with the sales effectiveness of Strategy A versus Strategy B. This is a reflection of improved methods of evaluating alternative strategies both in the laboratory and in the field and of improved electronic equipment for processing the data quickly and accurately. Of course, there is still much questioning of which appeal will communicate the message best. Researchers still wonder under what conditions illustrations communicate the message better than long copy, when color adds impact to the televised or printed message.

WHICH TEST IS BEST?

There is a continuing debate going on among researchers and would-be researchers to determine which method is best. Much of this comes down to a question of what it is you want to find out. One method will be best for one type of problem, another for a different type. One method will be perfectly satisfactory for a rough idea of which ad communicates best, but for something more precise, you may have need for a more elaborate method.

Perhaps the most useful approach is to consider the various types of tests and to attempt to assess the conditions under which each will be most useful. One useful and commonly used method of classifying them is to divide them into two general classes: pretesting, which is conducted before the advertising is exposed to an audience, and posttesting —which is done after exposure. This is the general division used in two books published by the National Industrial Conference Board in which these methods are described.[2] This approach will be used in this chapter.

Another method of classifying tests is in terms of *limited objective* and *sales-objective* tests. Although most persons would like to know the sales effectiveness of a proposed message or media plan, many contend that in practice we have to settle for some communication criterion (such as awareness and recall). It can reasonably be expected that the more effective an advertising message is in communicating, the more effective it will be in selling the product. Among the most important communications criteria are the following:

1. *Awareness* Did the test increase awareness of the message, product, theme, and so on?
2. *Recall* Can the respondents recall something that can be related to the specific message or medium?
3. *Attitudes and opinions* Was the person's attitude changed as a result of the advertisement?
4. *Belief* Does the consumer believe what is said in the ad?
5. *Inquiries* Which ad produced the most inquiries?

EXPERIMENT OR SURVEY?

Another approach to testing is on the basis of the technique or research design. Two quite different approaches are used in the study of communications—the *experiment* and the *survey*.[3]

In the experimental approach individuals are given a controlled exposure to the message and the effects are evaluated in terms of the amount of change of opinion or attitude or some measurable action. These experiments may take place in the laboratory, as they do with the tachistoscope (a device used by psychologists in laboratory experiments to measure the speed with which ideas are perceived) or in the field, as they do in some elaborate studies made by automobile companies. Some sort of base line is obtained through the use of a control group not exposed to the message or medium. As Banks points out, "The key to these (experimental) research procedures is the realization

[2]Harry D. Wolfe *et al., Measuring Advertising Results* (1961), and his *Pretesting Advertising* (1963), both published by the National Industrial Conference Board.
[3]See Carl I. Hovland, "Reconciling Conflicting Results Derived from Experimental and Survey Studies of Attitude Change," in Harper W. Boyd, Jr., and Joseph W. Newman, eds., *Advertising Management: Selected Readings* (Homewood, Ill.: Richard D. Irwin, Inc., 1965).

that, in almost all situations in which experiments are used, the fundamental interest is in a comparison of alternatives, not in the establishment of absolute values."[4]

In sample surveys, information is secured through interviews or
questionnaires regarding the person's exposure to the message or the
media and to changes in his attitudes or actions. The effectiveness is
appraised on the basis of correlations obtained between the reports of
exposure and the changes in attitude and action. For panels, a fixed
sample is used and interviews or mail contacts are made over a period
of time.

PRETESTING THE ADVERTISING

The idea of testing the effectiveness of an advertisement *before* it is run
in the media is obviously an attractive one to any marketing man. Most
persons would prefer to know how effective an advertisement is likely
to be before money has been spent to place it in the media and to merchandise it, and before the advertising man responsible for it has had to
commit himself. Unfortunately, no sure-fire method of predicting
success has been developed. However, there are certain methods of
pretesting that can be of considerable help to the advertiser if used
wisely. All have built-in limitations as well as advantages. In this
section an attempt will be made to appraise some of the pretesting
methods most commonly used today.

Consumer Opinion or Awareness (Print). This catchall classification includes everything from asking the girls in the office to evaluate
a proposed layout, to a systematic and rigorously controlled exposure of
advertising material to an audience of prospective consumers. Actually,
almost every copywriter does some testing of his creations on consumers. Sometimes an agency will merely send a boy down to Grand Central Station to ask persons in the waiting room which of two advertisements they like best. Sometimes it will send the material to thousands
of homes.

One of the more elaborate methods of pretesting has been used at
Young & Rubicam since 1945 when George Gallup was director of
research there. The agency publishes a magazine of its own called *New
Canadian World*. This is a real magazine with an appearance similar to
Life and *Look*. (The agency acquired the rights to the editorial content
of a discontinued Canadian publication.) Each issue (which contains a
full complement of advertisements, both black and white and full color)
is placed in a representative sample of homes in five areas of the United
States. The recipients are asked to read the "magazine" exactly as they
would read any American magazine they subscribe to or usually buy, to
read the articles, features, and ads that interest them. So that their
reactions will be as normal as possible, no extra emphasis is placed on
the advertising. The magazine is used to test new basic ideas, new
approaches, new formats, and new techniques. The interviewer takes
each respondent through a page-by-page examination of the advertise-

[4]Seymour Banks, *Experimentation in Marketing* (New York: McGraw-Hill, Inc.,
1965), p. 1.

ments and asks questions designed to find out whether the advertisement made any lasting impression. Unaided and aided recall research techniques are used but are not relied on exclusively.

Batten, Barton, Durstine & Osborn has used real magazines in somewhat the same way. Through a special arrangement with two of the major national weeklies the agency gets about a thousand first-off press advance copies of coming issues. The agency's production department removes some of the legitimate ads from the issues and "strips in" proofs of the ads that BBDO wants to test. Usually alternative versions of each ad will be substituted for the existing pages; and then 700 copies of the altered magazine will be given away on the day the real issue hits the newsstands—350 of each sample. Two or three days later interviewers are sent to query respondents by aided and unaided recall. Martin Mayer, in describing this method, says,

> The comparative ratings of the two ads on all three tests (aided, unaided recall, and readership) will guide the agency in deciding which advertisements to run, but the test is most useful in deciding technical questions—such as, shall we use one big picture of a cake made with Betty Crocker mix or two smaller pictures of two goodies made with two different kinds of mix?[5]

Another interesting device is that used from time to time by the Philip Morris Company. The interviewer asks matched samples of respondents which of two cigarettes tastes better, showing the ad for a Philip Morris brand as well as that of the competition. It is assumed that the respondent's answer on taste correlates with the effectiveness of the advertisement.

To test which headlines should be used in a series of advertisements for Johnson's Wax, its Chicago agency devised an "advertising puzzle game."[6] The company had just brought out a new self-polishing wax which was particularly strong on resistance to water spots and spills. The problem was to find out which headlines and illustrations registered this advantage the best. In this "game" a layout was shown to each housewife. It was blank where the main illustration was to appear. She had several headlines that she could fit in the blank spaces for the heads and six pictures she could use. She switched pictures and headlines around until she decided which combination seemed to fit the ad best.

Another variation of the consumer jury, "the sales conviction test," has been popularized by McCann-Erickson. First of all, the agency finds the "heavy-user category" for the product, the people who use most of it. A number of heavy users are asked which of two ads presented would be most likely to "convince" them to buy the product. The respondent picks one of the advertisements and the interviewer goes on for forty minutes or more asking the respondent how he came to his decision, whether he disliked any part of the ad, and so forth. Each relative sales conviction test involves at least 1,800 interviewers in New York, Chicago, and Los Angeles, and in a distant suburb of each. The final

[5]Martin Mayer, *Madison Avenue, U.S.A.* (New York: Harper & Row, Publishers, 1958), p. 279.
[6]Perham Nahl, "Researcher Gives Case Histories of Speedy, Inexpensive Pretests of Ads," *Advertising Age*, November 10, 1958, p. 83.

score, however, comes from an analysis of the respondents' comments rather than a straight counting of the votes for each ad. Verification has come from split-run tests (explained later in this chapter), sales from department store advertisements, and various direct-mail material sent out on a controlled basis. The agency claims that it was able to predict the ranking of ads correctly more than 98 percent of the time through the use of this test.

Joel Axelrod made an interesting study of ten measures of attitude that are commonly used in advertising to differentiate good advertisements from poor ones:

The lottery measure This is explained in the following pages in connection with broadcast opinion testing.

The +5 to −5 rating scale This is a variation of the semantic differential scales described in Chapter 13.

The predisposition-to-buy scale Respondents are asked which of the following statements describes their feelings about each brand as it is named: I will definitely buy the brand. . . I would not use this brand under any circumstances.

The constant sum scale Respondents are given a sheet on which are listed several brands. Next to each is a pocket. Respondents are asked to distribute cards in the pocket next to the brands to indicate how likely it is that they would buy each. They can put several or no cards in front of any brand.

Paired comparisons Respondents are asked to tell which brand they would be most likely to buy in each pair named by the interviewer.

Forced switching This measure is similar to the lottery measure except respondents are asked to name any brand except their regular one as the one they prefer to receive as a free gift. The lottery is used to determine whether they win this gift.

Advertising recall Respondents are asked to recall what brands they have seen or heard advertised within the past three months.

First and second choices Respondents are asked to name the brand they would be most likely to buy in a particular product class if they went shopping immediately. They are then asked to name the one they would substitute if their first choice were not available.

Awareness Respondents are asked to tell all the brands of a particular class they can think of.

Buying game The interviewer gives the respondents cards showing different situations they might encounter in shopping. Prices and brands vary from card to card. Respondents are asked to tell which brands they would be most likely to purchase.[7]

Axelrod concluded that "several measures commonly used in advertising research should be eliminated . . . because they have almost no predictive power: Second Choice, Second Brand Awareness, Total Brand Awareness, Forced Switching, Second Advertising Recall, and Total Advertising Recall." Recommendations regarding the others seemed to depend on the context in which they were used. For example, *constant sum scale* and *buying game* should be used only if personal interviews

[7]Joel N. Axelrod, "Attitude Measures that Predict Purchase," *Journal of Advertising Research*, March 1968, pp. 3–17.

can be obtained. If telephone interviews were used, *first choice, first brand awareness, lottery measure, paired comparison,* and *first advertising recall* were recommended. In general, *first brand awareness* was found to be the best predictor of short-term purchase behavior. However, where researchers want not only short-term predictions but also diagnostic information (for example, what attitudes are held by those who are going to buy), the *constant sum* was superior.

Most users of these tests, whatever the form or whatever the measure used, agree that the number of advertisements or other test material should be limited to six and that prospective consumers for the product advertised should be used wherever possible.

Advantages. There are four main advantages of the opinion or attitude test:

1. Its low cost. Since only rough layouts are usually used, the cost can be quite low.
2. Its speed. Once the respondents are selected, it takes only a short period to find out which advertisements rate the highest—and even the reasons for the preferences.
3. Its contact with typical consumers. The advertiser or agency can get a lot of information on consumer buying habits.
4. Its use of the complete ad. Unlike the tests that show only part of an ad or merely try out an idea, the consumer–jury test usually shows the whole ad, and, in such cases as the *New Canadian World*, shows it in a fairly natural setting.

Limitations. Against these advantages we must set certain important limitations:

1. Its difficulty in getting true opinions. People can report fairly accurately on what they *did*, but it is more difficult to obtain accurate information about their opinions. The man in the street does not always have any strong opinion on an ad shown to him, and he is likely to make up something on the spur of the moment just to get rid of an aggressive interviewer. Sometimes he probably does not want to admit that he might be influenced by the ad.

2. Its artificial situation. No matter how careful the interviewer is or how skillfully the scene is set, the situation is certain to be somewhat abnormal.

3. Its emphasis on noticing. Research indicates that consumers tend to pick the ad that makes the best first impression and then rationalize their choice. The advertisement that is easily noticed may not do the best over-all advertising job.

4. Its inadequacy for the negative appeal. A series of tests supervised by the author indicated that dentifrice ads that had a negative appeal did not do as well with a jury of consumers as ads with a positive appeal. Subsequent split-run tests indicated that the ad with the negative appeal was actually superior.

5. Its limitation to relative ranking. All the advertisements shown may have been very good, or all very poor.

Consumer Opinion or Awareness (Broadcast). Several interesting innovations of the consumer-jury approach have been devised for use in radio and television. Probably the earliest was the Program Analyzer developed by Paul Lazarsfeld and Frank Stanton. A transcription of the proposed program is given to a jury of consumers seated in a studio. Each jury member is given one handle to hold in his right hand and one in his left. Each handle is equipped with buttons connected to a recording machine. When the juror likes what he hears he presses the button in his right hand; when he dislikes it, the button in his left. (If neither is pressed, it is assumed he is indifferent.) A profile of listener reactions can then be made.

The Schwerin Corporation is a commercial organization that pretests commercials and programs for its clients by using the consumer-jury system. The respondents are solicited by mail (mainly from New York and the surrounding area) through a letter sent to a random selection of homes with telephones. Each person contacted receives four tickets and a letter inviting him and his friends to a theater in New York to see the films of two new television shows and to participate in testing to "help improve television programs and commercials." The letter states that valuable prizes will be awarded the winners of a drawing held in the theater.

Upon entering the theater each person is handed two attached tickets, each bearing the same number. He tears these apart, keeps one, and deposits the other in a box. Next, the audience members hear a short talk by the test director, accompanied by slides to orient them and make them feel at home. They then fill out a detailed questionnaire covering such characteristics as age, sex, and education. Respondents are asked also to indicate which brand of product they want to receive if they are winners in the drawing. Price differentials are eliminated by offering a dollar value rather than a set number of packages.

FIG. 32.1 *Audience watching test commercials and programs during a Schwerin Research Corporation session.* COURTESY SCHWERIN RESEARCH CORPORATION.

The show is a half-hour television program with three one-minute commercials. At certain intervals while the film is running, a number flashes on the screen and the spectators are asked to make a pencil mark in their program opposite the space indicating positive, neutral, or negative response. After the program, spectators are asked to recall each commercial and to write down anything they happen to remember about each. Next comes a second drawing and prize awards. The objective is to discover any changes in choice of brands that took place while the commercials were shown. The meeting is then thrown open for a general discussion. A client can expect to find out how many people remember the brand name, how many people remember at least one sales point, how many remember each idea, how many were motivated to prefer the brand after seeing the commercial, and how many believe key claims.

Some agencies pretest their commercials in storyboard form. Because it is difficult for viewers to visualize what the commercial will look like in finished form, care must be exercised in using storyboards of commercials. A straight selling commercial is not especially difficult for a respondent to visualize. But, Dr. Nahl points out the following dangers in commercials using a more subtle approach:

> A commercial which depends in large part for its success on its effectiveness in creating mood—and especially where this mood depends heavily on the video—is a questionable candidate for testing at the storyboard level. Likewise, the style of finished presentation—as in commercials with full animation—cannot be pretested without having the animation.[8]

Evaluation. In general, the consumer-jury approaches commonly used for the broadcast media have the same strong and weak points as approaches used for print advertising. The Schwerin system has the virtue of providing some evidence of the motivating power of commercials, although it seems at times a little too pat. We know from experience that the ultimate sale is a complicated process; consequently, an advertiser may find himself in trouble if he takes consumer-jury evaluations too literally and assumes that they always predict actual sales. We must realize, too, that every television campaign has a cumulative effect that may not be indicated by tests of only a few commercials.

Direct-Mail Test. Several variations of the basic direct-mail test are used. Probably the simplest is the "post-card test." In this test different copy appeals are condensed and printed on post cards. Each card makes some sort of free offer, the same on all cards. The post cards are sent to a large and representative sample of consumers of the product involved. The percentage of people who write in to take advantage of the offer is regarded as an indication of the effectiveness of the appeal. Instead of a post card, a letter, booklet, or other promotional literature may be mailed to prospects.

Advantages. The principal advantage of this test is that it measures action rather than opinion. The respondents take a positive action, presumably as a result of the advertisement. Also it minimizes variables, because everyone receives the message under much the same conditions. Obviously, it is relatively inexpensive.

[8]Nahl, p. 83.

Limitations. One limitation is that this method can never test more than a general appeal. It does not necessarily follow that the most effective appeal in mail promotion will also be best for the mass media. It would probably not be a valid test of an advertisement designed to build images rather than to stimulate direct action.

Sales Experiments. We have already discussed the simulated sales situation that Schwerin and various other researchers use to help measure the sales impact of television commercials. There are also several tests in which the respondent has to buy the product. One is to have the proposed copy spoken by salespeople either in the store or house-to-house. The sales talk that produces the most direct sales from a representative sample is presumed to be the most effective for advertising purposes. In a variation of this approach the salesman has the prospect listen to a recorded message of the talk and wait to see whether it makes her want to buy the product. Another variation is the "blind-product" test. Packages of the product (with identifying marks removed) are grouped side by side on a table in a store. Behind each group is a descriptive card bearing a different copy appeal or theme. The card that moves the most merchandise is assumed to be the best for advertising purposes. Martin Mayer points out:

> More can be done along these lines than most advertising men realize. In many specific areas of marketing interest – day of week, size of store, inventory, price, display area, activity of competitors, development in adjacent product categories, etc. (sales) data can be observed and fitted to curves, and then different ways of eliminating these variations mathematically can be tried out to see if any of them explain known results.[9]

Advantages. The selling tests provide an idea – rough though it may be – of the sales effectiveness of various approaches. They may help you eliminate totally unbelievable or ineffective appeals.

Limitations. Even at best, these tests represent little more than a preliminary step in the sorting out of the ads, because in none of these is there anything like normal exposure. If interviewers are used, the effectiveness of the advertisement may vary according to the attractiveness and force with which it is delivered.

Mechanical Methods. Advertising people have long been intrigued by the possibility of a machine or mechanical device that would perform as a sort of Geiger counter on ads – tell you clearly and objectively in a laboratory experiment when there was "pay dirt" in the ad. Of the many tried and discarded through the years, three – the tachistoscope, eye camera, and psychogalvanometer – are worthy of special note.

The tachistoscope has long been used by psychologists to measure perception. It is a mechanical device that controls exposure to a message in order that the tester can tell at what point it is perceived. Advertising researchers can thus find out how long it takes a respondent to get the intended point of the illustration, the headline, and so on. They can tell which of two alternative layout treatments gets the point across more quickly.

The eye camera was introduced at the Chicago World's Fair in 1890 to photograph the movement of people's eyes while they were reading.

[9]Mayer, *The Intelligent Man's Guide to Sales Measures of Advertising*, p. 10.

Among other things, it established the fact that the eyes do not move smoothly along a line of type and that people's reading habits differ widely. However, it was not until the late 1930s that the advertising industry took a serious interest in the eye camera. Since that time it has been used sporadically to gain information on the placement of headlines, on the proper length of copy for a particular advertisement, and on many other phases of advertising creation.

The third mechanical device, the psychogalvanometer, is one part of the lie-detector apparatus so widely publicized in criminology. The galvanometric method consists of attaching two zinc electrodes to the person being tested, one on the palm of the hand and the other on the forearm. Perspiration on the palm results in lower electrical resistance, which is duly recorded on a revolving drum apparatus. The theory is that the subject cannot control perspiration resulting from tension. It is assumed that the more tension an ad creates, the more successful it is likely to be.

Advantages. Although these mechanical methods play a relatively minor role in the over-all copy testing picture, they have certain advantages. They have a mechanistic sort of objectivity that appeals to many advertising people who are concerned about the subjective element in the other approaches. They sometimes uncover information perhaps not obtainable by other approaches. Although it is not clear just what extreme fluctuations indicate, it is likely that advertisements which produce little galvanic change are too neutral to cause much reaction or response under normal circumstances. Lucas and Britt cite a case in which it was hypothesized that initial reaction might correspond with initial attention.[10] Twelve Chicago transportation advertisements already measured for audience size were tested with a galvanometer. The evidence of attention in the market survey correlated moderately well (+.51) with the laboratory results from the galvanometer, but the correlation was not high enough to justify predictions of audience size for individual advertisements.

Limitations. It is not entirely clear just what the ratings on these mechanical devices indicate. Do they mean sales effectiveness, depth of penetration, or what? Their validity is doubtful because they put the respondent in an unusual atmosphere, surrounded by strange-looking gadgets. Finally, they are all rather costly in terms of the ads and the people one can accommodate.

Psychological Scoring. Some would call the various rating scales a means of copy testing. However, they serve more as preliminary check lists for creative people than as research tools. Actually, almost everyone who has ever created advertising copy devises for himself some sort of check list. This comprises the qualities he tries to include in every advertisement and those he tries to avoid. At one large agency, Kenyon and Eckhardt, ads are checked against the agency's "bible." Most check lists are based on some research evidence. For example, a check list devised by Richard Manville is based primarily on the ability of certain ads to produce inquiries. The Thompson-Luce method is based on the

[10]D. B. Lucas and S. H. Britt, *Measuring Advertising Effectiveness.* (New York: McGraw-Hill, Inc., 1963), pp. 156–158.

correlation between readership and certain elements. A much publicized check list of judging "advertising effectiveness" was devised by the Townsend Brothers in 1938. For several years it was much used by advertisers and agencies. Today's more sophisticated advertising people are not inclined to accept anything so rigid.

POSTTESTING THE ADVERTISING

In practice there is a lot more information collected these days *after* the advertising has been run than *before*. Although the potential is great in the pretesting methods, their limitations are still enough to discourage many. Although posttesting methods have distinct limitations, they have provided a somewhat more practical guide to the preparation of advertising. Several of them are conducted on a regular basis by leading research organizations, and the findings are available to agencies, advertisers, and the media. They are postmortem assessments but, they tell the communicator *who* listened to his message and thereby provide a basis for planning future messages. The most widely used methods of posttesting fall into four general categories—readership, recall, sales, and inquiry tests.

Readership (Recognition). The readership (or recognition) test was described in some detail in Daniel Starch's *Principles of Advertising*.[11] Dr. Starch has always been one of its strongest proponents, and he has built a sizable business dedicated to the proposition of providing a wealth of readership data on a regular basis, quickly and cheaply. The test was not widely used until George Gallup conducted a series of tests in the late 1920s, indicating its validity. Both Starch and Gallup were trying to tell advertising people that the mere presence of an advertisement in a publication did not mean that the readers had noticed it.

As the test is commonly used, the method is quite simple. For example, the Starch organization sends to interviewers copies of a recent issue of the magazine (or newspaper) to be tested. The interviewers have to find (within ten days after the date of publication for weeklies) a certain number of persons who have seen the magazine. The interviewer goes through an unmarked copy of the publication with the respondent and asks her to indicate the ads she has read. When ads are a half page or larger the interviewer will ask the respondent whether she saw the illustration, the headline, the copy, and so forth. No respondent is asked to commit herself on more than one hundred ads. The interviewer starts each session at a different point in the magazine, so that every ad will catch an equal proportion of fresh and tired respondents. Interviewers are scattered throughout the country, and the number of persons interviewed is determined by the geographical distribution of the magazine's circulation.

Most of the major national magazines are covered regularly by Starch. The expense is borne partly by the publishers, who use the data as a sales tool. Thus the cost to the advertising agency is fairly low. Figure 32.2 is a sample of Starch reports that the advertiser receives. He also receives a copy of the magazine, with a set of stickers on each advertisement, showing what percentage of men and women observed each

[11]Daniel Starch, *Principles of Advertising* (Chicago: A. W. Shaw Company, 1923.)

SATURDAY EVENING POST

Starch Advertisement Readership Service—Current Issue Report

49 Ads

MEN READERS

Advertiser (Page / Size & Color)	Noted %	Seen-Asso %	Read Most %	Seen-Noted #	Seen Asso #	Read Most #	Noted Ratio	Noted Rank	Seen Asso Ratio	Seen Asso Rank	Read Most Ratio	Read Most Rank
Alcoholic Beverages												
Early Times — 49, 1P4CBJ	36	36□	5	58	58	8	105	21	118	13	133	18
Auto Access/Gas												
Guardian Mainten GM — 10, 1P2C	26	24	2	45	41	3	82	36	84	32	50	36
Valvoline Motor Oil — 55, 1/2P4C	36	32	1	87	77	2	158	6	157	7	33	37
Goodrich Tires — 81, 1PBW	27	24	8	57	51	17	104	23	104	23	283	5
Goodrich Tires — 82, 1PBW	28	25	5	59	53	11	107	19	108	19	183	10
Bldg/Decorating												
Kentile Vinyl Fl — 25, 1P4CB	51	35	1	63	43	1	115	14	88	29	17	42
Cars/Trucks												
Plymouth — 2C, 1P4CB	75	73	12	92	90	15	167	5	184	3	250	6
Cadillac — 13, 1P4CB	74	72	12	94	91	15	171	4	186	2	250	6
Cadillac — 14, 1P4CB / 1P4CB	68	62	9	43	39	6	78	38	80	34	100	22
Pontiac — 22, 1P4C	63	61	9	42	41	6	76	39	84	32	100	22
Buick — 26, 2P4CB	74	70	14	47	44	9	85	35	90	27	150	15
Chevrolet — 46, 2P4C	76	75	15	55	55	11	100	24	112	16	183	10
GMC Trucks & Ata — 50, 2PBW	45	35	13	49	38	14	89	32	78	36	233	9
Rambler — 61, 1P4C	42	39	6	61	57	9	111	17	116	15	150	15
Rambler — 62, 2P4CB	62	60	12	38	37	7	69	43	76	38	117	20
Rambler — 64, 1P4CB	60	55	9	76	70	11	138	9	143	8	183	10
Oldsmobile — 76, 2P4CB	67	62	9	42	39	6	76	39	80	34	100	22
Volkswagen — 89, 1PBWB	53	48	13	98	88	24	178	3	180	4	400	2
Dodge Dart — 3C, 1P4C	61	60	7	86	85	10	156	8	173	5	167	13
Clothing Men												
Duofold Underwear — 54, DIG2CB	16	12	2	50	38	6	91	31	78	36	100	22
Nunn Bush Shoes — 66, 1/2HPBW	32	25	6	123	96	23	224	1	196	1	383	3

WOMEN READERS

Advertiser (Page / Size & Color)	Noted %	Seen-Asso %	Read Most %	Seen-Noted #	Seen Asso #	Read Most #	Noted Ratio	Noted Rank	Seen Asso Ratio	Seen Asso Rank	Read Most Ratio	Read Most Rank
Alcoholic Beverages												
Early Times — 49, 1P4CBJ	18	18□	2	32	32	4	55	41	76	30	133	21
Auto Access/Gas												
Guardian Mainten GM — 10, 1P2C	12	8	1	23	15	2	40	47	36	47	67	30
Valvoline Motor Oil — 55, 1/2P4C	17	11	*	45	29		78	27	69	34		
Goodrich Tires — 81, 1PBW	11	5	1	26	12	2	45	45	29	48	67	30
Goodrich Tires — 82, 1PBW	1·1	10	1	26	24	2	45	45	57	41	67	30
Bldg/Decorating												
Kentile Vinyl Fl — 25, 1P4CB	71	55	5	97	75	7	167	4	179	6	233	15
Cars/Trucks												
Plymouth — 2C, 1P4CB	50	47	4	68	64	5	117	17	152	13	167	19
Cadillac — 13, 1P4CB	56	50	2	78	70	3	134	13	167	7	100	24
Cadillac — 14, 1P4CB / 1P4CB	57	46	2	40	32	1	69	32	76	30	33	39
Pontiac — 22, 1P4C	51	37	3	38	28	2	66	36	67	36	67	30
Buick — 26, 2P4CB	45	38	1	32	27	1	55	41	64	37	33	39
Chevrolet — 46, 2P4C	46	38	2	37	30	2	64	37	71	33	67	30
GMC Trucks & Ata — 50, 2PBW	34	21	7	41	25	8	71	30	60	40	267	11
Rambler — 61, 1P4C	24	21	*	39	34		67	33	81	28		
Rambler — 62, 2P4CB	33	26	*	22	18		38	48	43	44		
Rambler — 64, 1P4CB	28	24	*	39	34		67	33	81	28		
Oldsmobile — 76, 2P4CB	52	41	3	36	29	2	62	38	69	34	67	30
Volkswagen — 89, 1PBWB	39	28	6	80	57	12	138	11	136	17	400	7
Dodge Dart — 3C, 1P4C	38	27	2	59	42	3	102	24	100	25	100	24
Clothing Men												
Duofold Underwear — 54, DIG2CB	8	3	1	28	10	3	48	43	24	49	100	24
Nunn Bush Shoes — 66, 1/2HPBW	10	4	1	42	17	4	72	29	40	45	133	21

												Clothing Women														
9	2□	1	35	8	4	64	45	16	49	67	31	6	1/2HPBW	DuPont Cantrece	21	16□	7	89	68	30	153	8	162	9	1000	2
												Drugs/Remedies														
15	11	1	32	23	2	58	47	47	45	33	37	2	1PBW	Contac	21	19	6	49	45	14	84	26	107	24	467	6
												Tobacco														
													1P2C													
38	38	*	37	37		67	44	76	38			70	1PBW	Pall Mall	25	24	*	27	26		47	44	62	38		
47	45□	3	58	55	4	105	21	112	16	67	31	87	1P4CB	Lucky Strike	48	41□	3	65	56	4	112	19	133	18	133	21
69	65	4	65	61	4	118	12	124	10	67	31	4C	1P4CB	Camel	58	53	1	60	55	1	103	23	131	19	33	39
												Toilet Gds Men														
32	28	1	59	52	2	107	19	106	20	33	37	5	1PBWB	Personna Bl Sweeps	20	12	3	41	24	6	71	30	57	41	200	17
												Misc														
44	36□·	15	54	44	18	98	26	90	27	300	4	97	1P4CB	Polaroid Cameras	58	49□	27	79	67	37	136	12	160	10	1233	1
			55	49	6							MEDIAN READERS/DOLLAR						58	42	3						

NUMBER OF READERS MEN 5,530,000
WOMEN 6,115,000
COMBINED 11,645,000

U.S. CIRCULATION A.B.C. 6,505,788
READERS PER COPY FROM STARCH CONSUMER MAGAZINE REPORT 1966

SPACE RATES USED IN DETERMINING READERS PER DOLLAR ARE ONE TIME RATES WITHOUT BENEFIT OF DISCOUNT
NOTED % OF MEN & WOMEN COMBINED EQUAL % FOR MEN X 47 PLUS % FOR WOMEN X 53

MEN & WOMEN COMBINED READERS PER DOLLAR EQUALS MEN READERS PER DOLLAR PLUS WOMEN READERS PER DOLLAR

FIG. 32.2 *Typical page from Starch readership report on* The Saturday Evening Post. COURTESY DANIEL STARCH AND STAFF.

part. Each advertisement is rated in terms of several criteria. The "noted" includes the percentage who remembered seeing the advertisement, the "seen-associated" includes the percentage who associated the name of the product with the advertisement, and "read most," the percentage who read 50 percent or more of the reading matter. The "cost ratio" measures the ad's readership per dollar against the average for all other ads in the magazine. Each ad is also given a ranking on the basis of its cost ratio for each of the three criteria Starch uses.

Readership testing is based on the premise that there is a significant correlation between noticing an advertisement for a product and buying the product (obviously, there is no communication if the ad is not seen). This problem has been investigated at some length both by the research organizations that sell readership data and by their customers.

Starch reports the following based on "data obtained in 400,000 interviews concerning (a) the readership of 45,000 advertisements in two large weekly magazines and (b) the buying acts of the readers and nonreaders of these advertisements":

A method has been developed which measures with reasonable accuracy the *relative* selling effect of different advertisements. The method is called the Netapps (net-ad-produced purchases) or Buyometer Method. The central technique of this method consists of two steps. The first is measurement of product purchases made by *perceivers* of advertisements, compared with purchases made by *nonperceivers*. The second step is to determine how much of the spread in buying rate between perceivers and nonperceivers is attributable to the reading of specific advertisements.[12]

In general, it was found that there was an increase in purchases of a given product by readers of a publication after that publication began to carry advertisements for the product. Conversely, there was a decrease when a publication stopped carrying them.

Advantages. One of the major advantages of readership testing is the information it provides on comparative ratings of different advertisements. It is possible, for example, to compare the effect of size and color on readership. A copywriter who has prepared a food advertisement for a particular magazine may find it helpful to see how his copy is making out in readers per dollar in comparison with his competition in the same issue of the magazine. He will have to be careful, however, if he compares his ad in one magazine with the competitor's ad in another, because the magazine itself may influence readership ratings.

Another advantage of the readership test is its focus on ways of getting attention. Attention-getting can be overemphasized, but the readers still have to select the message before it can be communicated to them. It is a fairly simple test to conduct accurately because it requires no highly specialized knowledge on the part of the researcher.

[12]Daniel Starch, *Measuring Product Sales Made by Advertising* (Mamaroneck, N.Y.: Daniel Starch and Staff, 1961), p. 93. (*See* Daniel Starch, *Measuring Advertising Readership and Results* [New York: McGraw-Hill, Inc., 1966], Chapter 18, for a detailed explanation of this method.)

Limitations. Probably the most important limitation is the assumption that readership means sales or penetration of an idea. Although more readers than nonreaders of an advertisement buy the product, it does not necessarily follow that the advertisement was the sole motivating force.

Another limitation is the danger that readership scores will put the pressure on creative people to use trick (although irrelevant) means of getting high readership. Most of them know that trick pictures, illustrations of scantily clad, pretty young women, or cute cocker spaniels will increase "noting" of the ad. But they know, too, that these may detract from its ultimate penetration power. Most readership studies show only general readership. The breakdown of audiences may be important for an advertiser.

Confusion among readers is often high. Readers are understandably unsure whether they saw a particular ad in one magazine or another, or really saw it at all. Then, too, some people will say they saw an ad merely to appear well-read and to impress the interviewer. Starch's small sample is sometimes criticized. However, a study by the Advertising Research Foundation supported his procedure. The ARF duplicated Starch interviews with a probability sample of 6,000 families and came up with a correlation of .85 with Starch's reported results.

Unaided Recall Test. The recall test is closely related to the readership test. Both depend on the memory of the respondent. However, in the readership test specific advertisements are shown. The unaided recall test, on the other hand, attempts to measure the penetration of the advertisement; therefore little aid is normally given. Some observers distinguish between the two by calling readership an "aided recall" test. In practice, many researchers (for example, Gallup and Robinson) combine the two.

The "Impact" service of Gallup and Robinson was designed to show which ads were best in getting and holding the attention of respondents. It was first used as a means of pretesting advertisements. Special magazines were created for testing purposes, but these were subsequently abandoned, and main attention was concentrated on posttesting the advertising. Gallup and Robinson—Total Prime Time reports on the evening viewing habits of a sample of 2,800 Philadelphia adults. With the aid of a program roster and a list of products viewers are asked to recall programs and commercials they saw "last night."

This is the way the "Impact" method works. Before the respondent is interviewed he must prove he has read the issue of the magazine to be tested by giving some details of at least one article or feature in that particular issue. If he passes this test, he is handed cards showing the names of all products advertised in full or double pages in the issue (such as "Ford"). After he has listed each advertisement he thinks he has seen, he is asked to tell "what it looks like." He is next asked to tell all he possibly can about what the advertiser said—what the sales points were, what message the advertiser tried to get across, and the like. He is also asked to tell the interviewer what he got out of the advertisement. The percentage of readers who successfully associate the brand or advertiser with sales points is called the "Proved Name Registration" (PNR). Next, he is asked whether the advertisement made him want to buy the product or to find out more about it. And finally, the interviewer asks questions to find out whether the person interviewed is a prospect for the product advertised. The interview ends with a conventional readership test of the publication.

The "Impact" method is designed to measure the depth of impression an advertisement leaves on the reader's mind. Three dimensions of an ad's impression are reported: proved name registration (percent of qualified readers who can recall the ad and describe it with the magazine closed); idea penetration (playback of the contents of the advertisement); and conviction ("want to see, try, or buy the product").

A variation of the recall test is the "triple associates" test developed by Henry C. Link. It is used primarily to find out how well a sales theme or slogan has penetrated consumers' minds. It thus focuses attention on the communication power of a series of advertisements. An interviewer might ask you, "Which brand of soft drinks advertises 'The light refreshment'?" You thus would have two associates—the generic product and the theme or slogan. It is up to you to provide the third (in this case "Pepsi-Cola").

Advantages. The recall tests provide information on the penetration of copy—not just surface impressions. They thus give the advertiser a guide to whether the audience got the point. Where "playback" information is recorded, the writers have some indication of the audience's language and frame of reference. Recall tests supply information on incorrect, as well as correct, impressions of the message.

Limitations. For small advertisers the major limitation is often the out-of-pocket cost of making a good study. Because it is a memory test, it is subject to the usual variations in human memory. Some persons have better memories than others, and some are better able to express what they do remember. It is difficult to interpret the results because there is no nice, neat statistical package of data as in some of the other approaches. And it does not isolate the effect of advertising from other communication variables.

Attitude Change. In general, attitude measurement tests (when used for posttesting) attempt to measure the effectiveness of advertising or other promotion on creating a favorable opinion toward the company, its products, or its brands. It is assumed that a favorable change in attitude predisposes people to buy the product. According to Wolfe, the principal kinds of information sought in attitude measurement include the following:

> General assessment of a company, product or brand.
> Loyalty to, acceptance of, preference for, or intent to buy a product or brand.
> Comparative ratings of a company and other companies on products, service, and other attributes.
> Determination of the images the company product and brand are associated with in the consumers mind.[13]

They are often made in connection with awareness or recall tests.

Attitudes are measured by a variety of techniques ranging from the direct question ("Do you like this brand?") to completely unstructured

[13]Wolfe *et al.*, p. 140.

questions or depth interviews. One popular technique is the semantic differential or polar adjectival test, which was discussed earlier in this book in connection with brand imagery.

Advantages. The main advantages of attitude tests are these:

1. Attitude change is closer to the purchase than is mere recall and therefore is a better measure of sales effectiveness.
2. They are relatively easy and inexpensive to make in that they can be made by phone or mail.

Limitations. There are three principal limitations:

1. A true recollection of people's attitudes is so difficult to obtain that the results of advertising campaigns or media mixes are often not clear-cut.
2. A favorable attitude does not necessarily mean ultimate purchase of the product or service, although an unfavorable attitude is certainly a serious barrier to product purchase.
3. Researchers have not agreed on just what an attitude is and what is to be measured.

Sales Tests. Most advertising people sigh wistfully for a test that will definitely indicate the sales impact of their advertisements. Lacking this, however, they have certain posttesting methods that provide useful information on the sales-producing value of certain campaigns, even, at times, of certain ads. There are three general types—measures of past sales, field experiments or local-area sales tests, and matched samples.

Measures of Past Sales. The big catalogue houses such as Sears, Roebuck and Montgomery Ward put out catalogues containing hundreds of ads. Some of these are productive, some are not. However, these houses, like most experienced mail order advertisers, can trace their sales to specific advertisements. If the advertisement for an item does not produce sales, it goes out, and a new approach is tried.

The average general advertiser, of course, sells through retail stores. Some attempt to correlate advertising with sales is made by having the A. C. Nielsen Company, the Market Research Corporation of America, or some other similar research organization furnish information on sales by brand and area. You examine your advertising and you correlate sales, trying to interpret the figures in the light of other variables you think might have influenced sales.

Field Experiments. In a sense field experiments are pretests in that the promotional campaign is tried out on a miniature basis. Mayer describes them as follows:

Usually a field study tries to determine the desirability of change in one of four aspects of marketing—price, advertising weight, advertising media, or advertising copy. In the simplest and most common test, the proposed change is studied by investigation in two markets, which are matched as closely as possible in population characteristics, shopping patterns, media habits, climate, and what have you. One of these is taken as the "control" and the existing advertising and marketing arrangements are continued intact. The other city is taken as the "test" and the one factor to be examined is changed—a new advertising message is introduced, television is substituted for newspapers, total pressure is increased, etc. Sales are audited as carefully as possible in both markets.[14]

[14]Mayer, *The Intelligent Man's Guide to Sales Measures of Advertising*, pp. 16–17.

It is extremely difficult to generalize on the basis of one market since the weather, a strike, a special offer by the competition or any of a number of factors may disturb the results.

One possible way out is to divide the country (or even individual cities) into test and control areas, with each area assigned one treatment or the other at random. Two of the major automobile companies have conducted tests along this line—obviously very expensive tests—in an attempt to gain information that might be used for years to come. In another study Fort Wayne, Indiana, was divided into four sections with each section exposed randomly to the variable to be tested and sales checked periodically.

The most certain (but also very expensive) way of eliminating variables is to try out different treatments with the same experimental subjects. Each market or group of subjects serves at different times during the test as both control and test. For example, the "double changeover" Latin Square design has been extensively used by the Department of Agriculture in testing the effectiveness of types of promotion for farm products. In a dairy promotion study, for example, an attempt was made to measure the effects of different promotional allocations on the sale of milk. Three were evaluated—2 cents per capita (shown as A below), 17 1/2 cents per capita (shown as B), and 32 cents per capita (shown as C). Six areas were involved (I–VI below), and each received all three treatments, six months at a time in the following pattern.

TIME PERIODS	MARKETS AND TREATMENTS					
	I	II	III	IV	V	VI
March–August	A	B	C	A	B	C
September–February	B	C	A	C	A	B
March–August	C	A	B	B	C	A
September–February	C	A	B	B	C	A

The basic measure of effectiveness here was sales, although other information, such as price changes and display, was gathered.[15]

The test is widely used for package goods. It is well suited to testing a campaign for toothpaste or packaged dessert but not so well suited for refrigerators or fur coats.

Matched Samples of Consumers. It is often possible to select two or more groups of consumers matched in age, education, occupation, and other socioeconomic factors. It is presumed that these samples are matched (or identical) in everything except the thing to be tested. Thus you may have two samples of consumers, one of which saw your message, one of which did not. You then may attribute the excess of sales in the first group over the second to your advertising message. Starch does this when he matches samples of readers and nonreaders of ads in order to explore the sales impact of the ads. It is important that the samples

[15]Seymour Banks, *Experimentation in Marketing* (New York: McGraw-Hill, Inc., 1965). Chapters 4–6 show additional examples of sales experiments.

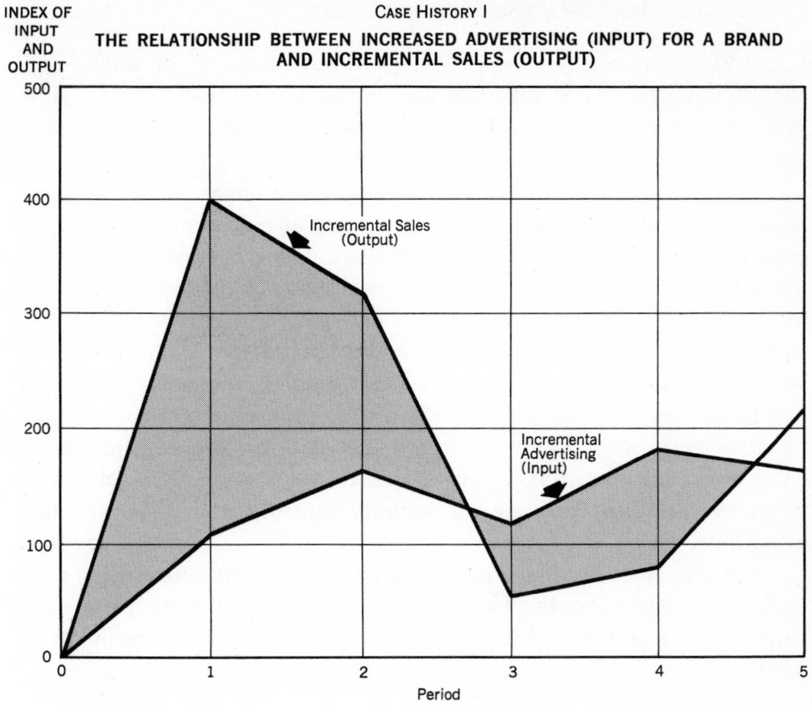

CASE HISTORY I

THE RELATIONSHIP BETWEEN INCREASED ADVERTISING (INPUT) FOR A BRAND
AND INCREMENTAL SALES (OUTPUT)

FIG. 32.3 *Example of data compiled by the Milwaukee Advertising Laboratory. Note that during certain periods the incremental advertising exceeded the incremental sales it generated.* COURTESY THE JOURNAL COMPANY.

be chosen with great care so that the only difference is the exposure to the advertisement.

One of the most ambitious uses of matched samples in recent years is the Milwaukee Advertising Laboratory sponsored by *The Milwaukee Journal* and run under the watchful eye of the Advertising Research Foundation. It is designed to overcome some of the deficiencies of other sales tests by incorporating more rigorous controls than one usually finds in such tests. It was designed "first of all to measure the cumulative sales results of alternative advertising strategies through time . . . to measure the cumulative sales result of alternative promotional strategies . . . and to offer diagnostic information which explains how different strategies work as they do and upon what groups of the marketing population."[16] Input of advertising is controlled by dividing the four metropolitan counties in the Greater Milwaukee Market into two identical halves based both on conventional demographic characteristics and on actual rates of purchase as measured by the *Journal's* consumer analysis. Advertising messages can then be exposed to one market and not the other through control of magazine, newspaper, and direct-mail circulation and through the electronic muter which, when installed to the chassis of a television set, permits a sending station to mute the commercial out of a particular household. Sales data are collected through a weekly diary of all purchases of packaged branded products that each family completes. An example of the type of data compiled is shown in Figure 32.3.

[16]G. Maxwell Ule, "Two Years of the Milwaukee Ad Lab: First Report," *Proceedings: 12th Annual Conference*, Advertising Research Foundation, New York, October 5, 1966.

Advantages of Sales Tests. The great advantage of the sales test is that it is based on the ultimate goal of most advertisers — sales. However, the advertiser should be careful that he does not let the magic of the word "sales" blind him to certain important limitations.

Limitations. The most important limitation of the sales-result test is that an advertisement (or even a series of advertisements) is seldom expected to increase sales directly. Instead, its job is to communicate to a given audience. It is in terms of the communication objective that the most satisfactory testing takes place. The sales test is thus of little use in any advertisements that are supposed to contribute to an image. It works best for products, such as razor blades and soaps, that are purchased fairly frequently and when the communication power of the advertising is most likely to be translated fairly quickly into sales. Even when sales are the objective, the ultimate sale is still influenced by more variables than one can usually control, even under the best conditions.

Finally, these tests are most expensive and time consuming, especially field experiments. They can be used only for complete campaigns, never to test individual advertisements or the elements of an advertisement.

Inquiry Tests. The idea of checking the effectiveness of advertisements through inquiries is an old and obvious one. The thinking behind the test is simple enough. You run a certain number of advertisements and offer some inducement to the people to reply to them. The offer may be a booklet, a sample of the product, or something else of value. The usual approach is to divide the cost of the advertisement by the number of inquiries to find the cost per inquiry. In a print advertisement the offer may be hidden deep in the copy or it may be strongly emphasized. Similarly, in TV or radio the offer may be played up or played down.

Inquiry testing may be used to check media, as well as individual ads or campaigns. If you want to check the effectiveness of two advertisements, you might run one ad one day and one the next in the local paper. You assume that the one that produced the most inquiries per dollar is the better. On the other hand, if you wanted to check the effectiveness of various media, you would use the same advertisement in two or more media. The point is that you should not try to test more than one factor at a time. If the samples are identical except for the element being tested, you attribute the difference to that element.

One variation of the inquiry test that appeals to many advertisers is the split-run test. Two or more versions of an advertisement are published in the *same* issue of a publication. The first advertisement may differ from the second in copy approach or headline or some other element. However, each advertisement is published in the same position in each issue. If two advertisements are tested, half the papers will contain one advertisement and half the other. Consequently, with the exception of the test advertisements, copies of that issue of the paper are the same. Keyed addresses are given in each advertisement, so that the advertiser will know which ad caused the inquiry.

One of the staunchest defenders of inquiry testing, particularly in split-run form, is John Caples of BBDO, famous also in advertising circles as the man who wrote the headline, "They Laughed When I Sat Down at the Piano, but When I Started to Play. . . ." Caples tests ads that the agency is considering by inserting them in newspapers providing split-runs. (Of the 1,530 U.S. daily newspapers listed by SRDS in 1968, 372 offered split runs.) The best ads are then used for full-page or half-page ads in national magazines. To sell the Revised Standard Version of the Bible, BBDO tried such headlines as "The Bible Jesus Would Have Loved," "How This Bible Can Bring You Closer to God," et cetera; the winner—"Biggest Bible News in 346 Years."

A recent development in the magazine field is a service whereby three ads may be tested nationally in the same publication. The normal procedure, however, is to test only two ads within a given geographical area. Because this test introduces geographical variables, you have to use one control ad in each section and then test the other ads against it. (In 1968, 53 consumer magazines and 20 farm publications were offering alternate-copy split-run facilities for advertising.)

Advantages. The consumer is motivated to take a positive action, somewhat in the same way that he buys the product or service. Replies indicate that the reader has seen (or heard) the advertising message. It is possible to test the reading and comprehension of the advertisement, as well as its attention value if the offer is buried in the copy. Furthermore, it gives a fairly good control of the variables that influence action, especially if a split-run is used. Unlike most other methods, it can be used fairly effectively to test small advertisements.

Limitations. The inquiry may not represent a sincere interest in either the product or the reward it offers. This defect may, however, be exaggerated. One analysis showed that 16 percent of the replies from a newspaper ad came from people who had replied to ads in a previous test, and 12 percent sent in two replies to the same ad; this is not high, but it may pose a problem.[17]

Unless you are testing a single element, such as one headline or illustration against another, results normally do not tell why one ad is better than the other. Sometimes results of ads are a standoff, so you have not learned anything. In fact, the number of replies for both versions of an ad are sometimes surprisingly low.

It is difficult to use this type of test for indirect-action advertising. Finally, it tends to be time consuming (the bulk of responses in a monthly magazine inquiry offer, for example, are not available for three or four months).

SUMMARY

In today's advertising world the user of advertising has a variety of techniques to provide feedback from his advertising. Imperfect though these are, they provide the best approach we have thus far for finding out whether our ads are communicating—and sometimes why. Testing need not inhibit the best creative efforts of advertising people—instead, it should make the efforts more productive. Of course, the advertising

[17]Richard M. Seitz, "Vicks Researcher Explores Advantages and Failings of Split-Run Advertising Tests," *Advertising Age*, May 11, 1959.

person has to know the limitations, as well as the strong points, of the various methods.

Advertising testing methods may be divided into pretesting (those used before the ad is placed in the media) and posttesting methods (those used after placement). The most commonly used methods of pretesting are consumer opinion and attitude tests, direct-mail tests, sales experiments, and mechanical tests of various types. The most important types of posttesting are readership (recognition), unaided recall, attitude, sales, and inquiry tests.

QUESTIONS FOR DISCUSSION

1. Is the measurement of advertising effectiveness more likely to hamper or to encourage originality in advertising? Why?
2. Why is it easier to posttest an advertisement than to pretest it?
3. To what extent has the improvement of experimental techniques made it easier to measure the effectiveness of an advertisement or campaign on the basis of its ability to stimulate sales?
4. Is it logical to assume that a change in favorable attitude would be related to a change in sales effectiveness?
5. To what extent are computers likely to influence the testing of advertising?
6. What are the advantages and disadvantages of exposing a print advertisement or a commercial to a test audience? Are the reactions of such an audience likely to be typical of the entire audience?
7. Clip from a current magazine or newspaper two advertisements that you think would obtain a high "Noted" rating on a Starch recognition test. Clip two which you think would obtain a low rating.
8. A large pharmaceutical company conducted a series of tests in which certain print advertisements were tested on both a recognition and an inquiry basis with split-runs used for the inquiry tests. Some of the advertisements that did well on the recognition tests did poorly when tested by inquiries. What are some possible reasons for this discrepancy?

SUGGESTED READINGS

Banks, Seymour, *Experimentation in Marketing.* New York: McGraw-Hill, Inc., 1965.

Barton, Roger, *Advertising Media.* New York: McGraw-Hill, Inc., 1964. Chapter 3.

Boyd, Harper W., Jr., and Joseph W. Newman, *Advertising Management: Selected Readings.* Homewood, Ill.: Richard D. Irwin, 1965. Part VI.

Dalbey, Homer M., Irwin Gross, and Yoram Wind, *Advertising Measurement and Decision Making.* Boston: Allyn & Bacon, Inc., 1968.

Lucas, D. B., and S. H. Britt, *Measuring Advertising Effectiveness.* New York: McGraw-Hill, Inc., 1963.

Mayer, Martin, *The Intelligent Man's Guide to Sales Measures of Advertising.* New York: Advertising Research Foundation, 1965.

Nafziger, Ralph O., and David M. White, *Introduction to Mass Communications Research*, 2nd ed. Baton Rouge: Louisiana State University Press, 1963.

Sandage, C. H., and Vernon Fryburger, *Advertising Theory and Practice*, 7th ed. Homewood, Ill.: Richard D. Irwin, Inc., 1967. Chapters 24–27.

Starch, Daniel, *Measuring Advertising Readership and Results*. New York: McGraw-Hill, Inc., 1966.

Wolfe, Harry D., James K. Brown, and G. Clark Thompson, *Measuring Advertising Results*. New York: National Industrial Conference Board, 1962.

———, *Pretesting Advertising*. New York: National Industrial Conference Board, 1964.

Index

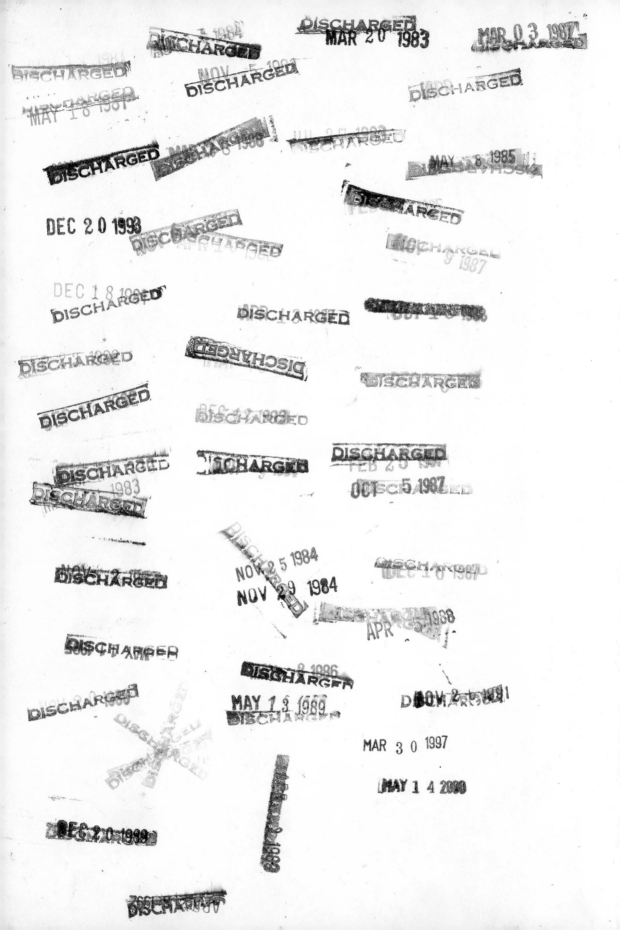